You'll experience the thrill of piping a perfect bouquet of Wilton Roses!

The kids will be amazed as you decorate a fun birthday cake before their eyes!

You'll be able to impress every guest with a personal-size cake finished with flowers!

Take a Wilton Method Course today and start the fun!

Wilton Method Courses bring a

Everyone loves cupcakes—and your decorated cupcakes will be the talk of the party!

You'll create a fondant birthday cake kids will never forget!

Finish your cake with homemade flowers and listen to the compliments!

lifetime of smiles!

You will make her dreams come true with a magical princess cake!

For details about these exciting cakes, course schedules and more, visit **www.wilton.com**

Every party needs a cake!

Cakes are a big part of the fun at any celebration. What a great feeling it is when you bring a cake you decorated to the table. Watching the smiles and hearing the compliments is something you always remember, no matter how many cakes you've made.

As you look at all the amazing cakes inside the 2011 Wilton Yearbook, think of all the smiles they will bring to your guests. Imagine being able to take our big top cover cake to the birthday party. It's filled with birthday cheer any kid will love. With its companion circus carousel cake, we couldn't fit all the fun on the cover!

You'll find many more fantastic circus and jungle theme designs in our special section, "Party Animals!". With these sensational cakes, you can really make a birthday boy or girl feel special. Check out the multi-level Amazon cake with a river of color flow connecting tiers topped with cookie lions, zebras, giraffes and other jungle pals. Wouldn't it feel great to decorate cakes that create this much excitement?

This Yearbook is packed with great designs for every occasion. Create the perfect holiday centerpiece with our gingerbread skating village. Charm shower guests with the cake that brings a nursery rhyme to life. Whatever you are celebrating, there's a perfect design for you in the 2011 Yearbook!

The excitement for 2011 extends beyond the great cake designs found in this Yearbook. The new Wilton Method Courses are here—there's never been a better time to experience the fun of cake decorating. We've added terrific new techniques and organized each lesson to make it even easier to achieve decorating success. You'll have a great time in Wilton Method Courses, and the skills you'll learn will help you make all your celebrations more memorable for years to come.

Now the fun begins as you discover all the fantastic cakes and desserts inside. As you plan a year of great celebrations, count on this Yearbook and our new Wilton Method Courses to help you create something great.

Marvin Oakes

Marvin Oakes
President
Wilton Enterprises

Totally Tooned In! .... p. 26

The kids will get very animated when their favorite character pops in for the party! Mickey has many ways to arrive in style, including a candy-filled balloon, cookie car and locomotive cake. Other big movers are here: Buzz Lightyear, patrolling the planets, Dora the Explorer on a jungle journey and Spider-Man, bouncing from building to building. And for the first time, you can let your little girl say, Hello Kitty!

Bright Birthday Smiles! ....p. 6

Light the candles and watch the smiles light up the room! No matter whose birthday it is, there's a cake here with their name on it! A sweet fondant blanket for the 1-year old. Silly snakes, dazzling divas in concert and karate-kicking kids for the youngsters. Or, make birthday treats to please young and old, like colossal smiling cupcakes and colorful candle-shaped loaf cakes.

Milestone Moments........... p. 68

Relax—your cake will live up to the exceptional occasion you're celebrating. How can you miss with a baby shower cake set to the theme of "Hey Diddle Diddle"? For religious events, you'll find designs that are meaningful and memorable, including communion cross cookies and petits fours, La Quinceañera rose tiers and a holy village cake for the bar/bat mitzvah celebration.

It's Always Party Season!...... p. 40

With these cakes and treats, you'll have something to look forward to any time of year! Skeletons and bats are creeping about on spooky cookies, cakes and cereal treats. For wintertime, you'll love to display a frosty, frilly gingerbread house with all the trimmings. Spring brings bunnies and butterflies, along with fondant-flower topped cookies. And top off your patriotic picnic with starred and striped cupcakes—some with foil fireworks!

CREATIVE DIRECTOR
Daniel Masini

SENIOR ART DIRECTOR/CAKE DESIGNER
Steve Rocco

DECORATING ROOM SUPERVISOR
Cheryl Brown

SENIOR CAKE DECORATORS
Mary Gavenda
Susan Matusiak

CAKE DECORATORS
Jenny Jurewicz
Kathy Krupa
Diane Knowlton
Mark Malak
Andrea Nickels
Michele Poto
Valerie Pradhan
Amber Spiegel
Tracey Wurzinger

EDITOR/WRITER
Jeff Shankman

WRITER/COPY EDITOR
Jane Mikis

WRITERS
Mary Enochs
Marita Seiler

PRODUCTION MANAGER
Challis Yeager

ASSOCIATE PRODUCTION MANAGER
Mary Stahulak

GRAPHIC DESIGN/PRODUCTION
Courtney Kieras
Drew Pistilli
RNB Graphics

PHOTOGRAPHY
Peter Rossi-PDR Productions
DeBolt Photography
Black Box Studios

PHOTO STYLIST
Carey Thornton

CREATIVE SERVICES ASSISTANT
Judi Graf

PRODUCT DEVELOPMENT/PUBLICATIONS
Tina Celeste

IN U.S.A.
Wilton Industries, Inc.
2240 West 75th Street, Woodridge, IL 60517
www.wilton.com

Retail Customer Orders:
Phone: 800-794-5866 • Fax: 888-824-9520
Online: www.wilton.com

Class Locations:
Phone: 800-942-8881
Online: www.wilton.com/classes/classlocator.cfm

IN CANADA
Wilton Industries Canada Company
98 Carrier Drive, Etobicoke, Ontario M9W5R1 Canada
Phone: 416-679-0790

Class Locations:
Phone: 416-679-0790, ext. 200
E-mail: classprograms@wilton.ca

¡SE HABLA ESPAÑOL!
Para mas informacion, marque 800-436-5778
In Mexico: www.wiltonenespanol.com

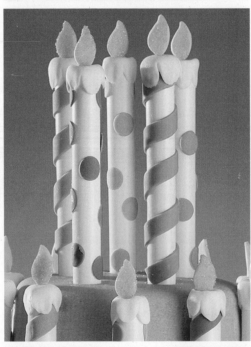

Bright Birthday Smiles!

Everyone's gathered to celebrate another great year and even the treats are grinning from ear to ear! When guests see the crowd of cupcakes below stand up and cheer, they can't help but share the excitement. As you can see, there's a smile waiting to greet birthday boys and girls of any age. Lollipops for your little leaguer, brownie blossoms and cookie wands for a princess, a colossal candle-topped cake in blazing colors for young and old. And for that all-important first birthday cake, meet an adorable toddler peeking out from a fondant blanket—the perfect way to start a lifetime of unforgettable celebrations.

Standing O!

Pans: 10 x 2 in. Round, p. 157; Dimensions Large Cupcake, p. 164; Cookie Sheet, Cooling Grid, p. 203

Tips: 1A, 9, 12, p. 134

Colors:* Rose, Lemon Yellow, Golden Yellow, Black, p. 146

Fondant: White Ready-To-Use Rolled Fondant (65 oz.), p. 147; 20 in. Rolling Pin, Roll & Cut Mat, Easy-Glide Fondant Smoother, p. 148; Brush Set, p. 149

Recipe: Buttercream Icing, p. 116

Also: 2011 Pattern Book (Large, Small Mouths), p. 130; Silly Feet! Silicone Baking Cups, p. 168; Jumbo Confetti Sprinkles, Flowerful Medley 6-Mix Sprinkles (confetti), p. 144; Wooden Dowel Rods (2 pks.), p. 139; Cake Circles, Fanci-Foil Wrap, p. 241; scissors, tape, knife, pedestal cake stand

Main Cakes: Bake and cool 2-layer round and 2-part large cupcake. Tint fondant: 36 oz. yellow, 24 oz. pink, 2 oz. black. Roll out ⅛ in. thick as needed. Prepare and cover round cake with yellow rolled fondant (p. 117) and cupcake bottom with pink rolled fondant. Prepare cakes for Stacked Construction (p. 114). Position round cake on foil-covered board, 1 in. larger than cake on all sides. Position cupcake on board cut to fit. Roll a 32 x ½ in. diameter yellow log; attach around cake base. Attach Jumbo Confetti to sides using icing dots. Roll 3½ x ¾ in. diameter logs for legs; bend and attach using damp brush. Attach 1¼ in. long oval feet; wrap ¼ in. diameter logs around feet at ankles. Cut dowel rod for two 5 in. lengths. Insert into cake sides for arms, leaving 2 in. exposed. Cover 1½ in. with ⅛ in. thick fondant strips. For each hand, roll and flatten a 1 in. ball; cut slits to shape fingers. Push onto tip of dowel rod. For cupcake top, use spatula to build up icing mound. Use tip 1A to pipe a continuous spiral, from bottom to tip. Roll out small amounts of pink, white and black fondant ⅛ in. thick. Use pattern to cut large mouth. Use wide end of tip 1A to cut eyes and cheeks; use narrow end of tip 1A to cut pupils. Attach features with icing dots. Position small confetti.

Cupcakes: Bake and cool cupcakes in silicone cups supported by cookie sheet. Build up icing mound using a spatula. Use tip 12 to pipe a continuous spiral, from bottom to tip. Roll out small amounts of pink, white and black fondant. Use pattern to cut small mouth. Use tip 12 to cut eyes; use tip 9 to cut pupils and cheeks. Attach features with icing dots. Position small confetti. Round cake serves 28, large cupcake serves 12, each small cupcake serves 1.

*Combine Lemon Yellow with Golden Yellow for yellow shown.

▲ Cupcakes That Crunch!

Pans: Cookie Sheet, Cooling Grid, p. 203

Tips: 3, 4, 10, 12, p. 134

Colors: Lemon Yellow, Rose, Sky Blue, Leaf Green, Black, Christmas Red, p. 146

Recipes: Royal Icing, Roll-Out Cookies, p. 116

Also: Party 4 Pc. Colored Metal Cutter Set, p. 202; Meringue Powder, p. 143; Flowerful Medley 6-Mix Sprinkles (confetti), p. 144; Spatula, p. 139; Parchment Triangles, p. 136

In advance: Make cookies. Prepare and roll out dough. Cut cookies using cupcake cutter from set. Bake and cool cookies. Outline ribbed bottom area with tip 4 and tinted, full-strength icing; flow in with thinned icing (p. 128). Let dry.

Decorate cookies using full-strength icing. Pipe tip 10 swirls for icing tops; blend and shape with spatula. Immediately position confetti sprinkles. Pipe tip 12 dot cherry. Pipe tip 3 dot eyes and nose; pipe outline smile and immediately attach confetti cheeks. Each serves 1

▲ Roof-Raising Birthday

Pan: 12 x 18 x 2 in. Sheet, p. 157

Tips: 1, 5, p. 134

Colors:* Leaf Green, Lemon Yellow, Golden Yellow, Violet, Orange, Rose, Royal Blue, p. 146

Fondant: White Ready-To-Use Rolled Fondant (112 oz.), p. 147; Happy Birthday Fondant Imprint Mat, 20 in. Rolling Pin, Roll & Cut Mat, Easy-Glide Fondant Smoother, p. 148; 10 Pc. Fondant/ Gum Paste Tool Set, Brush Set, p. 149

Recipe: Buttercream Icing, p. 116

Also: 101 Cookie Cutters (letters), p. 201; Light Green Colored Sugar, p. 144; 13 x 19 in. Cake Boards, Fanci-Foil Wrap, p. 241; tape, scissors, ruler, cornstarch, knife

In advance: Make letters. Tint 8 oz. fondant green. Roll out ⅛ in. thick. Cut letters. Brush with damp brush and sprinkle on Colored Sugar. Let dry on cornstarch-dusted board.

Bake and cool 1-layer cake. Prepare and cover with 80 oz. yellow rolled fondant (p. 117). Prepare imprinted top. Roll out 24 oz. white fondant ⅛ in. thick. Cut an 11 x 17 in. rectangle; imprint Happy Birthday design using Imprint Mat. Use shell tool from set to fray edges. Brush cake top with water and position imprinted top. Use tip 1 to outline and fill in designs using icing in assorted colors. Attach letters with dots of icing. Pipe tip 5 bead bottom border. Serves 36.

*Combine Lemon Yellow with Golden Yellow for yellow shown. Combine Leaf Green with Lemon Yellow for green shown. Combine Violet with Rose for violet shown.

▲ Cheesecakes to Celebrate

Pan: 10 x 2.75 in. Springform, p. 165

Tip: 6, p. 134

Colors:* Lemon Yellow, Golden Yellow, Pink, Leaf Green, Royal Blue, p. 146

Candy: Orange Candy Melts, p. 194; Stars Candy Mold, Candy Melting Plate, p. 197; Primary Candy Color Set (orange) p. 195

Recipe: Orange Cheesecake, p. 116

Also: Parchment Triangles, p. 136; 10 in. Cake Boards, p. 241; knife, ruler, small bowls, toothpicks

Mold candies. For each slice, mold 1 star and 7 round candies (10 in. cheesecake yields 8 slices). Mold stars in candy mold; mold rounds in Candy Melting Plate, filling cavities ½ in. deep. Prepare pan, crust and cheesecake batter. For each dot color, remove ¼ cup batter and tint. Pour remaining batter into pan. Use tip 6 to pipe random dots into batter. Bake, cool and unmold cheesecake per instructions. At serving time, cut into wedges; smooth sides with wet spatula. Position candies. Each slice serves 1.

*Combine Lemon Yellow with Golden Yellow for yellow shown.

▼ Birthday Bright Lights

Pans: 9 x 13 x 2 in. Sheet, p. 157; Cookie Sheet, Cooling Grid, p. 203

Tip: 2A, p. 134

Candy: White (2 pks.), Blue, Yellow Candy Melts, p. 194; Primary (orange, yellow, blue), Garden (pink, green) Candy Color Sets, p. 195; 4 in. Lollipop Sticks, p. 198

Recipes: Candy Clay, p. 116; favorite crisped rice cereal treats (3 batches)

Also: Cutter/Embosser, p. 150; 9 in. Rolling Pin, Roll & Cut Mat, p. 148; Leaf Cut-Outs, p. 151; Orange, Pink, Blue, Green, Yellow Colored Sugars, p. 144; Disposable Decorating Bags, p. 136; waxed paper, cornstarch, knife

In advance: Make 1 white candy clay recipe. Let set up overnight before tinting. Divide into 5ths; tint portions orange, pink, blue, green and yellow. **Also:** Make 3 batches of cereal treats; press mixture into prepared 9 x 13 in.

pan. Unmold onto waxed paper-covered board. Cut into three 3 x 13 in. sections. Let cool completely.

Place treat on cooling grid over cookie sheet. Cover with melted candy (p. 128) using a cut bag. Tap grid to remove air bubbles; chill until firm and repeat. Insert then remove lollipop stick in top of treat where flame will go. Repeat for remaining treats. Make candy clay decorations. Roll out candy clay ⅛ in. thick. For all decorations, after cutting, brush with water and sprinkle with matching colored sugar, shake off excess then attach with damp brush. Cut 30 circles using wide end of tip 2A. For vertical stripes, cut ½ in. wide strips using straight-edge wheel of Cutter/Embosser; for horizontal stripes, cut ¾ in. wide strips. Attach verticals ½ in. apart, horizontals ¾ in. apart. Cut 3 flames using largest leaf Cut-Out; let dry. Attach to lollipop stick with melted candy. Insert flames in treat tops. Each candle serves 12.

▼ Tiny Cakes, Big Wishes

Cookie: 10.5 x 15.5 x 1 in. Jelly Roll/Cookie, p. 157; Cooling Grid, p. 203; 101 Cookie Cutters, p. 201

Also: Flowerful Medley 6-Mix Sprinkles (confetti), p. 144; Celebrate! Icing Decorations, p. 175; White Candy Melts

(2 pks.), p. 194; Parchment Triangles, p. 136; Cake Boards, p. 241; waxed paper, knife

Bake and cool 1-layer cake. Imprint cake top with smallest round cutter; cut out cake rounds using knife. Cover with melted candy (p. 128). Chill until firm and repeat. Attach confetti to cake sides and icing decoration on top with dots of melted candy in a cut parchment bag. Each serves 1.

▲ Birthday Candlepower

Pans: 6, 8, 10 x 2 in. Round, p. 157

Colors:* Rose, Orange, Leaf Green, Lemon Yellow, Sky Blue, Violet, p. 146

Fondant: White Ready-To-Use Rolled Fondant (241 oz.), p. 147; 20 in. Rolling Pin, Roll & Cut Mat, Easy-Glide Fondant Smoother, p. 148; 10 Pc. Fondant/Gum Paste Tool Set, Brush Set, p. 149; Stepsaving Rose Bouquets Flower Cutter Set, Round and Leaf Cut-Outs, p. 151

Recipes: Buttercream Icing, p. 116; Thinned Fondant Adhesive, p. 117

Also: Cake Dividing Set, p. 136; Piping Gel, p. 143; Yellow Colored Sugar, p. 144; Plastic Dowel Rods (15 pks. for candles; forty 6 in. lengths), Wooden Dowel Rods, p. 239; Cake Circles, Boards, Fanci-Foil Wrap, 14 in. Silver Cake Bases (2), p. 241; toothpicks, ruler, knife, tape, scissors, cornstarch

Tint fondant: 5 oz. each rose, orange, green, yellow, violet, blue for candles; 36 oz. rose, 48 oz. orange, 72 oz. green to cover cakes; 36 oz. yellow for base board. Roll out ⅛ in.

thick unless otherwise specified. Reserve any excess fondant.

A week in advance: Make fondant flames. Cut 40 using smallest Leaf Cut-Out from set. Brush with damp brush; sprinkle on Yellow Sugar. Insert toothpick at bottom, leaving 2 in. exposed to insert into candle. Let dry 48 hours on cornstarch-dusted board. **Also:** Make candles (p. 121). **And:** Prepare base. Tape 2 cake bases together; brush with Piping Gel and cover with rolled fondant (p. 120). Use Cake Dividing Wheel to divide base into 12ths. Roll out remaining yellow fondant. Cut 5 x ½ in. strips. Twist and attach between marks. Roll ½ in. diameter balls; attach to cover ends.

Bake and cool three 2 in. high layers for each size cake. Prepare and cover with rolled fondant (p. 117). Prepare for Stacked Construction (p. 114). Attach candles to cake sides, 1½ in. apart, using thinned fondant adhesive. Push 5 candles into cake top. Serves 60.

*Combine Violet with Rose for violet shown.

▼ Covered in Cute!

Pans: #1, p. 160; 11 x 15 x 2 in. Sheet (girl's cake), p. 157

Tips: 2A, 6, 8, p. 134

Colors:* Rose, (Sky Blue for boy's cake), p. 146

Fondant: White Ready-To-Use Rolled Fondant (90 oz.), Natural Colors Fondant Multi Pack (pink used for skin tone shown), p. 147; 20 in. Rolling Pin, Roll & Cut Mat, Easy-Glide Fondant Smoother, p. 148; Brush Set, p. 149; Cutter/Embosser, p. 150

Recipe: Buttercream Icing, p. 116

Also: Mini Romantic (girl's), Mini Noah's Ark (boy's) Metal Cutter Sets, p. 202; Round Comfort-Grip Cutter, p. 200; Piping Gel, p. 143; Cake Boards, Fanci-Foil Wrap, p. 241; 16½ x 23½ in. plywood or foamcore board (½ in. thick), ruler, scissors, waxed paper, cornstarch, knife

2 days in advance: Prepare head using fondant from Multi Pack. (p. 121)

Girl's cake: Bake and cool two 1-layer sheet

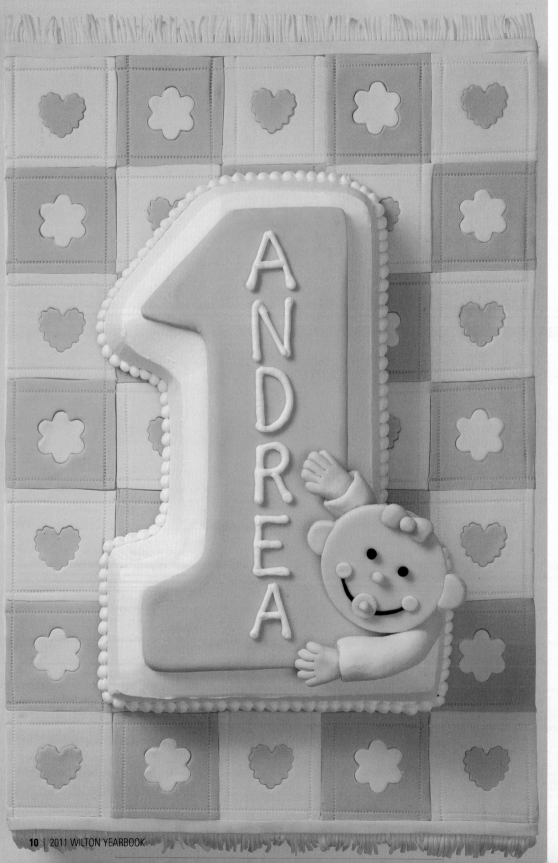

cakes. Position side-by-side on foil-wrapped base board. Ice smooth. Prepare for Stacked Construction (p. 114). Tint fondant: 54 oz. dark pink, 36 oz. light pink. (Reserve 18 oz. dark pink for #1.) Roll out ⅛ in. thick as needed. Use Cutter/Embosser with straight wheel to cut 3 in. squares (18 light, 17 dark); leave squares on mat. Use mini cutters to cut out center designs in 1 light square and 1 dark square. Switch fondant pieces and smooth edges with fingertip for 2-tone inlay. Repeat, making 4 or 5 of each design in each color. Attach squares to cakes, alternating colors and designs. Begin top row ½ in. down from edge; last row should end ½ in. from bottom edge. Use Cutter/Embosser with ridged wheel to make stitching marks ¼ in. from edges. For fringe, cut two 1¼ x 15 in. strips. Use scissors to cut ⅛ in. wide slits, ⅞ in. deep and attach. For blanket hem, cut two ⅜ x 15 in. strips. Attach at top of fringe with Piping Gel.

Boy's cake: Prepare blanket. Tint fondant: 54 oz. dark blue, 36 oz. light blue. (Reserve 18 oz. dark blue for #1.) Follow directions above for girl's cake to cover board with fondant blanket. Attach pieces using Piping Gel.

Bake and cool #1 cake. Position on cut-to-fit cake board and ice smooth. Roll out reserved dark fondant ¼ in. thick. Press into cake pan to shape #1; remove and trim edges as needed. Position on cake top. For hands, begin with ¾ in. balls of reserved skin tone fondant; flatten and shape, cutting slits for fingers. For sleeves, roll 1 in. diameter logs, 1½ and 3 in. long. Cut opening in end of sleeve; insert and attach hand using damp brush. Attach arms and head to cake top (support head with ball of fondant). Pipe tip 8 name. Position #1 cake on blanket; pipe tip 6 bead bottom border.

Girl's cake serves 66; boy's cake serves 12.

*Note: For boy's cake, we used Sky Blue instead of Rose, animal cutters instead of geometrics. Blanket squares are attached to base board without sheet cakes.

▶ Wonderful One!

Pans: #1, p. 160; 4 Pc. Oval Set (largest pan used), p. 156; Standard Muffin, p. 158

Tip: 5, p. 134

Colors: Leaf Green, Royal Blue, Lemon Yellow, Rose, p. 146

Candy: White (2 pks.), Light Cocoa (2 pks.) Candy Melts, p. 194; Primary (yellow, blue), Garden (pink, green) Candy Color Sets, p. 195; Candy Melting Plate, p. 197

Recipe: Buttercream Icing, p. 116

Also: Letters & Numbers Gum Paste & Fondant Mold Set, p. 151; White Standard Baking Cups, p. 184; Parchment Triangles, p. 136; Plastic Dowel Rod, p. 239; Cake Boards, Fanci-Foil Wrap, p. 241; ruler, knife

In advance: Mold #1 candy plaque (p. 128). Begin with 1 pk. melted light cocoa candy; fill to 1st level, tap to settle and chill 5 minutes to set. Add 14 oz. blue tinted candy. Tap, chill until firm. Attach dowel rod to back using melted candy; leave 3 in. exposed at bottom to insert into cake. **Also:** Make candy letters and 2-tone numbers using Letters & Numbers Set and Piping or Painting Method (p. 128). **And:** Make 72 candy dots (18 of each color). Mold tinted candy in Candy Melting Plate cavities; fill only ⅛ in. deep.

Bake and cool 2-layer cake (bake 1½ in. high layers for a 3 in. high cake) and cupcakes. Ice cake smooth. Pipe tip 5 bead bottom border. Attach letters to plaque using melted candy. Position candy dots; insert plaque. Spatula ice cupcakes; position numbers. Cake serves 44; each cupcake serves 1.

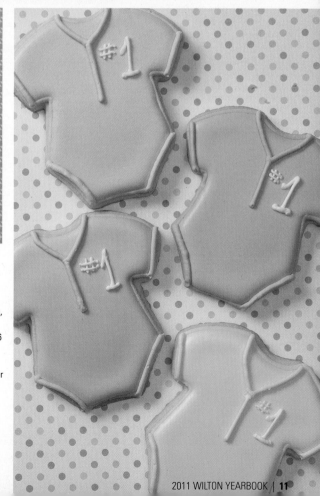

▲ Peek-a-Boo Pops

Pan: Round Cookie Treat, p. 203

Candy: White, Light Cocoa Candy Melts, p. 194; Primary (orange, blue), Garden (pink, black) Candy Color Sets, p. 195; Candy Melting Plate, p. 197; 8 in. Lollipop Sticks, p. 198

Also: Parchment Triangles, p. 136; Cake Boards, p. 241; ¼ in. wide ribbon (18 in. for each bow), waxed paper

Use white candy and treat pan to mold pops on sticks. Tint portion of melted white candy orange for skin tone shown. Fill Melting Plate cavities to mold heads. Chill until firm. Decorate and assemble using melted candy in cut parchment bags. Tint portions of melted white candy blue, pink and black. Pipe scallop border and message on base candy. Set heads on waxed paper-covered board. Add 1-2 drops of water to small amount of pink to thicken for piping. Immediately pipe bow loops, let set, then add center dot. Pipe facial features and hair curl. Let set. Attach heads to base. Pipe hands. Let set. Tie ribbon around stick. Each serves 1.

▶ Romper Rainbow

Pans: Cookie Sheet, Cooling Grid, p. 203

Tips: 1, 2, 3, p. 134

Colors: Sky Blue, Rose, Lemon Yellow, Leaf Green, p. 146

Recipes: Color Flow Icing, Roll-Out Cookies, p. 116

Also: Baby Colored Metal Cutter Set (onesie), p. 203; Color Flow Mix, p. 143; Cake Boards, p. 241; Parchment Triangles, p. 136; waxed paper

Make cookies. Prepare and roll out dough. Cut cookies using cutter from set. Bake and cool. Pipe tip 3 outline with full-strength icing; flow in with thinned icing (p. 128). Let dry. Decorate with full-strength icing. Use tip 3 to pipe lines at neck, sleeves and leg openings. Pipe tip 1 number sign, tip 2 number. Let dry. Each serves 1.

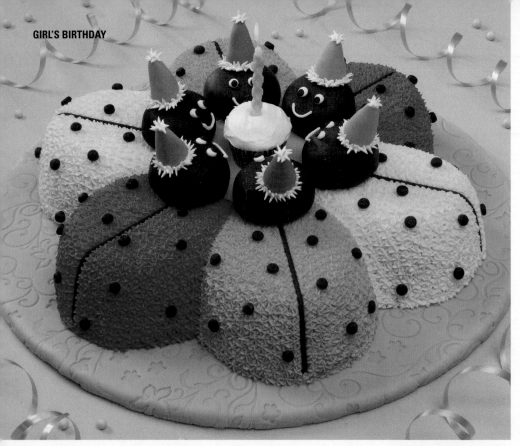

◀ Drawn to the Flame

Pans: Dancing Daisy, p. 163; Mini Muffin, p. 158

Tips: 2, 6, 16, p. 134-135

Colors:* Leaf Green, Lemon Yellow, Golden Yellow, Red-Red, Christmas Red, Orange, Rose, Violet, Royal Blue, Black, p. 14

Fondant: White Ready-To-Use Rolled Fondant (38 oz.), p. 14 Graceful Vines Fondant Imprint Mat, 20 in. Rolling Pin, R & Cut Mat, Easy-Glide Fondant Smoother, p. 148; Brush Set, p. 149

Recipes: Buttercream Icing, p. 116; Thinned Fondant Adhesive, p. 117

Also: White Mini Baking Cups, p. 184; Hot Colors Lattice Candles, p. 183; Piping Gel, Meringue Powder, p. 143; 14 in. Diameter Cake Circles (2), Fanci-Foil Wrap, p. 241; scissors, tape, ruler, cornstarch

In advance: Make fondant heads (p. 121). **Also:** Prepare base board. Tape 2 Cake Circles together. Tint 24 oz. fondant green. Roll out 1/8 in. thick. Imprint design using Fondant Imprint Mat. Cover with rolled fondant (p. 120).

Bake and cool Daisy cake and 1 mini muffin. Ice cake cente smooth with green icing. Pipe tip 6 black center lines. Cove bodies with tip 16 stars. Add tip 6 dots; flatten slightly with fingertip dipped in cornstarch. Position heads. Using tip 2, pipe pull-out fringe and pompom, dot eyes and pupils and outline mouth. Ice mini muffin and position in center. Insert candle. Serves 12.

*Combine Leaf Green with a little Lemon Yellow for green shown. Combine Red-Red with Christmas Red for red shown. Combine Lem Yellow with Golden Yellow for yellow shown.

▶ 'Shroom with a View

Pans: Mini Ball, p. 162; Non-Stick Cookie Sheet, p. 165

Colors:* Leaf Green, Lemon Yellow, p. 146

Candy: White Candy Melts (9 oz. per treat), p. 194; Primary (yellow), Garden (pink, green, black) Candy Color Sets, Cordial Cups Candy Mold, p. 195

Recipe: Truffles, p. 116

Also: White Ready-To-Use Rolled Fondant (1 oz. per treat), p. 147; Round Comfort-Grip Cutter, p. 200; Parchment Triangles, p. 136; Pastry Brush, p. 153; Brush Set, p. 149; shredded coconut, ruler, knife, waxed paper, zip-close plastic bag

In advance: Make candy pieces (p. 128). **Also:** Tint coconut (p. 120).

Prepare truffles recipe. Spoon or pipe into mushroom cap and stem; seal with melted candy. Chill until firm. Assemble mushroom on base using melted candy. Brush base with melted candy and immediately sprinkle on coconut. Tint fondant green. Roll 5 balls, decreasing in size from 1/2 in. diameter head to 1/4 in. diameter tail. Use dots of melted candy to assemble and attach caterpillar. Tint small amount of candy black; use cut parchment bag to pipe dot eyes and smile. Each serves 1.

*Combine Leaf Green with Lemon Yellow for green fondant and coconut.

◀ Beaming Birthday Butterfly

Pans: Cookie Sheet, Cooling Grid, p. 203

Tips: 2, 3, p. 134

Colors:* Orange, Violet, Rose, Leaf Green, Lemon Yellow, Black, p. 146

Recipes: Royal Icing, Roll-Out Cookies, p. 116

Also: 4 Pc. Butterflies Metal Nesting Cutter Set, p. 202; Oval, Round Cut-Outs, p. 151; Meringue Powder, p. 143; Parchment Triangles, p. 136; cornstarch, black shoestring licorice, knife, ruler

In advance: Make cookies. Prepare and roll out dough. For each treat cut 1 large butterfly, 1 round and 1 oval using largest cutters from sets plus 1 medium oval. Bake and cool. Set cookies on cooling grid over cookie sheet. Working with 1 color at a time, cover with thinned royal icing (p. 128). Immediately pipe on lighter orange dots or darker violet stripes. Let dry overnight.

Use full-strength icing to decorate and assemble cookies. Pipe tip 3 dot eye; flatten with finger dipped in cornstarch. Using tip 2, outline and pipe in eyelid; pipe dot pupils, nos and cheeks; outline mouth and add curved lashes. Let dry. Cut 1½ in. lengths of licorice. Attach to back of head. Pipe tip 2 balls on tips Let dry. Attach body and medium oval, center oval above body to support head. Attach hea Each serves 1.

*Combine Violet with Rose for violet shades shown. Combine Leaf Green with Lemon Yellow for green show

▶ The Garden Girls

Pans: Silicone Round Brownie Pops Mold, p. 171; Cookie Sheet, Cooling Grid, p. 203

Colors:* Violet, Rose, Lemon Yellow, Golden Yellow, Brown, Red-Red, Black, Copper (for light skin tone shown), Leaf Green, p. 146

Fondant: White Ready-To-Use Rolled Fondant (6 oz. per treat), Fine Tip FoodWriter Edible Color Markers (black), p. 147; 9 in. Rolling Pin, Roll & Cut Mat, p. 148; Brush Set, p. 149; Leaf Cut-Outs, p. 151

Recipes: Buttercream Icing, p. 116; Thinned Fondant Adhesive, p. 117; Favorite brownie recipe or mix

Also: Cake Boards, p. 241; knife, ruler, waxed paper, cornstarch

See instructions on p. 121.

*Combine Violet with Rose for violet shown. Combine Lemon Yellow with Golden Yellow for yellow shown. Combine Brown with Red-Red for darker skin tone shown. Combine Leaf Green with Lemon Yellow for green shown.

▼ Spritely Celebration

Pans: Dimensions Large Cupcake, p. 164; 4 Pc. Oval Set (2nd largest pan used), p. 156; Silicone Round Brownie Pops Mold, p. 171; Cookie Sheet, Cooling Grid, p. 203

Tips: 2, 3, 16, p. 134-135

Colors:* Leaf Green, Rose, Violet, Orange, Lemon Yellow, Golden Yellow, Red-Red, Christmas Red, p. 146

Fondant: White Ready-To-Use Rolled Fondant (55 oz.), Natural Colors Fondant Multi Pack (pink for skin tone shown, black), p. 147; 20 in. Rolling Pin, Roll & Cut Mat, Easy-Glide Fondant Smoother, p. 148; Brush Set, p. 149; Floral Collection Flower Making Set, Round and Heart Cut-Outs, p. 151

Recipes: Buttercream Icing, p. 116; Thinned Fondant Adhesive, p. 117; favorite brownie recipe or mix

Also: 4 in. Lollipop Sticks, p. 198; Cake Boards, Circles, Fanci-Foil Wrap, p. 241; Dowel Rods, p. 239; White Sparkling Sugar, p. 144; Piping Gel, p. 143; black shoestring licorice, scissors, tape, ruler, knife, cornstarch, waxed paper

In advance: Tint all fondant and make flowers and wings (p. 121). **Also:** Make brownie pop fairies. Bake and cool pops in silicone mold supported by Cookie Sheet. Prepare and cover with rolled fondant. Decorate (p. 121). **And:** Prepare base board. Using pan as a guide, cut 2 Cake Boards ½ in. wider than pan on all sides. Tape together and wrap with foil (p. 110).

Bake and cool 1-layer oval cake; ice smooth. Bake and cool 2-piece cupcake. Cut 2 in. off top half; position base upside down. Prepare and cover with rolled fondant (p. 116). Reserve excess yellow. Prepare cakes for Stacked Construction (p. 114), positioning house toward back of oval for 3 in. clearance in front. Make and attach house trims (p. 121). Pipe tip 16 pull-out grass around house and bottom border. Position flowers. Position fairies. Serves 27.

*Combine Lemon Yellow with Golden Yellow for yellow shown. Combine Violet with Rose for violet shades shown. Combine Red-Red with Christmas Red for red shown.

▲ Potted Pops

Pans: Dimensions Multi-Cavity Mini Flower Baskets, p. 164; Non-Stick Cookie Sheet, p. 165

Color: Leaf Green, p. 146

Candy: White Candy Melts (1 pk. makes 2 treats), p. 194; Garden (pink, violet), Primary (yellow) Candy Color Sets, p. 195; Dancing Daisies Lollipop Mold, p. 197; 4 in. Lollipop Sticks, p. 198; Decorator Brush Set, p.149

Recipes: Favorite crisped rice cereal treats

Also: Pastry Brush, p. 153; Cake Circles, p. 241; shredded coconut, knife, ruler, zip-close plastic bag

In advance: Mold 7 lollipops per treat using Painting Method (p. 128). Chill until firm. **Also:** Make candy baskets. Spoon ¼ cup melted candy into basket cavity; immediately brush candy all the way up sides using pastry brush. Chill until firm. Repeat. Chill completely then unmold. Smooth top edge by sliding over warmed Cookie Sheet.

Prepare cereal treat mixture. Let cool to touch. While still soft, press into prepared baskets to within ½ in. of top edge. Let cool completely. Insert pops, trimming sticks to vary heights. Tint coconut (p. 120). Sprinkle inside basket. Each serves 1.

◄ Birthday Girl's Galaxy

Pan: Star, p. 162

Tips: 1, 1A, 12, p. 134

Colors:* Lemon Yellow, Rose, Copper (for skin tone shown), Brown, Black, Red-Red, p. 146

Fondant: White Ready-To-Use Rolled Fondant (54 oz.), p. 147; Star Power Fondant Imprint M 20 in. Rolling Pin, Roll & Cut Mat, Easy-Glide Fondant Smoother, p. 148; Brush Set, p. 149

Recipe: Buttercream Icing, p. 116

Also: 2011 Pattern Book (Princess), p. 130; Star Plastic Nesting Cutter Set, p. 201; Yellow Colored Sugar, p. 144; Piping Gel, p. 143; Cake Circles, Fanci-Foil Wrap, p. 241; knife, cornstarch, waxed paper, ruler

Bake and cool cake. Prepare and cover with whi rolled fondant (p. 117). Tint fondant: 18 oz. yellow, 4 oz. skin tone, 4 oz. brown, 2 oz. light pink, 1 oz. dark pink, 1 oz. black. Roll out yellow ⅛ in. thick. Cut 14 in. diameter circle; set on Imprint Mat and imprint design. Using Star Pan as pattern, cut star shape. Cut yellow stars using smallest and 2nd smallest cutters from set (5 each). Brush imprinte designs and individual stars with Piping Gel; sprinkle with Colored Sugar. Attach imprinted sta to cake top using damp brush. For girl, roll out ski tone, brown and light pink fondant ³⁄₁₆ in. thick. Us pattern to cut head, hair and crown; position on cake top. Roll out remaining dark pink, black and brown ⅛ in. thick. Cut ⅛ in. wide strips and positi for smile, crown loop and hair details; attach usin damp brush. Using tip 12, cut eyes with narrow en cheeks with wide end; attach. Cut 1 tip 12 dot and 4 tip 1A dots for crown tips; attach. Serves 12.

*Combine Brown with Red-Red for brown shown.

▲ Cookie Pop Princesses

Pans: Cookie Sheet, Cooling Grid, p. 203

Candy: White, Yellow, Light Cocoa Candy Melts, p. 194; Primary (orange, red), Garden (black) Candy Color Sets, p. 195; Candy Melting Plate, p. 197

Recipe: Roll-Out Cookies, p. 116

Also: Princess Icing Decorations, p. 173; Star Plastic Nesting Cutter Set, p. 201; 8 in. Cookie Treat Sticks, p. 203; Yellow Sparkling Sugar, p. 144; Parchment Triangles, p. 136; Cake Boards, p. 241; waxed paper

In advance: Make cookies. Prepare and roll out dough. Cut stars using 3rd smallest cutter from set. Bake and cool cookies. Cover with melted yellow candy (p. 128). Let set 3-5 minutes, then sprinkle on Sparkling Sugar. Chill until firm. Attach Cookie Stick to back using melted candy. **Also:** Mold heads. Melt candy and tint for various skin tones. For heads, fill Candy Melting Plate cavities; chill until firm.

Decorate and assemble using melted candy in cut parchment bags. Set heads on waxed paper-covered cake board. Pipe curly hair; attach crown icing decorations. Pipe dot eyes and outline smile. Let set. Attach to cookie. Each serves 1.

▶ Skate and Celebrate!

Pan: Skate, p. 162

Tips: 1A, 3, 6, 8, 12, 18, p. 134-135

Colors:* Violet, Rose, Black, p. 146

Recipe: Buttercream Icing, p. 116

Also: Cake Boards, Fanci-Foil Wrap, p. 241; cornstarch

Bake and cool cake. Ice wheels, tongue and background areas smooth. Pipe tip 1A dot wheel centers; flatten and smooth with finger dipped in cornstarch. Use tip 3 to outline tongue and pipe bead flower with dot center on axles. Pipe in heel and platform with tip 12. Cover skate with tip 18 stars. Pipe tip 8 bow, tails and laces. Pipe tip 12 dot buttons; flatten and smooth with finger dipped in cornstarch. Pipe tip 3 pull-out pompoms in alternating colors. Print tip 6 name. Serves 12.

*Combine Violet with Rose for violet shades shown.

◄ Colorfully Crowned

Pans: Cookie Sheet, Cooling Grid, p. 203

Tips: 1, 2, 10, p. 134

Colors:* Rose, Violet, Sky Blue, Lemon Yellow, Golden Yellow, Copper (for light skin tone shown), Brown, Black, Christmas Red, p. 146

Fondant: White Ready-To-Use Rolled Fondant (12 oz. makes 4-5 treats), p. 147; 9 in. Rolling Pin, Roll & Cut Mat, p. 148; Brush Set, p. 149; Round Cut-Outs, p. 151

Recipes: Color Flow Icing, Roll-Out Cookies, p. 116

Also: 2011 Pattern Book (Hair, Bangs, Bow Loop, Knot), p. 130; Princess Candy Pick Mold (crown), p. 173; 4 Pc. Party Cutter Set (hat), p. 202; Color Flow Mix, p. 143; Cake Boards, p. 241; Parchment Triangles, p. 136; scissors, cornstarch, ruler, knife, waxed paper

In advance: Make cookies. Prepare and roll out dough. For each treat, cut 1 party hat (bottom becomes scalloped skirt) using cutter from set and 1 brace, ½ x 1½ in. Bake and cool. Outline hat cookies using tip 2 and full-strength icing; flow in using thinned icing (p. 128). Let dry 24 hours. **Also:** Make fondant features (p. 121).

Assemble and decorate cookies using full-strength icing. Position brace cookie at tip of hat. Attach head and crown. Attach arms. For belt, cut ¼ x 2¼ in. strip; attach. Use pattern to cut 2 bow loops; use narrow end of tip 10 to cut knot. Attach. Cut ⅛ in. wide strip for scalloped trim; attach. Pipe tip 1 dot and outline smile, crown details, facial features (flatten cheeks slightly), necklace and dress trim. Let dry. Each serves 1.

*Combine Violet with Rose for violet shades shown. Combine Brown with Christmas Red for brown shades shown. Combine Lemon Yellow with Golden Yellow for yellow shown.

► Rope-Skippin' Kitten

Pan: Ballerina Bear, p. 161

Tips: 3, 7, 16, 126, p. 134-135

Colors:* Violet, Rose, Lemon Yellow, Black, p. 146

Fondant: White Ready-To-Use Rolled Fondant (4 oz.), p. 147; 9 in. Rolling Pin, Roll & Cut Mat, p. 148; Alphabet/Numbers Cut-Outs, p. 151

Recipe: Buttercream Icing, p. 116

Also: 13 x 19 in. Cake Boards, Fanci-Foil Wrap, p. 241; cornstarch, ruler, knife

In advance: Prepare base board. Use pan as a guide; allow an extra 4 in. above head to hold jump rope and name. Cut and wrap Cake Board (p. 110).

Bake and cool cake. Trim ears for triangular shape. Ice cake sides and background areas smooth. Use tip 3 to outline and fill in eyes, nose, mouth and inner ears; pat smooth with fingertip dipped in cornstarch. Outline body, dress and shoes using tip 3. Cover with tip 16 stars. Pipe tip 126 ruffle. Pipe tip 7 waistband; pat smooth. Pipe tip 3 bead heart tongue and buttons. Pipe tip 7 bead bottom border. Tint fondant rose. Roll out small amount ⅛ in. thick; use alphabet cutters from set to cut out name; position on prepared board. Roll remaining fondant into 22 in. long x ½ in. diameter rope; position on board with ends in hands. Pipe tip 3 outlines over rope for fingers; cover fingers with tip 16 stars. Serves 12.

*Combine Violet with Rose for violet shown.

► Jumping Kitty Cookies

Pans: Cookie Sheet, Cooling Grid, p. 203

Tips: 2, 3, 7, p. 134

Colors:* Violet, Rose, Black, p. 146

Recipes: Color Flow Icing, Roll-Out Cookies, p. 116

Also: Teddy Bear Comfort-Grip Cutter, p. 200; Color Flow Mix, p. 143, Ready-To-Use Gum Paste (1 oz. per treat), p. 147; Parchment Triangles, p. 136; Cake Boards, p. 241; waxed paper, cornstarch

In advance: Make cookies. Prepare and roll out dough. Cut cookies using bear cutter, trim ears to point; bake and cool. Use tip 3 to outline cookies with full-strength icing; flow in with thinned icing (p. 128). Let dry on waxed paper-covered boards.

Decorate with full-strength color flow. Using tip 3 to outline and fill in shirt and skirt; pat smooth with finger dipped in cornstarch. Pipe in inside ears with tip 2. Pipe tip 3 outline suspenders and waistband. Add tip 2 bead hearts on suspenders. Pipe tip 7 ball muzzle, tip 2 dot nose and whiskers, outline mouth and eyes. Pipe in tip 3 bow and dot knot. Tint gum paste rose and roll a 9 x ¼ in. diameter rope. Curve rope and position on arms. Pipe tip 3 bead paws. Each serves 1.

*Combine Violet with Rose for violet shown.

◄ Sassy Shades

Pan: 10 x 2 in. Round, p. 157

Tip: 1A, p. 134

Colors:* Lemon Yellow, Golden Yellow, Rose, Viol█ Black, Copper (for skin tone shown), p. 146

Fondant: White Ready-To-Use Rolled Fondant (49 oz.), p. 147; 20 in. Rolling Pin, Roll & Cut Mat, Easy-Glide Fondant Smoother, p. 148; Brush Set, p. 149; Star Cut-Outs, p. 151

Recipes: Buttercream Icing, p. 116; Thinned Fondant Adhesive, p. 117

Also: 2011 Pattern Book (Sunglasses, Hair, Ponytail, Ear), p. 130; Pink, Lavender Sugars, p. 144; Piping Gel, p. 143; 4 in. Lollipop Sticks, p. 198; 13 x 19 in. Cake Boards, Circles, Fanci-Foil Wrap, p. 241; knife, cornstarch, ruler, scissors, tape

In advance: Prepare base board. Use cake pan, ponytail and ear patterns to trace shape. Cut out board and wrap with foil (p. 110). **Also:** Prepare fondant trims (p. 121).

Bake and cool 1-layer cake. Roll out fondant ⅛ thick unless otherwise specified. Prepare and cover cake with rolled fondant (p. 117). Make bangs and hair details (p. 121). Insert ears in ca█ sides, securing with fondant adhesive. Roll out violet ⅛ in. thick. Cut 2 earrings using medium s█ Cut-Out and a 1¼ x 2½ in. strip for ponytail ban█ Brush earrings and sunglasses with Piping Gel and sprinkle with colored sugars; attach. Positi█ sunglasses. For nose, roll ¾ in. ball. For smile, c█ ⅛ x 4 in. strip. For cheeks, cut 2 circles using w█ end of tip 1A. Attach features. Serves 14.

*Combine Lemon Yellow with Golden Yellow for yellow█ shown. Combine Violet with Rose for violet shown.

▼ Go Girls!

Pan: 9 x 13 x 2 in. Sheet, p. 157

Tips: 2A, 12, p. 134

Colors:* Orange, Rose, Violet, Lemon Yellow, Red-Red, Golden Yellow, Black, p. 146

Fondant: White Ready-To-Use Rolled Fondant (42 oz. for 4), Fine Tip FoodWriter Edible Color Markers (black), Gum-Tex, p. 147; 9 in. Rolling Pin, Roll & Cut Mat, p. 148; 10 Pc. Fondant/Gum Paste Tool Set, Silver Pearl Dust, Brush Set, p. 149

Recipes: Buttercream Icing, p. 116; Thinned Fondant Adhesive, p. 117

Also: Mini Doll Picks, p. 160; Cake Boards, p. 241; Clear Vanilla Extract, p. 143; knife, ruler, waxed paper, small rubber bands, cornstarch

In advance: Prepare fondant and make windshield and steering wheel (p. 121).

Bake and cool cake using firm-textured batter such as pound cake. Cut a 2½ x 4½ in. rectangle for each treat. Make cars (p. 121). Cut picks off bottom of dolls. Arrange hair in ponytail; secure with rubber band. Cover with thin strip of fondant. Cut and attach 1 x 2½ in. strip to cover bodice; trim to fit. Attach ¼ in. wide strips for shoulder straps. Cut ¾ x ¼ in. strips; cut and shape for sunglasses. Use black FoodWriter to draw in lenses. Attach to face and add thin strips for side pieces. Roll a ¼ in. ball of black fondant; shape and attach for steering column. Attach steering wheel and windshield using fondant adhesive. Position driver. Each serves 1.

*Combine Violet with Rose for violet shown. Combine Lemon Yellow with Golden Yellow for yellow shown.

▲ Posing on Pops

Pan: Non-Stick Cookie Sheet, p. 165

Candy: White, Light Cocoa Candy Melts, p. 194; Primary (yellow, orange), Garden (green and black) Candy Color Sets, p. 195; 2 Pack Girl Pov█ Candy Mold Set (glasses), p. 196; 6 in. Lollipop Sticks, p. 198; Decorator Brush Set, p. 197

Also: Circle Metal Cutter, p. 202; Parchment Triangles, p. 136; Cake Boards, p. 241; waxe█ paper, ruler

In advance: Make candy glasses. Use Painting or Piping Method (p. 128) to cover lens areas; fill frames (but not earpieces). **Also:** Make candy heads. Set Circle Cutter on non-stick pan. Fill ¼ in█ deep with melted candy. Tap to settle; chill until fir█

Set head on waxed paper-covered board. Usin█ melted candy in cut parchment bags, outline a█ fill in hair; chill until firm. Overpipe thin outline details. Pipe dot nose and outline smile. Attach glasses. Chill until firm. Attach Lollipop Stick to back using melted candy. Chill until Set. Each serves 1.

◄ Prepping the Princess

Pan: Classic Wonder Mold, p. 160

Tips: 1, 2, p. 134

Colors:* Rose, Leaf Green, Sky Blue, Violet, Orange, Lemon Yellow, Copper (for skin tone shown), Black, p. 146

Fondant: White Ready-To-Use Rolled Fondant (48 oz.), Fine Tip FoodWriter Edible Color Markers (black), Gum-Tex, p. 147; Happy Birthday Fondant Imprint Mat, 20 in. Rolling Pin, Roll & Cut Mat, p. 148; Orchid Pink Pearl Dust, Brush Set, p. 149

Recipes: Buttercream, Royal Icings, p. 116; Thinned Fondant Adhesive, p. 117

Also: 2011 Pattern Book (Sleeves, Wings, Front Tie Dry Line), p. 130; Teen Doll Pick, p. 160; 6 in. Lollipop Sticks, p. 198; Meringue Powder, p. 143; Flowerful Medley 6-Mix Sprinkles (confetti), p. 144; Cake Circles, Fanci-Foil Wrap, p. 241; 28-gauge wire (3 in.), cornstarch, ruler, knife, scissors, tape

2-3 days in advance: Make curved front tie. Tape dry line pattern to Cake Board to achieve correct curve; cover with waxed paper. Tint 3 oz. fondant rose. Roll out small amount ⅛ in. thick; reserve remainder for decorators. Cut a 3½ x ⅜ in. strip. Stand on edge over pattern and let dry 24 hours. **Also:** Make fondant decorators (p. 122).

Bake and cool cake. Roll out white fondant ⅜ in. thick. Use Imprint Mat to imprint design (p. 148). Prepare and cover cake with rolled fondant (p. 117). Cover Doll Pick with fondant; use knife to cut and shape bodice. Use pattern to cut 2 sleeves; raise arms and attach sleeves using damp brush. Style hair and secure with wire. Insert pick into cake. Use tip 1 and buttercream to fill in imprinted details using assorted colors. Pat larger areas smooth. Attach confetti over dots. Roll out reserved rose fondant ⅛ in. thick. Cut two 4 x ⅜ in. strips; attach one for waistband, the other for curved back tie. Insert decorators. Serves 12.

*Combine Violet with Rose for violet shown.

► Diva's Debut

Pan: 12 x 2 in. Round, p. 157

Tips: 2A, 3, p. 134

Colors:* Violet, Royal Blue, Black, Lemon Yellow, Golden Yellow, Sky Blue, Orange, Leaf Green, Rose, p. 146

Fondant: White Ready-To-Use Rolled Fondant (72 oz.), Gum-Tex, p. 147; 20 in. Rolling Pin, Roll & Cut Mat, Easy-Glide Fondant Smoother, p. 148; Pink, Silver, Gold Pearl Dust, Brush Set, p. 149; Alphabet/Number, Star Cut-Outs, p. 151

Recipes: Buttercream Icing, p. 116; Thinned Fondant Adhesive, p. 117

Also: 2011 Pattern Book (Crowd Silhouette, Small, Medium, Large Back Panels), p. 130; Mini Doll Picks, p. 160; Orange, Pink, Lavender, Blue, Yellow, Black Colored Sugars, White, Orange Cake Sparkles, p. 144; Piping Gel, Clear Vanilla Extract, p. 143; 11¾ in. Lollipop Sticks, p. 198; 14 in. Silver Cake Base, Cake Circles, Boards, p. 241; scissors, tape, ruler, knife, cornstarch, waxed paper, 28-gauge cloth-covered wire (8 in.)

2-3 days in advance: Prepare panels and stars (p. 121). **Also:** Decorate figures (p. 121).

Bake and cool 2-layer cake (bake 1½ in. layers for a 3 in. high cake). Tint fondant: 24 oz. violet, 17 oz. black. Prepare and cover cake with violet fondant (p. 117). Cut 12 in. diameter black circle; attach to cake top using damp brush. Use pattern to cut out 2 sets of silhouettes; attach to front of cake. For spotlight bases, roll out black ¼ in. thick. Cut 8 circles using wide end of tip 3. Shape small cones and attach to back to prop up bases at an angle. Roll out yellow ¹⁄₁₆ in. thick. Use narrow end of tip 2A to cut 8 lenses; attach to spotlights and slightly indent centers with rounded end of brush handle. Pipe tip 3 bead border between figures.

At party: Insert back panels and figures. Arrange spotlights. Serves 40.

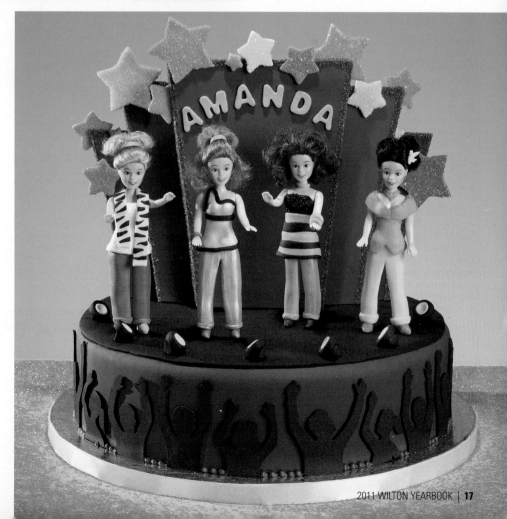

*Combine Violet with Royal Blue for violet shown. Combine Leaf Green with Lemon Yellow for green shown.

◄ Cookies for the Kickoff

Pans: Cookie Sheet, Cooling Grid, p. 203

Tip: 3, p. 134

Colors: Royal Blue, Brown, Orange, Lemon Yellow, Violet, p. 146

Recipes: Royal Icing, Roll-Out Cookies, p. 116

Also: Football Colored Metal Cutter Set, p. 202; Meringue Powder, p. 143; 6 in. Lollipop Sticks, p. 198; Cake Boards, p. 241; Parchment Triangles, p. 136; waxed paper

In advance: Make cookies. Prepare and roll out dough. Cut cookies using cutters from set. Bake and cool cookies. Outline with tip 3 and full-strength icing; flow in with thinned icing (p. 128). Let dry on waxed paper-covered boards.

Using full-strength icing, pipe tip 3 outline details, names and numbers.; attach Lollipop Sticks to back of pennants. Let dry. Each serves 1.

◄ Cornerback Cake

Pans: Helmet, p. 162; 9 x 2 in. Round, p. 157

Tips: 1, 2A, p. 134

Colors:* Lemon Yellow, Golden Yellow, Black, Copper (for skin tone shown), p. 1

Fondant: White Ready-To-Use Rolled Fondant (24 oz.), p. 147; 20 in. Rolling Pin, Roll Cut Mat, Easy-Glide Fondant Smoother, p. 148; Brush Set, p. 149

Recipe: Buttercream Icing, p. 116

Also: Red (2 pks.), White Candy Melts, p. 194; A-B-C and 1-2-3 50 Pc. Cutter Set p. 201; Parchment Triangles, p. 136; ruler, knife, cornstarch

In advance: Make candy plaque helmet. Use melted white candy in cut parchment bag to fill earpiece and face guard sections of cake pan; chill until firm. Overpipe face guard for strength; chill. Fill helmet area with red candy to ¾ in. deep. Chill until firm.

Bake and cool 1-layer round cake. Prepare and cover with 16 oz. skin tone fondant (p. 117). Position candy helmet on cake. Tint 4 oz. fondant yellow, ¼ oz. black; reserve ¼ oz. white. Roll out ⅛ in. thick as needed. Cut number using small size cutter from set; attach using damp brush. Cut 1 x 8 in. long stripe; attach, trimming as needed. Cut eye with wide end of tip 1. Cut pupil with narrow end of tip 2A; cut 1 in. long eyebrow. Roll 1 in. ball nose. Attach features. Cake serves 1

*Combine Lemon Yellow with Golden Yellow for yellow shown.

▶ Black Belt Birthday

Pans: Teddy Bear, p. 161; Cookie Sheet, Cooling Grid, p. 203

Tips: 1A, 3, 16, 18, p. 134-135

Colors: Black, Red-Red, Copper (for skin tone shown), p. 146

Recipes: Buttercream, Royal Icings, Roll-Out Cookies, p. 116

Also: 2011 Pattern Book (Hand, Foot, Headband Tie), p. 130; Meringue Powder, p. 143; 4 in. Lollipop Sticks, p. 198; Cake Boards, Fanci-Foil Wrap, p. 241; cornstarch, knife, ruler

In advance: Make and decorate cookies with royal icing. Prepare and roll out dough. Use patterns to cut 2 hands (reverse pattern for 2nd; fold over thumb of left hand), 2 feet (reverse pattern for 2nd) and 1 tie. Use wide end of tip 1A to cut 1 circle; cut in half for 2 ears. Bake and cool cookies. Cover hands and feet with tip 16 stars. Let dry on waxed paper-covered boards. Outline and pipe in headband ties; let dry. Attach Lollipop Sticks to back of hands with royal icing, leaving 2½ in. of stick exposed to insert into cake. Let dry.

Bake and cool cake. Cut off ears. Decorate using buttercream icing. Using tip 3, outline and pipe in outfit edging, belt, headband, eyes, pupils, mouth, teeth; smooth with fingertip dipped in cornstarch. Pipe tip 3 outline details on outfit and headband. Cover outfit and head with tip 16 stars. Pipe tip 18 pull-out stars for hair. Insert hands. Insert ears; cover with tip 16 stars. Attach feet and headband ties with icing. Cake serves 12; each cookie serves 1.

◀ Ballpark Bouquet

Pan: Non-Stick Cookie Sheet, p. 165

Candy: * White, Peanut Butter, Green, Yellow, Light Cocoa, Red Candy Melts, p. 194; 10 Pack Candy Mold Set, p. 197; Primary Candy Color Set (blue), p. 195; 11¾ in. Lollipop Sticks, p. 198

Also: 2011 Pattern Book (Red and White Box Ovals), p. 130; Parchment Triangles, p. 136; Popcorn Treat Boxes, p. 217; White Ready-To-Use Rolled Fondant (5 oz. per treat), p. 147; Round Cut-Out, p. 151; red cardstock, red and black markers, popped popcorn, ruler, glue, pencil, scissors, knife, plastic wrap

In advance: Make candies. Tint candy assorted colors. Use Painting or Piping Method (p. 128) to mold candies in Sports Champ and Snack Time molds from 10 Pack Set. Chill until firm. For face, set medium round Cut-Out on non-stick pan. Fill ¼ in. deep with melted candy. Tap to settle; chill until firm. Pipe features using melted candy in cut parchment bag. Attach hat using melted candy; chill until firm. Attach sticks to backs using melted candy. Chill until firm.

Use red marker and ruler to draw vertical lines on Popcorn Boxes, beginning each line at bottom of scallop in top edge. Trace red oval on red card stock; Make copy of white oval pattern on white paper. Cut out ovals. Glue white oval to red oval. Use black marker to add message. Glue ovals to box. Wrap 5 oz. fondant in plastic wrap; place in bottom of box for weight. Fill to top with popcorn. Position candies, trimming sticks to vary heights. Fill to top with popcorn. Each candy serves 1.

*Combine Orange and White candy for skin tone shown. Combine Light Cocoa and Peanut Butter for dark brown shown. Combine White and Peanut Butter for medium and light brown shown.

▶ Play of the Day

Pans: Baseball Mitt, p. 162; 16 x 2 in. Round, p. 157

Colors: * Kelly Green, Leaf Green, p. 146

Fondant: White Ready-To-Use Rolled Fondant (80 oz.), p. 147; 20 in. Rolling Pin, Roll & Cut Mat, Easy-Glide Fondant Smoother, p. 148; Brush Set, p. 149

Candy: White and Peanut Butter (2 pks. each), Light Cocoa, Dark Cocoa, Red (1 pk. each) Candy Melts, p. 194; 10 Pack Candy Mold Set (alphabet), p. 197; Sports Large Lollipop Mold, p. 196

Recipe: Buttercream Icing, p. 116

Also: Cake Dividing Set, p. 136; ULTIMATE Cake Leveler, p. 152; Piping Gel, p. 143; Parchment Triangles, p. 136; Cake Circles, Fanci-Foil Wrap, p. 241; Baseball Topper Set, p. 181; 18 in. diameter foamcore circle (¼ in. thick), knife, ruler, toothpicks

In advance: Make candy plaque (p. 128) using mitt pan and Candy Melts: 5 oz. white, 2 oz. red, 2 oz. dark cocoa, 18 oz. peanut butter mixed with 2 oz. light cocoa for lighter brown shown. **Also:** Mold 12 candy baseballs using Piping Method (p. 128) and Lollipop Mold without sticks. Pipe red stitching after unmolding using melted candy in cut parchment bag. **And:** Mold candy message using alphabet mold from 10 pack set.

Bake and cool 2-layer cake (trim layers to 1½ in. for a 3 in. high cake) and place on foil-wrapped board. Prepare and cover cake with 72 oz. light green rolled fondant (p. 117); reserve excess green. Use Dividing Wheel to divide cake into 12ths. Attach baseball candies at marks using melted candy. Tint remaining green and 8 oz. white fondant dark green and roll out ⅛ in. thick. Cut 1 x 5 in. strips. Use knife to cut away triangular grass blades at upper edge, about ¾ in. deep. Roll strip and separate random blades. Attach around cake using Piping Gel. Repeat to complete border. Position candy plaque, message and players. Serves 77.

*Combine Leaf Green with Kelly Green for green shades shown.

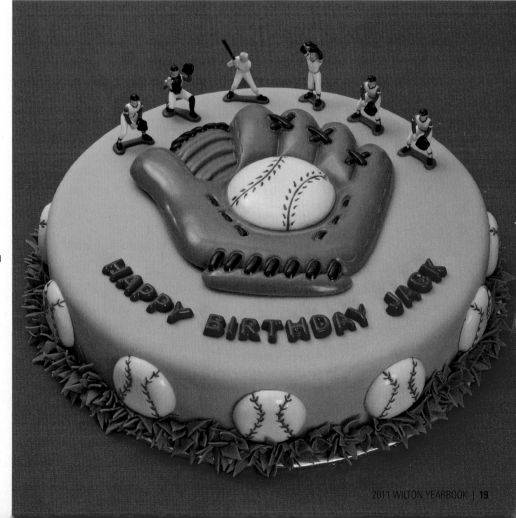

◄ Triple-Track Treat

Pans: 6, 8, 10 x 2 in. Round, p. 157; Cookie Sheet, Cooling Grid, p. 203
Tips: 1, 2, 3, 6, p. 134
Colors:* Sky Blue, Kelly Green, Leaf Green, Royal Blue, Christmas Red, Red-Red, Lemon Yellow, Orange, Violet, Rose, Brown, Black, p. 146
Fondant: White Ready-To-Use Rolled Fondant (56 oz.), Fine Tip Primary Colors FoodWriter Edible Color Markers (black), p. 147; 20 in. Rolling Pin, Roll & Cut Mat, Easy-Glide Fondant Smoother, p. 148; Brush Set, p. 149
Recipes: Buttercream, Royal Icings, Roll-Out Cookies, p. 116
Also: 101 Cookie Cutters, p. 201; Meringue Powder, Piping Gel, p. 143; Cake Dividing Set, p. 136; Pastry Brush, p. 153; Cakes 'N More 3-Tier Party Stand, p. 236; White Candy Melts, p. 194; 4 in. Lollipop Sticks, p. 198; Cake Boards, Circles, Fanci-Foil Wrap, p. 241; ULTIMATE Cake Leveler, p. 152; Parchment Triangles, p. 136; knife, ruler, waxed paper, cornstarch, toothpicks

2-3 days in advance: Make cookies. Prepare and roll out dough. Using cutters from set, cut 4 large trees, 2 small trees, 3 train engines (flip 1 before baking), 5 trucks (cut off cabs to make train cars). Bake and cool. Outline tree and train cookies using tip 6 and full-strength royal icing; flow in using thinned royal icing. Let dry 24 hours on waxed paper-covered boards. Pipe details using full-strength royal icing. Outline and fill-in windows; pipe tip 3 zigzag tree trunks, tip 6 dot headlights, tip 2 and tip 1 outline wheels and spokes. Let dry. Use melted candy to attach 2 Lollipop Sticks to each cookie. Let dry.

Bake and cool 2-layer cakes (bake 1½ in. high layers for 3 in. high cakes). Tint fondant: 32 oz. green, 24 oz. blue. Prepare cakes and cover with blue fondant (p. 117). Roll out green ⅛ in. thick. Use plates from stand to mark sizes; cut fondant to cover tops of plates and attach with Piping Gel, trimming as needed. For hills, cut 1¾ in. wide strips: one 19 in. long for 6 in. cake; two 13 in. long for 8 in. cake; two 16 in. long for 10 in. cake. Cut wavy top edge; attach to cake sides using damp brush. For tracks, mark 2 circles, 1 in. apart, on cake tops; begin outer circle ½ in. from outer edge. For ties, use Cake Dividing Wheel to divide 6 in. cake into 16ths, 8 in. and 10 in. cakes into 12ths (add an additional line in between for 24 lines). Cover marks using black FoodWriter. Pipe tip 6 message.

At party: Position cakes on stand. Position cookies. Pipe tip 6 bead borders. Serves 60.

*Combine Leaf Green with Lemon Yellow for lighter green shown. Combine Christmas Red with Red-Red for red shown. Combine Violet with Rose for violet shown.

► Underwater Wonders

Pans: First and Ten Football, p. 162; Cookie Sheet, Cooling Grid, p. 203
Tips: 2, 3, 8, 12, 16, p. 134-135
Colors:* Black, Violet, Orange, Leaf Green, Lemon Yellow, Rose, Royal Blue, Brown, Copper (for skin tone shown), Christmas Red, p. 146
Candy: White Candy Melts, p. 194; Primary (yellow, orange), Garden (pink, green, black) Candy Color Sets, p. 195; Sea Creatures Lollipop Mold, Decorator Brush Set, p. 197
Recipes: Buttercream, Color Flow Icings, Roll-Out Cookies, p. 116
Also: 2011 Pattern Book (Propeller, Periscope, Window), p. 130; Animal Pals 50 Pc. Cutter Set, p. 201; Color Flow Mix, p. 143; Parchment Triangles, p. 136; Cake Boards, Fanci-Foil Wrap, p. 241; knife, waxed paper, toothpicks, cornstarch

2-3 days in advance: Make and decorate cookies (p. 122). **Also:** Pipe bubbles. Use thinned color flow to pipe assorted puddle dots (p. 120), ¼ to ¾ in. using tip 3 and 1¾ in. diameter for name using tip 12, on waxed paper-covered board. Let dry 48 hours. Pipe tip 3 name. **And:** Mold candies. Use Painting or Piping Method (p. 128) and candy mold to make starfish, turtle and 3 fish. Pipe dot pupils and outline facial features after unmolding.

Bake and cool cake. Use icing to stack 2 propeller and 2 periscope cookies. Position next to cake. Use pattern to mark windows; ice areas smooth. Pipe tip 3 section lines. Outline windows with tip 12. Cover cake with tip 16 stars. Pipe tip 3 dot rivets; pipe lines and large dots (flatten with finger dipped in cornstarch) on periscope. Pipe tip 12 ball heads; flatten and smooth. Pipe tip 3 pull-out hair and dot eyes, pupils, nose and mouth; flatten with finger dipped in cornstarch. Position cookies, candies and bubbles. Cake serves 12; each cookie and candy serves 1.

*Combine Orange with Christmas Red for orange icing shown. Combine Leaf Green with Lemon Yellow for green icing shown. Combine Violet with Rose for light violet shown. Combine Violet with Royal Blue for dark violet shown. Combine Black with Violet and Royal Blue for blue/gray shark shown. Combine Brown with Christmas Red for brown shown.

▲ Treats Stop Traffic!

Pan: Standard Muffin, p. 158

Tip: 44, p. 135

Colors: * Royal Blue, Violet, Kelly Green, Rose, Black, p. 146

Fondant: White Ready-To-Use Rolled Fondant (12 oz.), Gum-Tex, p. 147; 9 in. Rolling Pin, Roll & Cut Mat, p. 148

Recipes: Buttercream, Royal Icings, p. 116

Also: 2011 Pattern Book (Building), p. 130; Wheels Icing Decorations (3 pks.), p. 174; 13 Count Standard Cupcakes 'N More Dessert Stand, p. 167; White Standard Baking Cups, p. 184; 4 in. Lollipop Sticks, p. 198; Meringue Powder, p. 143; Cake Boards, p. 241; knife, cornstarch, waxed paper

2-3 days in advance: Make buildings. Mix 1 teaspoon Gum-Tex into 12 oz. white fondant. Tint ⅓ each violet, blue, green. Roll out ⅛ in. thick. Use pattern to cut 13 buildings in various colors. Let dry overnight on waxed paper-covered boards dusted with cornstarch. Use royal icing to pipe tip 44 windows and doors. Let dry. Use royal icing to attach Lollipop Sticks to backs of buildings and backs of 13 stop sign Icing Decorations. Let dry.

Bake and cool cupcakes. Ice tops with gray buttercream. Insert buildings and stop signs; trim sticks as needed. Position vehicles. Position on stand. Each serves 1.

*Combine Violet with a little Rose for violet shown.

▼ Happy Hauling

Pans: Dump Truck, p. 163; Cookie Sheet, Cooling Grid, p. 203

Tips: 1, 2, 2A, 3, 5, 8, 18, 21, p. 134-135

Colors: * Christmas Red, Red-Red, Lemon Yellow, Golden Yellow, Royal Blue, Orange, Brown, Violet, Rose, Leaf Green, Black, Copper (for skin tone shown), p. 146

Recipes: Buttercream, Color Flow Icings, Roll-Out Cookies, p. 116

Also: A-B-C and 1-2-3 50 Pc. Cutter Set (number), p. 201; Square Cut-Outs, p. 151; Flowerful Medley 6-Mix Sprinkles (confetti), p. 144; White Candy Melts, p. 194; 4 in. Lollipop Sticks, p. 198; Tapered Spatula, p. 139; Color Flow Mix, p. 143; Cake Boards, Fanci-Foil Wrap, p. 247; Parchment Triangles, p. 136; curling ribbon, scissors, cornstarch, knife, ruler, waxed paper

1-2 days in advance: Make cookies. Prepare and roll out dough. Cut 2 medium and 4 large squares using cutters from set. Trim ½ in. off one large square to make rectangle. Cut out number using cutter from set. Bake and cool cookies. Using full-strength color flow, outline cookies with tip 3; flow in with thinned color flow (p. 128). Let dry overnight on waxed paper-covered boards. Decorate with full-strength color flow. Pipe tip 3 or tip 5 ribbons; pat smooth with fingertip dipped in cornstarch. Use tip 5 to pipe beads for bow loops and dot for center knot. Let dry. Attach Lollipop Sticks to backs using melted candy; allow stick to extend at bottom to insert into cake.

Bake and cool cake. Decorate truck (p. 122) using buttercream. Cake serves 12; each cookie serves 1.

*Combine Lemon Yellow with Golden Yellow for yellow shown. Combine Violet with Rose for violet shown. Combine Leaf Green with Lemon Yellow for green shown. Combine Brown with Red-Red for brown shown.

◀ Grabbing All the Goodies

Pans: Sports Ball Set, p. 162; Cookie Sheet, Cooling Grid, p. 203

Tip: 1M, p. 134

Colors: * Leaf Green, Lemon Yellow, Golden Yellow, Rose, Violet, Black, Royal Blue, p. 146

Fondant: White Ready-To-Use Rolled Fondant (50 oz.), p. 147; 20 in. Rolling Pin, Roll & Cut Mat, Easy-Glide Fondant Smoother, p. 148; Brush Set, p. 149

Recipe: Buttercream Icing, p. 116

Also: Pastel Round Silicone Baking Cups, p. 168; Lavender Candy Melts (2 pks.), p. 194; Flowerful Medley 6-Mix Sprinkles (confetti), p. 144; Soft Colors Round Candles, p. 183; Piping Gel, p. 143; Cake Boards, 16 in. Cake Circles (2), Fanci-Foil Wrap, p. 241; ice cream sugar cone, waxed paper, scissors, knife, tape, warming tray (optional), ruler, cornstarch

In advance: Make candy shell for head (p. 128). **Also:** Prepare base board. Tape two 16 in. Cake Circles together. Prepare and cover with 24 oz. blue fondant tinted (p. 120). **And:** Make fondant-covered hat (p. 122).

Bake and cool cupcakes in silicone cups supported by Cookie Sheet. Top with tip 1M icing swirl; sprinkle on confetti. Tint fondant: 16 oz. violet, 1 oz. black; reserve 3 oz. white. For each arm, roll 2 oz. fondant into a 10 in. long, slightly tapered rope; make 8 and position on board. Position candy shell flat side down in center. For features, shape 1½ x ½ in. thick eyes, ½ in. diameter flattened ball pupils and ¼ x 4½ in. rope smile. Attach features and hat using melted candy. Position cupcakes. Insert candles. Each serves 1.

*Combine Leaf Green with Lemon Yellow for green shown. Combine Lemon Yellow with Golden Yellow for yellow shown. Combine Violet with Rose and a little Black for violet shown.

◄ Celebrate with Shipmates

Pans: Soccer Ball, p. 162; Classic Wonder Mold, p. 160; 9 x 2 in. 2-Pa[n]
Round Set, p. 157

Tips: 3, 16, p. 134-135

Colors:* Royal Blue, Christmas Red, Red-Red, Leaf Green, Lemon
Yellow, Violet, Rose, Orange, Copper (for skin tone shown), Blac[k]
Ivory, p. 146

Fondant: White Ready-To-Use Rolled Fondant (168 oz.), Fine Tip
FoodWriter Edible Color Markers (black), p. 147; 20 in. Rolling Pi[n]
Roll & Cut Mat, Easy-Glide Fondant Smoother, p. 148; Brush Set,
p. 149; Leaf, Round Cut-Outs, p. 151

Recipe: Buttercream Icing, p. 116

Also: 2011 Pattern Book (Shoe, Eye Patch, Hand), p. 130; Pirate
Candy Pick Mold, p. 177; White Candy Melts, p. 194; Hidden
Pillars, p. 237; Piping Gel, p. 143; Pastry Brush, p. 153; Fanci-Foil
Wrap, p. 241; 26 x 20 in. plywood or foamcore board (½ in. thick)[,]
foil-wrapped candy coins (18), ruler, knife, cornstarch, toothpic[k,]
tape, scissors

In advance: Make candies (p. 128). Use melted candy to mold 18 skull[s]
and crossbones candies. Tap to settle; chill until firm. Cut off pick area[s.]
Also: Prepare base board. Tint fondant: 120 oz. blue, 24 oz. black. Roll
out ⅛ in. thick as needed. Cover board with blue fondant (p. 120). Cut
1¾ in. wide black strips; use damp brush to attach for border.

Bake and cool 1-layer cake (bake 9 in. round just 1 in. high). Positio[n]
Soccer Ball on board for head. Cut Wonder Mold in half vertically;
position half for upper body. Cut 9 in. round into 2 semi-circles; sta[ck]
with icing and attach cut side down under Wonder Mold for lower
body. Insert 2 pillars for legs, leaving 4 in. exposed; insert 2 pillars f[or]
arms, leaving 3½ in. exposed. Use patterns to mold fondant hands
1 in. thick and shoes 1¼ in. thick (flip patterns for opposite side). Fo[r]
parchment, tint 4 oz. fondant ivory (leave color slightly marbleized).
Roll out ⅛ in. thick. Cut a 6 x 4 in. section with irregular edges, sligh[t]
tears and ripples. Push shoes and hands onto dowel rods; position
parchment in 1 hand and fold fingers over. For bandana tie, roll out
fondant ½ in. thick, cut 2 leaves using largest Cut-Out and 1 round
using medium Cut-Out; attach to board using damp brush. For ear,
1 round using medium Cut-Out; trim to fit curve of head and attach [to]
board. Use medium round cutter to mark dots on scarf. Use pattern
and tip 3 to outline and fill in eye patch; smooth with fingertip. Use
tip 3 to outline and fill in eye and pupil; pat smooth. Pipe tip 3 outline[s]
mouth, eye patch string, shirt neckline and scarf edge. Cover cake
and features with tip 16 stars. Overpipe nose and belt with tip 16 sta[rs]
for dimension. Use FoodWriter to print message. Attach candies to
border using dots of melted candy. Serves 30.

*Combine Christmas Red with Red-Red for red shown. Combine Leaf Green w[ith]
Lemon Yellow for green shown. Combine Violet with Rose for violet shown.

► Buccaneer Headgear

Pan: Crown, p. 160
Color: Black, p. 146
Fondant: White Ready-To-Use Rolled Fondant (24 oz.),
p. 147; 20 in. Rolling Pin, Roll & Cut Mat, Easy-
Glide Fondant Smoother, p. 148; Brush Set, p. 149;
Alphabet/Number Cut-Outs, p. 151
Recipe: Buttercream Icing, p. 116
Also: 2011 Pattern Book (Skull Features), p. 130; 3 Pc.
Haunted Halloween Cutter Set (skull), p. 207; Cake
Boards, Fanci-Foil Wrap, p. 241; knife, cornstarch,
ruler, toothpicks

Bake and cool cake. Trim 1½ in. off bottom edge; trim off
crown points at left and right of center point. Prepare
and cover with 20 oz. fondant tinted black. Roll out white
fondant ⅛ in. thick. Cut a 26 x ½ in. wide strip. Attach
around edge of hat using damp brush; trim ends as
needed. Cut skull using cutter from set. Using pattern,
cut out facial features. Attach skull to hat. For bones, cut
2 strips, 3 x ¼ in. Attach 1; cut 2nd in half diagonally and
attach on sides of 1st bone. Roll 8 balls, ¼ in. diameter;
attach to bone ends. Use alphabet cutters to cut out
name; attach. Serves 12.

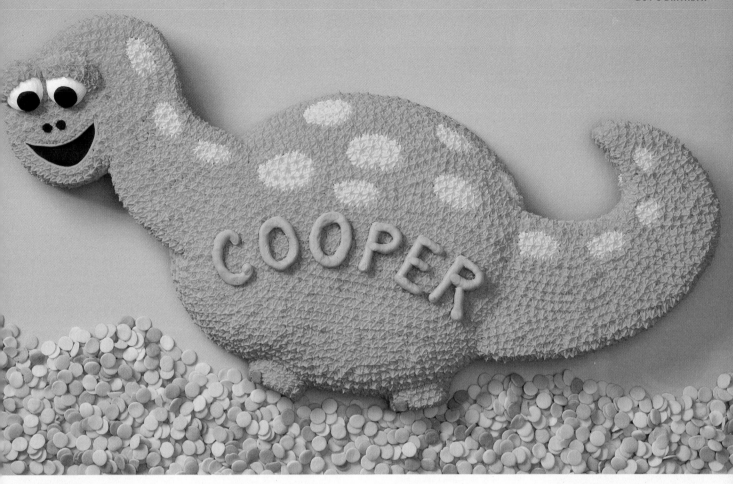

▲ Brontosaurus Birthday

Pans: Lady Bug, p. 161; Cookie Sheet, Cooling Grid, p. 203

Tips: 2A, 3, 4, 8, 18, p. 134-135

Colors:* Orange, Lemon Yellow, Golden Yellow, Violet, Rose, Leaf Green, Black, p. 146

Recipes: Buttercream Icing, Roll-Out Cookies, p. 116

Also: 2011 Pattern Book (Head, Tail), p. 130; Cake Boards, Fanci-Foil Wrap, p. 241; Jumbo Confetti Sprinkles, p. 144; 30 x 14 in. plywood or foamcore board (½ in. thick), knife, scissors, toothpicks, cornstarch

In advance: Make cookies. Prepare and roll out dough. Use patterns to cut 4 each heads and tails. Bake and cool. **Also:** Prepare base board. Use cake pan, head and tail patterns to mark shape of finished cake on board. Cut out and wrap with foil (p. 110).

Bake and cool cake. Position on prepared base board. Sandwich head and tail cookies with icing so finished stacks match height of cake. Attach to board with icing. Ice mouth smooth; pipe tip 4 outline. Use toothpick to mark various spots on back. Cover dinosaur with tip 18 stars; overpipe feet. Pipe tip 3 dot toenails; flatten. Pipe tip 2A eyeballs. Pipe tip 18 star lids. Add tip 4 dot pupils (flatten slightly) and nostrils. Pipe tip 8 name. Cake serves 12; each cookie serves 1.

*Combine Lemon Yellow with Golden Yellow for yellow shown. Combine Leaf Green with Lemon Yellow for green shown. Combine Violet with Rose for violet shown.

▶ Dino Cookie Delights

Pans: Cookie Sheet, Cooling Grid, p. 203

Tips: 2, 3, p. 134

Colors:* Sky Blue, Violet, Christmas Red, Leaf Green, Orange, Black, p. 146

Recipes: Color Flow Icing, Roll-Out Cookies, p. 116

Also: Dinosaur Plastic Cutter, p. 201; Color Flow Mix, p. 143; Cake Boards, p. 241; Parchment Triangles, p. 136; waxed paper

In advance: Make cookies. Prepare and roll out dough. Cut cookies using dinosaur cutter. Bake and cool. Use full-strength icing to pipe tip 3 outline; flow in with thinned icing (p. 128). Use lighter shade of thinned icing to immediately add assorted tip 2 dots for spots. Let dry on waxed paper-covered boards.

Use full strength icing to pipe tip 3 dot eye and tip 2 pupil. Each serves 1.

*Combine Violet with Rose for violet shown.

◀ **Sending Hissss Best**

Pan: Horseshoe, p. 162

Tips: 3, 21, p. 134-135

Colors:* Leaf Green, Lemon Yellow, Violet, Rose, Red-Red, Black, p. 146

Fondant: White Ready-To-Use Rolled Fondant (11 oz.), 9 in. Rolling Pin, Roll & Cut Mat, p. 147; Brush Set, p. 149

Recipe: Buttercream Icing, p. 116

Also: 2011 Pattern Book (Tongue), p. 130; Hot Colors Wavy "Trick" Sparklers, p. 183; Piping Gel, p. 143; Cake Boards, Fanci-Foil Wrap, p. 241; cornstarch, ruler, tape, scissors, knife, 20 x 14 in. plywood or foamcore board (¼ in. thick), sugar ice cream co candy-coated chocolates.

In advance: Make Hat (p. 122).

Bake and cool 2 cakes. Cut 6 in. off right-side end of each cake and trim other ends for rounded head and tail. Ice cut edges and attach cakes in S-shape Pipe tip 3 outline mouth. Use tip 21 stars to pipe 1¼ diameter dots over body; cover cake with tip 21 sta Tint fondant: ½ oz. black, 1½ oz. red; reserve 3 oz. white. For features, roll 1½ in. diameter eyes, ½ in. diameter pupils, ⅜ in. diameter nostrils; attach usin damp brush. Roll out red ⅛ in. thick. Use pattern to cut tongue. Attach under mouth. Attach candle wit piece of damp fondant. Position hat and chocolates Serves 20.

*Combine Leaf Green with Lemon Yellow for green shown Combine Violet with Rose for violet shown.

▼ A Surprise Before Your Eyes!

Pans: Cookie Sheet, Cooling Grid, p. 203

Tips: 2A, 3, 4, 5, 8, 12, 234, p. 134-135

Colors:* Orange, Leaf Green, Lemon Yellow, Royal Blue, Violet, Rose, Black, p. 146

Recipes: Royal Icing, Roll-Out Cookies, p. 116

Also: Daisy Comfort-Grip Cutter, p. 200; Blossom Nesting Cutter Set, p. 201; Meringue Powder, p. 143; Parchment Triangles, p. 136; White Candy Melts, p. 194; Cake Boards, p. 241; jellied fruit slices, colored licorice twists, scissors, waxed paper, knife, granulated sugar, cornstarch

In advance: Make cookies. Prepare and roll out dough. Cut bodies using daisy cutter and 2nd largest blossom cutter from set. Bake and cool. Also: Cover blossom cookies with icing. Outline cookie with tip 3 and full-strength icing; flow in with thinned icing (p.128). Let dry overnight.

To complete blossom cookies, with full-strength icing, pipe tip 2A ball eyes, tip 5 dot irises and tip 4 dot pupils. Pipe tip 8 outline eyelids, tip 12 dot nose. Outline mouth with tip 3; pipe in with thinned icing. Let set. For daisy cookies, pipe tip 234 pull-out fur, working from edge to center. Pipe tip 2A ball eye, tip 8 dot iris and tip 5 dot pupil and mouth. Let set. For all arms and legs, cut 3 in. lengths of licorice. Flatten fruit slices slightly and cut shapes for hands and feet with knife. Cut a small slit and insert on licorice. Attach to cookie backs with melted candy. Each serves 1.

*Combine Leaf Green with Lemon Yellow for green shown. Combine Violet with Rose for violet shown.

▲ A Rainbow of Boas

Pans: Cookie Sheet, Cooling Grid, p. 203

Tips: 2, 7, p. 134

Colors:* Sky Blue, Lemon Yellow, Orange, Violet, Rose, Christmas Red, Leaf Green, Black, p. 146

Recipes: Color Flow Icing, Roll-Out Cookies, p. 116

Also: A-B-C and 1-2-3 50 Pc. Cutter Set, p. 201; Color Flow Mix, p. 143; Parchment Triangles, p. 136; Cake Boards, p. 241; waxed paper

In advance: Make cookies. Prepare and roll out dough. Cut snakes using "S" cutter from set. Bake and cool. Cover cookies with thinned icing (p. 128). Immediately pipe on stripes or dots using a lighter color. Let dry 24 hours on waxed paper-covered boards.

Use full-strength icing to pipe tip 7 dot eyes, tip 2 dot pupils and nostrils. Let dry. Each serves 1.

*Combine Violet with Rose for violet shades shown.

▲ Brownie Bogeymen

Pans: Silicone Round Brownie Pops Mold, p. 171; Cookie Sheet, Cooling Grid, p. 203

Tips: 12, p. 134-135

Colors:* Violet, Leaf Green, Orange, Rose, Lemon Yellow, Black, p. 146

Fondant: White Ready-To-Use Rolled Fondant (1¼ oz. per treat), p. 147; 9 in. Rolling Pin, Roll & Cut Mat, p. 148; Brush Set, p. 149

Recipes: Buttercream Icing, p. 116; favorite brownie recipe or mix

Also: White Candy Melts (2 oz. per treat), p. 194; Primary (orange), Garden (violet, green, black) Candy Color Sets, p. 195; pretzel sticks, knife, rule

In advance: Prepare pops. Bake and cool brownie pops in silicone mold supported by Cookie Sheet. Cover pops with melted, tinted candy (p. 128). Repeat 2-3 times for smooth finish. Let set.

Decorate treats with fondant (p. 122).

*Combine Violet with Rose for violet shown. Combine Leaf Green with Lemon Yellow for green shown.

◄ Hobgoblin Hug!

Pan: Stand-Up Cuddly Bear Set, p. 161
Tips: 2A, 5, 16, p. 134-135
Colors:* Leaf Green, Lemon Yellow, Violet, Rose, Royal Blue, Orange, Black, p. 146
Fondant: White Ready-To-Use Rolled Fondant (17 oz.), p. 147; 9 in. Rolling Pin, Roll & Cut Mat, p. 148; Brush Set, p. 149
Recipe: Buttercream Icing, p. 116
Also: Wooden Dowel Rods (two 5 in. lengths), p. 239; Cake Circles, Fanci-Foil Wrap, p. 241; scissors, tape, ruler, cornstarch, toothpicks, knife

Bake and cool cake using firm-textured batter such as pound cake. Trim off arms and face; ice cut areas lightly to contain crumbs. Pipe tip 2A ball eyes; flatten and smooth with fingertip dipped in cornstarch. Using tip 5, pipe dot pupils; pipe in mouth and teeth, pat smooth. Tint fondant: 2 oz. blue, 3 oz. light purple, 4 oz. each yellow, dark purple, green. For nose, roll 1 in. ball; attach. For soles of feet, roll out yellow and a small amount of dark purple ⅛ in. thick. Cut 3¼ x 2¼ in. yellow ovals; attach with icing. Cut about 14 dots using narrow end of tip 2A; attach using damp brush. Roll 6 cone-shaped toenails 1 in. long; attach with icing. For 3½ in. long tapered horns, roll flattened disks in alternating colors, beginning with a 1½ in. diameter circle, ½ in. thick, and ending with a ¾ in. high tip. Mark a 4 in. diameter circle on belly with tip 16 stars. Cover body with tip 16 pull-out star fur. For arms, cover dowel rod with 1 x 1½ in. fondant strip, leaving 3 in. and ½ in. of rod exposed on either side of fondant. For hands, begin with a rounded triangle 2 in. high, ½ in. thick. Cut slits 1 in. deep and separate fingers. Push onto exposed ½ in. of arm. Roll and attach ⅝ in. long cone nails using damp brush. Insert arms into cake. Roll ¼ in. diameter log for number; shape and attach. Serves 12.

*Combine Lemon Yellow with Leaf Green for green shown. Combine Violet with Rose for violet shades shown.

► Mesmerized Monster

Pan: Princess Carriage, p. 160
Tips: 2, 3, 5, 8, 12, 21, p. 134-135
Colos:* Violet, Rose, Lemon Yellow, Golden Yellow, Leaf Green, Orange, Royal Blue, Red-Red, Black, p. 146
Fondant: White Ready-To-Use Rolled Fondant (11 oz.), Gum-Tex, p. 147; 9 in. Rolling Pin, Roll & Cut Mat, p. 148; Brush Set, p. 149; Cutter/Embosser, p. 150
Recipes: Buttercream Icing, p. 116; Thinned Fondant Adhesive, p. 117
Also: 2011 Pattern Book (Hat, Nose), p. 130; 8 in. Lollipop Sticks, p. 198; Cake Boards, Fanci-Foil Wrap, p. 241; knife, ruler, cornstarch, waxed paper, marshmallows

Several days in advance: Make fondant hat (p. 122). **Also:** Make fondant nose and teeth. Tint fondant: 1 oz. orange; reserve 1 oz. white. For nose, use pattern to cut 1 each yellow and orange. Cut curved strips from orange nose and attach over yellow nose using damp brush. For teeth, cut irregular triangles: three ½ in. high and two each ¾, 1, 1⅛, 1¼ in. high. Let all dry on waxed paper-covered board dusted with cornstarch. **And:** Prepare and wrap cut-to-fit board (p. 110).

Bake and cool cake. Smooth out top and sides with white buttercream, covering carriage details and building up eyeballs (pat smooth with fingertip dipped in cornstarch). Pipe tip 8 dot irises and pupils; flatten with finger dipped in cornstarch. Pipe tip 2 dot highlights and tip 3 zigzag veins. Cover cake with tip 21 stars. Pipe outline mouth and lower eyelids with tip 12. Position nose and teeth, larger sizes on the outside. Push hat into cake top; position marshmallows for support. Roll out reserved blue fondant ⅛ in. thick. Cut 8-10 strips, 1 x 2 in. wide. Cut ¾ in. deep slits, ⅛ in. wide. Roll into tufts and attach for hat brim using thinned fondant adhesive. Pipe tip 5 number. Serves 12.

*Combine Violet with Rose for violet shown. Combine Lemon Yellow with Golden Yellow for yellow shown. Combine Leaf Green with Lemon Yellow for green shown.

Totally Tooned In!

We're showing kids' favorite characters in 3-D! There's no better way to get their attention than with birthday cakes and treats featuring the names they love, big as life. Just watch as Mickey Mouse stops traffic with his lively locomotive that carries a special greeting for the birthday boy or girl. Whoever your kids are into, whether it's action heroes such as Transformers, cute companions like Hello Kitty or good-time guys like SpongeBob SquarePants and Elmo, we have the ideal star-studded treats to get kids focused on fun!

Engineering a Great Birthday!

Pans: *Mickey Mouse Clubhouse*, p. 186; Classic Wonder Mold, p. 160; 12 x 18 x 2 in. Sheet, 10 x 2 in. Square, p. 157; Jumbo Muffin, p. 158; Cookie Sheet, Cooling Grid, p. 203

Tips: 3, 5, 6, 12, 18, p. 134-135

Colors:* Leaf Green, Lemon Yellow, Golden Yellow, Royal Blue, Red-Red, No-Taste Red, Black, p. 146

Candy: White (2 pks.), Dark Cocoa Candy Melts, p. 194; Garden (black), Primary (orange, red) Candy Color Sets, p. 195

Recipes: Buttercream, Color Flow Icings, Roll-Out Cookies, p. 116

Also: 2011 Pattern Book (Smoke Cloud), p. 130; Round Cut-Outs, p. 151; Color Flow Mix, p. 143; White Jumbo Baking Cups, p. 184; Parchment Triangles, p. 136; Wooden Dowel Rods (four 2 in. lengths), p. 239; 6 in., 8 in. Cake Circles, Cake Boards, Fanci-Foil Wrap, p. 241; two 24 x 36 in. foamcore boards (¼ in. thick), ruler, knife, waxed paper, toothpicks, tape

In advance: Make *Mickey* candy plaque (p. 128). **Also:** Make cookies. Prepare and roll out dough. Use pattern to cut smoke. Use Cake Circles as a guide to cut one 8 in. and two 6 in. circles for wheels. Use medium Cut-Out to cut 11 rounds for axles and lug nuts. Cut 2 strips, 1 x 13 in., for roof trim. Cut ½ x 8 in. strip for connecting rod. Bake and cool cookies. **And:** Ice cookies by pouring on color flow icing (p. 128). For large wheel, use largest Cut-Out to mark center circle; outline with tip 3, fill in and let set before covering outer area. Cover wheels, axles, lug nuts and 8 in. connecting rod with thinned icing. Cover cloud with full-strength icing. Let all dry overnight on waxed paper-covered boards. Use full-strength icing and tip 6 to pipe smoke outline and message. Let dry. **And:** Prepare double-layer base board. Use cake pans as a guide. Sheet cake is positioned vertically for cab; square cake becomes front of engine. Wheels extend 8 in. beyond bottom; cloud extends 6 in. above roof; cowcatcher extends 5 in. in front. Cut 2 foamcore boards to fit, tape together and wrap with foil (p. 110).

Bake and cool Wonder Mold cake (use firm-textured batter, such as pound cake), 1-layer square and sheet cakes, 13 cupcakes. Position and decorate cakes (p. 122). Position candy plaque. Pipe tip 12 shirt. Cakes serve 63; each cupcake and cookie serves 1.

*Combine Golden Yellow with Lemon Yellow for yellow cab shown. Combine Leaf Green with Lemon Yellow for green shades shown. Combine Royal Blue with a little Black for blue shades shown.

▶ *Mickey* in the Driver's Seat

Pans: Cookie Sheet, Cooling Grid, p. 203

Tips: 1, 3, 4, p. 134

Colors:* No-Taste Red, Red-Red, Black, p. 146

Recipes: Color Flow Icing, Roll-Out Cookies, p. 116

Also: 101 Cookie Cutters (car), p. 201; *Mickey Mouse Clubhouse* Icing Decorations, p. 186; Color Flow Mix, p. 143; Cake Boards, p. 241; waxed paper, cornstarch

In advance: Make cookies. Prepare and roll out dough. Cut cookies using car cutter from set. Bake and cool cookies. Outline lower car body using tip 3 and full-strength red color flow; flow in using thinned icing. Let dry on waxed paper-covered boards.

Decorate using full-strength color flow. Pipe in tip 3 white background areas for windshield and front grill; pat smooth with finger dipped in cornstarch. Use gray to pipe in tip 3 grill interior (pat smooth), dot lights, windshield and steering wheel outlines and zigzag convertible top. Use black to pipe tip 1 lattice grillwork, tip 3 light border, tip 4 outline tires and arm. Pipe tip 4 dot glove; flatten with finger. Pipe tip 1 outline finger details. Pipe tip 3 outline hubcaps and dot axle. Pipe tip 3 front bumper. Attach icing decoration with icing dot. Each serves 1.

*Combine No-Taste Red with Red-Red for red shown.

◀ Multi *Mickey* Celebration

Pan: Standard Muffin, p. 158

Recipe: Buttercream Icing, p. 116

Also: 13 Count Standard Cupcakes 'N More Dessert Stand, p. 167; Flowerful Medley 6-Mix Sprinkles (confetti), p. 144; *Mickey Mouse Clubhouse* Candle, Toppers, Baking Cups, p. 186

Bake and cool 12 cupcakes. Ice smooth. Sprinkle on confetti. Position on stand. Position toppers. Position candle in top position. Each serves 1.

◀ Up, Up & Away with *Mickey*

Pan: Standard Muffin, p. 158; Cookie Sheet, Cooling Grid, p. 203

Tips: 2, 16, p. 134-135

Colors:* Leaf Green, Kelly Green, Royal Blue, Violet, Burgundy, Red-Red, Black, p. 146

Recipes: Buttercream, Color Flow Icings, Roll-Out Cookies, p. 116; favorite crisped rice cereal treats

Also: *Mickey Mouse Clubhouse* Icing Decorations, p. 186; Yellow Candy Melts (1 pk. makes 4 treats), p. 194; Decorator Brush Set, p. 197; Standard Baking Cups, p. 184; Round Comfort-Grip Cutter, p. 200; 8 in. Cookie Treat Sticks (cut to 5 in. long), p. 203; Color Flow Mix, p. 143; Cake Boards, p. 241; regular, mini candy-coated chocolates, toothpicks, ruler, waxed paper

In advance: Make cookie balloon. Prepare and roll out dough. Cut rounds using cutter. Bake and cool cookies. Use ruler and edge of cookie cutter to mark sections. Use tip 2 and full-strength color flow to outline each section, then flow in with thinned color flow (p. 128). Let dry on waxed paper-covered boards. **Also:** Make yellow candy shells in muffin pan (p. 128).

Prepare cereal treats mixture and press into bottom of candy shells, ¾ in. deep. Attach mini candies around top edge using melted candy. Fill center with regular candies. Push 2 cookie sticks into base; attach cookie balloon using melted candy. Pipe tip 16 buttercream rosettes. Position *Mickey*. Each serves 1.

*Combine Leaf Green with Kelly Green for green shown. Combine Royal Blue with Black for light blue shown. Combine Royal Blue with Violet for dark blue shown. Combine Burgundy with Red-Red and a little Black for red shown.

©Disney

◀ *Hello Kitty* Birthday Cake

Pans: *Hello Kitty*, p. 188; 16 x 2 in. Round, p. 157

Tips: 3, 16, p. 134-135

Colors:* *Hello Kitty* Icing Color Kit (pink, red, black, yellow), p. 188; Rose, Burgundy, p. 146

Fondant: White Ready-To-Use Rolled Fondant (78 oz.), p. 147; Easy-Glide Fondant Smoother, 9, 20 in. Rolling Pins, Roll & Cut Mat, p. 148; Brush Set, p. 149

Recipe: Buttercream Icing, p. 116

Also: A-B-C and 1-2-3 50 Pc. Cutter Set, p. 201; Dowel Rods, p. 239; Cake Board, Fanci-Foil Wrap p. 241

Bake and cool *Hello Kitty* and 2-layer round cake (bake two 1½ in. layers for a 3 in. high cake). Prepare for Stacked Construction (p. 114). Position *Hello Kitty* cake on cut-to-fit foil-wrapped cake board (p. 110). Using tip 3, outline bow and whiskers, pipe in eyes, nose and bow openings. Pat smooth with fingertip. Fill in cake with tip 16 stars.

Tint 72 oz. fondant pink, 4 oz. rose, reserve 2 oz. white. Prepare and cover round cake with pink fondant (p. 117). Reserve remaining fondant. Position *Hello Kitty* cake on round cake. Roll out rose fondant ⅛ in. thick and cut out letters; attach using damp brush. For bottom border, roll ½ in. diameter balls of reserved pink fondant; attach with damp brush. Roll out white fondant ⅛ in. thick. Cut circles with wide end of tip 3 and attach to cake sides with damp brush. Serves 89.

*Combine Rose with *Hello Kitty* Red and a little Burgundy for rose letter shade shown.

▶ *Hello Kitty* Cupcakes

Pan: Standard Muffin, p. 158

Colors: *Hello Kitty* Icing Colors Set (pink, dark pink, yellow), p. 188; Royal Blue, p. 146

Fondant: White Ready-To-Use Rolled Fondant (¼ oz. per treat), p. 147; 9 in. Rolling Pin, Roll & Cut Mat, p. 148; Brush Set, p. 149

Recipe: Buttercream Icing, p. 116

Also: *Hello Kitty* Standard Baking Cups, Toppers, p. 188; Blossom Plastic Nesting Cutter Set, p. 201

Bake and cool cupcakes. Ice smooth. Tint fondant yellow, blue and pink. Roll out ⅛ in. thick as needed. Cut blossom using 3rd smallest cutter from set. Position on cupcake. Position topper. Each serves 1.

▲ *Hello Kitty* Cookies

Pans: Cookie Sheet, Cooling Grid, p. 203

Tips: 1, 2, 3, p. 134

Colors:* *Hello Kitty* Icing Color Set (pink), p. 188; Royal Blue, Sky Blue, p. 146

Recipes: Royal Icing, Roll-Out Cookies, p. 116

Also: 2011 Pattern Book (Plane), p. 130; *Hello Kitty* Icing Decorations, p. 188; Meringue Powder, p. 143; Cake Boards, p. 241; waxed paper, knife, ruler

In advance: Make cookie planes. Prepare and roll out dough. Use pattern to cut out planes. Bake and cool. Cover cookies with thinned royal icing (p. 128). Let dry overnight on waxed paper-covered boards.

Decorate on waxed paper-covered boards. Using full-strength icing, pipe tip 2 body and steering wheel; let dry. Overpipe tip 2 arm and hand; position icing decoration in wet icing. Pipe stripes with tips 1 and 3. Using tip 2, pipe dot and bead propeller; outline oval wing and 2 tail fins. Fill in wing and fins with thinned icing. Let dry. Each serves 1.

*Combine Royal Blue with Sky Blue for blue shown.

© 1976, 2010 SANRIO CO., LTD.

◀ *Hello Kitty* Mini Cakes

Pans: Non-Stick Cookie/Jelly Roll, p. 165; Cooling Grid, p. 203

Tips: 1, 3, p. 134

Colors: *Hello Kitty* Icing Color Set (pink), p. 188

Also: *Hello Kitty* Icing Decorations, p. 188; White Ready-To-Use Decorator Icing (2 cans cover 6 treats), p. 147; Round Cut-Outs, p. 151; 101 Cookie Cutters (small round), p. 201; Nesting Blossoms Metal Cutter Set, p. 202; White Candy Melts (1 pk.), p. 194; Primary (red), Garden (pink, violet) Candy Color Sets, p. 195; ULTIMATE Cake Leveler, p. 152; Cake Boards, p. 241; waxed paper, knife, ruler

In advance: Make candy base using second smallest blossom cutter from set. Melt candy and tint using red, pink and a little violet candy color. Set cutter on non-stick pan. Fill to ⅛ in. deep. Tap to settle; chill until firm.

Bake and cool 1-layer cake using firm-textured batter such as pound cake. Trim cake to ¾ in. high as needed. Cut base cakes using medium round Cut-Out; cut top cakes using smallest round from 101 Cookie Cutters. Reserve ¼ cup white icing. Tint remaining icing using *Hello Kitty* pink. Reserve ¼ cup pink for borders. Individually cover cakes with heated icing (p. 128). Let set. Stack cakes on candy blossom. Pipe tip 1 bead borders. Pipe tip 3 dots. Attach *Hello Kitty* Icing Decoration. Each serves 1.

◄ Tower of Toys!

Pans: 12 x 18 x 2 in. Sheet, p. 157; Cookie Sheet, Cooling Grid, p. 203

Tips: 2, 3, 44, p. 134-135

Colors:* Sky Blue, Royal Blue, Leaf Green, Lemon Yellow Orange, Violet, Brown, Black, p. 146

Recipes: Color Flow Icing, Roll-Out Cookies, p. 116

Also: *Disney/Pixar Toy Story* Candle, Toppers (2 pks.), p. 187; Cake Leveler, p. 152; 101 Cookie Cutters (car, truck, bear, ball), p. 201; White Candy Melts (4 pks.), p. 194; Color Flow Mix, p. 143; Parchment Triangles, p 136; Cake Boards, p. 241; knife, ruler, waxed paper

2 days in advance: Make cookies. Prepare and roll out dough. Cut car, truck, bear and ball using cutters from set. Bake and cool cookies. Outline colors using tip 2 and full-strength icing; flow in using thinned icing (p. 128). For bear, immediately after flowing in, flow in tummy and inside ears with light brown. Let dry 24 hour on waxed paper-covered boards. Add details using full-strength icing. Use tip 2 to outline and fill in tires; add tip 2 dot axles. Pipe tip 2 outline car details. Pipe tip 3 dot bear muzzle, tip 2 outline mouth, dot eyes and nose. Pip tip 3 dot button on ball; flatten with finger.

Bake and cool 1-layer cake, 1½ in. high, using firm-textured batter such as pound cake. Cut into 32 squares 1½ x 1½ in. Using a spatula, swipe bottoms with melted candy; let set. Cover with melted candy (p. 128); let set. Decorate with full-strength icing. Using tip 44, outline al edges in assorted colors; let dry on waxed paper. Pipe tip 3 letters on all 4 sides; let dry. Stack cakes. Position cookies, toppers and candles. Each serves 1.

*Combine Leaf Green with Lemon Yellow for green shown.
Combine Royal Blue with Violet for darker blue shown.

◄ Rex in the Box

Pan: 9 x 13 x 2 in. Sheet, p. 157

Tips: 1M, 2 p. 135

Colors:* Royal Blue, Lemon Yellow, Sky Blue, Leaf Green, Orange, p. 146

Fondant: White Ready-To-Use Rolled Fondant (5 oz. per treat), Gum-Tex, p. 147; 9 in. Rolling Pin, Roll & Cut Mat, p. 148; Brush Set, p. 149; Cutter/Embosser, p. 150

Recipes: Buttercream, Royal Icings, p. 116; Thinned Fondant Adhesive, p. 117

Also: *Disney/Pixar Toy Story* Icing Decorations, p. 187; Meringue Powder, p. 143; Cake Board, Fanci-Foil Wrap, p. 241; mini candy-coated chocolates, ruler, cornstarch, waxed paper, cotton balls

In advance: Make fondant box panels. Add ½ teaspoon Gum-Tex to 5 oz. fondant; tint half blue. Roll out ⅛ in. thick as needed. Cut: 2 side panels, 2¼ x 2¼ in.; front and back panels, 2½ x 2½ in.; blue lid, 2¾ x 2¾ in.; toy block, ¾ x ¾ in.; and toy ball using wide end of tip 1M. Let all dry on waxed paper-covered boards dusted with cornstarch. Reserve excess blue fondant.

Bake and cool 1-layer cake (2 in. high) using firm-textured batter such as pound cake. For each treat, cut a 2 x 2 in. square; use icing to attach cake square to wrapped, cut-to-fit cake board (p. 110). Ice smooth with buttercream. Attach front, back and side panels, securing corners with fondant adhesive. Roll out reserved blue fondant for trims. Cut 2½ x ¼ in. strips. Attach to top and outer edges using damp brush; trim as needed to fit. Decorate using tip 2 and royal icing. Print letters on box and block; outline block. Outline and fill in stars and ball swirls; pat smooth with finger. Attach lid using fondant adhesive; prop lid with cotton balls until set. Fill with candies and position icing decoration. Each serves 1.

*Combine Leaf Green with Lemon Yellow for green shown.

▲ Toy Topper Treats

Pans: Standard Muffin, p. 158; Cooling Grid, p. 203

Recipe: Buttercream Icing, p. 116

Also: *Disney/Pixar Toy Story* Standard Baking Cups, Toppers, p. 187

Bake and cool cupcakes. Ice smooth; position toppers. Each serves 1.

©Disney/Pi

◄ Space Faces

Pans: Silicone Round Brownie Pops Mold, p. 171; Cookie Sheet, Cooling Grid, p. 203

Colors:* Sky Blue, Royal Blue, Lemon Yellow, Leaf Green, Violet, Rose, p. 146

Fondant: White Ready-To-Use Rolled Fondant (1 oz. per treat), p. 147; 9 in. Rolling Pin, Roll & Cut Mat, p. 148; Brush Set, p. 149

Also: *Disney/Pixar Toy Story* Icing Decorations, p. 187; White Candy Melts (1 oz. per treat), p. 194; Primary (blue, yellow) Candy Color Set, p. 195; Parchment Triangles, p. 136; knife, ruler, waxed paper, scissors

In advance: Make candy bodies. Melt and tint candy blue using candy color from set. Mold bodies in Brownie Pops pan supported by cookie sheet. Tap to settle; chill until firm. Attach Icing Decoration head with melted candy; let set.

Assemble alien with melted candy. Tint fondant: ¼ oz. each light blue, dark blue, green, violet. Roll out dark blue and violet 1⁄16 in. thick. Cut 4 x 3⁄16 in. strips and attach for collar and belt; trim to fit. For arms, roll ¼ x ¼ in. logs; flatten ends and attach. For hands, roll ¼ in. balls; flatten, cut slits for fingers and attach. For shoes, roll ½ in. balls; flatten, shape and attach. Pipe insignia using melted candy in cut parchment bag. Each serves 1.

*Combine Sky Blue with Royal Blue and Black for light blue shown. Combine Lemon Yellow with Leaf Green for green shown. Combine Violet with Rose for violet shown.

▼ It's *Buzz's* World!

Pans: *Disney/Pixar Toy Story*, p. 187; Cookie Sheet, Cooling Grid, p. 203

Tips: 1, 3, 5, 13, p. 134-135

Colors:* *Disney/Pixar Toy Story* Icing Color Set (*Buzz* skin tone, green, violet, black), p. 187; Sky Blue, Royal Blue, Lemon Yellow, Brown, Juniper Green, Christmas Red, Red-Red, Orange, p. 146

Fondant: White Ready-To-Use Rolled Fondant (32 oz.), p. 147; 20 in. Rolling Pin, Roll & Cut Mat, Easy-Glide Fondant Smoother, p. 148; Brush Set, p. 149

Recipes: Buttercream, Royal Icings, Roll-Out Cookies, p. 116

Also: 2011 Pattern Book (Planet), p. 130; Star Plastic Nesting Cutter Set, p. 201; Piping Gel, p. 143; 16 in. Cake Circle, 13 x 19 in. Cake Boards, Fanci-Foil Wrap, p. 241; 34 x 24 in. plywood or foamcore board (¼ in. thick), cornstarch, ruler, waxed paper, tape, scissors, knife

In advance: Prepare and cover base board (p. 122). **Also:** Make cookie stars. Prepare and roll out dough. Cut about 16 stars using 2 smallest cutters from set. Bake and cool cookies. Pour on tinted thinned royal icing to cover (p. 128). Let dry on waxed paper-covered boards.

Bake and cool *Buzz* cake. Position on wrapped, cut-to-fit Cake Board. Ice sides smooth with buttercream matching blue planet. Use tip 3 to fill in eyes and teeth; pat smooth with finger dipped in cornstarch. Use tip 1 to fill in iris; pat smooth. Use tip 1 to outline iris and pipe dot pupil. Using tip 3, outline remaining details and fill in buttons, patches and blue and violet bolts; pat fill-ins smooth. Fill in design with tip 13 stars. Pipe tip 3 eyebrows; pat smooth. Pipe tip 5 bead bottom border. Position Buzz on planet and surround with stars. Each cookie serves 1; cake serves 12.

*Combine Royal Blue with Black for blue shown. Combine Lemon Yellow with *Disney/Pixar Toy Story* Green for green planet ring. Combine Brown with Juniper Green for eyebrows. Combine Christmas Red with Red-Red for red shown. Combine Lemon Yellow with Orange for gold shown.

◄ Dora's Island Adventure

Pans: Dora the Explorer, p. 193; Long Loaf, p. 158; Mini Ball, p. 162

Tips: 2, 3, 8, 16, 21, p. 134-135

Colors:* Dora the Explorer Icing Color Set (Dora skin tone, pink, brown, purple), p. 193; Sky Blue, Leaf Green, Kelly Green, Rose, Violet, Orange, Lemon Yellow, Royal Blue, Red-Red, Black, p. 146

Fondant: White Ready-To-Use Rolled Fondant (94 oz.), Gum-Tex, p. 147 20 in. Rolling Pin, Roll & Cut Mat, Easy-Glide Fondant Smoother, p. 148; Flower Former Set, Brush Set, p. 149; Leaf Cut-Outs, p. 151

Recipes: Buttercream, Royal Icings, p. 116

Also: 2011 Pattern Book (Small, Medium Fern, Large Leaf), p. 130; 101 Cookie Cutters (alphabet), Mini Romantic Cutter Set (bell) p. 202; Flower Comfort-Grip Cutter, p. 200; Meringue Powder, Piping Gel, p. 143; Cake Boards, Fanci-Foil Wrap, p. 241; 15 x 20 in foamcore board (½ in. thick), aluminum foil, ruler, knife, waxed paper, cornstarch

1-2 days in advance: Make fondant flowers (p. 122). **Also:** Make fonda leaves. Tint 28 oz. fondant leaf green. Add ¼ teaspoon Gum-Tex to 5 oz of fondant (reserve 23 oz. to cover loaf cake and to make vines and medium fern). Roll out ⅛ in. thick. Use largest cutter from set to cut 24 leaves. Set on Large Flower Formers, alternating curved side up, curved side down. Use royal icing to pipe tip 3 outlines and center veir Let dry. **And:** Prepare base board. Tint fondant: 48 oz. sky blue. Roll out ⅛ in. thick as needed. Wrap board in foil and cover with rolled fondant (p. 120). Tint 3 oz. kelly green, 1½ oz. light leaf green, 1 oz. dark violet; use 1½ oz. of reserved leaf green. Using patterns, cut 1 large leaf and 1 medium fern; attach to corners of base board using damp brush. Use royal icing to pipe tip 2 outlines. Use pattern to cut 2 small ferns, use smallest Cut-Out to cut 22 vine leaves and use alphabet cutters to cut out name. Outline vine leaves with tip 2. Set pieces on waxed paper-covered board until needed.

Bake and cool 1-layer (2 in. high) loaf cake; trim to 13 in. long. Prepare and cover with reserved leaf green fondant (p. 117). Positio on prepared base board, 1 in. from bottom edge.

Bake and cool Dora cake. Ice cake sides and background areas smooth; ice underside of hair smooth in black. Use tip 3 for the following: outline details, outline and fill in Dora and pocket map eyes, irises, inside mouth, pipe dot pupils, eye highlights, bracelet and map pupils and tongue; smooth with fingertip dipped in cornstarch. Cover cake with tip 16 stars. Position cake on board above loaf cake. Pipe tip 21 shell border. Attach name and small ferns to board using damp brush. For vines, use remaining leaf gree fondant to roll 4¼ x 14 in. logs. Loosely intertwine 2 vines together o either side of Dora. Roll two logs, 5 x ¼ in. and position above name Attach leaves and flowers over loaf cake, securing with buttercrear icing. Serves 24.

*Combine Violet with Rose for violet shown.

► Floral Dora

Pans: Cookie Sheet, Cooling Grid, p. 203

Tip: 3, p. 134

Colors: Rose, Orange, Lemon Yellow, p. 146

Recipes: Royal Icing, Roll-Out Cookies, p. 116

Also: Dora Icing Decorations, p. 193; Flower Comfort-Grip Cutter, p. 200; Leaf Cut-Outs, p. 151; 8 in. Cookie Treat Sticks, p. 203; Meringue Powder, p. 143; Cake Boards, p. 241; card stock, scissors, markers, tape, waxed paper, ruler

In advance: Make cookies. Prepare and roll out dough. Cut cookies using flower cutter. Bake and cool cookies. Using full-strength icing and tip 3, outline petals and a 1¾ in. diameter center circle; flow in using thinned icing (p. 128), a lighter shade for petals, yellow for center circle. Let dry on waxed paper-covered boards. Using full-strength icing, pipe tip 3 petal details and attach icing decoration. Let dry. Attach Cookie Stick to back. Let dry.

Trace largest leaf Cut-Out as pattern for cutting cardstock name tags. Outline in dark green; print name in black. Use tape to attach to stick. Each serves 1.

◀ *Elmo* On Safari Cake

Pans: *Elmo* Face, p. 193; 12, 16 x 2 in. Round, p. 157

Tips: 1, 5, p. 134

Colors:* Royal Blue, Leaf Green, Kelly Green, Brown, Lemon Yellow, Golden Yellow, Orange, Copper, Red-Red, Christmas Red, Violet, Rose, Ivory, Black, p. 146

Fondant: White Ready-To-Use Rolled Fondant (274 oz.), Gum-Tex, p. 147; 20 in. Rolling Pin, Roll & Cut Mat, Easy-Glide Fondant Smoother, p. 148; 10 Pc. Fondant/Gum Paste Tool Set, Fondant Shaping Foam, Flower Former Set, Brush Set, p. 149; Leaf Cut-Outs, p. 151

Candy: Red (2 pks.), White (1 pk.) Candy Melts, p. 194; Primary (orange), Garden (black) Candy Color Sets, p. 195

Recipes: Buttercream, Royal Icings, p. 116

Also: 2011 Pattern Book (Helmet, Right and Left Brim, Right and Left Band, Giraffe, Elephant, Rhino, Zebra), p. 130; Piping Gel, p. 143; Plastic Dowel Rods, p. 239; Cake Circles, Boards, Fanci-Foil Wrap, p. 241; 20 in. diameter foamcore board (½ in. thick), tape, scissors, knife, cornstarch, waxed paper, ruler

3-4 days in advance: Make *Elmo* candy plaque (p. 128) and helmet (p. 122). **Also:** Make fondant leaves (p. 122). **And:** Make fondant animals. Tint 2 oz. fondant each: yellow for giraffe, gray for elephant, violet for rhino; reserve 2 oz. white for zebra. Add ¼ teaspoon Gum-Tex to each. Roll out ⅛ in. thick. Use patterns to cut out animals. Let dry 2 days. Pipe outline and dot details using royal icing and tip 1; outline and fill in larger areas, patting smooth with fingertip. **And:** Prepare base. Wrap foamcore circle with foil (p. 110). Tint 48 oz. fondant green. Roll out ⅛ in. thick. Cover top only with fondant (p. 120). Reserve excess fondant.

Bake and cool 2-layer cakes. Tint 156 oz. fondant blue. Prepare and cover cakes with rolled fondant (p. 117). Prepare for Stacked Construction (p. 114). Pipe tip 5 bead border on 12 in. cake. Roll out reserved green fondant ⅛ in. thick. Cut out assorted shapes up to 2 x 2 in. high for trees and bushes on side of 16 in. cake; attach using damp brush. Use royal icing to attach animals; attach 50 small and 25 medium leaves around animals, cake sides and on board. Pipe tip 5 name.

Insert *Elmo* into cake top. For hands, tint 14 oz. fondant red. Divide into 2 balls; flatten and make cuts for fingers; continue shaping by hand, then position on cake. Use royal icing to attach remaining leaves. Serves 117.

*Combine Red-Red with Christmas Red and a little Black for red hands. Combine Leaf Green with Kelly Green for green leaves and trees. Combine Brown with Red-Red for light brown in helmet and dark brown shades shown. Combine Orange with Golden Yellow and Copper for giraffe spots. Combine Royal Blue with Violet for colors in elephant. Combine Violet with Royal Blue for colors in rhino. Combine Lemon Yellow with Golden Yellow for yellow message. Combine Golden Yellow with Ivory for giraffe body.

▶ Safari So Good!

Pan: Standard Muffin, p. 158

Tips: 1, 3, 352, p. 134-135

Colors:* Leaf Green, Christmas Red, Red-Red, Brown, p. 146

Recipes: Buttercream, Royal Icings, p. 116

Also: 2011 Pattern Book (Small Helmet), p. 130; *Elmo* Standard Baking Cups, Icing Decorations, p. 193; Green Candy Melts, p. 194; Meringue Powder, p. 143; Cake Board, p. 241; Rolling Pin, p. 148; pretzel sticks, spearmint leaves, waxed paper, tape, granulated sugar, scissors

One day in advance: Tape helmet pattern to cake board and cover with waxed paper. Attach *Elmo* icing decoration to waxed paper with tip 3 dot of royal icing. Use royal icing and tip 3 to pipe helmet and outline with tip 1; let dry. **Also:** Make palm tree leaves. Roll out spearmint leaves on waxed paper sprinkled with sugar; use scissors to cut 1¼ x ³⁄₁₆ in. notched leaf shapes. Let dry. Attach leaves to pretzel sticks with melted candy.

Bake and cool cupcakes. Using buttercream and tip 352, cover top with leaves. Position icing decoration. Pipe tip 3 dot fingers. Insert tree. Each serves 1.

*Combine Christmas Red with Red-Red for red shown. Combine Brown with Red-Red for brown shown.

SESAME STREET `123`

◀ *Tinker Bell's* Flowing Flower Garden

Pans: 6, 8, 10 x 3 in. Round, p. 157
Tip: 3, p. 134
Colors:* Leaf Green, Royal Blue, Violet, Rose, Lemon Yellow, Golden Yellow, Burgundy, p. 146
Fondant/Gum Paste: White Ready-To-Use Rolled Fondant (72 oz.), Ready-To-Use Gum Paste (20 oz.), p. 147; 20 in. Rolling Pin, Roll & Cut Mat, Easy-Glide Fondant Smoother, p. 148; Flower Forming Cups, Flower Former Set, Brush Set, p. 149; Floral Collection Flower Making Set, White Pearl Dust, Flower Cut-Outs, p. 151
Recipes: Buttercream Icing, p. 116; Thinned Fondant Adhesive, p. 117
Also: 2011 Pattern Book (Small, Large Waterfalls), p. 130; *Tinker Bell* Candle, p. 191; Cake and Treat Display Set, p. 235; Piping Gel, p. 143; Fresh Flower Cake Spikes, p. 240; White Candy Melts, p. 194; Parchment Triangles, p. 136; Cake Circles, Fanci-Foil Wrap, p. 241; 18-gauge florist wire (12 ft.), florist tape, tea strainer, non-toxic pastel green chalk, waxed paper, ruler, knife, tape, scissors, wire cutters, cornstarch

In advance: Make gum paste flowers and leaves (p. 122). **Also:** Prepare wires. Cut wire into 7 varied lengths from 9 to 17 in. Curl 1 end into spiral. Attach some of prepared flowers and leaves using melted candy in cut parchment bag.

Bake and cool 2-layer cakes (bake two 1½ in. high layers for 3 in. high cakes). Prepare and cover with 56 oz. green fondant (p. 117). Pipe tip 3 bead bottom borders. Use patterns to cut small and large waterfalls from Cake Boards. Bend for curved shape; cover with foil (p. 110). Tint 16 oz. fondant blue; roll out ⅛ in. thick as needed. Brush waterfalls with Piping Gel and cover tops with fondant. Cut 3 ponds (2½, 5 and 6½ in. diameter for 6, 8 and 10 in. cakes respectively) with wavy edges. Attach to cake tops using damp brush.

At reception: Position cakes on stand; position waterfalls. Brush ponds and waterfalls with Piping Gel tinted blue. Position candle. Insert Flower Spikes 2 in. behind small pond, 1 in. behind medium pond. Position wires in spikes, trimming ends as needed. Use fondant adhesive to attach flowers and leaves to cakes and edges of waterfalls. Serves 60.

*Combine Violet with Rose for violet shown. Combine Lemon Yellow with Golden Yellow for yellow shown.

▶ *Tinker Bell's* Wishing Wand

Pans: Cookie Sheet, Cooling Grid, p. 203
Tips: 2, 4, p. 134
Colors:* Christmas Red, Sky Blue, Violet, p. 146
Recipes: Royal Icing, Roll-Out Cookies, p. 116
Also: Daisy Comfort-Grip Cutter, p. 200; *Tinker Bell* Icing Decorations, p. 191; White Candy Melts, p. 194; Meringue Powder, p. 143; Tapered Spatula, p. 139; 8 in. Cookie Treat Sticks, p. 203; Cake Boards, p. 241; waxed paper

In advance: Make cookies. Prepare and roll out dough. Cut cookies using daisy cutter. Bake and cool cookies. Attach Cookie Treat Stick to back using melted candy. Let dry.

Ice cookies smooth. Attach icing decoration to center. Pipe tip 4 lines; add tip 2 dots. Each serves 1.

*Combine Violet with a little Christmas Red for lavender shown.

©Disney

▶ *Ariel's* Sea Castle

Pans: 8, 14 x 3 in. Round, 9 x 13 x 2 in. Sheet, p. 157; King Size Muffin, p. 158

Tips: 6, 16, 67, p. 134-135

Colors:* Royal Blue, Leaf Green, Lemon Yellow, Golden Yellow, Orange, Teal, Rose, p. 146

Fondant: White Ready-To-Use Rolled Fondant (60 oz.), p. 147; 20 in. Rolling Pin, Roll & Cut Mat, Easy-Glide Fondant Smoother, p. 148; 10 Pc. Fondant/Gum Paste Tool Set, Brush Set, p. 149

Recipes: Buttercream, Royal Icings, p. 116; favorite crisped rice cereal treats

Also: *Ariel* Candle, p. 191, Yellow, Green Candy Melts, p. 194; 4 in., 8 in. Lollipop Sticks, p. 198; Meringue Powder, p. 143; Parchment Triangles, p. 136; Plastic Dowel Rods, p. 239; Cake Boards, Circles, Fanci-Foil Wrap, p. 241; 18 in. diameter plywood or foamcore circle (½ in. thick), plastic drinking straws, waxed paper, knife, ruler, tape

2-3 days in advance: Make castle (p. 122). **Also:** Make fondant clam shells. Tint 3½ oz. fondant blue. Roll into 10 ovals, 1 in. diameter. Flatten bottoms and shape rounded top. Use knife tip to cut center slit. Use veining tool to open slit, pressing tool upward in several spots and imprint top ridges. Let dry on waxed paper-covered board. **And:** Make royal icing seaweed. Use tip 67 to pipe 30 zigzags (make extras to allow for breakage), 2½ to 4 in. high, on waxed paper-covered boards. Let dry. Attach 4 in. Lollipop Sticks to back bottom using melted green candy, leaving 3 in. of stick exposed at bottom to insert into cake. Let set. **And:** Cover base board with 42 oz. fondant tinted green (p. 120). Reserve excess fondant.

Bake and cool 2-layer cakes (bake two 1½ in. layers for 3 in. high cakes). Prepare for Stacked Construction (p. 114); position dowel rods to support 8 in. cake 1 in. from back left edge of 14 in. cake. Ice smooth using buttercream. Pipe assorted tip 16 elongated reverse shell and curving branches of coral around cake sides; pipe tip 6 wavy seaweed. Using reserved green fondant, roll ¼ in. diameter logs, ¼ x 12 in. long. Pinch up then down to form scallops; attach for bottom borders.

At party: Position castle, ¼ in. from back edge. Use Lollipop Stick to make holes, ½ in. apart, where candy straws for curved front railing will go. Build railing; decreasing length by ½ in. for each piece as you go from front to back. Use melted candy to attach ¼ x 8 in. diameter fondant log for top railing. Insert seaweed; position clams and *Ariel* candle. Cakes serve 83; cereal treats serve 8; candy pieces each serve 1.

*Combine Golden Yellow with Orange for gold fondant shown. Combine Leaf Green with Lemon Yellow for lighter green shown.

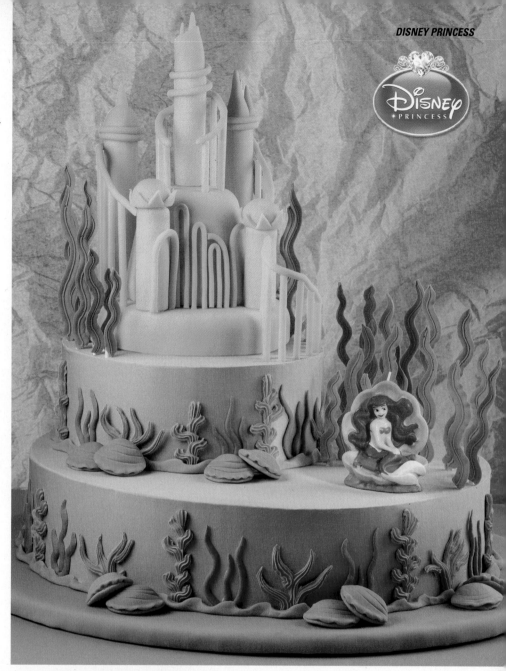

◀ Sea-nic Placecards

Pans: Non-Stick 13.25 x 9.25 x .5 in. Small Cookie, p. 165

Candy: White Candy Melts (1 pk. makes 3 treats), p. 194; Primary (yellow, blue, red), Garden (pink, green, black) Candy Color Sets, p. 195

Also: *Ariel* Icing Decorations, p. 191; 101 Cookie Cutters, p. 201; Tapered Spatula, p. 139; Parchment Triangles, p. 136; Cake Boards, p. 241; granulated brown sugar, ruler, waxed paper

In advance: Make 2 candy circles. Tint candy: 5 oz. light blue. Place largest round cutter from set on pan. Fill ⅛ in. deep with melted candy. Tap to settle; chill until firm. Reserve excess candy. Trim off about ¼ in. from upright circle for a flat edge. **Also:** Make 4 coral pieces per treat. Tint candy: 3 oz. dark green (mix green with blue and black). Use melted candy in cut parchment bag to pipe assorted shapes, about 1 x 1½ in. high, on a waxed paper-covered board. Chill until firm. Reserve excess candy.

Tint candy: 1 oz. each pink, dark blue, golden yellow (mix yellow with a little red), tan (mix yellow with pink and green). For upright circle, use tapered spatula to paint on golden yellow candy sand; let set. Decorate and assemble using melted candy in cut parchment bags. Attach icing decoration. Chill until firm. Pipe stones, clam shell, smaller coral, name, starfish and bubbles. Attach upright round to base; hold until set. Use spatula to ice bottom round with blue candy. Attach upright coral pieces and sprinkle on brown sugar before candy sets. Each serves 1.

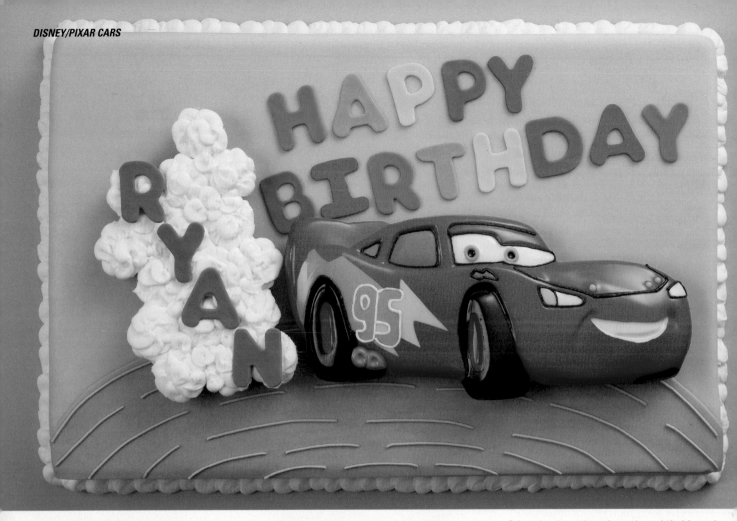

▲ *Cars!* Birthday Rally

Pans: *Disney/Pixar Cars,* p. 190; 11 x 15 x 2 in. Sheet, p. 157; Mini Muffin, p. 158

Tips: 3, 12, p. 134

Colors:* Royal Blue, Kelly Green, Orange, Violet, Rose, Lemon Yellow, Christmas Red, Black, p. 146

Fondant: White Ready-To-Use Rolled Fondant (116 oz.), p. 147; 20 in. Rolling Pin, Roll & Cut Mat, Easy-Glide Fondant Smoother, p. 148; Brush Set, p. 149

Candy: Dark Cocoa (1 pk.), White (1 pk.), Red (3 pks.) Candy Melts, p. 194; Primary (orange, yellow, blue), Garden (black)

Candy Color Sets, Decorator Brush Set, p. 195

Recipe: Buttercream Icing, p. 116

Also: 101 Cookie Cutters (letters), p. 201; White Mini Baking Cups, p. 184; Piping Gel, p. 143; Plastic Dowel Rods (3 pieces, 3 in. long), p. 239; Parchment Triangles, p. 136; Cake Boards, Fanci-Foil Wrap, p. 241; 24 x 16 in. plywood or foamcore board (¼ in. thick), craft knife, knife, ruler, cornstarch, waxed paper, tape, toothpicks, soft towel

In advance: Make *Cars* candy plaque (p. 128). **Also:** Make fondant letters. Tint 1 oz. each green, orange, violet, yellow, red and blue. Roll out ⅛ in. thick. Cut letters using cutters from set. Let dry on cornstarch-dusted board.

Bake and cool two 1-layer sheet cakes and 16 mini cupcakes. Trim 1 in. off each sheet cake then set cakes side-by-side on wrapped board to create a 22 x 14 in. rectangle. Tint fondant: 90 oz. blue, 20 oz. gray. Roll out ⅛ in. thick as needed. Prepare and cover cakes with blue rolled fondant (p. 117). Cut a 22 x 5 in. curve for track; attach using damp brush. Pipe tip 3 curved outline details. Cover mini cupcakes with tip 12 swirls for smoke effect. Position mini cupcakes, letters and candy plaque. Pipe tip 12 large bead "smoke" bottom border. Cake serves 54; each cupcake serves 1.

*Combine Violet with Rose for violet shown.

▶ You Get a Car!

Pans: Cookie Sheet, Cooling Grid, p. 203

Tips: 2, 3, p. 134

Colors: *Disney/Pixar Cars* Icing Color Set, p. 190

Recipes: Color Flow Icing, Roll-Out Cookies, p. 116

Also: 2011 Pattern Book (Flag), p. 130; *Disney/Pixar Cars* Toppers, p. 190; Round Comfort-Grip Cutter, p. 200; Color Flow Mix, p. 143; Cake Boards, p. 241; knife, toothpicks, ruler, waxed paper

In advance: Make cookies. Prepare and roll out dough. Use pattern to cut flags; use round cutter to cut bases. Bake and cool cookies. **Also:** Ice flags. Use toothpick to mark 4 horizontal rows of ⅜ in. wide checks. Pipe tip 2 outlines using black full-strength icing; flow in alternating checks using thinned black and white icing (p. 128). Let dry. **And:** Ice bases. Pipe tip 3 outlines using full-strength icing; flow in using thinned icing. Let dry.

Trim and assemble using full-strength icing and tip 3. Print name on flag. Pipe outline track details on base. Attach flag to base; position Topper. Each serves 1.

©Disney/Pixar

▶ Well Done, SpongeBob!

Pan: SpongeBob SquarePants, p. 189

Tips: 3, 16, 21, p. 134-135

Colors: SpongeBob SquarePants, Icing Color Set (yellow, red, blue, brown), p. 189; Royal Blue, Sky Blue, Brown, Black, p. 146

Fondant: White Ready-To-Use Rolled Fondant (19 oz.), Gum-Tex, p. 147; 20 in. Rolling Pin, Roll & Cut Mat, p. 148; Silver, Sapphire Blue Pearl Dust, Brush Set, p. 149

Recipe: Buttercream Icing, p. 116

Also: 2011 Pattern Book (Grill, Hat, Spatula), p. 130; Piping Gel, p. 143; 8 in. Lollipop Sticks, p. 198; Wooden Dowel Rod, p. 239; Cake Boards, Fanci-Foil Wrap, p. 241; cornstarch, waxed paper, knife, ruler

In advance: Make fondant grill, burgers, hat and spatula (p. 123). Tint fondant: 6 oz. dark gray (add ¼ teaspoon Gum-Tex); 4 oz. light brown; 1½ oz. dark brown; 3 oz. light gray (add ⅛ teaspoon Gum-Tex); 2 oz. black; ½ oz. each sky blue, green; reserve 1 oz. white (add ⅛ oz. Gum-Tex). **Also:** Prepare cut-to-fit Cake Board; wrap in foil (p. 110).

Bake and cool cake. Position on board. Ice sides and background areas smooth. Using tip 3, outline and fill in: sponge holes; teeth, mouth and tongue; eyes, irises and pupils; tie. Pat smooth with finger dipped in cornstarch. Using tip 3, outline all details except hand holding spatula; pipe shoelaces and stripes on socks. Cover remaining cake with tip 16 stars. Pipe tip 3 outline chin and cheeks, dot freckles and outline eyelashes. Pipe tip 21 shell bottom border. Position spatula sections. Use tip 3 to outline fingers over handle; fill in with tip 16 stars. Insert 2 Lollipop Sticks to support hat. Position hat, grill and Krabby Patties. Serves 12.

*Combine Brown with SpongeBob Red for buns and patties. Combine Black with Royal Blue for dark gray grill.

◀ Fry Guy SpongeBob

Pan: 10.5 x 15.5 x 1 in. Jelly Roll/Cookie, p. 158

Tips: 2, 4, p. 134

Colors: Brown, Black, Sky Blue, Royal Blue, Orange, Red-Red, Leaf Green, p. 146

Fondant: White Ready-To-Use Rolled Fondant (10 oz. per treat),Fine Tip Primary Colors FoodWriter Edible Color Markers, p. 147; Sapphire Blue Pearl Dust, Brush Set, p. 149; 9 in. Rolling Pin, Roll & Cut Mat, p. 148

Recipes: Buttercream Icing, p. 116; Thinned Fondant Adhesive, p. 117; favorite crisped rice cereal treats

Also: SpongeBob SquarePants Toppers, p. 189; knife, ruler

Prepare cereal treats and press 1 in. thick into prepared pan. Cut into 2½ x 3 in. pieces. For each treat, tint fondant as follows: 6 oz. marbleized brown (p. 120), 2 oz. gray, ½ oz. black ½ oz. sky blue; reserve 1 oz. white. Cover treat and base of SpongeBob topper with marbleized brown fondant. Use knife to score lines ⅜ in. apart for floorboards. Roll out white and black fondant ⅛ in. thick. Cut a ¾ x 1¼ in. white strip; cover hat. Cut a ¼ x 1¼ in. black hat band and shape a ⅜ x ⅜ in. blue brim; attach with damp brush. Pipe tip 2 anchor. For grill base, shape a blue 1½ x 1 x ⅝ in. high rectangle. Roll out gray ⅛ in. thick; cut a 1½ x 1 in. grill top and attach with fondant adhesive. Brush with Pearl Dust. In buttercream, pipe and overpipe tip 4 circles to build sandwiches; add tip 2 outline lettuce. For barrels, roll ⅝ x ⅝ in. brown logs; score lines with knife. Roll thin logs in lighter shade of brown and white; attach around top and sides with fondant adhesive. Position fondant pieces and topper on treat. Each serves 1.

*Combine Brown with Black for marbleized brown shown. Combine Royal Blue with Black for blue grill base. Combine Black with a little Royal Blue for gray grill top. Combine Brown with Orange for brown buns. Combine Brown with Red-Red and Black for dark brown patties.

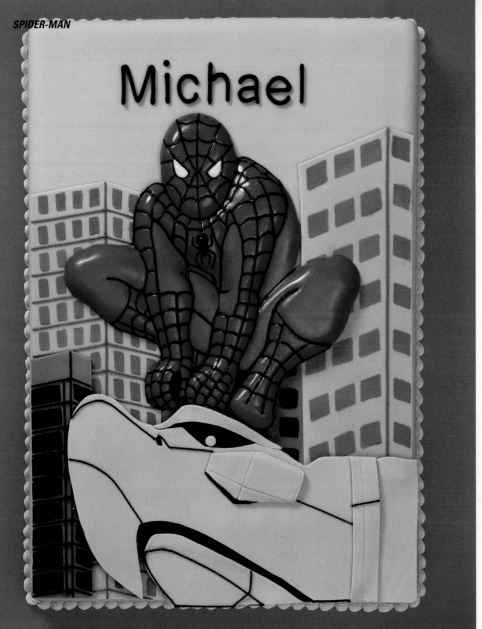

Michael

◄ *Spidey's* Bird's-Eye View

Pans: *Spider Sense Spider-Man*, p. 192; 11 x 15 x 2 in. Sheet, p. 157
Tips: 2, 3, 18, p. 134-135
Colors: Royal Blue, Black, p. 146
Fondant: White Ready-To-Use Rolled Fondant (200 oz.), Gum-Tex, p. 147; 20 in. Rolling Pin, Roll & Cut Mat, Easy-Glide Fondant Smoother, p. 148; Brush Set, p. 149
Candy: White, Red Candy Melts (2 pks. each), p. 194; Primary (red, blue), Garden (black, violet) Candy Color Sets, p. 195
Recipes: Buttercream, Royal Icings, p. 116
Also: 2011 Pattern Book (Bird, Buildings), p. 130; Parchment Triangles, p. 136; Meringue Powder, p. 143; Cake Boards, Fanci-Foil Wrap, p. 241; 22 x 15 in. plywood or foamcore board (½ in. thick), knife, scissors, tape, ruler, cornstarch, waxed paper

In advance: Make *Spider-Man* candy plaque (p. 128). Combine Blue and Violet candy colors for blue candy shown. **Also:** Make buildings. Tint fondant: 18 oz. dark gray, 30 oz. light gray. Add ¼ teaspoon Gum-Tex to dark gray, 1 teaspoon to light gray. Roll out ⅛ in. thick as needed. Use patterns to cut 2 dark gray small buildings, 2 light gray large buildings. Let dry on cornstarch-dusted boards. Using royal icing and tip 2, pipe building details; outline and fill in windows (smooth with fingertip dipped in cornstarch. **And:** Make bird. Tint 40 oz. fondant medium gray; add 2 teaspoons Gum-Tex. Roll out ⅛ in. thick. Use pattern to cut 2 birds. Position 2-layer bird on cornstarch-dusted board. Cut and remove eye socket, nostril and mouth area with shadow from top layer; fill in cut out areas using black royal icing. Replace cut out area from mouth. Use pattern to cut extra fondant pupil, cheek, eyebrow and collar; attach using damp brush. Use knife to imprint texture lines on cheek and collar. Pipe tip 2 outline details and shadow under cheek. Let dry.

Bake and cool two 1-layer sheet cakes. Position side-by-side on foil-wrapped base board (p. 110). Prepare and cover cakes with 108 oz. fondant tinted blue. Position buildings and bird on cake. Position *Spider-Man*. Pipe tip 3 name and tip 18 shell border. Serves 54.

► *Spider-Man's* Cityscape

Pan: Standard Muffin, p. 158
Tip: 1, p. 134
Colors: Royal Blue, Black, p. 146
Recipes: Buttercream, Royal Icings, p. 116; Thinned Fondant Adhesive, p. 117
Also: *Spider Sense Spider-Man* Toppers, Baking Cups, p. 192; Cakes 'N More 3-Tier Party Stand, p. 236; Meringue Powder, p. 143; Cake Boards, p. 241; cornstarch, knife, ruler

2-3 days in advance: Make fondant buildings. Tint 6 oz. each light gray, dark gray, blue; add ½ teaspoon Gum-Tex to each. Roll out ⅛ in. thick as needed. Cut 3 buildings in each color: 2¼ x 4 in. high light gray, 2¼ x 6 in. high dark gray, 2 x 7 in. blue. Also cut 3 triangular supports (2 x 1¼ in.) in each color. Let dry overnight on cornstarch-dusted boards. **Also:** Pipe royal icing windows. Use tip 1 and black icing. On light gray, pipe horizontal lines ½ in. apart; add ¼ in. square windows. On dark gray, pipe horizontal lines 1 in. apart and vertical lines ¾ in. apart; add ½ in. square windows. On blue, pipe vertical and horizontal lines ½ in. apart; add ⅜ in. square windows. Let dry overnight. **And:** Attach supports to backs of buildings using fondant adhesive.

Bake and cool cupcakes. Ice tops smooth. Position toppers in center of cupcakes. Use tip 1 to pipe straight lines extending from topper to outside edge. Add curved webbing between lines. Position buildings on stand and surround with cupcakes. Each serves 1.

◀ Tracking the *Transformers*

Pans: *Transformers*, p. 192; 16 x 2 in. Round, p. 157

Tips: 4, 10, 18, 101s, p. 134-135

Colors: Transformers Icing Color Set (blue, black), p. 192; Red-Red, p. 146

Candy: White Candy Melts (2 pks.), p. 194; Primary (blue), Garden (violet, black) Candy Color Sets, p. 195; Decorator Brush Set, p. 197

Recipe: Buttercream Icing, p. 116

Also: *Transformers* Icing Decorations (2 pks.), p. 192; Parchment Triangles, p. 136; Silver Classic Candles, p. 183; Dowel Rods, p. 239; Cake Boards, Fanci-Foil Wrap, p. 241; 18 in. diameter foamcore board (½ in. thick), knife, scissors, tape

In advance: Make candy plaque using candy color set (p. 128). Tint candy: 12 oz. dark blue (mix blue with black and violet), 10 oz. gray, 1 oz. each black, light blue.

Bake and cool 2-layer cake. Ice smooth. Cut and insert dowel rods where candy plaque will rest. Use tip 101s to pipe top and bottom zigzag tire tracks, ¾ in. wide. Use brush to pat smooth. Position candy plaque. Pipe tip 10 message. Pipe tip 18 rosettes above message; insert candles. Pipe tip 4 bead bottom border. Attach icing decorations to cake sides. Cake serves 77.

Licensed By:

▶ Traveling *Transformers*

Pans: 17.25 x 11.5 x 1 in. Large Cookie/ Jelly Roll, Cookie Sheet, Cooling Grid, p. 165

Candy: Red, Violet, Dark Cocoa Candy Melts, p. 194; Garden (black) Candy Color Set, p. 195

Also: *Transformers* Toppers, p. 192; Circle Metal Cutter, p. 202; Parchment Triangles, p. 136; Cake Boards, p. 241; waxed paper, knife, ruler

In advance: Make wheels. Bake and cool 1-layer cake using firm-textured batter such as pound cake. Cut wheels using Circle Cutter. Pour or pipe on melted candy to cover (p. 128). Add 2nd layer if necessary for smooth finish. Let set on waxed paper-covered boards.

Tint dark cocoa candy black. Add a drop or 2 of water to thicken candy for piping. Use cut parchment bag to outline and fill in zigzag tire treads, ⅛ in. wide, ⅛ in. apart. Chill until firm. Attach topper with melted candy. Each serves 1.

IT'S ALWAYS PARTY SEASON!

You don't have to look far to find a reason to celebrate. Just flip through the calendar! There's always a fun holiday to look forward to—and with the amazing treats we're showing in this section, you'll want to start planning now! We'll help you make a big impression at the party with ideas like the eerie crypt cake below or the enchanting Santa's gingerbread workshop with cookie elves turning out the toys. Of course, little treats can be big hits too. You'll find treats-for-one to celebrate every season, including stand-up spring chicks in sunglasses and star-topped flag mini cakes for the 4th of July.

Bat Hang-Out

Pans: 6, 8, 10 x 2 in. Square, p. 157
Tips: 2, 3, p. 134
Colors:* Black, Orange, Violet, Rose, p. 146
Fondant/Gum Paste: White Ready-To-Use Rolled Fondant (144 oz.), Ready-To-Use Gum Paste, p. 147; 20 in. Rolling Pin, Roll & Cut Mat, Easy-Glide Fondant Smoother, p. 148; Brush Set, p. 149
Recipes: Buttercream, Royal Icings, p. 116; Chocolate Fondant, Thinned Fondant Adhesive, p. 117
Also: 2011 Pattern Book (Gate, Tree, Bat), p. 130; Dark Cocoa Candy Melts (4 pks.), p. 194; Meringue Powder, Piping Gel, p. 143; 6 in. Cookie Treat Sticks, p. 203; Dowel Rods, p. 239; Cake Boards, Fanci-Foil Wrap, p. 241; 12 x 12 in. plywood or foamcore board (½ in. thick), tape, ruler, knife, scissors, cornstarch, toothpicks

3 days in advance: Make gate, tree and bat. Tint Gum Paste: 8 oz. black, 8 oz. gray. Roll out ⅛ in. thick. Use patterns to cut out shapes. Let dry on cornstarch-dusted boards. **Also:** Decorate gate. Follow pattern to pipe tip 3 details in royal icing. Let dry. **And:** Decorate bat (p. 123). **And:** Cover base board with 24 oz. violet fondant. (p. 120).

Bake and cool 2-layer 6 in. and 10 in. square cakes, 3-layer 8 in. square cake (trim 1 layer for 5 in. high tier). Prepare 4 recipes of Chocolate Fondant; tint black. Prepare and cover cakes with fondant (p. 117). Prepare for Stacked Construction (p. 114). Stack cakes on board. Attach gate to center front with fondant adhesive. Using full-strength royal icing and tip 3, pipe vertical fence posts, ¾ in. apart. Pipe pointed bead on top of each post. Pipe horizontal lines 3 in. and 2¼ in. from bottom. Pipe a circle inside each square. Using tip 3, pipe message and bead borders on top 2 tiers. Attach tree. Insert bat. Serves 62.

*Combine Violet with Rose for violet shown.

▼ Crispy Cranium

Pans: Guitar, p. 162; Cookie Sheet, Cooling Grid, p. 203
Candy: White Candy Melts (2 pks.), p. 194; Garden Candy Color Set (black), p. 195
Recipes: Favorite crisped rice cereal treats
Also: 2011 Pattern Book (Facial Features), p. 130; Parchment Triangles, p. 136; Cake Boards, Fanci-Foil Wrap, p. 241; tape, scissors, knife, waxed paper, toothpicks

Prepare cereal treats mixture and press into lightly greased pan (do not press into guitar neck area). Let cool; unmold. Tape pattern to cake board and cover with waxed paper. Outline and fill in facial features using 3 oz. melted, tinted candy in cut parchment bag; chill until firm. Place skull on cooling grid set over cookie sheet. Melt remaining white candy and pour over to cover top and sides (p. 128); tap to settle. Chill until firm. Repeat and position facial features, smooth side up. Pipe black outline mouth using melted candy in cut parchment bag; use toothpick to pull black candy into lines for teeth. Chill until firm. Serves 12.

▲ Laying the Groundwork for Fun

Pan: Standard Muffin, p. 158
Color: Black, p. 146
Recipe: Chocolate Buttercream Icing, p. 116
Also: Pick Your Poison Cupcake Combo Pack, p. 205; 3-D Skulls Candy Mold, p. 206; Black Colored Sugar, p. 205; Parchment Triangles, p. 136; Cake Boards, p. 241; White Candy Melts, p. 194; pretzel sticks, waxed paper, ruler, knife

In advance: Mold candy skulls (p. 128). Attach halves together with melted candy. **Also:** Make arms. Dip pretzels in melted candy; set on waxed paper-covered board. Chill until firm. Trim pretzel to 2½ in. long. Attach pick to pretzel stick with candy; let set. Using melted candy in cut parchment bag, pipe hand, fingers and thumb around stick. Chill until firm.

Bake and cool cupcakes. Ice smooth with chocolate buttercream tinted black and immediately cover with black sugar. Position candy skulls. Insert arms. Each serves 1.

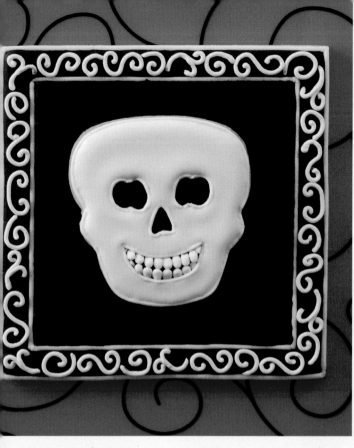

◀ Skullful Snack

Pans: Cookie Sheet, Cooling Grid, p. 203
Tips: 2, 3, p. 134
Color: Black, p. 146
Recipes: Royal Icing, Roll-Out Cookies, p. 116
Also: 2011 Pattern Book (Facial Features), p. 130; 3 Pc. Haunted Halloween Cutter Set, p. 207; Meringue Powder, p. 143; knife, ruler, 3 x 5 in. cardstock, craft knife

In advance: Make cookies. Prepare and roll out dough. Cut skulls using cutter from set. Cut a 5 in. square background for each treat.

Bake and cool cookies. **Also:** Ice squares. Outline cookie and ½ in. inside border with tip 3 and full-strength white icing; flow in with thinned black icing (p. 128). Let dry. **And:** Ice skulls. Use pattern and cardstock to cut a stencil for facial features. Set over cookie and ice features smooth using black full-strength icing; remove stencil. Outline skull and facial features with tip 2 and full-strength icing; flow in with thinned icing. Let dry.

Attach skull to square with icing. Pipe tip 2 scrolls inside square border. Pipe tip 2 teardrop-shaped teeth. Let dry. Each serves 1.

▶ Bone Appetite!

Pans: Cookie Sheet, Cooling Grid, p. 203
Tip: 3, p. 134
Color: Black, p. 146
Recipes: Color Flow Icing, Roll-Out Cookies, p. 116
Also: Halloween Cupcake and Cookie Stencils, p. 207; Round Comfort-Grip Cutter, p. 200; Color Flow Mix, p. 143; Silver Pearlized Jimmies, p. 205; Tapered Spatula, p. 139

In advance: Make cookies. Prepare and roll out dough. Cut using round cutter. Bake and cool. Outline cookies using tip 3 and full-strength black icing; flow in with thinned icing (p. 128). Let dry.

Decorate with full-strength white icing. Set stencil over cookie; use tapered spatula to spread icing. Remove stencil. Pipe tip 3 outline around cookie edge; roll edge in jimmies. Each serves 1.

◀ The Bat-tallion Lands!

Pans: Cookie Sheet, Cooling Grid, p. 203
Tips: 1, 2, 2A, 3, 5, 8, 10, 12, p. 134
Color: Black, p. 146
Recipes: Color Flow Icing, Roll-Out Cookies, p. 116
Also: 4 Pc. Grippy Cutter Set (large bat), p. 206; 9 Pc. Halloween Cutter Set (small bat), p. 207; Color Flow Mix, p. 143; Cake Boards, p. 241; waxed paper, cornstarch

In advance: Make cookies. Prepare and roll out dough. Cut large and small bats using cutters from sets. Bake and cool. Cover cookies with thinned color flow icing (p. 128). Let dry.

Decorate cookies with full-strength icing. For large bats, use tip 2A to figure pipe teardrop-shaped body and head; smooth with fingertip dipped in cornstarch. Add tip 10 pull-out ears. Pipe tip 8 outline arms. Pipe tip 5 pull-out thumbs, outline legs and pull-out feet. Pipe tip 3 outline wing ribbing. Use tip 1 to pipe outline ear details, eyebrows and mouth, dot eyes and nose, pull-out fangs. For small bats, repeat as above, changing to tip 12 for head and body, tip 8 for ears, tip 5 for arms, tip 3 for thumbs, legs and feet, tip 2 for ribbing. Let dry. Each serves 1.

Pan: Standard Muffin, p. 158
Tip: 16, p. 135
Colors: Leaf Green, Lemon Yellow, Royal Blue, Violet, p. 146
Recipe: Buttercream Icing, p. 116
Also: Polka Dot Pumpkin Cupcake Combo Pack, p. 205; Natural Colors Fondant Multi Pack (dark brown), p. 147; Brush Set, p. 149; ruler

Bake and cool cupcakes. For pumpkin cupcakes, pipe tip 16 pull-out star grass. Insert picks. For owl cupcakes, spatula ice tops. Use brown fondant to roll logs for branches, about ¼ in. diameter, tapering toward tips. Attach pieces with damp brush. Position on cupcakes. Insert picks. Each serves 1.

*Combine Leaf Green with Lemon Yellow for green shown. Combine Royal Blue with Violet for blue shown.

▼ Pumpkin Paradise

Pans: 13 x 9 x 2 in. Sheet, p. 157; Non-Stick Cookie Sheet, Cooling Grid, p. 165
Colors: Leaf Green, Lemon Yellow, p. 146
Fondant: White Ready-To-Use Rolled Fondant (2 oz. per treat), p. 147; 9 in. Rolling Pin, Roll & Cut Mat, p. 148
Candy: White, Orange, Yellow Candy Melts, p. 194; Garden Candy Color Set (green, black, violet), p. 195; Decorator Brush Set, p. 197
Recipe: Favorite crisped rice cereal treats
Also: Parchment Triangles, p. 136; Circle Metal Cutter, p. 202; Pumpkins 4 Pc. Nesting Cutter Set (smallest used), p. 207; Cake Boards, p. 241; knife, scissors, ruler, waxed paper

In advance: Mold candy pumpkins. Set pumpkin cutter on non-stick cookie pan. Fill ¼ in. deep with melted orange candy. Chill until firm. **Also:** Make round bases. Prepare cereal treats mixture. Press into lightly greased sheet cake pan, 1½ in. deep; let cool. Cut rounds using metal cutter. Cover with melted candy (p. 128); tap to settle, chill until set.

Make fondant grass (p. 123). Decorate pumpkins with melted candy in cut parchment bags. Attach to base with melted candy. Each serves 1.

*Combine Leaf Green with Lemon Yellow for green fondant shown.

▲ A Hoot and a Howl!

Pan: 10 x 3 in. Round, p. 157
Tips: 1, 12, p. 134
Colors: Orange, Golden Yellow, Lemon Yellow, Violet, Rose, Leaf Green, p. 146
Fondant/Gum Paste: White Ready-To-Use Rolled Fondant (60 oz.), Ready-To-Use Gum Paste (32 oz.), p. 147; 20 in. Rolling Pin, Roll & Cut Mat, Easy-Glide Fondant Smoother, p. 148; Brush Set, p. 149
Recipes: Buttercream Icing, p. 116; Gum Paste Adhesive, p. 117
Also: 2011 Pattern Book (Tree, Moon, Owl, Pumpkin Face), p. 130; Pumpkin Comfort-Grip Cutter, p. 206; 8 in. Lollipop Sticks, p. 198; Orange Candy Melts, p. 194; Cake Boards, Fanci-Foil Wrap, p. 241; cornstarch, knife, ruler, toothpicks, waxed paper

1 week in advance: Make gum paste trims for cake top (p. 123).

Bake and cool 2-layer cake (bake two 1½ in. high layers for a 3 in. high cake). Tint fondant: 34 oz. green, 16 oz. orange; reserve 3 oz. white. Roll out ⅛ in. thick as needed, unless otherwise specified. Prepare and cover cake with 24 oz. green fondant. Use cutter to cut pumpkin stem; cut out 1 in. long leaf shape. Cut thin strips for stem and leaf details and attach using damp brush. Reserve remaining green. Tint a small amount of icing dark violet; pipe tip 1 eyelids. Cut 32 x 3 in. high orange strip; attach around cake using damp brush. Roll out white fondant ⅛ in. thick. Using narrow end of tip 12, cut 300 white dots; attach in 5 staggered rows, about ½ in. apart. For grass, roll out reserved green ¼ in. thick. Cut 18 assorted strips, 1 in. to 4 in. wide and ½ to 1¼ in. high. Cut triangle-shaped blades on top edge. Attach using damp brush. Insert tree; position pumpkin to hide sticks supporting moon. Serves 28.

*Combine Golden Yellow with Lemon Yellow and Orange for yellow shown. Combine Leaf Green with Lemon Yellow for green shown. Combine Violet with Rose for violet shown.

▼ Owl Be There!

Pans: Round Cookie Treat, Cookie Sheet, Cooling Grid, p. 203

Tips: 1, 1A, 2, 10, 12, p. 134

Colors:* Golden Yellow, Lemon Yellow, Orange, Red-Red, Violet, Rose, p. 146

Recipe: Color Flow Icing, Roll-Out Cookies, p. 116

Also: White Ready-To-Use Rolled Fondant (2 oz. for each treat), p. 147; Color Flow Mix, p. 143; 8 in. Cookie Treat Sticks, p. 203; cornstarch, knife, ruler

In advance: Make cookies. Prepare dough and press into Cookie Treat pan; position sticks. Bake and cool. Cover with thinned color flow icing (p. 128); tap to settle, then let dry. **Also:** Shape fondant tree (p. 123). **And:** Figure pipe owl (p. 123). Let dry. Each serves 1.

*Combine Golden Yellow with Lemon Yellow for yellow shown. Combine Orange with Red-Red for orange shown. Combine Violet with Rose for violet shown.

▶ Perky Pumpkin

Pan: Iridescents! Jack-O-Lantern, p. 204

Tips: 3, 16, p. 134-135

Colors:* Orange, Golden Yellow, Lemon Yellow, Violet, Rose, Leaf Green, Black, p. 146

Fondant: White Ready-To-Use Rolled Fondant (24 oz.), p. 147; 20 in. Rolling Pin, Roll & Cut Mat, Easy-Glide Fondant Smoother, p. 148; Brush Set, p. 149

Recipe: Buttercream Icing, p. 116

Also: 2011 Pattern Book (Pumpkin Features), p. 130; 16 in. Cake Circles (2), Fanci-Foil Wrap, p. 241; Piping Gel, p. 143; tape, scissors, toothpicks, cornstarch

In advance: Prepare board. Tape cake circles together. Cover with 22 oz. fondant (p. 120).

Bake and cool cake. Position on prepared board. Decorate cake and base board (p. 123). Serves 12.

*Combine Golden Yellow with Lemon Yellow for yellow shown. Combine Violet with Rose for violet shown.

▲ Pumpkin Polka Dot Cookies

Pans: Cookie Sheet, Cooling Grid, p. 203

Tips: 2, 3, p. 134

Colors:* Orange, Lemon Yellow, Violet, Leaf Green, Black, p. 146

Recipes: Color Flow Icing, Roll-Out Cookies, p. 116

Also: 101 Cookie Cutters (largest round), p. 201; Pumpkins 4 Pc. Nesting Cutter Set (smallest used), p. 207; 6-Mix Halloween Pumpkin Sprinkles (Halloween Confetti), p. 205; Color Flow Mix, p. 143; cornstarch

In advance: Make cookies. Prepare and roll out dough. Cut 1 round and 1 pumpkin for each treat. Bake and cool. For round, outline with tip 3 and full-strength icing; flow in with thinned icing (p. 128). For pumpkin, outline, then add section lines with tip 2 and full-strength icing; flow in with thinned icing. Let dry.

Assemble and decorate with full-strength icing. Attach pumpkin to round with icing. Use tip 2 to outline and pipe in stem and facial features; pat smooth with fingertip dipped in cornstarch. Attach confetti with icing. Each serves 1.

*Combine Leaf Green with Lemon Yellow for green shown.

▼ Halloween Dreams

Pans: Cookie Sheet, Cooling Grid, p. 203

Tips: 2, 3, 366, p. 134-135

Colors:* Violet, Rose, p. 146

Recipes: Color Flow Icing, Roll-Out Cookies, p. 116

Also: Color Flow Mix, p. 143; Oval Cut-Outs, p. 151; Parchment Triangles, p. 136; Cake Boards, p. 241; ruler, knife, cornstarch, waxed paper

In advance: Make cookies. Prepare and roll out dough. For each treat, cut 2 ovals using large cutter from set. Cut curve in top of heads, about ¼ in. deep, using narrow end of cutter. Bake and cool. Outline cookies with tip 3 and full-strength icing; flow in with thinned icing (p. 128). Let dry overnight.

Decorate and assemble owl using full-strength icing (p. 123). Each serves 1.

*Combine Violet with Rose for violet shades shown.

Pans: Silicone Round Brownie Pops Mold, p. 171; Cookie Sheet, Cooling Grid, p. 203

Colors:* Violet, Rose, Leaf Green, Lemon Yellow, Orange, Black, p. 146

Fondant: White Ready-To-Use Rolled Fondant (8 oz. for 3 treats), p. 147; 9 in. Rolling Pin, Roll & Cut Mat, p. 148

Recipes: Buttercream Icing, p. 116; favorite brownie recipe or mix

Also: 2011 Pattern Book (Lapels), p. 130; 3-D Skulls Candy Mold, p. 206; White Candy Melts, p. 194; Cake Boards, p. 241; pretzel sticks, ruler, cornstarch, knife, waxed paper

In advance: Mold candy skulls. Attach halves.

Bake and cool brownie pops in silicone mold supported by cookie sheet. Ice lightly. Make and attach fondant details (p. 123). Each serves 1.

*Combine Violet with Rose for violet shown. Combine Leaf Green with Lemon Yellow for green shown.

▲ Pie-romaniacs!

Pans: 9 x 1.5 in. Non-Stick Pie, p. 165; Non-Stick Cookie Sheet, p. 165

Tip: 1A, p. 134

Colors:* Moss Green, Lemon Yellow, Golden Yellow, p. 146

Candy: Spooky Green, Dark Cocoa Candy Melts, p. 194; 6 in. Lollipop Sticks, p. 198

Recipe: favorite custard or firm cream pie

Also: Ghosts 4 Pc. Nesting Cutter Set, p. 207; 9 in. Rolling Pin, p. 148; Whipped Icing Mix, p. 143; Parchment Triangles, p. 136; Piping Gel, p. 143; 16 in. Disposable Decorating Bag, p. 136; Decorator Brush Set, p. 148; 10 in. Cake Circle, p. 241, or serving plate; orange and yellow spice drops, pretzel rods, granulated sugar, waxed paper, scissors, knife

In advance: Make candy ghosts. Place largest and 2 smallest ghost cutters on cookie sheet. Fill ¼ in. deep with melted candy. Tap to settle then chill until firm. Attach Lollipop Sticks to backs using melted candy; let set. Use melted cocoa candy in cut parchment bag to pipe facial features; let set. **Also:** Make candy spirals. Use melted candy in cut parchment bag to pipe assorted spirals on cookie sheet; chill until firm. Turn over and overpipe backs; let set.

Prepare pie, tinting filling a fun color if desired. Tint Piping Gel and whipped icing 2 shades of green. Fit Disposable Bag with tip 1A; stripe sides with gel (p. 111) then fill with whipped icing. Pipe assorted size balls over pie, overpiping toward center for height. Chill until serving time. Flatten spice drops by rolling between sheets of waxed paper sprinkled with sugar. Cut leaf-shaped flames in various sizes. Arrange pretzel rods and flames on serving plate for fire; set pie pan on top. Insert candy ghosts and spirals, trimming as needed. Serves 8.

*Combine Moss Green with Lemon Yellow and Golden Yellow for green shown.

◄ A Field of Corn

Pans: Silicone Round Brownie Pops Mold, p. 171; Cookie Sheet, Cooling Grid, p. 203

Tip: 12, p. 134

Candy: White, Orange, Yellow Candy Melts (1 pk. of each covers 4-5 treats), p. 194

Recipes: Buttercream Icing, p. 116; favorite brownie recipe or mix

Also: Parchment Triangles, p. 136; Cake Boards, p. 241; Spatula, p. 136; waxed paper

Bake and cool brownie pops in silicone mold supported by cookie sheet. Using tip 12, pipe icing to build up point; smooth with spatula. Set on waxed paper-covered board; freeze until icing is firm. Ice bottoms with melted white candy; chill until firm. Stand on cooling grid set over cookie sheet. Cover with melted white candy (p. 128). Chill until firm, then cover again. Let coated treat return to room temperature before adding additional coats of candy. Hold pop by tip and dip to coat with melted orange candy, leaving top ⅓ white; set on cooling grid, tap then chill until firm. Dip to coat bottom ⅓ with melted yellow candy; set on cooling grid, tap then chill. Let set completely. Each serves 1.

▶ Candy-Gobbling Goblin

Pans: Mini Ball, p. 162; Non-Stick Cookie Sheet, p. 165

Candy: Midnight Black, Spooky Green Candy Melts, Halloween Candy Kit MEGA PACK (mouth mold), 3-D Eyes Candy Mold, p. 206

Also: Leaf Cut-Outs, p. 151; Parchment Triangles, p. 136; Pastry Brush, p. 153; black shoestring licorice, assorted candy

In advance: Make two ¼ in. thick green candy shells (p. 128) using Mini Ball Pan. **Also:** Make candies. Mold eyes and mouth using Piping Method (p. 128), filling mouth only halfway full.

For ears, place medium Leaf Cut-Out on non-stick sheet pan and fill ⅛ in. deep with green candy; chill until firm. Turn over Cut-Out and repeat for other ear. Attach features to top shell with melted candy. Cut 3 in. pieces of licorice for hair; attach with melted candy. Fill bottom shell with candy. Position top. Each serves 1.

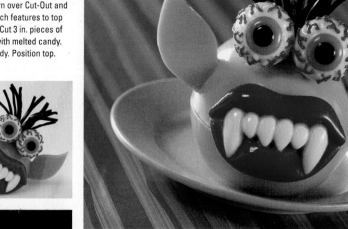

◀ An Eye for Beauty

Pans: Cookie Sheet, Cooling Grid, p. 203
Tips: 3, 4, 6, 9, 47, p. 134-135
Color: Black, p. 146
Candy: White (1 pk. makes 36-40 eyes), Light Cocoa Candy Melts, p. 194; Primary (red), Garden (green) Candy Color Sets, p. 195; 3-D Eyeballs Candy Mold, p. 206
Recipes: Royal Icing, Roll-Out Cookies, p. 116
Also: 3 Pc. Haunted Halloween Cookie Set (skull), p. 207; Parchment Triangles, p. 136; Meringue Powder, p. 143; Cake Boards, p. 241; waxed paper

In advance: Mold candy eyeballs. Use Piping Method (p. 128); filling front of eyeball mold halfway. **Also:** Make cookies. Prepare and roll out dough. Cut heads using skull cutter from set. Bake and cool. Outline mouth with tip 3 and full-strength icing; flow in with thinned icing (p. 128). Outline head with tip 3 and full-strength icing; flow in with thinned icing. Let dry overnight.

Set cookies on waxed paper-covered board to decorate. Attach candy eye with icing dots. Pipe tip 9 pull-out ears and 3-part dot nose (pat smooth) with smaller dot wart. Pipe tip 4 outline eyebrow. Pipe tip 47 teeth (smooth side up). Pipe tip 6 pull-out hair. Let dry. Each serves 1.

▶ Bat Intentions

Pans: Animal Crackers, p. 161; 4 Pc. Heart Set (10 x 2 in. used); 4 Pc. Oval Set (7.75 x 5.5 x 2 in. used), p. 156

Tips: 3, 19, p. 134-135

Colors: Violet, Black, p. 146

Fondant: White Ready-To-Use Rolled Fondant (48 oz.), p. 147; 20 in. Rolling Pin, Roll & Cut Mat, Easy-Glide Fondant Smoother, p. 148; Brush Set, p. 149; Oval Cut-Outs, p. 151

Recipes: Buttercream Icing, Roll-Out Cookies, p. 116

Also: 2011 Pattern Book (Ears), p. 130; 6 in. Cake Circles, Cake Boards, p. 241; Piping Gel, p. 143; 20 x 18 in. plywood or foamcore board (¼ in. thick), scissors, tape, knife, ruler

In advance: Make wings. Prepare cookie dough. Press half into bottom of Heart Pan. Bake and cool; repeat. Tint 24 oz. fondant black. Roll out ⅛ in. thick. Brush cookies with Piping Gel; cover with rolled fondant. Reserve remaining fondant.

Bake and cool cakes using smallest oval and Animal Crackers pans. Trim ears for more pointed shape. Make and attach fondant facial features with icing (p. 123). Cover head and oval body with tip 19 stars. Cut 2 large teeth (1 in. long) and 5 small teeth (⅝ in. long). Position on cake. Roll 2 x ¼ in. logs for eyebrows; attach. Position wings. Tape 6 in. Cake Circles together, 2 or 3 thick, to build supports for head and body that equal height of wings. Position supports, head and body. Roll thin logs for wing ribbing (⅜ in. diameter for main ribs, ¼ in. diameter for others). Attach using damp brush. Cake serves 16. Each cookie serves 1.

▲ Winterized Guy

Pans: 6 x 2 in. Round, p. 157; 4 Pc. Oval Set (2nd smallest pan used), p. 156

Tip: 12, p. 134

Colors:* Leaf Green, Red-Red, Christmas Red, Sky Blue, Orange, Black, Lemon Yellow, Golden Yellow, p. 148

Fondant: White Ready-To-Use Rolled Fondant (48 oz.), Gum-Tex, p. 147; 20 in. Rolling Pin, Roll & Cut Mat, Easy-Glide Fondant Smoother, p. 148; Brush Set, p. 149; Cutter/Embosser, p. 150; Round Cut-Outs, p. 151

Recipes: Buttercream Icing, p. 116; Thinned Fondant Adhesive, p. 117

Also: 2011 Pattern Book (Scarf, Hat, Hat Band, Buckle, Nose), p. 130; 13 x 19 in. Cake Board, Cake Circles, Fanci-Foil Wrap, p. 241; Piping Gel, p. 143; ruler, cornstarch, waxed paper, tape, scissors, toothpicks, knife

In advance: Make fondant trims (p. 123). **Also:** Cut and wrap base board (p. 110). Use cake pans as a pattern, allowing 1 in. extra on all sides and overlapping 1 in. at bottom of round onto oval.

Bake and cool 1-layer cakes. Trim 1 in. off round cake at bottom edge. Prepare and cover with rolled fondant (p. 117). Position on wrapped board. Use fondant adhesive to attach braces to back of hat; let dry several minutes. Attach fondant pieces to cake with icing. Serves 16.

*Combine Leaf Green with a little Lemon Yellow and Sky Blue for green shown. Combine Red-Red with Christmas Red for red shown. Combine Lemon Yellow with a little Golden Yellow and Red-Red for gold shown.

▼ Fir Trader

Pans: 6 x 2 in. Round, p. 157; Cookie Sheet, Cooling Grid, p. 203

Tips: 2, 3, 4, 7, 12, p. 134

Colors:* Leaf Green, Kelly Green, Sky Blue, Royal Blue, Violet, Lemon Yellow, Golden Yellow, Christmas Red, Red-Red, Orange, Black, p. 146

Fondant: White Ready-To-Use Rolled Fondant (24 oz.), p. 147; 20 in. Rolling Pin, Roll & Cut Mat, Easy-Glide Fondant Smoother, p. 148; Brush Set, p. 149; Cutter/Embosser, p. 150

Recipes: Buttercream, Color Flow Icings, Roll-Out Cookies, p. 116; favorite crisped rice cereal treats

Also: 2011 Pattern Book (Snowman's Hat, Large and Small Stars), p. 130; 18 Pc. Holiday Cutter Set (snowman), p. 212; Christmas Tree Comfort-Grip Cutter, 4 Pc. Grippy Cutter Set (tree), p. 211; Color Flow Mix, p. 143; 6 in. Lollipop Sticks, p. 198; 6 and 8 in. Cake Circles, Boards, Fanci-Foil Wrap, p. 241; White Candy Melts (1 pk.), p. 194; waxed paper, cornstarch, knife, tape, non-stick pan spray

2-3 days in advance: Make and decorate cookies (p. 123). **Also:** Make 1 large and 2 small icing stars. Tape patterns to board and cover with waxed paper. Outline and fill in stars using tip 2 and full-strength icing. When dry, attach to tree tops with icing. **And:** Make hat. Tint a 1 in. ball of fondant black; roll out ⅛ in. thick. Cut out hat using pattern and let dry.

Prepare cereal treat and immediately st in melted Candy Melts. Press firmly into sprayed pan. Unmold onto foil-wrapped Cake Circle; secure with melted candy. Let cool completely. Prepare and cover treat with 10 oz. blue rolled fondant (p. 117). Make snow drift and snowflake dots (p. 123). Using full-strength icing, pipe tip 2 outline hat band, hat buckle, pull-out nose, dot eyes and tip 3 dot buttons. Attach hat to snowman using icing. Outline and pipe in tip 3 scarf; pat smooth with fingertip dipped in cornstarch. Insert cookies. Treat serves 12; each cookie serves 1.

*Combine Leaf Green with Lemon Yellow for light green shown. Combine Christmas Red with Red-Red for red shown. Combine Royal Blue with Violet for blue fondant shown.

◄ Picking Their Pine

Pans: Holiday Cookie Shapes, p. 214; Cookie Sheet, Cooling Grid, p. 203

Tips: 1, 2, 3, p. 134

Colors:* Leaf Green, Kelly Green, Christmas Red, Red-Red, Teal, Orange, Black, Golden Yellow, p. 146

Recipes: Buttercream, Color Flow Icings, Shortbread and Roll-Out Cookies, p. 116

Also: 3 Pc. Trees Cutter Set, p. 212; Color Flow Mix, p. 143; cornstarch

2-3 days in advance: Make trees. Prepare and roll out Roll-Out cookie dough. Cut using classic fir cutter from set. Bake and cool cookies. Outline using tip 3 and full-strength color flow; let set. Flow in with thinned color flow (p. 128). Let dry 24 hours. **Also:** Make snow people. Prepare shortbread dough. Press into snowman cavity of pan. Bake and cool.

Decorate snow people with buttercream (p. 123). Each serves 1.

*Combine Christmas Red with Red-Red for red shown.

▲ Flurry Friend

Pans: Non-Stick Large Loaf, Cooling Grid, p. 165

Colors:* Black, Golden Yellow, Orange, Sky Blue, Christmas Red, Leaf Green, Lemon Yellow, p. 146

Fondant: White Ready-To-Use Rolled Fondant (2 oz. per treat), p. 147; Round Cut-Outs, p. 151; 9 in. Rolling Pin, Roll & Cut Mat, p. 148; Cutter/Embosser, p. 150; Brush Set, p. 149

Recipe: Favorite pound cake recipe or mix

Also: White Candy Melts, p. 194; Round Comfort-Grip Cutter, p. 200; White Sparkling Sugar, p. 144; waxed paper, ruler

In advance: Make cakes. Bake and cool cake using firm-textured batter such as pound cake. Cut ¾ in. thick slices. Use large and medium Cut-Outs to cut body and head for each treat. Cover with melted candy (p. 128). Let set. **Also:** Make base. Place Comfort-Grip Cutter in loaf pan; pour in melted candy to ¼ in. thick. Chill until firm; unmold.

Assemble snowman, make features and clothes (p. 123). Spread melted candy over base and sprinkle with Sparkling Sugar. Each serves 1.

*Combine Leaf Green with Lemon Yellow for green shown.

▲ Rompin' Reindeer

Pans: 3 Pc. Paisley Set (smallest and largest used), p. 156; Cookie Sheet, Cooling Grid, p. 203; Standard Muffin, p. 158

Tips: 3, 12, 16, p. 134-135

Colors:* Brown, Christmas Red, Red-Red, Leaf Green, Black, p. 148

In advance: Make royal icing antlers (p. 123). **Also:** Make cookie pieces. Prepare and roll out dough. Use pattern to cut out hat. Use smallest Paisley Pan as pattern to cut out head. Use largest oval Cut-Out to cut tail and 2 ears (trim ¾ in. off base of ears). Bake and cool. **And:** Cut 2 Lollipop Sticks to 3 in. and attach to back of ears and tail with melted candy,

Recipes: Buttercream, Royal Icings, Roll-Out Cookies, p. 116

Also: 2011 Pattern Book (Hat, Antlers), p. 130; Oval Cut-Outs, p. 151; White Standard Baking Cups, p. 184; Light Cocoa Candy Melts, p. 194; 6 in. Lollipop Sticks, p. 198; Cake Boards, p. 241; Meringue Powder, p. 143; pretzel rods, waxed paper, non-stick pan spray, facial tissue, tape, knife

leaving excess exposed at bottom, attach 2 Lollipop Sticks to top of head to support hat. With candy, Attach hat and ears to head; attach back antler.

Bake and cool 1-layer cake with largest paisley pan and 3 cupcakes; spatula ice cupcake tops. Position head on body, using 2 cupcakes under hat and face for support. Use tip 3 to outline and fill in nose; pipe dot eyes and outline mouth. Cover head, ears, hat, body and tail with tip 16 stars. Insert tail and pretzel rod legs. Position and attach front antler with icing. Cake serves 20; each cupcake and cookie serves 1.

*Combine Brown with Red-Red for light brown shown. Combine Christmas Red with Red-Red for red shown.

◄ King of the Forest

Pans: Standard Muffin, p. 158; Cookie Sheet, Cooling Grid, p. 203

Colors:* Leaf Green, Lemon Yellow, Sky Blue, Red-Red, p. 146

Recipes: Buttercream, Color Flow Icings, Roll-Out Cookies, p. 116

Also: Christmas Cookie Tree Cutter Kit, p. 216; Woodland Friends Cupcake Combo Pack, p. 210; Flowerful Medley 6-Mix Assortment (confetti), White Sparkling Sugar, Red Cake Sparkles, p. 144; Color Flow Mix, p. 143; Cake Boards, 8 in. Cake Circles, Fanci-Foil Wrap, p. 241; waxed paper

In advance: Make cookies. Prepare 3 recipes cookie dough; roll out as needed. Use all cutters from set except largest;

cut 1 small star and 3 of each remaining size. Bake and cool. Cover cookies with color flow icing (p. 128) using red for smallest star, green for the rest. Sprinkle red star with Cake Sparkles after it has set 15 minutes. Let all dry overnight on waxed paper-covered boards.

Assemble tree on foil-wrapped 8 in. Cake Circle using full-strength color flow. Alternate position of points as you stack stars. Attach standing top star and confetti ornaments. Bake and cool cupcakes. Ice smooth with buttercream. Sprinkle with Sparkling Sugar; insert Fun Pix. Position cupcakes around tree. Each cupcake and cookie serves 1.

*Combine Leaf Green with Lemon Yellow and a little Sky Blue for green shown.

◀ Noël Nesters

Pans: 6, 8 x 2 in. Square, p. 157

Tip: 2, p. 134

Colors: * Christmas Red, Red-Red, Kelly Green, Brown, Black, p. 146

Fondant: White Ready-To-Use Rolled Fondant (96 oz.), Gum-Tex, p. 147; 20 in. Rolling Pin, Roll & Cut Mat, Easy-Glide Fondant Smoother, p. 148; Brush Set, p. 149

Recipes: Buttercream Icing, p. 216; Thinned Fondant Adhesive, p. 217

Also: 2011 Pattern Book (Bird), p. 130; Piping Gel, p. 143; White Sparkling Sugar, p. 144; 6 Pc. Holiday Mini Cutter Set (holly leaf), p. 212; 6 in. Cookie Treat Sticks, p. 203; Dowel Rods, p. 239; Cake Boards, p. 241; 10 in. square foamcore board (½ in. thick), cornstarch, ruler, knife

In advance: Make fondant pieces. Tint fondant: 6 oz. red (add ½ teaspoon Gum-Tex), 2 oz. light green, 2 oz. dark green. Roll out ⅛ in. thick as needed. Use pattern to cut 3 birds (reverse pattern for 1). Use cutter to make 4 dark green and 5 light green holly leaves (after cutting, adjust cutter, position and recut to vary sizes). Roll 13 red berries, about ¼ in. diameter. Let dry on cornstarch-dusted board. Attach Cookie Treat Stick to back of top bird using fondant adhesive. Pipe tip 2 dot eyes. **Also:** Cover base board with rolled fondant (p. 120).

Bake and cool 2-layer cakes. Prepare and cover with rolled fondant (p. 117). Prepare for Stacked Construction (p. 114). Brush top areas with Piping Gel and sprinkle on Sparkling Sugar. Tint 3 oz. fondant brown and roll out ⅛ in. thick. Cut 2 tapered branches, 9 in. and 12 in. long, about ⅜ in. wide. Use Piping Gel to attach fondant branches, holly leaves, berries and 2 birds to cake sides. Insert top bird. Serves 32.

*Combine Christmas Red with Red-Red for red shown. Combine Brown with Red-Red for brown shown.

▶ Her Holly Home

Pan: Standard Muffin, p. 158

Tips: 2, 13, 352, p. 134-135

Colors: * Christmas Red, Red-Red, Kelly Green, Black, p. 146

Recipes: Buttercream, Royal Icings, p. 116

Also: 2011 Pattern Book (Bird), p. 130; Meringue Powder, p. 143; White Sparkling Sugar, p. 144; White Standard Baking Cups, p. 184; Cake Boards, p. 241; pretzel sticks, waxed paper, tape

2-3 days in advance: Make royal icing birds. Tape patterns to Cake Board and cover with waxed paper. Pipe tip 2 outlines with full-strength icing; flow in with thinned icing (p. 128). Let dry. Use full-strength icing to pipe tip 13 elongated shell wings and tip 2 dot eye. Let dry.

Bake and cool cupcakes. Ice smooth with buttercream; roll tops in Sparkling Sugar for heavy coating. Position bird; cut pretzels in half and insert for branches. Pipe tip 352 leaves and tip 2 dot berries with buttercream. Each serves 1.

*Combine Christmas Red with Red-Red for red shown.

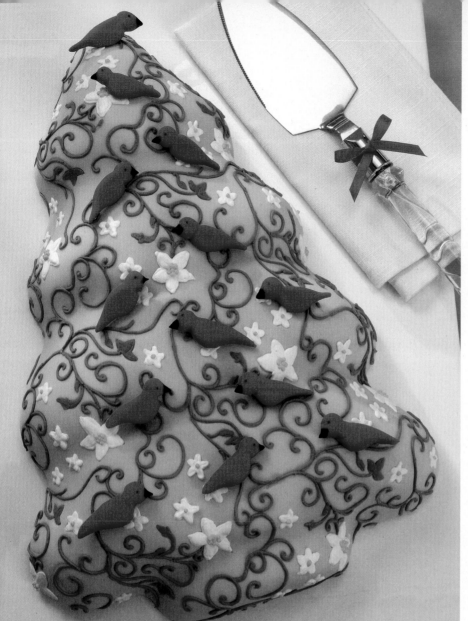

▼ Season's Tweetings

Pans: Cookie Sheet, Cooling Grid, p. 203

Tips: 1, 2, 3, 8, p. 134

Colors:* Kelly Green, Leaf Green, Christmas Red, Red-Red, Black, p. 146

Recipes: Color Flow Icing, Roll-Out Cookies, p. 116

Also: 18 Pc. Holiday Cutter Set (holly leaf), p. 212; Cake Boards, p. 241; Color Flow Mix, p. 143; waxed paper, tape, toothpicks, ruler, cornstarch

In advance: Make cookies. Prepare and roll out dough. Cut using holly leaf from set. Bake and cool cookies. Outline using tip 3 and full-strength icing; flow in using thinned icing (p. 128). Immediately overpipe 2 veins using lighter green thinned icing; use toothpick to draw tips to a point. Pipe tip 2 dot berries using thinned icing. Let dry. **Also:** Make birds. Figure pipe birds using tip 8 and full-strength icing on waxed paper-covered boards. Pipe bead for body, about 1¼ in. long, drawing end into curved tail. Pipe dot head and continue squeezing as you pull away to form beak. Add tip 1 dot eye and tip 8 bead wing. Let dry.

Attach bird to holly leaf using full-strength icing. Let dry. Each serves 1.

*Combine Kelly Green with Leaf Green for both greens shown. Combine Christmas Red with Red-Red for red shown.

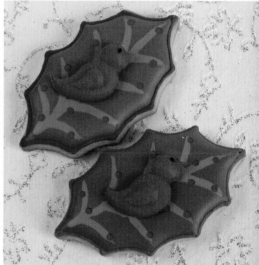

In advance: Make candy clay pieces. Make 1 recipe each red and green candy clay. Roll out ⅛ in. thick. Cut 1 bird and 4 leaves for each treat. Use small end of veining tool to imprint details on leaves. Use melted candy in cut parchment bag to outline wings, tail and pipe dot eye details on bird. Let dry.

Assemble using melted white candy in a cut parchment bag. Cut pretzel rod for 3, 3½ and 1¾ in. branches. Attach to full-length pretzel rod. Attach leaves and bird. Pipe candy snow; sprinkle with Sparkling Sugar. Attach Cinnamon Drops. Each serves 1.

▲ Flocked Tree

Pan: Iridescents! Tree Pan, p. 209

Tips: 1, 2, p. 134

Colors: Kelly Green, Golden Yellow, p. 146

Fondant: White Ready-To-Use Rolled Fondant (24 oz.), Primary Colors Fondant Multi Pack (red), Fine Tip FoodWriter Edible Color Markers (black), p. 147; 20 in. Rolling Pin, Roll & Cut Mat, Graceful Vines Fondant Imprint Mat, p. 148

Recipe: Buttercream Icing, p. 116

Also: Cake Boards, Fanci-Foil Wrap, p. 241; tape, cornstarch, knife, ruler

Bake and cool cake. Prepare to cover with fondant (p. 117). Tint fondant and roll out ⅛ in. thick. Imprint design using Imprint Mat. Transfer fondant to cake and smooth using hands; trim excess as needed. Pipe tip 2 vines and leaves in imprinted areas; add additional scrolls as needed. Use tip 2 to outline and fill in flowers; add tip 1 dot centers. Shape birds from ⅝ in. balls of fondant; some facing left, some right. Use FoodWriter to draw black beak and dot eye. Position on cake, attach with icing. Serves 12.

▼ Perfect Perch

Candy: White, Red, Green Candy Melts, p. 194; Garden Candy Color Set (black), p. 195

Recipes: Candy Clay (2 recipes for 12-14 treats), p. 116

Also: Animal Pals 50 Pc. Cutter Set (bird), p. 130; 6 Pc. Holiday Mini Cutter Set (holly leaf), p. 212; 10 Pc. Fondant/Gum Paste Tool Set, p. 149; 9 in. Rolling Pin, Roll & Cut Mat, p. 148; Cinnamon Drops Sprinkles, White Sparkling Sugar, p. 144; Parchment Triangles, p. 136; pretzel rods, knife, ruler, cornstarch, waxed paper

◀ Saucer Sledders

Pans: Silicone Round Brownie Pops Mold, p. 171; Mini Ball, p. 162; Cookie Sheet, Cooling Grid, p. 203

Colors:* Violet, Rose, Brown, Red-Red, Golden Yellow, Lemon Yellow, Royal Blue, Black, Copper (for light skin tone shown), p. 146

Fondant: White Ready-To-Use Rolled Fondant (6 oz. per treat), Fine Tip FoodWriter Edible Color Markers, p. 147; 9 in. Rolling Pin, Roll & Cut Mat, p. 148; Brush Set, p. 149

Recipe: Buttercream Icing, p. 116

Also: Red, Green Candy Melts, p. 194; 6 in. Lollipop Sticks (cut to 3 in.), p. 198; Cake Boards, p. 241; Wooden Dowel Rods, p. 239; knife, ruler, cornstarch, waxed paper

In advance: Make ¼ in. thick candy shells (p. 128) in Mini Ball pan. Use hot knife to trim off top edge for a 1 in. high sled.

Bake and cool brownie pops (1 for each body) in silicone mold supported by cookie sheet. Make fondant sledding figures (p. 124). Each serves 1.

*Combine Violet with Rose for violet shown. Combine Brown with Red-Red for dark skin tone shown. Combine Golden Yellow with Lemon Yellow for yellow shown.

▶ Star Gazers

Pan: Non-Stick Cookie Sheet, p. 165

Candy: Primary (yellow, orange), Garden (black) Candy Color Sets, p. 195; Christmas Candy Kit for Pretzels, Christmas Candy Making Kit MEGA PACK (kit includes snowman and tree molds, Red, White, Green, Light Cocoa Candy Melts used; additional Candy Melts may be required), p. 211

Also: 101 Cookie Cutters (largest round), p. 201; White Sparkling Sugar, Flowerful Medley 6-Mix Sprinkles (confetti), p. 144; Parchment Triangles, p. 136; tape, knife, ruler

In advance: Mold candy pieces using Painting or Piping Method (p. 128). Tint portions of candy yellow, orange and black. For base, place largest round cutter from set on cookie sheet; fill ¼ in. deep with melted candy. Tap to settle; chill until firm. Mold trees without stick. For snowmen, tape cavity closed below figures. After unmolding, use warm knife to cut off snowball. Use melted candy to pipe eyes and mouth.

Assemble using melted white candy. Attach tree and snowmen to base; let set. Spread candy over top of base; immediately sprinkle on Sparkling Sugar snow. Attach confetti ornaments to hand, tree and snow. Each serves 1.

◀ Cookies, Candy & Canes!

Candy: Winter Cookie Candy Mold, p. 211; White, Red, Green, Light Cocoa Candy Melts, p. 194; Primary Candy Color Set (blue), p. 195; Decorator Brush Set, p. 197

Also: Parchment Triangles, p. 136; Cake Boards, p. 241; 2 in. sandwich cookies, candy canes, ¼ in. wide ribbon (13 in. per treat), waxed paper, knife

Mold tree and Santa sections of mold using Painting or Piping method (p. 128). Chill until firm. Fill cavities half full with melted candy in background color. Press in cookie. Pipe melted candy over cookie to seal. Chill until firm. Trim curve off candy cane; attach to back of cookie using melted candy; set on waxed paper-covered board and chill until firm. Tie ribbon around candy cane, securing with dot of melted candy. Each serves 1.

▲ Pinwheel Pops

Pan: Silicone Bite-Size Gingerbread Boy Mold, p. 209

Candy: White, Red, Green, Light Cocoa Candy Melts, p. 194; Pinwheel Large Lollipop Mold, p. 196; 6 in. Lollipop Sticks, p. 198

Also: Parchment Triangles, p. 136

Mold pinwheel lollipops using Piping Method (p. 128). Chill until firm. Mold gingerbread boys in silicone mold, filling cavities ¼ in. deep. Chill until firm. Unmold. Using melted candy in cut parchment bag, add dot, zigzag and outline details. Attach gingerbread boys to pinwheels; let set. Each serves 1.

▼ Toymaker Treats

Pan: Non-Stick Cookie Pan, p. 165

Candy:* White, Green, Red Candy Melts, p. 194; Party/Birthday Large Lollipop Mold, p. 196; Primary (orange), Garden (pink) Candy Color Sets, p. 195; Decorator Brush Set, p. 197; 6 in. Lollipop Sticks, p. 198

Also: Round Cut-Outs, p. 151; Parchment Triangles, p. 136; White Nonpareils Sprinkles, p. 144; Cake Boards, p. 241; waxed paper, ruler

Mold hats without sticks using lollipop mold and Painting Method (p. 128). Chill until firm.

Place on waxed paper-covered board. Brush brim and pompom with melted candy and immediately sprinkle on nonpareils. Mold heads. Set largest round Cut-Out on cookie sheet; fill ¼ in. deep with melted candy. Tap to settle; chill until firm. Place on waxed paper-covered board. Use melted candy in cut parchment bags to pipe pull-out ears and nose, outline mouth, dot eyes and cheeks. Let set. Attach hat to head and Lollipop Stick to back using melted candy. Let set. Each serves 1.

*Tint portion of white candy light orange for skin tone shown.

◄ Delivered in the Nick of Time

Pan: Non-Stick Cookie Sheet, p. 165

Candy: Christmas Candy Making Kit MEGA PACK (Santa, present; includes Red and Light Cocoa Candy Melts used; additional Candy Melts may be required), p. 211; Green, White Candy Melts, p. 194; Primary Candy Color Set (blue, yellow), p. 195

Also: Christmas Tree Comfort-Grip Cutter, p. 211; 101 Cookie Cutters (large round), p. 201; Star Cut-Outs, p. 151; Parchment Triangles, p. 136; Quick Ease Roller, Cake Boards, p. 241; waxed paper, yellow jellied candy, granulated sugar, ruler, tape

In advance: Mold candy pieces using Painting or Piping Method (p. 128). For base

and tree: Set cutters on Cookie Sheet. Fill ¼ in. deep with melted candy. Chill until firm. For Santa and separate present, mold shapes from candy kit without lollipop sticks. Chill until firm. Pipe dot eyes and mouth after unmolding.

Set trees on waxed paper-covered board. Using melted candy in cut parchment bag, pipe zigzag branches across bottom section. Chill until firm. Repeat with additional rows of branches to reach top. Let set completely. For star, roll out jellied candy on waxed paper sprinkled with sugar. Cut star using medium Cut-Out. Arrange candies on base and attach with melted candy. Let set. Attach star. Each serves 1.

◄ The Celebration's Afoot!

Pan: Horseshoe, p. 162

Colors:* Leaf Green, Lemon Yellow, Kelly Green, Violet, Rose, Orange, Red-Red, Christmas Red, p. 146

Fondant: White Ready-To-Use Rolled Fondant (48 oz.), p. 147; 20 in. Rolling Pin, Roll & Cut Mat, p. 148; Brush Set, p. 149; Fondant Ribbon Cutter/Embosser Set, p. 150

Recipe: Buttercream Icing, p. 116

Also: White Sparkling Sugar, p. 144; 4 in. Lollipop Sticks, p. 198; Cake Board, Fanci-Foil Wrap, p. 241; cornstarch, waxed paper, ruler, knife, scissors

Bake and cool cake. Cut rounded toe about 2 in. left of center. Prepare for rolled fondant (p. 117). Tint fondant: 18 oz. light green, 10 oz. violet, 6 oz. kelly green, 3 oz. each red, yellow, orange. Roll out ⅛ in. thick as needed. Cover cake with light green fondant. Cut 4 x 8 in. kelly green section for toe and 5 strips, 1 x 8 in. for stripes; trim to fit and attach using damp brush. Fit roller handle with 2 zigzag wheels (no spacers). Cut six 8 in. long zigzag details and attach. For cuff, cut a 5 x 8 in. rectangle. Use scissors to cut away 6 triangles; curl edges up slightly. Attach. Repeat with a 4 x 8 in. rectangle. Roll twelve ½ in. diameter balls; brush with water and roll in Sparkling Sugar. Attach to cuff tips. Roll a 1¼ in. diameter ball and insert on a 3 in. Lollipop Stick. Brush with water, roll in sugar and insert in toe. For each candy cane, roll 1 white and 1 colored log, 11 x ½ in. diameter. Roll to twist and smooth together; curve into shape. Position above stocking, trimming as needed. Serves 8.

*Combine Leaf Green with Lemon Yellow for light green shown. Combine Violet with Rose for violet shown. Combine Red-Red with Christmas Red for red shown.

► Neon on Your Tree!

Pan: 10 x 2 in. Round, p. 157

Tip: 1A, p. 134

Colors:* Violet, Rose, Leaf Green, Lemon Yellow, Sky Blue, p. 146

Fondant: White Ready-To-Use Rolled Fondant (34 oz.), Gum-Tex, p. 147; 20 in. Rolling Pin, Roll & Cut Mat, Easy-Glide Fondant Smoother, p. 148; Brush Set, p. 149

Recipe: Buttercream Icing, p. 116

Also: Cake Board, Fanci-Foil Wrap, p. 241; Circle Metal Cutter, p. 202; Purple, Yellow Cake Sparkles, p. 144; facial tissue, waxed paper, knife, cornstarch

In advance: Make bow and streamers (p. 124).
Also: Make hook. Tint 3 oz. fondant blue. Roll a ½ x 10 in. long log; shape into a hook and let dry on cornstarch-dusted board.

Tint remaining fondant: 18 oz. violet, 5 oz. yellow. Bake and cool 1-layer round cake. Prepare and cover cake with violet fondant (p. 117). Roll out yellow and remaining violet fondant ⅛ in. thick. Use wide end of tip 1A to cut approximately 12 violet circles; use circle metal cutter to cut 7 yellow circles. Brush circles with water; sprinkle with matching Cake Sparkles. Attach to cake with damp brush. Attach bow and streamers. Position hook. Serves 14.

*Combine Violet with Rose for violet shown.

◄ Let the Flakes Fly

Pans: Mini Ball, p. 162; Standard Muffin, p. 158

Tips: 8, 12, p. 134

Colors:* Black, Orange, Sky Blue, Rose, Violet, Red-Red, Christmas Red, Leaf Green, Lemon Yellow, Brown, p. 146

Fondant: White Ready-To-Use Rolled Fondant (5 oz. per treat), p. 147; 9 in. Rolling Pin, Roll & Cut Mat, p. 148; Brush Set, p. 149; Round Cut-Outs, p. 151

Recipe: Buttercream Icing, p. 116

Also: 4 in. Lollipop Sticks, p. 198; sugar ice cream cones, ruler, knife, cornstarch

Bake and cool ball cakes and cupcakes. Cut cupcake in half for body. Ice smooth. For each pair of snowmen, tint fondant: 4 oz. black, 2 oz. violet, 1 oz. green, 1 oz. blue and ½ oz. each pink, orange, red and brown. Roll out ⅛ in. thick as needed. Make and position hats (p. 124). Using narrow end, cut eyes and buttons with tip 8, cut cheeks with tip 12. Cut ⅛ x 1¼ in. strip for mouth; shape small cone for nose. Attach features using damp brush. For scarf, cut ¼ x 4 in. strip for around neck, ¼ x ¾ in. and ¼ x 1½ in. strips for ends. Use knife to fringe ends; attach. Roll thin logs for 1½ in. long arms. Roll ¾ in. balls and shape into shoes. Push shoes onto 3 in. Lollipop Sticks and insert in body. Each serves 1.

*Combine Violet with Rose for violet shown. Combine Leaf Green with Lemon Yellow for green shown.

◀ Glittering Getaway

Cookie: Pre-Baked Gingerbread House Kit (2104-1903; includes icing mix, assorted candies, decorating bag and tip, cardboard base and complete instructions), p. 215

Colors:* Rose, Leaf Green, Lemon Yellow, Christmas Red, Orange, Sky Blue, Violet, p. 146

Fondant: White Ready-To-Use Rolled Fondant (96 oz.), Gum-Tex, p. 147; 9 in. Rolling Pin, Roll & Cut Mat, p. 148; Brush Set, p. 149

Also: 2011 Pattern Book (Door, Large and Small Windows, Large and Small Curls, Loop, Shingle Line, Side Windows), p. 130; White Sparkling Sugar, p. 144; Piping Gel, p. 143; 10 x 14 in. Cake Boards, p. 241; knife, ruler

Two days in advance: Make assorted fondant trims (p. 124).**Also:** Make house: Trim cardboard base to 10 x 9 in. and cover with white fondant; brush with Piping Gel and coat with Sparkling Sugar. Tint 24 oz. fondant rose, 24 oz. green, 6 oz. violet, 1 oz. blue. Brush house pieces with Piping Gel and attach rose or green fondant. Let dry. Assemble house following package directions; let dry.

Make house trims and attach with Piping Gel. Roll ¼ in. diameter rose logs; attach under eaves. Roll out fondant ⅛ in. thick; cut out blue door and yellow windows using patterns; attach. Cut ⅛ in. wide violet strips and attach for windowpanes. Roll ¼ in. diameter logs for window and door frames, ⅛ in. diameter violet and rose logs for window trims and ¼ in. ball for doorknob; attach. Brush window frames and trims with Piping Gel and coat with Sparkling Sugar. For shingles and roof peak, roll ⅜ in. diameter logs; attach roof peak log. Shape shingles following shingle line pattern and attach. Brush with Piping Gel and coat with Sparkling Sugar. Use icing to attach swirl pieces to roof, loops to front and back roof peaks, candy cane logs to house corners and gumdrops around base.

*Combine Violet with Rose for violet shown.

▶ His Sleigh's on the Way!

Pan: Baby Buggy, p. 160

Tip: 5, p. 134

Colors:* Christmas Red, Violet, Rose, Lemon Yellow, Orange, Sky Blue, Leaf Green, p. 146

Fondant: White Ready-To-Use Rolled Fondant (48 oz.), Gum-Tex, p. 147; 20 in. Rolling Pin, Roll & Cut Mat, p. 148; Brush Set, p. 149

Recipe: Buttercream Icing, p. 116

Also: 2011 Pattern Book (Presents, Sleigh, Runner), p. 130; Piping Gel, p. 143; White Sparkling Sugar, p. 144; Cake Boards, Fanci-Foil Wrap, p. 241; knife, cornstarch, waxed paper, ruler, tape

Two days in advance: Make presents. Tint fondant: 3 oz. each pink, violet, green and orange; 2 oz. yellow; 1 oz. each light pink, light violet, light green, light orange, light yellow. Roll out ⅛ in. thick as needed. Use patterns to cut 9 presents (including bow) in assorted colors. Cut ribbon and bow trims; attach using damp brush. Let dry on cornstarch-dusted boards. **Also:** Make sleigh. Tint 12 oz. fondant red; reserve 10 oz. white. Roll out ¼ in. thick. Use patterns to cut sleigh and trim. Let dry on cornstarch-dusted board. Tape runner pattern to board and cover with waxed paper. Roll 1 red and 1 white log, 12 x ½ in. diameter. Twist and roll together for striped bottom runner, then trim to 17 in. (log will expand when rolled together). Position over pattern. Roll 1 red and 1 white log, 3½ x ¼ in. diameter. Repeat as above, cut and position for runner supports. Let dry.

Bake and cool cake. Ice smooth. Pipe tip 5 bead bottom border. Attach sleigh, runner and presents. Brush sleigh trim with Piping Gel and sprinkle with Sparkling Sugar. Position on sleigh. Serves 12.

*Combine Violet with Rose for violet shades shown. Combine Leaf Green with Lemon Yellow for green shades shown.

▲ Season's Greeting Cards

Pans: Cookie Sheet, Cooling Grid, p. 203

Tips: 2, 3, p. 134

Colors:* Violet, Royal Blue, Red-Red, Christmas Red, Leaf Green, Kelly Green, Black, Brown, Orange, p. 146

Recipes: Color Flow Icing, Roll-Out Cookies, p. 116

Also: 18 Pc. Holiday Cutter Set, p. 212; Color Flow Mix, p. 143; Pastry Wheel, p. 153; knife, toothpicks, ruler

In advance: Make cookies. Prepare and roll out dough. Cut 5 in. squares; bake and cool. Use cutters from set to cut 1 reindeer, snowman or tree for each square; bake and cool. **Also:** Decorate cookies. Using full-strength icing and tip 3, outline square and ½ in. inner border; flow in border with thinned icing (p. 128). Flow in centers with tinted thinned icing. While still wet, pipe tip 2 dot snowflakes, about ½ to ¾ in. apart. Outline shaped cookies with tip 3 and full-strength icing; flow in centers with thinned icing. Let all dry 24 hours.

Add reindeer and snowman features using tip 2 dots and outlines and full-strength icing. Attach figures to squares with icing. Let dry. Each serves 1.

*Combine Red-Red with Christmas Red for red shown. Combine Leaf Green with Kelly Green for green shown. Combine Brown with Red-Red for tan shown. Combine Orange with Red-Red for orange shown.

◄ The Cookie Kid

Pans: Cookie Sheet, Cooling Grid, p. 203

Tips: 2, 3, p. 134

Colors: Red-Red, Kelly Green, Brown, p. 14

Recipes: Color Flow Icing, Roll-Out Cookies, p. 116

Also: Blossom Plastic Nesting Cutter Se p. 201; 6 Pc. Holiday Mini Cutter Set, p. 212; Color Flow Mix, p. 143

In advance: Make cookies. Prepare and roll out dough. For each treat cut 1 gingerbread boy and 1 blossom using 2 largest cutter from set. Bake and cool. Using full-strength icing, outline blosso with tip 3, gingerbread boy with tip 2; flo in with thinned icing (p. 128). Let dry.

Decorate and assemble using full-strength icing. Attach gingerbread boy to blossom. Use tip 2 to pipe blossom outline, dot buttons and dot and outline facial features; pipe tip 3 bow tie. Let dr Each serves 1.

*Combine Brown with Red-Red for brown shown.

◄ Tree Artistry

Pans: Cookie Sheet, Cooling Grid, p. 203

Tips: 1, 2, 3, p. 134

Colors:* Violet, Royal Blue, Kelly Green, Leaf Green, Red-Red, Rose, Christmas Red, Golden Yellow, Lemon Yellow, p. 146

Recipes: Color Flow Icing, Roll-Out Cookies, p. 116

Also: 3 Pc. Trees Cookie Cutter Set, p. 212; Gold, Bronze Pearl Dust, p. 149; Sugar Pearls Sprinkles, p. 145; Color Flow Mix, Clear Vanilla Extract, p. 143; Brush Set, p. 149; cornstarch

Prepare and roll out dough. Cut using straight-sided cutter. Bake and cool. Outline with tip 3 and full-strength icing; flow in with thinned icing (p. 128). For blue tree, add Sugar Pearls immediately after flowing in. For violet tree with dots, pipe tip 2 green branches immediately after flowing in. Let dry. Decorate all trees using full-strength icing. For violet scroll tree, pipe tip 1 white scrolls; let dry. Paint with bronze Pearl Dust/vanilla mixture (p. 120). For violet tree with green branches, pipe tip 2 dot ornaments. For green tree, pipe tip 2 zigzag garland; let dry. Pipe tip 2 dot ornaments; use fingertip dipped in cornstarch to flatten large top dot. For red scroll tree, pipe tip 2 white center line and scrolls; let dry. Paint with gold Pearl Dust/vanilla mixture (p. 120). Pipe tip 2 dot ornaments; use fingertip dipped in cornstarch to flatten large top dot. For leaf tree, outline leaves and pipe center branch with tip 2; flow in leaves with thinned icing. Pipe tip 2 pull-out star points. Let dry. Each serves 1.

*Combine Kelly Green with Leaf Green for green shown. Combine Red-Red with Christmas Red for red shown. Combine Golden Yellow with Lemon Yellow for yellow shown. Combine Violet with Rose for violet shown.

▶ Stand-Out Snowflakes

Pans: Cookie Sheet, Cooling Grid, p. 203
Tip: 2, p. 134
Color: Christmas Red, p. 146
Recipes: Color Flow Icing, Roll-Out Cookies, p. 116
Also: 3 Pc. Snowflake Cookie Cutter Set, p. 212; Color Flow Mix, p. 143; Decorator Brush Set, p. 197; White Pearl Dust, p. 149; Cake Boards, p. 241; waxed paper, tape, ruler

In advance: Make cookies. Prepare and roll out dough. Cut cookies using light blue cutter from set. Bake and cool. Outline cookies with tip 2 and full-strength icing; flow in with thinned icing (p. 128). Let dry. **Also:** Make puddle dots (p. 120). Pipe tip 2 dots on waxed paper-covered board using thinned icing. Pipe 1 center dot and 6 lines of 5 more dots (from 5/16 in. to 1/16 in. diameter) for each cookie. Let dry. Brush dots with Pearl Dust (p. 120).

Attach dots to cookies using dots of full-strength icing. Let dry. Each serves 1.

◀ Making Winter Bearable

Pans: Cookie Sheet, Cooling Grid, p. 203
Tips: 2, 3, p. 134
Color: Black, p. 146
Fondant: Primary Colors Fondant Multi Pack, p. 147; 9 in. Rolling Pin, Roll & Cut Mat, p.148; Brush Set, p.149
Recipes: Color Flow Icing, Roll-Out Cookies, p. 116
Also: Teddy Bear Plastic Cutter, p. 201; Color Flow Mix, p. 143; knife, ruler

In advance: Make cookies. Prepare and roll out dough. Cut cookies using bear cutter. Bake and cool. Outline cookie with tip 3 and full-strength icing; flow in with thinned icing (p. 128). Let dry.

Decorate and assemble using full-strength icing. Shape 1½ in. high fondant hat; attach with icing. For scarf, roll out fondant ⅛ in. thick. Cut 2 tails, ¼ x 1 in. long; cut slits for fringed ends and attach with damp brush. Cut one strip 2¼ in. long and attach around neck with damp brush. Using tip 2, pipe dot eyes, ball nose and outline mouth; pipe zigzag hat brim and swirl pompom. Let dry. Each serves 1.

▶ Sleigh Team Captain

Pans: Cookie Sheet, Cooling Grid, p. 203
Tips: 2, 3, 4, p. 134
Colors:* Brown, Black, p. 146
Recipes: Color Flow Icing, Roll-Out Cookies, p. 116
Also: 101 Cookie Cutters (football), p. 201; 3 Pc. Holiday Cutter Set (reindeer head), p. 212; Color Flow Mix, p. 143; pretzel sticks

In advance: Make cookies. Prepare and roll out dough. For each treat, cut 1 reindeer head and 1 football body. Bake and cool. Outline cookies with tip 3 and full-strength icing; flow in with thinned icing (p. 128). Let dry.

Decorate using full-strength icing. Attach head to body. Attach pretzel legs to back. Pipe tip 4 dot nose and pull-out tail, tip 2 outline mouth and dot eyes. Let dry. Each serves 1.

*Combine Brown with Black for brown shades shown.

▲ Busy Building!

Cookie: Pre-Baked Gingerbread House Kit (2104-1509; includes house pieces, icing mix, assorted candies used), Gingerpops Cookie Kit, p. 215

Tips: 2, 5, 12, 13, p. 134-135

Fondant: White Ready-To-Use Rolled Fondant (18 oz.), Primary and Natural Colors Fondant Multi Packs, Fine Tip Primary Colors FoodWriter Edible Color Markers, Gum-Tex, p. 147; 9 in. Rolling Pin, Roll & Cut Mat, p. 148; Brush Set, p. 149; Alphabet/Numbers Cut-Outs, p. 151

Recipes: Royal Icing (plus icing mix from kit), p. 116; Thinned Fondant Adhesive, p. 117

Also: 2011 Pattern Book (Peaked Wall Trim), p. 130; Meringue Powder, Piping Gel, p. 143; 13 x 19 in. Cake Boards, Fanci-Foil Wrap, p. 241; White Sparkling Sugar, p. 144; candy canes (6), ruler, straight pins, toothpicks, knife, small embroidery scissors, card stock, pencil, waxed paper, cornstarch, tape, heavy jars or cans for support

2-3 days in advance: Make tables and toys (p. 124). **Also:** Decorate Gingerpop figures (p. 124). For light brown bases under figures, mix 4 oz. white fondant with light brown fondant pouch from Multi Pack. Roll out ¼ in. thick. Cut 7 rectangles, 2 x ½ in.; reserve remaining mixed light brown fondant. Let bases dry overnight on cornstarch-dusted board. Attach figures using fondant adhesive. **And:** Prepare sign. Add ½ teaspoon Gum-Tex to reserved green fondant; roll out ⅛ in. thick. Cut 2 x 7 in. rectangle. Let dry overnight. Roll out reserved red ⅛ in. thick. Cut letters using

cutters from set. Attach to sign using damp brush. **And:** Prepare base board. Cut 2 Cake Boards to 11 x 16½ in.; tape together and cover with foil (p. 110). Begin decorating and assembling workshop wall and roof panels 4 days in advance. Gingerbread House Kit side walls and roof panels will be lined up end to end to create open house. Front and back walls from kit are used as your side walls here.

Decorate inside of workshop walls using blue from Multi Pack plus reserved light and dark brown. Roll out ⅛ in. thick as needed. Use pattern to cut 2 dark brown peaked wall trims. Attach at peaks of side walls using Piping Gel. Cut 4 blue windows, 2 x 1½ in.; attach ¾ in. from bottom edge. Edge windows and panes with ¼ in. wide light brown strips. Cut and attach 4½ in. long beams to 2 roof panels. Begin with a ¼ in. wide beam on each side, 1¼ in. from outside edge; add 3 more moving towards center from each, ½ in. wide, 1 in. apart. Using royal icing, attach 2 rectangle panels to create long wall; add 2 side wall panels at 90° angles. Support on prepared base to hold in position until dry.

Cut 2 x 3 in. high dark brown door; attach using damp brush. Cut and attach 1 x ¾ in. blue door window. Edge window and door with ¼ in. wide light brown strips. Roll thin log for door handle; shape and attach. Cover corner seams and edge below scalloped eaves with ¼ in. wide dark brown vertical strips. Roll out reserved mixed light brown ⅛ in. thick. Cut 11 x 5 in. floor; use knife with ruler to score floor planks, ¼ x 2½ in. long. Brush open floor area lightly with Piping Gel; position floor.

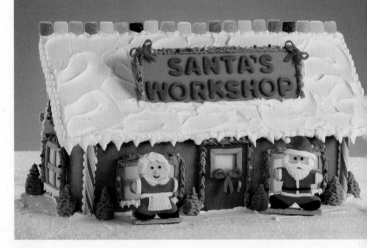

Add windows and door to outside of house same as above but with yellow "glass" and omitting outside door trim. Pipe tip 5 zigzags over outside corners and top edge of back panels; trim 4 candy canes to 2¾ in. high and attach to corners. Use icing to attach roof panels to each other and to walls, with excess extending past peak. Trim 2 candy canes to 3½ in. and attach for inside support; let dry.

Cut 1 x 4½ in. dark brown beam and attach over roof seam using damp brush. Spatula ice rooftop and base board. Attach sign using 3 teardrop-shaped 1 in. long balls of fondant to maintain angle. Cut spice drops from kit in half. Pipe tip 5 zigzag over roof edge and peak. Position spice drop halves. For garland trims, roll logs, then use small

scissors to make random, partial cuts for branches. For windows and door garlands, begin with logs 5-7 in. long, ¼ in. diameter. For 2 wreaths, use 3 x ½ in. diameter logs; for rooftop sign, use two 6 x ¼ in. diameter logs. For 5 bows, roll out red 1⁄16 in. thick. Cut ⅛ x 3½ in. strips; fold into bows. Use dots of Piping Gel to attach bows and nonpareil sprinkles from Gingerpop Kit for lights on all garlands and wreaths. Attach spice drop half to top of back candy canes. Pipe pull-out icicles using tip 2 under windows, tip 5 at roof edge. For 8 trees, roll 1 in. high fondant cones; cut as for wreaths to make branches. Spatula ice front and sides of house base. Cover with Sparkling Sugar. Position trees around workshop. Position figures, tables and toys.

▶ Gingerpop-ulation

Cookie: Gingerpops Cookie Kit, p. 215

Tips: 1, 2, 101, p. 134-135

Colors:* Kelly Green, Rose, Royal Blue, Black, Brown, Sky Blue, Lemon Yellow, Golden Yellow, Violet, Rose, Christmas Red, Red-Red, p. 146

Recipe: Buttercream Icing, p. 116

Also: Cornstarch

Assemble gingerpops using icing mix, sticks and instructions in kit.

For all, use round tip from kit to pipe facial features, including outline mouths, dot eyes, nose, pupils and cheeks. Use same tip to outline and pipe in all clothing (smooth with finger dipped in cornstarch). Pipe tip 2 outline, curly or pull-out hair. Add clothing details using tips 1 and 2, including outline stripes, waistbands, pockets, cuffs, neck ruffles, dot buttons and skirt pattern. Pipe tip 2 outline braids and bows. Pipe ruffled skirt with tip 101; pipe tip 2 trim on ruffle. Each cookie serves 1.

*Combine Lemon Yellow with Golden Yellow for yellow shown. Combine Violet with Rose for violet shown. Combine Christmas Red with Red-Red for red shown. Combine Brown with Red-Red for brown shown.

▼ Skating Village

Pans: 12 x 18 x 2 in. Sheet, p. 157; Non-Stick Cookie Pan, p. 165

Cookie: Pre-Baked Gingerbread Mini Village Kit, p. 215

Candy: Christmas Trees Pretzel Mold, p. 211; Green (1 pk. makes 12-14 trees), White Candy Melts (2 pks.), p. 194; Primary, Garden (violet) Candy Color Sets, p. 195

Recipe: Favorite crisped rice cereal treats (5 batches needed to fill 12 x 18 x 2 in. pan)

Also: Mini Gingerbread Boy Icing Decorations, p. 210; White Sparkling Sugar, p. 144; Parchment Triangles, p. 136; Wooden Dowel Rods, p. 239; 13 x 19 in. Cake Boards, Fanci-Foil Wrap, p. 241; Blue, White Pearl Dust, Brush Set, p. 149; Vanilla Whipped Icing Mix, p. 143; pretzel rods, non-stick pan spray, waxed paper, freezer paper, scissors, knife, ruler, tape

In advance: Assemble and decorate village following package directions. **Also:** Make 6 candy trees in Christmas Trees Pretzel Mold. After unmolding, use melted candy and piping method (p. 128) to pipe zigzag snow. **And:** Prepare figures. Cut ½ in. long slivers of jellied candy from village kit for skates on 7 figures; press to attach. For men in snow, pipe ½ in. line of melted white candy on cookie sheet; stand icing decoration in candy. Chill until firm. **And:** Make candy pond and bridge (p. 128). **And:** Prepare board. Tape two 13 x 19 in. cake boards together. Cover with foil (p. 110).

Spray sheet pan with non-stick spray. Prepare cereal treat mixture and press firmly into pan. Immediately unmold onto wrapped board. Let cool. Spatula ice top with prepared whipping icing, shaping icicles down sides. Position pond; sprinkle Sparkling Sugar snow over top. Position houses, bridge and gingerbread figures. Use dowel rod to make holes for trees. Trim pretzels to various heights and position trees. Serves 48.

▶ Smooch from a Pooch

Pans: 17.25 x 11.5 x 1 in. Non-Stick Large Cookie/Jelly Roll, Cooling Grid, p. 165

Candy: White, Light Cocoa Candy Melts, p. 194; 8 in. Lollipop Sticks, p. 198

Recipe: Roll-Out Cookies, p. 116

Also: Hearts Plastic Nesting Cutter Set, p. 220; Parchment Triangles, p. 136; ⅛ in. wide ribbon (8 in. per treat), cardstock, hole punch, ruler, waxed paper, knife, marker, scissors

In advance: Make cookies. Prepare and roll out dough. Cut heads using 3rd smallest heart cutter from set. Bake and cool cookies. Cover with melted white candy (p. 128). Tap to settle; chill until set. **Also:** Mold candy ears and mouths. Set 3rd smallest and smallest heart cutters from set on non-stick pan. Fill ¼ in. deep with melted light cocoa candy. Tap to settle; chill until firm. Use warm knife to cut larger hearts in half and to cut off curves from smaller heart, ¾ in. deep.

Assemble and decorate using melted candy in cut parchment bag. Attach 2 curved pieces behind head: 1 below cookie division for mouth, 1 above mouth for support. Attach larger halves for ears. Pipe dot features and outline lip. Attach Lollipop Stick to back. Cut 1 x 1½ in. card and punch out hole; print message. Tie on card with ribbon. Each serves 1.

▼ Amorous Angels

Pans: Cookie Sheet, Cooling Grid, p. 203

Tips: 2, 3, 8, 10, p. 134

Colors:* Copper (for light skin tone shown), Brown, Red-Red, Black, Lemon Yellow, Golden Yellow, p. 146

Recipes: Color Flow Icing, Roll-Out Cookies, p. 116

Also: 4 Pc. Baby Colored Metal Cutter Set (Bear), p. 245; 6 Pc. Mini Romantic Metal Cutter Set (Heart), p. 202; Color Flow Mix, p. 143; White Pearl Dust, p. 149; Hearts Remembered Icing Decorations, p. 219; Parchment Triangles, p. 136; Brush Set, p. 149, cornstarch

Prepare and roll out dough. Cut 1 bear and 2 heart wings for each cookie; trim ears off bear. Bake and cool cookies. Outline angels with tip 3 and full-strength color flow; let set. Flow in angels and cover wings with thinned color flow (p. 128); let dry. Brush wings with Pearl Dust. Complete decorating with full-strength color flow. Outline and pipe in diapers with tip 3 (pat smooth). Pipe tip 8 outline arms. Position heart icing decoration between arms; Pipe tip 2 dot hand and fingers. Pipe tip 10 ball feet; smooth with finger dipped in cornstarch. Pipe tip 2 dot toes. Add tip 2 outline mouth, dot eyes, nose and cheeks. Pipe tip 3 pull-out hair. Attach heart wings with dots of icing. Each serves 1.

*Combine Lemon Yellow with Golden Yellow for yellow shown. Combine Brown with Red-Red for dark skin tone shown.

◀ Cubby Love

Pan: Standard Muffin, p. 158

Tips: 1, 1A, 2A, 3, 10, p. 134

Colors:* Rose, Brown, Red-Red, Black, p. 146

Recipes: Buttercream, Royal Icings, p. 116

Also: Valentine Combo Pack, p. 219; Micro Hearts Sprinkles, p. 220; Meringue Powder, p. 143; Cake Boards, p. 241; Disposable Decorating Bags, p. 136; ruler, waxed paper

In advance: Figure pipe royal icing bear (p. 124).

Bake and cool cupcakes. Spatula ice with buttercream. Add heart sprinkles. Position bear. Each serves 1.

*Combine Brown with Red-Red for brown shown.

◀ Valentine Variety

Pans: Cookie Sheet, Cooling Grid, p. 203
Tip: 3, p. 134
Colors: Rose, Christmas Red, p. 146
Recipe: Color Flow Icing, Roll-Out Cookies, p. 116
Also: 3 Pc. Valentine Cutter Set, Micro Hearts Sprinkles, Jumbo Hearts Sprinkles, Valentine 6-Mix Sprinkles (red, pink sugars, sweetheart nonpareils), p. 220; Hearts Remembered Icing Decorations, p. 219; White Pearl Dust, Brush Set, p. 149; Pink, White Sparkling Sugars, p. 144; White Sugar Pearls, Pink Posies Icing Flowers, Daisy Icing Flowers, p. 145; Color Flow Mix, Piping Gel, Clear Vanilla Extract, p. 143

In advance: Make cookies. Prepare and roll out dough. Cut hearts using classic heart cutter from set. Bake and cool cookies. Outline cookies using tip 3 and full-strength icing; flow in using thinned icing (p. 120). For white-on-pink wavy stripes, overpipe white immediately after adding an all-over pink layer. Let all dry 24 hours before adding trims and sprinkles.

For Colored Sugar, Sparkling Sugar or Nonpareils, brush tops, edges or specific designs with Piping Gel; immediately sprinkle on trims and shake off excess. For Icing Flowers, Heart Decorations, Sugar Pearls and large Heart Sprinkles, attach trims one piece at a time using dots of full-strength icing. For white scrolls and overpiped pink outlines, pipe designs using tip 3 and full-strength icing. Paint various white areas with Pearl Dust/vanilla mixture (p. 120). Let all dry. Each serves 1.

▶ Love's Bubbling Over

Pans: Cookie Sheet, Cooling Grid, p. 203
Colors: * Rose, Leaf Green, Violet, Sky Blue, p. 146
Recipes: Royal Icing, Roll-Out Cookies, p. 116
Also: 7 Pc. Hearts Cutter Set, p. 220; Meringue Powder, p. 143; Parchment Triangles, p. 136; White Pearl Dust, Brush Set, p. 149; Cake Board, p. 241; waxed paper

In advance: Make puddle dots (p. 120). On waxed paper-covered board, using thinned icing in cut parchment bag, pipe approximately 9 at ⅜ in. diameter, 28 at ¼ in. diameter and 24 at ⅛ in. diameter per cookie. Make extras in each size to allow for breakage; let dry.

Prepare and roll out dough. Cut cookies using stylized cutter; bake and cool. Cover cookies with thinned royal icing (p. 128); let set. Attach dots with full-strength royal icing. Brush cookies with Pearl Dust. Each serves 1.

*Combine Violet and Rose for violet shown.

▼ Petite Pastel Hearts

Pans: Silicone Petite Heart Mold, p. 218; Cookie Sheet, Cooling Grid, p. 203
Colors: * Royal Blue, Rose, Kelly Green, Lemon Yellow, Golden Yellow, p. 146
Also: Blue, Pink, Green, Yellow Sugar Pearls, p. 145; White Ready-To-Use Decorator Icing (1 can covers 12-15 treats), p. 143; waxed paper, knife

Bake and cool hearts in silicone mold supported by cookie sheet. Heat icing (p. 128), then tint portions rose, blue, yellow and green. Working 2-3 treats at a time, cover with tinted icing (p. 128); let set briefly. Position Sugar Pearls before icing sets, being careful to maintain heart shape. Each serves 1.

*Combine Lemon Yellow with Golden Yellow for yellow shown.

▲ Daisy Declaration

Pans: Silicone Mini Heart Mold, p. 218; Cookie Sheet, Cooling Grid, p. 203
Tip: 2, p. 134
Colors: * Violet, Rose, Lemon Yellow, Kelly Green, p. 146
Also: White Ready-To-Use Decorator Icing (1 can makes 15 treats), p. 143; Daisy Icing Flowers, p. 145; Disposable Decorating Bags, p. 136

Bake and cool heart cakes in silicone mold supported by cookie sheet. Heat icing (p. 128), then tint portions violet, rose, yellow and green. Cover treats with heated icing (p. 128). Pipe tip 2 lattice lines ³⁄₁₆ in. apart; let set. Attach daisy with dots of icing. Each serves 1.

*Combine Violet and Rose for violet shown.

▶ Lovable Lamb

Pans: Cookie Sheet, Cooling Grid, p. 203

Tip: 3, p. 134

Color: Black, p. 146

Recipe: Color Flow Icing, Roll-Out Cookies, p. 116

Also: 18 Pc. Easter Cutter Collection, p. 223; White Nonpareils, p. 144; Color Flow Mix, p. 143; Cake Boards, p. 241; Parchment Triangles, p. 136; waxed paper

In advance: Make cookies. Prepare and roll out dough. Cut cookies using lamb cutter from set. Bake and cool cookies. Use tip 3 to outline cookies with full-strength icing, leaving hooves open; flow in with thinned icing (p. 128). Sprinkle body and top of head with nonpareils while icing is wet. Let dry on waxed paper covered boards.

Use tip 3 and full-strength icing to pipe dot eye, outline mouth and hooves; pat smooth. Let dry. Each serves 1.

◀ Treats that Tweet

Pans: Standard Muffin, p. 158; Cookie Sheet, Cooling Grid, p. 203

Tips: 1, 2, p. 134

Colors:* Leaf Green, Lemon Yellow, Golden Yellow, Orange, Sky Blue, p. 146

Recipes: Buttercream, Royal Icings, Roll-Out Cookies, p. 116

Also: Hop 'N Tweet Standard Baking Cups, p. 222; Parchment Triangles, p. 136; Round Cut-Outs, p. 151; 6 in. Lollipop Sticks (3 in. lengths), p. 198; Meringue Powder, p. 143; Cake Boards, p. 241; shredded coconut, zip-close plastic bag, knife, waxed paper

In advance: Make cookie chicks. Prepare and roll out dough. Cut heads using medium Cut-Out from set. Bake and cool cookies. Ice cookie with royal icing. Use royal icing to pipe tip 2 curly hair and tip 1 dot eyes and fill-in beak. Attach 3 in. Lollipop Stick to back with royal icing, leaving excess extended at bottom to insert into cupcake. Let dry overnight on waxed paper-covered boards. **Also:** Tint coconut (p. 120).

Bake and cool cupcakes. Ice smooth with buttercream. Sprinkle on coconut. Insert chick. Each serves 1.

*Combine Lemon Yellow with Golden Yellow for yellow shown.

▲ Fluttering on Flowers

Pans: Standard Muffin, p. 158; Cooling Grid, p. 203

Tip: 1M, p. 135

Colors:* Rose, Violet, Lemon Yellow, p. 146

Fondant: White Ready-To-Use Rolled Fondant (6 oz. makes 18-20 butterflies), p. 147; 9 in. Rolling Pin, Roll & Cut Mat, p. 148; Brush Set, p. 149

Recipe: Buttercream Icing, p. 116

Also: Pink, Lavender, Yellow, Petal Baking Cups, p. 184; 6 Pc. Easter Mini Cutter Set (butterfly), p. 223; 6-Mix Easter Sprinkles, p. 222; Disposable Decorating bags, p. 136; cornstarch, 4 x 6 in. or larger cardstock

In advance: Make butterflies (p. 124).

Bake and cool cupcakes in petal cups. Pipe tip 1M swirl; sprinkle with colored sugars. Attach butterflies with dots of icing. Each serves 1.

*Combine Violet with Rose for violet shown.

▶ Eclectic Egg Cookies

Pans: Cookie Sheet, Cooling Grid, p. 203

Tips: 2, 44, p. 136

Color:* Violet, Rose, Leaf Green, Lemon Yellow, Orange, Sky Blue, p. 146

Recipes: Color Flow Icing, Roll-Out Cookies, p. 116

Also: 4 Pc. Easter Grippy Cutter Set, p. 223; White Pearl Dust, Brush Set, p. 149; Color Flow Mix, Clear Vanilla Extract, p. 143; Cake Boards, p. 241; Parchment Triangles, p. 136; waxed paper, ruler

In advance: Make cookies. Prepare and roll out dough. Cut cookies using egg cutter from set. Bake and cool. Outline cookies using tip 2 and full-strength icing; flow in with thinned icing (p. 128). Let dry on waxed paper-covered boards. **Also:** Make puddle dots (p. 120). Use tip 2 and thinned icing to pipe ¼ in. wide dots on waxed paper-covered board (about 14 per cookie). Let dry.

Decorate with full-strength icing. Pipe tip 44 stripes and tip 2 spirals. Attach puddle dots with icing. Let dry. Paint trims with Pearl Dust/vanilla mixture (p. 120). Let dry. Each serves 1.

*Combine Leaf Green with Lemon Yellow for green shown. Combine Violet with Rose for violet shown.

Quick Chick

Pans: Silicone Mini Decorated Egg, p. 221; Cookie Sheet, Cooling Grid, p. 203

Tips: 2, 9, 352, p. 134-135

Colors:* Golden Yellow, Lemon Yellow, Sky Blue, Orange, p. 146

Recipe: Buttercream Icing, p. 116

Also: Cake Boards, Fanci-Foil Wrap, p. 241; Parchment Triangles, p. 136; black shoestring licorice, orange spice drops, scissors, ruler, waxed paper, granulated sugar

Bake and cool mini eggs in silicone mold supported by cookie sheet. Place on foil-wrapped board, cut to fit. Ice smooth. Pipe tip 9 beads side-by-side for hair and wings. Pipe tip 2 dots where legs will go; flatten slightly. For feet, cut spice drop in half vertically. Cut away V-shapes to make toes. Roll in granulated sugar to cover edges. Insert 1½ in. long licorice string into foot; insert into cake. Pipe tip 2 dot eyes; flatten slightly. Pipe tip 352 leaves for lips; pinch outside corners to blend. Each serves 1.

*Combine Lemon Yellow with Golden Yellow for yellow shown.

▲ Upsy Daisy Cookies

Pans: Cookie Sheet, Cooling Grid, p. 203

Tip: 2, p. 136

Colors:* Violet, Rose, Kelly Green, Lemon Yellow, Royal Blue, p. 148

Recipes: Color Flow Icing, Roll-Out Cookies, p. 116

Also: 101 Cookie Cutters, p. 202; Daisy Icing Flowers, p. 147; Color Flow Mix, p. 143; Parchment Triangles, p. 136

Roll out dough. Cut cookies using medium circle cutter. Bake and cool cookies. Using tip 2 and white full-strength color flow, outline cookies; let dry. Tint portions of remaining icing rose, yellow, blue, green and violet. Flow in cookies with thinned icing (p. 128); immediately pipe tip 2 white lattice lines, ¼ in. apart. Let dry. Attach daisy icing decoration with dots of icing.

*Combine Violet with Rose for violet shown.

▲ One Chic Chick

Pans: 12 x 18 x 1 in. Jelly Roll/Cookie, p. 158; Cooling Grid, p. 203

Candy: Girl Power 2-Pk. Candy Mold Set, p. 196; Yellow, Lavender, White Candy Melts, p. 194; Garden Candy Color Set (black), p. 195

Also: Circle Metal Cutter, p. 202; Parchment Triangles, p. 136; Cake Leveler, p. 152; large spice drops (yellow, orange), scissors, granulated sugar, waxed paper, ruler

In advance: Mold sunglasses in candy mold using Painting or Piping Method (p. 128), making frames, then filling in lenses. Chill until firm. **Also:** Prepare body. Bake and cool cake. Trim to ¾ in. high. Cut circles using cutter. Cover with melted candy (p. 128). Chill until firm.

For wings, cut yellow spice drop in half lengthwise; cut 2 V-shaped slits in top. For hair, cut spice drop into 4ths. Using ¼ piece, cut slits and separate tufts. For feet, cut orange spice drop lengthwise in half. Cut a ¼ in. flat slice off each half and back (reserve curved pieces). Flatten slightly; cut slits for toes. Use reserved orange piece to shape beak; cut slit for opening. Roll all pieces in sugar to coat. Attach features and sunglasses using melted candy. Each serves 1.

▲ The Picture of Spring

Pans: Cookie Sheet, Cooling Grid, p. 203

Tips: 1, 2, p. 134

Colors:* Violet, Rose, Lemon Yellow, Leaf Green, Orange, Black, p. 146

Recipes: Color Flow Icing, Roll-Out Cookies, p. 116

Also: 101 Cookie Cutters (large, small circles), p. 202; 9 Pc Easter Cutter Collection (bunny), p. 223; Color Flow Mix, p. 143; Cake Boards, p. 241; Parchment Triangles, p. 136; waxed paper, ruler, knife

In advance: Make cookies. Prepare and roll out dough. Cut bunny using cutter from 9 Pc. Set; cut a 4 x 5 in. rectangle for base. Cut chick using small round from 101 Pc. Set; cut base using largest round from set. Bake and cool cookies. Using tip 2 and full-strength icing, outline borders of all cookies (⅜ in. wide for rectangle cookies); let dry. On rectangle cookies, pipe tip 2 violet outlines inside border, ⅜ in. apart; let dry. Flow in heads, rounds and stripes using thinned icing (overpipe dark green dots on rounds before green icing sets). Let dry on waxed paper-covered boards.

Assemble and pipe details using full-strength icing (p. 124). Each serves 1.

*Combine Violet with Rose for violet shades shown. Combine Leaf Green with Lemon Yellow for green shades shown.

◀ Bounding Bunny

Pans: Step-By-Step Bunny, p. 221; Cookie Sheet, Cooling Grid, p. 203

Tips: 5, 8, 18, p. 134-135

Colors: Rose, Sky Blue, Leaf Green, p. 146

Recipe: Buttercream Icing, Roll-Out Cookies, p. 116

Also: 2011 Pattern Book (bunny body), p. 130; Cake Board, Fanci-Foil Wrap, p. 241; 17 x 16 in. plywood or foamcore board (¼ in. thick), shredded coconut, jelly beans, zip-close plastic bag

In advance: Make cookies. Prepare and roll out dough. Using pattern, cut 2 bunny body shapes. Bake and cool. **Also:** Prepare base board. Using pan and pattern, cut foamcore board to shape; wrap with foil. **And:** Tint coconut (p. 120).

Bake and cool cake. Ice inside ears and facial area of cake smooth, building up face to cover pan details. Sandwich body cookies with icing. Position body and head on base board. Cover with tip 18 stars. Pipe tip 8 dot eyes and nose. Pipe tip 5 outline whiskers. Cover tail with tip 18 rosettes. Position coconut and jelly beans. Cake serves 12; cookies serve 4.

▶ Spring Football

Pan: Dimensions Multi-Cavity Mini Cupcakes, p. 164

Color: Leaf Green, p. 146

Recipe: Favorite crisped rice cereal treats

Also: 2011 Pattern Book (basket handle), p. 130; White Candy Melts (1 pk. makes 4 treats), p. 194; Football Icing Decorations, p. 181; Cake Boards, p. 241; Disposable Decorating Bags, p. 136; Spring Confetti Sprinkles, p. 122; shredded coconut, zip-close plastic bag, waxed paper

In advance: Make candy basket and handle. For baskets, make candy shells (p. 128) using white Candy Melts and cupcake bottom cavities of pan. For handles, tape pattern to board and cover with waxed paper. Pipe in pattern area using melted candy in cut bag; chill until firm. Turn handle over and overpipe; chill until firm. **Also:** Tint coconut (p. 120).

Prepare cereal treats and press into basket. Attach handle to basket with melted candy; hold until secure. Cover with tinted coconut. Position icing decorations and sprinkles. Each serves 1.

◀ Happy Hopper

Pans: 9 x 5 in. Loaf, p. 158; Cookie Sheet, Cooling Grid, p. 203

Candy: Fuzzy Bunny Lollipop Mold, p. 222; White Candy Melts (1 pk. makes 3-4 treats), p. 194; Primary (blue) and Garden (pink) Candy Color Sets, p. 195

Also: 9 Pc. Easter Cutter Collection, p. 223; Parchment Triangles, p. 136, knife

In advance: Mold candy bunny heads without sticks using Piping Method (p. 128). Chill until firm. Using a cut parchment bag, outline mouth.

Bake and cool a 3 in. high cake using firm-textured batter like pound cake. Cut into 1 in. thick slices. Cut shapes using bunny cutter from set. Trim ½ in. off tip of ear and face. Dip back of cake into melted candy to seal; chill until firm. Cover cakes with melted candy (p. 128). Using cut parchment bag, pipe candy tails. Attach candy heads to cakes with melted candy. Each serves 1.

Cookies for Launch

ns: Cookie Sheet, Cooling Grid, p. 203

s: 1, 2, 4, p. 134

lors: Orange, Leaf Green, Lemon Yellow, Rose, Christmas Red, Black, p. 146

cipes: Color Flow Icing, Roll-Out Cookies, p. 116

so: 3 Pc. Spring Colored Cutter Set, p. 223; Color Flow Mix, p. 143; Cake Boards, p. 241; Parchment Triangles, p. 136; Jumbo Star Sprinkles, p. 144; waxed paper, cornstarch

advance: Make cookies. Prepare and roll out dough. Cut okies using carrot from set. Bake and cool. Outline window, rrot and base using tip 2 and full-strength icing; flow in with nned icing (p. 128). Let dry on waxed paper-covered boards.

corate with full-strength icing. Pipe tip 4 ball bunny head; pat oth with finger dipped in cornstarch, outline ears. Pipe tip 2 tline inner ears and dot cheeks, tip 1 dot eyes and nose. Using 2, outline red flames; overpipe with yellow outlines. Add tip 2 dot ets. Let dry. Position stars. Each serves 1.

ombine Leaf Green with Lemon Yellow for green shown.

Bunny and Bouquets

ns: 3-D Bunny, p. 221; 9 x 13 x 2 in. Sheet, Cooling Grid, p. 157

s: 3, 47, p. 134-135

lors: Leaf Green, Kelly Green, p. 146

ndy: White (5 pks.), Light Cocoa Candy Melts, p. 194; Garden Candy Color Set (pink, green), p. 195

cipe: Buttercream Icing, p. 116

so: Pink, Purple Posies, Daisy Icing Flowers, Icing Leaves (2 pks.), p. 145; Round Cut-Outs, p. 151; Parchment Triangles, p. 136; Cake Boards, Fanci-Foil Wrap, p. 241; cake pedestal, waxed paper, warming tray, toothpicks

advance: Make candy bunny. Tint 1 oz. candy pink; melt z. light cocoa. Fill in eye and nose of pan (reserve excess k); chill until firm. Use 3 pks. white candy to make candy ell (p. 128) in both halves of pan. Chill until firm; unmold. Use served pink candy in cut parchment bag to outline and fill ear. Attach halves with melted candy. Slide bunny across arming tray to smooth bottom so bunny will stand. Attach nny to wrapped cake board cut-to-fit, with melted candy.

ke and cool 1½ in. high cake using firm-textured batter such pound cake. Cut 12 rounds using largest Cut-Out. Cover with elted candy tinted green (p. 128). Let set. Repeat if necessary smooth finish. Let set. Use candy to attach cakes to wrapped, t-to-fit boards, ½ in. wider than cakes. Divide cakes into 8ths. pe tip 47 vertical lines. Pipe tip 3 pull-out grass. Attach icing wers and leaves to cakes with dots of icing. Position bunny pedestal and surround with additional flowers and leaves. sition cakes. Each serves 1.

ombine Leaf Green with a little Kelly Green for green shown.

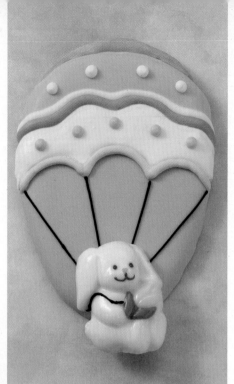

◀ Hare in the Air

Pans: Cookie Sheet, Cooling Grid, p. 203

Tips: 1, 3, 4, 5, p. 134

Colors:* Royal Blue, Lemon Yellow, Golden Yellow, Violet, Rose, Leaf Green, Black, p. 146

Candy: Hoppy Easter Lollipop Mold, p. 222; White, Yellow, Green, Pink, Light Cocoa Candy Melts, p. 194

Recipe: Royal Icing, Roll-Out Cookies, p. 116

Also: Egg Comfort-Grip Cutter, p. 223; Meringue Powder, p. 143; Parchment Triangles, p. 136; Cake Boards, p. 241; ruler, waxed paper, tape

In advance: Make bunny candies in lollipop mold. Tape over opening for stick. Mold candies using Painting or Piping Method (p. 128). Tap to settle; chill until firm. Pipe facial features after unmolding using melted candy in cut parchment bag. **Also:** Make cookies. Prepare and roll out dough. Cut cookie background using egg cutter. Bake and cool cookies. Pour thinned blue icing over cookies to cover (p. 128). Let dry overnight on waxed paper-covered boards.

Pipe 3 tip 4 bottom pink scallops 2¾ in. up from narrow end of egg using full-strength icing. Add other colors using thinned icing. Pipe tip 5 yellow wavy band ¾ in. wide. Pipe tip 4 violet wavy stripe, then tip 3 yellow wavy stripe. Pipe tip 5 green band ½ in. wide with curved top. Use tip 5 to fill in violet top. Let dry at least 4 hours. Pipe tip 3 dot trims. Using full-strength icing, pipe tip 1 outline ropes. Attach bunny candy with icing. Pipe tip 1 rope over bunny. Each serves 1.

*Combine Lemon Yellow with Golden Yellow for yellow shown. Combine Violet with Rose for violet shown.

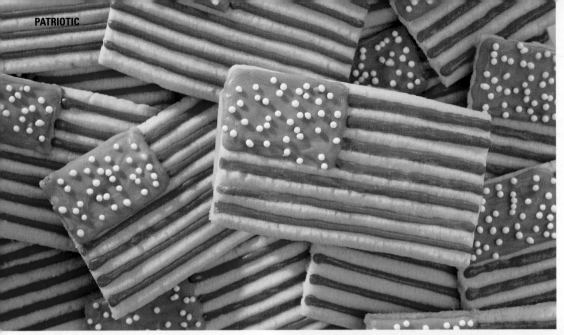

◀ **Spritz Stars & Bars**

Pans: Cookie Sheet, Cooling Grid, p. 203
Candy: White, Red Candy Melts, p. 194; Primary Candy Color Set (blue), p. 195
Recipe: Spritz Cookies, p. 116
Also: Comfort Grip Cookie Press, p. 213; White Nonpareils, p. 144; Disposable Decorating Bags, p. 136; ruler

In advance: Make cookies. Prepare dough. Press 3 in. long cookies using bar disk. Bake and cool cookies.

Melt white candy and tint blue. Using melted candy in disposable decorating bag, fill in 1¼ x ⅞ in. corner rectangle. Tap to settle candy in ridges; add candy if necessary to level surface. Sprinkle on nonpareils. Using melted red candy, pipe stripes in spritz indentations. Let set. Each serves 1.

▶ **Standing Up For Their Country**

Pans: Standard Muffin, p. 158; Cookie Sheet, Cooling Grid, p. 203
Tip: 3, p. 134
Colors:* Christmas Red, Red-Red, Royal Blue, Black, p. 146
Recipes: Buttercream, Royal Icings, Roll-Out Cookies, p. 116
Also: Patriotic Standard Baking Cups, p. 226; Patriotic Mix Sprinkles, p. 226; 101 Cookie Cutters, p. 201; Meringue Powder, p. 143; White Candy Melts, p. 194; 20 in. Rolling Pin, p. 153; black shoestring licorice, black and white spice drops, uncooked spaghetti, knife, granulated sugar, waxed paper

In advance: Make cookies. Prepare dough, roll out and cut using smallest star cutter from set. Bake and cool. Cover with thinned royal icing (p. 128); let dry overnight. Use tip 3 and royal icing to pipe dot eyes, noses and pupils, outline mouths. For each cookie, cut four 1¼ in. pieces of black licorice and attach to backs of stars for arms and legs with melted candy; let set. On waxed paper sprinkled with sugar, roll out white spice drops ⅛ thick, black spice drops ¼ in. thick. Cut into hand and shoe shapes with knife. Insert into licorice arms and legs. Cut uncooked spaghetti into 2½ in. lengths and attach to backs of legs for support with melted candy, leaving 1¼ in. open on one end to insert into cupcakes; let set.

Bake and cool cupcakes. Ice smooth with spatula and add sprinkles. Insert cookies. Each serves 1.

*Combine Christmas Red with Red-Red for red shown.

◀ **BBQ All-Stars**

Pan: 9 x 13 x 2 in. Sheet, p. 157
Colors: Royal Blue, Red-Red, p. 146
Fondant: White Ready-To-Use Rolled Fondant (14 oz. covers 6 treats), p. 147; 9 in. Rolling Pin, Roll & Cut Mat, p. 148; Brush Set, p. 149; Round, Star Cut-Outs, p. 151
Recipe: Buttercream Icing, p. 116
Also: White Sparkling Sugar, p. 144; White Candy Melts, p. 194; 6 in. Lollipop Sticks (cut to 3 in. lengths), p. 198; Cake Board, p. 241; cornstarch, ruler, knife

In advance: Make fondant stars. Roll out fondant ⅛ in. thick. Cut stars using largest Cut-Out. Let dry overnight on cornstarch-dusted board. Attach Lollipop Stick to back using melted candy, leaving 1½ in. extended. Chill until firm. Brush front with damp brush; sprinkle on Sparkling Sugar. Let dry.

Bake and cool 1-layer cake, 1½ in. high, using firm-textured batter such as pound cake. Cut rounds with knife using largest Cut-Out as a guide. Ice lightly. Tint fondant: 3 oz. each blue, red; reserve 6 oz. white. Roll out ⅛ in. thick as needed. For top, cut blue round using largest Cut-Out; attach using damp brush. For side, cut a white 1½ x 8 in. strip; attach. For stripes, cut three ¼ x 8 in. red strips; attach, about ¼ in. apart. Insert stars. Each serves 1.

◀ Lady Liberty and Uncle Sam

Pans: Silicone Round Brownie Pops Mold, p. 171; Cookie Sheet, p. 203

Colors:* For Her: Kelly Green, Teal, Brown, Red-Red, Lemon Yellow, Copper (for skin tone shown); For Him: Royal Blue, Christmas Red, Black, Copper (for skin tone shown), p. 146

Fondant: White Ready-To-Use Rolled Fondant (6-7 oz. per treat), Fine Tip FoodWriter Edible Color Markers (black), p. 147; 9 in. Rolling Pin, Roll & Cut Mat, p. 148; Brush Set, p. 149

Recipes: Buttercream Icing, p. 116; Thinned Fondant Adhesive, p. 117; favorite brownie recipe or mix

Also: Stars and Stripes Party Picks (for him), p. 226; pretzel sticks, ruler, cornstarch, scissors, knife

Bake and cool brownie pops in silicone mold supported by cookie sheet. Lightly ice brownie. Tint fondant as follows: For her: 3 oz. green, 1½ oz. skin tone, 1 oz. brown, ½ oz. yellow. For him 1 ½ oz. skin tone, 1 oz. each red and blue, ½ oz. black, reserve 3 oz. white. Decorate following directions (see p. 124). Each serves 1.

*Combine Kelly Green with Teal for green shown. Combine Brown with Red-Red for brown shown.

▶ Patriotism on Parade!

Pans: Standard Muffin, p. 158; Cookie Sheet, Cooling Grid, p. 203

Tips: 1, 2, p. 143

Colors:* Sky Blue, Christmas Red, Black, Brown, Lemon Yellow, Copper (for light skin tone shown), p. 146

Recipes: Buttercream Icing, Royal Icing, Roll-Out Cookies, p. 116

Also: Meringue Powder, p. 143; Metal Gingerbread Boy Cutter, p. 202; Parchment Triangles, p. 136; 13 Ct. Standard Cupcakes 'N More Dessert Stand, p. 167; Stars and Stripes Party Picks, Patriotic Foil Pix (2 pks.), Patriotic Standard Baking Cups, p. 226; cornstarch

In advance: Make cookies. Tint dough desired skin tone. Roll out and cut 5 gingerbread boy cookies; and 10 triangle easel backs, 2 x 1¼ in., bake and cool. Decorate with royal icing: Use tip 2 to outline and pipe in clothes; smooth with finger dipped in cornstarch. Add tip 2 outline and pull-out hair. Pipe tip 1 dot and outline facial features and clothing details. Attach flags to hands with icing. Let dry overnight. Attach easel backs to backs of legs with royal icing. Let dry.

Bake and cool cupcakes. Ice smooth in buttercream. Insert foil pix. Position cupcakes on stand and cookies around stand. Each serves 1.

*Combine Brown with Christmas Red for brown shown.

Milestone Moments

Pure joy! It's what everyone at the big event is feeling, and it's the mood you'll capture on your decorated dessert. When the teddy bear pulls up at the baby shower on his wagon filled with a rainbow of gift cakes, he creates smiles that will last the rest of the day. For Communion guests, a centerpiece stand that holds their personal petits fours is the perfect touch for an inspiring event. And what better way to cap off the graduate's celebration than with our cap-tossing class of 2011, featured on a tall 3-tier fondant cake? Count on these and every design in this section to do you proud—and your guest of honor too!

The Big Wheel Arrives!

Pans: 6, 8, 10 x 2 in. Square, p. 157

Tip: 6, p. 134

Colors:* Lemon Yellow, Sky Blue, Rose, Leaf Green, Brown, Ivory, Red-Red, Black, p. 146

Fondant: White Ready-To-Use Rolled Fondant (324 oz.), Fine Tip FoodWriter Edible Color Markers (black), Gum-Tex, p. 147; 20 in. Rolling Pin, Roll & Cut Mat, Easy-Glide Fondant Smoother, p. 148; Brush Set, p. 149; Fondant Ribbon Cutter/Embosser Set, p. 150; Star, Round, Heart Cut-Outs, p. 151

Recipes: Buttercream Icing, p. 116; Thinned Fondant Adhesive, p. 117

Also: 2011 Pattern Book (Handle, Base Hitch), p. 130; Piping Gel, p. 143; Cookie Treat Sticks, p. 203; 101 Cookie Cutters (letters), p. 201; 3 in. Grecian Pillars (4), p. 237; 3 in. Globe Base Set, p. 238; Wooden, Plastic Dowel Rods, p. 239; Cake Boards, Fanci-Foil Wrap, p. 241; 12 x 22 in. foamcore board (½ in. thick), hot glue gun, knife, ruler, facial tissue, waxed paper, cornstarch, tape, toothpicks, pencil

Begin about 1 week in advance: Make fondant wagon (p.124). Tint fondant: 60 oz. light brown (add 2 tablespoons Gum-Tex) and 24 oz. dark brown (add 1 tablespoon Gum-Tex) for wagon; 20 oz. dark brown (add 2 teaspoons Gum-Tex) for bear; plus ½ oz. black for trims. Reserve 2 oz. white. Roll out ⅛ in. thick unless otherwise specified. **Also:** Make fondant bear (p. 124). **And:** Prepare wagon support base. Use hot glue gun to attach Grecian Pillars to bottom of 10 x 14 in. cake board, about 1 in. from corners.

Bake and cool 3-layer cakes. Trim one 6 in. and one 8 in. layer to make 5 in. high squares in yellow and blue. Bake five 10 x 2 in. cakes; use 3 for rose cake, cut two lengthwise in half and stack three halves to make 5 x 10 x 6 in.

high green rectangle. Tint fondant: 36 oz. light yellow, 36 oz. light green, 48 oz. light blue, 72 oz. light rose to cover cakes; 8 oz. dark rose, 6 oz. each dark yellow and dark green and 4 oz. dark blue. Prepare cakes and cover with rolled fondant (p. 116); reserve excess fondant for trims. Prepare for Stacked Construction (p. 114).Make cake trims (p. 124). Make letters. Roll out small amount of reserved dark blue, pink, green and yellow. Cut letters using cutters from set; attach to wagon using damp brush.

At reception: Position wagon on base. Use fondant adhesive to attach wheels to sides of wagon to hide pillars. Position cakes. Attach loops and curls with icing dots. Position bear. Attach wagon handle, trimming bottom if needed to create angle. Serves 77.

*Combine Brown with Ivory and a little Red-Red for light brown shown. Combine Brown with Red-Red and a little Black for dark brown shown.

◀ Party Time Nursery Rhyme

Pan: 10 x 2 in. Round, p. 157

Tips: 1, 2, p. 134

Colors:* Violet, Royal Blue, Brown, Red-Red, Daffodil Yellow, Pink, No-Taste Red, Black, p. 146

Fondant: White Ready-To-Use Rolled Fondant (60 oz.), Gum-Tex, p. 147; 20 in. Rolling Pin, Roll & Cut Mat, Easy-Glide Fondant Smoother, p. 148; Brush Set, p. 149; Star Cut-Outs, p. 151

Recipes: Buttercream, Royal Icings, p. 116

Also: 2011 Pattern Book (Cow, Dog, Moon, Dish, Spoon, Cloud), p. 130; Meringue Powder, p. 143; White Candy Melts, p. 194; 11¾ in. Lollipop Sticks, p. 198; Cake Circles, Boards, Fanci-Foil Wrap, p. 241; 10 in. pedestal cake stand, knife, cornstarch, waxed paper, toothpicks

3 or more days in advance: Make fondant pieces. Tint fondant: 10 oz. light periwinkle, 3 oz. light yellow, 3 oz. dark yellow, 1 oz. dark pink (moon hat), 2 oz. light pink (plate base and spoon bow tie), 4 oz. white. Add 1 teaspoon Gum-Tex to periwinkle; ⅛ to ¼ teaspoon to other colors. Roll out ⅛ in. thick as needed. Make fairy tale figures (p. 125). Reserve excess light periwinkle and yellow fondant. **Also:** Make clouds and stars. Use reserved light periwinkle fondant and pattern to cut 2 clouds for cake top; reserve remaining fondant. Use reserved yellow fondant and medium star Cut-Out to cut 4 stars; use smallest Cut-Out to cut 20 stars. Let pieces dry overnight on cornstarch-dusted boards. Using melted candy, attach 4 medium stars and 2 small stars to clouds; cut 1 Lollipop Stick in half and attach 1 half to back of each cloud. Let dry.

Bake and cool 2-layer cake. Prepare and cover with 36 oz. dark periwinkle fondant. Position on stand. Roll out reserved light periwinkle fondant ⅛ in. thick. Use pattern to cut 8 clouds. Use damp brush to attach around cake bottom, extending past edge of cake stand. Use melted candy to attach dog, plate and spoon to cake sides. Insert clouds, moon and cow in cake top; trim sticks if needed. Pipe tip 2 message. Serves 28.

*Combine Royal Blue with Violet for light and dark periwinkle shown. Combine Brown with Red-Red and Black for light brown shown. Combine a small amount of No-Taste Red with White fondant for dark pink shown.

The invitations go with the party garlands which match the fun favor boxes which complement the cake—everything rhymes at this baby shower! Our Nursery Rhyme accessories and stationery products (p. 242-244) make it easy to create a sweet celebration that will send your guests over the moon.

Baby Face

Pans: 4 Pc. Petal Set (15 x 2 in. used), p. 156; Soccer Ball, p. 162

Tip: 2D, p. 134

Colors: Copper (for skin tone shown), Rose, Black, p. 146

Fondant: White Ready-To-Use Rolled Fondant (80 oz.), Gum-Tex, p. 147; 20 in. Rolling Pin, Roll & Cut Mat, Easy-Glide Fondant Smoother, p. 148; Brush Set, p. 149

Recipes: Buttercream Icing, p. 116; Thinned Fondant Adhesive, p. 117

Also: ULTIMATE Cake Leveler, p. 152; Dowel Rods, p. 138; Cake Boards, p. 241; waxed paper, cornstarch, knife, ruler, facial tissue

In advance: Make fondant bow (p. 125).

Bake and cool 1-layer 15 in. petal and soccer ball cakes. Prepare and cover with 40 oz. copper and 48 oz. white fondant. Prepare for Stacked Construction (p. 114). Make fondant accents (p. 125). Attach using damp brush. Assemble bow and secure with fondant adhesive. Serves 36.

▼ Tot Pops

Pans: Cookie Sheet, Cooling Grid, p. 203

Tips: 2, 3, p. 134

Colors:* Pink, Brown, Red-Red, Black, p. 146

Recipes: Color Flow Icing, Roll-Out Cookies, p. 116

Also: Nesting Blossoms Metal Cutter Set, p. 202; Round Cut-Outs, p. 151; White Candy Melts, p. 194; Color Flow Mix, p. 143; 8 in. Cookie Treat Sticks, p. 203; Cake Boards, p. 241; ¼ in. wide ribbon (10 in. for each bow), waxed paper, cornstarch

2-3 days in advance: Prepare and roll out dough. For each treat cut 1 bonnet using 2nd largest blossom cutter from set and 1 face using medium round Cut-Out. Bake and cool cookies. Decorate cookies (p. 125). Tie ribbon around stick. Each serves 1.

*Combine Brown with Red-Red for dark skin tone shown.

◄ Darling Duckling

Pans: 3D Rubber Ducky, p. 160; Soccer Ball, p. 162

Tips: 7, 21, p. 134-135

Colors:* Lemon Yellow, Golden Yellow, Orange, Black, p. 146

Recipe: Buttercream Icing, p. 116

Also: White Ready-To-Use Rolled Fondant (4 oz.), p. 147; 9 in. Rolling Pin, Roll & Cut Mat, p. 148; Metal 7 Pc. Hearts Cutter Set, p. 202; 13 x 19 in. Cake Boards, Fanci-Foil Wrap, p. 241; knife, ruler, tape

Bake and cool Soccer Ball cake and 1 side of Rubber Ducky cake. Trim head off duck and 1 in. off bottom of ball. Position cakes together on foil-wrapped cake board cut to fit or plate; secure with icing. Tint fondant orange and roll out ¾ in. thick. Cut beak using non-symmetrical heart cutter from set; secure in place with icing. Pipe tip 7 dot eye. Cover cakes with tip 21 stars. Overpipe tip 21 pull-out wings and hair. Serves 18.

*Combine Lemon Yellow with Golden Yellow for yellow shown.

Cookie Quackers

Pans: Cookie Sheet, Cooling Grid, p. 203

Tips: 2, 3, 16 p. 134-135

Colors: Lemon Yellow, Orange, Black, p. 146

Recipes: Color Flow Icing, Roll-Out Cookies, p. 116

Also: Round Cut-Outs, p. 151; 101 Cookie Cutters (duck), p. 201; Cake Boards, p. 241; cornstarch, waxed paper, tape

In advance: Make cookies. Prepare and roll out dough. For each treat cut 1 round using medium Cut-Out and 1 duck using cutter from set. Bake and cool. Cover with thinned icing (p. 128); let dry on waxed paper-covered boards. **Also:** Decorate round heads. Secure to waxed paper-covered boards with icing. Use tip 3 and full-strength icing to outline heart-shaped beak; pipe center and let dry. Overpipe until beak is same height as cookie, outlining, then filling in with thinned icing. Pipe tip 16 pull-out hair and tip 2 dot eye. Let dry.

Attach head to body with full-strength icing. Pipe tip 16 pull-out wing. Let dry. Each serves 1.

◀ Candy Dish Cubs

Pans: Petite Loaf, p. 158; Non-Stick Biscuit/ Brownie, p. 165

Candy: White (2 pks. make 3-4 treats), Light Cocoa Candy Melts, p. 194; Primary, Garden Candy Color Sets, p. 195; Decorator Brush Set, p. 197; Baby 2-Pack Candy Mold Set, p. 196; Pillow Mints, Mint Drops Favor Candy, p. 233

Also: 2011 Pattern Book (Box Lid), p. 130; Oval Cut-Outs, p. 151; Cutesy Bear Centerpiece, p. 242; Parchment Triangles, p. 136; Cake Boards, p. 241; knife, waxed paper

In advance: Make yellow candy boxes. Melt and tint candy. For lids, pour candy in non-stick pan 3/16 in. deep. Tap to settle; chill until firm. Unmold onto waxed paper-covered board;

return to room temperature before cutting. Use pattern and warm knife to cut out box lids. For bottoms, use Petite Loaf Pan to make 1/8 in. thick candy shells (p. 128). **Also:** Mold bears using candy mold and Painting Method (p. 128). For light brown, add a small amount of Light Cocoa candy to White. Overpipe eyes and inner ears after unmolding. **And:** Mold candy message plaques. Place medium oval Cut-Out on non-stick pan. Fill 1/8 in. deep with melted candy. Tap to settle; chill until firm. Pipe letters onto shiny side using melted candy in cut parchment bag. Let set.

To assemble, attach bear inside bottom using melted candy. Position lid; attach using melted candy. Hold until set. Attach plaque to front. Add candies. Position centerpiece. Each serves 1.

▶ Infants Love Elephants!

Pans: Teddy Bear, p. 161; Cookie Sheet, Cooling Grid, p. 203

Tips: 2, 5, 16, p. 134-135

Colors:* Violet, Pink, Royal Blue, Brown, Red-Red, p. 146

Recipes: Buttercream Icing, p. 116; Roll-Out Cookies, p. 117

Also: 2011 Pattern Book (Ear, Trunk), p. 130; 4 in. Lollipop Sticks, p. 198; White Candy Melts, p. 194; knife, toothpicks, cornstarch

In advance: Make trunk and ears. Prepare and roll out cookie dough. Use pattern to cut out trunk and 2 ears (flip pattern for 2nd ear).

Bake and cool. Attach Lollipop Sticks to back of ears using melted candy; allow 2 in. to extend at bottom to insert into cake. Let set.

Bake and cool cake. Trim ear areas to 1 in. high; trim edges as needed to match shape of cookie ears. Ice smooth inside of ears and trunk opening on cookies and paw pads on cake. Pipe tip 5 dot eyes; flatten slightly with fingertip dipped in cornstarch. Add tip 2 dot highlights. Cover cake with tip 16 stars; position trunk and ear cookies and trim with tip 16 stars. Add tip 2 outline stitching details. Cake serves 12; each cookie serves 1.

*Combine Violet with Pink and Royal Blue for violet shown. Combine Pink with Royal Blue for pink shown. Combine Brown with Red-Red for brown shown.

◀ Bitty Bear Cookies

Pans: Cookie Sheet, Cooling Grid, p. 203

Tips: 1, 2, p. 134

Colors:* Kelly Green, Brown, Red-Red, Lemon Yellow, Ivory, p. 146

Recipes: Color Flow Icing, Roll-Out Cookies, p. 116

Also: 4 Pc. Baby Cutter Set, p. 202; Color Flow Mix, p. 143; knife, ruler

At least 1 day in advance: Make cookies. Prepare and roll out dough. Cut bears using cutter from set. Cut 2 x 1¼ in. wide triangle easel backs. Bake and cool. Use tip 2 and

full-strength icing to outline features; bear in dark brown; tummy, muzzle and 4 paw pads in light brown; inner ears in green. Let set. Flow in (p. 128) using thinned color flow; let set.

Decorate and assemble using full-strength icing. Use tip 1 to pipe dark brown stitches around light brown sections. Pipe tip 2 dots for inner ears, eyes and nose. Use tip 2 to outline and fill-in bow; add dot knot and pull-out streamers. Let set. Attach easel to back with full-strength icing; let set. Each serves 1.

*Combine Brown with Red-Red for dark brown shown. Combine Lemon Yellow with Ivory for yellow shown.

▲ Sew Adorable Cake!

Pan: 4 Pc. Oval Set (largest pan used), p. 156

Tips: 2, 3, 7, p. 134

Colors:* Brown, Red-Red, Pink, Royal Blue, Violet, Lemon Yellow, Ivory, Kelly Green, p. 146

Fondant: White Ready-To-Use Rolled Fondant (84 oz.), p. 147; 20 in. Rolling Pin, Roll & Cut Mat, Easy-Glide Fondant Smoother, p. 148

Recipes: Buttercream, Color Flow Icings, p. 116; Chocolate Fondant, p. 117

Also: 2011 Pattern Book (BABY Letters), p. 130; Color Flow Mix, p. 143; Dark Cocoa Candy Melts, p. 194; Cake Boards, Fanci-Foil Wrap, p. 241; Piping Gel, p. 143; Parchment Triangles, p. 136; 18 x 15 in. plywood or foamcore board (½ in. thick), waxed paper, sugar cubes, tape, non-stick pan spray, facial tissue

At least 3 days in advance: Make color flow letters (p. 128). Tape patterns to cake board and cover with waxed paper; spray lightly with pan spray and wipe with tissue. Outline letters with tip 3 and full-strength color flow; flow in with thinned color flow in cut parchment bag. Make extras to allow for breakage and let dry 3 days. Pipe tip 2 outline stitching in full-strength color flow. Let dry. **Also:** Prepare base board. Using pan as a guide, cut board ½ in. larger than pan on all sides; cover with chocolate fondant (p. 120).

Bake and cool 2-layer cake, 3 in. high. Prepare and cover cake with 60 oz. pink fondant (p. 116). Position cake on base board; pipe tip 7 bead bottom border in buttercream.

At party: Position letters. Raise B's with sugar cubes to overlap other letters, attaching with dots of full-strength color flow. Serves 48.

*Combine Brown with Red-Red for brown shown. Combine Pink with Royal Blue for pink shown. Combine Royal Blue with Violet for blue shown. Combine Lemon Yellow with Ivory for yellow shown. Combine Violet with Royal Blue and Pink for violet shown.

▼ Tot's Trotter

Pan: Party Pony, p. 161

Tips: 3, 16, p. 134-135

Colors:* Brown, Lemon Yellow, Ivory, Pink, Red-Red, p. 146

Fondant: White Ready-To-Use Rolled Fondant (48 oz.), p. 147; 20 in. Rolling Pin, Roll & Cut Mat, p. 148

Recipe: Buttercream Icing, p. 116

Also: Plastic Dowel Rods (1), p. 239; Cake Board, Fanci-Foil Wrap, p. 241; knife, ruler, toothpicks, cornstarch

Bake and cool cake. Trim off back ear; trim neck area, leaving 4½ in. wide squared-off neck shape. Tint fondant brown. To give mane dimension, roll

12 fondant logs, 4 x ½ in. diameter. Position logs starting on cake top and running down sides, about 1 to 1½ in. apart; secure with icing if necessary. Roll out fondant ⅛ in. thick. Cut a 4 x 20 in. rectangle. Position over logs and smooth with hands, trimming if necessary. Trim fondant away from ear. Pipe tip 3 zigzag inner ear, pat smooth. Cover head with tip 16 stars. Shape ½ in. fondant eye; flatten and attach. Cut ⅝ in. wide strips for bridle; attach. Cover dowel rod with fondant, leaving 1½ in. exposed to insert into cake. Insert dowel rod. Serves 10.

*Combine Lemon Yellow with Brown and Red-Red for tan shown. Combine Lemon Yellow with Ivory for yellow shown.

◀ A Bear with Flair

Pans: 4 Pc. Oval Set (2 medium pans used), p. 156

Tip: 2A, p. 134

Colors:* Royal Blue, Lemon Yellow, Pink, Brown, Ivory, p. 146

Fondant: White Ready-To-Use Rolled Fondant (64 oz.), p. 147; 20 in. Rolling Pin, Roll & Cut Mat, Easy-Glide Fondant Smoother, p. 148; Brush Set, p. 149

Recipes: Buttercream Icing, p. 116; Thinned Fondant Adhesive, p. 117

Also: 101 Cookie Cutters (largest round used), p. 201; Circle Metal Cutter, p. 202; ruler, knife, cornstarch, 4 in. diameter dish or circle

Bake and cool 1-layer cakes. Tint fondant: 42 oz. blue, 16 oz. yellow, 3 oz. light brown, 2 oz. pink, 1 oz. brown. For ears, cut 2 circles from smaller cake, using outside edge of

largest circle cutter from 101 Cutter Set as guide. Trim 1 in. off bottoms to match curve of head. Use icing to attach ears to oval head on serving plate or board. Prepare and cover with rolled fondant (p. 117). Roll out pink ⅛ in. thick; use metal cookie cutter to cut 2 circles for inner ears. Trim to 1¾ in. deep; attach using damp brush. Roll out brown ¼ in. thick. Cut eyes using wide end of tip 2A; attach. Roll out light brown ½ in. thick. Cut muzzle using largest round from set; attach. Shape 1½ x 1 x ¼ in. thick oval nose; attach. Roll out yellow ¼ in. thick. Cut two 5 x 8 in. rectangles for bow tie. Form pleats and pinch to gather at center. Cut 4 x 1½ in. strip; attach over center for knot. Attach under head with fondant adhesive. Serves 17.

*Combine Royal Blue with Ivory and Lemon Yellow for blue shown. Combine Lemon Yellow with Ivory for yellow shown. Combine Pink with a little Royal Blue for pink shown. Combine Ivory with a little Brown for light brown shown.

▶ Declaration of Faith

Pan: Cross, p. 224

Tips: 2, 4, p. 134

Colors:* Royal Blue, Brown, Red-Red, Black, p. 146

Fondant: White Ready-To-Use Rolled Fondant (96 oz.), Natural Colors Fondant Multi Pack (dark brown used), p. 147; 20 in. Rolling Pin, Roll & Cut Mat, Easy-Glide Fondant Smoother, Graceful Vines Fondant Imprint Mat, p. 148; Brush Set, p. 149

Recipes: Buttercream, Royal Icings, p. 116

Also: Cake Boards, Fanci-Foil Wrap, p. 241; Piping Gel, Meringue Powder, p. 143; 16 x 20 in. plywood or foamcore board (¼ in. thick), ruler

In advance: Prepare base board. Using pan as guide, cut board 1¾ in. larger on all sides. Tint 48 oz. of fondant blue, roll out ⅛ in. thick and imprint design using Imprint Mat. Cover base board (p. 120). Use tip 2 and dark brown royal icing to pipe in imprint design. Work from outer edge of frame and in 2¼ in. from edge. Do not pipe in area where cross cake will be positioned. Let dry.

Bake and cool cake. Prepare and cover with rolled fondant (p. 117). Tint remaining fondant light blue; roll out ¼ in. thick. Cut out cross shape using top area of pan as pattern. Brush back with damp brush and attach. Score lines across center using edge of spatula. Roll out dark brown fondant from Multi Pack ⅛ in. thick. Cut ½ in. wide strips for center cross, 11 and 7 in. long. Attach. Imprint lines. Position cake on base board. Pipe tip 4 white bead bottom border in buttercream. Serves 12.

*Combine Brown with Red-Red and a small amount of Black for brown shown.

◀ Heaven's Blessings

Pan: Book, p. 162

Tips: 1, 2, 5, p. 134

Colors:* Pink (or Sky Blue), Brown, Red-Red, p. 146

Fondant: White Ready-To-Use Rolled Fondant (80 oz.), Gum-Tex, p. 147; 20 in. Rolling Pin, Roll & Cut Mat, Easy-Glide Fondant Smoother, p. 148; Brush Set, White Pearl Dust, p. 149; Cutter/Embosser, p. 150; Floral Collection Flower Making Set, Round Cut-Outs, p. 151

Recipes: Buttercream, Royal Icings, p. 116

Also: 2011 Pattern Book (Christ and Child), p. 130; Italic Make-Any-Message Letter Press Set, Decorating Comb, p. 140; Meringue Powder, Clear Vanilla Extract, Piping Gel, p. 143; Cake Boards, Fanci-Foil Wrap, p. 241; knife, waxed paper, cornstarch, ruler, toothpicks, straight pin, scissors, tape

Several days in advance: Make fondant plaque (p. 125). **Also:** Make flowers. Roll out fondant ⅛ in. thick. Cut 3 flowers using pansy and 2 using apple blossom cutters from Flower Making Set. Add tip 2 embroidery details (p. 120) using royal icing. Let dry on cornstarch-dusted surface. Paint with Pearl Dust/vanilla mixture (p. 120). Let dry. **And:** Prepare base board. Cut double-thick Cake Board 13 x 17 in.; allow 1 extra inch on all sides. Prepare and cover with 40 oz. fondant (p. 120).

Bake and cool cake. Ice smooth with buttercream. Comb sides using small tooth edge of comb. Position on prepared board.

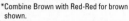

Decorate cake top (p. 125). Attach plaque and flowers using dots of buttercream. Pipe tip 5 bead bottom border. Serves 30.

*Combine Brown with Red-Red for brown shown.

Christening Commemoration

Pans: Cookie Sheet, Cooling Grid, p. 203
Tips: 1, 2, 3, 101, 101s, 102, p. 134-135
Colors: Copper (for skin tone shown), Black, Brown, Red-Red, p. 146
Fondant: White Ready-To-Use Rolled Fondant (4 oz. per treat), p. 147; 9 in. Rolling Pin, Roll & Cut Mat, p. 148; Round Cut-Outs, p. 151; White Pearl Dust, Brush Set, p. 149
Recipes: Color Flow Icing, Roll-Out Cookies, p. 116; Thinned Fondant Adhesive, p. 117
Also: 2011 Pattern Book (Baby, Dress), p. 130; Nesting Blossoms Metal Cutter Set, p. 202; Color Flow Mix, p. 143; Piping Gel, Clear Vanilla Extract, p. 143; Cake Boards, Circles, p. 241; cornstarch, knife, ruler, waxed paper, toothpicks

In advance: Make cookies. Prepare and roll out dough; Use pattern to cut babies. Bake and cool. **Also:** Add dress. Roll out fondant ⅛ in. thick. Use pattern to cut out dress. Brush cookie with Piping Gel and attach dress; trim if needed. **And:** Add head and hands. Tint color flow skin tone. Outline head and hands using tip 3 and full-strength icing; let set. Flow in centers using thinned icing (p. 128). Let dry. **And:** Add bonnet. Roll out fondant ³⁄₁₆ in. thick. Cut using 2nd smallest blossom cutter from set. Use medium round Cut-Out to cut away center. Use knife to cut away 3 bottom scallops. Attach bonnet around head using fondant adhesive.

Decorate using full-strength color flow. For face, pipe tip 1 dot eyes, outline mouth and hair curl. Pipe tip 2 dot cheeks; flatten slightly. For sleeves, pipe tip 101 outer ruffles and tip 101s inner ruffles. For bottom trim, pipe tip 102 ruffles; add tip 1 bead and dot details. For collar, use tip 3 to outline and fill in 2 sections; pat smooth with fingertip dipped in cornstarch. Add bow loops, center dot and streamers in same way. Pipe tip 1 scallop details. Let dry. Paint dress details with Pearl Dust/vanilla mixture (p. 120). Each serves 1.

*Combine Brown with Red-Red for brown shown.

▼ Cross Cookies

Pans: Cookie Sheet, Cooling Grid, p. 230
Tips: 2, 3, 5, p. 134
Colors: Pink, Sky Blue, p. 146
Fondant: White Ready-To-Use Rolled Fondant (for daisy), p. 147; 9 in. Rolling Pin, Roll & Cut Mat, p. 148; White Pearl Dust, Brush Set, p. 149; Daisy Cut-Outs. p. 151
Recipes: Color Flow Icing, Roll-Out Cookies, p. 116
Also: Metal Cross Cutter, p. 202; Sugar Pearls Sprinkles, p. 145; Color Flow Mix, Clear Vanilla Extract, p. 143; Cake Boards, p. 241; cornstarch, waxed paper, tape, ruler

In advance: Make cookies. Prepare and roll out dough. Cut crosses using metal cutter. Bake and cool. Outline using full-strength color flow and tip 3 (use pink and tip 5 for daisy version); let set. Fill in using thinned color flow. Let dry overnight. Add details on monogram, pearl and daisy designs (p. 125). Each serves 1.

◀ Collective Spirit

Pans: 12 x 18 x 2 in. Sheet p. 157; Cooling Grid, p. 203
Tip: 3, p. 134
Color: Pink, p. 146
Fondant: White Ready-To-Use Rolled Fondant (3 oz. for 36 flowers), p. 147; 9 in. Rolling Pin, Roll & Cut Mat, p. 148; White, Orchid Pink Pearl Dust, Brush Set, p. 149; Floral Garland Cutter/Ejector Set, Round Cut-Outs, p. 151
Candy: Cross/Bible Lollipop Mold, p. 224; White Candy Melts (1 pk. for 36 treats), p. 194; 6 in. Lollipop Sticks (cut into 3 in. lengths), p. 198
Also: Graceful Tiers Cake Stand, p. 235; Ready-To-Use Decorator Icing (1 can for 6 to 8 treats), p. 143; Sugar Pearls Sprinkles, p. 145; ULTIMATE Cake Leveler, p. 152; Cake Board, p. 241; Clear Vanilla Extract, p. 143; waxed paper, cornstarch, ruler, knife

In advance: Mold candy crosses in small cross cavity of lollipop mold (p. 128). Tap to settle; chill until firm. Paint cross with White Pearl Dust/vanilla mixture (p. 120). Paint top only with Orchid Pink Pearl Dust/vanilla mixture; let dry. **Also:** Make fondant flowers. Roll out fondant ⅛ in. thick. Cut 1 flower for each cross using Cutter/Ejector with flower cutter. Brush with white Pearl Dust. Let dry on waxed paper-covered board dusted with cornstarch. **And:** Complete crosses using melted candy. Attach stick to back, leaving 1½ in. of stick exposed at bottom; let set. Attach Sugar Pearl to flower center; let set. Attach flower to center of cross; let set.

Bake and cool cake using firm-textured batter, such as pound cake. Trim to 1½ in. high. Cut circles using largest Cut-Out as guide. Cover with heated Decorator Icing (p. 128); let dry. Repeat if necessary; let dry. Trim bottoms with knife to smooth. Using tip 3 and Decorator Icing, pipe 4 equally spaced dots at midpoint of cake sides; pipe scrolls between dots.

At reception: Insert crosses and position petits fours on stand. Each serves 1.

The Quinceañera girl has captured everyone's heart. Now give guests a little heart to take home, using our Heart Favor Kit (p. 232), including see-through containers, ribbon, tulle and printable tags. We've filled the containers with our Peppermint Pearls (p. 233) and topped each with a Pink Posy Icing Flower (p. 145).

◄ Blooms for La Quinceañera

Pans: 6, 8, 10, 12, 14, 16 x 2 in. Round, p. 157
Tips: 1A, 2, 12, 127, p. 134-135
Color: Rose, p. 146
Fondant/Gum Paste: White Ready-To-Use Rolled Fondant (36 oz.), Ready-To-Use Gum Paste (1 pkg.), p. 147; 20 in. Rolling Pin, Roll & Cut Mat, Easy-Glide Fondant Smoother, p. 148; White Pearl Dust, Brush Set, p. 149
Recipes: Buttercream, Royal Icings, p. 116
Also: Dowel Rods, p. 239; Decorating Nail Set (2½ in. used), p. 138; Meringue Powder, Piping Gel, p. 143; Sugar Pearls Sprinkles, p. 145; Cake Circles, Fanci-Foil Wrap, p. 241; 6 in. Cookie Treat Sticks (2), p. 203; 18 in. diameter plywood or foamcore board (½ in. thick), 3½ in. waxed paper squares, ruler, cornstarch, tape

At least 1 week in advance: Make royal icing roses (p. 119). Use large flower nail to pipe 77 tip 127 roses with tip 1A centers. Make extras to allow for breakage. Let dry. **Also:** Make gum paste initial. Tint gum paste and roll out ⅜ in. thick. Cut initial (up to 5 in. wide, 10 in. tall). Let dry 3 to 4 days on waxed paper-covered board dusted with cornstarch. Using royal icing, pipe tip 2 dots to attach Sugar Pearls to edges. Brush center of letter with Pearl Dust (p. 120). Let dry. Use royal icing to attach 2 Cookie Treat Sticks to back of letter. Trim as needed to leave 3 in. extended at bottom to insert into cake. **And:** Cover base board with 36 oz. rolled fondant (p. 120).

Bake and cool 2-layer cakes (bake two 1½ in. layers for 3 in. high cakes). Use buttercream to ice tops white and sides pink. Prepare for Stacked Construction (p. 114).

At reception: Stack tiers. Attach roses to sides using tip 12 dots of buttercream icing. Use 7 on top tier, then 10, 12, 14, 16 and 18 on descending tiers. Insert initial. Serves 240.

▶ A Spiritual Journey

Pans: 8, 10, 12, 14 x 2 in. Square, p. 157

Tips: 2, 16, p. 134-135

Colors: Royal Blue, Black, p. 146

Fondant: White Ready-To-Use Rolled Fondant (458 oz.), Gum-Tex, p. 147; 20 in. Rolling Pin, Roll & Cut Mat, Easy-Glide Fondant Smoother, p. 148; Brush Set, Gold Pearl Dust, p. 149

Recipes: Buttercream, Royal Icings, p. 116; Thinned Fondant Adhesive, p. 117

Also: 2011 Pattern Book (Star, Buildings), p. 130; Meringue Powder, Piping Gel, Clear Vanilla Extract, p. 143; ULTIMATE Cake Leveler, p. 152; Pastry Brush, p. 153; 8 in. Cookie Treat Stick, p. 203; Dowel Rods, p. 239; Cake Boards, Fanci-Foil Wrap, p. 241; 20 in. square plywood or foamcore board (½ in. thick), cornstarch, ruler, knife, waxed paper, tape, scissors, toothpicks

Several days in advance: Make star. Add 3 tablespoons Gum-Tex to 84 oz. fondant. Roll out ⅛ in. thick. Use pattern to cut 2 stars. Cut away center of 1 star, leaving ¼ in. border; attach border to first star using damp brush. Let dry overnight on cornstarch-dusted board. Attach Cookie Treat Stick to back using thinned fondant adhesive; leave 4 in. of stick extended at bottom. Let dry. **Also:** Make buildings using remaining fondant. Roll out ⅛ in. thick as needed. Use patterns to cut out shapes in number indicated on patterns. Let dry on cornstarch-dusted boards. **And:** Cover base board (p. 120) with 80 oz. fondant tinted black. Reserve excess fondant.

Bake and cool 3-layer cakes (trim 1 layer to 1 in. high for 5 in. high cakes). Prepare and cover with 294 oz. fondant tinted blue. Prepare for Stacked Construction (p. 114). Attach buildings around cake sides using royal icing, overlapping for dimension. Use royal icing to pipe tip 2 outlines and tip 16 stars. Roll out reserved black fondant ⅛ in. thick. Cut assorted shapes for doors and windows; attach using damp brush. Paint building outlines, stars and large star border with Pearl Dust/vanilla mixture (p. 120). Pipe tip 2 message. Insert star. Serves 161.

▲ Milestone Monogram Cookies

Pans: Cookie Sheet, Cooling Grid, p. 203

Tips: 2, 3, p. 134

Colors:* Royal Blue, Brown, Red-Red, p. 146

Recipes: Color Flow Icing, Roll-Out Cookies, p. 116

Also: Round Comfort-Grip Cutter, p. 200; Color Flow Mix, p. 143; Parchment Triangles, p. 136

In advance: Make cookies. Prepare and roll out dough. Cut cookies; bake and cool. Outline using tip 3 and full-strength color flow; let set. Flow in with thinned color flow; let set.

Decorate cookies using full-strength color flow. Pipe tip 3 monogram, tip 2 scallops and dots. Each serves 1.

*Combine Brown with Red-Red for brown shown.

▼ Smart Cookies

Pans: Cookie Sheet, Cooling Grid, p. 203

Tips: 2, 3, 4, p. 134

Colors:* Royal Blue, Black, Brown, Red-Red, Golden Yellow, Copper (for skin tone shown), p. 146

Fondant: White Ready-To-Use Rolled Fondant (3 oz. for each figure), p. 147; 9 in. Rolling Pin, Roll & Cut Mat, p. 148; Brush Set, p. 149

Recipes: Color Flow Icing, Roll-Out Cookies, p. 116

Also: 2011 Pattern Book (Mortarboard), p. 130; 101 Cookie Cutters (large gingerbread girl), p. 201; Color Flow Mix, Piping Gel, p. 143; Graduation Icing Decorations (diplomas), p. 227; Cake Boards, p. 241; knife, ruler, cornstarch

In advance: Make cookies. Prepare and roll out dough. Use large gingerbread girl cutter from set to cut figures. Bake and cool. Outline head and hands using tip 3 and full-strength icing; flow in using thinned icing (p. 128). Let dry. **Also:** Make fondant caps. Reserve a ¾ in. ball of white fondant for trims on each figure; tint remaining fondant favorite school color. Roll out ⅛ in. thick. Use pattern to cut out mortarboard; let dry. Shape a 1⅜ x ½ x ⁵⁄₁₆ in. high oval for cap base. Attach mortarboard using damp brush; let dry on cornstarch-dusted board. Reserve remaining fondant.

Roll out fondant ⅛ in. thick as needed. Use cookie cutter to cut gown; set over cookie and trim at head, hands and feet to shape gown. Lightly brush gown cookie area with Piping Gel and attach. Use knife tip to score center line. Cut ¾ in. wide semi-circles or triangles for collars; attach using damp brush. Cut thin strips for sleeve trims and small semi-circles for girl's shoes; attach. Add details using full-strength color flow. Use tip 2 to outline and fill in boy's tie and shoes; pipe tip 2 dot eyes and outline mouth; pipe tip 4 zigzag girl's hair and tip 2 e-motion boy's hair. Attach cap; pipe tip 2 outline tassel and dot knot. Attach diploma. Each serves 1.

*Combine Brown with Red-Red for brown shown.

▲ Capping Off Their Education!

Pans: 6, 8, 10 x 2 in. Round, p. 157

Tip: 4, p. 134

Colors:* Black, Red-Red, Christmas Red, p. 146

Fondant: White Ready-To-Use Rolled Fondant (76 oz.), Gum-Tex, p. 147; 20 in. Rolling Pin, Roll & Cut Mat, Easy-Glide Fondant Smoother, p. 148; Brush Set, p. 149; Alphabet/Number Cut-Outs, p. 151

Recipes: Buttercream Icing, p. 116; Thinned Fondant Adhesive, p. 117

Also: 2011 Pattern Book (Graduates, Cap), p. 130; 101 Cookie Cutters, p. 201; 8 in. Lollipop Sticks, p. 198; Cake Circles, Boards, p. 241; Dowel Rods, p. 239; knife, cornstarch, waxed paper

Two days in advance: Make numbers and caps for top. Tint fondant: 20 oz. red, 14 oz. black. Separate 2 oz. of each color and add ½ teaspoon Gum-Tex to each (reserve remaining tinted fondant). Roll out ⅛ in. thick. Use cutters from set to cut 4 numbers; use pattern to cut 5 caps. Let dry 24 hours. Attach 4 numbers and bottom 3 hats to lollipop sticks using fondant adhesive; attach 2 hats to top of numbers. Let dry.

Bake and cool 2-layer 6 and 8 in. cakes and 1-layer 10 in. cake. Prepare and cover with rolled fondant (p. 117). Prepare for Stacked Construction (p. 114). Roll out black fondant ⅛ in. thick. Use patterns to cut 10 graduates and 10 caps. Attach to cake sides using damp brush. Use alphabet Cut-Outs to cut message; attach. Pipe tip 4 bead bottom borders. Insert hats and numbers into cake top, trimming sticks as needed. Serves 48.

*Combine Red-Red with Christmas Red for red shown.

▼ Sticking with Their Studies!

Pans: Cookie Sheet, Cooling Grid, p. 203

Tips: 1, 2, 3, p. 134

Colors: Black, Royal Blue, Kelly Green, Christmas Red, Golden Yellow, p. 146

Recipes: Color Flow Icing, Roll-Out Cookies, p. 116

Also: 3 Pc. Graduation Cutter Set, p. 227; 6 in. Lollipop Sticks, p. 198; Gold Pearl Dust, p. 149; Decorator Brush Set, p. 197; Color Flow Mix, Clear Vanilla Extract, p. 143; knife, ruler

In advance: Make cookies. Prepare and roll out dough. For each treat, cut 1 complete cap using cutter from set. Cut 1 mortarboard area only; use knife to trim ⅛ in. off all sides. Bake and cool all cookies. For complete cap, outline with tip 3 and full-strength icing; flow in center using thinned icing (p. 128). Let dry. For mortarboard cookies pour on thinned icing to cover (p. 128). Let dry.

Assemble and decorate caps using full-strength icing (p. 125). Attach lollipop stick to back. Let dry. Each serves 1.

▲ Delicious Diplomas

Pan: 10 x 2 in. Square, p. 157

Candy: White (3 pks. make 10-12 treats), Red Candy Melts, p. 194

Recipe: Wilton Fudge, p. 116

Also: 3 Pc. Graduation Cutter Set, p. 227; Non-Stick Parchment Paper, p. 152; Parchment Triangles, p. 136; Cake Boards, p. 241; non-stick pan spray, scissors

In advance: Make fudge. Prepare pan by lightly spraying with pan spray (to hold parchment in place) and lining with parchment paper. Pour in fudge; chill at least 2 hours to set. Let return to room temperature before cutting.

Lift parchment paper to remove fudge square from pan. Cut diplomas using cutter from set (spray inside of cutter with pan spray before each cut for easier release). Set diplomas on parchment paper-covered board. Decorate with melted candy in cut parchment bag. Pipe white outline. Outline and fill in red bow. Chill until firm. Store in airtight container at room temperature until serving time. Each serves 1.

▶ Paging All Your Friends

Pan: Book, p. 162

Tips: 2, 6, p. 134

Colors:* Royal Blue, Violet, Rose, Brown, Red-Red, Black, Lemon Yellow, Ivory, Copper (for light skin tone shown), p. 146

Fondant: White Ready-To-Use Rolled Fondant (96 oz.), Fine Tip Primary Colors FoodWriter Edible Color Markers (black, blue), p. 147; 20 in. Rolling Pin, Roll & Cut Mat, Easy-Glide Fondant Smoother, p. 148; Brush Set, p. 149; People, Square Cut-Outs, p. 151

Recipe: Buttercream Icing, p. 116

Also: Decorating Comb, p. 140; Piping Gel, p. 143; Pastry Brush, p. 153; 13 x19 in. Cake Boards (3), Fanci-Foil Wrap, p. 241; ruler, knife, tape, toothpicks

In advance: Prepare base board. Cut 2 Cake Boards to 13 x 17 in. Tape together, wrap in foil and cover with 40 oz. brown rolled fondant (p. 120).

Bake and cool cake. Position on cut-to-fit Cake Board. Ice smooth. Comb sides using small tooth edge of comb. Position on board. Roll out 24 oz. fondant ⅛ in. thick; place on top of pan and trim to size. Transfer to cake top and smooth. Tint fondant: 6 oz. violet, 6 oz. blue (or gown color), 3 oz. gray, 3 oz. various skin tones (p. 146), 1 oz. red. Roll out ⅛ in. thick as needed. For individual pictures, cut 18 squares using medium Cut-Out; for trio picture, cut a 3 x 5 in. rectangle. Attach backgrounds using damp brush. Using People Cut-Outs cut 21 heads in various skin tones; attach. Use shirt cutter to cut 3 shirts; adjust to fit trio and attach. Cut just top portion of shirt for 18 individual pictures; trim to fit and attach. Cut ¾ x ½ in. diamonds for hats; attach. Pipe tip 2 outline, pull-out and swirl hair. Use FoodWriters to print names and messages, draw eyes and mouths. Roll thin log, 8 in. long; attach around guest of honor's picture. Pipe tip 6 bead bottom border. Serves 36.

*Combine Violet with Rose for violet shown. Combine Brown with Red-Red for brown hair and darker skin tones and base board shown.

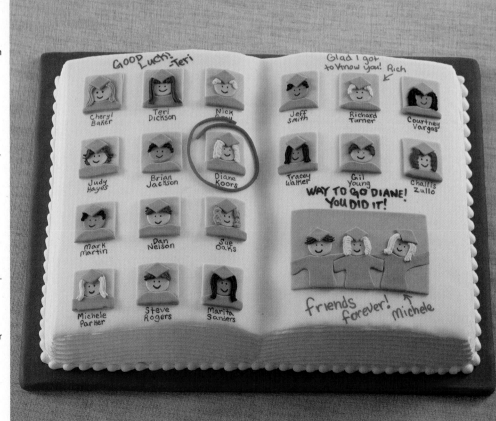

A Window to Your Wedding

The wedding cake tells guests everything about the way you feel on this amazing day. Our collection lets your style, your personality, shine through! Embrace tradition with the simple beauty of the wrapped fondant roses below or the pretty carnation-topped petits fours at left. Choose fresh new shapes like our stacked pillow cakes in a trio of textures or exciting color combos including hot pink tiers with a chocolate heart topper. Or just have fun with our globe pillar people designs, which are easy to customize with fondant details—you can even take your cat and dog for a walk down the aisle!

Rose Unity

Pans: 6, 8, 10 x 2 in. Round, p. 157
Tip: 3, p. 134
Colors:* Rose, Kelly Green, Leaf Green, p. 146
Fondant: White Ready-To-Use Rolled Fondant (105 oz.), Gum-Tex, p. 147; 20 in. Rolling Pin, Roll & Cut Mat, Easy-Glide Fondant Smoother, p. 148; 10 Pc. Fondant/Gum Paste Tool Set, Flower Former Set, Fondant Shaping Foam, p. 149; Leaf Cut-Outs, p. 151
Recipe: Buttercream Icing, p. 116

Also: Cake and Treat Display Set, p. 235; Cake Circles, Boards, p. 241; ⅝ in. wide ribbon (3 yards), cornstarch, waxed paper, knife, toothpicks, ruler, double stick tape

In advance: Make wrapped roses (p. 125). Tint 24 oz. fondant rose; add 2 teaspoons Gum-Tex. Roll out ⅛ in. thick. Make 3 large and 5 small roses. **Also:** Make leaves. Tint 3 oz. fondant green; add ¼ teaspoon Gum-Tex. Roll out ⅛ in. thick. Use large leaf cutter from set to cut 7 leaves. Set on thin foam and use ball

tool to soften edges; use veining tool to add details. Set on large Flower Formers dusted with cornstarch to dry.

Bake and cool 2-layer cakes. Prepare and cover with rolled fondant (p. 117). Position on plates. Attach ribbon around bottom edges, overlapping ends and securing with double stick tape. Pipe tip 3 bead bottom borders. Attach flowers and leaves with icing. Serves 62.**

*Combine Kelly Green with Leaf Green for green shown.

▼ Natural Wonders

Pans: 9 x 13 x 2 in. Sheet, p. 157; Cookie Sheet, Cooling Grid, p. 203
Tips: 2, 3, 5, p. 134
Colors:* Sky Blue, Orange, Leaf Green, Lemon Yellow, Violet, Rose, Brown, Red-Red, p. 146
Fondant: White Ready-To-Use Rolled Fondant (4 oz. will make about 200 flowers), p. 147; 9 in. Rolling Pin, Roll & Cut Mat, p. 148; Brush Set, p. 149; Floral Collection Flower Making Set, p. 151
Recipes: Buttercream, Royal Icings, p. 116
Also: 2011 Pattern Book (Small Butterfly), p. 130; White Mini Baking Cups, p. 184; Light Cocoa Candy Melts (1 pk. covers 5-6 treats), p. 194; Chocolate Ready-To-Use Decorator Icing, Meringue Powder, p. 143; Circle Metal Cutter, p. 202; Cake Boards, p. 241; waxed paper, tape, scissors, cornstarch, cotton balls, ruler, knife, non-stick pan spray

At least 3 days in advance: Make royal icing small butterflies (p. 125). **Also:** Make fondant apple blossoms (p. 125), 4 for each treat.

Bake and cool sheet cake using firm-textured batter, such as pound cake. To cut treats use 3 in. circle cutter. Cover with melted candy (p. 128). Transfer to waxed paper-covered board and chill until firm. Recoat if needed for smooth finish. Set each treat on a flattened baking cup. Use Decorator Icing to pipe tip 5 bead bottom border. Use buttercream to pipe tip 3 light brown and tip 2 green scrolls. Attach apple blossoms and butterfly with icing. Each serves 1.

*Combine Leaf Green with Lemon Yellow for green shown. Combine Violet with Rose for violet shown. Combine Brown with Red-Red for light brown shown.

▲ Garden Guests

Pans: 3 Pc. Paisley Set, p. 156
Tips: 4, 5, 6, 7, p. 134
Colors:* Sky Blue, Orange, Leaf Green, Lemon Yellow, Violet, Rose, Brown, Red-Red, p. 146
Fondant: White Ready-To-Use Rolled Fondant (56 oz.), p. 147; 20 in. Rolling Pin, Roll & Cut Mat, Easy-Glide Fondant Smoother, p. 148; Brush Set, p. 149; Floral Collection Flower Making Set, p. 151
Recipes: Buttercream, Chocolate Buttercream, Royal Icings, p. 116; Chocolate Fondant (2 recipes), p. 117
Also: 2011 Pattern Book (Large Butterfly, Side Scrolls), p. 130; Piping Gel, p. 143; Dark Cocoa Candy Melts (2 pks.), p. 194;

Meringue Powder, p. 143; Fresh Flower Cake Spikes, p. 240; Dowel Rods, p. 239; Cake Boards, Fanci-Foil Wrap, p. 241; 22-gauge green cloth-covered florist wire (2 pieces, each 7 in. long), 20 x 15 in. plywood or foamcore board (½ in. thick), waxed paper, tape, scissors, cornstarch, cotton balls, ruler, knife, toothpicks, non-stick pan spray

At least 3 days in advance: Make 2 large royal icing butterflies on wires (p. 125). **Also:** Make fondant flowers (p. 125). Use assorted colors to make 10-12 each: apple blossoms, daisies and pansies using cutters from set. **And:** Prepare base board. Using largest pan as a guide, cut board 1 in. larger than pan on all sides. Cover with chocolate fondant (p. 120).

Bake and cool 2-layer cakes. Ice smooth with chocolate buttercream and prepare for Stacked Construction (p. 114). Use pattern to mark side scrolls: 1 on top tier, 1½ on middle tier, 2 on bottom tier. Use light brown buttercream icing to cover main stems with tip 7 outlines. Use green to add tip 4 side stems. Pipe tip 6 bead bottom borders. Attach flowers with icing dots.

At reception: Fill 2 Flower Spikes with chocolate fondant; insert butterflies, trimming wires as needed to vary heights. Insert spikes into cake. Serves 94.**

*Combine Leaf Green with Lemon Yellow for green shown. Combine Violet with Rose for violet shown. Combine Brown with Red-Red for light brown shown.

▶ The Family Tree Branches Out

Pans: 6, 8, 10 x 2 in. Square, p. 157
Tips: 1s, 5, 17, 101, 101s, p. 134-135
Colors:* Brown, Ivory, Rose, Red-Red, p. 146
Fondant: White Ready-To-Use Rolled Fondant (132 oz.), p. 147; 20 in. Rolling Pin, Roll & Cut Mat, Easy-Glide Fondant Smoother, p. 148
Recipes: Buttercream, Royal Icings, p. 116; Chocolate Fondant, p. 117
Also: 2011 Pattern Book (Branch), p. 130; Flower Nail No. 7, p. 138; Meringue Powder, Piping Gel, p. 143; Pastry Brush, p. 153; Dark Cocoa Candy Melts, p. 194; Cake Boards, Fanci-Foil Wrap, p. 241; Dowel Rods, p. 239; ULTIMATE Cake Leveler, p. 152; 12 x12 in. plywood or foamcore board (½ in. thick), waxed paper, tape, non-stick pan spray, facial tissue

In advance: Make branches. Tape 3 patterns to board; cover with waxed paper. Spray with pan spray; wipe off excess with a tissue. Use royal icing with tip 17 to outline branches; make extras to allow for breakage. Let dry. **Also:** Make royal icing flowers. Use tip 101s to pipe 19 white and 21 rose apple blossoms (p. 120). Use tip 101 to pipe 13 white and 11 rose apple blossoms. Add tip 1s dot centers. Let dry. Attach flowers to branches with dots of royal icing. **And:** Cover base board with Chocolate Fondant (p. 120).

Bake and cool 3-layer cakes (bake 2 in. high layers; trim 1 to 1 in. high for 5 in. high tiers). Prepare and cover with rolled fondant (p. 117). Prepare for Stacked Construction (p. 114). Pipe tip 5 bead bottom borders.

At reception: Carefully remove branches from waxed paper. Attach to cake sides using royal icing. Serves 82.**

*Combine Ivory with Brown for ivory shown. Combine Brown with Red-Red for brown shown. Combine Rose with Ivory for rose shown.

◀ Taking That Big Step

Pans: 6, 8, 10 x 2 in. Square, p.157
Tips: 2, 6, p. 134
Colors:* Lemon Yellow, Daffodil Yellow, p. 146
Fondant/Gum Paste: White Ready-To-Use Rolled Fondant (132 oz.), Gum-Tex, p. 147; 20 in. Rolling Pin, Roll & Cut Mat, Easy-Glide Fondant Smoother, p. 148; White Pearl Dust, Brush Set, p. 149; Floral Collection Flower Making Set, p. 151
Ornament: Clay Topper, p. 234
Recipes: Buttercream Icing, p. 116; Thinned Fondant Adhesive, p. 117
Also: Sugar Pearls Sprinkles, p. 145; Dowel Rods, p. 239; Cake Boards, Circles, Fanci-Foil Wrap, p. 241; Piping Gel, p. 143; 12 x 12 in. plywood or foamcore board (½ in. thick), waxed paper, cornstarch, knife

Two days in advance: Make flowers. Add ⅛ teaspoon Gum-Tex to 3 oz. fondant. Roll out 1⁄16 in. thick. Use cutters from set to cut 10 pansies, 20 apple blossoms and 10 forget-me-nots; make extras to allow for breakage. Cup flowers on thick foam using rounded end of wooden modeling tool. Use thinned fondant adhesive to attach Sugar Pearl to center. Let dry on cornstarch-dusted board. Brush flowers with Pearl Dust. **Also:** Cover base board with 21 oz. white fondant (p. 120).

Bake and cool 2-layer cakes. Prepare and cover with 108 oz. tinted rolled fondant (p. 117). Prepare for Stacked Construction (p. 114). Pipe tip 6 bead bottom borders. Attach flowers with tip 2 icing dots, using larger flowers at the top, smaller flowers at the bottom.

At reception: Position ornament.†
Serves 82.**

*Combine Lemon Yellow with Daffodil Yellow for yellow shown.

**The smallest tier is often saved for the first anniversary. The number of servings given does not include the smallest tier.

†Always place a separator plate, or cake board cut to fit, on the cake where you position any figurine or topper. This protects both the cake and your keepsake. For extra stability, secure your figurine to the plate with double-stick craft tape.

◀ Plush Patterns

Pans: 3-Tier Pillow Set, p. 156
Tips: 1A, 2A, 12, p. 134
Colors:* Red-Red, Violet, Rose, Kelly Green, Ivory, p. 146
Fondant: White Ready-To-Use Rolled Fondant (168 oz.), p. 147; 20 in. Rolling Pin, Roll & Cut Mat, Easy-Glide Fondant Smoother, p. 148; Gold Pearl Dust (4 pks.), Brush Set, p. 149
Recipes: Buttercream Icing, p. 116; Thinned Fondant Adhesive, p. 117
Also: Dowel Rods, p. 239; Cake Boards, Fanci-Foil Wrap, p. 241; Clear Vanilla Extract, p. 143; knife, ruler, cornstarch

Bake and cool 2-layer cakes using firm-textured batter such as pound cake.†† Tint fondant: 72 oz. ivory, 36 oz. green, 24 oz. violet, 12 oz. red. Assemble cake layers on cut-to-fit cake boards. Ice cakes smooth. Cover top layer with ivory fondant; smooth with Fondant Smoother and trim at seam. Place cake board on top of cake and carefully flip to position ivory layers at bottom. Cover top layers with tinted fondant; smooth with Fondant Smoother. Prepare for Stacked Construction (p. 114). Roll white fondant into ¼ in. diameter ropes. Twist 2 together and attach over center seams using fondant adhesive. For spirals, roll ropes in various lengths from 4 to 10 in. long. Brush backs with damp brush and attach. For rings, roll out fondant ⅛ in. thick. Cut circles using both ends of tips 2A and 12 and narrow end of tip 1A. Reserve center cut-outs for top pillow cake. Attach with damp brush. For dots, use reserved pieces and cut additional circles using wide and narrow ends of tips. Attach. For tassels, roll out fondant ¹⁄₁₆ in. thick. Cut a 2 x 2½ in. wide rectangle. Leaving top ½ in. uncut, use knife to cut ⅛ in. wide slits 1½ in. deep. Roll and pinch at top. Roll a ½ in. diameter ball; cut hole into bottom, brush with damp brush and insert tassel. Cut a ¼ x 1 in. strip; attach over seam. Paint all white decorations with Pearl Dust/vanilla mixture (p. 120).

At reception: Stack cakes. Serves 128.**

*Combine Violet with Rose for violet shown.

**The smallest tier is often saved for the first anniversary. The number of servings given does not include the smallest tier.

▶ Double Ring Ceremony

Pan: 3-Tier Pillow Set (10 x 10 x 2 in. used), p. 156
Tip: 2, p. 134
Fondant: White Ready-To-Use Rolled Fondant (48 oz.), Gum-Tex, p. 147; 20 in. Rolling Pin, Roll & Cut Mat, Easy-Glide Fondant Smoother, p. 148; White Pearl Dust, Brush Set, p. 149; Floral Collection Flower Making Set, p. 151
Ornament: Two Rings, p. 234
Recipe: Buttercream Icing, p. 116; Thinned Fondant Adhesive, p. 117
Also: Sugar Pearls Sprinkles, p. 145; Cake Boards, Fanci-Foil Wrap, p. 241; knife, ruler, cornstarch, waxed paper, tape, toothpicks

In advance: Make fondant flowers (p. 125).

Bake and cool 2-layer cake using firm-textured batter such as pound cake.†† Assemble cake layers on cut-to-fit cake boards. Ice cakes smooth. Cover top layer with white fondant; smooth with Fondant Smoother and trim at seam. Place cake board on top of cake and carefully flip to position covered layer at bottom. Cover top layer with white fondant; smooth with Fondant Smoother. Brush Pearl Dust over top half (p. 120). Lightly mark where ornament will sit. Roll 2 logs, ¼ x 11 in., for each side. Twist together to form rope. Use thinned fondant adhesive to attach rope over center seam. Roll out fondant ⅛ in. thick. Cut 2 strips, ¼ x 2 in., for each corner. Attach at an angle for corner ribbons. Use icing to attach flowers to pillow top, leaving center open for ornament; attach 3 flowers at each corner. Attach Sugar Pearls to flower centers and randomly over background.

At reception: Position ornament.† Serves 40.

†Always place a separator plate, or cake board cut to fit, on the cake where you position any figurine or topper. This protects both the cake and your keepsake. For extra stability, secure your figurine to the plate with double-stick craft tape.

††Each pan will need to be baked twice, iced and stacked together to achieve the full pillow effect shown.

◄ Pillows to Dream On

Pans: 3-Tier Pillow Set, p. 156

Tips: 2, 3, p. 134

Fondant: White Ready-To-Use Rolled Fondant (168 oz.), Gum-Tex, p. 147; 20 in. Rolling Pin, Roll & Cut Mat, Easy-Glide Fondant Smoother, p. 148; White Pearl Dust, Brush Set, p. 149; Cutter/Embosser, p. 150; Stepsaving Rose Bouquets Flower Cutter Set, Leaf Cut-Outs, p. 151

Recipes: Buttercream, Royal Icings, p. 116; Thinned Fondant Adhesive, p. 117

Also: White Candy Melts, p. 194; 4 in. Lollipop Sticks, p. 198; Piping Gel, Meringue Powder, Clear Vanilla Extract, p. 143; Dowel Rods, p. 239; Cake Boards, Fanci-Foil Wrap, p. 241; favorite alphabet font for initial pattern, tape, scissors, knife, ruler, cornstarch, waxed paper, toothpicks

Several days in advance: Make royal icing puddle dots (p. 120). Pipe 160 dots ³⁄₁₆ in. diameter for top tier. Pipe 50 each ³⁄₁₆, ³⁄₈ and ½ in. diameter for middle tier. Pipe 130 dots ½ in. diameter for bottom tier. Make extras to allow for breakage and let dry. Paint all dots with Pearl Dust/vanilla mixture (p. 120). **Also:** Make fondant initial (p. 125).

Bake and cool 2-layer cakes using firm-textured batter such as pound cake. †† Assemble cake layers on a cut-to-fit cake board. Ice cake smooth and cover top layer with fondant; smooth with Fondant Smoother and trim at seam. Place cake board on top of cake and carefully flip to position covered layer at bottom. Cover top layer with fondant; smooth with Fondant Smoother. Prepare cakes for Stacked Construction (p. 114). Decorate cake tops (p. 125).

At reception: Stack cakes. Insert initial. Serves 128.**

► Finding The Perfect Fit

Pan: 3-Tier Pillow Set (10 x 10 x 2 in. used), p. 156

Tips: 2, 8, p. 134

Colors:* Violet, Rose, p. 146

Fondant/Gum Paste: White Ready-To-Use Rolled Fondant (48 oz.), Ready-To-Use Gum Paste, p. 147; Floral Fantasy Fondant Imprint Mat, 20 in. Rolling Pin, Roll & Cut Mat, Easy-Glide Fondant Smoother, p. 148; Brush Set, p. 149

Recipe: Buttercream Icing, p. 116

Also: 2011 Pattern Book (Slipper Front/Back, Heart), p. 130; White Candy Melts, p. 194; 6 in. Lollipop Sticks, p. 198; White Sparkle Gel, p. 142; Cake Boards, Fanci-Foil Wrap, p. 241; knife, ruler, waxed paper, cornstarch

Several days in advance: Make gum paste slipper (p. 125). **Also:** Make fondant tassels (p. 125).

Bake and cool 2-layer cake using firm-textured batter such as pound cake.†† Assemble cake layers on cut-to-fit cake boards. Ice cake smooth. Cover top layer with tinted fondant imprinted using Imprint Mat. Trim fondant at seam. Fill in imprint designs using white icing and tip 2. Place cake board on top of cake and carefully flip to position imprinted layer at bottom. Cover top layer with white fondant; smooth with Fondant Smoother. Pipe tip 8 bead border over seam. Pipe tip 2 scrolls on top layer about 1½ in. from seam.

At reception: Insert tassels into cake at corners. Position slipper on top, trimming sticks if needed. Serves 40.

*Combine Violet with Rose for violet shown.

▶ Sticking Together

Pan: Heart Cookie Treat, p. 203

Tips: 2A, 12, p. 134

Color: Pink, p. 146

Fondant: White Ready-To-Use Rolled Fondant (½ oz. per treat), Natural Colors Fondant Multi Pack (dark brown), p. 147; 9 in. Rolling Pin, Roll & Cut Mat, p. 148; Letters & Numbers Gum Paste & Fondant Mold Set, Heart Cut-Outs, p. 151

Candy: White, Light Cocoa Candy Melts, p. 194; Garden Candy Color Set (pink), p. 195; 6 in. Lollipop Sticks, p. 198; Decorator Brush Set, p. 197

Also: ¼ in. wide ribbon (10 in. for each bow)

In advance: Mold candy pops with sticks. Melt white and light cocoa candy; tint white candy pink. Mold pops in Cookie Treat Pan (p. 128). Tap to settle; chill until firm. **Also:** Mold candy monograms. Use letter mold from set, filling cavities only ⅛ in. deep. Chill until firm.

Roll out white fondant ⅛ in. thick. Use largest heart Cut-Out to cut 1 heart for each treat. Tint small amount of fondant pink. For dots, roll out pink, white and dark brown fondant from Multi Pack ⅛ in. thick. Cut assorted dots using narrow end of tips 12 and 2A. Using dots of melted candy, attach fondant heart, dots and candy monogram. Tie ribbon around stick. Each serves 1.

◀ Bubbly Bliss

Pans: Flower Fun Silicone Baking Cups, p. 168; Cookie Sheet, Cooling Grid, p. 203

Tips: 2, 3, p. 134

Colors:* Copper (for skin tone shown), Lemon Yellow, Golden Yellow, Brown, Red-Red, p. 146

Fondant: White Ready-To-Use Rolled Fondant (4 oz. for each treat), Fine Tip FoodWriter Edible Color Markers (black), Gum-Tex, p. 147; White Pearl Dust, Brush Set, p. 151

Recipes: Buttercream, Royal Icings, Wilton Fudge, p. 116

Also: Meringue Powder, p. 143; 4 in. Lollipop Sticks, p. 198; knife, cornstarch, waxed paper, ruler, craft block

In advance: Make heads. Tint 1 oz. fondant skin tone for each treat; add ⅛ teaspoon Gum-Tex. Roll 2 heads, 1 in. diameter. Insert Lollipop Sticks cut to 3 in. Roll tiny ball noses; attach using damp brush. Insert sticks into craft block and let dry. U[se] FoodWriter to draw eyes and mouths. Pipe royal icing pull-out hair; use tip 3 for her, tip 2 for him.

Prepare fudge and pour in silicone cups support[ed] by cookie sheet; chill until firm. Insert heads. Rol[l] fondant bubbles in various sizes from ⅛ to ⅜ in. diameter. Layer and attach over fudge using tip 3 and buttercream. Attach a few bubbles to hair using icing. Brush with Pearl Dust (p. 120). Each serves 1.

*Combine Lemon Yellow with Golden Yellow for yellow shown. Combine Brown with Red-Red for brown show[n].

▶ Petaled Petits Fours

Pans: 10.5 x 15.5 x 1 in. Jelly Roll/Cookie Pan, p. 158; Cookie Sheet, Cooling Grid, p. 203

Tip: 2, p. 134

Colors:* Pink, Leaf Green, Orange, Lemon Yellow, Golden Yellow, p. 146

Recipe: Royal Icing, p. 116

Also: White Ready-To-Use Decorator Icing, Meringue Powder, p. 143; Brush Set, p. 149; Stepsaving Rose Bouquets Flower Cutter Set, p. 151; Circle Metal Cutter, p. 202; waxed paper, toothpicks

Bake and cool 1 in. high cake using firm-textured batter such as pound cake. Cut circles using cutter. Set on cooling grid placed over cookie sheet. Cover with heated, tinted Decorator Icing (p. 128). Let set. Imprint outer petals using small rose cutter from set. Use royal icing to cover imprint with tip 2 zigzag. Immediately create Brush Embroidery (p. 120), using square-tipped brush. Work in quick, short strokes, 1 treat at a time. Use toothpick to mark 3 center petals. Repeat as above. Pipe tip 2 swirl in center. Each serves 1.

*Combine Lemon Yellow with Golden Yellow for yellow shown.

► Colorful Purse-onalities

Pan: 10.5 x 15.5 x 1 in. Jelly Roll/Cookie, p. 158

Colors: Sky Blue, Rose, Moss Green, p. 146

Fondant: White Ready-To-Use Rolled Fondant (24 oz. makes 4 treats), Gum-Tex, p. 147; 9 in. Rolling Pin, Roll & Cut Mat, p. 148; 10 Pc. Fondant/Gum Paste Tool Set, Brush Set, p. 149; Letters & Numbers Gum Paste & Fondant Mold Set, p. 151

Recipes: Buttercream Icing, p. 116; Thinned Fondant Adhesive, p. 117

Also: 2011 Pattern Book (Purse Flap, Strap Curve), p. 130; Cake Boards, p. 241; knife, cornstarch, toothpicks, waxed paper, ruler

In advance: Make straps. For each purse, tint 2 oz. fondant; add ¼ teaspoon Gum-Tex to each color. Roll out ⅛ in. thick. For each purse, cut 2 straps 5¾ x ¼ in. (reserve remaining tinted fondant). Use pattern to shape curve. Let dry 24 hours.

Bake and cool 1 in. high cake using firm-textured batter such as pound cake. Cut a 3¼ x 2½ in. rectangle for each purse. Prepare and cover with rolled fondant (p. 117) in upright position. Use pattern to cut out fondant purse flaps; use serrated quilting wheel from set to imprint stitching line ¼ in. from curved edge. Attach to cakes using damp brush. Cut ¼ in. wide strips and attach at 4 corners, trimming to fit. Attach straps with fondant adhesive. Roll a small ball of tinted fondant; flatten and attach for button. Mold initial, filling only the first level of mold cavity with fondant; attach using damp brush. Each serves 1.

▼ Perfect Attendants!

Pans: Silicone Round Brownie Pops Mold, p. 171; Cookie Sheet, Cooling Grid, p. 203

Tip: 1, p. 134

Colors: * Rose, Copper (for skin tone shown), Lemon Yellow, Golden Yellow, Brown, Red-Red, p. 146

Fondant: White Ready-To-Use Rolled Fondant (10 oz. for 4 to 5 treats), Gum-Tex, Neon Colors Foodwriter Edible Color Markers (pink, black); 9 in. Rolling Pin, Roll & Cut Mat, p. 148; Orchid Pink Pearl Dust, Brush Set, p. 149; Floral Collection Flower Making Set, p. 151

Recipes: Buttercream Icing, p. 116; favorite brownie recipe or mix

Also: 4 in. Lollipop Sticks, p. 198; knife, ruler, waxed paper, toothpicks, cornstarch

Bake and cool brownie pops in silicone mold supported by cookie sheet. Tint fondant: 1½ oz. light pink; 1½ oz. dark pink, ½ oz. light brown, ½ oz. dark brown, ½ oz. yellow, 3 oz. skin tone; reserve 2 oz. white. Add ¼ teaspoon Gum-Tex to skin tone. Decorate bride and bridesmaids (p. 126). Use pansy cutter from set to cut flowers; set on thick foam and cup centers using rounded end of modeling stick from set. Roll small ball centers, flatten and attach. Attach flowers with icing. Each serves 1.

*Combine Brown with Red-Red for brown shown. Combine Lemon Yellow with Golden Yellow for yellow shown.

▲ Cookies Capture the Day

Pans: Cookie Sheet, Cooling Grid, p. 203

Tips: 3, 12, p. 134

Colors: * Pink, Royal Blue, Leaf Green, p. 146

Fondant: White Ready-To-Use Rolled Fondant (12 oz. for 24-30 cookies), p. 147; 9 in. Rolling Pin, Roll & Cut Mat, p. 148; White, Silver Pearl Dust, Brush Set, p. 149; Round, Heart Cut-Outs, Floral Collection Flower Making Set, p. 151

Recipes: Buttercream, Color Flow Icings, Roll-Out Cookies, p. 116

Also: 101 Cookie Cutters (largest round cutter used), p. 201; Wedding Colored Metal Cutter Set (dress), p. 202; White Sparkling Sugar, p. 144; Piping Gel, Clear Vanilla Extract, Color Flow Mix, p. 143; cornstarch, ruler, knife, waxed paper, toothpicks

In advance: Make cookies. Prepare and roll out dough. Turn largest round cutter over; trace outer rim with toothpick and cut with knife. Bake and cool cookies. Divide color flow recipe into 3rds. Tint 1 portion light pink, 1 dark pink; reserve 1 white. Use tip 3 to outline cookies with full-strength color flow. Flow in center using thinned color flow in a different color. Let dry overnight. Brush light pink cookies with Piping Gel; sprinkle on Sparkling Sugar.

Make assorted trims (p.126). Each serves 1.

*Combine Pink with a little Royal Blue for pink shown.

Your bridal shower invitations are as tastefully done as your cookies! Our Bridal Shower Fun Invitation Kit (p. 229) has all the elements in place to match your treats, including a wedding dress silhouette, sparkling engagement ring and a pastel bouquet.

◄ Calla Lily Classic

Pans: 6 x 2 in. Round, p. 157; 4 Pc. Hexagon Set (12 x 2 in. used), p. 156
Tips: 5, 8, p. 134
Colors:* Ivory, Lemon Yellow, Moss Green, p. 146
Fondant/Gum Paste: Ready-To-Use Gum Paste (1 lb.), White Ready-To-Use Rolled Fondant (48 oz.), p. 147; Calla Lily Former Set, p. 150; 20 in. Rolling Pin, Roll & Cut Mat, Easy-Glide Fondant Smoother, p. 148; Leaf Green, White and Yellow Pearl Dust, Brush Set, p. 149
Recipes: Buttercream Icing, p. 116; Gum Paste Adhesive, p. 117
Also: 2011 Pattern Book (Scalloped Ribbon), p. 130; Yellow Colored Sugar, p. 144; Piping Gel, p. 143; Plastic Dowel Rods, p. 239; Cake Circles, Fanci-Foil Wrap, p. 241; 15 x 14 in. plywood or foamcore board (¼ in. thick), 22-gauge cloth-covered florist wire (50 pieces, 6 in. long), green florist tape, 2 in. high craft block, knife, ruler, cornstarch, waxed paper, toothpicks, ½ in. wide white satin ribbon (2 feet), double stick tape

In advance: Make 50 gum paste calla lilies (p. 119). **Also:** Prepare base board. Using pan as a guide, cut board 1 in. larger than pan on all sides. Cover base board with 24 oz. ivory tinted fondant (p. 120); reserve remaining fondant.

Bake and cool 2-layer cakes. Ice smooth and prepare for Stacked Construction (p. 114). Tint 24 oz. fondant ivory and knead in any reserved fondant. Roll out ⅛ in. thick. Use pattern to cut scalloped ribbons (cut one 19 in. long for round cake; two 18 in. long for hexagon cake). Use narrow end of tip 8 to cut a hole in each scallop, about ¼ in. from edge. Roll up ribbons; unroll as you attach to cake sides with icing dots. Pipe tip 5 bead bottom borders. For side flowers on board, use florist tape to secure 3 lilies together at staggered heights. Use remaining lilies and florist tape to assemble bouquet. Wrap stems with ribbon and secure with tape.

At reception: Insert dowel rod cut to 4 in. long into center of round cake. Push 1 in. ball of fondant into top end. Insert bouquet at desired height in cake top. Postition 3 lilies on base board. Serves 40.**

*Combine Ivory with Lemon Yellow for yellow shown.

**The smallest tier is often saved for the first anniversary. The number of servings given does not include the smallest tier.

To complement the graceful beauty of lilies on your wedding cake, choose our Calla Lily Bouquet Invitation Kit (p. 229). The elegant eyelet-edged band presents a lovely lily trio tied with a neat satin bow.

► Carnation Spotlight

Pans: 9 x 13 x 2 in. Sheet, p. 157; Cookie Sheet, Cooling Grid, p. 203
Tip: 2A, p. 134
Colors:* Leaf Green, Violet, Brown, Rose, Royal Blue, Red-Red, p. 146
Fondant/Gum Paste: Ready-To-Use Gum Paste (1 pk. makes about 30 carnations), White Ready-To-Use Rolled Fondant (1 oz. per treat), p. 147; 9 in. Rolling Pin, Roll & Cut Mat, p. 148; 10 Pc. Fondant/Gum Paste Tool Set, Fondant Shaping Foam, Brush Set, p. 149; Round Cut-Outs, p. 151
Recipe: Gum Paste Adhesive, p. 117
Also: White Candy Melts (1 pk. covers about 6-8 treats), p. 194; 101 Cookie Cutters Set (smallest round used), p. 201; Dusting Pouches, p. 149; vegetable shortening, knife, ruler

In advance: Make gum paste carnations (p. 126).

Bake and cool 2 in. high sheet cake using firm-textured batter like pound cake. Cut cakes using smallest round cookie cutter as cutting guide. Set cakes on cooling grid over drip pan. Cover with melted candy (p. 128); chill until firm. Tint fondant and roll out ⅛ in. thick. Cut 2 x 7 in. strips but do not lift. Cut and remove dots using narrow end of tip 2A. Lift strips and brush backs with damp brush; wrap around petits fours and smooth seams. Attach carnation to each using dot of melted candy. Each serves 1.

*Combine Violet with Rose and a little Royal Blue for violet shown. Combine Brown with Red-Red for brown shown.

◀ Petals on a Pedestal

Pan: Standard Muffin, p. 158
Tips: 5, 6, 101, 352, p. 134-135
Colors: Pink, Leaf Green, p. 146
Recipes: Buttercream, Royal Icings, p. 116
Also: 2011 Pattern Book (Single, Double Vines), p. 130; Cupcake Pedestals, p. 168; White Standard Baking Cups, p. 184; Meringue Powder, p. 143; Decorating Nail Set, p. 138; Cake Boards, p. 241; non-stick pan spray, waxed paper, scissors, tape, facial tissue, ruler

2 days in advance: Make vines. Tape patterns to board; tape waxed paper over. Spray with pan spray; use tissue to wipe off excess. Use royal icing to pipe tip 6 vines, 2 for each treat. Let dry. **Also:** Make royal icing roses (p. 119). Use smallest flower nail and tip 101 to make 8 dark pink and 10 light pink roses for each treat, all with tip 5 bases. Let dry.

Bake and cool cupcakes. Ice smooth with green buttercream icing. Attach roses. Pipe tip 352 leaves. Set on pedestals. Insert vines. Each serves 1.

▶ More Memories in Store!

Pans: 6, 8, 10 x 2 in. Round, p. 157; 4 Pc. Hexagon Set (15 x 2 in. used), p. 156
Tips: 2, 3, 4, 5, 7, 12, 101s, 102, 104, 349, 352, p. 134-135
Colors: Ivory, Moss Green, p. 146
Fondant: White Ready-To-Use Rolled Fondant (96 oz.), Gum-Tex, p. 148; 20 in. Rolling Pin, Roll & Cut Mat, Graceful Vines Fondant Imprint Mat, Easy-Glide Fondant Smoother, p. 148; Orchid Pink, White, Gold Pearl Dust, Color Tray, Brush Set, p. 149
Ornament: 50th Anniversary Pick, p. 235
Recipes: Buttercream, Royal Icings, p. 116; Thinned Fondant Adhesive, p. 117
Also: Decorating Nail Set, p. 138; Piping Gel, Meringue Powder, Clear Vanilla Extract, p. 143; Cake Boards, Circles, Fanci-Foil Wrap, p. 241; Plastic Dowel Rods, p. 239; 8 in. Lollipop Sticks, p. 198; 20 x 23 in. plywood or foamcore board (½ in. thick), green cloth-covered florist wire (6 in. lengths: 30 in 22-gauge, 22 in 24-gauge), green florist tape, 2 in. high craft block, knife, scissors, ruler, waxed paper, cornstarch

At least 7 days in advance: Make white royal icing roses (p. 119): 84 with tip 101s on tip 3 bases; 30 with tip 102 on tip 7 bases; 30 with tip 104 on tip 12 bases. Make extras to allow for breakage; let dry. Mix orchid pink with small amount of white Pearl Dust. Brush onto roses (p. 120) for subtle color variations. **Also:** Make green royal icing calyxes and leaves. Make 30 calyxes by piping a ¾ in. high tip 12 cone onto waxed paper. Insert hooked length of 22-gauge wire; let dry. Make 22 tip 352 leaves on 24-gauge wire (p. 120). Let dry. Paint edges (p. 120) of all roses and leaves with a mixture of gold Pearl Dust/vanilla mixture; let dry. Later, assemble bouquet (p. 126). **And:** Make drawers and front panels (p. 126). Later, decorate and assemble drawers. **And:** Prepare base board. Using pan as a guide, cut board 3½ in. wider than pan on all sides. Cover with 60 oz. white fondant (p. 120).

Bake and cool 2-layer cakes. Ice smooth. Prepare for Stacked Construction (p. 114). Pipe tip 4 curving vines around sides of round cakes. Attach tip 102 roses using 8 on 6 in., 10 on 8 in. and 12 on 10 in. cake. Pipe tip 352 leaves; when icing crusts, paint edges with gold Pearl Dust/vanilla mixture. Pipe tip 5 bead borders on top and bottom of round cakes, top only of hexagon.

At reception: Push 1 in. ball of fondant into top of dowel rod cut to 7 in. Push into cake top. Insert bouquet and pick. Position open drawers and attach drawer fronts with icing. Add mementos. Serves 108.

▲ The Wedding Party Makes the Rounds

Pans: 8, 10, 12 x 2 in. Round, p. 157

Tips: 2, 3, p. 134

Colors:* Violet, Rose, Black, Copper (for skin tone shown), Golden Yellow, Brown, Red-Red, p. 146

Fondant: White Ready-To-Use Rolled Fondant (180 oz.), Neon Colors (pink, black) FoodWriter Edible Color Markers, Brush Set, p. 149; 10 Pc. Fondant/Gum Paste Tool Set, p. 149; 20 in. Rolling Pin, Roll & Cut Mat, Easy-Glide Fondant Smoother, p. 148; Floral Collection Flower Making Set, p. 151

Recipes: Buttercream, Royal Icings, p. 116

Also: 2011 Pattern Book (Shirt, Lapels), p. 130; Cake Dividing Set, p. 136; Candy Melting Plate, p. 197; Piping Gel, p. 143; 4 in. Lollipop Sticks, p. 198; Wooden Dowel Rods, p. 239; Cake and Treat Display Set, p. 235; 2 in. (1 set shown), 2.5 in. (4 sets shown) Globe Pillar Sets, p. 238; Cake Circles, p. 241; Meringue Powder, p. 143; 26-gauge white florist wire (2 in.), 6 x 10 in. white tulle, tape, knife, ruler, cornstarch, toothpicks

At least 3 days in advance: Make people (p. 126). Tint fondant as follows: 34 oz. skin tone, 16 oz. black, 14 oz. violet, 6 oz. yellow, 4 oz. dark brown, 4 oz. light brown; reserve 100 oz. white. Roll out ⅛ in. thick as needed. **Also:** Make flowers. For all flowers, roll out fondant ⅛ in. thick and cut using cutters from set. For bride and each bridesmaid, make 1 apple blossom and 5 forget-me-nots in white for bride and violet for bridesmaids (6 for flower girl). For groom and each groomsman, make 1 forget-me-not; white for groom, violet for groomsmen. For cakes, make 30 white pansies. Set all flowers on thick foam and shape using ball tool. In royal icing, pipe tip 3 dot centers on pansies and tip 2 dot centers on all other flowers. Let pansies dry in melting plate.

Bake and cool 2-layer cakes (bake two 1½ in. layers for 3 in. cakes). Prepare and cover with rolled fondant (p. 117). Use dividing wheel to divide cakes: 12 in. into 12ths, 10 in. into 10ths, 8 in. into 8ths. For each side drape, cut a 3 x 5 in. rectangle. Gather into folds and pinch ends together. Use damp brush to attach in curve between division marks, trimming ends at an angle to fit. Pipe tip 3 bead bottom borders in buttercream. Attach pansies with icing dots. Trim pillars to 7 in. for 2.5 in. globe adults and 6 in. for 2 in. globe kids. Push into cakes. Slide on people. Serves 94.**

*Combine Violet with Rose for violet shown. Combine Brown with Red-Red for light and dark brown shown.

**The smallest tier is often saved for the first anniversary. The number of servings given does not include the smallest tier.

▶ Black Tie and Tails

Pans: 3-Tier Diamond Set (2 largest pans used), p. 156

Tips: 3, 6, p. 134

Colors:* Sky Blue, Copper (for skin tone shown), Black, Brown, Red-Red, Golden Yellow, p. 146

Fondant: White Ready-To-Use Rolled Fondant (164 oz.), Neon Colors (pink, black) FoodWriter Edible Color Marker Set, p. 147; 20 in. Rolling Pin, Roll & Cut Mat, Easy-Glide Fondant Smoother, p. 148; Brush Set, 10 Pc. Fondant/Gum Paste Tool Set, p. 149; Floral Collection Flower Making Set, p. 151

Recipe: Buttercream Icing, p. 116

Also: 2011 Pattern Book (Shirt, Lapel), p. 130; Decorator Favorites Pattern Press Set, p. 140; 2 in., 2.5 in. Globe Pillar Sets, p. 238; Candy Melting Plate, p. 197; Dowel Rods, p. 239; Piping Gel, p. 143; Cake Boards, Fanci-Foil Wrap, p. 241; 24 x 18 in. plywood or foamcore board (½ in. thick), 6 x 10 in. fabric tulle, 26 gauge white florist wire (2 in.), knife, ruler, tape, cornstarch, waxed paper

In advance: Prepare base board. Using largest pan as a guide, cut board 1 in. wider than pan on all sides. Tint 136 oz. fondant blue. Use 36 oz. to cover board (p. 120); reserve remaining blue. **Also:** Make figures (p. 126). Tint fondant: 8 oz. skin tone, 4 oz. black (suit), 4 oz. dark brown (hair, dog ears), 4 oz. yellow (cat), 4 oz. brown (dog). Reserve 4 oz. white. **And:** Make flowers. Roll out white fondant ⅛ in. thick. Cut 2 pansies using cutter from Set. Set on thick foam and shape using ball tool. Pipe 3 dot centers; let dry in melting plate.

Bake and cool 2-layer cakes. Prepare and cover with reserved blue fondant. Prepare for Stacked Construction (p. 114). Set cakes on turntable or cake pan to raise above counter. Imprint sides using open heart, medium C-scroll and vine pattern presses. Stack cakes on base board. Use tip 6 outlines to cover imprints and add extra scrolls; overpipe with tip 3 outlines. Pipe tip 6 bead bottom borders. Trim 2 pillars to 8 in. for bride and groom; trim 2 pillars to 5 in. for cat and dog. Insert in top layer to rest on cake board. Slide figures over pillars. Attach white flower where bride and groom's arms meet and on veil. Serves 66.**

*Combine Brown with Red-Red and Black for brown hair shown.

◀ Their New Horizon

Pans: 4 Pc. Oval Set (3 smallest pans used), p. 156

Tip: 4, p. 134

Colors:* Brown, Red-Red, Black, Rose, p. 146

Fondant: White Ready-To-Use Rolled Fondant (132 oz.), Neon Colors (pink, black) Foodwriter Edible Color Markers, p. 147; 20 in. Rolling Pin, Roll & Cut Mat, Easy-Glide Fondant Smoother, p. 148; Floral Collection Flower Making Set, p. 151; 10 Pc. Fondant/Gum Paste Tool Set, Brush Set, p. 149

Recipe: Buttercream Icing, p. 116

Also: 2011 Pattern Book (Shirt, Lapel, Tiara), p. 130; 2.5 in. Globe Pillar Set, p. 238; Dowel Rods, p. 239; Sugar Pearls Sprinkles, p. 145; Candy Melting Plate, p. 197; Piping Gel, p. 143; Cake Boards, Fanci-Foil Wrap, p. 241; 15 x 11 in. plywood or foamcore board (½ in. thick), knife, ruler, tape, cornstarch, waxed paper

In advance: Make bride and groom (p. 126). Tint fondant: 8 oz. light rose, 8 oz. black, 8 oz. skin tone; reserve 72 oz. white. **Also:** Make pansies. Tint 8 oz. fondant light rose. Roll out ⅛ in. thick. Cut 100 light rose and 1 white pansy using cutter from set. Set on thick foam and shape using ball tool. Roll small balls for centers; attach using damp brush. Let dry in melting plate. **And:** Prepare base board. Using 13.5 x 9.8 in. pan as a guide, cut board ¾ in. larger then pan on all sides. Cover with 36 oz. dark rose fondant (p. 120).

Bake and cool 1-layer cakes. Prepare for Stacked Construction (p. 114). Prepare and cover with rolled fondant (p. 117). Pipe tip 4 bead bottom borders. Position pansies. Trim 2 pillars to 6 in.; insert in top layer. Slide bride and groom over pillars. Attach white pansy in bride's hands with dots of icing. Serves 43.**

*Combine Brown with Red-Red and Black for skin tone shown.

▶ Love, Lilies and Lace

Pans: 6, 10, 14 x 2 in. Round, p. 157
Tips: 2, 7, 16, 366, p. 134-135
Fondant/Gum Paste: Ready-To-Use Gum Paste, p. 147; 10 Pc. Fondant/Gum Paste Tool Set, Brush Set, p. 149; Floral Collection Flower Making Set, p. 151
Recipes: Buttercream, Royal Icings, p. 116; Gum Paste Adhesive, p. 117
Also: Lily Nail Set, Flower Stamen Assortment (9 pks., using only Pearl Stamens), Flower Former Set, p. 138; Meringue Powder, Piping Gel, p. 143; Foil Wrappers, p. 198; 8, 12, 16 in. Decorator Preferred Smooth Edge Plates (2 of each size used), 4 in. Fillable Pillars (3 sets), p. 237; Fresh Flower Cake Spikes, p. 240; Dowel Rods, p. 239; Cake Circles, p. 241; 26-gauge white cloth-covered florist wire (6 pieces, 6 in. long), waxed paper, knife, ruler, toothpicks, tape, scissors, cornstarch

In advance: Make royal icing lilies (p. 126). Use 1⅝ in. Lily Nail to make 72 lilies with tip 366 petals, tip 16 star center and 7 pearl stamens each. **Also:** Make gum paste lily (p. 126) for cake top.

Bake and cool 2-layer cakes. Ice smooth and prepare for Separator Plate (2-Plate) and Pillar Construction (p. 114). Pipe tip 7 bead bottom borders. Attach icing lilies around plates.

At reception: Allow 1 hour or more for piping suspended drop strings. Assemble cakes on pillars. Use royal icing to pipe tip 2 scallops from plate edges, working from top tier down. All scallops are ¾ in. wide and ½ in. deep; start successive rows between midpoints of scallops in row above. For top tier, begin with 2 complete rows. Pipe suspended drop strings centered between pillars, decreasing from 7 scallops to 1. Skip 1 scallop then repeat. For middle tier, begin with 2 complete rows. Pipe suspended drop strings centered between pillars, decreasing from 6 scallops to 1. Pipe suspended drop strings between previous drops, decreasing from 4 scallops to 1. For bottom tier, begin with 3 complete rows. Pipe suspended drop strings centered over each pillar, decreasing from 5 scallops to 1. Fill with a drop that decreases from 3 scallops to 1, another with just 1 scallop, then another that decreases from 3 scallops to 1. Position gum paste lily in Flower Spike, securing with ball of gum paste if needed; insert in cake top. Serves 116.**

**The smallest tier is often saved for the first anniversary. The number of servings given does not include the smallest tier.

◀ Waterfall Wedding

Pans: 6, 8, 10 x 2 in. Round, p.157
Tips: 2, 4, p. 134
Color: Sky Blue, p. 146
Fondant/Gum Paste: White Ready-To-Use Rolled Fondant (78 oz.), Ready-To-Use Gum Paste (3 pks.), p. 147; 20 in. Rolling Pin, Roll & Cut Mat, Easy-Glide Fondant Smoother, p. 148; 10 Pc. Fondant/Gum Paste Tool Set, Brush Set, p. 149; Stepsaving Rose Bouquets Flower Cutter Set, Floral Collection Flower Making Set, p. 151
Ornament: First Kiss, p. 234
Recipes: Buttercream, Royal Icings, p. 116; Gum Paste Adhesive, p. 117
Also: 10.25 in. Roman Columns (2 pks.), 12 in. Decorator Preferred Smooth Edge Plates (2), p. 237; Sugar Pearls Sprinkles, p. 145; Meringue Powder, p. 143; Cake Boards, Circles, p. 241; Dowel Rods, p. 239; 14½ yards ¼ in. wide white satin ribbon (40 pieces, 13 in. long), craft block, knife, ruler, toothpicks, waxed paper, cornstarch, tape

At least a week in advance: Make 66 full-bloom gum paste roses (p. 120). **Also:** Make gum paste flowers. Roll out gum paste 3/16 in. thick. Use Flower Making Set to cut 260 small flowers with apple blossom cutter and 260 large flowers with pansy cutter. Let dry on waxed paper-covered board dusted with cornstarch. Attach Sugar Pearl centers using tip 2 dot of royal icing. Let dry. **And:** Prepare and decorate stand (p. 126).

Bake and cool 2-layer cakes. Prepare and cover with 78 oz. tinted rolled fondant (p. 117). Prepare for Stacked Construction (p. 114). Roll ¼ in. diameter ropes; use damp brush to attach around base of each cake. Position roses around 6 in. and 8 in. tiers.

At reception: Stack cakes on stand. Position roses around 10 in. tier, trimming toothpicks as needed. Position ornament.† Serves 62.**

Imperial Presence

ns: 8, 12, 16 x 2 in. Square, p. 157

: 2, p. 134

lors:* Violet, Rose, p. 146

ndant: White Ready-To-Use Rolled Fondant (462 oz.), Gum-Tex, . 147; 20 in. Rolling Pin, Roll & Cut Mat, Easy-Glide Fondant Smoother, p. 148; Brush Set, p. 149; Oval Cut-Outs, p. 151

nament: Monogram Topper, p. 234

cipes: Buttercream, Royal Icing, p. 116

so: 2011 Pattern Book (Borders, Base Board Middle and Corner Triangles, Draped Triangles, Small, Medium and arge Swags), p. 130; Meringue Powder, Piping Gel, . 143; 4 in. Fillable Pillars (2 pks.), 10 in., 14 in. Decorator Preferred Square Plates (2 each), p. 237; Cake Boards, Circles, Fanci-Foil Wrap, p. 241; waxed paper, cornstarch, knife, ruler, 20 x 20 in. plywood or foamcore board (½ in. hick), 4 in. high square box or container, toothpicks, cornstarch, tape

ays in advance: Make fondant trims. Tint 40 oz. light violet, oz. dark violet. Roll out ⅛ in. thick (unless otherwise ecified) as needed; reserve remaining tinted fondant. Use tern to make 8 draped triangles (p. 126); make extras to w for breakage. Let dry. Make 8 each small, medium and ge ribbon swags (p. 126). Let dry. Make 12 cameos. Cut se using largest oval Cut-Out. Cut top using medium oval -Out; attach using damp brush. Pipe royal icing tip 2 ball der. Let dry. **Also:** Cover base board with fondant (p. 120). serve remaining fondant. **And:** Prepare monogrammed ament following package directions.

ke and cool 3-layer cakes (bake 2 in. high layers; trim 1 to . high for 5 in. high cakes). Prepare and cover with rolled dant (p. 117). Prepare for Separator Plate (2-Plate) and Pillar nstruction (p. 114). Roll out reserved light violet fondant n. thick. For borders, cut 1¼ in. high strips; use damp brush attach around base of cakes, trimming ends as needed. base board, use patterns to cut 4 each middle and corner ngles. Attach to base board with damp brush. Use patterns d toothpick to transfer designs onto borders and base board ngles. Using royal icing, cover marks with tip 2 outlines, ds and curls. Attach swags to cake sides using royal icing; sition at a slight angle so ends at center extend 1 in. above e of 8 in. cake and 1¼ in. above 12 and 16 in. cakes. Trim needed to fit. Attach cameos using royal icing. Roll ¼ in. meter fondant logs; flatten slightly and attach at corners to er seams.

reception: Stack cakes on pillars. Attach draped triangles lates with royal icing. Position ornament.† Serves 200.**

mbine Violet with Rose for light and dark violet shown.

ways place a separator plate, or cake board cut to fit, on the cake here you position any figurine or topper. This protects both the cake d your keepsake. For extra stability, secure your figurine to the plate th double-stick craft tape.

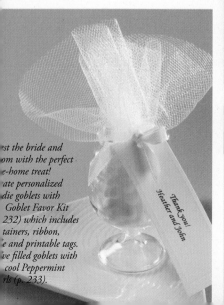

st the bride and
om with the perfect
e-home treat!
ate personalized
die goblets with
Goblet Favor Kit
232) which includes
tainers, ribbon,
e and printable tags.
ve filled goblets with
cool Peppermint
rls (p. 233).

◀ A Pedestal of Petals

Pan: Dimensions Large Cupcake, p. 164

Tips: 2, 6, 45, p. 134-135

Colors:* Violet, Pink, p. 146

Fondant: White Ready-To-Use Rolled Fondant (8 oz.), Gum-Tex, p. 147; 20 in. Rolling Pin, Roll & Cut Mat, p. 148; White Pearl Dust, Brush Set, p. 149; Flower Cut-Outs, p. 151

Ornament: Our Day, p. 234

Recipes: Buttercream Icing, p. 116; Thinned Fondant Adhesive, p. 117

Also: Candy Melting Plate (4), p. 197; Sugar Pearls Sprinkles, p. 145; Cake Circles, Boards, p. 241; ruler, knife, cornstarch, toothpicks, waxed paper

Several days in advance: Make flowers. Add ½ teaspoon Gum-Tex to 8 oz. fondant; roll out ¹⁄₁₆ in. thick. Cut 80 flowers using medium Flower Cut-Out. Make extras to allow for breakage. Let dry in Candy Melting Plate dusted with cornstarch. When flowers have dried, brush on Pearl Dust (p. 120). Use fondant adhesive to attach Sugar Pearl centers.

Bake and cool cake. Stack top and bottom; trim 3 x 2 in. of top flat where ornament will sit. Using violet icing, pipe 2 tip 6 vertical lines into each indentation of cupcake bottom. Pipe vertical center line using white icing and tip 45. Pipe tip 2 violet bead hearts, about ½ in. apart, beginning at bottom and working upward. Ice top of cupcake smooth. Attach large flowers, beginning at bottom edge and working upward; leave center open for ornament.

At reception: Position ornament.† Serves 24.

*Combine Violet with Pink for violet shown.

†Always place a separator plate, or cake board cut to fit, on the cake where you position any figurine or topper. This protects both the cake and the keepsake. For extra stability, secure your figurine to the plate with double-stick craft tape.

▶ Cupcake Courtship

Pan: Standard Muffin, p. 158

Colors:* Violet, Pink, p. 146

Fondant: White Ready-To-Use Rolled Fondant (3 oz. makes 6-8 hearts with flowers), Gum-Tex, p. 147; 20 in. Rolling Pin, Roll & Cut Mat, p. 148; 10 Pc. Fondant/Gum Paste Tool Set, White Pearl Dust, Fondant Shaping Foam, Brush Set, p. 149; Flower Cut-Outs, p. 151

Recipes: Buttercream Icing, p. 116; Thinned Fondant Adhesive, p. 117

Also: 6 Pc. Nesting Hearts Cutter Set, p. 220; White Standard Baking Cups, p. 184; White Sparkling Sugar, p. 144; Sugar Pearls Sprinkles, p. 145; Cake Circles, Boards, p. 241; ruler, knife, cornstarch, toothpicks, waxed paper

In advance: Make hearts. Tint 2 oz. fondant violet; add ⅛ teaspoon Gum-Tex. Roll out ⅛ in. thick. Cut heart using 2nd smallest cutter from set. Let dry on cornstarch-dusted boards. **Also:** Make flowers. Add ⅛ teaspoon Gum-Tex to 1 oz. fondant; roll out ¹⁄₁₆ in. thick. Cut flower using smallest Cut-Out from set. Set on thick foam and cup centers using ball tool. Let dry on cornstarch-dusted surface. Brush with Pearl Dust (p. 120). Attach Sugar Pearl centers with fondant adhesive.

Bake and cool cupcakes. Ice tops; sprinkle with Sparkling Sugar. Position heart, add icing in back for support. Each serves 1.

*Combine Violet with Pink for violet shown.

Easy and elegant! Our see-through Square Heart Boxes, filled with sweet Pastel Jordan Almonds (both p. 233) are the ideal favor to honor a couple whose love shows through in everything they do.

▲ Beak to Beak

Pan: 3 Pc. Paisley Set (9 x 6 in. used), p. 156

Tips: 2, 3, p. 134

Colors:* Rose, Black, Red-Red, Christmas Red, p. 146

Fondant: White Ready-To-Use Rolled Fondant (75 oz.), p. 147; 20 in. Rolling Pin, Roll & Cut Mat, p. 148; Cutter/Embosser, p. 150; Brush Set, p. 149

Recipe: Buttercream Icing, p. 116

Also: 6 Pc. Nesting Hearts Cutter Set, p. 220; Piping Gel, p. 143; 13 x 19 in. Cake Boards (2), Fanci-Foil Wrap, 10 in. Diameter Cake Circles (2), p. 241; cornstarch, ruler, tape, knife, toothpicks

In advance: Prepare base board. Tape 13 x 19 in. Cake Boards together and wrap with Fanci-Foil. Tint fondant: 20 oz. light rose, 20 oz. dark rose, 4 oz. red; reserve 30 oz.

white. Roll out ⅛ in. thick as needed. Roll out 2 shades of rose. Cut 10 x 1¾ in. wide strips. Use Piping Gel to attach strips to board, starting with center light rose strip and alternating colors. Wrap outer edges over sides and trim with knife. Shape triangle fondant beaks, ¾ x ½ in. wide, ³⁄₁₆ in. thick; insert toothpick for support. Let dry.

Bake and cool two 1-layer cakes. Position facing opposite directions on

cut-to-fit cake boards. Prepare and cover with fondant (p. 117). Position on prepared base board. Roll out red fondant. Cut hearts using largest (cut 1), smallest (cut 5) and 2nd smallest (cut 4) cutters from set. Attach using damp brush. Pipe tip 2 message. Insert beaks in cakes. Outline birds and pipe outline eyes, wings and feet using tip 3. Serves 13.

*Combine Red-Red with Christmas Red for red shown.

▶ On the Road to Romance

Pan: 12 x 2 in. Square, p. 157

Tips: 1s, 7, p. 134

Colors:* Pink, Ivory, Royal Blue, Black, Christmas Red, Red-Red, p. 146

Fondant: White Ready-To-Use Rolled Fondant (65 oz.), Gum-Tex, p. 147; 20 in. Rolling Pin, Roll & Cut Mat, Easy-Glide Fondant Smoother, p. 148; Silver Pearl Dust, Brush Set, p. 149

Recipe: Buttercream Icing, p. 116

Also: 2011 Pattern Book (Car, Hearts, Can), p. 130; Piping Gel, Clear Vanilla Extract, p. 143; Cake Boards, Fanci-Foil Wrap, p. 241; 14 x 14 in. plywood or foamcore board (½ in. thick), knife, cornstarch, waxed paper, toothpick, tape

In advance: Make car. Tint fondant: 3 oz. pink, 1 oz. gray, 1 oz. dark pink, 1 oz. black. Add ⅛ teaspoon Gum-Tex to each color. Add ½ teaspoon Gum-Tex to 6 oz. white fondant. Tint small amount red. Roll out all ⅛ in. thick as needed. Using pattern as a guide, cut white base, sign and license plate background. Cut pink car back, license plate and fender, dark pink hearts, black roof and wheels, gray wheel wells and cans. Paint wheel wells and cans with silver Pearl Dust/vanilla mixture (p. 120). Use toothpick to mark line for can top. Let all pieces dry flat on cornstarch-dusted boards. **Also:** Prepare base board and cover with 24 oz. black fondant (p. 120).

Bake and cool 1-layer cake. Prepare and cover with pale pink rolled fondant (p. 117). Attach fondant pieces using damp brush. Use tip 1s to print message and license plate; outline strings and knots to cans. Pipe tip 7 bead bottom border. Serves 24.

*Combine Pink with Ivory for pale pink covering cake. Combine Pink with a little Royal Blue for darker pink hearts. Combine Christmas Red with Red-Red for red shown.

The limo is here to shift your shower into high gear! Our Save The Date Post Cards (p. 229) will deliver everyone to the celebration with a smile—especially when they see the matching cake.

▶ Baroque Beauty

Pans: 6, 10, 14 x 2 in. Round, p. 157
Tip: 5, p. 134
Colors: Moss Green, Black, p. 146
Fondant: White Ready-To-Use Rolled Fondant (72 oz.), p. 147; 20 in. Rolling Pin, Roll & Cut Mat, Easy-Glide Fondant Smoother, p. 148
Ornament: First Kiss, p. 234
Recipes: Buttercream, Royal Icings, p. 116
Also: Tailored Tiers Cake Display Set, p. 238; Designer Pattern Press Set (Corner Flourish, Small Fleur-de-Lis), p. 140; Meringue Powder, p. 143; Cake Dividing Set, p. 136; Cake Circles, p. 241; Dowel Rods, p. 239; cornstarch, toothpicks, knife

Bake and cool 2-layer cakes. Prepare for Tailored Tiers Construction (p. 115). Place tiers on same-size cake circles; ice smooth with buttercream. Tint 36 oz. fondant light and 36 oz. dark moss green; roll out ⅛ in. thick as needed. Cut 5 x 1 in. wide strips; attach to cake sides with dots of icing,

alternating colors and trimming ends to match cake height. Use Cake Dividing Set to divide top tier into 5ths, middle into 8ths, bottom into 12ths. Using Corner Flourish, imprint design on right and left of division marks; there will be about ½ in. between design ends. Use small Fleur-de-Lis to imprint 4 flourishes inside each design, positioning straight center line between center and outside points; there will be a ¼ to ½ in. gap at center. Outline imprints using tip 5 and royal icing. Pipe center and scrolls with dots to connect all designs.

At reception: Position tiers on plates and pipe tip 5 bead top and bottom borders. Assemble tiers with separators from cake display set; position ornament.† Serves 116.**

†Always place a separator plate, or cake board cut to fit, on the cake where you position any figurine or topper. This protects both the cake and your keepsake. For extra stability, secure your figurine to the plate with double-stick craft tape.

◀ Hot Chocolate!

Pans: 6, 8, 10, 12 x 3 in. Rounds p. 157, 6 x 2 in. Heart, p. 218
Color: Rose, p. 146
Recipe: Buttercream Icing, p. 116
Also: Dark Cocoa Candy Melts (2 pks.), p. 194; 8 in. Cookie Treat Sticks, p. 203; Heart Plastic Nesting Cutter Set, p. 201; Parchment Triangles, p. 136; Dowel Rods, p. 239; Cake Circles, Fanci-Foil Wrap (optional), p. 241; waxed paper, tape, scissors, ruler, knife, malted milk ball candies, 14 in. diameter plate or ½ in. thick plywood or foamcore board, 4 in. diameter bowl or craft block

In advance: Make candy heart. Set 3rd largest heart cutter inside 6 in. heart pan. Pour in melted Candy Melts between cutter and pan sides, to ¼ in. deep. Tap to settle then chill until firm. Cut Cookie Stick to 6½ in. long and attach to back with melted candy, leaving excess at bottom to insert into cake. Let set.

Bake and cool 2-layer cakes; trim 1 layer to 2 in. high to make 5 in. high cakes. Ice smooth and prepare for Stacked Construction (p. 000) but do not stack. Set each cake on a slightly smaller cake pan or bowl to elevate. Cut waxed paper strips: a 5 x 19 in. strip for 6 in. tier, two 5 x 13 in. strips for 8 in. tier, two 5 x 16 in. strips for 10 in. cake, two 5 x 19 in. strips for 12 in. cake. Using melted candy in cut parchment bag, pipe random circles and swirls over and beyond edge of waxed paper strip (work with 1 strip at a time). Let set briefly then wrap around cake sides paper side out, pressing to transfer candy to icing. Chill until set then carefully remove waxed paper. If using plywood or foamcore board, wrap with foil. Stack cakes. Attach malted milk balls with icing for bottom borders.

At reception: Insert candy heart. Serves 118.**

**The smallest tier is often saved for the first anniversary. The number of servings given does not include the smallest tier.

◄ Scrolling Down the Aisle

Pans: 6, 8, 10 x 2 in. Round, p. 157

Tips: 2, 9, p. 134

Fondant: White Ready-To-Use Rolled Fondant (115 oz.), p. 147; Floral Fantasy Fondant Imprint Mat, 20 in. Rolling Pin, Roll & Cut Mat, Easy-Glide Fondant Smoother, p. 148; Brush Set, White Pearl Dust, p. 149

Recipes: Buttercream, Royal Icings, p. 116; Thinned Fondant Adhesive, p. 117

Also: 2011 Pattern Book (6, 8, 10 in. Double Scrolls and Singles Side Scrolls, 6, 8, 10 in. Cake Ribbons), p. 130; Cake Dividing Set, p. 136; Clear Vanilla Extract, Meringue Powder, p. 143; Cake & Treat Display Set, p. 235; 2.5 in. Globe Pillar Set, p. 238; Cake Boards, Cake Circles, p. 241; Dowel Rods, p. 241; ruler, knife, cornstarch, non-stick pan spray, waxed paper, tape, facial tissue

At least 3 days in advance: Use patterns to make royal icing scrolls (p. 127). Make 30 single scrolls for cake sides; 8 small double scrolls for top of 6 in. cake, 10 medium for 8 in. cake and 12 large for 10 in. cake.

Bake and cool 2-layer cakes. Cover with rolled fondant (p. 117). Insert dowel rods into centers (5 in. will be exposed). Roll out fondant ⅛ in. thick. Cut 4 in. wide strips to wrap around bottom of exposed dowel rods: cut strips 3¼ in. high for 6 in. cake, 4 in. high for 8 in. cake, 4½ in. high for 10 in. cake. Smooth to hide seams. Use Cake Dividing Set to divide 6 in. cake into 8ths, 8 in. cake into 10ths, 10 in. cake into 12ths. Roll out fondant ¼ in. thick; imprint pattern using Fondant Imprint Mat (p. 148). Use patterns to cut ribbons (8 small, 10 medium, 12 large), making sure patterns are centered over matching rows of flower imprints. Attach to cake at division marks using damp brush. Tape top hole of 3 globes closed. Cut a 6 in. fondant circle; wrap around globe, leaving bottom hole clear. Slide globes over dowel rods until bottom of globe rests against fondant covered section of dowel rod. Pipe various-size tip 2 scrolls over globes. Paint globes and ribbons with Pearl Dust/vanilla mixture (p. 120).

At reception: Attach side and top scrolls between ribbons using fondant adhesive. Serves 62.**

► Queen of Hearts

Pans: Oval Pan Set (7.75 x 5.5, 10.75 x 7.8, 16.5 x 12.38 in. used), p. 156

Colors:* Black, Red-Red, Christmas Red, Orange, p. 146

Fondant: White Ready-To-Use Rolled Fondant (226 oz.), Gum-Tex, p. 147; 20 in. Rolling Pin, Roll & Cut Mat, p. 148; 10-Pc. Fondant/Gum Paste Tool Set, Easy-Glide Fondant Smoother, Brush Set, p. 149; Heart Cut-Outs, p. 151; Fondant Shaping Foam, p. 149

Recipes: Buttercream Icing, p. 116; Thinned Fondant Adhesive, p. 117

Also: 2011 Pattern Book (Heart, Rising Scallops), p. 130; Red Colored Sugar, p. 144; Piping Gel, p. 143; 8 in. Cookie Treat Sticks, p. 203; Dowel Rods, p. 239; 13 x 19 in. Cake Boards, Cake Circles, Fanci-Foil Wrap, p. 241; 18 x 14 in. plywood or foamcore board (½ in. thick), knife, ruler, cornstarch, waxed paper, toothpicks

Several days in advance: Tint fondant: 12 oz. light red, 72 oz. dark red, 8 oz. black; reserve remaining white. Make heart (p. 127). **Also:** Using largest oval pan as a guide, cut foamcore or plywood board 1 in. larger on all sides. Wrap with foil and cover with red fondant (p. 120).

Bake and cool cakes: 2-layer 7.75 x 5.5 in. oval (4 in. high), 3-layer 10.75 x 7.8 in. oval (6 in. high) and 1-layer 16.5 x 12.38 in. oval (2 in. high). Place on cut-to-fit Cake Circles and cover with white fondant (p. 117). Prepare for Stacked Construction (p. 114). Using Rising Scallops pattern, mark left half of scallop on front of middle cake; reverse pattern and mark right half. Roll out light red fondant ⅛ in. thick; cut a 6 x 18 in. rectangle. Use pattern to mark left half of scallop; flip pattern and mark right half. Cut as single piece. Roll ends toward center, lift and unroll as you insert in position. Roll out dark red ¹⁄₁₆ in. thick. Cut hearts using medium cutter; brush with damp brush and sprinkle with red sugar. Starting at top center, attach to insert, about ¾ in. apart in staggered rows. Stack cakes on prepared base board. Shape and attach drapes (p. 127). Roll out black fondant ⅛ in. thick. Cut ¾ x 5 in. strips. Brush backs with damp brush and attach to bottom layer, about 1 in. apart; trim ends to fit. Make ribbon roses (p. 127). Make 1 large using 4 x 14 in. strip; make 4 small using 2 x 8 in. strips. Attach with thinned fondant adhesive.

At reception: Insert heart. Serves 96.**

*Combine Red-Red with Christmas Red and Orange for red shown.

PARTY ANIMALS!

Step right up for the best birthday party of all! Get ready for treats that take the celebration under the big top, with kids' favorite animal friends ready to let the fur fly! Presenting show-stopping cakes like the circus of stars at right, featuring brownie pop animals on a 3-ring fondant cake, and the colorful carousel with fondant-trimmed horses under a rainbow canopy. Or, bring the party on safari, with a cool multi-level Amazon waterfall cake, featuring cookie gorillas, zebras and giraffes under fondant palm trees. Whatever you choose, it's going to be a wild time!

Center Ring Salute!

Pans: 6, 12 x 2 in. Round, 18 x 3 in. Half Round, p. 159; Cookie Sheet, Cooling Grid, p. 203; Silicone Round Brownie Pops Mold, p. 171

Tips: 2A, 12, p. 134

Colors:* Sky Blue, Orange, Golden Yellow, Lemon Yellow, Leaf Green, Christmas Red, Red-Red, Brown, Violet, Rose, Copper (for skin tone shown), Black, p. 146

Fondant: White Ready-To-Use Rolled Fondant (337 oz.), Fine Tip FoodWriter Edible Color Marker (black), p. 147; 20 in. Rolling Pin, Roll & Cut Mat, Easy-Glide Fondant Smoother, p. 148; Brush Set, p. 149; Round, Star, Heart Cut-Outs, p. 151

Recipe: Buttercream Icing, p. 116; favorite brownie recipe or mix

Also: 6 in. Cookie Treat Sticks (3 in. lengths), p. 203; Wooden Dowel Rods, p. 239; Cake Circles, Fanci-Foil Wrap, p. 241; 20 in. diameter plywood or foamcore circle (½ in. thick), knife, cornstarch, ruler, waxed paper, tape, scissors

2 days in advance: Make fondant heads. Tint fondant: 56 oz. dark brown; 37 oz. blue; 34 oz. orange; 28 oz. golden yellow; 18 oz. red; 11 oz. skin tone; 8 oz. green; 6 oz. black, 8 oz. lemon yellow; 3 oz. violet; 4 oz. light brown; 2 oz. pink. Reserve 122 oz. white. For each head (1 ringmaster, 2 clowns, 4 each lions, elephants, monkeys, tigers and bears.), roll 3½ oz. tinted fondant into a ball. Flatten slightly at bottom. Let dry 24 hours on waxed paper-covered board. Reserve excess tinted fondant. **Also:** Make bodies. Bake and cool 23 brownie pops in silicone mold supported by cookie sheet. Lightly ice and cover with reserved tinted fondant rolled ⅛ in. thick. Insert 3 in. Cookie Stick. Slide on head. **And:** Complete figures (p. 127). Reserve excess tinted fondant for cake trims.

Bake and cool cakes (bake two 1½ in. high 6 and 12 in. rounds for 3 in. high cakes; bake two 2 in. high half-rounds to make 18 x 2 in. base cake). Prepare and cover cakes with 122 oz. white rolled fondant (p. 117). Prepare for Stacked Construction (p. 114). Roll out reserved tinted fondant ⅛ in. thick as needed. For bottom layer, cut 26 rounds using largest Cut-Out from set; cut 26 stars using medium Cut-Out from set. Attach using damp brush. For middle layer, cut 25 red strips, 3 x ½ in.; attach, 1 in. apart. For top layer, cut 10 diamonds, 3 x 2 in. wide; attach with points touching. Position figures around cake. Each figure serves 1; cake serves 107.

*Combine Leaf Green with Lemon Yellow for green shown. Combine Christmas Red with Red-Red for red shown. Combine Violet with Rose for violet shown. Combine Brown with Red-Red and Black for brown shown.

Carousel Celebration

Pan: 10 x 2 in. Round, p. 157

Colors:* Orange, Royal Blue, Lemon Yellow, Leaf Green, Red-Red, p. 146

Fondant: White Ready-To-Use Rolled Fondant (80 oz.), p. 147; 20 in. Rolling Pin, Roll & Cut Mat, Easy-Glide Fondant Smoother, p. 148; Brush Set, p. 149; Star Cut-Outs, p. 151

Recipes: Buttercream Icing, p. 116; Thinned Fondant Adhesive, p. 117

Also: Carousel Cake Set, p. 185; Yellow Colored Sugar, p. 144; Piping Gel, p. 143; 12 in. Silver Cake Base, 10 in. Cake Circle, p. 241; ruler, knife

In advance: Prepare carousel. Tint fondant: 8 oz. each dark orange, light orange, red, green, dark blue; 10 oz. light blue, 6 oz. yellow; reserve 24 oz. white. Roll out ⅛ in. thick as needed; reserve excess fondant. Cut six 3 x 4½ in. triangles to fit canopy; brush top sections with Piping Gel and attach, trimming as needed. Cut 4 x 36 in. blue strip to wrap over canopy edge; attach. Roll red ropes, ⅛ in. diameter; attach over seams using fondant adhesive. For ball border, roll 32 balls, ¼ in. diameter, in each of 4 colors; attach with fondant adhesive. For dark blue trim, roll ⅛ in. diameter ropes, 5 in. long, and ¼ in. diameter balls; attach. Roll 1¼ in. diameter red ball; attach inside finial. Cover pillar bases. Decorate horses with fondant, trimming as needed. **Also:** Make stars. Roll out yellow fondant. Cut 12 stars using medium Cut-Out. Brush with Piping Gel and sprinkle with colored sugar.

Bake and cool 2-layer cake (bake two 1½ in. high layers for a 3 in. high cake). Prepare and cover with white fondant (p. 117). Prepare for Push-In Pillar Construction (p. 114), using 10 in. plate from kit to mark position for pillars. Cut 1 x 3 in. fondant strips and attach to cake sides using damp brush, alternating colors. For ball border, roll 15 balls, 1 in. diameter, in each of 3 colors; attach with fondant adhesive. Roll very thin ropes, 2 in. long, and attach for spiral trim. Attach stars.

At party: Slide horses on pillars, then bases. Insert pillars. Position canopy. Serves 28.

*Combine Leaf Green with Lemon Yellow for green shown.

Seals of Approval

Pans: Jumbo Muffin, p. 158; Cookie Sheet, Cooling Grid, p. 203

Tips: 2, 4, 10, p. 134

Colors: Black, Royal Blue, Lemon Yellow, Red-Red, p. 146

Recipes: Color Flow Icing, Roll-Out Cookies, p. 116; favorite crisped rice cereal treats

Also: 2011 Pattern Book (Easel Support), p. 130; Animal Pals 50 Pc. Cutter Set, p. 201; Yellow Candy Melts (3 oz. per treat), p. 194; Jumbo Stars Sprinkles, p. 144; Color Flow Mix, p. 143; Cake Boards, p. 241; Parchment Triangles, p. 136; waxed paper, knife, ruler, toothpicks

In advance: Make cookies. Prepare and roll out dough. Cut seals using cutter from set. Use pattern to cut 1 easel support per treat. Bake and cool cookies. Use tip 2 and full-strength icing to outline seals. Flow in using thinned icing (p. 128). Let dry on waxed paper-covered boards. Decorate and assemble using full-strength icing. Pipe tip 10 hats; pat smooth with finger. Pipe tip 2 dot eye and nose, outline whiskers and pull-out hat fringe. Let dry. Attach easel support to back with full-strength icing. Let dry. **Also:** Make bases. Use Jumbo Muffin Pan to make ¼ in. thick candy shells (p. 128), 1½ in. high. Prepare cereal treats and fill shells. Seal tops with melted candy; chill until firm.

Decorate and assemble treats using full-strength icing. Divide top of base into 4ths; mark bottom edge midway between top marks. Use tip 4 outlines to connect marks. Attach sprinkles and position seals. Each serves 1.

◄ **Big Top Big Cat**

Pans: Stand-Up Cuddly Bear Set, p. 161; 10 x 2 in. Round, p. 157; Cookie Sheet, Cooling Grid, p. 203

Tips: 4, 5, 17, p. 134-135

Colors: Golden Yellow, Sky Blue, Black, p. 146

Fondant: White Ready-To-Use Rolled Fondant (30 oz.), Primary (red, yellow), Neon (orange) Fondant Multi Packs, p. 147; 20 in. Rolling Pin, Roll & Cut Mat, Easy-Glide Fondant Smoother, p. 148; Brush Set, p. 149; Round, Star Cut-Outs, p. 151

Recipes: Buttercream Icing, Roll-Out Cookies, p. 116; Thinned Fondant Adhesive, p. 117

Also: 2011 Pattern Book (Paw), p. 130; Yellow Colored Sugar, p. 144; Cake Dividing Set, p. 136; White Candy Melts, p. 194; 6 in. Cookie Treat Sticks, p. 203; Plastic Dowel Rods, p. 239; Cake Circles, Fanci-Foil Wrap, p. 241; ruler, knife, tape, waxed paper, cornstarch, toothpicks

In advance: Make lion's mane (p. 127). **Also:** Make cookie paws. Prepare and roll out dough. Use pattern to cut paw; reverse pattern for 2nd paw. Bake and cool cookies. Cut 2 Cookie Treat Sticks to 4 in. long. Attach to paws with melted candy; allow 3 in. at bottom to insert into cake.

For round stand: Bake and cool 2-layer cake. If desired, trim sides to angle from 9 in. diameter top to 10 in. diameter bottom. Tint 24 oz. fondant blue. Prepare and cover round with rolled fondant (p. 117). Prepare for Stacked Construction (p. 114). Roll out red from Multi Pack ⅛ in. thick; cut 2 strips ½ x 32 in.; attach to cake sides using damp brush. Use Cake Dividing Set to divide cake into 10ths. Roll out 2 oz. white and yellow from Multi Pack ⅛ in. thick. Cut 10 rounds using medium Cut-Out; center and attach at marks. Cut 10 stars using medium Cut-Out; brush with water and sprinkle with Colored Sugar. Attach to rounds.

For lion cake: Bake and cool cake using firm-textured batter such as pound cake. Trim off arms and trim ears to a point. Cut dowel rod for two 5 in. lengths. Push into cake sides for arms, leaving 1½ in. extended. Roll 2 fondant logs, ⅝ x 1½ in.; push into dowel rods. Insert paws. Use tip 4 to pipe dot eyes, outline and pipe-in nose and mouth; pat smooth with fingertip dipped in cornstarch. Ice inside of ears and bottom of feet smooth. Cover lion with tip 17 stars. Pipe tip 5 dot foot pads; flatten with fingertip. Pipe tip 4 dot whiskers. Position lion on base cake. Position curls for mane, trimming as needed. Cake serves 40; each cookie serves 1.

▶ Well-Balanced Birthday

Pans: 6, 8 x 2 in. Round, p. 157; Standard Muffin, p. 158

Tips: 2A, 3, 10, p. 134

Colors:* Red-Red, Christmas Red, Lemon Yellow, Golden Yellow, Sky Blue, Leaf Green, Copper (for skin tone shown), Black, p. 146

Fondant: White Ready-To-Use Rolled Fondant (56 oz.), Fine Tip FoodWriter Edible Color Marker (black), p. 147; 20 in. Rolling Pin, Roll & Cut Mat, Easy-Glide Fondant Smoother, p. 148; Gold Pearl Dust, Brush Set, p. 149

Recipes: Buttercream Icing, p. 116; Thinned Fondant Adhesive, p. 117

Also: Jungle Pals Candle Picks, p. 176; Big Top Standard Baking Cups, p. 172; 2 in. Globe Pillar Set, p. 238; Cake Dividing Set, p. 136; White Candy Melts, p. 194; Clear Vanilla Extract, p. 143; 4 in. Lollipop Sticks, p. 198; Wooden Dowel Rods, p. 239; Cake Circles, Fanci-Foil Wrap, p. 241; ruler, tape, knife

In advance: Tint fondant: 24 oz. red; 8 oz. each black, skin tone; 6 oz. golden yellow; 3 oz. lemon yellow; ½ oz. each blue, green. Reserve 6 oz. white. **Also:** Make acrobats (p. 127). **And:** Make fondant mini cake (p. 127).

Bake and cool 1-layer cakes and cupcakes. Prepare and cover cakes with rolled fondant (p. 117). Prepare for Stacked Construction (p. 114). Roll out golden yellow ⅛ in. thick. For bottom borders, cut ½ in. wide strips, 21 and 24 in. long; attach around cakes using damp brush. Cut 48 circles using narrow end of tip 2A; attach to borders using fondant adhesive. Divide 6 in. cake into 8ths, 8 in. cake into 10ths. Use tip 3 to pipe 2¼ in. wide scrolls between marks. Let dry 1 hour. Paint scrolls and borders with Pearl Dust/vanilla mixture (p. 120). Insert pillar from Globe Set into 6 in. cake only. Slide on people. Attach miniature cake with fondant adhesive. Insert candle. Ice cupcake tops with tip 2A swirl. Insert candles. Cake serves 16; each cupcake serves 1.

*Combine Red-Red with Christmas Red for red shown.

◀ Circus Train Cars

Pans: 9 in. Square Covered Brownie, p. 171; Non-Stick Cookie Sheet, p. 165

Tip: 4, p. 134

Candy: Red, Green, Yellow, White Candy Melts, p. 194; Primary (orange, blue) Candy Color Set, p. 195

Recipes: Buttercream Icing, p. 116; favorite brownie recipe or mix

Also: 2011 Pattern Book (Roof Top), p. 130; Big Top Icing Decorations, p. 172; Round Cut-Outs, p. 151; Disposable Decorating Bags, p. 136; Cake Boards, p. 241; regular and mini candy-coated chocolates, knife, ruler, waxed paper, tape

In advance: Make candy pieces. For roof top, copy pattern and tape to board; cover with waxed paper. Using melted candy in disposable decorating bags, outline and fill in design. Tap to settle; chill until firm. Pipe zigzag trim; chill. For wheels, place medium round Cut-Out on Cookie Sheet. Fill to ¼ in. deep. Tap to settle; chill until firm. Make 2 per treat. For bottom edge, pipe 2 x ¼ in. wide stripe. Chill until firm. Attach candy-coated chocolates with dots of candy.

Bake and cool brownies. Cut into 3 x 2¾ in. wide rectangles. Pipe tip 4 outlines, ⅝ in. apart, for bars. Attach candy pieces and animal icing decorations. Each serves 1.

◀ The Whole Circus Turned Out!

Pans: 4 Pc. Petal Set (largest pan used), p. 156; 10 x 2 in. Round, p. 157
Tips: 1, 3, p. 134
Colors:* Orange, Lemon Yellow, Leaf Green, Sky Blue, Red-Red, Christmas Red, Violet, Royal Blue, Brown, Golden Yellow, Black, p. 146
Fondant: White Ready-To-Use Rolled Fondant (86 oz.), Gum-Tex, p. 147; 9 in., 20 in. Rolling Pins, Roll & Cut Mat, Easy-Glide Fondant Smoother, p. 148; Brush Set, p. 149; Round, Star Cut-Outs, p. 151
Recipes: Buttercream, Royal Icings, p. 116; Thinned Fondant Adhesive, p. 117
Also: Carousel Cake Set, p. 185; Animal Pals 50 Pc. Cutter Set, p. 201; Meringue Powder, Piping Gel, p. 143; Wooden Dowel Rods, p. 239; Cake Boards, Circles, Fanci-Foil Wrap, p. 241; 16 in. diameter plywood or foamcore circle (½ in. thick), knife, ruler, cornstarch, waxed paper, tape, scissors

1-2 days in advance: Make fondant animals. Tint fondant: 4 oz. each gray, violet, yellow. Add ¼ teaspoon Gum-Tex to each color. Roll out ⅛ in. thick as needed. Use cutters from set to cut 8 animals (2 each, lion, giraffe, seal and elephant). Decorate with royal icing. Use tip 1 to outline animals and pipe features. Outline and fill in elephant ear and giraffe spots; pat smooth with fingertip dipped in cornstarch. Pipe tip 1 dot and outline facial features, dot nails, fill in tusk, pull-out lion's mane. Let dry on waxed paper-covered boards. **Also:** Cover base board with 26 oz. red fondant (p. 120). Reserve excess fondant. **And:** Prepare carousel. Tint fondant: 4 oz. lemon yellow, 8 oz. sky blue, 16 oz. each orange and green; also use reserved red. Roll out ⅛ in. thick as needed. Cut six 3 x 4½ in. triangles (3 green, 3 blue) to fit canopy top; brush top with Piping Gel and attach, trimming as needed. Cut yellow strips, ¼ in. wide; attach over seams with fondant adhesive. Cut 4 x 36 in. strip to wrap over canopy edge; attach. Roll 1¼ in. diameter ball; attach inside finial. Cover pillar bases. Reserve excess fondant. **And:** Paint carousel horses. Thin red and yellow royal icing with small amount of water. Use brush to paint saddle and bridle, mane, tail and hooves. Let dry.

Bake and cool 1-layer petal cake and 2-layer round (bake two 1½ in. high layers for a 3 in. high cake). Ice smooth (tops white, sides blue or yellow); prepare for Stacked Construction (p. 114). Pipe tip 3 dot trim and bead borders. Roll out reserved green, red, yellow and orange fondant ⅛ in. thick. For petal cake, cut ¾ in. wide green strips and attach to cake sides with icing. For medallions, cut 8 yellow, 8 orange rounds using medium Cut-Out. Attach to carousel roof and cake sides using damp brush. Cut 16 stars using medium Cut-Out; attach to rounds. Attach animals with icing. Position carousel at party. Serves 52.

*Combine Leaf Green with Lemon Yellow for green shown. Combine Red-Red with Christmas Red for red shown. Combine Violet with Royal Blue for elephant violet shown. Combine Black with Violet and Royal Blue for seal gray shown. Combine Brown with Red-Red for brown shown. Combine Golden Yellow with Lemon Yellow and Orange for lion yellow shown.

▶ Big Top Place Cards

Pan: Mini Loaf, p. 158
Candy:* White, Red, Orange Candy Melts, p. 194; Primary (blue, yellow), Garden (green) Candy Color Sets, p. 195; Big Top Candy Pick Mold, p. 172
Also: Parchment Triangles, p. 136; Brush Set, p. 149, knife

Make candy plaques (p. 128), filling Mini Loaf cavities ¼ in. deep with white Candy Melts. Make an extra plaque for every 4 treats to cut into easel backs. Make tent candies in picks mold using Painting Method (p. 128), filling and chilling each color area one at a time, then filling with white candy. Chill until firm.

Using melted candy in cut parchment bag, pipe scallop border and dots, leaving tent area open. Chill until firm. Attach tent and print name with melted candy; chill until firm. Cut four 1 x 1½ in. triangle easel backs from each extra plaque. Trim one side at slightly less than 90° angle so that plaque will lean back. Attach to left side of plaque to support tent. Chill until firm. Each serves 1.

*Combine green and yellow candy colors with melted white Candy Melts for green shown.

◀ Step Right Up!

Pans: Wonder Mold, p. 160; 8 x 3 in., 14 x 2 in. Round, p. 159

Tips: 1, 2, 3, p. 134

Colors:* Violet, Rose, Christmas Red, Red-Red, Lemon Yellow, Golden Yellow, Sky Blue, Leaf Green, Orange, Royal Blue, Black, Brown, p. 146

Fondant: White Ready-To-Use Rolled Fondant (130 oz.), p. 147; 20 in. Rolling Pin, Roll & Cut Mat, Easy-glide Fondant Smoother, p. 148; Brush Set, p. 149

Recipes: Buttercream, Color Flow Icings, Roll-Out Cookies, p. 116; Thinned Fondant Adhesive, p. 117

Also: 2010 Pattern Book (Flag, Roof Triangle), p. 130; Animal Pals 50 Pc. Cutter Set, p. 201; Color Flow Mix, p. 143; Cake Dividing Set, p. 136; 4 in. Lollipop Sticks, p. 198; Candy Melts, p. 194; Wooden Dowel Rods, p. 139; Cake Boards, Circles, 16 in. Silver Cake Base, p. 241; knife, ruler, waxed paper, cornstarch, toothpicks

1-2 days in advance: Make cookie animals. Prepare and roll out dough. Use cutters from set to cut 6 animals (2 of each lion, giraffe and bear). Bake and cool. Ice and decorate cookies (p. 127). When dry, cut Lollipop Sticks into 3 in. lengths. Attach sticks to cookie backs using melted candy, leave 2 in. of stick exposed below cookie.

Bake and cool Wonder Mold cake, 1-layer 14 in. round and 2-layer 8 in. round (bake 2½ in. high layers for a 5 in. high cake). Cut 1 in. off bottom of Wonder Mold cake; use icing to build up and shape top point. Prepare and cover cakes with white fondant (p. 117). Prepare for Stacked Construction (p. 114). Tint fondant: 16 oz. red, 6 oz. violet, 6 oz. yellow, 3 oz. sky blue, 3 oz. green. Roll out ⅛ in. thick (unless otherwise specified). Use roof pattern to cut 6 white and 6 red triangles; attach to roof using damp brush, smoothing edges and trimming as needed. Divide 8 in. cake into 6ths. Roll out remaining red fondant ¹⁄₁₆ in. thick. For swags, cut six 3 x 3½ in. wide strips. Shape pleats using dowel rods (p. 127); pinch ends, curve and attach at top border. For drapes, cut six 4 x 3½ in. wide strips. Shape pleats using dowel rods and attach below swags, trimming as needed to fit. Roll out fondant ⅛ in. thick: 8 each yellow, green and blue, 24 violet. Use knife to cut 2 x 2 in. wide triangles. Attach all violet triangles, then 3 alternating colors, trimming as needed to fit. Roll ⅝ in. diameter yellow balls; attach above swags using fondant adhesive. Use pattern to cut flag; wrap around Lollipop Stick and secure using damp brush. Push stick through 1 in. ball of fondant leaving ¼ in. space; insert in cake top. Insert animals. Cake serves 63, each cookie serves 1.

*Combine Violet with Rose for violet shown. Combine Christmas Red with Red-Red for red shown. Combine Lemon Yellow with Golden Yellow for yellow shown. Combine Brown with Red-Red for brown shown.

▶ Little Big Tops

Pan: Dimensions Multi-Cavity Mini Cupcake, p. 164

Tip: 16, p. 135

Colors:* Christmas Red, Royal Blue, Orange, Leaf Green, Lemon Yellow, Golden Yellow, p. 146

Recipe: Buttercream Icing, p. 116

Also: Jungle Pals Icing Decorations, p. 176; 4 in. Lollipop Sticks, p. 198; Cake Dividing Set, p. 136; Cake Circles, p. 241; colored construction paper, scissors, ruler, marker, toothpicks, clear tape

Bake and cool mini cakes. Ice bottom cakes smooth with white icing, wide end of cakes down. Pipe tip 16 lines for tent sides, leaving 2¼ in. wide opening at the front. Attach Icing Decoration in opening. Position top cake on bottom cake. Use Cake Dividing Wheel to divide top cake into 8ths. Cover sections with tip 16 stars. Cut 1 x 2 in. triangle for paper flag. Print name. Tape to end of Lollipop Stick. Insert flag. Each serves 1.

*Combine Lemon Yellow with Golden Yellow for yellow shown.

▶ Animal Tracks

Pans: Choo Choo Train Set, p. 163; 9 x 5 in. Loaf, p. 158

Tips: 1, 1A, 2, 2A, 3, 8, 10, 16, p. 134-135

Colors:* Sky Blue, Violet, Lemon Yellow, Golden Yellow, Orange, Leaf Green, Christmas Red, Red-Red, Rose, Pink, Brown, Black, Copper (for skin tone shown), p. 146

Fondant: White Ready-To-Use Rolled Fondant (18 oz.), p. 147; 9 in. Rolling Pin, Roll & Cut Mat, p. 148; Brush Set, p. 149; Cutter/Embosser, p. 150

Recipes: Buttercream, Royal Icings, p. 116; Thinned Fondant Adhesive, p. 117

Also: 101 Cookie Cutters (round, star), p. 201; Meringue Powder, p. 143; Tapered Spatula, p. 139; Cake Boards, p. 241; cornstarch, knife, waxed paper, ruler, candy sticks, toothpicks

In advance: Make royal icing heads (p. 127). **Also:** Make fondant wheels. Tint fondant: 10 oz. violet, 6 oz. green, 1 oz. blue, 1 oz. yellow. Roll out ⅛ in. thick as needed. Cut 10 rounds using medium cutter from set. For spokes, cut 2½ x ⅛ in. strips; attach using damp brush. For axle, roll small ball and press onto center. For rims, cut 10 medium rounds; use top edge of smallest round cutter as a guide to cut away center. Attach rims to wheels. Position 2 wheels side by side; attach a 3 in. candy stick connecting rod with royal icing. Let dry on cornstarch-dusted boards. Reserve excess fondant. **And:** Make rooftop scallops. Cut 1 round using large cutter from set. Cut in half

and trim each to 1½ in. high. Cut 2 rounds using medium cutter. Cut in half and trim all pieces to ⅞ in. high. For large spirals (make 2), roll yellow fondant into 4 x 3/16 in. diameter rope. Roll violet into 4 x ⅛ in. diameter rope. Lay ropes side by side then wind into spiral. Flatten slightly for a 1¼ in. wide spiral. For small spirals (make 4), roll ropes 3 in. long for a ½ in. wide spiral. Attach spirals to scallops, flat side up with damp brush. Reserve excess fondant.

Bake and cool train cake using firm-textured batter such as pound cake. Trim off bell. For train car, bake and cool 2-layer loaf cake (trim cakes to 2½ in. high for a 5 in. high cake). Trim sides straight. Use toothpicks to mark 2¼ in. square windows, ½ in. from top edge. Use tapered spatula to ice smooth in black. Pipe tip 8 outline borders; pat smooth with finger dipped in cornstarch. Use knife to score corners. For engine, divide cowcatcher into 5 parts; using tip 10, pipe in areas in alternating colors. Pat smooth. Mark 1 in. wide stripes. Cover cake with tip 16 stars. Roll ¼ in. diameter fondant balls; attach around cab roof and smokestack. Attach boy. Attach wheels. Roll out remaining yellow fondant ⅛ in. thick. Cut star using smallest cutter from set; attach to front. For train car, cover cake with tip 16 stars. Attach wheels and animals. Position scallops on roof. Connect cakes with candy stick. Serves 24.

*Combine Violet with Rose for violet shown. Combine Lemon Yellow with Golden Yellow for yellow shown. Combine Leaf Green with Lemon Yellow for green shown. Combine Brown with Red-Red for brown shown.

▶ A Roaring Good Time!

Pans: 4 Pc. Petal Set (largest pan used), p. 156; 8 x 2 in. Heart, p. 159; Non-Stick Cookie Sheet, p. 165

Tips: 3, 18, p. 134-135

Color: Orange, p. 146

Candy: Yellow, Light Cocoa Candy Melts, p. 194

Recipe: Buttercream Icing, p. 116

Also: Circle Metal Cutter, p. 202; Parchment Triangles, p. 136; Cake Circles, Fanci-Foil Wrap, p. 241; ruler, knife, vegetable peeler, tape

In advance: Make candy pieces. Make candy plaque in heart pan, filling to ¼ in. deep (p. 128). For ears, set Circle Cutter on non-stick sheet; fill to ¼ in. deep. Tap to settle; chill until firm. For lip, pipe candy inside Circle Cutter to make a 2½ in. long curve. Let set, then repeat to build up to ¼ in. thick.

Bake and cool 1-layer cake. Lightly ice top and sides. Position heart plaque, shiny side up. For ears, cut candy circle in half using warm knife; shave cut edge to match curve of head. Attach ears and lip with melted candy. Using melted candy in cut parchment bag with tip 3 taped over the outside, pipe outline whiskers; outline and pipe in nose and mouth; attach Candy Melts disks for eyes. Let set. Cover cake with tip 18 pull-out stars, working from bottom up to candy face. Serves 24.

◀ Lion Lineup

Pan: Non-Stick Cookie Sheet, p. 165

Tip: 2, p. 134

Candy: Orange, Yellow, Light Cocoa Candy Melts, p. 194; 8 in. Lollipop Sticks, p. 198

Also: Heart Plastic Nesting Cutter Set, p. 201; Nesting Blossoms Metal Cutter Set, p. 202; Parchment Triangles, p. 136; tape, ruler

In advance: Make candies. For face, use 3rd smallest heart cutter from set; for mane, use 2nd largest blossom cutter from set. Set cutters on non-stick cookie sheet. Fill to ⅛ in. deep with melted candy. Tap to settle; chill until firm. Attach face to mane, shiny sides up, using melted candy. Let set.

Decorate using melted candy in cut parchment bags with tip 2 taped over the outside. Pipe dot ears and outline lip. Pipe outline whiskers, dot eyes and nose; fill in inside mouth. Let set. Attach Lollipop Stick to back using melted candy. Each serves 1.

◀ Pachyderm Takes His Turn

Pans: 6, 12 x 2 in. Round, p. 157; Standard Muffin, p. 158

Tip: 1M, p. 134

Colors:* Sky Blue, Lemon Yellow, Leaf Green, Orange, Red-Red, Rose, Royal Blue, Black, p. 146

Fondant: White Ready-To-Use Rolled Fondant (102 oz.), Fine Tip FoodWriter Edible Color Markers (black), p. 147; 20 in. Rolling Pin, Roll & Cut Mat, Easy-Glide Fondant Smoother, p. 148; Brush Set, p. 149; Heart Cut-Outs, p. 151

Recipes: Buttercream Icing, p. 116; Thinned Fondant Adhesive, p. 117

Also: Big Top Cupcake Wraps 'N Pix, p. 172; White Standard Baking Cups, p. 184; Blue Candy Melts, p. 194; 2 in., 2½ in. Globe Pillar Sets, p. 238; Dowel Rods, p. 239; 14 in. Round Silver Cake Base, Cake Boards, Circles, Fanci-Foil Wrap, p. 241; ruler, knife, tape, cornstarch

In advance: Make elephant topper (p. 127). Tint fondant: 8 oz. sky blue, 4 oz. orange, 3 oz. royal blue, ½ oz. each rose, black. Roll out ⅛ in. thick as needed; reserve excess royal blue and orange.

Bake and cool 1-layer 12 in. round, 2-layer 6 in. round and 6 cupcakes. Prepare and cover rounds with white rolled fondant (p. 117). Prepare for Stacked Construction (p. 114). Tint fondant: 10 oz. yellow, 8 oz. green; 6 oz. red; use reserved royal blue and orange. Roll out ⅛ in. thick as needed. Cut 10 strips, 1 x 4 in.; use damp brush to attach to sides of 6 in. cake, 1 in. apart. Cut a 2 x 20 in. strip of yellow; cut into 2 in. triangles. Repeat with green. Attach triangles to 12 in. cake sides, trimming if needed. For borders, roll ½ in. diameter balls. For 6 in. cake: 19 green, 19 blue, 38 yellow. For 12 in. cake: 80 orange. Attach using fondant adhesive. Ice cupcake tops with tip 1M swirl. Attach wraps and insert picks. Position on cake. Insert plastic dowel rod through center. Slide on orange ball. Shape four ¾ in. squares for feet. Attach around dowel rod. Slide on elephant. Cake serves 32, each cupcake serves 1.

*Combine Leaf Green with Lemon Yellow for green shown.

▼ Trunk Talking

Pans: Elephant, p. 161; 16 x 2 in. Square, p. 157
Tips: 2, 5, 8, 10, 18, 366, p. 134-135
Colors:* Kelly Green, Sky Blue, Brown, Rose, Lemon Yellow, Orange, Red-Red, Royal Blue, Black, p. 146
Candy: Monkey Large Lollipop Mold, p. 196; Blue (2 pks.), White, Light Cocoa, Green, Peanut Butter Candy Melts, p. 194; Primary (blue, yellow), Garden (green) Candy Color Sets, p. 195; Decorator Brush Set, p. 197
Recipes: Buttercream, Royal Icings, p. 116
Also: Flowerful Medley 6-Mix Sprinkles (confetti, 2 pks.), p. 144; Meringue Powder, p. 143; Parchment Triangles, p. 136; Cake Boards, Fanci-Foil Wrap, p. 241; Wooden Dowel Rods, p. 239; 17 x 17 in. plywood or foamcore board (½ in. thick), knife, ruler, waxed paper, cornstarch

In advance: Make elephant candy plaque (p. 128). **Also:** Make candy monkeys. Use melted candy in cut parchment bags with Piping Method (p. 128) to mold candies without sticks. Chill until firm. Place on waxed paper-covered board. Using royal icing, pipe tip 10 hats; add tip 2 pull-out fringe and pompom. Let dry overnight.

Bake and cool 1-layer cake. Ice smooth (sky in sky blue, grass in green) and decorate with buttercream. Pipe tip 10 bead tree trunks, starting at bottom of trees. Pipe tip 366 leaves. Insert dowel rods in area where elephant will sit for support. Position elephant and monkeys. For bottom border, pipe tip 5 blue beads or tip 18 green pull-out star grass following cake top color position. Pipe tip 18 pull-out grass details. Position confetti for message and trims. Serves 40.

*Combine Brown with Red-Red for brown icing shown. Combine Sky Blue with Royal Blue and a little Black for gray icing on elephant.

▲ Leafy & Lively Cookies

Pans: Cookie Sheet, Cooling Grid, p. 203
Tip: 3, p. 134
Color: Leaf Green, p. 146
Recipes: Color Flow Icing, Roll-Out Cookies, p. 11
Also: Football Colored Metal Cutter Set, p. 202; Jung Pals Icing Decorations, p. 176; Color Flow Mix, p. 143; Parchment Triangles, p. 136; waxed paper

In advance: Make cookies. Prepare and roll out dou Cut leaves using football cutter from set. Bake and cool cookies. Using full-strength dark green icing in parchment bag, outline cookies with tip 3; let set. Flo in with thinned light green icing (p. 128); immediately overpipe dark green vein lines. Let dry overnight.

Attach icing decorations with icing dots. Each serves

▲ Treetop Greetings

Pans: Guitar, p. 162; Mini Loaf, p. 158
Tips: 3, 16, p. 134-135
Colors:* Lemon Yellow, Golden Yellow, Orange, Kelly Green, Leaf Green, Royal Blue, Black, p. 146
Fondant: White Ready-To-Use Rolled Fondant (94 oz.), Gum-Tex, p. 147; 9 in., 20 in. Rolling Pins, Roll & Cut Mat, Easy-Glide Fondant Smoother, p. 148; Fondant Shaping Foam, 10 Pc. Gum Paste Tool Set, p. 149; Flower Former Set, p. 138; Brush Set, p. 149; Leaf Cut-Outs, p. 151
Recipe: Buttercream Icing, p. 116
Also: 2011 Pattern Book (Ear), p. 130; 101 Cookie Cutters (alphabet, numbers), p. 201; 6 in. Cookie Treat Sticks, p. 203; Piping Gel, p. 143; Jumbo Confetti Sprinkles, p. 144; Cake Boards, Fanci-Foil Wrap, p. 241; 17 x 23 in. plywood or foamcore board (½ in. thick), knife, ruler, tape, scissors, cornstarch, craft block, waxed paper, toothpicks

In advance: Make ears and horns (p. 127). **Also:** Make leaves. Tint 12 oz. fondant green. Add 1½ teaspoons Gum-Tex. Roll out ⅛ in. thick. Cut 35 leaves using largest Cut-Out. Place leaves on thin foam and draw veins with veining tool. Let dry in various positions on cornstarch-dusted large Flower Formers. Reserve excess fondant. **And:** Cover base board with 70 oz. blue fondant (p. 120); reserve remaining blue.

Bake and cool guitar cake and 2 mini loaves. Cut 3½ in. off neck of guitar. Position guitar on a cut-to-fit Cake Board; position on prepared base board, 5½ in. from top edge. For eyeballs, using 2 oz. reserved white fondant, roll 1½ in. diameter balls; attach with icing. Mark muzzle area; build up and round area with icing, about 1 in. thick. Cover cake and edges and sides of ears with tip 16 stars. Attach ears to board. Pipe tip 3 dot pupils, nostrils and outline mouth. Insert horns in cake. Prepare loaf cakes and cover with green fondant; position horizontally at bottom of neck, centered. Attach leaves with icing. Tint reserved blue fondant a darker shade; roll out ⅛ in. thick. Cut name and age. Attach to board using damp brush. Sprinkle on confetti. Serves 14.

*Combine Kelly Green with Leaf Green for green shown. Combine Lemon Yellow with Golden Yellow for yellow shown.

◀ Hip Hippo, Hurray!

Pans: Lady Bug, p. 161; Cookie Sheet, Cooling Grid, p. 203

Tips: 3, 12, 16, p. 134-135

Colors:* Royal Blue, Violet, Orange, Pink, Black, p. 146

Recipes: Buttercream, Royal Icings, Roll-Out Cookies, p. 116

Also: 2011 Pattern Book (Hippo Head), p. 130; Meringue Powder, p. 143; 13 x 19 in. Cake Boards, Fanci-Foil Wrap, p. 241; knife, cornstarch

In advance: Make cookie head. Prepare and roll out dough. Use pattern to cut out head; with knife, cut 2 x 2 in. supports for head. Bake and cool cookies.

Bake and cool cake. Level head area. On cookie, use tip 3 to outline and fill in inner ears; pat smooth. Pipe tip 12 dot eyes, tip 3 dot nostrils, outline smile. Attach supports to back of head with royal icing. On cake, pipe tip 3 outline nails and tip 16 star spots. Cover remainder of cookie and cake with tip 16 stars. Pipe tip 16 e-motion tail. Position cookie on cake. Cookie serves 1; cake serves 12.

*Combine Royal Blue with Violet for blue shown.

Animals of the Amazon

Pans: 6, 8, 10 x 2 in. Round, p. 157; Cookie Sheet, Cooling Grid, p. 203

Tips: 1, 2, 3, 16, p. 134-135

Colors:* Leaf Green, Kelly Green, Lemon Yellow, Golden Yellow, Orange, Royal Blue, Pink, Brown, Red-Red, Black, p. 146

Fondant: White Ready-To-Use Rolled Fondant (120 oz.), Gum-Tex, p. 147; 20 in. Rolling Pin, Roll & Cut Mat, Easy-Glide Fondant Smoother, p. 148; 10 Pc. Fondant/Gum Paste Tool Set, Flower Former Set, Brush Set, p. 149; Leaf Cut-Outs, p. 151

Recipes: Buttercream, Color Flow Icings, Roll-Out Cookies, p. 116

Also: Animal Pals 50 Pc. Cutter Set, p. 201; Cakes 'N More 3-Tier Party Stand, p. 236; Color Flow Mix, Piping Gel, p. 143; Cake Boards, Circles, Fanci-Foil Wrap, p. 241; Wooden Dowel Rods (six 7 in. long), p. 239; Green Candy Melts, p. 194; 4 in. Lollipop Sticks, p. 198; knife, scissors, tape, ruler, cornstarch, craft block

In advance: Make animal cookies. Prepare and roll out dough. Use cutters from set to cut giraffe and 1 each lion, zebra/horse, rhino, hippo, gorilla, snake, alligator (use lizard cutter, cutting off 2 top feet). Bake and cool. Ice and decorate cookies (p. 127). When dry, attach Lollipop Sticks to back of each animal (except snake and alligator) using melted candy; allow 1½ in. to extend at bottom to insert into cake. **Also:** Make leaves and trees (p. 127).

Bake and cool 1-layer cakes. Prepare and cover with 56 oz. light green fondant (p. 117). Tint 36 oz. fondant medium green. Roll out half ⅛ in. thick. Cover top of plates. Position cakes on plates. Roll out remaining medium green fondant ⅛ in. thick. Cut 2 in. high strips to wrap around cake sides: 21 in. long for 6 in., 27 in. for 8 in., 34 in. for 10 in. cake. Cut wavy top edge ¾ to 1½ in. high. Attach strips to cake sides using damp brush. Use buttercream to pipe tip 16 pull-out grass; attach 22 medium leaves. For ponds, roll out white fondant ⅛ in. thick. Cut wavy shapes: 2 x 4 in. for 6 in. cake, 5½ x 3½ in. for 8 in. cake, 5 x 4 in. for 10 in. cake; attach to cake tops. For waterfalls, cut a cake board into strips, 2½ in. wide, 5 and 6 in. long. Curve slightly. Brush with Piping Gel and wrap with fondant strips, 5 in. wide, 5 and 6 in. long. Tint 4 oz. fondant gray. Roll about 50-55 assorted rocks, ⅜ to ¾ in. diameter and attach to sides of waterfalls and ponds using damp brush. **At Party:** Position plates on stand. Position waterfalls; cover with tinted Piping Gel for water. Insert animals and trees; attach alligator and snake to sides with icing. Each animal serves 1; cakes serve 30.

*Combine Leaf Green with Lemon Yellow for green shades shown. Combine Brown with Red-Red for brown shown. Combine Lemon Yellow with Golden Yellow for yellow shades shown. Combine Black with Royal Blue for gray shades shown.

▲ Buddies on the Block

Pans: Mini Stand-Up Bear Set, p. 161; 6 x 2 in. Square, p. 157

Tips: 2A, 3, 13, 16, p. 134-135

Colors:* Royal Blue, Lemon Yellow, Leaf Green, Pink, Violet, Golden Yellow, Orange, Brown, Christmas Red, Black, p. 146

Fondant: White Ready-To-Use Rolled Fondant (108 oz.), p. 147; 20 in. Rolling Pin, Roll & Cut Mat, Easy-Glide Fondant Smoother, p. 148; Brush Set, p. 149

Recipe: Buttercream Icing, p. 116

Also: 2011 Pattern Book (Tiger, Monkey, Elephant, Lion Ears), p. 130; Jumbo Confetti Sprinkles, p. 144; A-B-C and 1-2-3 50 Pc. Cutter Set, p. 201; Tapered Spatula, p. 139; Cake Boards, Fanci-Foil Wrap, p. 241; knife, ruler, cornstarch

In advance: Make fondant ears. Roll out 1 oz. white fondant ⅛ in. thick. Use patterns to cut animal ears (flip pattern for 2nd ear). Let dry on cornstarch-dusted board.

For animals: Bake and cool mini bear cakes. Cut off ears. Shape feet using ¾ in. fondant ovals; attach with icing. Pipe tip 2A elephant trunk. Pipe tip 16 star tiger stripes. For all, ice smooth soles of feet and inside areas of fondant ears. Attach ears with icing. Pipe tip 3 dot eyes, outline mouths and dot or fill-in noses. Cover animals with tip 13 stars; overpipe arms for dimension. Pipe tip 16 pull-out star lion's mane.

For blocks: Bake and cool 2-layer cakes. Tint fondant: 4 oz. violet; 24 oz. each blue, yellow, green, pink. Roll out ⅛ in. thick as needed. Prepare and cover cakes with rolled fondant (p. 117). Cut letters; attach using damp brush. Attach confetti using icing dots. Each block with animal serves 15.

*Combine Orange with Christmas Red for dark orange on tiger. Combine Brown with Christmas Red for brown shown. Combine Lemon Yellow with Golden Yellow for yellow lion; combine Orange with Golden Yellow for orange mane. Combine Violet with Pink for violet shown.

▶ A Zebra in Party Colors

Pans: 3 Pc. Paisley Set (medium pan used), p. 156; Cookie Sheet, Cooling Grid, p. 203

Tips: 3, 16, p. 134-135

Colors:* Violet, Rose, Black, p. 146

Recipes: Buttercream, Royal Icings, Roll-Out Cookies, p. 116

Also: 2011 Pattern Book (Head, Tail, Legs), p. 130; Meringue Powder, p. 143; Tapered Spatula, p. 139; 6 in. Lollipop Sticks, p. 203; Cake Boards, Fanci-Foil Wrap, p. 241; knife, ruler, toothpicks

In advance: Make cookie pieces. Prepare and roll out dough. Use patterns to cut out head, tail and 2 legs. Use knife to cut 3 supports, each 2 x 2 in. Bake and cool cookies. **Also:** Decorate and assemble cookie pieces using royal icing. Use tip 3 to outline and fill-in eyes and nostrils (pat smooth); pipe outline smile. Ice inner ears smooth. Cover head, tail and feet with tip 16 stars. Finish tail end with tip 16 pull-out stars. Let dry. Attach Lollipop Stick to back of tail, leaving 4 in. exposed to insert into cake. Attach support cookies to back of head behind ears and to right of smile. Let all dry overnight.

Bake and cool 1-layer cake. Using buttercream, cover with tip 16 stars. Insert tail. Position head and legs. Cookies serve 1; cake serves 14.

*Combine Violet with Rose for violet shown.

▶ Zoo Keepers

Pans: Cookie Sheet, Cooling Grid, p. 203
Tips: 1, 2, 5, p. 134
Colors: Pink, Royal Blue, Leaf Green, Lemon Yellow, Golden Yellow, Brown, Black, p. 146
Recipes: Royal Icing, Roll-Out Cookies, p. 116
Also: 3 Pc. Jungle Pals Cutter Set, p. 176; Parchment Triangles, p. 136; Meringue Powder, p. 143; Cake Boards, p. 241; knife, ruler, waxed paper

In advance: Make cookies. Prepare and roll out dough. For each treat, cut one 4¼ in. square and 1 animal using cutters from set. Bake and cool cookies. **Also:** Ice squares. Outline cookies using tip 5 and full-strength white icing; flow in with thinned tinted icing (p. 128). Immediately add white dots using thinned icing in cut parchment bag. Let dry on waxed paper-covered boards. **And:** Ice animals. For

elephant, outline cookie, inner ears and trunk with tip 2 and full-strength icing; flow in gray areas with thinned icing. Flow in inner ear with thinned pink icing. For monkey, outline cookie and inner ears with tip 2 and full-strength icing; flow in dark brown areas with thinned icing. Flow in inner ears with thinned pink icing. Let dry. Outline muzzle with tip 2 and full-strength icing; flow in with thinned icing. For lion, outline face, ears, triangle nose and inner ears with tip 2 and full-strength yellow icing; flow in with thinned icing. Outline mane with tip 2 and full-strength golden icing; flow in with thinned icing. Flow in inner ears with thinned pink icing. Let all dry on waxed paper-covered boards.

Assemble and decorate using full-strength icing. Attach animal cookies to squares. Pipe tip 1 dot and outline facial features on all. Each serves 1.

▶ Monkey Messenger

Pans: Monkey, p. 176; 16 x 2 in. Round, p. 157
Tip: 21, p. 135
Colors: Violet, Orange, p. 146
Fondant: White Ready-To-Use Rolled Fondant (72 oz.), Pastel Fondant Multi Pack, p. 147; 20 in., 9 in., Rolling Pins, Roll & Cut Mat, Easy-Glide Fondant Smoother, p. 148; Brush Set, p. 149
Candy: Light Cocoa (2 pks.), Peanut Butter, White Candy Melts, p. 194; Garden Candy Color Set (black), p. 195
Recipe: Buttercream Icing, p. 116
Also: 101 Cookie Cutters (alphabet), p. 201; Parchment Triangles, p. 136; Wooden Dowel Rods, p. 239; Cake Boards, Circles, Fanci-Foil Wrap, p. 241; waxed paper, cornstarch

In advance: Make monkey candy plaque (p. 128). **Also:** Prepare fondant trims. Tint fondant: 1 oz. each orange, violet. Roll out orange, violet and blue, pink and green from Multi Pack ⅛ in. thick. Cut 8-10 dots of each color using wide end of tip 21. Cut letters using cutters from set. Let fondant trims dry on cornstarch-dusted boards.

Bake and cool 2-layer cake (bake 1½ in. high layers for a 3 in. high cake). Mix 1 pouch of yellow fondant from Multi Pack with 70 oz. white fondant for pale yellow shown. Place dowel rods where candy plaque will sit for support. Prepare and cover with rolled fondant (p. 117). Position candy plaque. Attach letters and dots using damp brush. Pipe tip 21 shell border. Serves 77.

◀ Chocolate Chimps

Pans: Silicone Round Brownie Pops Mold, p. 171; Cookie Sheet, Cooling Grid, p. 203
Candy: White, Light Cocoa Candy Melts, p. 194; Garden Candy Color Set (pink, green), p. 195; Animals Cookie Candy Mold, p. 176
Recipes: Buttercream Icing, p. 116; favorite brownie recipe or mix
Also: Natural Colors Fondant Multi Pack, p. 147; Parchment Triangles, p. 136; Cake Boards, p. 241; thick uncooked spaghetti (three 2½ in. lengths per treat), ruler, waxed paper, knife

In advance: Make candy heads. Tint small amounts of candy pink and green. Using melted candy in cut parchment bag, fill in nose and ear details in candy mold. Chill until firm. Fill in head section with melted light cocoa candy. Tap to settle; chill until firm. Pipe eyes and mouth after unmolding; let set. Dip spaghetti in melted candy; attach to back of head, leaving 1 in. exposed at bottom to insert into body. Chill until firm.

Bake and cool brownie pops in silicone mold supported by Cookie Sheet. Trim off bottom to make 1½ in. high body. Ice bottom with melted candy; let set on waxed paper-covered board.

Cover with melted candy (p. 128). Repeat if necessary for smooth finish. Let set. Roll out dark brown fondant ⅛ in. thick. Cut a 1 x 1½ in. strip for each arm; wrap around spaghetti, leaving 1 in. exposed to insert into body. Roll ⅜ in. balls for hands. Flatten and shape; use knife to cut fingers. Attach to arms with melted candy. Use tip of knife to cut holes through candy shell for head and arms; insert head and arms, trimming spaghetti if needed. Shape legs from ½ x 2¼ in. fondant logs; cut slits for toes. Attach with melted candy. Each serves 1.

Step-By-Step
Decorating Guide

Decorating help starts here! Whatever cake you want to make from this Yearbook, you'll find out how to make it happen on the following pages. Whether you're creating a cake for the first time or need a quick brush-up on a technique, it's easy when you use this handy guide as you decorate.

 Want to learn more?

Find Wilton Cake Decorating Classes in your area or register for The Wilton School in Darien, Illinois online at **www.wilton.com**. Our website is also a great place to explore decorating techniques, find recipes and chat with other decorators. Visit us regularly!

Cake Preparation

Think of your cake as the canvas on which you will create beautiful icing decorations. To achieve the masterpiece you want, it is essential that your canvas be smooth and free of crumbs. These steps for preparing and icing your cake will result in the perfect decorating surface essential for your work of art.

BAKING THE CAKE

Follow recipe directions for specific baking instructions and recommended batter amounts for the pan size you choose.

Prepare the pan by generously greasing the inside using a pastry brush or paper towel and solid vegetable shortening. For best results, do not use butter, margarine or liquid vegetable oil. Spread the shortening so that all indentations are covered. Sprinkle about 2 tablespoons of flour inside the pan and shake so that the flour covers all greased surfaces. Turn pan upside down and tap lightly to remove excess flour. If any uncovered spots remain, touch up with shortening and flour. Or use Bake Easy Non-Stick Spray or Cake Release (p. 152) to coat the pan—no grease or flour needed. Pour batter into pan and place in pre-heated oven.

After cake has baked the specified time, remove it from the oven and let it cool in the pan on a cake rack for 10 minutes. Run a thin knife between the cake and side of the pan. Unmold from pan by placing cooling rack against cake and turning both cooling rack and pan over. Lift pan off carefully. Cool at least one hour and brush off loose crumbs prior to icing.

CUTTING AND WRAPPING A CAKE BOARD

For round and sheet cakes, you don't need to cut a cake board. Simply buy a ready-made board that is 2 in. larger than your cake. (For example, if the cake is 8 in. diameter, buy a 10 in. round board.) For shaped cakes and squares, cut a board to fit. Turn pan upside down and trace outline onto your cake board. Cut board with a craft knife, leaving 1 in. extra around outline.

To wrap, trace your cut board onto Fanci-Foil, making the outline 3-4 in. larger than the board. Cut Fanci-Foil along the outline. Place your board, white side down, on top of your cut foil. Cut deep slits at several points along foil edge, creating tabs of foil to wrap neatly around the board. Secure foil tabs to the board with tape.

LEVELING THE CAKE

After the cake has cooled at least one hour, you'll need to level the top of the cake. This can be done using a serrated knife or the Cake Leveler (p. 152).

Using a Serrated Knife

Place the cake on a cake board, then place the board on a Trim 'N Turn Cake Plus Turntable (p. 139). While slowly rotating the turntable, move the knife back and forth across the top of cake in a sawing motion to remove the crown. Try to keep knife level as you cut.

Using the Wilton Cake Leveler

Position the ends of the cutting wire (or feet on large leveler) into the notches at the desired height. With legs standing on the work surface, cut into the crusted edge using an easy sawing motion, then proceed by gently gliding wire through the cake.

TORTING THE CAKE

Torting adds extra height, drama and taste to the cake when the layers are filled with icing, pudding or fruit filling. A serrated knife or the Cake Leveler may be used to cut a cake into multiple layers.

Using a Serrated Knife

Divide cake sides and mark equal horizontal points with dots of icing or toothpicks all around. Place one hand on top of the cake to hold it steady and rotate the stand. While slowly turning the cake, move the knife back and forth to cut the cake along the measured marks. Repeat for each additional layer.

Using the Cake Leveler

Torting is easily accomplished with the Cake Leveler. Simply follow the same directions as for leveling.

Separating the Layers

Carefully slide the top torted layer onto a cake board to keep it rigid and safe from breakage. Repeat for each additional layer.

FILLING THE LAYERS

Fill a decorating bag with medium consistency icing and use a large round tip, like tip 12. Or simply use the coupler without mounting a tip.

Starting with the bottom layer, leveled side up, create a dam of icing just inside the edge of the cake (about ¾ in. high and ¼ in. from the outside edge). Fill with icing, preserves or pudding. Place next layer on top, level; repeat. Finish with top layer leveled side down.

ICING THE CAKE

For better results, use a revolving turntable like professional decorators do…see our Trim 'N Turn Plus Cake Turntables on p. 139.

Using a Spatula

The trick to keeping crumbs out of your icing is gliding your spatula on the icing—*never allow it to touch the surface of the cake.* Place a large amount of thin consistency icing on the center of the cake.

Spread icing across the top, pushing toward edges. Smooth the top using the edge of the spatula.

Sweep the edge of the spatula from the rim of the cake to its center then lift it off and remove excess icing.

Cover the sides with icing. Smooth sides by holding the spatula upright with the edge against the icing and slowly spinning the turntable without lifting the spatula from the icing surface. Return excess icing to the bowl and repeat until sides are smooth.

Rotate the cake slightly and repeat the procedure, starting from a new point on the rim until you have covered the entire top surface. Smooth the center of the cake by leveling the icing with the edge of your spatula. For easier smoothing, it may help to dip the spatula into hot water, wipe dry and glide it across the entire surface. Set the cake aside and allow the icing to crust over for at least 15 minutes before decorating. At that point you may also lay Non-Stick Parchment Paper (p. 152) on the iced cake top and gently smooth with the palm of your hand.

Using a Decorating Tip

Trim a 16 in. Featherweight bag to fit tip 789. Fill bag half full with icing. Hold bag at 45° angle and lightly press tip against cake. Squeeze a ribbon of icing in a continuous spiral motion to cover cake top, with last ribbon forcing icing over edge of cake top.

To ice the sides, squeeze icing as you turn the cake slowly. Repeat the process until the entire cake side is covered.

Smooth sides and top with spatula, same as above.

Icing Basics

In this section, we've listed general descriptions of icings, their uses, qualities and consistencies. Use this information to determine the right icing for your cake. Refer to our recipes for homemade icings (p. 118) along with color instructions below, to create the look and taste you want.

ICING USAGE GUIDE

Icing Type	Flavor/Description	Consistency	Best Used For…	Coloring	Storage/Freshness	Special Information
Buttercream (Wilton Mix or homemade)	Sweet, buttery flavor. Tastes/looks great for most decorating.	Thin-to-stiff depending on amount of corn syrup or sugar added (sugar stiffens).	Icing cakes smooth. Borders, writing, flowers, decorations.	Yields all colors. Most deepen upon setting. Let set 2-3 hours for deep color. Some may fade in bright light.	Can be refrigerated in airtight container for 2 weeks. Iced cake stores at room temperature for 2-3 days.	Flowers remain soft enough to be cut with a knife.
Snow-White Buttercream (homemade)	Sweet, almond flavor. Ideal for wedding cakes.	Thin-to-stiff depending on amount of corn syrup or sugar added (sugar stiffens).	Icing cakes smooth. Borders, writing, flowers, decorations.	Yields truer colors due to pure white base color. Creates deep colors. Most colors deepen upon setting.	Can be refrigerated in airtight container for 2 weeks. Iced cake stores at room temperature for 2-3 days.	Air-dried flowers have translucent look. Flowers remain soft enough to be cut with knife.
Wilton Ready-To-Use Decorator White (4½ lb. tub)	Sweet, vanilla flavor. Convenient, ready-to-spread icing. Pure white color ideal for tinting.	Thin-to-medium. No need to thin for spreading.	Spreading on cakes right from the can. Piping stars, shells, messages and more.	Yields truer colors due to pure white base color. Creates deep colors. Most colors deepen upon setting.	Leftover icing can be refrigerated for 2 weeks. Iced cake stores at room temperature for 2-3 days.	Available for purchase through Wilton Yearbook, at www.wilton.com or any authorized Wilton retailer.
Wilton Ready-To-Use Decorator White (1 lb. can)	Sweet, vanilla flavor. Convenient, ready-to-spread icing. Pure white color ideal for tinting.	Stiff. Make roses right from the can.	Shells, stars, flowers—use from container. Icing cakes, writing, leaves—thin with milk, water or corn syrup.	Yields truer colors due to pure white base color. Creates deep colors. Most colors deepen upon setting.	Leftover icing can be refrigerated for 2 weeks. Iced cake stores at room temperature for 2-3 days.	Available for purchase through Wilton Yearbook, at www.wilton.com or any authorized Wilton retailer.
Wilton Ready-To-Use Decorator Chocolate (1 lb. can)	Sweet chocolate flavor. Convenient ready-to-spread icing.	Stiff. Make roses right from the can.	Shells, stars, flowers—use from container. Icing cakes, writing, leaves—thin with milk, water or corn syrup.	Recommended when black or brown icing is needed. Add a little black icing color to chocolate for a better tasting black icing.	Leftover icing can be refrigerated for 2 weeks. Iced cake stores at room temperature for 2-3 days.	Available for purchase through Wilton Yearbook, at www.wilton.com or any authorized Wilton retailer.
Royal (made with Wilton Meringue Powder)	Very sweet flavor. Dries candy-hard for lasting decorations.	Thin-to-stiff, depending on the amount of water added.	Flower making, figure piping, making flowers on wires. Decorating cookies and gingerbread houses.	Yields deep colors. Some colors may fade in bright light. Requires more icing color than buttercream to achieve the same intensity.	Icing can be stored in airtight, grease-free container at room temperature for 2 weeks. Air-dried decorations last for months.	Bowls and utensils must be grease-free. Cover icing with damp cloth to prevent crusting.
Rolled Fondant (homemade or Wilton Ready-To-Use Rolled Fondant)	Covers cakes with a perfectly smooth, satiny surface. Easy and fast to use. Knead in flavor of your choice.	Dough-like. Fondant Is rolled out before being applied to cake. Stays semi-soft on cake.	Any firm-textured cake, pound cake or fruit cake. Cutting, molding and modeling decorations.	White yields pastels to deep colors. Wilton pre-colored fondant is also available in Multi Packs for fondant decorations in a variety of colors.	Excess can be stored 2 months in an airtight container. Do not refrigerate or freeze. Iced cake stores at room temperature for 3-4 days.	Prior to applying fondant, cake should be lightly covered with a glaze or buttercream icing to seal in freshness and moisture.
Whipped Icing Mix (Wilton Mix)	Light, delicate vanilla flavor. Holds shape like no other mix. **For chocolate icing,** add ½ cup of sifted cocoa powder.	Velvety, perfect for stars, roses, borders, garlands and writing.	Icing cakes. Most decorations. Toppings on pies, puddings, tarts and more.	Yields any color.	Can be refrigerated in airtight container. Iced cake stores at room temperature for 2-3 days.	Exclusive Wilton formula. Available for purchase through Wilton Yearbook, at www.wilton.com or any authorized Wilton retailer.
Stabilized Whipped Cream (homemade)	Creamy, delicate sweetness.	Light, thin-to-medium.	All cakes but especially those decorated with fruits. Borders, large tip work, writing.	Yields pastels only.	Use immediately. Iced cake must be refrigerated.	Texture remains soft on decorated cake.

COLORING ICING

Mixing Colors

Begin with white icing and use concentrated Icing Colors (p. 146) which will not affect your icing consistency. (Using ordinary liquid food colors can thin your icing and affect your ability to pipe certain decorations.) If you are tinting icing dark brown or black, begin with chocolate icing—your icing will not have the aftertaste that large amounts of icing color can produce. If you are tinting a large area red, use No-Taste Red.

Dip a fresh toothpick into the color, then swirl it into the icing. Add color a little at a time until you achieve the shade you desire. Always use a new toothpick each time you add color; you want to avoid getting icing in your jar of color. Blend the icing well with a spatula.

Consider the type of icing you are using when mixing color. Icing colors intensify or darken in buttercream icing about 1-2 hours after mixing. Royal icing requires more color than buttercream icing to achieve the same color intensity.

Always mix enough of each icing color to complete your entire cake. For example, if you are going to decorate a cake with pink flowers and borders, color enough icing for both. It is difficult to duplicate an exact shade of any color, and you will want to keep your colors consistent on your cake.

Bag Striping Effects

You can easily pipe two-tone decorations just by adding a different color inside the bag before you put in your tinted icing. This is how you pipe flowers with natural light and dark tones or make a rainbow-colored clown suit to brighten up the party.

Brush Striping

Produces more intense multiple colors because it is done with straight icing color brushed into the bag. Apply one or more stripes of icing color with a decorating brush, then fill the bag with white or pastel-colored icing. As the icing is squeezed past the color, your decorations will come out striped.

Spatula Striping

Produces two-tone and realistic pastel tones for flowers and figure piping. It is done with pastel-colored icing, striped inside the decorating bag with a spatula. After striping, fill the bag with white icing or another shade of the same color as the striping. Squeeze out decorations with soft contrasts.

Brush Striping

Spatula Striping

FILLING THE DECORATING BAG

Hold bag with 1 hand and fold down the top with the other hand to form a generous cuff over your hand.

Fill bag with approximately ½ cup of icing. It is very important not to overfill the bag. Overfilling may result in icing squeezing out the top of the bag.

Squeeze bag with spatula between your thumb and finger while removing spatula.

Close bag by unfolding the cuff and twisting the bag closed. This forces the icing down into the bag.
Use an Icing Bag Tie to secure the bag and ensure that the icing does not squeeze out of the top of the bag.

Place the twisted part of the bag between your thumb and forefinger.
Close your hand around the bag so you can squeeze the icing in the bag between your palm and fingers.

Three Essentials of Cake Decorating

Every decoration you make is the result of three things working together: the consistency of your icing, the position of the bag (that is, the way you are holding it) and the amount and type of pressure you apply to the bag. You'll know when you have everything right because you'll get perfect results time after time. This will take practice. The more you concentrate on perfecting these three essentials, the sooner you will achieve perfect results.

ICING CONSISTENCY

If the consistency of your icing is not right, your decorations will not be right either. Just a few drops of liquid can make a great deal of difference in your decorating results. Many factors can affect icing consistency, such as humidity, temperature, ingredients and equipment. You may try using different icing consistencies when decorating to determine what works best for you. As a general guideline, if you are having trouble creating the decorations you want and you feel your icing is too thin, add a little more confectioners' sugar; if you feel your icing is too thick, add a little more liquid. In royal icing recipes, if adding more than ½ cup confectioners' sugar to thicken icing, also add 1-2 additional teaspoons of Meringue Powder (p. 143).

Stiff icing is used for figure piping and stringwork and for decorations like roses, carnations and sweet peas with upright petals. If icing is not stiff enough, flower petals will droop. If icing cracks when piped out, icing is probably too stiff. Add light corn syrup to icing used for stringwork to give strings greater elasticity so they will not break.

Medium icing is used for decorations such as stars, shell borders and flowers with flat petals. If the icing is too stiff or too thin, you will not get the uniformity that characterizes these decorations.

Thin icing is used for decorations such as printing and writing, vines and leaves. Leaves will be pointier, vines will not break and writing will flow easily if you add 1-2 teaspoons light corn syrup to each cup of icing. Thin icing is used to ice cakes smooth. Begin with your prepared icing recipe, then add small amounts of the same liquid used in the recipe (usually milk or water) until the proper spreading consistency is reached.

CORRECT BAG POSITION

The way your decorations curl, point and lie depends not only on icing consistency but also on the way you hold the bag and the way you move it. Bag positions are described in terms of both angle and direction.

Angle

Angle refers to the position of the bag relative to the work surface. There are two basic angle positions, 90° (straight up) and 45° (halfway between vertical and horizontal).

90° angle
or straight up, perpendicular to the surface.

45° angle
or halfway between vertical and horizontal.

Direction

The angle in relation to the work surface is only half the story on bag position. The other half is the direction in which the back of the bag is pointed.

Correct bag direction is easiest to learn when you think of the back of the bag as the hour hand of a clock. When you hold the bag at a

45° angle to the surface, you can sweep out a circle with the back end of the bag by rolling your wrist and holding the end of the tip in the same spot. Pretend the circle you formed in the air is a clock face. The hours on the clock face correspond to the direction you point the back end of the bag.

Back of bag at 6:00 **Back of bag at 3:00**

The technique instructions in this Decorating Guide will list the correct direction for holding the bag. When the bag direction differs for left-handed decorators, that direction will be listed in parentheses. For example, when a bag is to be held at 3:00 for a right-handed decorator, it should be held at 9:00 for a left-handed decorator.

One more thing…since most decorating tip openings are the same shape all the way around, there's no right side and wrong side up when you're squeezing icing out of them. However, some tips, such as petal, ruffle, basketweave and leaf have irregularly shaped openings. So you must watch your tip position as well as your bag position. If the tip opening must be in a special position, the instructions will tell you.

PRESSURE CONTROL

In addition to having the proper icing consistency and the correct bag position, you'll need to master three types of pressure control: heavy, medium and light. The size and uniformity of your icing designs are affected by the amount of icing pressure you apply to the bag and the steadiness of that pressure. (In other words, how you squeeze and relax your grip on the decorating bag.) Your goal is to learn to apply pressure so consistently that you can move the bag in a free and easy glide while just the right amount of icing flows through the tip. Practice will help you achieve this control.

Heavy Pressure **Medium Pressure** **Light Pressure**

Storing Cakes

Take some final precautions and store your cake the best way possible. After all, your time, effort and creativity have made it very special! Beware of the following factors, which can affect the look of your decorated cake.

Sunlight and fluorescent lighting will alter icing colors. Keep your cake stored in a covered box and out of direct sunlight and fluorescent lighting.

Humidity can soften royal icing, fondant and gum paste decorations. If you live in a climate with high humidity, prepare your royal icing using only pure cane confectioners' sugar (not beet sugar or dextrose), add less liquid and add 1 more teaspoon Meringue Powder (p. 145) to the recipe.

Heat can melt icing and cause decorations to droop. Keep your decorated cake as cool as possible and stabilize buttercream icing by adding 2 teaspoons Meringue Powder per recipe. Protect your cake by placing it in a clean, covered cake box. Avoid using foil or plastic wrap to cover a decorated cake—these materials can stick to icing and crush delicate decorations. The icing that covers your cake determines how it should be stored—in the refrigerator, at cool room temperature, or frozen, if storing for longer than 3 days. If you want to store your iced cake in a different way than noted, make a small test cake.

Icing type determines care. See chart on p. 111 for storage information.

NOTE: Cakes with thoroughly-dried royal icing decorations should be stored according to the type of icing that covers the cake. However, if royal icing decorations are to be put on a cake that will be frozen, it is recommended that these decorations be placed on the cake after thawing so that they don't bleed from condensation or become soft.

Transporting Tiered Cakes

Moving a tiered cake from one location to another does not have to be difficult. It can be quite easy! Following some simple guidelines ensures that your cake will arrive safely—whether you are traveling hundreds of miles or just a few.

Before Moving Cakes

Be certain the cake is constructed on a sturdy base made of three or more thicknesses of corrugated cardboard. Base tiers of very heavy cakes should be placed on a foamcore or plywood base, ½ in. thick. Cakes on pillars must be transported unassembled. Toppers, candles and ornaments should be removed from cakes when they are being moved. For stacked tiers, move the entire assembled cake. Or, for a larger quantity of tiers, transport unassembled and assemble at the reception. Be sure to have with you the equipment and icings you will need to finish any decorating needed after assembly at the reception.

For a cake which combines stacked and 2-plate construction, take tiers apart, keeping stacked tiers as units. Boxing the cake makes transportation easier. Not only does it protect the tiers from damage, but it keeps the tiers clean—free from dirt, dust and bugs. Place the boxes on carpet foam or a non-skid mat on a level surface in the vehicle to prevent shifting. Keep the boxes flat; never place on a car seat. Boxed cakes can also be transported in the trunk of the car, except in hot weather, because air conditioning will not reach the trunk area. It's also important to find out about the reception location before the event. Knowing what to expect when you arrive can make your delivery and setup so much easier. Call the reception hall a few days before the event to get an idea of the conditions you will encounter there. Ask whether the room is located upstairs or downstairs. Find out what is the best location for bringing the cake into the building. That way you can park in the right place the first time and minimize the distance your cake has to travel from your car. Also ask how far in advance the cake can be set up so that you can plan your day and reduce the stress.

At Your Destination

Before you bring in the cake from your car, walk the path you will have to travel to the set-up site. Be alert for any bumps along the way and note any tight spaces you will have to maneuver around. Make sure the cake table is level—it's a good idea to bring a level to check this on setup day. Request a cart on wheels to move the cake into the reception area. This is easier and safer than carrying by hand. Remove the cakes from the boxes on the reception table by cutting the sides of the boxes and sliding the cakes out. Bring along a repair kit, including extra icing, prepared decorating bags and tips, flowers and spatulas, just in case it is necessary to make any repairs. Once the cake is assembled, take a picture to establish that the cake was in perfect condition when you left it.

In Pan

Take tiers apart if constructed in Center Column or Push-In Leg method. Leave columns or legs in place. Position the plates on crumpled foil or in shallow pans if they do not sit level. Remove pillars from tier plates; plates stay in position.

In Box

Place the cakes in clean, covered, sturdy boxes that are sized to the base board of each cake. This prevents shifting within the box and possibly crushing the sides of the cake. If the box is too big, roll pieces of masking tape sticky side out and attach to the inside bottom of the box. Position the cake base on top of the tape, securing the base in the box. For taller decorations, prop up box top and sides, secure with masking tape.

On Non-Skid Foam

If tiers cannot be boxed, they can be transported on large pieces of non-skid foam. Place the foam on the floor of the vehicle, then carefully place the tiers centered on each piece of foam. Remove any ornament or fragile decorations before transporting.

Cake Baking and Serving Guides

The charts below are based on baking recommendations from the Wilton Test Kitchen; your results may vary depending on oven performance or altitude in your area. For large cakes, always check for doneness after they have baked for 1 hour.

Serving amounts are based on party-sized portions of 1.5 x 2 in. or smaller wedding-sized portions of approximately 1 x 2 in. Cakes from 3 to 6 in. high, baked in the same size pan, would yield the same number of servings because they follow the same pattern of cutting. Cakes shorter than 3 in. would yield half the number of servings indicated for that pan. Number of servings are intended as a guide only.

Icing amounts are very general and will vary with consistency, thickness applied and tips used. Icing amounts allow for top and bottom borders.

4 IN. HIGH CAKES (using 2 in. high pans)

The figures for 2 in. pans are based on a 2-layer, 4 in. high cake. Fill pans ½ to ⅔ full.

PAN SHAPE	SIZE	NUMBER SERVINGS PARTY	NUMBER SERVINGS WEDDING	CUPS BATTER 1 LAYER, 2 IN.	BAKING TEMP. (F.)	BAKING TIME MINUTES	APPROX. CUPS ICING TO ICE AND DECORATE
Round	6 in.	12	12	2	350°	25-30	3
	8 in.	20	24	3½	350°	30-35	4
	9 in.	24	32	5½	350°	30-35	4½
	10 in.	28	38	6	350°	35-40	5
	12 in.	40	56	7½	350°	35-40	6
	14 in.	63	78	10	325°	50-55	7½
	16 in.	77	100	15	325°	55-60	9
Square	6 in.	12	18	2	350°	25-30	3½
	8 in.	20	32	4	350°	35-40	4½
	10 in.	30	50	6	350°	35-40	6
	12 in.	48	72	10	350°	40-45	7½
	14 in.	63	98	13½	325°	45-50	9½
	16 in.	80	128	15½	325°	50-55	11
Heart	6 in.	8	14	1½	350°	25-30	3½
	8 in.	18	22	3½	350°	30-35	4½
	9 in.	20	28	4	350°	30-35	6
	10 in.	24	38	5	350°	30-35	8½
	12 in.	34	56	8	325°	45-50	9
	14 in.	48	72	10	325°	45-50	10
	15 in.	50	74	11	325°	40-45	11
	16 in.	64	94	12½	325°	40-45	12
Petal	6 in.	6	8	1½	350°	25-30	4
	9 in.	14	18	3½	350°	35-40	6
	12 in.	38	40	7	350°	35-40	9
	15 in.	48	64	12	325°	50-55	11
Hexagon	6 in.	10	12	1¾	350°	30-35	3
	9 in.	20	26	3½	350°	35-40	5
	12 in.	34	40	6	350°	40-45	6
	15 in.	48	70	11	325°	40-45	9
Oval	7.75 x 5.5 in.	9	13	2½	350°	25-30	3
	10.75 x 7.8 in.	20	26	5	350°	25-30	4
	13.5 x 9.8 in.	30	45	8	350°	35-40	5½
	16.5 x 12.4 in.	44	70	11	325°	40-45	7½
Sheet	7 x 11 in.	24	32	5½	350°	30-35	5
	9 x 13 in.	36	50	7	350°	35-40	6
	11 x 15 in.	54	74	11	325°	35-40	8
	12 x 18 in.	72	98	14	325°	45-50	10
Paisley	9 x 6 in.	9	13	3	350°	35-40	5
	12.75 x 9 in.	28	38	7	350°	45-50	6
	17 x 12 in.	40	56	10½	325°	55-60	8
Diamond	10.25 x 7.4 in.	12	18	3¼	350°	20-25	2½
	15 x 11	20	32	7¼	350°	40-45	5
	19.25 x 14.25	42	66	13¼	350°	65-70	8
Pillow	6.75 x 6.75 in.	13	19	5	350°	33-38	3
	10 x 10 in.	30	40	11	350°	34-39	6½
	13.25 x 13.25 in.	64	88	19	350°	42-47	9½

3 IN. HIGH CAKES (using 3 in. high pans)

The figures for 3 in. pans are based on a 1-layer cake which is torted and filled to reach 3 in. high; fill pans ½ full.

PAN SHAPE	SIZE	NUMBER SERVINGS PARTY	NUMBER SERVINGS WEDDING	CUPS BATTER 1 LAYER, 2 IN.	BAKING TEMP.	BAKING TIME MINUTES	APPROX. CUPS ICING TO ICE AND DECORATE
Round	6 in.	12	12	3	350°	35-40	3
	8 in.	20	24	5	350°	55-60	4
	10 in.	28	38	8	325°	65-75	5
	12 in.	40	56	10½	325°	60-65	6
	14 in.	63	78	15	325°	75-85	8
	16 in.	77	100	18	325°	75-85	9
	18 in. Half, 2 layer	110*	146*	9**	325°	60-65	10½
	18 in. Half, 3 layer	110*	146*	12**	325°	60-65	10½
Sheet	9 x 13 in.	36	50	11½	325°	70-75	5
	11 x 15 in.	54	74	16	325°	80-85	6½
	12 x 18 in.	72	98	20	325°	85-90	8
Square	8 in.	20	32	6½	350°	60-65	4½
	10 in.	30	50	9	325°	65-75	6
	12 in.	48	72	14	325°	65-75	7½
	14 in.	63	98	19	325°	65-75	9½
Contour	7 in.	6	11	3½	350°	45-50	2
	9 in.	11	17	5½	350°	45-50	2½
	11 in.	16	24	8	325°	80-85	3
	13 in.	22	39	13	325°	75-80	4
	15 in.	32	48	16	325°	75-80	5

For pans 10 in. and larger, we recommend using a heating core (p. 158) to insure even baking. Use 2 cores for 18-in. pans.

*Two half rounds.   **For each half round pan.

For additional pan information, check out www.wilton.com

General Cake Cutting Guides

The diagrams below will give you a general plan for cutting the most popular cake shapes. They will help you serve more attractive, uniform pieces while reaching your targeted number of servings. Diagrams show only one size in each shape; you will use the same general technique to cut each size cake in that shape.

WEDDING CAKES—1 x 2 in. slices

The diagrams show how to cut popular shaped wedding tiers into slices approximately 1 x 2 in. and 2 layers high (about 4 in.) For cakes shorter than 3 in. you will need to cut wider slices to serve a proper portion; even if a larger serving size is desired, the order of cutting is still the same. Before cutting the cake, remove the top tier, which is usually saved for the first anniversary and is not included in our serving amounts for wedding cakes in this book. Begin by cutting the 2nd tier, followed by the 3rd, 4th and so on.

Square Tiers:
Move in 2 in. from the outer edge and cut vertically, top to bottom. Slice and serve 1 in. pieces of cake. Now move in another 2 in. and repeat process until the entire tier is cut.

12 in.

Round Tiers:
Move in 2 in. from the tier's outer edge and cut a circle. Slice and serve 1 in. pieces from around the circle. Now move in another 2 in. and cut another circle. Repeat process until the tier is completely cut. The center core of each tier and the small top tier can be cut into 4ths, 6ths, or more, depending on size.

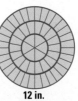

12 in.

Paisley Tiers:
Move in 2 in. from the outer edge and cut across. Slice and serve 1 in. pieces of cake, similar to oval tiers as diagram shows. Now move in another 2 in., repeat process until the entire tier is cut.

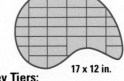

17 x 12 in.

Diamond Tiers:
Move in 2 in. from any outer edge and cut across. Slice and serve 1 in. pieces of cake. Now move in another 2 in. and repeat process until the entire tier is cut.

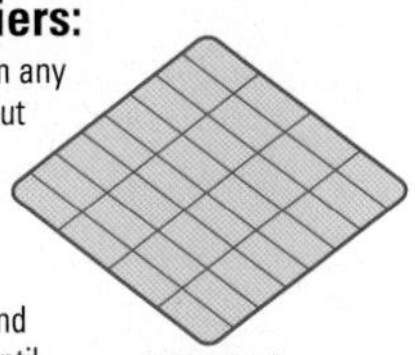

15 x 11 in.

Heart Tiers:
Divide the tiers vertically into 2 in. wide rows. Within rows, slice and serve 1 in. pieces of cake.

12 in.

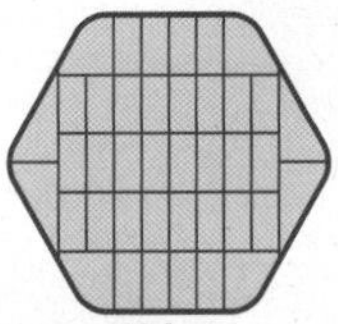

12 in.

Hexagon Tiers:
Move in 2 in. from the outer edge and cut across. Slice and serve 1 in. pieces of cake. Now move in another 2 in., repeat process until the entire tier is cut.

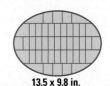

13.5 x 9.8 in.

Oval Tiers:
Move in 2 in. from the outer edge and cut across. Slice and serve 1 in. pieces of cake. Now move in another 2 in., repeat process until the entire tier is cut.

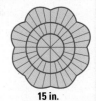

Petal Tiers:
Cut similar to round tiers as diagram shows.

15 in.

Pillow Tiers:
Cut similar to square tiers as diagram shows.

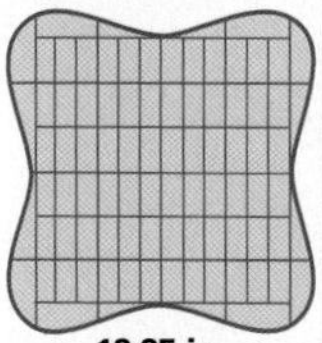

13.25 in.

PARTY CAKES— 1.5 x 2 in. slices

Follow the diagrams above to cut party cakes (from 3 to 6 in. high), but adjust for the larger party-size slices. For cakes shorter than 3 in. you will need to cut wider slices to serve a proper portion; even if a larger serving size is desired the order of cutting is still the same.

Rounds:
To cut round cakes, move in 2 in. from the cake's outer edge; cut a circle and then slice approximately 1.5 in. pieces within the circle. Now move in another 2 in. and cut another circle; slice approximately 1.5 in. pieces. Continue until the cake is completely cut. Note: 6 in. diameter cakes should be cut in wedges, without a center circle. Cut petal and hexagon cakes similar to round cakes.

Squares:
To cut square cakes, move in 2 in. from the outer edge and cut top to bottom, then slice approximately 1.5 in. pieces. Now move in another 2 in. and continue until the entire cake is cut.

Sheets:
Cut sheet cakes similar to square cakes.

Tiered Cake Construction

There are many methods of constructing tiered cakes. Here are some used in this book. Visit www.wilton.com for more construction methods.

TO PREPARE CAKE FOR ASSEMBLY

Place base tier on a sturdy base plate of 3 or more thicknesses of corrugated cardboard. For heavy cakes, use foamcore or plywood ½ in. thick. Base can be covered with Fanci-Foil Wrap and trimmed with Tuk-'N-Ruffle or use Ruffle Boards (p. 241). Each tier of your cake must be on a cake circle or board cut to fit. Place a few strokes of icing on boards to secure cake. Fill and ice layers before assembly.

Adding Dowel Rods to Tiered Cakes

Use the upper tier for size reference when determining dowel rod placement. All the dowel rods must be placed within the area you will mark (see steps below) to provide adequate support.

1. Center a cake board the same size as the tier above it on base tier and press it gently into icing to imprint an outline. Remove. Use this outline to guide the insertion of the dowel rods.

2. Insert one dowel rod into cake straight down to the cake board. Make a knife scratch on the rod to mark the exact height. Pull dowel rod out.

3. Cut the suggested number of rods (see note below) the exact same length, using the mark on the first one as a guide.

4. Insert rods into tier, spacing evenly 1½ inches in from the imprinted outline. Push straight down until each touches the cake board. Repeat this procedure for every stacked or pillared tier on the cake.

NOTE: The larger and more numerous the tiers, the more dowels needed. If the tier above is 10 in. or less, use six ¼ in. wooden dowels. Use 8 dowel rods for 16 in. and 18 in. cakes; on these larger tiers, use ½ in. plastic dowel rods in the base tier. When using white plastic dowel rods that are wider and provide more support, the number needed may be less.

Stacked Construction

Stacking is the most architectural method of tiered cake construction. Tiers are placed directly on top of one another and pillars are not used. Cakes are supported and stabilized by dowel rods and cake boards.

1. Dowel rod all tiers except top tier.

2. Position the middle tier on the base tier, centering exactly.*

3. Repeat with the top tier.

4. To stabilize tiers further, sharpen one end of a long dowel rod and push it through all tiers and cake boards to the base of the bottom tier. To decorate, start at the top and work down.

*Finely shredded coconut or confectioners' sugar, placed in area where cake circles or plastic plates will rest, helps prevent icing on the cake from sticking.

Separator Plate (2-Plate) and Pillar Construction

This most dramatic method features 2, 3 or more single cakes towered together. Use separator plates and pillars (p. 237). Check pillars and plates for correct fit before constructing your cake.

1. Set cake tiers on separator plates 2 in. larger in diameter than cakes.

2. Dowel rod cakes and position separator plates on tiers with feet up. (Note: Connect only same size separator plates with pillars.)

3. Position pillars over feet on separator plates.

4. Carefully set cake plate on pillars. Continue adding tiers this way.**

**Assemble cakes when you arrive at the reception or party.

Push-In Pillar Construction

Simple assembly—no dowel rods needed! Use any type of Wilton push-in pillars and plates (p. 237). Check pillars and plates for correct fit before constructing your cake.

1. Mark tier for push-in pillar placement. Use the separator plate for the next tier above, gently pressing it onto the tier, feet down, making sure it is centered. Lift plate away. The feet will leave marks on the icing to guide the position of pillars when you assemble the tier. Repeat this process for each tier, working from largest to smallest tier. The top tier is left unmarked.

2. Place each tier on its separator plate, securing with icing.

3. Position push-in pillars at marks, and insert into tiers. Push straight down until pillars touch the cake plate.

4. To assemble, start with the tier above the base tier. Place the feet of the separator plate on the pillar openings. Continue adding tiers in the same way until the cake is completely assembled.**

Center Column Construction (Tall Tier Stand) (p. 239)

1. Use boards the same size as tiers, or if tiers are shaped, cut boards to fit. Make a waxed paper pattern for each tier except the top tier in order to find the exact center for the columns. Fold the pattern in quarters. Snip the point to make a center hole. Test the hole for size by slipping it over a column, adjust size if necessary. Trace hole pattern on prepared cake board and cut out. Also cut a hole in the top tier board to allow for the column cap nut. Save patterns for marking cake tops later.

2. The base tier of the cake will rest on a 14, 16 or 18 in. plate. (18 in. plate is footed. Do not use a bottom plate smaller than 14 in.) To add legs to bottom plate, turn it upside down; using extra-strength glue designed for plastic, attach the six legs, positioning the legs over each of the ribs on the plate.

3. Prepare and ice tiers and position on prepared cake boards. Make the center holes for the columns in all tiers except the top tier. Mark the top of the cakes with corresponding waxed paper pattern. Cut the hole by pressing a Hidden Pillar (p. 237) through the tier right down to the bottom. Hold the pillar upright, remove pillar and push the cake out of center pillar.

4. Screw in a column to the prepared base plate and bottom column bolt from underneath the plate. Slip the next size tier on its plate over the column.

5. Add a second column and position the next size tier on its plate, slipping it over the column. Finally, add on the top plate only, securing the top column nut. Place the top tier on the plate and decorate bottom border.**

Globe Pillar Set Construction

These elegant pearl-look globes (p. 238) are available in separate sets of four 2 in., 2½ in. or 3 in. globes. The 3 in. globes are to be used to support the base cake only. They have a reinforced center channel which eliminates the need for pillars. The 2 and 2½ in. sets should be used with 9 in. "Hidden" Pillars (included in set); do not use these sets to support the base cake. Your cake design may use a base board instead of the 3 in. globes to support the base cake as shown below.

1. Position separator plate holding base cake on 3 in. Globe Base Set or a thick base board. Using the separator plate which will hold the cake above, mark base cake for pillar placement (see Push-In Pillar construction, p. 114). Lift plate away.

2. Insert pillars through cake centered over marked area to rest on its separator plate or base board. Place the correct size globe (2½ in. for cake shown here) over the pillars. Mark pillars where they extend above globes. The cut pillars should be equal to the height of the base cake plus the height of each globe.

3. Trim pillars at markings with craft knife or serrated edge knife.

4. Insert pillars in base cake. Position globes over pillars.

5. Position the tier above on globes.

6. Add additional sets for more tiers.

Tailored Tiers Construction

Our Tailored Tiers Cake Display Set (p. 238) features fabric-wrapped separators which add great texture to your tiered design. The top 2 tiers are decorated on same-size boards, then transported to the reception on larger boards, so that cakes can be easily transferred to the separator plates during assembly. Bottom borders are then added to these tiers. The recommended display for Tailored Tiers separators includes a 14 in. base cake, a 10 in. center cake and a 6 in. top cake.

1. Ice cakes; place 14 in. base cake on 16 in. base board wrapped in foil or 16 in. Silver Cake Base (p. 241). Place 10 in. center and 6 in. top cakes on same size boards. Mark 14 in. and 10 in. cakes for placement of dowel rods. Center the 8 in. plate from the Tailored Tiers set on top of the 14 in. cake and press it gently into icing to imprint an outline. Remove. Use this outline to guide the insertion of dowel rods.

2. Dowel rod 14 in. cake (see page 114). Place the 6 in. plate from set on top of the 10 in. cake and repeat process for marking and inserting dowel rods. Complete decorating on cakes, except bottom borders of 10 in. center and 6 in. top cakes, which will be done at reception. Attach 10 in. and 6 in. cakes to larger boards before transferring to reception.

3. Place the 12 in. plate (spikes up) on table. Center the large (7¼ in.) separator over the plate and press down over the spikes. Position one 8 in. plate (spikes down) on top of the large separator. Place the second 8 in. plate (spikes up) on table. Center the small (4¼ in.) separator over the plate and press down over the spikes. Position the 6 in. plate (spikes down) on top of the small separator.

4. At reception: Position the large separator, with 8 in. plate on bottom and 12 in. plate on top, on the base cake. Remove 10 in. and 6 in. cakes from their larger boards. Position 10 in. cake on large separator.

5. Add bottom border to 10 in. cake. Position the small separator, with 6 in. plate on bottom and 8 in. plate on top, on the 10 in. cake. Position 6 in. cake on small separator. Add bottom border.

To Use Acetate Wrap for Tailored Tiers

1. Insert photos, patterned paper or fabric in pockets of acetate wrap. Trim inserted items as needed to fit.
2. Wrap acetate around separator and fasten hook and loop ends.

Alternate 2-Plate Set-Ups

The Fluted Bowl and Spiral Separator Sets shown below are assembled similar to 2-Plate and Pillar Construction (p. 114)—the separators provide support instead of pillars; each set includes 2 separator plates. Cakes must still use dowel rods to support cakes and secure the separators.

Fluted Bowl Separator Set (p. 238)

Spiral Separator Set (p. 238)

Dowel rod base cake as for 2-Plate & Pillar Construction. Position smaller plate from set on base cake (spikes up). Position Fluted Bowl or Spiral Separator over spikes. Position next tier on larger plate from set. Position plate (spikes down) on separator.

Recipes

The cakes, cookies and other desserts in this Yearbook were made using our favorite kitchen-tested recipes. Follow these instructions for decorated desserts that look and taste their best!

ICING RECIPES

Buttercream Icing (Medium consistency)*

½ cup solid vegetable shortening
½ cup (1 stick) butter or margarine, softened
1 teaspoon Clear Vanilla Extract**
4 cups sifted confectioners' sugar (about 1 lb.)
2 tablespoons milk

In large bowl, cream shortening and butter with electric mixer. Add vanilla. Gradually add sugar, one cup at a time, beating well on medium speed. Scrape sides and bottom of bowl often. When all sugar has been mixed in, icing will appear dry. Add milk and beat at medium speed until light and fluffy. Keep bowl covered with a damp cloth until ready to use. For best results, keep icing bowl in refrigerator when not in use. Refrigerated in an airtight container, this icing can be stored 2 weeks. Rewhip before using. Makes about 3 cups.

For thin (spreading) consistency icing, add 2 tablespoons light corn syrup, water or milk.

For Pure White Icing (stiff consistency), omit butter; substitute an additional ½ cup vegetable shortening for butter and ½ teaspoon No-Color Butter Flavor (p. 145). Add up to 4 tablespoons light corn syrup, water or milk to thin for icing cakes.

Chocolate Buttercream Icing

Add ¾ cup cocoa powder (or three 1 oz. squares unsweetened chocolate, melted) and an additional 1-2 tablespoons milk to buttercream icing. Mix until well blended.

Chocolate Mocha Icing: Substitute brewed strong coffee for milk in Chocolate Buttercream recipe.

Darker Chocolate Icing: Add an additional ¼ cup cocoa powder (or 1 additional 1 oz. square unsweetened chocolate, melted) and 1 additional tablespoon milk to Chocolate Buttercream Icing.

Snow-White Buttercream Icing (Stiff consistency)*

⅔ cup plus 3 tablespoons water, divided
¼ cup Meringue Powder**
12 cups sifted confectioners' sugar (about 3 lbs.), divided
1¼ cups solid vegetable shortening
3 tablespoons light corn syrup
¾ teaspoon salt
¾ teaspoon No-Color Almond Extract**
¾ teaspoon Clear Vanilla Extract**
½ teaspoon No-Color Butter Flavor**

In large bowl, combine ⅔ cup water and meringue powder; whip with electric mixer at high speed until peaks form. Add 4 cups sugar, one cup at a time, beating at low speed after each addition. Add remaining 8 cups sugar and 3 tablespoons water, shortening and corn syrup in 3 additions, blending well after each. Add salt and flavorings; beat at low speed until smooth. Makes about 7 cups.

For thin (spreading) consistency icing, add up to 4 more tablespoons each water and corn syrup.

NOTE: Recipe may be doubled or halved.

Royal Icing

3 tablespoons Meringue Powder**
4 cups sifted confectioners' sugar (about 1 lb.)
6 tablespoons water [1]

Beat all ingredients at low speed for 7-10 minutes (10-12 minutes at high speed for portable mixer) until icing forms peaks. Makes about 3 cups.

[1] When using large countertop mixer or for stiffer icing, use 1 tablespoon less water.

*Changes in Wilton's traditional recipes have been made due to Trans Fat Free Shortening replacing Hydrogenated Shortening.
** p. 143

Thinned Royal Icing: To thin for pouring, add 1 teaspoon water per cup of royal icing. Use grease-free spoon or spatula to stir slowly. Add ½ teaspoon water at a time until you reach proper consistency.

Stabilized Whipped Cream Icing

½ pint (1 cup) heavy whipping cream
2 tablespoons confectioners' sugar
2 tablespoons Piping Gel**
½ teaspoon Clear Vanilla Extract**

In large bowl, combine whipping cream and sugar with electric mixer, whip to soft peak stage. Add Piping Gel and vanilla, then continue to whip until stiff peaks form. Do not overbeat. Makes 1½ to 2 cups.

As an alternative, you can use frozen non-dairy whipped topping or packaged topping mix. Thaw frozen whipped topping in refrigerator before coloring or using for decorating. Use packaged topping mix immediately after preparing. Do not allow either to stay at room temperature, as they become too soft for decorating. Store decorated cake in refrigerator until ready to serve.

Heated Wilton Ready-To-Use Decorator Icing**

Open icing container, remove foil. Microwave at 30% (Defrost) Power for 20-30 seconds, stirring at least once, until ready to pour. If a microwave is unavailable, icing container can be heated on a warming tray or in a pan of hot water on a stove.

Color Flow Icing Recipe (full-strength for outlining)

¼ cup + 1 teaspoon water
4 cups sifted confectioners' sugar (about 1 lb.)
2 tablespoons Color Flow Mix**

With electric mixer, using grease-free utensils, blend all ingredients on low speed for 5 minutes. If using hand mixer, use high speed. Color Flow icing "crusts" quickly, so keep bowl covered with a damp cloth while using. Stir in desired icing color. Makes about 2 cups.

Thinned Color Flow: To fill in an outlined area, the recipe above must be thinned with ½ teaspoon of water per ¼ cup of icing (just a few drops at a time as you near proper consistency). Use grease-free spoon or spatula to stir slowly. Color Flow is ready for filling in outlines when a small amount dropped into the mixture takes a count of ten to disappear.

NOTE: Color Flow designs take a long time to dry, so plan to do your Color Flow piece at least 2 or 3 days in advance.

Poured Cookie Icing

This icing dries to a shiny, hard finish. Great to use as icing or to outline and fill in with tip 2 or 3.

1 cup sifted confectioners' sugar
2 teaspoons milk
2 teaspoons light corn syrup

Place sugar and milk in bowl. Stir until thoroughly mixed. Add corn syrup; mix well. For filling in areas, use thinned icing (add small amounts of light corn syrup until desired consistency is reached). Makes about ½ cup.

COOKIE RECIPES

Roll-Out Cookies

1 cup (2 sticks) unsalted butter, softened
1½ cups granulated sugar
1 egg
1½ teaspoons Clear Vanilla Extract**
½ teaspoon No-Color Almond Extract**
2¾ cups all-purpose flour
2 teaspoons baking powder
1 teaspoon salt

Preheat oven to 400°F. In large bowl, beat butter and sugar with electric mixer until light and fluffy. Add egg and extracts; mix well. Combine flour, baking powder and salt; add to butter mixture 1 cup at a time, mixing after each addition. Do not chill dough. Divide dough into 2 balls. On a floured surface, roll each ball into a circle approximately 12 in. wide and ⅛ in. thick. Dip cookie cutter in flour before each use. Bake cookies on ungreased cookie sheet 6-7 minutes or until cookies are lightly browned.

Makes about 3 dozen cookies. Recipe may be doubled.

Spritz Cookies

1½ cups (3 sticks) butter, softened
1 cup granulated sugar
1 egg
2 tablespoons milk
1 teaspoon Clear Vanilla Extract**
½ teaspoon No-Color Almond Extract**
3½ cups all-purpose flour
1 teaspoon baking powder

Preheat oven to 350°F. In large bowl, beat butter and sugar with electric mixer until light and fluffy. Add egg, milk, extracts; mix well. Combine flour and baking powder; gradually add to butter mixture, mixing to make a smooth dough. Do not chill. Place dough into cookie press and press cookies onto ungreased cookie sheet.

Bake 10-12 minutes or until lightly browned around edges. Remove cookies from cookie sheet; cool on cooling grid. Makes 7-8 dozen cookies.

Grandma's Gingerbread

5 to 5½ cups all-purpose flour
1 teaspoon baking soda
1 teaspoon salt
2 teaspoons ground ginger
2 teaspoons ground cinnamon
1 teaspoon ground nutmeg
1 teaspoon ground cloves
1 cup solid vegetable shortening
1 cup granulated sugar
1¼ cups unsulphured molasses[2]
2 eggs, beaten

Preheat oven to 375°F. Thoroughly mix flour, baking soda, salt and spices. Melt shortening in large saucepan. Cool slightly. Add sugar, molasses and eggs to saucepan; mix well. Add 4 cups dry ingredients and mix well.

Turn mixture onto lightly floured surface. Knead in remaining dry ingredients by hand. Add a little more flour, if necessary, to make firm dough.

On floured surface, roll out ⅛ to ¼ in. thick for cut-out cookies. Bake on ungreased cookie sheet; small and medium-sized cookies for 6-10 minutes, large cookies for 10-15 minutes. Makes 40 medium-sized cookies.

NOTE: If you're not going to use your gingerbread dough right away, wrap in plastic and refrigerate. Refrigerated dough will keep for a week.

[2] Substitute 1¼ cups light corn syrup for molasses to make Blonde Gingerbread.

SPECIALTY RECIPES

Orange Cheesecake

Crust:

1¾ cups graham cracker crumbs
¼ cup + 2 tablespoons granulated sugar
4 tablespoons (½ stick) butter, melted

Cut Cake Board to fit over inside bottom of springform pan. Wrap outside of pan with foil to waterproof. Grease inside sides of pan. Mix crust ingredients. Press firmly into pan for bottom crust.

Cheesecake:

1¾ lbs. cream cheese, room temperature
⅔ cup granulated sugar
4 eggs
1 package (14 oz.) White Candy Melts, coarsely chopped
1 teaspoon Clear Vanilla Extract**
½ teaspoon orange candy flavoring
2-3 teaspoons orange zest (optional)
1⅓ cups heavy whipping cream

Preheat oven to 300°F. In large bowl, place cream cheese and sugar. With electric mixer, cream mixture until smooth. Add eggs, 1 at a time, and mix. Melt candy following package directions. Cool 7-10 minutes (candy should still be liquid). Add cooled candy, vanilla, orange flavoring, orange zest and whipping cream to cream cheese mixture. Blend well. Pour into prepared pan. Place prepared pan into larger ovenproof pan (there should be at least 1 in. clearance on all sides). Add hot water to outer pan to ½ in. deep. Place pans in center of oven for about 1¾ to 2 hours. To test for doneness, gently shake pan. Top of cake should move as one solid piece with no soupy movement in the center. (Cake will set completely when refrigerated.) Remove from oven and bring to room temperature. Cover and refrigerate overnight. To unmold, run a metal spatula around edge of pan. Release spring and remove outer ring. Smooth sides of cheesecake with wet spatula. Refrigerate for up to 1 week.

Shortbread Cookies

1½ cups (3 sticks) butter, softened
1 cup granulated sugar
½ teaspoon salt
6 egg yolks
2 teaspoons Pure Vanilla Extract**
4 cups all-purpose flour

In large bowl, beat butter, sugar and salt with electric mixer until light and fluffy. Add egg yolks one at a time, mixing well after each addition. Add vanilla. Add flour: mix just until combined. (**Note:** Dough can be tinted with Wilton Icing Color. Add small amounts until desired color is reached.) Divide dough in half. Press dough to flatten; wrap with plastic wrap. Refrigerate at least 2 hours or overnight. Preheat oven to 375°F. Work with one dough disk at a time. Let chilled dough stand at room temperature for 10 minutes. Lightly flour work surface and roll dough ⅛ to ¼ in. thick. Depress imprint disk into flour, then cut and imprint cookies. Gather scraps and roll dough again to make more cookies. For best results, depress disk into flour after each use. Carefully transfer cookies to an ungreased cookie sheet, leaving 1 in. between cookies. Bake 14-16 minutes or until edges are lightly browned. Remove cookies from cookie sheet and cool completely on cooling grid.

Makes about 2 dozen cookies.

Sugar Cookies (for pan-shaped cookies)

1 cup (2 sticks) butter, softened
1½ cups granulated sugar
1 egg
1½ teaspoons Vanilla Extract**
½ teaspoon Almond Extract (optional)**
2¾ cups all-purpose flour
1 teaspoon salt

Preheat oven to 350°F. Lightly spray pan or mold cavities with vegetable pan spray. In large bowl, beat butter and sugar with electric mixer at medium speed until well blended. Beat in egg and extracts; mix well. Combine flour and salt; add to butter mixture. Beat until well blended. Press dough into prepared mold or pan, filling to ¼ in. deep. Bake 12-15 minutes or until light brown around edges. Cool in pan 10 minutes. Carefully remove cookies. Cool completely on cooling grid. Makes about 3 dozen cookies.

CANDY RECIPES

Basic Ganache and Truffles

1 package (14 oz.) Candy Melts (p. 194)
½ cup heavy whipping cream

Chop candy (you can use a food processor). Heat whipping cream in saucepan just to boiling point. Do not boil. Remove from heat and add chopped candy, stir until smooth and glossy.

Whipped Ganache: Follow recipe above, using 1 cup whipping cream. Allow mixture to set and cool to room temperature (mixture will have the consistency of pudding; this may take 1-2 hours). Whip on high speed with an electric mixer until light and soft peaks form.

Truffles: Add 1 tablespoon liqueur for flavor, if desired. Stir until smooth and creamy. Refrigerate until firm. Roll into 1 in. diameter balls. Can be used as center for dipped candies, served plain or rolled in nuts, coconut or cocoa powder. Store truffles in refrigerator up to 3 weeks. Makes about 2 dozen (1 in.) balls.

Ganache Glaze: If mixture is too thick, add 1 to 2 tablespoons whipping cream. Position cake on wire rack over drip pan. Pour glaze onto center and work out toward edges.

NOTE: Cake may be iced first in buttercream. Let icing set, then pour on ganache glaze. If cake has a perfect surface, no other icing is needed.

Candy "Clay"

1 package (14 oz.) Candy Melts (p. 194)
⅓ cup light corn syrup

Melt candy following package directions. Add corn syrup and stir to blend. Turn out mixture onto waxed paper and let set at room temperature to dry. Wrap well and store at room temperature until needed. Candy clay handles best if hardened overnight.

To Use: Candy clay will be very hard at the start; knead a small portion at a time until workable. If candy clay gets too soft, set aside at room temperature or refrigerate briefly. When rolling out candy clay, sprinkle work surface with cornstarch or cocoa (for cocoa clay) to prevent sticking; roll to approximately ⅛ in. thick.

To Tint: White candy clay may be tinted using Candy Color or Icing Color. Knead in color until well blended.

To Store: Prepared candy clay will last for several weeks at room temperature in an airtight container.

Wilton Fudge

2 packages (14 oz. ea.) Wilton Candy Melts (White, Light or Dark Cocoa)
1 can (14 oz.) sweetened condensed milk (not evaporated milk)
1 cup chopped nuts (optional)
1½ teaspoons Wilton Clear Vanilla** (optional)

In heavy saucepan over low heat, melt Candy Melts in condensed milk, stirring until smooth. Remove from heat. Stir in nuts and vanilla, if desired. Spread evenly into 8- or 10-inch square pan lined with parchment paper and sprayed with vegetable pan spray. Chill 2 hours or until firm. Lift parchment paper to remove fudge from pan. Cut into squares or shapes as desired. Store in airtight container at room temperature. Make approximately 2 lbs.

To microwave, use High power to heat Candy Melts and sweetened condensed milk in 2-quart glass bowl for 2½ to 3½ minutes; remove bowl and stir until smooth. (Note: Since microwaves vary, cooking time may need to be adjusted.)

ROLLED FONDANT AND GUM PASTE RECIPES

Fondant is rolled out and used as a covering for any firm-textured cake, pound cake or fruit cake, which is traditionally first covered with a layer of marzipan to seal in flavor and moistness of the cake. A light layer of buttercream icing or apricot glaze may also be used. Cakes covered with rolled fondant can be decorated with royal or buttercream icing. Wilton also offers convenient Ready-To-Use Rolled Fondant (p. 147) for easy-to-handle fondant with no mixing.

Rolled Fondant

1 tablespoon plus 2 teaspoons
  unflavored gelatin
¼ cup cold water
½ cup Glucose (p. 147)
2 tablespoons solid vegetable shortening
1 tablespoon Glycerin (p. 147)
Icing color and flavoring, as desired
8 cups sifted confectioners' sugar
  (about 2 lbs.)

Combine gelatin and cold water; let stand until thick. Place gelatin mixture in top of double boiler and heat until dissolved. Add glucose, mix well. Stir in shortening and just before completely melted, remove from heat. Add glycerin, flavoring and color. Cool until lukewarm. Next, place 4 cups confectioners' sugar in a bowl and make a well. Pour the lukewarm gelatin mixture into the well and stir with a wooden spoon, mixing in sugar and adding more, a little at a time, until stickiness disappears. Knead in remaining sugar. Knead until the fondant is smooth, pliable and does not stick to your hands. If fondant is too soft, add more sugar; if too stiff, add water (a drop at a time). Use fondant immediately or store in airtight container in a cool, dry place. Do not refrigerate or freeze. When ready to use, knead again until soft. This recipe makes approx. 36 oz., enough to cover a 10 x 4 in. round cake.

Chocolate Fondant

1 package (14 oz.) Dark Cocoa Candy Melts
  (p. 194)
½ cup light corn syrup
24 oz. White Ready-To-Use Rolled Fondant
  (p. 147)
Brown or Black Icing Color (p. 146, optional)

Melt Candy Melts following package directions. Add corn syrup; stir to blend. Turn out mixture onto waxed paper; let stand at room temperature to dry and harden several hours. Wrap well and store at room temperature until ready to continue with recipe.
Knead small portions of candy mixture until soft and pliable. Knead softened mixture into fondant until smooth and evenly colored. If darker color is desired, knead in icing color.

Extra-Firm Rolled Fondant

Use this recipe for a fondant with the extra body and pliability ideal for making drapes, swags and elaborate decorations.

1 to 2 teaspoons Gum-Tex (p. 147)
24 oz. Ready-To-Use Rolled Fondant (p. 147)

Knead Gum-Tex into fondant until smooth. Store in an airtight container or tightly wrapped in plastic.

Apricot Glaze

Ideal for preparing a cake for fondant or for crumb-coating cakes before icing.

1 cup apricot preserves

Heat preserves to boiling, strain. Brush on cake while glaze is still hot. Let dry. Glaze will dry to a hard finish in 15 minutes or less. Makes enough to cover a 10 x 4 in. cake.

Thinned Fondant Adhesive

Use this mixture when attaching dried fondant to other fondant decorations or for attaching freshly-cut fondant pieces to lollipop sticks or florist wire.

1 oz. Ready-To-Use Rolled Fondant (p. 147)
  (1½ in. ball)
¼ teaspoon water

Knead water into fondant until it becomes soft and sticky. To attach a fondant decoration, place mixture in decorating bag fitted with a small round tip, or brush on back of decoration. Recipe may be doubled.

Quick-Pour Fondant Icing

6 cups sifted confectioners' sugar
  (about 1½ lbs.)
½ cup water
2 tablespoons light corn syrup
1 teaspoon No-Color Almond Extract (p. 143)
Wilton Icing Colors (p. 146)

Cakes should be covered with apricot glaze (see recipe) or a thin coating of buttercream icing. Let set 15 minutes before covering with fondant.
Place sugar in saucepan. Combine water and corn syrup. Add to sugar and stir until well mixed. Place over low heat. Don't allow temperature to exceed 100°F. Remove from heat, stir in flavor and icing color. To cover, place cake or cookies on cooling grid over a drip pan. Pour fondant into center and work towards edges. Touch up bare spots with spatula. Let set. Excess fondant can be reheated. Makes about 2½ cups.

Gum Paste

Clay-like gum paste can be rolled thinner than fondant for finer detail. Gum paste dries hard and is meant for decoration only; remove from cake before serving. For perfectly mixed gum paste whenever you need it, try Wilton Ready-To-Use Gum Paste (p. 147)

1 tablespoon Gum-Tex (p. 147)
3 cups sifted confectioners' sugar (about ¾ lb.)
1 heaping tablespoon Glucose (p. 147)
4 tablespoons warm water
1 cup sifted confectioners' sugar
  (save until ready to use)

In a large bowl, mix Gum-Tex into 3 cups confectioners' sugar. Make a well in the center and set aside. Mix water and glucose in a glass measuring cup and blend; heat in microwave on high for about 30 seconds until mixture is clear. Pour into well of 3 cups confectioners' sugar and mix until well blended (mixture will be very soft). Place mixture in a plastic bag and seal tightly; let mixture rest at room temperature for 8 hours or overnight. Knead remaining confectioners' sugar into gum paste when you are ready to use it. As you work it in, gum paste will whiten and soften.

Gum Paste Adhesive

This easy-to-make "glue" will hold your gum paste flowers and other decorations together.

1 tablespoon Wilton Meringue Powder (p. 143)
1 tablespoon water

Mix Meringue Powder and water together; add more water if mixture is too thick. Brush on decorations.

HOW TO COLOR AND FLAVOR FONDANT

You can easily tint our White Ready-To-Use Rolled Fondant (p. 147) or the Rolled Fondant recipe (above) using Wilton Icing Colors (p. 146). Using a toothpick, add icing color, a little at a time, and knead into fondant until color is evenly blended. Wilton Ready-To-Use Rolled Fondant has a mellow flavor which can be enhanced using Wilton No-Color Butter Flavor, Clear Vanilla Extract or No-Color Almond Extract (p. 143). Knead flavor into fondant until well blended.

Using Rolled Fondant

The dough-like consistency of fondant makes it the perfect medium for creating ruffles and braids, stately molded accents, distinctive borders, fun trims and beautiful flowers. Decorators agree that fondant is an icing that is truly easy to work with. It's even easier with Wilton Ready-To-Use Rolled Fondant (p. 147)—no mixing, no mess!

COVERING THE CAKE

Just follow our instructions for the right ways to knead, roll out and lift the fondant, and you'll find that covering a cake is easy. For instructions on covering Square, Petal and other cake shapes, see the *Celebrate With Fondant* book, available on p. 131.

1. Prepare cake by lightly covering with buttercream icing.

2. Before rolling out fondant, knead it until it is a workable consistency. If fondant is sticky, knead in a little confectioners' sugar. Lightly dust your smooth work surface or the Roll & Cut Mat and your rolling pin with confectioners' sugar to prevent sticking. Roll out fondant sized to your cake (see "Fondant Amounts," at right). To keep fondant from sticking, lift and move as you roll. Add more confectioners' sugar if needed.

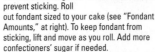

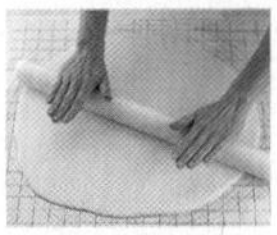

3. Gently lift fondant over rolling pin and position on cake. We recommend using the Smoother because the pressure of your hands may leave impressions on the fondant.

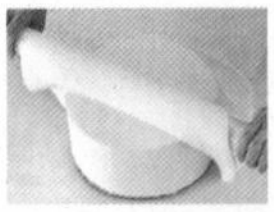

4. Smooth and shape fondant on top and sides of cake using Easy-Glide Smoother (p. 148) 1. Beginning in the middle of the cake top, move the Smoother outward and down the sides to smooth and shape fondant to the cake and remove air bubbles. If an air bubble appears, insert a pin on an angle, release air and smooth the area again. Use the straight edge of the Smoother to mark fondant at the base of cake. Trim off excess fondant using a spatula or sharp knife.

COVERING LARGE CAKES

In most cases, the smaller your cake, the easier it will be to cover with rolled fondant. However, there is an easy way to position and smooth fondant on cakes that are 12 in. diameter or larger. Follow the steps below to lift fondant onto the cake without tearing.

1. Cover cake lightly with buttercream icing. Roll out fondant sized to fit your cake.

2. Slide a large cake circle that has been dusted with confectioners' sugar under the rolled fondant. Lift the circle and the fondant and position over cake. Gently shake the circle to slide the fondant off and into position on the cake. Smooth and trim as described above.

COVERING PILLOW PAN CAKES WITH FONDANT

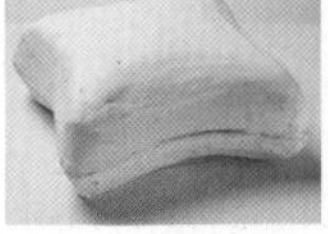

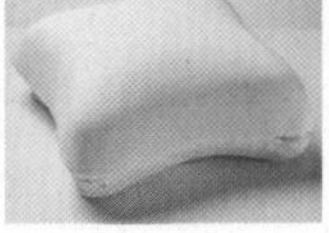

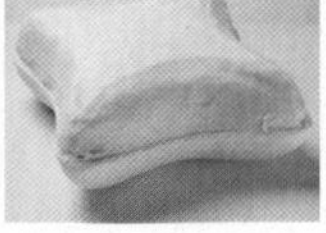

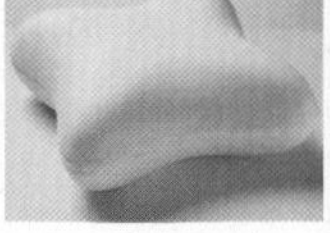

Each pan will need to be baked twice, iced and stacked together to achieve the full pillow effect. Assemble cake layers on cut to fit cake boards. Ice cakes smooth. Cover top layer with fondant in chosen color. Smooth with Fondant Smoother and trim at seam. Place cake board on top of cake and carefully flip to position covered layer at bottom. Cover top layer with fondant; smooth with Easy-Glide Smoother.

FONDANT AMOUNTS

Use this chart to determine how much Ready-To-Use Rolled Fondant to buy. Wilton Fondant is available in 24 oz. (1 lb., 8 oz.) or 80 oz. (5 lb.) packages. Amounts listed do not include decorations.

Cake Shape	Cake Size	Fondant
Rounds 4 in. high	6 in.	18 oz.
	8 in.	24 oz.
	10 in.	36 oz.
	12 in.	48 oz.
	14 in.	72 oz.
	16 in.	108 oz.
	18 in.	140 oz.
Rounds 3 in. high	6 in.	14 oz.
	8 in.	18 oz.
	10 in.	24 oz.
	12 in.	36 oz.
	14 in.	48 oz.
	16 in.	72 oz.
	18 in.	108 oz.
Sheets 2 in. high	7 x 11 in.	30 oz.
	9 x 13 in.	40 oz.
	11 x 15 in.	60 oz.
	12 x 18 in.	80 oz.
Ovals 4 in. high	7.75 x 5.5 in.	24 oz.
	10.75 x 7.8 in.	36 oz.
	13.5 x 9.8 in.	48 oz.
	16.5 x 12.4 in.	72 oz.
Hearts 4 in. high	6 in.	18 oz.
	8 in.	26 oz.
	9 in.	32 oz.
	10 in.	36 oz.
	12 in.	48 oz.
	14 in.	72 oz.
	16 in.	96 oz.
Petals 4 in. high	6 in.	18 oz.
	9 in.	30 oz.
	12 in.	48 oz.
	15 in.	72 oz.
Squares 4 in. high	6 in.	24 oz.
	8 in.	36 oz.
	10 in.	48 oz.
	12 in.	72 oz.
	14 in.	96 oz.
	16 in.	120 oz.
Hexagons 4 in. high	6 in.	18 oz.
	9 in.	36 oz.
	12 in.	48 oz.
	15 in.	84 oz.
Paisley 4 in. high	9 x 6 in.	20 oz.
	12.75 x 9 in.	48 oz.
	17 x 12 in.	72 oz.
Diamond 4 in. high	10.25 x 7.4 in.	24 oz.
	15 x 11 in.	36 oz.
	19.25 x 14.25 in.	60 oz.
Pillow 4 in. high	6.75 x 6.75 in.	16 oz.
	10 x 10 in.	28 oz.
	13.25 x 13.25 in.	48 oz.

Tip Techniques

Your icing turned out great—now you're ready to learn how to pipe beautiful shapes on your cake. Stars, shells, dots, lines and other techniques are the foundation of your decorating knowledge. We'll tell you step-by-step how to pipe each one, including the angle, pressure and movement to use for a uniform look. With practice, you can build on these basics to create many other impressive designs.

ROUND TIPS

Dot

Pipe dots for flower centers, faces, figure piping and border effects. When making large dots, lift the tip as you squeeze to allow icing to fill out completely.

Practice With: Tip 3
Icing Consistency: Medium
Bag Position: 90°
Hold Tip: Slightly above surface

1. Hold the bag straight up with the tip slightly above the surface. Squeeze the bag and keep point of the tip in icing until the dot is the size you want.
2. Stop squeezing the bag completely before you lift the tip from the dot.
3. Lift tip up and pull away from piped dot.

Ball

An important technique to master, the ball shape makes bold borders and is the first step to learn for figure piping. Vary the basic look by adding stars, dots or spirals on the ball shapes.

Practice With: Tip 9
Icing Consistency: Medium
Bag Position: 90°
Hold Tip: Slightly above surface

1. Squeeze the bag, applying steady even pressure. As the icing begins to build up, raise the tip with it, but keep the tip end buried in the icing.
2. Stop squeezing as you bring the end of the tip to the surface.
3. Lift the tip up and pull away from your piped ball. Use the edge of the tip to shave off any point so that your ball is nicely rounded.

Bead

If you can pipe a shell, you can pipe a bead—the movements are similar. To pipe a bead heart, simply pipe one bead, then a second, joining the tails. Smooth together using a decorator brush.

Practice With: Tip 5
Icing Consistency: Medium
Bag Position†: 45° at 3:00 (9:00)
Hold Tip: Slightly above surface

1. Squeeze as you lift tip slightly so that icing fans out.
2. Relax pressure as you draw the tip down and bring the bead to a point.
3. To make a bead border, start the end of your next bead so that the fanned end covers the tail of the preceding bead to form an even chain.

†The technique instructions in this Decorating Guide will list the correct direction for holding the bag. When the bag direction differs for left-handed decorators, that direction will be listed in parentheses. For example, when a bag is to be held at 3:00 for a right-handed decorator, it should be held at 9:00 for a left-handed decorator.

Printing

Practice With: Tip 3 with message press
Icing Consistency: Thin
Bag Position: 45° at 3:00 (9:00)
Hold Tip: Lightly touching surface

You may pipe letters freehand, pipe over a pattern traced with a toothpick, or pipe after imprinting letters with a message press. If you are using a message press, let icing crust slightly, then imprint the message. With a steady, even pressure, squeeze out a straight line, lifting the tip off the surface to let icing string drop. To prevent tails from forming, be careful to stop squeezing before you touch tip to surface and pull away. Be sure the end of the tip is clean before you go on to another line.

Writing

Practice With: Tip 5
Icing Consistency: Thin
Bag Position†: 45° at 3:00 (6:00)
Hold Tip: Lightly touching surface

You may pipe letters freehand, pipe over a pattern traced with a toothpick, or pipe after imprinting letters with a message press. If you are using a message press, let icing crust slightly, then imprint the message. Steadily squeeze, gliding along the surface in a smooth, continuous motion. Use your arm, not your fingers, to form each line, letter or word. Keep your wrist straight, moving your entire forearm as a single unit. After you begin to master the curves and swings of the letters, lift the tip up slightly as you write. You'll find you have more control if you let the icing draw out slightly over the surface as you write.

Note: Left-handed decorators may have to adjust the bag position to fit their writing style.

Outline

Characters or designs are often outlined first, then piped in with stars or zigzags. Outlines are used for facial features, too. Color flow plaques are also outlined before icing is flowed into the shape.

Practice With: Tip 3
Icing Consistency: Thin
Bag Position†: 45° at 3:00 (9:00)
Hold Tip: Slightly above surface

1. Touch tip to surface. Raise the tip slightly and continue to squeeze.
2. The icing will flow out of the tip while you direct it along the surface.
3. To end, stop squeezing, touch tip to surface and pull away.

To Pipe-In
After outlining, using the same tip, squeeze out rows of lines to fill area. Pat icing down with fingertip dipped in cornstarch or smooth with dampened art brush.

Drop Strings

These flowing strings are a beautiful way to adorn the sides of a cake. The trick to making drop strings is to pull the bag toward you as the string drapes down. If you "draw" the string with the tip, you won't achieve a pretty curve and your strings will tend to break. Pipe at eye level to your cake so that strings line up evenly. The Cake Dividing Set (p. 136) is a great help in accurately dividing and marking your cake for even drop strings.

Single Drop Strings

Practice With: Tip 3
Icing Consistency: Stiff
Bag Position†: Shoulder level at 4:30 (7:30)
Hold Tip: Lightly touching surface to attach

1. With a toothpick, mark horizontal divisions on cake in the width you desire. Touch tip to first mark and squeeze, pausing momentarily so that icing sticks to surface.
2. While squeezing, pull the bag toward you. Continue squeezing to allow the icing to drape naturally into an arc. Icing will drop by itself—do not move the tip down with the string. The end of the tip should be the same distance from the surface as the width from point to point on your cake.
3. Stop pressure before you touch tip to second mark to end string. Repeat, keeping drop strings uniform in length and width.

STAR TIPS

Star

Practice With: Tip 16
Icing Consistency: Medium
Bag Position: 90°
Hold Tip: Between ⅛ and ¼ in. above surface

1. Hold the decorating bag straight up, with the tip between ⅛ and ¼ in. above the surface, while using your other hand to hold the tip steady. Squeeze the bag to form a star. Increasing or decreasing the pressure changes the size of the star.
2. Stop squeezing the bag completely before you lift the tip from the star.
3. Lift the tip up and pull away from piped star.

Pull-out stars add even more dimension to your cake. To make them, hold bag at a 45° angle to surface. As you squeeze out icing, pull tip up and away from cake. When your mound is high enough, stop pressure and pull tip away. Work from bottom to top of area to be covered with pull-out stars.

Star Fill In

Because these close-together stars require so much piping from the same bag, it's a good idea to keep replenishing the icing. Replenish icing when it gets soft or stars will be poorly defined.

Practice With: Tip 16
Icing Consistency: Medium
Bag Position: 90°
Hold Tip: ¼ in. above surface

1. Pipe a row of stars evenly and close together, adjusting the tip position slightly each time so that the points of the stars interlock and cover the area without gaps.
2. Pipe a row of stars beneath the first, again adjusting tip position to close any gaps.
3. Continue to fill in entire area.

Zigzag

A quick and popular way to fill in outlined areas, perfect for ribbed sweater and cuff effects. You can use tight zigzags to cover the entire side of your cake—they look great!

Practice With: Tip 16
Icing Consistency: Medium
Bag Position†: 45° at 3:00 (9:00)
Hold Tip: Lightly touching surface

1. Steadily squeeze and move your hand in a tight up and down motion.
2. Continue piping up and down with steady pressure. To end, stop pressure and pull tip away. For more elongated zigzags, move your hand to the desired height while maintaining a steady pressure. For a more relaxed look, just increase the width as you move the bag along.
3. Repeat as you move in a straight line with consistent up/down motion.

Shell

Most popular icing technique of all, the shell is the basis for many borders. Lift tip slightly when piping shells to avoid a bumpy look.

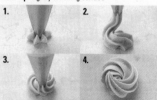

Practice With: Tip 21
Icing Consistency: Medium
Bag Position: 45° at 6:00
Hold Tip: Slightly above surface

1. Hold the bag in the 6:00 position so that you can pull the bag toward you. The tip should be slightly above the surface.
2. Squeeze hard, letting the icing fan out generously as it lifts the tip—do not lift the bag. Gradually relax your pressure as you lower the tip until it touches the surface.
3. Stop pressure and pull the tip away, without lifting it off the surface, to draw the shell to a point.
4. To make a shell border, start the end of your next shell so that the fanned end covers the tail of the preceding shell to form an even chain.

Rosette

Practice With: Tip 16
Icing Consistency: Medium
Bag Position: 90°
Hold Tip: Lightly touching surface

1. Keeping the tip slightly above the surface, squeeze out icing to form a star and, without releasing pressure, move the tip in a tight, complete rotation, starting at 9:00 (3:00), moving to 12:00. . .
2. then to 3:00 (9:00) and 6:00. . .
3. and ending back at 9:00 (3:00).
4. Stop pressure and lift tip away.

MULTIPLE TIPS

Swirl Drop Flower

The swirled look adds a nice motion effect to the cake. You must squeeze and turn at the same time.

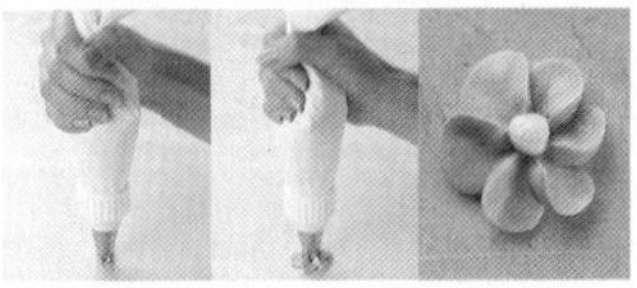

Practice With: Tips 2D, 3; use Large Coupler
Icing Consistency: Use royal icing: medium for flower, thin for center
Bag Position: 90°
Hold Tip: Slightly above surface

1. Turn your wrist in toward you before piping. Hold bag straight up, just touching the surface. You will turn wrist a full twist. Starting with the flat of your knuckles at 9:00 (3:00). As you squeeze out the icing, slowly turn your hand, with knuckles ending at 12:00.
2. Stop squeezing and lift the tip away.
3. Make a tip 3 dot flower center, holding your bag straight up and keeping the tip buried as you squeeze. Stop squeezing, then pull your tip up and away.

PETAL TIPS

Ruffle

Everyone loves a ruffle's graceful motion—ruffles always add interest to your cake. Use them as a top border, to frame a plaque or to trim doll dresses and baby bonnets.

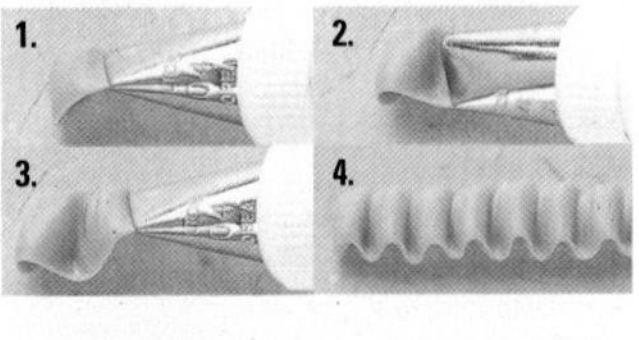

Practice With: Tip 104
Icing Consistency: Medium
Bag Position†: 45° at 3:00 (9:00)
Hold Tip: Wide end lightly touching surface with narrow end facing down and away from surface

1. Keep the wide end of your tip touching the cake with the narrow end down. Move wrist up to pull up icing.
2. Move wrist down to complete one curl of the ruffle.
3. Repeat up and down motion.
4. Raise and lower the narrow end as you move around the cake. Repeat this motion for the entire ruffle.

BORDER

Fondant Rope Border

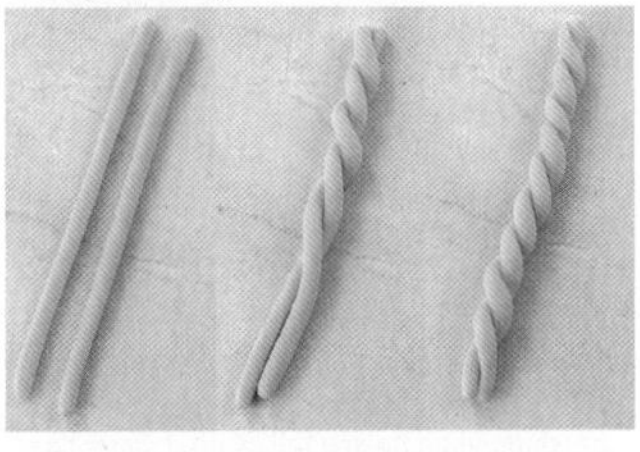

1. Use palms of hands to roll fondant logs, ¼ in. diameter. You will need 4 pieces 36 in. long for cake border; twist 2 ropes together to make each rope section. Lay pieces side by side and gently press together at one end to join.
2. Holding the joined end in a stationary position, twist the other end 2 to 3 complete turns. Continue twisting as needed.
3. Attach rope to bottom border using a damp brush. Moisten cake slightly and position rope, pressing ends lightly to secure.

Flower-Making Techniques

Explore beautiful flowers and leaves, which add lovely color to your cake design. Create the magnificent rose—the most popular icing flower of all. With practice, your flowers will have the just-picked look of real garden flowers.

FLOWER NAIL FLOWERS

Using a Flower Nail

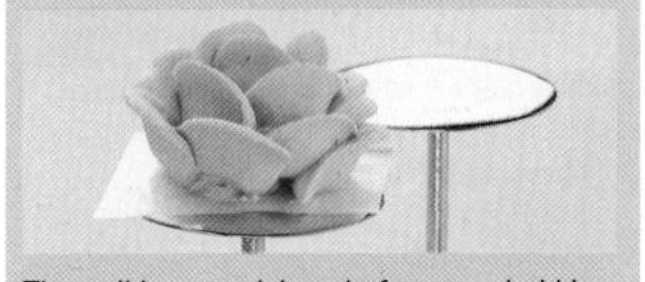

The nail is a revolving platform you hold in your hand to conveniently build roses and other flowers. It allows you to work close up, to turn for easy piping and to remove your completed flowers without damage, to dry.

The key to making the flower on the nail is to coordinate the turning of the nail with the formation of each petal.

Attach a square of waxed paper on the flat surface of the flower nail using a dot of icing. Pipe your flower directly on the waxed paper. Hold the flower nail between the thumb and forefinger of your left (right) hand (use other fingers to support nail) and roll it slowly counterclockwise (clockwise for lefties) as you press out icing with the decorating bag held in the right (left) hand. Your right (left) hand moves in and out, or up and down, as it holds the decorating bag and tip at just the right angle (in most cases 45°) and keeps the icing flowing at an even speed. After piping, slide the waxed paper with flower off the nail to dry.

The Wilton Rose

NOTE: If you are going to be placing your roses on your cake immediately, waxed paper squares are not needed. To remove finished roses, use the Flower Lifter (p. 138). Slide flower from lifter onto cake, using a spatula.

Practice With: Tips 104, 12
Icing Consistency: Royal or stiff buttercream
Bag Position†: Base 90° (straight up); petals 45° at 4:30 (7:30)
Hold Tip: For base, slightly above nail; for petals, wide end touching base
Flower Nail: #7

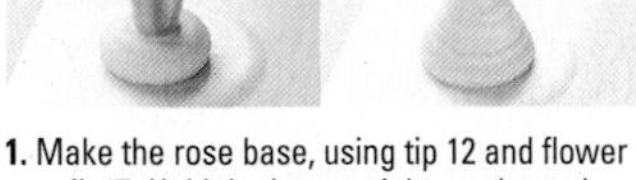

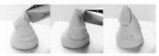

1. Make the rose base, using tip 12 and flower nail #7. Hold the bag straight up, the end of tip 12 slightly above the center of your waxed paper-covered flower nail, which is held in your other hand. Using heavy pressure, build up a base, remembering to keep your tip buried as you squeeze. Start to lift the tip higher, gradually raise the tip, and decrease the pressure.
2. Stop pressure, pull up and lift away. The rose base should be 1½ times as high as the rose tip opening.

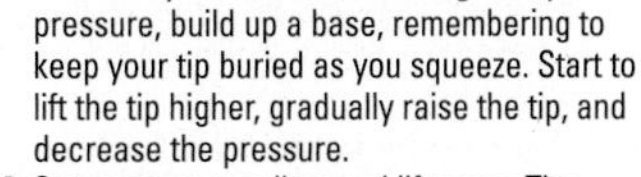

3. Make the center bud, using tip 104. Hold nail containing base in your left (right) hand and bag with rose tip 104 in right (left) hand. Bag should be at a 45° angle to the flat surface of the nail and in the 4:30 (7:30) position. The wide end of the tip should touch the cone of the icing base at or slightly below the midpoint, and the narrow end of the tip should point up and angled in over top of base.
4. Now you must do 3 things at the same time: squeeze the bag, move the tip and rotate the nail. As you squeeze the bag, move the tip up from the base, forming a ribbon of icing. Slowly turn the nail counterclockwise (clockwise for lefties) to bring the ribbon of icing around to overlap at the top of the mound, then back down to starting point. Move your tip straight up and down only; do not loop it around the base.
5. Now you have a finished center bud.

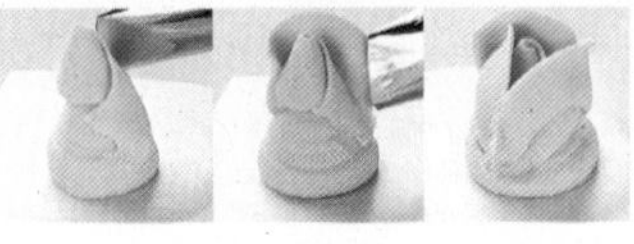

6. Make the top row of 3 petals. Touch the wide end of tip to the midpoint of bud base, narrow end straight up.
7. Turn nail, keeping wide end of tip on base so that petal will attach. Move tip up and back down to the midpoint of mound, forming the first petal.
8. Start again, slightly behind end of first petal, and squeeze out second petal. Repeat for the third petal, ending by overlapping the starting point of the first petal. Rotate the nail ⅓ turn for each petal.

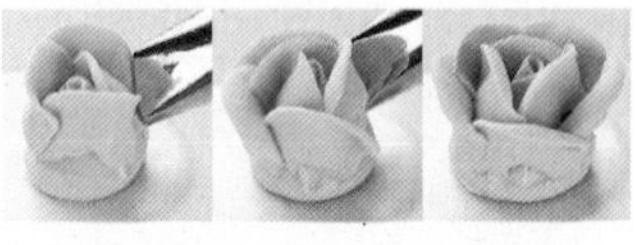

9. Make the middle row of 5 petals. Touch the wide end of tip slightly below center of a petal in the top row. Angle the narrow end of tip out slightly more than you did for the top row of petals. Squeeze bag and turn nail moving tip up, then down, to form first petal.
10. Repeat for a total of 5 petals, rotating the nail ⅕ turn for each petal.
11. The last petal end should overlap the first's starting point.

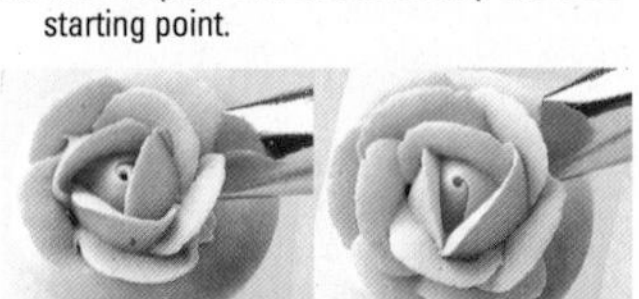

12. Make the bottom row of 7 petals. Touch the wide end of tip below the center of a middle row petal, again angling the narrow end of tip out a little more. Squeeze bag and turn nail to end of fingers, moving tip up, then down to form first petal.
13. Repeat for a total of 7 petals, rotating the nail ⅐ turn for each petal.

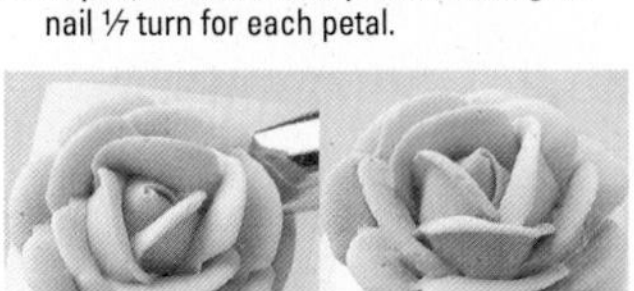

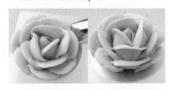

14. The last petal end should overlap the first's starting point.
15. Slip waxed paper and completed rose from nail. This is the completed Wilton Rose.

Gum Paste Calla Lilies

(see Calla Lily Classic, p. 88)

For Flower

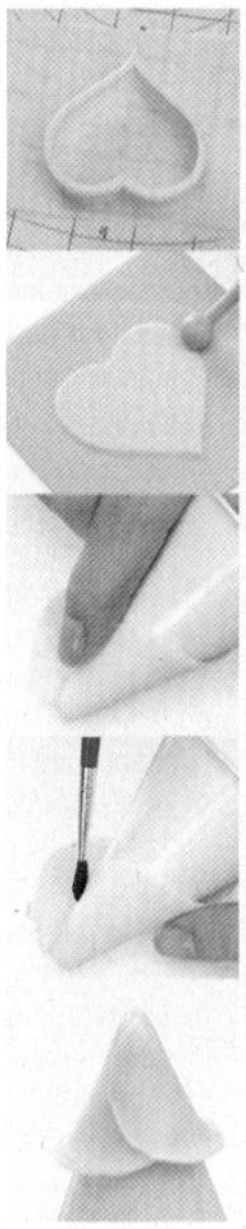

1. Roll out white gum paste less than 1⁄16 in. thick. Cut with Calla Lily Cutter.
2. Move to thin foam. Use the ball tool to thin edges. Position tool on the foam and slide around the petal, keeping it mostly on the foam, to "outline" the petal. The ball tool should only touch the petal edge.
3. Dust Calla Lily Former with cornstarch to avoid sticking. Position former over petal with the wide end toward the point of the petal and the pointed end of the former at the indented end of the petal.
4. Wrap one side of the petal around the former. Brush edge of rounded portion with gum paste adhesive.
5. Wrap the other side of petal so it overlaps the first petal and attach to make a cone-shaped flower, leaving a small opening for wired center to pass through. With fingertip, gently curl the edge of the overlapping petal. Stand former upright and set aside to dry.

For Centers

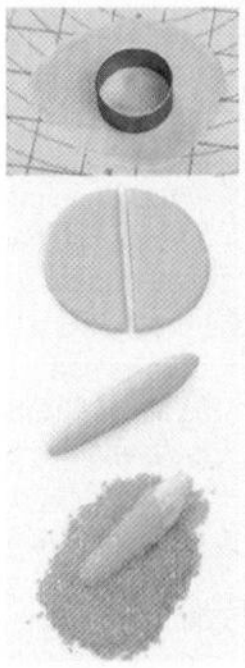

1. Tint a 1½ in. ball of gum paste yellow. Make calla lily center on 22-gauge wire. Roll a 3⁄16 in. log and cut lengths of ¾ to 1 in.
2. Brush one end of wire with gum paste adhesive and insert into ¾ of center length.
3. Brush center with adhesive and dip in yellow colored sugar. Insert in craft block and let dry.

Assembling Calla Lily with Calyx

1. When dry, remove flowers from formers. Roll a ⅛ in. ball of gum paste and drop inside flower. Brush with gum paste adhesive and insert wired center, pulling wire through ball to hold center in place.

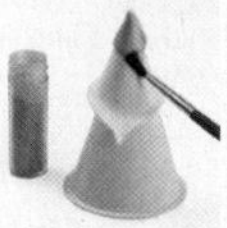

2. For calyx, roll out a small amount of green gum paste less than 1⁄16 in. thick. Use the medium Round Cut-Out to cut one circle.
3. Cut the gum paste circle in half. Brush a small amount of gum paste adhesive on one of the half circles.
4. Using the half circle, position the center of the flat edge so it overhangs the point of the cone on the side opposite the seam of the flower; the rounded edge is on the flower. Wrap around the base of the calla lily and press gently to attach. Line up the overlap of the calyx with the overlap of the flower. Set aside to dry.

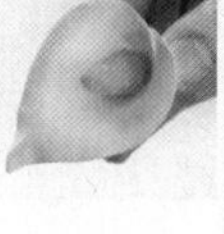

5. Brush calla lily flower inside and out with white Pearl Dust. Brush yellow Pearl Dust on inside where center is positioned. Brush a little green Pearl Dust on top point of calla lily and at base above calyx. Tape wires with florist tape.

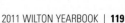

Gum Paste Roses
(see Waterfall Wedding, p. 92)

1. In advance: Make the rose center. Roll a ½ in. ball of gum paste and form into a teardrop shape. Dip toothpick end into gum paste adhesive and insert at bottom of rose center, inserting halfway through base. Press bottom of center to shape and smooth against toothpick. Let dry at least 48 hours.

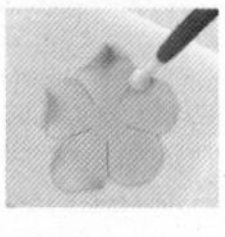

2. Roll out gum paste ¹⁄₁₆ in. thick. Using the large rose cutter from the Stepsaving Kit (p. 151), cut blossom shape. Use a knife to make a ½ in. cut between each petal toward middle of blossom. Place on thin foam and use ball tool from 10-Pc. Fondant/Gum Paste Tool Set to soften edges of petals. Move blossom to thick foam and cup center by pressing in middle with ball tool.

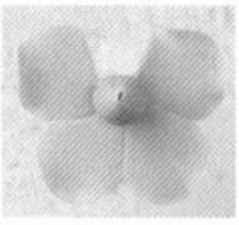

3. Apply gum paste adhesive to rose center. Insert the toothpick holding the rose center into the middle of the blossom and thread blossom up to the bottom of the rose center. Visualize the 5-petal blossom as a stick figure, with petals corresponding to "head", "arms" and "legs". Wrap the head petal around rose center.

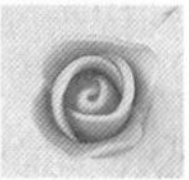

4. Brush bottom half of one "arm" and opposite "leg" with adhesive and wrap around the center bud. Repeat for remaining petals. Gently press bottom to shape. Petals should overlap each other. Pinch off any excess gum paste from bottom. Furl back petal edges of the outer layer of petals.

5. Prepare the next blossom; cut slits and soften edges as above. Transfer to thick foam and use ball tool to cup the 2 "arm" petals. Turn over blossom and cup 2 "leg" petals and "head" petal. Turn over blossom again and cup the center. Brush adhesive on bottom of rose center; thread blossom onto toothpick. Brush the 2 "arm" petals with adhesive and attach, centering over the seams of the previous 2 petals.

6. Brush bottom half of remaining petals and attach, spacing evenly. Press bottom to shape; pinch off excess if needed.

7. Add a third blossom; cut slits and soften edges as in step 2. Transfer to thick foam. Using the ball tool, cup all petals. Turn blossom shape over and cup center. Brush adhesive on bottom of rose center. Push toothpick through the center of the blossom shape. Brush adhesive on bottom half of petals as needed.

8. Turn rose over and let petals fall naturally into place. Gently press petals against the rose center to attach.

9. Roll out gum paste ¹⁄₁₆ in. thick and cut calyx using calyx cutter from the Stepsaving Set. Brush bottom of rose center with adhesive and thread toothpick through center of calyx. Brush adhesive on bottom half of sepals and press to attach. Bend top half of wire stem down and let rose hang down to dry in craft foam block.

Attaching Royal Icing Leaves to Wire Stems
(see More Memories in Store, p. 89)

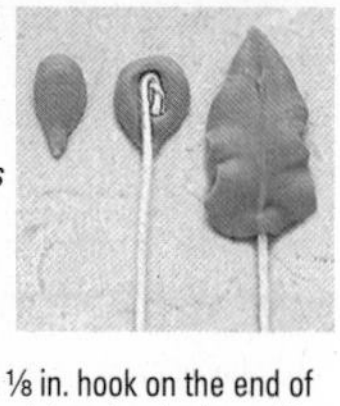

On a 1¼ in. waxed paper square, using royal icing, pipe a dot base with tip 4. Make a ⅛ in. hook on the end of florist wire and insert hook into the dot base. Use tip 352 and pipe leaf directly on top of wire. Push the other end of wire into craft block and let dry. Remove waxed paper square when dry.

Apple Blossom

Pipe apple blossoms about the size of a penny and dry them on Flower Formers (p. 138).

Practice With: Tips 101, 1
Icing Consistency: Stiff royal icing
Bag Position: 45° for petals; 90° for dots
Hold Tip: Wide end touching surface, with narrow end pointed out.
Flower Nail: #7

1. Use tip 101 and hold bag at a 45° angle to flower nail with wide end of tip touching nail center, narrow end pointed out ⅛ in. away from nail surface.
2. Squeeze bag and turn nail as you move tip ⅛ in. out from nail center and back, relaxing pressure as you return to starting point.
3. Repeat procedure to make 4 more petals. Add 5 tip 1 dots for center.

FLORAL GREENERY

Leaves

Practice With: Tips 352, 67, 366
Icing Consistency: Buttercream thinned with corn syrup
Bag Position: 45° at 6:00
Hold Tip: Lightly touching surface; wide opening parallel to surface

Basic Leaf Tip 352	Veined Leaf Tip 67	Large Leaf Tip 366 Use large coupler

1. Squeeze hard to build up the base and, at the same time, lift the tip slightly.
2. Relax pressure as you pull the tip toward you, drawing the leaf to a point.
3. Stop squeezing and lift away.

Vines

Practice With: Tip 3
Icing Consistency: Thin
Bag Position: 45° at 3:00 (9:00)
Hold Tip: Lightly touching surface

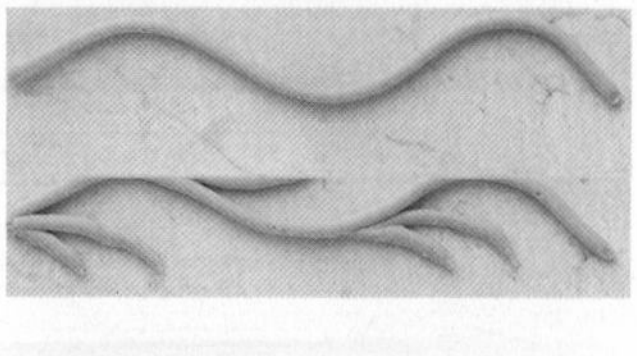

1. Touch your tip lightly to the surface as you start to squeeze, then lift slightly above the surface as you draw out the stem.
2. Move tip gently up and down to form "hills and valleys." To end the line, stop squeezing and pull the tip along the surface.
3. Add secondary curved stems, starting at main stem, stopping pressure as you pull to a point.

Other Decorating Techniques

Combing

Practice With: Icing Sculptor (p. 141), Decorating Comb or Triangle (p. 140), Trim 'N Turn Plus Cake Turntable (p. 139)
Icing Consistency: Medium-to-thin buttercream

Cover the cake with a slightly thicker coating of icing so the comb's ridges will not touch the cake. Hold comb at 45° angle. Comb immediately after icing cake, while icing is soft. Using a turntable helps to keep the movement smooth. Use the Icing Sculptor, Decorating Comb or Decorating Triangle to add different contoured effects to your iced cake. Choose the type of effect you want—wide or narrow—then run that edge around your cake to form ridges. Ridges will be deep or shallow depending on the Icing Sculptor blade or the side of Decorating Comb or Triangle you use.

Icing Sculptor

Select the sculpting blades you want and slide into holder. Press sculptor into iced cake as you rotate cake on turntable. Mix and match between the 64 blades to achieve the perfect look for your cake.

Pattern Press

The trick to uniform designs and steady writing and printing is using a pattern press (p. 140).

Simply imprint the press on any icing, including fondant.

Practice With: Tips 3, 16
Icing Consistency: Medium
Bag Position: 45° at 3:00
Hold Tip: Slightly above surface

1. Lightly press pattern onto your iced or fondant-covered cake to imprint the design.
2. Outline the imprinted design with icing, using the tip of your choice. Change the tip to change the look of each pattern.

Tinting Shredded Coconut

Place desired amount of coconut in plastic bag, add a little color with a toothpick and knead until color is evenly blended. Dry on waxed paper.

Marbleizing Fondant

Using Icing Color: Roll fondant into a ball, kneading until it's soft and pliable. Using a toothpick, add dots of icing color in several spots. Knead fondant slightly until color begins to blend in, creating marbleized streaks. Roll out fondant to desired shape.

Using Pre-Tinted Fondant and White Fondant: Roll a log each of tinted and white fondant. Twist one log around the other several times. Knead fondant slightly until color begins to blend in, creating marbleized streaks. Roll out fondant to desired shape.

Puddle Dots

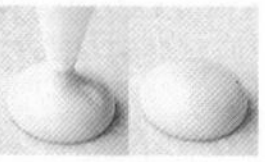

Thin royal icing (or color flow), adding ½ teaspoon water per ¼ cup of icing. Icing is ready for flowing when a small amount dripped back into mixture takes a count of 10 to disappear. On waxed paper, pipe a ball, ¼ to 1¼ in. diameter, depending on project instructions, using thinned icing in a cut parchment bag. Let dry 48 hours. Decorate following project instructions.

Covering Base Boards with Fondant

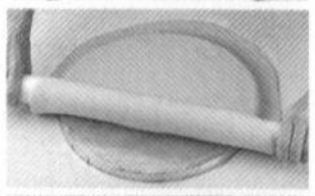

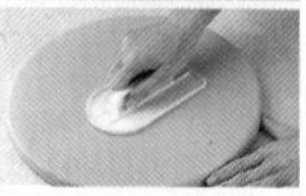

Cut cake boards 2 in. larger in diameter than your cake, unless otherwise directed, then roll out fondant about 1 in. larger than board size. Wrap board with foil.

1. Lightly coat board with piping gel to help the fondant stick to the foil.
2. Roll out fondant to desired size, ⅛ in. thick. Position over board using a rolling pin, draping fondant over edge.
3. Trim excess fondant from edges under bottom of board. Smooth top and sides with Easy-Glide Smoother.

Curliques

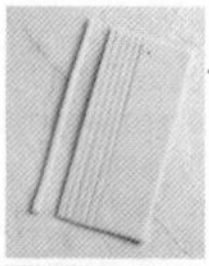

Toothpicks, Lollipop Sticks or dowel rods may be used for various sizes.

1. Roll out fondant ¹⁄₁₆ in. thick on Roll & Cut Mat lightly dusted with cornstarch. Cut into thin strips. 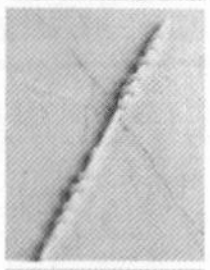
2. Loosely wrap strips around a Lollipop Stick several times to form curls. Let set 5 to 10 minutes. 
3. Slide curl off Lollipop Stick and let dry. Attach to cake with Thinned Fondant Adhesive (p. 119).

Brush Embroidery

Add textured flowers and leaves with the soft look of lace using this easy icing technique. Works best using the square tip brush from the Wilton Brush Set (p. 149).

1. Imprint shape on freshly rolled fondant (or on your covered cake) using a Cut-Out or cookie cutter. 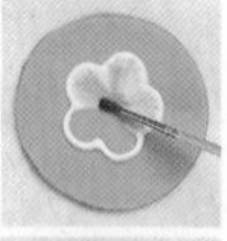
2. Thin royal or buttercream icing with Piping Gel. Using tip 2 or 3, outline shape. For large designs, outline one section of the design, brush out lines following step 3, then continue with the next design section. 
3. Before each outline can dry, immediately brush out lines of icing toward center of pattern area with damp brush. Work in quick, short strokes. Clean brush with water after brushing each design to create distinct lines of icing.

BRUSHING DECORATIONS WITH PEARL DUST

It's easy to add a shimmering touch to fondant and candy decorations with Wilton Pearl Dust (p. 149). This **food-safe** powder creates rich, lustrous highlights on flowers, bows, letters and more. To apply, just brush onto your decoration with a soft artist brush. Or, to paint decorations, pour a small amount of clear vanilla, lemon extract or vodka into a shallow cup, stir in a small decoration of Pearl Dust and brush onto your decoration.

Decorating Techniques for the 2011 Wilton Yearbook Cakes

We've organized our decorating techniques to make everything easier to find. Special techniques for this book are presented in the same order as our projects, beginning with the Birthday Section projects on page 6 up through our Special Section, ending at page 109.

Candles

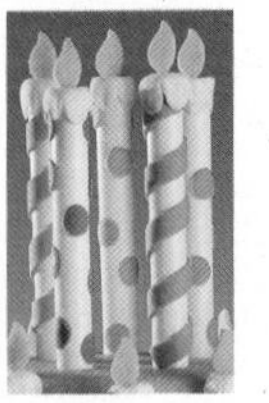

(see Birthday Candlepower, p. 9)
Make 4 dot and 4 striped candles in each color (pink, orange, violet, blue, green). Roll out fondant 1/16 in. thick. **For dots**, cut 6-8 using smallest Round Cut-Out for each candle. **For stripes**, cut 12 x ½ in. strips. Attach trims to 6 in. dowel rods using Piping Gel. Roll 40 white fondant logs, 1½ x 5/8 in. diameter. Brush inside top 1 in. of dowel rod with Piping Gel; push in 1 fondant log until even with top. For wax drips, roll out white fondant ⅛ in. thick. Use small rose cutter from set to cut 40 flowers. Set on thin foam and use small ball tool to slightly elongate petals. Attach over top of dowel rod using Piping Gel; shape with fingers. Insert flame. Let dry 2 days.

Baby Heads

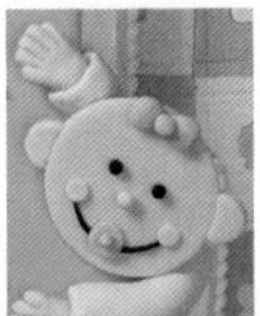

(see Covered in Cuteness, p. 10)
Roll out pink fondant from Multi Pack 3/16 in. thick. Use Comfort-Grip Cutter to cut head, wide end of tip 2A to cut ears; trim 3/8 in. off one side and attach using damp brush. Set on waxed paper-covered board dusted with cornstarch. Roll tiny ball nose (reserve remaining pink for hands), tiny black balls for eyes, ⅛ x 3 in. long log for smile; attach using damp brush. Tint small amount dark pink and roll out. Cut cheeks using narrow end of tip 2A; attach. **For girl**: Cut pacifier base using wide end of tip 8; roll tiny ball for tip. **For bow**, shape 2 loops from 3/8 in. balls; roll ¼ in. diameter ball for knot. Assemble pacifier and bow and attach to head. Let dry. **For boy:** Roll thin log 3 in. long; shape into curl and attach. Let dry.

Ladybug Heads

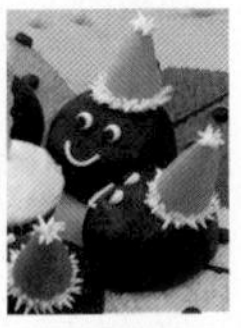

(see Drawn to the Flame, p. 12)
Tint 12 oz. fondant black, ¾ in. ball each pink, violet, blue. Roll and shape 2 oz. black fondant into 1 in. wide head. For hat, shape fondant into a 1¼ in. high cone. Attach hat to head with thinned fondant adhesive.

Fondant Flower Girls

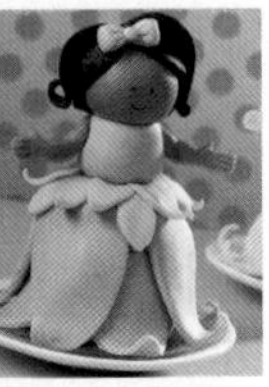

(see The Garden Girls, p. 13)
2 hours in advance:
Make head and arms. Tint 2 in. ball of fondant light or dark skin tone. Pinch off small amount to roll and shape 3/16 x 1¼ in. long arms. Flatten hands and use knife to mark fingers. Roll remaining fondant into ball for head; flatten bottom slightly. Let pieces dry on waxed paper-covered board.
Bake and cool brownie pops in silicone mold supported by Cookie Sheet. Tint fondant assorted colors; roll out ⅛ in. thick as needed. Prepare brownies for rolled fondant (p. 117). Cover with a 4 in. diameter circle of fondant in skirt color. Smooth with hands; cut away excess. **For skirt base**, cut 8 petals using largest leaf Cut-Out. Attach bottom 4 petals with damp brush, wide end down; leave about ½ in. extended beyond bottom edge and curl tips around brush handle. Attach next 4 petals between bottom petals, narrow end down, positioning so tips curve out to left and to right in front and again in back; curl tips as above. **For skirt top**, cut 12-14 leaves using smallest Cut-Out. Position as above but do not curl bottom layer and use 2 leaves in each gap for top layer. Shape bodice from a 1 in. diameter ball; attach to skirt using fondant adhesive. Use end of brush to make holes for arms. Insert and secure arms with adhesive. Attach head. **For bangs**, cut 2 leaves using smallest cutter from set; attach curved tip down, trimming as needed. **For hair**, cut 3 leaves using medium cutter from set; attach 2 to sides with curved tip down, attach 1 to back with curved tip up. **For bow**, roll two ¼ in. balls; flatten and pinch end to shape loops. Use knife to mark lines. Attach to head. Roll tiny ball for knot; flatten and attach. Use FoodWriter to draw dot eyes and smile. Each serves 1.

Brownie Pop Fairies

(see Spritely Celebration, p. 13)
Tint fondant as follows: 20 oz. yellow; 18 oz. dark rose; 6 oz. light rose; 3 oz. each light violet, light orange; 1 oz. each dark violet, dark orange, red. Roll out ⅛ in. thick unless otherwise specified. Reserve any excess fondant. **Make fondant flowers**, roll out fondant 1/16 in. thick. Cut light rose, orange and violet apple blossoms (24 each) using cutter from set.

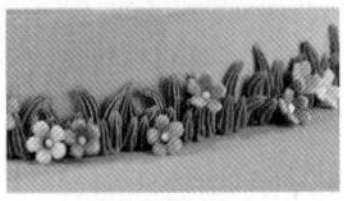

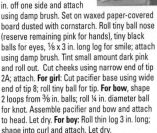

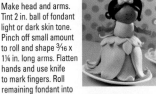

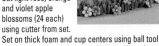

Set on thick foam and cup centers using ball tool from set. Let dry on cornstarch-dusted board. Pipe tip 2 dot centers in buttercream.
To make fondant wings, roll out white fondant 1/16 in. thick. Cut 6 wings using medium heart cutter from set. Let dry 24 hours on cornstarch-dusted board. Brush with Piping Gel; sprinkle with Sparkling Sugar.

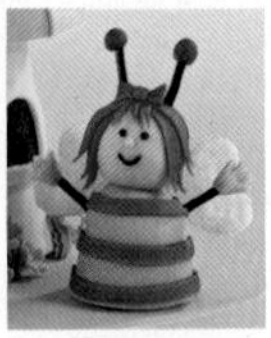

To make fairies, cover pops with tinted fondant per instructions. Decorate using darker fondant shades and pink fondant from Natural Multi Pack. Attach pieces using fondant adhesive. For each figure, cut 3 strips 5 x ¼ in. wide. Attach, trimming as needed to fit. Cut Lollipop Stick to 3 in. long. Roll 1¼ in. diameter ball heads. Insert stick and position in pop. Roll thin log mouth and tiny ball eyes and nose; attach. **For hair**, roll out small amount of fondant 1/16 in. thick. Cut various thin strips and attach for hair-dos. Shape bow from 2 triangles and center ball; attach. Cut licorice to 1 in. lengths. Insert for antennae and arms. Roll ¼ in. diameter balls for antennae tips; attach. Roll 3/8 in. flattened balls for hands. Use knife to separate fingers; attach. Attach 2 dried wings to back. **Make house trims**. Roll out pink fondant 1/16 in. thick. Cut 12 rounds using medium cutter from set; attach to roof using damp brush, trimming as needed. Roll out black fondant from Multi Pack. Cut 2 windows (1¼ x 1 in. high) and door (2 x 3¼ in. high). Attach to house. Cut ¼ in. wide yellow strips and attach around windows and door.

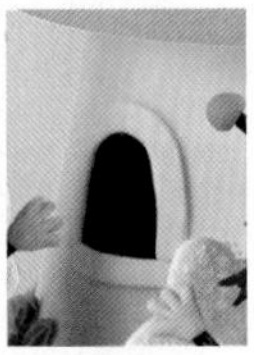

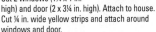

Princess Fondant Features

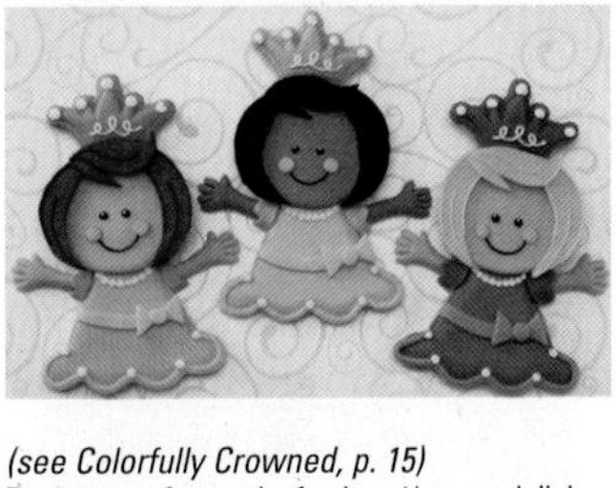

(see Colorfully Crowned, p. 15)
For 3 treats shown, tint fondant: ½ oz. each light pink, blue and violet; 1 oz. each dark pink, blue and violet, dark brown, black, yellow, light brown; 2 oz. copper. Roll out ⅛ in. thick as needed. Set on waxed paper-covered boards to decorate. Cut heads using largest round Cut-Out. Use patterns to cut out hair (flip pattern for opposite side) and bangs; attach using damp brush. **For arms**, roll 1½ x 3/8 in. diameter logs. Flatten hand and cut slits for fingers. **For sleeves**, cut 3/8 x ¾ in. long strips with wavy edge on one long side. Attach around end of arms. **For crowns**, press fondant into candy mold; unmold and set on waxed paper-covered board. Let all pieces dry 24 hours.

Windshield, Steering Wheel and Cars

(see Go Girls!, p. 16)

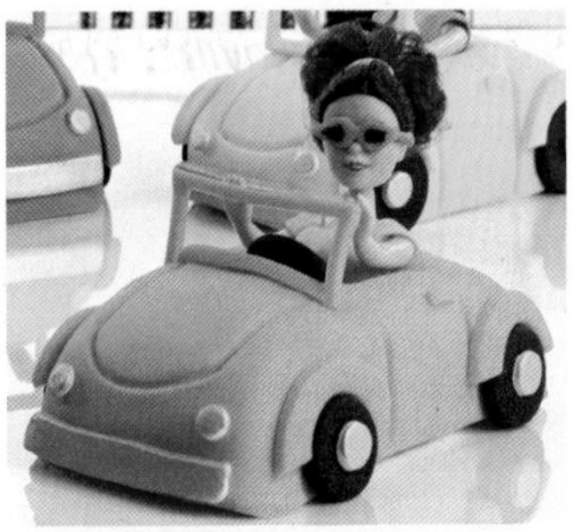

Tint 8 oz. fondant in each car color (we show yellow, orange, violet and rose) plus a 1 in. ball of red, 4 oz. black; reserve 5 oz. white. **For windshields**, combine ¼ teaspoon Gum-Tex with a small amount of fondant in matching car color. Roll out ⅛ in. thick. Cut ⅛ in. wide strips as follows: one 2¼ in. long top, one 2 in. long bottom and two ¾ in. long sides. Attach strips at corners using fondant adhesive. Let dry on waxed paper-covered board dusted with cornstarch. **For steering wheel**, roll out a portion of black fondant ⅛ in. thick. Cut wheel using wide end of tip 2A. Cut center using narrow end of tip 12 and gently remove; use knife to cut thin strips for grip areas. Attach to wheel with adhesive and let dry.
For cars, trim cakes to 1½ in. high; trim front and back to shape curved hood and angled trunk. Cut out 1½ x 1¼ x 1½ in. deep passenger area, starting 1¼ in. from back of car. Roll out fondant ⅛ in. thick as needed. Prepare and cover car with rolled fondant, using white for passenger area, colors for car. Use modeling tool from set to imprint details: hood, side doors, trunk. Roll out remaining black fondant. Use wide end of tip 2A to cut 4 wheels; attach using damp brush. Cut 4 colored strips ¼ x 2 in. and attach above wheels for wheel covers. Roll out white. Cut 2½ x 3/8 in. front and back bumpers using knife to round ends; 2 front white and 2 back red lights using narrow end of tip 12; 4 white hubcaps using narrow end of tip 2A. Attach using damp brush. Paint with silver Pearl Dust/vanilla mixture (p. 120).

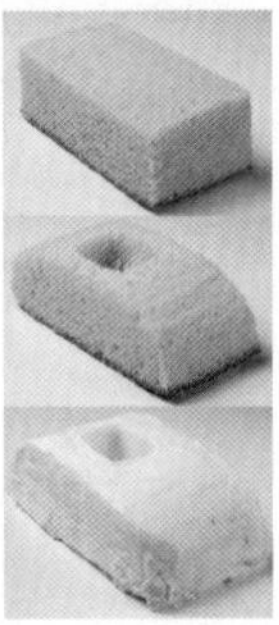

Fondant Trims

(see Sassy Shades, p. 16)
Tint fondant: 24 oz. skin tone, 16 oz. yellow, 6 oz. rose, 2 oz. black, 1 oz. light rose. **For ears**, roll out skin tone ¼ in. thick. Use pattern to cut 2 ears (flip pattern for 2nd ear). Roll out small amount 1/16 in. thick. Cut two ⅛ x 5 in. strip details; attach at top curve using damp brush. **For ponytail**, roll out yellow ½ in. thick. Use pattern to cut ponytail. **For sunglasses**, roll out rose ¼ in. thick and black 1/16 in. thick. Use pattern to cut sunglasses and lenses; attach lenses using damp brush. Brush sunglass frame with Piping Gel and sprinkle with Sparkling Sugar. Set all pieces on cornstarch-dusted surface to dry. Reserve excess fondant. Trim lollipop sticks to 3 in. Attach lollipop sticks to ears with Fondant Adhesive; let dry. **For bangs**, cover top ⅓ and sides of cake; position pattern and cut bang edge. Position cake and ponytail on prepared board. Roll out small amount of yellow 1/16 in. thick. Cut ⅛ in. wide strip details in 2 to 14 in. lengths; attach over bangs and ponytail using damp brush.

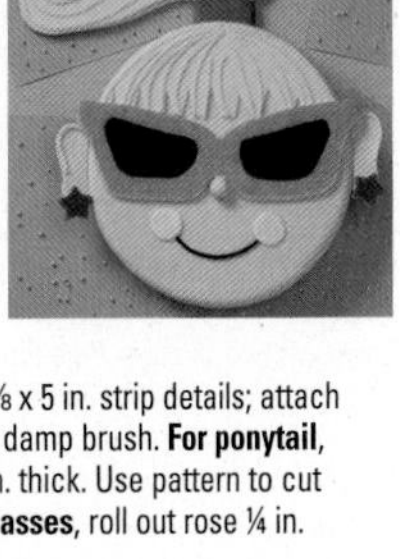

Panels, Stars, Singers

(see Diva's Debut, p. 17)

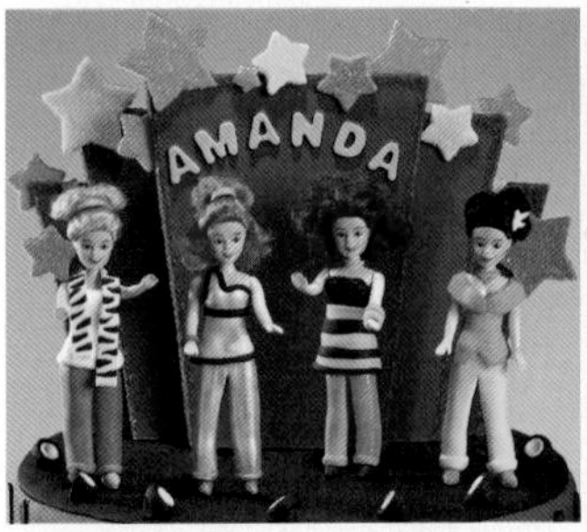

For panels, tint 12 oz. fondant violet. Add 1 teaspoon Gum-Tex. **For stars**, tint fondant: 3 oz. each rose, blue and yellow, 2 oz. each orange, green. Add ¼ teaspoon Gum-Tex to each. Roll out ⅛ thick as needed. Use patterns to cut 1 large, 2 medium, 2 small back panels. Cut stars using cutters from set: with large, 1 each orange, yellow, rose, blue; with medium, 2 each orange, yellow, rose plus 1 blue; with small, 1 each yellow, pink, blue. Let dry 2 days on waxed paper-covered boards. Reserve excess fondant for figures. **To complete back panels**: Brush panel edges and stars with Piping Gel and sprinkle on matching Colored Sugar. Assemble using thinned fondant adhesive. Attach Lollipop Sticks to back of panels; trim sticks, leaving 3 in. extended at bottom to insert into cake. Attach stars to panel edges. Cut name using Cut-Outs; attach to large panel. Let dry.
Tint additional fondant: 2 oz. gray, 1 oz. golden yellow, ½ oz. light violet (mix small amount of reserved violet with white to lighten); reserve 1 oz. white. Add ⅛ teaspoon Gum-Tex to each. Also use reserved fondant. Roll out ⅛ in. thick as needed.

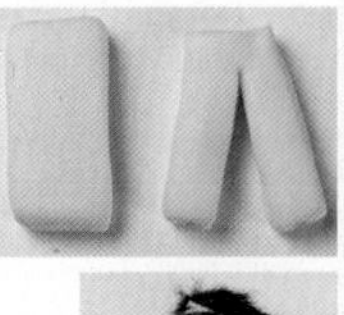

For lower body, begin with a 2½ x 1¼ x ½ in. thick rectangle. Cut 2 in. slit for legs. Smooth edges and shape by hand. Cut Lollipop Sticks into 5 in. lengths. Insert into bottom of each leg, leaving 3½ in. exposed. Let dry 2 days. Cut doll pick section to just ½ in. long; insert into lower body. Create assorted tops using a variety of colors and patterns. Roll fondant for base layers ⅛ in. thick, for trims just 1/16 in. thick. Attach to figures using Piping Gel. Secure ponytails with small lengths of wire. Attach fondant strips to cover wire and for pant cuffs, tiny logs for bracelets and necklaces. Roll ½ in. balls and shape into shoes; push onto sticks and attach to pants. Brush with Piping Gel and sprinkle on Cake Sparkle accents. Paint pants with Pearl Dust/vanilla mixture (p. 120).

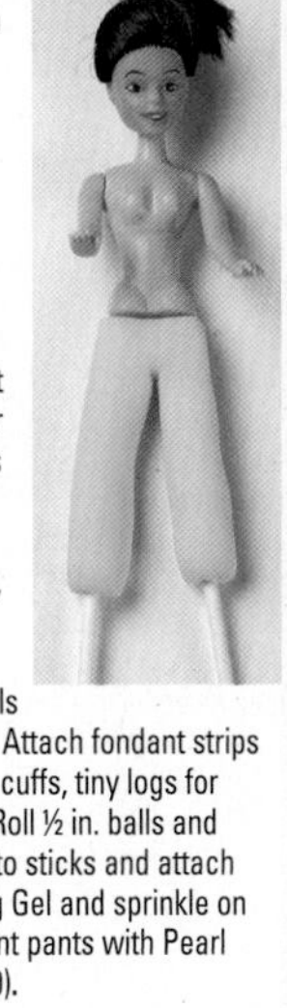

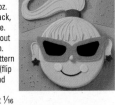

Fondant Decorators

(see Prepping the Princess, p. 17)

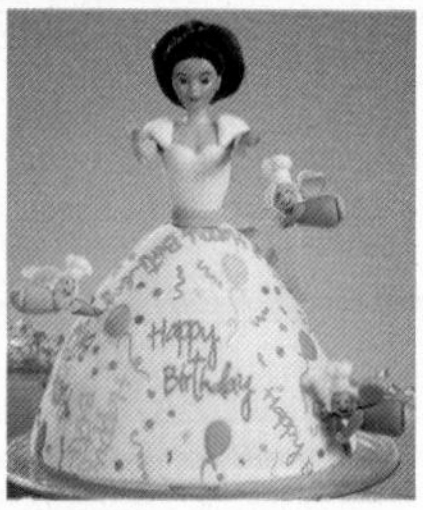

Tint fondant: 2 oz. each blue, violet and copper, ½ oz. each light pink, light blue and light violet; use reserved rose fondant from curved front tie and 2 oz. white. Add ½ teaspoon Gum-Tex to each.

For each decorator you will make: cone-shaped dress, 1½ x ¾ in. wide at hem; ¾ in. ball head; ½ in. ball for hat base, four ¼ in. balls for hat top. Shape pieces and attach with fondant adhesive. Let dry overnight. Use royal icing to pipe tip 2 pull-out hair. Use FoodWriter to draw eyes and smile. Roll and attach tiny ball nose. Brush cheeks with Pearl Dust. Use light colors for wings; roll out ⅛ in. thick. Use pattern to cut 2 wings (flip pattern for 2nd); attach with thinned fondant adhesive. Roll and flatten ¾ in. long oval feet; attach. Roll and attach tiny ball toes. Let dry overnight. **For blue decorator:** Insert 4½ in. Lollipop Stick into body. Attach curved front tie to stick, leaving 2 in. exposed to insert into cake. **For arms**, roll 1 x 3/8 in. logs; curve and attach. Roll and flatten tiny ball hands; use knife to cut fingers. Attach. **For pink decorator**: Insert stick. Roll cone-shaped decorating bag and tip; push onto stick, leaving 2 in. exposed. Roll and attach arms and hands as above. **For violet decorator**: Roll and attach arms and hands as above. Insert stick through 1 arm and into dress. Position confetti in hands. Reserve 1 oz. rose for waistband and back tie. Reserve remaining fondant.

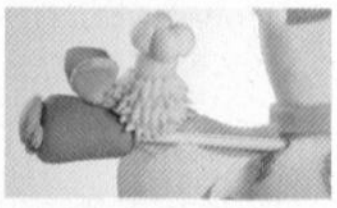

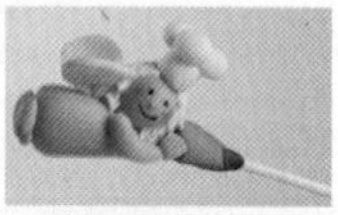

Sea Creature Cookies

(see Underwater Wonders, p. 20)

Prepare and roll out dough. Use animal cutters to cut octopus, whale and shark. Use patterns to cut 2 propellers and 2 periscopes. Bake and cool cookies. Outline fish cookies with tip 2 and full-strength color flow; flow in with thinned color flow (p. 128); on octopus, immediately pipe tip 8 spots. Let dry 24 hours. Use full-strength color flow to pipe tip 2 dot eyes and pupils, outline mouths and shark fin, pull-out teeth.

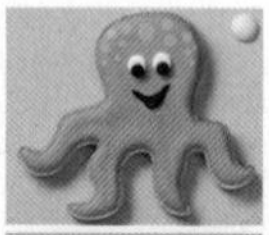

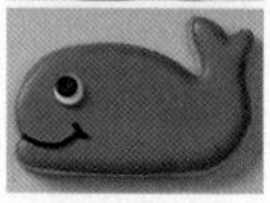

Truck

(see Happy Hauling, p. 21)

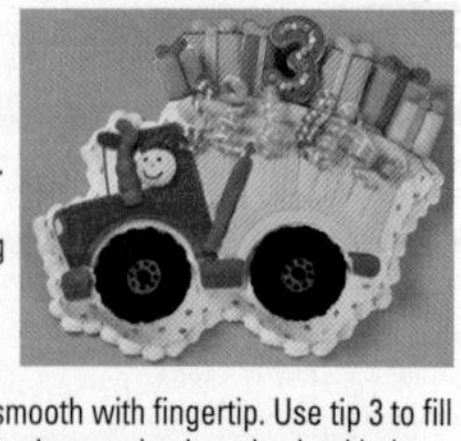

Ice cake sides, truck cab and background areas smooth. Outline features using tip 3. Use tip 8 to fill in smooth areas on truck; pat smooth with fingertip. Use tip 3 to fill in headlight, fender, running board, wheel hubs, bumper, smokestack and connecting shaft. Pipe tip 8 tires; smooth with fingertip. Pipe tip 5 dot lugnuts and axle (flatten with fingertip). Cover truck with tip 18 stars. Pipe tip 2A head; pipe tip 3 pull-out hair, tip 2 dot nose, tip 1 dot eyes and outline mouth. Pipe tip 21 shell bottom border. Attach confetti to cake sides and number cookie. Insert cookies. Curl 12 in. lengths of ribbon and attach.

Hat

(see Grabbing All the Goodies, p. 21 and Sending Hissss Best, p. 24)

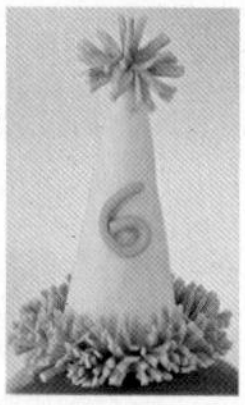

Tint fondant: 3 oz. green, 3 oz. yellow. Roll out ⅛ in. thick as needed. Cut a 5 x 4½ in. strip of yellow fondant. Brush cone with Piping Gel and wrap fondant around cone. Smooth and trim away excess. **For fringe**, cut 22 strips, 2 x ¾ in. wide. Cut slits ⅛ in. wide, ½ in. deep, across outer edge. Roll and separate to make a tuft of fringe. Attach to bottom of hat using damp brush. Repeat. **For pompom**, cut 4 additional strips and repeat as above. Let hat dry on waxed paper-covered board.

Bogeymen Fondant Decorations

(see Brownie Bogeymen, p. 24)

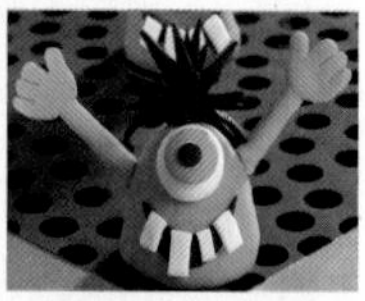

For each treat, tint fondant: ½ oz. black, ½ oz. in violet, orange or green; reserve ¼ oz. white. **For arms**, roll out fondant ⅛ in. thick. Cut strip 1 x 1¼ in. Wrap and attach around pretzel stick, leaving ¼ in. exposed at one end to insert into pop. **For hands**, roll out fondant 1/16 in. thick. Use wide end of tip 194 to cut circles. Use knife to cut slits and shape fingers. Attach to arm using damp brush. Use knife tip to poke small hole through candy shell; insert arms. **For eye**, roll and flatten 7/8 in. diameter disk; attach. Roll out black, white and tinted fondant ⅛ in. thick. Use wide end of tip 12 to cut iris, use narrow end to cut pupil; attach. Cut a 1¼ x 1 in. black scallop for smile; attach. Cut 4 assorted teeth, ¼ to 3/16 in. wide, 5/16 to 9/16 in. long; attach. **For hair**, cut a 1 x ¼ in. wide strip. Cut and remove thin triangles, leaving base with spiked teeth like on a comb. Roll and pinch at base; attach.

Monster Hat

(see Mesmerized Monster, p. 25)

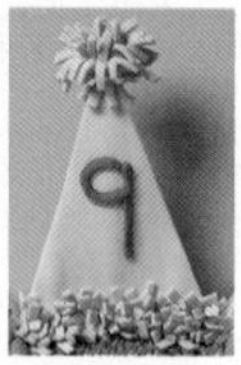

Tint fondant: 6 oz. yellow (add ½ teaspoon Gum-Tex), 3 oz. blue. Roll out ⅛ in. thick as needed. Use pattern to cut hat; let dry overnight on waxed paper-covered board. Reserve remaining fondant. Attach 2 Lollipop Sticks to back with thinned fondant adhesive, leaving 5 in. extended at bottom. **For pompom**, cut a 1½ x 6 in. wide strip (reserve remaining blue). Use Cutter/Embosser to make slits for fringe, 1 in. deep, ⅛ in. wide. Wrap uncut edge around tip of hat, securing with damp brush as you wrap. Let dry.

Mickey Train Cake

(see Engineering a Great Birthday, p. 28)

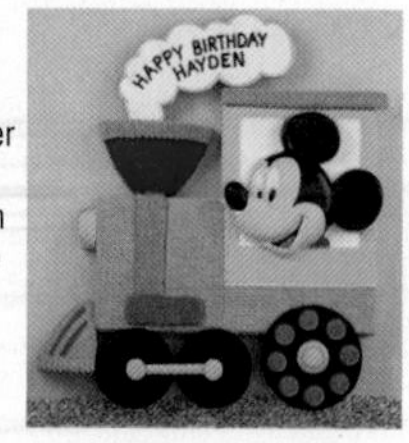

Position square and sheet cakes on prepared board. Cut Wonder Mold cake in half vertically; position 1 piece for smoke stack. Cut other piece in half and trim bottom for 5 in. high section; attach for cowcatcher. Remove baking cup and trim 1 cupcake to 1½ in. high for flat back; attach for light. Use toothpick to mark 9½ in. square window (begin 2 in. from top edge). Ice smooth window area and top of smoke stack. On 10 in. square, use toothpicks to mark 2 x 7½ in. vertical blue stripe (2½ in. from front edge), 2 x 6 in. horizontal dark green stripe, ½ in. wide stripes on cowcatcher. Outline window with tip 5. Cover cakes with tip 18 stars; overpipe engine stripes for dimension. Position roof trim cookie; cover with tip 18 stars. Pipe tip 18 zigzags on edge of cowcatcher and smoke stack. Spatula ice cupcake supports. Position 5 under smoke, 3 under large wheel, 2 for each small wheel. Position smoke and wheel cookies. Attach connecting rod, axles and lug nuts with full-strength color flow. Insert dowel rods to support candy plaque.

Planet Base Board

(see It's Buzz's World!, p. 31)

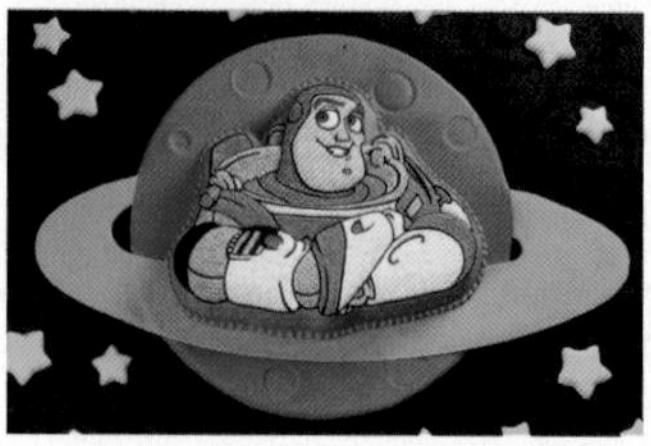

Increase planet pattern to 246% (round planet will be 24.6 x 10.4 in.). Cut foamcore board to fit; cover with foil. Tint fondant: 20 oz. blue, 8 oz. green, 4 oz. black. Roll out to ⅛ in. thick as needed. Cut blue fondant to cover top and sides of board; attach with Piping Gel. Set 16 in. Cake Circle over center to mark planet. Remove fondant from left and right extensions; replace with black fondant, covering top and sides. Remove cake circle. Use pattern to cut yellow/green ring; attach. Use ½ to 2 in. rounds (cans, cutters) to imprint craters.

Fondant Flowers

(see Dora's Island Adventure, p. 32)

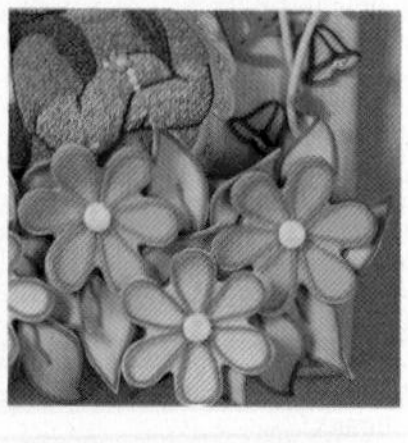

For large flowers, crumple foil to a height of 1 in. and place in bottom of Mini Ball cavities; cover with a 3 in. foil square, leaving a slightly curved depression only ¾ in. deep. Tint fondant: 5 oz. each orange, rose. Add ¼ teaspoon Gum-Tex to each. Roll out ⅛ in. thick. Use Comfort-Grip Cutter to cut 3 flowers in each color. Set in prepared pan. Using royal icing, pipe tip 3 outlines and tip 8 dot center. Let dry. **For small flowers**, tint 2 oz. light violet. Roll out ⅛ in. thick. Use bell cutter from Mini Romantic Set to cut 8 flowers. Cut off clapper using knife; use corner of cutter to cut notch at bottom. Use tip 2 to outline flower and pipe dot stamens. Let dry.

Safari Helmet

(see Elmo on Safari Cake, p. 33)

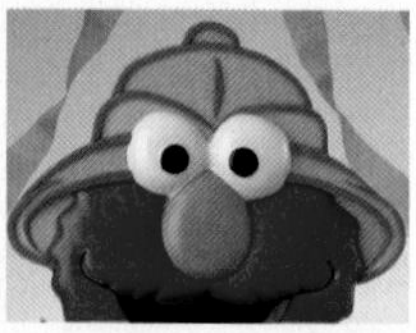

Mold Elmo Candy Plaque (p. 128). Tint 24 oz. fondant light brown; mix in 1 tablespoon Gum-Tex. Roll out to ⅛ in. thick. Using pattern, cut out whole helmet (flip pattern for 2nd half). Set on cornstarch-dusted Cake Board; let dry for 2 days. Position and attach candy plaque over helmet using melted candy. Cut out right and left bands; attach using damp brush. Cut out right and left brims; attach. Tint remaining light brown fondant dark brown. Cut thin strips (¼ in. wide, some tapering to 1/16 in. wide) and attach around edges and at middle for dimension. Let dry 1 to 2 days. Attach dowel rod to back using melted candy. Allow 4 in. to extend at bottom to insert into cake.

Fondant Leaves

(see Elmo on Safari Cake, p. 33)

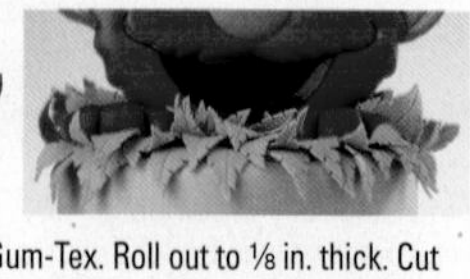

Tint 24 oz. fondant green. Add 1 tablespoon Gum-Tex. Roll out to ⅛ in. thick. Cut 50 each small, medium and large leaves using Cut-Outs set. Place on thin foam and mark center vein using veining tool. Cut random slits using scissors. Let dry in various positions on Flower

Gum Paste Flowers and Leaves

(see Tinker Bell's Flowing Flower Garden, p. 34)

Tint gum paste: 8 oz. green, 4 oz. violet, 4 oz. yellow, 2 oz. blue, 1 oz. pink, 1 oz. burgundy. Roll out 1/16 in. thick as needed for flowers, ⅛ in. thick for leaves. Use cutters and tools from Floral Collection Flower Making Set (unless otherwise specified). Attach pieces using damp brush. Roll ball centers; flatten and attach. Let flowers dry in Flower Forming Cups dusted with cornstarch; let leaves dry on large Flower Formers dusted with cornstarch. Brush flowers with Pearl Dust; brush leaves with a mixture of Pearl Dust and green chalk (rub over tea strainer to create a powdery texture).

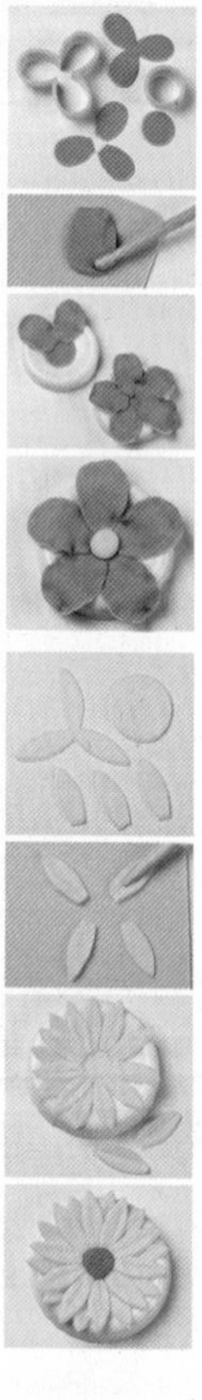

Violet flower (make 5): Cut 5 individual petals using tulip cutter. Place on thin foam and ruffle edges using wooden stick. Cut small carnation round base; attach petals.

Blue flower (make 7): Cut 5 large rose petals. Place on thin foam and make slightly larger by rolling over with wooden stick. Use wide end of tip 3 to cut base; ruffle edges. Attach petals.

Tri-color flower (make 5): Cut 3 layers using small, medium and large Flower Cut-Outs. Dry in small Forming Cups.

Yellow flower (make 6): Cut 20 individual petals using daffodil cutter. Place on thin foam and imprint center line using wooden stick. Cut base using small carnation cutter. Attach 2 rows of 10 petals each.

Leaves (make 60 small and 24 large): Cut small leaves using large rose petal cutter. Cut large leaves using tulip leaf cutter; vary sizes by moving cutter up and cutting leaf a 2nd time. Place on thin foam and add details with veining tool. Let dry on both sides of large Flower Formers.

Ariel's Castle

(see Ariel's Sea Castle, p. 35)

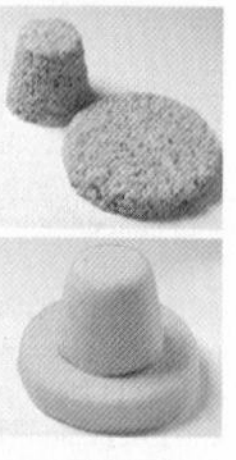

Prepare cereal treat mixture. Press into 9 x 13 in. pan to 1 in. thick. Cut a 6 in. circle for base. Press remaining treats into king size muffin pan; remove. Place treats on cooling grid; cover with melted yellow candy (p. 128); let set. Attach base to 6 in. Cake Circle. Tint 14 oz. fondant golden yellow. Roll out ⅛ in. thick as needed. Cover dome and base with fondant (p. 120). Attach dome to

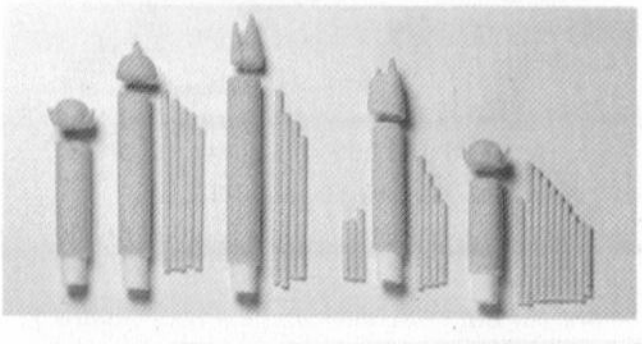

center of base using melted candy. **For turrets**, cut plastic dowel rods to 6, 5½, 4½, 4 and 3½ in. long; tape tops closed. Wrap in fondant, leaving bottom 1 in. bare. Insert 4½ in. turret in dome, about ⅛ in. from back; insert remaining turrets into base around dome, beginning with shortest at front right and increasing sizes in clockwise circle. **For trimmings at tops of 2 smallest turrets**, roll 2 fondant balls ¾ in.; flatten slightly and attach to pillars with buttercream. Cut 2 strips 3 ¾ x ½ in.; cut triangles ½ in. wide and attach to ball with damp brush. **For 3 tallest turrets**, roll teardrop shaped peaks; attach. Wrap 2 turrets with fondant strips around cones. Roll ¼ to ⅛

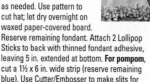

in. diameter fondant logs; wrap around turret tops and attach to dome front and left turret for decorative pattern. Reserve excess fondant. **For railings,** make yellow candy straw posts. Cut plastic drinking straws as follows: **For top of dome,** make 7 straws, 4 in. long. **For left and right curves,** make 10 straws, 5½ in. long. **For front railing** (inserted into cake at party), make 10 straws, 4½ in. long. Make extras to allow for breakage. Tape bottoms of straws closed. Use cut parchment bag to fill straws with melted candy; chill until firm. Use long Lollipop Stick to push out candy straws. Use knife to trim straws to exact length needed. Mark spacing for posts, curving between and

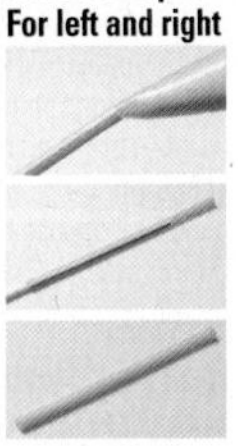

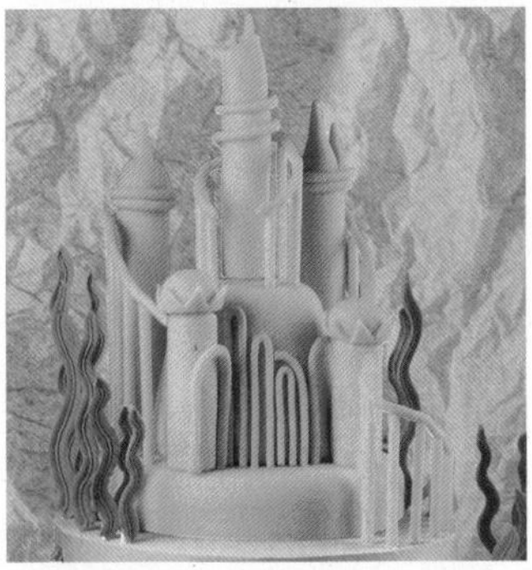

around turrets, ¾ in. apart. Use Lollipop Stick to make holes at marks, 1 in. deep into dome and base. Insert candy straws, trimming to gradually decrease length by ½ in. between posts. Begin with 5½ in. lengths at 2 tallest back turrets and 4 in. lengths at top turret. Roll ¼ in. diameter fondant logs; attach to top of posts for railings with melted candy. Reserve 1 in. ball of fondant for front railing.

SpongeBob Grill and Accessories

(see Well Done, SpongeBob, p. 37)

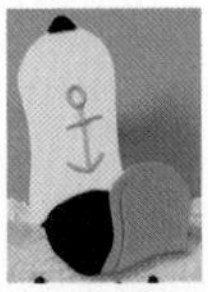

Tint and prepare fondant per instructions. Roll out ⅛ in. thick as needed unless otherwise specified. Let all pieces dry overnight on cornstarch-dusted Cake Boards.

For Hat: Use pattern to cut out complete hat in white. Cut and attach colored details using damp brush. Let dry. Pipe tip 3 anchor with icing.

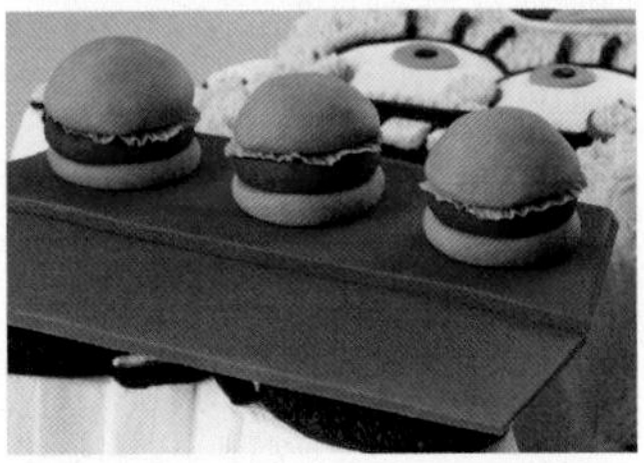

For Grill: Use pattern to cut out 5 in. high grill section in dark gray fondant. Cut additional top half; attach overlay using damp brush. Let dry. Brush grill top with blue Pearl Dust.

For Patties: Divide light brown into 6 balls. Roll and shape into bun halves, 1⅝ in. diameter; flatten 1 side. Divide dark brown into 3 balls. Flatten into 1⅝ in. diameter patties. Roll out green 1/16 in. thick. Cut 3 circles, 1¾ in. diameter, for lettuce. Use back of brush to thin and furl edges. Let dry. Stack pieces using damp brush.

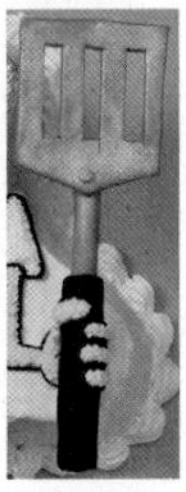

For Spatula: Use pattern to cut out flat end in light gray fondant. Roll tiny ball and flatten slightly for rivet; attach. Cut wooden dowel rod to 5 in. long. Brush with Piping Gel and wrap with light gray for handle . Cover bottom 3 in. with black fondant for handle grip. Let dry. Brush gray areas with silver Pearl Dust.

Gum Paste Bat

(see Bat Hang-Out, p. 42)

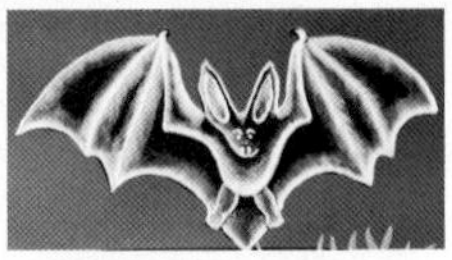

Decorate using Thinned Royal Icing. Work quickly, 1 section at a time, to prevent drying. Outline wings and legs with tip 2, body with tip 3. Outline section then immediately use damp brush to brush icing outward for shaded effect. Use tip 2 to pipe facial features and to overpipe main details. When dry, attach Cookie Stick to back with Thinned Fondant Adhesive. Let dry.

Grass

(see Pumpkin Paradise, p. 44)

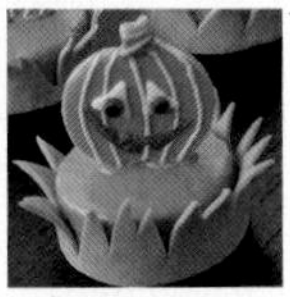

Tint fondant and roll out ⅛ in. thick. Cut 10 x 1½ in. strips. Make V-shaped cuts into top edge. Attach around base with melted candy. Shape edges for natural look.

Halloween Gum Paste Trims

(see A Hoot and a Howl!, p. 44)

Tint gum paste: 18 oz. yellow, 8 oz. orange, 4 oz. light violet, 2 oz. dark violet; reserve a small amount of white. Roll out ⅛ in. thick unless otherwise specified. Using patterns, cut out yellow moon with tree in 1 piece. Set on cornstarch-dusted board. Cut orange tree; attach over yellow base using Gum Paste Adhesive. Use cutter to cut out pumpkin; set on cornstarch-dusted board. Roll out violet 1/16 in. thick; use pattern to cut out owl. Attach. **For trims,** roll out gum paste 1/16 in. thick. Cut thin yellow and orange strips for pumpkin lines, white eyes for pumpkin and owl, light violet pumpkin nose, mouth and irises, dark violet owl wings, bow tie, nose and pupils for pumpkin. Attach all using Gum Paste Adhesive. Let dry 1 week. When dry, attach Lollipop Sticks with melted candy. Carefully turn gum paste pieces over onto waxed paper-covered cake boards. Attach three 3 in. lengths where tree branches connect to moon and on upper trunk section. Attach 6 in. length to tree trunk and 5 in. length to pumpkin, leaving 3 in. exposed at bottom to insert into cake. Attach two 8 in. lengths to back of moon, leaving 5 in. exposed at bottom.

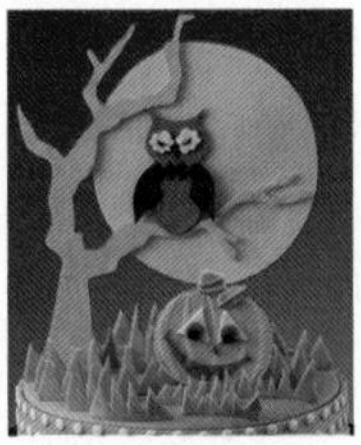

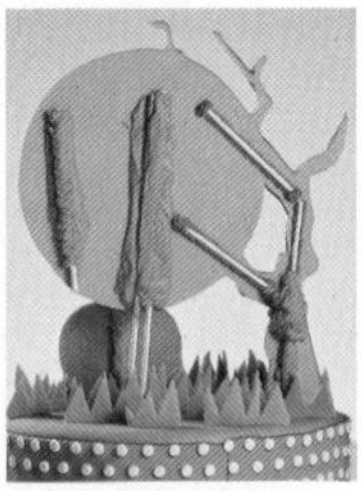

Decorated Pumpkin Cake and Base Board

(see Perky Pumpkin, p. 45)

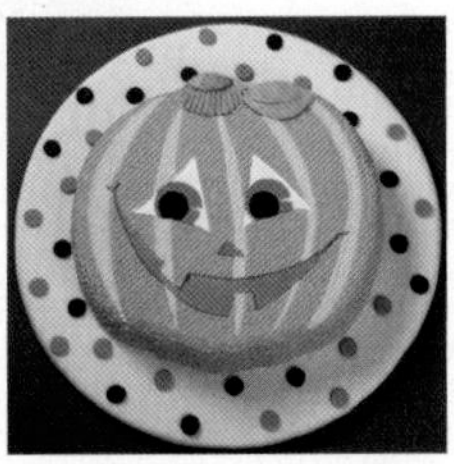

Use patterns to mark facial features. Use tip 3 to outline and fill in features, patting smooth with fingertip dipped in cornstarch. Cover cake with tip 16 stars. Pipe tip 16 lines and swirl for top stem. Use tip 3 to outline and pipe in leaf; pat smooth then add tip 3 center vein. Tint remaining fondant (½ black, ½ violet) and roll out ⅛ in. thick. Cut circles using wide end of tip 3. Attach to base board using damp brush.

Color Flow Owl and Fondant Tree

(see Owl Be There!, p. 45)

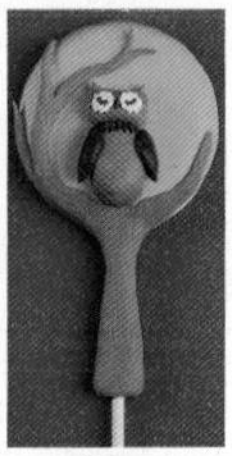

Use full-strength color flow icing to figure pipe owl on cookie. Pipe tip 1A teardrop shaped body, 1 x 1¼ in. long. Pipe tip 12 oval head and pull-out ears. Pipe 8 tip 2 dots in a circle for eyes; fill center and pat smooth. Pipe tip 1 bead beak and outline eyelashes, tip 10 teardrop-shaped wings and tip 2 pull-out dot feathers around neck. Let dry overnight. For fondant tree, wrap cookie stick with tinted fondant, leaving 3 in. exposed at bottom. Shape fondant to form tree trunk and branches. Use knife tip to imprint lines for bark texture.

Owl

(see Halloween Dreams, p. 45)

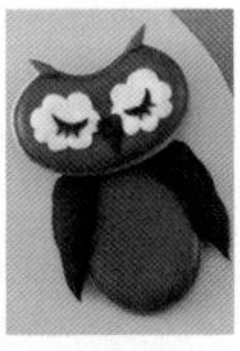

Using tip 2, outline and fill in ¾ in. wide scalloped eyes and ½ in. long nose; pat smooth with fingertip dipped in cornstarch. Pipe tip 2 eyelashes and tip 3 pull-out horns. Using tip 366, pipe pull-out wings. Attach head; support top with a section of Cake Board to hold level until icing dries.

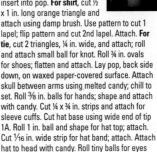

Headless Skeleton Fondant Details

(see Heads Up for Halloween!, p. 46)

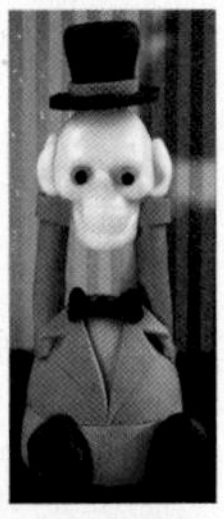

For every 3 treats, tint fondant as follows: 3 oz. violet, 2 oz. green, 2 oz. black, 1 oz. orange. Roll out 1/16 in. thick as needed. **For jacket,** cut 3 in. violet circle and cover pop top. **For pants,** cut 6 x ¾ in. green strip and wrap around bottom. **For sleeves,** cut 1 x 1½ in. strips and smooth around pretzel sticks, leaving bottom end exposed; insert into pop. **For shirt,** cut ½ x 1 in. long orange triangle and attach using damp brush. Use pattern to cut 1 lapel; flip pattern and cut 2nd lapel. Attach. **For tie,** cut 2 triangles, ¼ in. wide, and attach; roll and attach small ball for knot. Roll ¾ in. ovals for shoes; flatten and attach. Lay pop, back side down, on waxed paper-covered surface. Attach skull between arms using melted candy; chill to set. Roll ⅜ in. balls for hands; shape and attach with candy. Cut ¼ x ¾ in. strips and attach for sleeve cuffs. Cut hat base using wide end of tip 1A. Roll 1 in. ball and shape for hat top; attach. Cut 1/16 in. wide strip for hat band; attach. Attach hat to head with candy. Roll tiny balls for eyes and pupils; attach.

Bat Facial Features

(see Bat Intentions, p. 47)

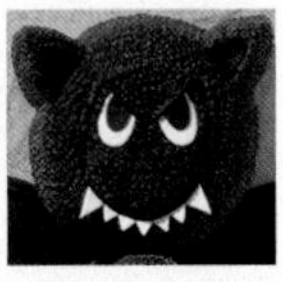

Roll out some white and reserved black fondant. Use pattern to cut 2 inner ears. Using Oval Cutter Set, cut whites of eyes using large cutter, pupils using medium cutter, nose using large cutter. Attach pupils to whites with damp brush, then cut at an angle. Trim nose to 1¼ in. long with slightly curved bottom edge; use tip 3 to indent nostrils. Roll 6½ x ¼ in. rope for mouth. Attach facial features with icing.

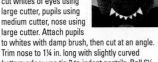

Snow People

(see Picking Their Pine, p. 48)

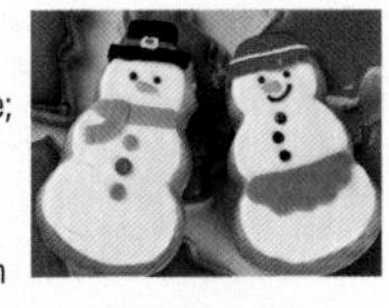

Ice smooth in white; tint icing for trims. Using tip 3, outline and fill in hats, patting smooth with fingertip. Using tip 3, pipe dot buttons; outline and fill in scarf and apron, patting smooth with fingertip. Using tip 1, pipe dot eyes, outline mouth, outline hat bands and hat buckle. Pipe tip 2 pull out noses.

Fondant Snowman Trims

(see Winterized Guy, p. 48)

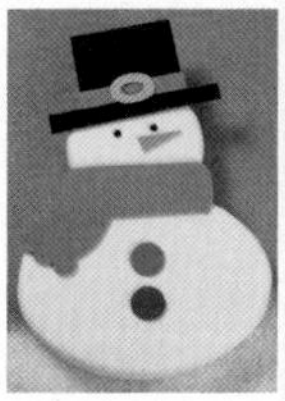

Tint fondant: 5 oz. black, 4 oz. green, ½ oz. each red, blue, orange, golden yellow. Add ½ teaspoon Gum-Tex to black and green. Roll out ⅛ in. thick as needed. Use patterns and Cutter/Embosser fitted with smooth edge wheel to cut scarf, hat, hat band, buckle and nose. Cut out center of buckle using knife. Use narrow end of tip 12 to cut 2 eyes. Use medium round Cut-Out to cut 2 buttons. Cut two 2½ in. squares to brace hat. Let all pieces dry on waxed paper-covered boards dusted with cornstarch.

Snowman and Tree Cookies

(see Fir Trader, p. 48)

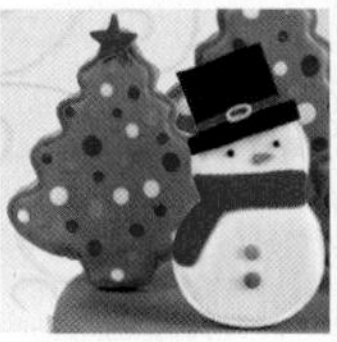

Prepare and roll out dough. Cut 1 snowman (cut off brim and sides of hat), 1 Comfort-Grip tree and 2 Grippy Cutter trees. Bake and cool cookies. Outline with tip 3 and full-strength icing; flow in with thinned icing (p. 128). For trees, immediately add tip 2 dots of thinned icing for ornaments. Let dry. Attach Lollipop Sticks to backs of cookies using full-strength icing; leave 2 in. extended at bottom to insert into base. Let dry.

Snowdrift and Snowflake Dots

(see Fir Trader, p. 48)

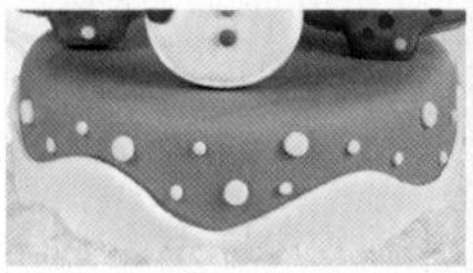

Roll out white fondant ⅛ in. thick. Cut a 1¾ x 18 in. strip of white fondant;use Cutter/Embosser to cut wavy topline 1 to 1½ in. deep. Attach snowdrift around base using damp brush. Cut snowflake dots using narrow end of tips 7 and 12; attach using damp brush.

Snowman Assembly, Features and Clothes

(see Flurry Friend, p. 49)

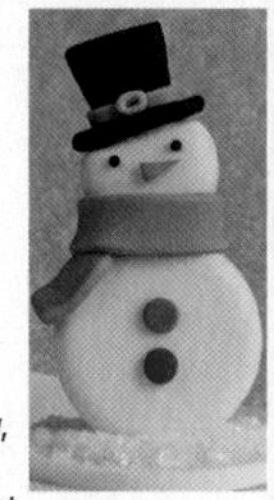

Slightly flatten body cake with knife; attach to candy base with melted candy. Let set. Trim ¼ in. off head cake for positioning hat. Attach head cake on an angle to body; let set. Make features and clothes. Tint portions of fondant black, golden yellow, orange, blue, red and green.

For hat: Roll out black fondant 3/16 in. thick; cut a 1½ x ¾ in. wide piece for brim, shape into oval. Roll out fondant ¼ in. thick; cut 1 x 1 in. piece for top of hat. Taper at bottom and attach to brim with water. Roll out green fondant ⅛ in. thick; cut ⅛ x 1½ in. long hat band. Attach. Use narrow opening of tip 12 to cut golden yellow buckle. Cut out center using narrow opening of tip 6. Shape into oval and attach. Roll out remaining colors ⅛ in. thick. Cut 2 eyes with small opening of tip 6. **For nose,** cut a ½ in. long triangle. For scarf, cut 2 pieces ½ x 1½ in. long for tail and 1 piece 4 in. long for neck. Cut buttons using narrow opening of tip 12.

Antlers

(see Rompin' Reindeer, p. 49)

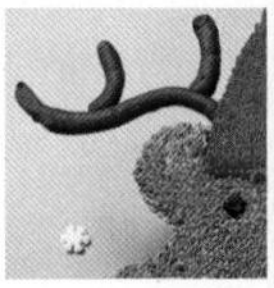

Tape patterns to board; cover with waxed paper. Spray with pan spray; wipe off excess with tissue. For back antler, tape Lollipop Stick into position so that 2 in. of stick will be inside antler bottom. Pipe tip 12 antlers. Let dry.

Sledding Figures

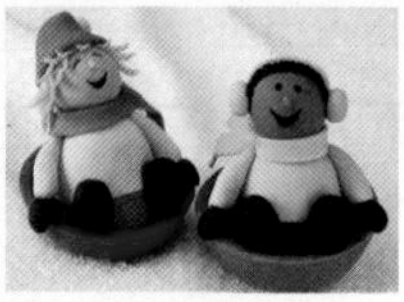

(see Saucer Sledders, p. 52)

For 2 figures shown, tint fondant: 2 oz. each black, rose, blue and violet; 1 oz. yellow; 1 oz. brown or copper for each head. **For scarf ends**, roll out yellow and violet 1/16 in. thick. Cut 3 x ⅜ in. strips. Fold into V-shape; cut 1/16 in. wide slits, ¼ in. deep, for fringed ends. Let dry on cornstarch-dusted wooden dowel rods. **To cover bodies**, ice smooth; roll out pink and blue ⅛ in. thick and cover. Cut a 3 in. circle for shirts; attach around top of brownie pop and smooth with hands. Roll out violet and black 1/16 in. thick; cut ⅝ x 6 in. strips for pants; attach around bottom. Position bodies leaning back slightly in candy shells; support with fondant if necessary. Roll ¾ in. balls of pink and blue (2 each); shape into 1½ in. long tapered sleeves and attach using damp brush. Roll four ¾ in. black balls; shape into shoes and attach. Roll four ½ in. black balls; shape into mittens and attach, resting on sled. Roll 1¼ in. balls in copper and brown; insert cut Lollipop Stick and attach for heads. **For straight hair**, attach individual strands, about ½ to ¾ in. long. **For curly hair**, attach tiny black balls. Shape 1½ in. high tapered hat with ⅜ in. diameter ball tip; roll ¼ in. ball for pompom; attach. Cut 1½ x ⅛ in. strip for earmuff band; attach. Roll ⅜ in. diameter balls for earmuffs; flatten and attach. **For scarf around neck**, roll small amount of violet and yellow 1/16 in. thick. Cut 3 x ⅜ in. strips; attach around neck. Attach prepared scarf ends with dot of melted candy. Roll tiny ball noses; attach. Use Black FoodWriter to draw eyes and mouth.

Snowman Hats

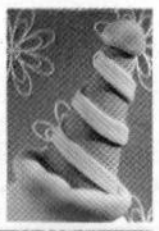

(see Let the Flakes Fly, p. 54)

For pointed hat, trim ice cream cone to 2¼ in.; for top hat, trim 2¼ in. off point and 1 in. off opening of cone, leaving a 1¼ in. piece. Cover with fondant. **For pointed hat**, cut a ¼ x 4 in. strip and wrap around. Push 3 in. Lollipop Stick into head and position hat on stick. Roll small ball for tip and log for brim; attach using damp brush. **For top hat**, use large round cutter to cut circle brim. Push stick into head and position brim and hat over stick. Cut ¼ x 2½ in. hat band; attach using damp brush.

Bow and Streamers

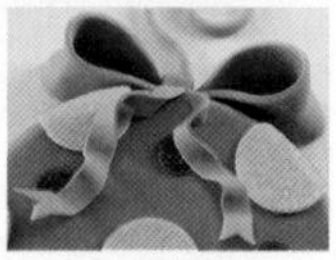

(see Neon On Your Tree!, p. 54)

Tint 8 oz. fondant green; add 1 teaspoon Gum-Tex. Roll out ⅛ in. thick. Cut 2 strips for loops, 2 ½ in. wide x 8 in. long. Brush ends with damp brush and press together. Cut ends to taper to 1½ in. Align on sides on cornstarch-dusted board, supporting openings with tissue. **For streamers**, cut 2 strips ¾ x 10 in.; cut v-shaped notch in ends. Shape and let dry on cornstarch-dusted board, supporting with tissue. Cut a ¾ x 2 in. strip for knot; wrap around ends of loops.

Fondant House Trims

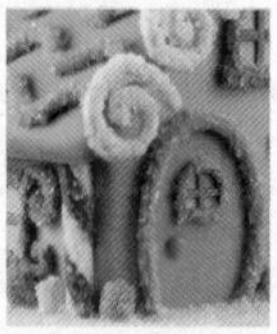

(see Glittering Getaway, p. 55)

Add 1 teaspoon Gum-Tex to 7 oz. fondant. Roll out a portion of white fondant ⅛ in. thick; cut 2 circles using wide end of tip. Roll remaining fondant into ¼ in. diameter logs. Following patterns, make 14 small and 2 large swirls and 2 loops. Tint 2 oz. fondant red. Roll ¼ in. diameter red and white logs together; twist and roll smooth. Cut four 3 in. candy cane logs. Tint 6 oz. fondant yellow and 2 oz. orange. Shape 13 gumdrops ½ in. high in each color; reserve remaining yellow. Let all pieces dry. Brush with piping gel, coat with Sparkling Sugar; let dry overnight.

Santa's Workshop

(see Busy Building, p. 58)

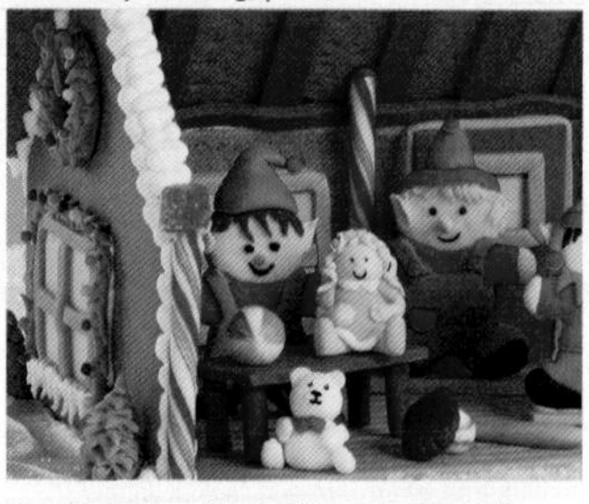

Prepare fondant. **For dark brown tables**: Mix 4 oz. white with dark brown pouch from Multi Pack. Mix ½ teaspoon Gum-Tex into 2 in. ball; reserve remaining fondant. **For toys**: Mix some white into yellow and blue from Multi Packs for softer shades. **For pink dress**, tint a ½ in. ball red and mix with a 1½ in. white ball. Assemble pieces using Piping Gel unless otherwise specified.

Tables: Roll out prepared dark brown ⅛ in. thick. Cut 1 x 2⅝ and 1¼ x 3½ in. rectangles for tabletops. Roll a ¼ in. diameter log. Cut 8 table legs, 1 in. long. Let dry 48 hours on cornstarch-dusted board. Attach legs using Fondant Adhesive.

Doll: Begin with ¾ in. high cone-shaped body and ½ in. ball head, using pink pouch from Natural Multi Pack Fondant. Shape 1 in. long legs and arms; use knife to indent fingers. Shape shoes and sleeves, collar and dress hem. For hair, roll out yellow 1/16 in. thick. Cut 1/16 in. wide strips, 1 to 1½ in. long; wrap around straight pin to curl. Roll tiny ball nose. Use FoodWriter to add eyes and smile.

Bear: Begin with ⅝ in. ball body and ½ in. ball head. Roll a ¼ in. diameter log; cut ¾ in. long arms, 1 in. long legs. Shape muzzle, ears and 2-pc. bow tie. Use FoodWriter to add facial features.

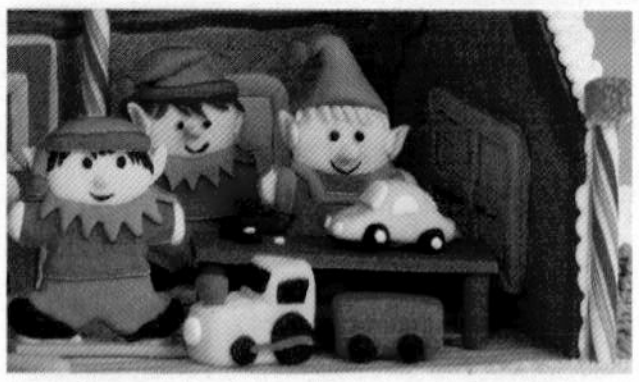

Car: Shape 1 car body from 1 in. ball. Roll out small amount of black and white 1/16 in. thick. Cut wheels using narrow end of tip 12. Cut windows with wide end of tip 12; trim to fit. Roll tiny balls of fondant and flatten for hubcaps, headlights and tail lights.

Train: Shape engine from 1½ in. ball, train car from 1 in. ball. Roll out small amounts of black, red and white 1/16 in. thick. Cut large wheels with wide end of tip 12; cut headlight and other wheels with narrow end of tip 12. Cut 1 in. long strip for axle; cut rectangular windows to fit. Roll ½ in. long cone for smokestack; use toothpick to make small opening in wide end using brush handle tip. Indent engine area for smokestack and attach. Roll ¼ in. ball for hitch to attach car.

Baseball, Bat, Mitt: Shape bat from ¼ x 1¾ in. log. Shape mitt from ¾ in. ball; use knife tip to indent fingers and open slit where hand would go. Roll ⅜ in. diameter baseball; let dry. Use red FoodWriter to add stitching.

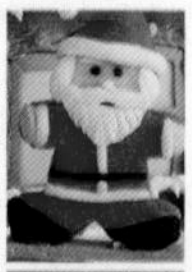

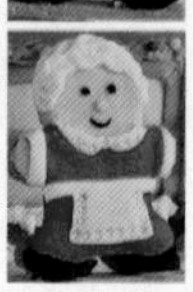

For Santa and Mrs. Claus: Cut and shape heads, outfits and shoes. Shape hat from ¾ in. ball. Shape hair-dos, beard and mustache. Use knife tip or toothpick to add texture. Shape hands, pompom, tiny ball eyes and nose, thin log mouth. Cut thin strips for hat and outfit trims, cuffs and belts. Cut rounded collar and 1 in. apron. Indent details using tip 13.

Gingerpop Figures: Mix 4 oz. white fondant with green fondant pouch from Multi Pack. Use pink from Natural Multi Pack for skin tone shown. Roll out ⅛ in. thick as needed; reserve remaining fondant. Attach fondant pieces to Gingerpops using Piping Gel; shape and smooth with fingers.

For Elves: Cut and shape head, shirts, pants, overalls, shoes and collars. Roll tiny spiked logs for hair. Shape pointed hats from ¾ in. balls. Shape hands, pointed noses and ears. Roll tiny ball eyes and log mouth. Cut pockets, buttons, hat brims and pompoms.

Figure Piped Bear

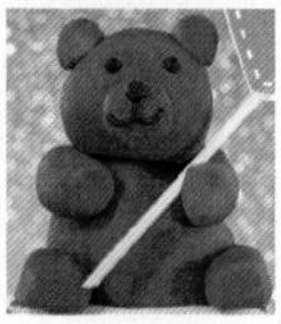

(see Cubby Love, p. 60)

Pipe figures on waxed paper-covered board. Use tip 1A to figure pipe dome-shaped body, 1¼ in. high. Pipe tip 2A ball head, 1 in. diameter. Using tip 10, pipe 1 in. long arms and legs curving around body; pipe ⅜ in. round muzzle. Pipe tip 3 ears; pinch to flatten slightly. Pipe tip 1 dot eyes and nose, outline mouth. Position pick in hand. Let dry 24 hours.

Fondant Butterflies

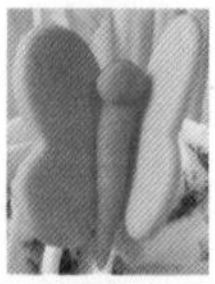

(see Fluttering on Flowers, p. 62)

Tint 1½ oz. portions of fondant rose, violet and yellow. Tint ½ oz. of each color in a darker shade. Roll out light fondant ⅛ in. thick. Cut butterflies using mini cutter. Fold cardstock accordion style; dust with cornstarch and position butterflies in folds to dry. Roll 3/16 in. diameter logs of dark fondant. Cut 1 in. lengths for bodies, taper ends and attach to butterflies with damp brush. Roll 3/16 in. diameter ball heads and attach. Let dry overnight.

Bunny and Chick Details

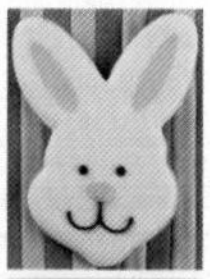

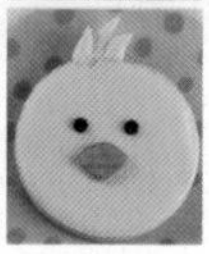

(see The Picture of Spring, p. 63)

Attach heads to bases. Pipe tip 1 dot eyes and bunny mouth; pipe tip 2 dot nose on bunny, fill in beak (indent with knife tip) and pull-out hair on chick.

Lady Liberty and Uncle Sam Decorations

(see Lady Liberty and Uncle Sam, p. 67)

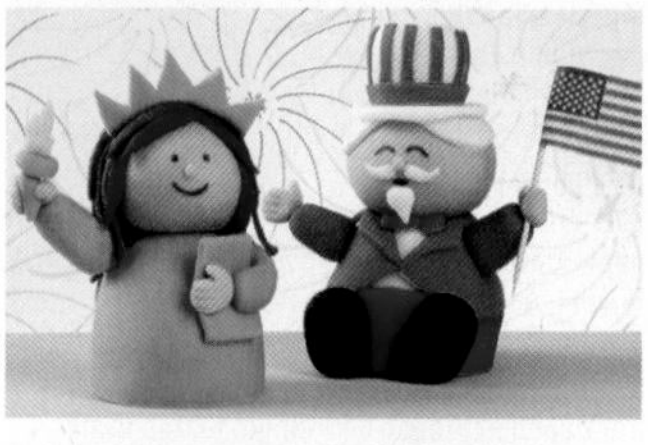

Roll out fondant as needed, ⅛ in. thick unless otherwise specified. **For her**: Cover brownie with green fondant. For head, roll a 1¾ in. ball. Flatten bottom slightly; insert pretzel stick, leaving 1 in. exposed. Insert head into body. For raised arm, trim pretzel stick to 1½ in. long. Insert, leaving ¾ in. exposed. For sleeve, roll ½ in. fondant ball and wrap around pretzel. Cut a 1 x 1½ in. rectangle for book. Roll a 1½ x ⅜ in. log for 2nd arm. For hands, roll ½ in. fondant balls; flatten and cut slits for fingers. Attach all using damp brush. For torch, shape a ½ in. high cone handle, ½ in. wide disk top and ⅝ in. high flame (use knife to score fondant). Assemble and secure in hand. **For hair**, cut 3/16 in. wide strips, 1 to 1½ in. long; attach. For crown, cut a 2 x ¾ in. strip; use knife to cut points. Attach. Roll small ball nose; attach. Use FoodWriter to draw eyes and mouth.

For him: Cover brownie with white fondant. For pants, cut a strip 1 x 7 in; attach using damp brush. For coat, cut a 1¼ x 6 in. strip; attach. Cut away front for V-neck and shaped bottom. Cut triangle lapels and bow tie; attach. **For shoes**, roll ½ in. diameter balls; shape and attach. **For head**, roll a 1¾ in. ball; flatten top for hat. Insert pretzel stick in bottom, leaving ½ in. exposed. Insert head into body. **For hair**, cut 2 circles, 1 in. diameter; attach. **For hat brim**, cut 1¾ in. diameter circle; attach. **For hat top**, roll a 1 in. ball; flatten ends and attach. Roll out red 1/16 in. thick. Cut 10 strips, ⅛ x 1 in. and attach for stripes. For hat band, cut ¼ x 3 in. blue strip; attach. **For arms**, trim pretzel sticks to 1½ in. long. Insert, leaving ¾ in. exposed. **For sleeves**, roll ½ in. fondant balls and wrap around pretzel. **For hands**, roll ⅜ in. fondant balls; flatten and cut slits for fingers. Attach. Wrap 1 hand around flag pick. Roll tiny ball nose, swirled moustache and beard; attach. Use FoodWriter to draw eyes and mouth. Each serves 1.

Baby's Wagon

(see The Big Wheel Arrives, p. 70)

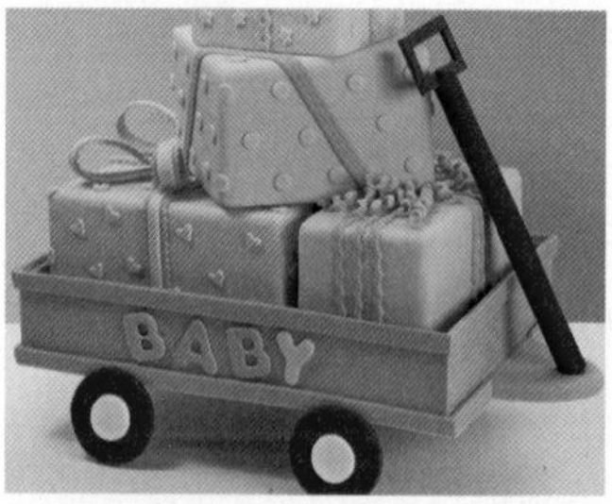

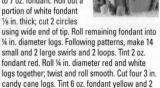

Begin 5 or more days in advance. Tint light and dark brown fondant per instructions. Roll out light brown ¼ in. thick. **For sides**, cut two 18 x 3 in. and two 11½ x 3 in. panels. **For side trims**, cut four strips each 18 ½ x ¾ in. and 12 x ¾ in. Let dry for 5 days on cornstarch-dusted board. Reserve excess fondant. **For base**, lightly mark a 12 x 18 in. rectangle on foamcore board; position Base Hitch pattern at center point of 1 end and mark outline. Cut foamcore and wrap with Fanci-Foil (p. 110). Roll out fondant ⅛ in. thick. Cut 4 x 5 in. rectangle to cover Base Hitch area only. Attach upright side panels and trims using fondant adhesive; let dry. Reserve remaining light brown for bear trims. Roll out half of dark brown 3/16 in. thick. Cut 4 wheels using largest round cutter from 101 Cutters Set. Roll out reserved white fondant; cut 4 wheel centers using smallest round cutter from set. Roll out remaining dark brown fondant. Use pattern to cut out handle. Use knife to cut a ¼ x ½ in. deep slot into 1 end of Plastic Dowel Rod to hold handle. Brush rod with Piping Gel; cover with 3 x 12 in. fondant rectangle, smoothing with hands and keeping slot clear. Let all pieces dry for 3-4 days on cornstarch-dusted boards. Attach handle to rod using fondant adhesive. Let dry. Attach handle and wheels to wagon at reception.

Baby Bear

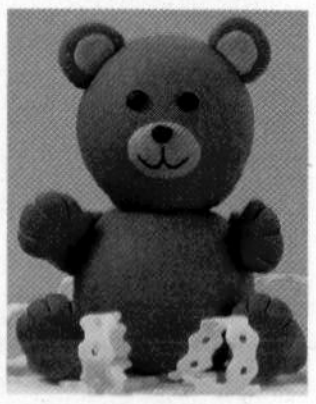

(see The Big Wheel Arrives, p. 70)

Begin 2 or more days in advance. Tint dark brown and black fondant per instructions; use reserved light brown fondant from wagon. Use small ball of fondant to close off top hole of 1 globe for head. Roll out dark brown fondant ⅛ in. thick. Cut 2 circles, 8 in. diameter. Brush head and body globes with Piping Gel, cover with fondant and smooth with hands. Brush neck area with damp brush and stack globes. Let dry overnight. Roll 1 x 3 in. logs for legs with feet, ¾ x 2½ in. logs for arms with hands. Flatten and taper ends; score edges for fingers and toes. Attach to body; support with tissue and let dry completely. Roll ⅝ in. balls for ears; flatten, trim bottom edge and attach. Roll 1 in. ball for muzzle; flatten, shape and attach. Roll ¼ in. balls for inner ears; flatten, trim bottom edge and attach. Roll 3/16 in. balls for eyes and nose; attach. Draw mouth with FoodWriter. Position on cake top at reception.

Cake Trims

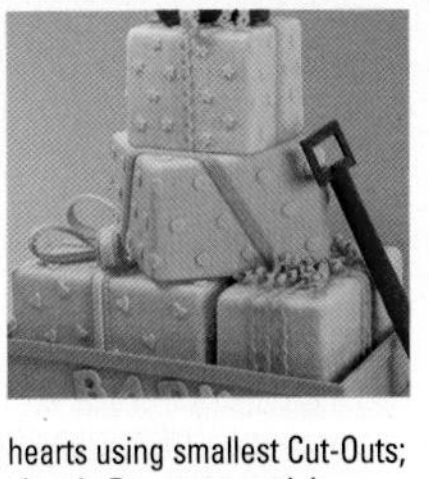

(see The Big Wheel Arrives!, p. 70)

Use reserved fondant to cut fondant ribbons using Ribbon Cutter/Embosser. Cut stars, rounds and hearts using smallest Cut-Outs; attach using damp brush. Reserve remaining fondant. **For yellow**: Cut 8 in. lengths for 4 flat ribbons and 4 loops using 2 wavy wheels with ¼ in. spacer; use narrow end of tip 6 to cut and remove center dots. Attach flat ribbons to cake. Form loops, pinch slightly and secure ends with damp brush; support with tissue and let dry on cornstarch-dusted board. Cut and attach about 60 stars. **For blue**: Cut 2 strips, 14 in. long, using 2 beaded wheels and no spacer; attach. Cut and attach about 45 rounds. **For pink**: Cut 10 in. lengths for flat ribbons and 8½ in. lengths for loops. Cut pink base using 2 zigzag wheels with ¾ in. spacer; cut light pink center strip using 2 straight wheels with ½ in. spacer. Attach layers. Attach flat ribbons to cake. Form loops, pinch slightly and secure ends with damp brush; support with tissue and let dry on cornstarch-dusted board. Cut and attach about 70 hearts. **For green**: Cut strips using 2 wavy wheels and no spacer. Cut six 10 in. lengths and six 7½ in. lengths for flat ribbons; attach. Cut 10 strips, 4 to 6 in. long, for curls. Wrap loosely around Cookie Sticks dusted with cornstarch; let set 15 minutes then slide off and let dry on cornstarch-dusted board.

Fairy Tale Figures

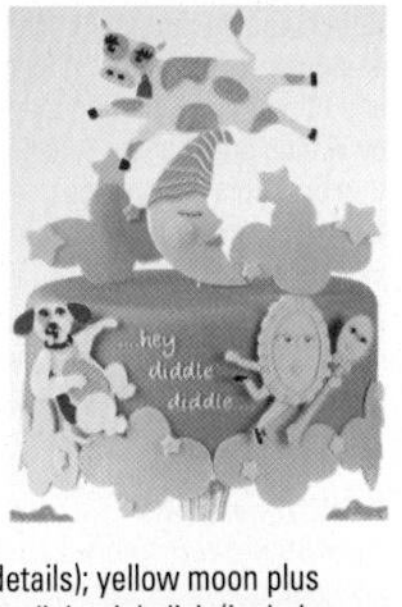

(see Party Time Nursery Rhyme, p. 70)

Tint fondant and roll out as specified in instructions. Use patterns to cut out: white cow; white dog plus leg and arm overlays (attach after icing details); yellow moon plus dark pink hat overlay; light pink dish (includes arms and legs) plus light and dark yellow oval overlays; periwinkle spoon; and 7 light periwinkle clouds. Use royal icing to attach cut Lollipop Sticks to back of spoon and plate arms; position spoon and curl arm over. Use royal icing and tip 1 to outline and fill in details; use finger to pat smooth large areas. Let dry on cornstarch-dusted surface. Turn cow over; reinforce legs and tail with royal icing; let dry. Use melted candy to attach moon and cow to same Lollipop Stick; allow 10 in. to extend at bottom to insert into cake. Let set.

Fondant Baby Accents

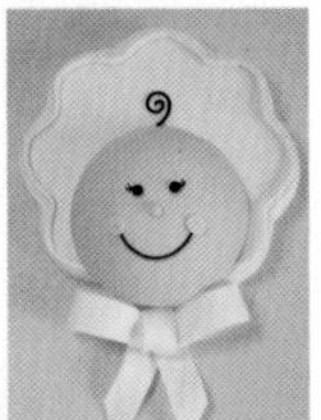

(see Baby Face, p. 71)

For Bonnet Bow, add 1 teaspoon Gum-Tex to 12 oz. fondant. Roll out 1/8 in. thick. Cut 2 strips 2 x 11 in. for bow loops, 2 strips 2 x 8 in. for streamers and a 2 x 5 in. strip for knot. Brush ends of loops and knot with damp brush, fold over and pinch lightly to secure. Set on sides on cornstarch-dusted board; use soft tissue in centers to maintain openings. Trim ends of streamers at an angle; set on board and use tissue to form waves. Let all dry. Assemble using fondant adhesive. **For Hat,** roll fondant rope 30 x ⅜ in. diameter. Attach for hat trim using damp brush. **For fondant features,** tint 1 in. ball rose and 1 in. ball black. Roll two ⅜ in. diameter balls and flatten slightly for eyes. Roll thin strips for lashes. Roll two 5 x ⅛ in. diameter ropes for smile and hair curl. Roll and flatten ½ in. wide nose. Roll out rose ⅛ in. thick. Use wide end of tip 2D to cut cheeks.

Baby and Bonnet Cookies

(see Tot Pops, p. 71)

Place round cookies on cooling grid and cover with thinned color flow (p. 128). Let dry overnight on waxed paper-covered boards. Attach head to bonnet cookie using full-strength icing. Use full-strength icing and tip 3 to outline bonnet outer edge; flow in with thinned icing (p. 128). Let dry. Attach cookies to cookie sticks with melted candy; let set. Decorate cookies with full-strength icing. Using tip 2, pipe hair curl, outline smile and dot eyes; pipe dot nose. Pipe tip 3 dot cheeks; flatten slightly with finger dipped in cornstarch. Let dry. Tie ribbon around stick. Each serves 1.

Fondant Plaque

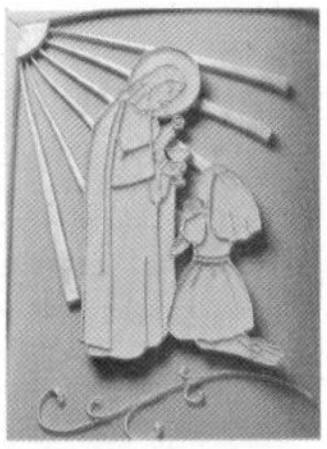

(see Heaven's Blessings, p. 74)

Add ½ teaspoon Gum-Tex to 6 oz. fondant. Roll out to ⅛ in. thick. Use knife and pattern to cut out figures. Use pin to poke holes to indicate inner details. Tape waxed paper over curved back of pan where figures will go; dust with cornstarch. Position figures over waxed paper; let dry 2 days. Use full-strength color flow to outline figures and inner details with tip 2 outlines (use tip 1 for smaller details); let dry. Paint plaque with Clear Vanilla and Pearl Dust mixture (p. 120)

Communion Book Cake Top

(see Heaven's Blessings, p. 74)

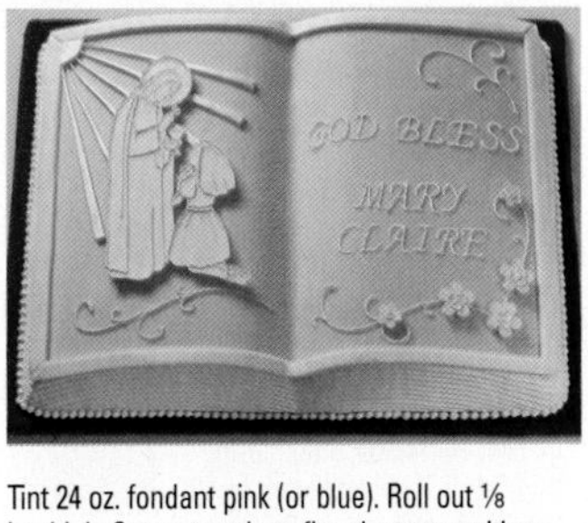

Tint 24 oz. fondant pink (or blue). Roll out ⅛ in. thick. Cut rectangle to fit cake top; position and smooth. Trim edges if necessary. Roll out white fondant 3/16 in. thick. Cut ½ in. wide strips to form outer border; attach to cake top using damp brush. Roll out white fondant ⅛ in. thick. Cut 6 light rays, 6 in. long, tapering from ¼ to ⅛ in. wide; attach. Cut circle using medium round Cut-Out from set. Cut off 1 quarter and attach over light rays for sun. Use letter press to imprint message. Pipe tip 2 message and scroll vines using royal icing; let dry, then brush with Pearl Dust.

Monogrammed and Daisy Cookies

(see Cross Cookies, p. 75)

For monogrammed version, outline blue cross using full-strength color flow and tip 2; fill-in with thinned color flow. Let dry. Also: Make monogrammed disk. Using thinned color flow, pipe 1⅛ in. diameter puddle dots (p. 120) on waxed paper-covered board. Use full-strength color flow to pipe tip 2 initial; let dry. Paint initial and blue cross section with Pearl Dust/Vanilla mixture (p. 120).

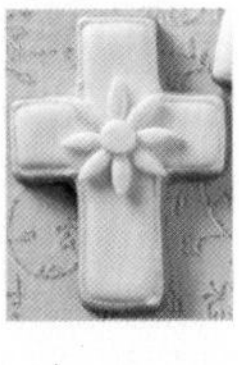

For daisy version, roll out fondant ⅛ in. thick. Cut using medium daisy cutter from set. Roll ¼ in. ball; attach to center using damp brush. Flatten ball and petals with fingertip dipped in cornstarch. Paint pink edges with Pearl Dust/Vanilla mixture. Attach daisies using full-strength color flow.

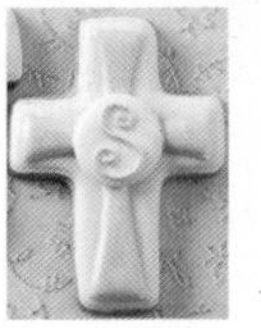

For monogrammed version, attach disks using full-strength color flow. **For all-white version,** paint outer edges with Pearl Dust/Vanilla mixture. Pipe center cross using full-strength color flow and tip 5 outlines. Flatten with fingertip dipped in cornstarch. Position Sugar Pearls; attach with dots of full strength icing.

Grad Caps

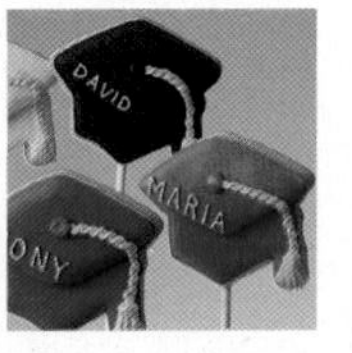

(see Sticking with Their Studies, p. 79)

Attach mortarboard to complete cap. Pipe tip 3 rope cording; add tip 2 pull-out tassels. Pipe tip 3 dot button; flatten slightly with fingertip. Pipe tip 1 name. Let all dry. Paint cord and tassel with Pearl Dust (p. 120); let dry.

Wrapped Roses

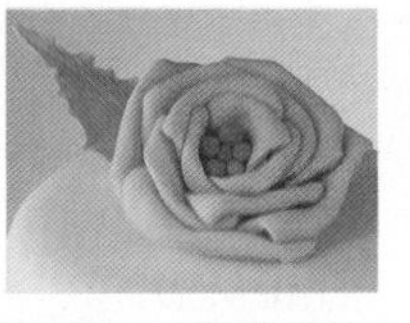

(see Rose Unity, p. 82)

Tint and roll out fondant per instructions. **For large rose**, cut 2 strips 2 x 1 ½ in.; fold to 1 x 1½ in. Curve and wrap for rose center, positioning fold at top. Secure with damp brush. Cut 5 strips 2 x 2 in.; fold to 1 x 2 in. curve and attach using damp brush, staggering petals and increasing angle as you add outer petals. Cut 4 strips 2 x 3 in.; fold to 1 x 3 in. Attach as above. **For small roses**, cut 4 strips 2 x 1¼ in.; fold to 1 x 1¼ in. Curve and attach as above. Cut 4 strips 2 x 2 in.; fold to 1 x 2 in. Attach as above. Tint small amount of fondant a darker shade of rose. Roll ¼ in. diameter balls for center of each rose; 3-6 balls for large roses, 1 for small roses.

Royal Icing Butterflies

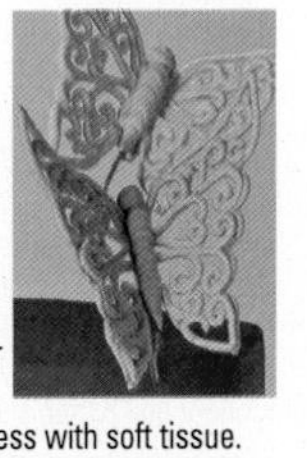

(see Garden Guests and Natural Wonders, p. 82)

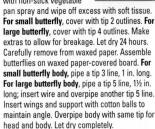

Tape wing patterns to cake board and cover with waxed paper. For easy release, spray waxed paper with non-stick vegetable pan spray and wipe off excess with soft tissue. **For small butterfly**, cover with tip 2 outlines. **For large butterfly**, cover with tip 4 outlines. Make extras to allow for breakage. Let dry 24 hours. Carefully remove from waxed paper. Assemble butterflies on waxed paper-covered board. **For small butterfly body**, pipe a tip 3 line, 1 in. long. **For large butterfly body**, pipe a tip 5 line, 1½ in. long; insert wire and overpipe another tip 5 line. Insert wings and support with cotton balls to maintain angle. Overpipe body with same tip for head and body. Let dry completely.

Fondant Flowers

(see Garden Guests and Natural Wonders, p. 82)

Tint 1 oz. portions of fondant blue, violet, orange and pink. Roll out 1/16 in. thick. Cut flowers specified in directions using cutters from set. Place on thick foam and cup centers using rounded end of modeling stick dipped in cornstarch. Roll small balls (⅛ to ¼ in. diameter) for centers. Attach using damp brush. Let dry.

Fondant Flowers

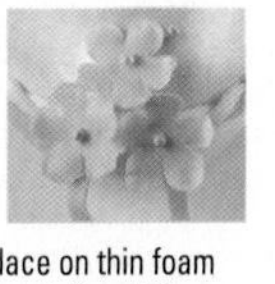

(See Double Ring Ceremony, p. 82)

Add ¼ teaspoon Gum-Tex to 3 oz. fondant. Roll out 1/16 in. thick. Cut 48 flowers using pansy cutter from set. Place on thin foam and thin edges using rounded end of modeling stick. Place on thick foam and cup center using rounded end of modeling stick. Let dry on cornstarch-dusted board.

Fondant Initial

(See Pillows to Dream On, p. 85).

Make pattern for initial, up to 5 in. wide, 5½ in. high. Mix 1½ teaspoons Gum-Tex into 12 oz. fondant. Roll out ¼ in. thick. Using pattern, cut out initial. Paint with Pearl Dust/vanilla mixture (p. 120). Let dry 2 to 3 days. Use melted candy to attach 2 Lollipop Sticks to back, trimming as needed to leave 2 in. exposed at bottom to insert into cake.

Cake Tops

(See Pillows to Dream On, p. 85)

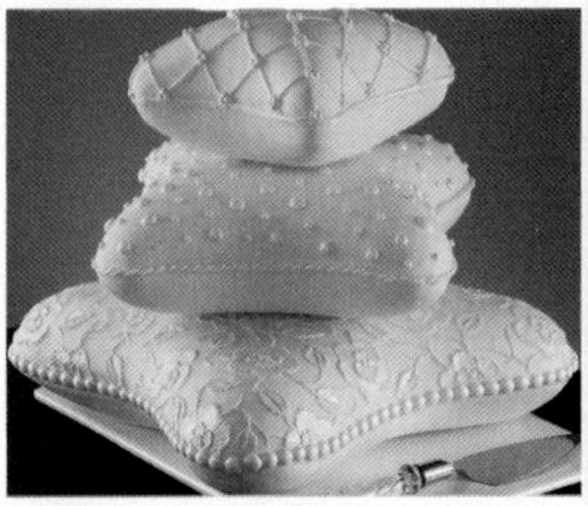

For top tier: Using a damp brush, attach ⅛ in. wide strips 1½ in. apart to create latticework top. Cut ¼ in. wide strips and attach over center seam using fondant adhesive. Using royal icing, attach 3/16 in. puddle dots (p. 120) at each latticework intersection. **For middle tier**: Use royal icing to attach various puddle dots to top, leaving a 4 in. square section open for top tier. Roll fondant into 3/16 in. thick ropes. Twist 2 together and attach over center seam using fondant adhesive. **For bottom tier**: Leave a 5 in. square section open in top center where middle tier will rest. Use large rose cutter to imprint roses. Outline imprint with tip 2 zigzags in royal icing; immediately brush lines inward using Brush Embroidery technique (p. 120). Repeat for center petals, outlining 3 free-hand petals. Use smallest leaf cutter to imprint leaves. Repeat as above. Pipe tip 2 vines. Use royal icing to attach ½ in. puddle dots over center seam. Paint Brush Embroidery details with Pearl Dust/vanilla mixture.

Slipper

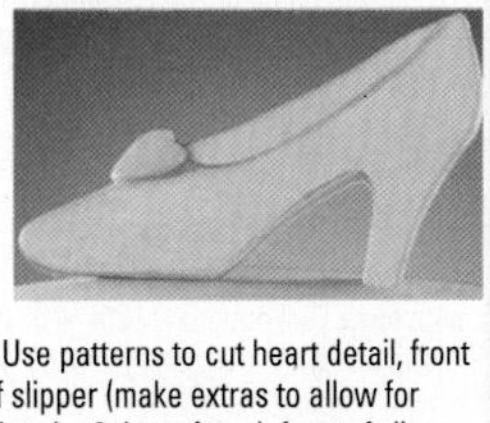

(see Finding the Perfect Fit, p. 85)

Roll out gum paste ⅛ in. thick. Use patterns to cut heart detail, front and back of slipper (make extras to allow for breakage). Let dry 3 days. Attach front of slipper to back using damp brush; let dry 24 hours. Use melted candy to attach 2 lollipop sticks to back, leaving excess extended at bottom to insert into cake; let set. Brush Sparkle Gel over shoe front and heart detail. Attach heart using melted candy; let set.

Fondant Tassels

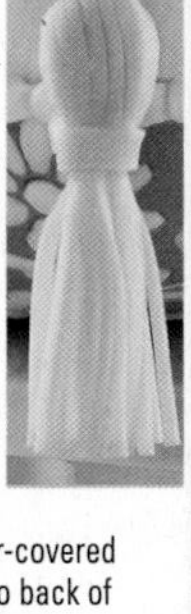

(see Finding the Perfect Fit, p. 85)

Roll a ¼ in. diameter ball for each tassel base. Roll out fondant 1/16 in. thick. Cut sixteen 1/16 x 6 in. strips for each tassel. Brush base with damp brush; attach 8 strips over top in one direction, then overlap 8 more strips. Gather strips under base. Cut a ¼ x 1 in. fondant strip for each tassel. Wrap and attach under base to secure strips. Trim ends to make tassels 2½ in. long. Let dry on waxed paper-covered board. Insert 3 in. lollipop sticks into back of tassels; secure with melted candy.

Bride and Bridesmaids

(see Perfect Attendants!, p. 87)
Roll out fondant ⅛ in. thick as needed. Cover brownie pops for skirts. Cut lollipop stick to 3½ in. and insert in center. Use ⅞ in. ball of copper to shape upper body; slide onto stick. Cut ¾ x 2½ in. strip for dress bodice. Wrap and attach, trimming ends to fit. Cut ¼ in. strips for straps; attach using damp brush. Roll ¼ in. ball of copper; flatten and slide over stick for neck. Roll 3/16 in. wide logs and cut 1½ in. lengths for arms; shape and attach. **For bride**, pipe tip 1 ball necklace; for bridesmaid necklace, roll very thin log and attach. Pipe tip 1 ball trim on all bodices. Roll ⅞ in. copper ball for head; slide over stick. Let set at least 1 hour. Draw eyes and mouth with FoodWriters; use Pearl Dust to brush on blush. Cut assorted strips for hair; attach using damp brush. **For veil**, roll out fondant 1/16 in. thick and cut 2 x 2¼ in. wide rectangle; use knife to round bottom corners and taper rounded top to just ¾ in. wide. Attach.

Cookie Trims

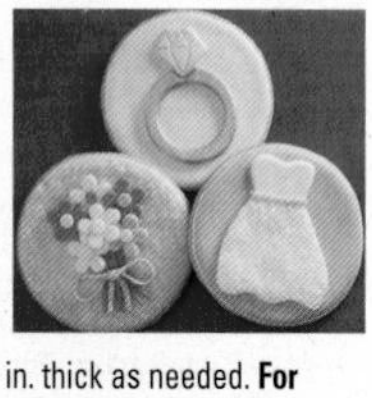

(see Cookies Capture the Day, p. 87)
Tint a 1 in. ball of fondant to make 3 to 4 bouquet cookies, each green and light, medium and dark pink. Roll out ⅛ in. thick as needed. **For wedding dress**, use cutter from wedding set to cut dress. Cut a ¼ x 1¼ in. strip for belt. Attach to cookie using damp brush. Brush bottom of dress with Piping Gel and sprinkle on Sparkling Sugar. **For ring**, cut band using 2 largest round Cut-Outs. **For diamond**, begin with a medium heart Cut-Out. Trim off curves by cutting straight across top and down each side at a 45° angle. Imprint facets using modeling stick from Flower Making Kit. Attach band to cookie; use medium heart Cut-Out to cut notch where diamond will sit. Paint with silver Pearl Dust/vanilla mixture (p. 120). Attach diamond; paint with white Pearl Dust/vanilla mixture. **For bouquet**, cut 6 flowers using apple blossom cutter from Flower Making Set. Use small opening of tip 12 to cut centers; attach using damp brush. For stems, cut 6 strips, 1/16 x 1¾ in.; attach to cookie. Attach flowers. **For bow loops**, cut a ⅛ x 4 in. strip; curve and attach. Cut 2 strips, ⅛ x ¾ in. for tails; attach. Roll tiny ball for knot; attach.

Gum Paste Carnation

(see Carnation Spotlight, p. 88)
Make base. Roll out gum paste ⅛ in. thick. Cut a circle using medium Round Cut-Out that has been coated with white vegetable shortening. Roll piece into a ball. Roll one side of ball between your fingers to form a golf tee shape about ¾ in. long. Flatten the round portion of ball around tee and place on dusted mat. Use modeling stick to roll flat portion very thin, rolling from center to edges. Center the medium Round Cut-Out over tee; cut out. Move base to thin foam dusted with Dusting Pouch. Using wide end of veining tool like a pencil, gently press the heel down and pull out the outer edge of the circle to form ruffled edge. Continue all the way around the circle, overlapping the impressions to create the torn, ruffled look desired. Let dry, flat side down.

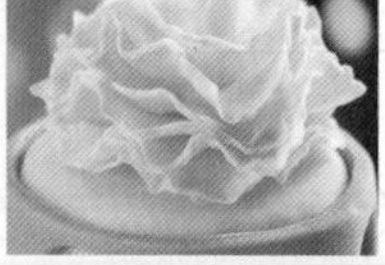

Make flower. Roll out gum paste less than 1/16 in. thick. Cut 5 or 6 circles for each Carnation using medium Round Cut-Out. Place 1 circle on thin foam and use wide end of veining tool to thin and pull edge away from center to form ruffled edge. Continue all the way around circle, overlapping impressions for a torn, ruffled look. Brush center of carnation base with gum paste adhesive. Gently press 1 circle on top of the base to attach. Repeat with additional circles. To help place last petal, fold it around the tip of veining tool before inserting into center. Trim extended tee base off carnations and let dry.

Rose Bouquet

(see More Memories in Store, p. 89)
Make royal icing flowers, calyxes and leaves as specified in directions; let dry. Attach tip 104 roses to calyxes using royal icing; let dry. Arrange roses and leaves to form bouquet. Wrap wires with green florist tape. Cut ends off 50th Anniversary Pick. Attach Lollipop Stick to back center area using thinned fondant adhesive; let dry.

Drawers and Front Panels

(see More Memories in Store, p. 89)
Cut panels. Tint 24 oz. fondant ivory; add 2 teaspoons Gum-Tex. Roll out ⅛ in. thick as needed. Cut 6 front panels, 4 x 7¼ in. Cut 2 drawer bottoms, 2¾ x 6½ in. Cut 4 drawer sides, 2¾ x 3¼ in. Let dry 48 hours.
Decorate front panels. Roll out 12 oz. white fondant ⅛ in. thick. Cut ½ in. wide strips; attach around all outer edges using damp brush. Roll out remaining fondant ⅛ in. thick; imprint using Graceful Vines Mat. Cut six 2 x 5 in. rectangles and attach to center of panels. Using royal icing, pipe tip 2 curving vines around white borders; attach tip 101s roses (14 per panel). Pipe tip 349 leaves. Roll six ½ in. diameter balls of ivory fondant and flatten slightly; attach to centers. Let dry.
Assemble drawers. Attach side panels to bottom and front panels using tip 3 and royal icing. Prop as needed; let dry.

Bride, Groom and Bridal Party People

(see The Wedding Party Makes the Rounds, p. 90, Their New Horizon and Black Tie and Tails, p. 91)

For Brides, Bridesmaids, Grooms, Groomsmen and Kids: Use 2.5 in. globes for heads and bodies of adults, 2 in. globes for kids. Tape top holes closed on globes for heads. Roll out fondant ⅛ in. thick. Brush globes lightly with Piping Gel. **For adult heads**, cut a 6 in. fondant circle; for body, cut a 2 ½ x 8 in. fondant strip. **For kids heads**, cut a 5 in. fondant circle; for body, cut a 2 x 6½ in. fondant strip. Attach fondant to globes; smooth with hand. Cut fondant away from open holes. Cut 3-6 in. diameter circles for adult hair; 2-3 in. diameter for kids' hair; position loosely. Use knife to cut hair line; carefully remove excess fondant. Attach hairline with damp brush; smooth. If desired, add 2nd layer or use veining tool to add detail (see below for specific hairdos). Let dry 1 hour before drawing facial features. Use FoodWriters to draw dot eyes and outline mouths.

For grooms and groomsmen: Use pattern to cut away shirt front; cut white shirt and insert. Cut small triangles for collar as needed. Use pattern to cut 1 lapel; reverse pattern for 2nd lapel. Attach using damp brush. Shape ¾ in. wide bow tie; or cut a 1¼ x ⅜ in. strip for straight tie; attach. Roll 2½ in. long logs, ½ in. wide for arms; shape and attach. Roll and flatten small balls for hands; cut slits for fingers and attach.

For brides and bridesmaids: Roll 2½ in long logs, ⅜ in. wide for arms (¼ in. wide for kids); shape and attach. Cut small ovals for sleeves or cut two white pansies; cut off 2 top petals. Attach sleeves above arms. For ring bearer's pillow, shape a ¾ in. square; attach. Shape very thin strips of gray fondant for 2 rings.
Hairdos:
For The Wedding Party Makes the Rounds: For bride's curls, cut ⅛ in. wide strips and wrap around lollipop stick to form curliques. Let set 5-10 minutes; slide off and let set again 5-10 minutes. Attach individual strands, trimming lengths as needed. **For groom's spikes**, roll and shape tiny logs; attach. **For flat blond spikes**, cut 5 starbursts and attach in layers. For hair bows, shape 2 loops from ½ x 1½ in. wide strips; roll small ball for center knot. Attach.

For *Their New Horizon* bride: Add hair curls. Roll out black fondant 1/16 in. thick. Cut ¼ in. wide strips from 4 to 6 in. long. Loosely wrap around wooden dowel rods to form curls. Let set 5-10 minutes. Slide off and let set another 10 minutes, then attach to top of hair. For tiara: Roll out white fondant ⅛ in. thick; cut shape using pattern. Attach Sugar Pearls for jewels with Piping Gel.
For Veils: Gather 6 x 10 in. tulle and wrap with florist wire. Insert in hair.

For Cat and Dog: Use 2 in. globes for bodies. Tape top holes closed. Roll out fondant ⅛ in. thick. Brush globes lightly with Piping Gel. Cut a 5 in. fondant circle to cover globes; attach and smooth with hand. Cut fondant away from open holes. Roll 1 in. balls for heads; attach using damp brush. Roll and flatten small balls for cheeks; attach. Roll tiny ball noses; attach. Shape ears; attach. Let dry 1 hour before drawing eyes. Use FoodWriter to draw dot eyes.

Royal Icing Lilies

(see Love, Lilies and Lace, p. 92)
If petals split while piping, widen tip slightly by inserting a thin spatula into the opening.

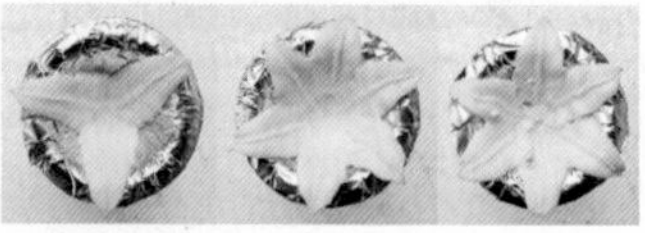

Practice With: Tips 366, 16
Icing Consistency: Stiff royal icing
Bag Position†: For petals 45° at 3:00 (9:00); for center 90°
Hold Tip: For petals, lightly touching surface of nail, wide opening parallel to surface; for center, slightly above flower line.

1. Line 1⅝ in. lily nail with foil. Use tip 366. Touch center well of nail with tip and squeeze, pulling petal up and over edge of foil cup. Decrease pressure as you reach end of petal and hesitate before you stop pressure and pull tip away, drawing petal to point.
2. Pipe 2 more petals.
3. Pipe 3 more petals between open spaces.
4. Add tip 16 star center and push in stamens.

NOTE: Stamens are not to be eaten.

Gum Paste Lily

(see Love, Lilies and Lace, p. 92)
Roll out gum paste 1/16 in. thick. Cut 6 petals using tulip leaf cutter from Floral Collection Flower Making Set. Ruffle edges of 3 petals by placing petal on thin foam and rolling ball tool over edges. Cut florist wire to 6 in. Brush 1½ in. of end with Gum Paste Adhesive. Wrap base of petal around wire; smooth. Repeat for all 6 petals. Set wire side down on large Flower Formers dusted with cornstarch to curve; let dry. Assemble lily, alternating smooth and ruffled petals, around 15 pearl stamens. Secure with white florist tape. Insert end in Flower Spike, securing with ball of gum paste if necessary.

Ribbon and Flower Stand

(see Waterfall Wedding, p. 92)

Secure pillars to plates using royal icing; let dry. Attach and decorate one 13 in. length of ribbon at a time. Tape 1 end of ribbon to top of top plate and other end under bottom plate (raise plate by setting stand on an 8 in. cake pan or circle). Use tip 4 dots of royal icing to attach gum paste flowers, beginning with a large flower and alternating large and small flowers as you go. Attach next ribbon as above, leaving about ½ in. between ribbons and beginning with a small flower this time. Repeat as needed to complete circle. Let dry.

Ribbon Swags

(see Imperial Presence, p. 93)

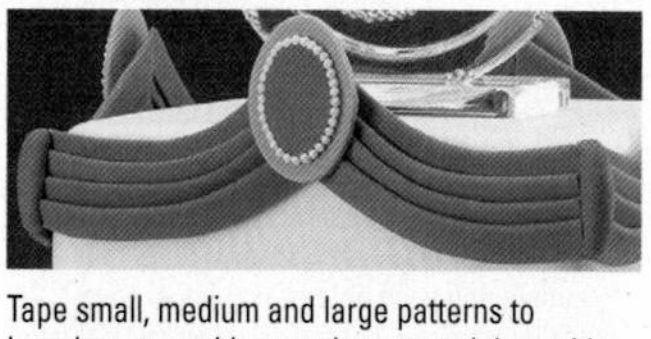

Tape small, medium and large patterns to boards; cover with waxed paper and dust with cornstarch. Add 2 tablespoons Gum-Tex to 36 oz. of prepared dark violet fondant. Roll out to 1/16 in. thick as needed. Make 8 small swags. For each, cut 4 strips, 1 x 6 in. wide. Fold each strip to ½ x 6 in. Attach in overlapping layers (folded edges on top) using damp brush. Place over small pattern to shape curve; let dry. Repeat using 1 x 8 in. strips for 8 medium swags and 1 x 10 in. strips for 8 large swags.

Draped Triangles

(see Imperial Presence, p. 93)

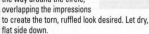

Prepare 4 in. high square box by covering with waxed paper and dusting with cornstarch. Add 1 tablespoon Gum-Tex to 20 oz. of prepared light violet fondant. Roll out to ⅛ in. thick. Use pattern to cut 8 triangles; cut extras to allow for breakage. Position over edge of box with top 1¾ in. laying flat and remainder hanging down. Let dry 2 days. Use pattern and toothpick to transfer design to triangles. Use royal icing to cover marks with tip 2 outlines. Let dry.

Royal Icing Scrolls

(see Scrolling Down the Aisle, p. 97)
Copy patterns and tape to cake boards; tape waxed paper over patterns. Spray with pan spray; wipe off excess with facial tissue. Use royal icing to cover scrolls with tip 9 outlines; pat smooth and flatten slightly. Let dry 24 hours. Turn scrolls over and overpipe backs; pat smooth and flatten slightly. Let dry 24 hours. Use brush to paint outer edges with thinned royal icing to hide seams. Let dry 24 hours.

Fondant Drapes and Ribbon Roses

(see Queen of Hearts, p. 97)

For drapes: Roll out fondant ⅛ in. thick. Cut 4 x 5 in. wide strips. Pinch ends and gather to form random pleats. Trim ends to fit. Attach using damp brush.
For ribbon roses: Roll out fondant ⅛ in. thick. Cut strips per instructions. Brush bottom (horizontal) long edge with damp brush. Fold in half horizontally and press edges lightly together; fold becomes outer edge. Brush sealed edge with damp brush. Begin lightly rolling from 1 end, pinching and folding at base, gradually loosening roll as rose gets larger. Trim base for desired height.

Heart

(see Queen of Hearts, p. 97)
Add 1 tablespoon Gum-Tex to 10 oz. dark red fondant. Roll out ¼ in. thick. Using 6 in. heart pan as pattern, cut out heart; imprint lines 1 in. apart by pressing with Cookie Stick. Roll ¼ in. balls of fondant; use damp brush to attach balls where lines cross and press lightly to flatten. Let dry overnight. Roll out fondant 1/16 in. thick. Cut 1x10 in. strips; place on thin foam and use ball tool to thin outer edge. Pinch and fold inside edge to form ruffle; attach to back of heart with damp brush. Let dry overnight. Attach Cookie Stick to back using thinned fondant adhesive, leaving 4 in. extended at bottom. Let dry overnight.

Elephant Topper

(see Pachyderm Takes His Turn, p. 105)
Tint and roll out fondant per instructions. Cut a 2½ x 8 in. orange strip; smooth around 2½ in. globe and attach using damp brush (keep both holes clear). Cut a ¾ x 6 in. royal blue strip; cut into eight ¾ in. squares. Attach around ball using fondant adhesive. Tape closed top hole of 2 in. globe (head) and 2½ in. globe (body). Cover with sky blue fondant, smoothing with hands (keep bottom holes clear). Assemble using melted candy. Attach head to body, holding in position until set. Roll and shape a 1½ in. log for trunk; attach. Indent tip. **For ears,** cut base using large heart Cut-Out, inside using medium heart Cut-Out. Attach layers using damp brush. Trim tips to match curve of head; attach. Roll tiny balls for eyes; attach. Use FoodWriter to draw smile. Roll and shape thin log for tail; attach.

Fondant Circus Figures

(see Center Ring Salute, p. 100)
Tint fondant and prepare bodies per instructions. Roll out fondant ⅛ in. thick unless otherwise specified. Attach trims using damp brush. Finally, use black FoodWriter to draw buttons, smiles, nostrils, muzzles and whiskers.

Ringmaster: For jacket, attach an 8 x 1¼ in. red strip; cut away "V" shapes at neck and bottom. Roll small amount of black very thin; cut ¾ in. long lapels. **For hair,** attach 5 in. circle, use knife to cut hairline details. **For hat base,** cut 1⅝ in. round using medium cutter from set. Add 1½ in. high hat top. Roll small balls for eyes, bow tie and nose, curved logs for mustache. Roll ¾ x ½ in. logs for arms. **For gloves,** flatten ½ in. balls; cut slits for fingers. Shape ¾ in. balls into shoes.

Clowns: For collar, cut a 5 x ⅝ in. strip with wavy edge. Shape a 1 in. high cone for hat. **For fringe,** cut ½ in. wide strips; cut ¼ in. deep slits, ⅛ in. apart. Roll ½ to ⅝ in. high cones for hair. Roll small balls for eyes, nose and cheeks (flatten for cheeks and eyes). Roll ¾ x ½ in. logs for arms. For gloves, flatten ½ in. balls; cut slits for fingers. Use narrow end of tip 12 to cut dots. Shape ¾ in. balls into shoes.

Lions: Attach ½ in. high triangles for ears. Shape muzzle and mouth from ½ in. ball. Roll 1¼ x ⅝ in. log arms and legs; flatten paws and cut slits for fingers and toes. Roll small ball eyes and nose. **For paw pads and inner ears,** roll small amount of fondant very thin; cut dots and triangles as needed. **For mane,** roll about 125 cones, ¼ to ½ in. long.

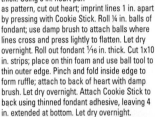

Tigers: Follow directions above for lion but omit inner ear trims and instead of mane, add triangular strips for stripes.

Bears: Follow directions above for lion, omitting paw pads and mane and changing to a rounded muzzle and ears.

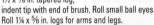

Elephants: For ears, cut hearts using large and medium Cut-Outs. Layer hearts and trim off points to match curve of head. **For trunk,** roll a 1½ x ⅝ in. tapered log; indent tip with end of brush. Roll small ball eyes. Roll 1¼ x ⅝ in. logs for arms and legs.

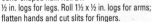

Monkeys: For **ears,** cut circle using wide end of tip 2A; cut in half. Cut inner ears using wide end of tip 12; trim to fit. Roll small amount of light brown very thin; cut 1¼ x 1 in. wide curved face. Roll small ball eyes and cone-shaped hair. Roll 2 x ½ in. logs for legs. Roll 1½ x ½ in. logs for arms; flatten hands and cut slits for fingers.

Globe Acrobats

(see Well-Balanced Birthday, p. 101)
Tint fondant per instructions. Roll out ⅛ in. thick as needed. Attach trims with fondant adhesive unless otherwise stated. Tape 1 opening of top globe closed where mini cake will sit; as you work, keep all remaining holes open by trimming away fondant with knife tip. Cover globes with 2 x 7 in. strips of fondant, using white for bodies, skin tone for heads. Attach with damp brush. **For shirt,** cut away front neckline and replace with skin tone. **For hair,** attach 5 in. circle; use knife to trim and shape hairline. Use narrow end of tip 10 to cut out eyes; attach. Roll small ball nose and tapered logs for mustache; attach. Use FoodWriter to draw smile. **For arms,** roll and shape 1¾ x ⅝ in. logs; flatten hand and cut slits for fingers. Attach. **For shoes,** roll and shape 1½ x 1 in. ovals; attach. Let individual globes dry on a waxed paper-covered board.

Fondant Mini Cake

(see Well-Balanced Birthday, p. 101)
Tint fondant per instructions. Shape 2-layer mini cake using 1 x 2 in. and 1 x 1½ in. diameter round layers; attach using fondant adhesive. **For bottom border,** roll a 8 x ¼ in. diameter log; attach. **For swags,** cut a circle using wide end of tip 10; move tip up ⅛ in. and cut again. Attach around cakes. Use narrow end of tip 10 for ball trims; attach. Marbleize (p.120) ⅜ in. ball of golden yellow with red. Shape flame; insert Lollipop Stick. Let dry on waxed paper-covered board.

Fondant Lion's Mane

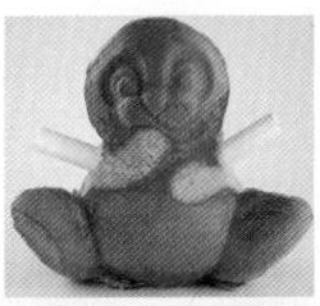

(see Big Top Big Cat, p.100)
Mix 4.4 oz. pack of orange from Multi Pack with 4 oz. white fondant. Roll out ⅛ in. thick. Cut thin strips ¼ x 4 to 6 in. long. Wrap loosely around Cookie Stick. Let set 10 minutes. Carefully slide off. Let curls dry in random curves on waxed paper-covered boards. Make 90 to 100 curls.

Figure Piped Boy and Animals

(see Animal Tracks, p. 104)
Figure pipe royal icing heads on waxed paper-covered boards. **For boy,** pipe a tip 1A dot, 1½ in. diameter; flatten and smooth with finger dipped in cornstarch. **For animals,** pipe a tip 1A dot, 2 in. diameter; flatten and smooth. **For boy,** pipe tip 3 pull-out hair and

dot nose, tip 2 dot eyes and outline smile. **For bear,** pipe tip 2A ears and muzzle. Pipe inner ears using tip 3; pat smooth. Outline ears with tip 3; smooth. Pipe tip 2 dot and outline muzzle, eyes, nose and mouth.
For tiger and lion, pipe tip 8 ears (shape with finger); pipe tip 3 inner ears; smooth. Pipe tip 3 outline stripes and pull-out mane. Pipe tip 2 dot and outline eyes, nose, mouth and whiskers.
For elephant, pipe tip 2A trunk; blend top with damp brush. Pipe tip 8 pull-out dot tusks and tip 2 dot eyes. Make ears separately. Outline and fill-in two 2 x 1 in. deep hearts without point; pat smooth. Outline and fill in center using tip 3; overpipe tip 8 outer edge. When dry, attach ears behind head.

Ears and Horns

(see Treetop Greetings, p. 106)

Tint 10 oz. fondant yellow. Roll out ¼ in. thick. Use pattern to cut 4 ears (flip pattern for 3rd and 4th). Attach matching layers, securing with damp brush. Let dry on waxed paper-covered board. Roll out remaining yellow ⅛ in. thick. Cut a 3 x 3 in. square. Set Cookie Treat Stick across fondant edge with ½ and 2½ in. exposed on either end. Brush fondant with damp brush. Roll up fondant to cover stick, being sure fondant adheres to stick. Cut off excess and smooth seam. Repeat for 2nd horn. Roll two 1¼ in. diameter balls; push onto exposed ½ in. of sticks for tips. Stand in craft block to dry.

Cookie Animals

(see Step Right Up, p. 103 and Animals of the Amazon, p. 107)
Bake and cool cookies per instructions. To ice cookies, outline using tip 3 and full-strength color flow (omit tail area on zebra); flow in using thinned color flow (p. 128). Let dry on waxed paper-covered boards.
Decorate animals on waxed paper using full-strength color flow. **For all**: Pipe tip 1 or 2 dot eyes, pupils and nose/nostrils, outline mouths.

For giraffe: Use tip 2 to outline and fill in spots; pat smooth. Pipe tip 2 pull-out tail tip. Pipe tip 2 outline ear and tail.

For rhino: Use tip 2 to outline and fill in horns and inner ear. Pipe tip 2 tail and details. **For lion**: Pipe tip 2 outline tail and ear; fill in inner ear (pat smooth). Pipe pull-out mane, claws and tail tip.

For gorilla: Pipe tip 2 outline details at tummy and leg. **For hippo**: Use tip 2 to fill in inner ear; pat smooth. Pipe outline tail and details.

For zebra: Use tip 2 to pipe pull-out mane (alternate colors), outline and fill in stripes (pat smooth) and outline tail with tip 2 and pull-out tip. **For snake**: Add tip 2 dots. **For alligator**: Pipe tip 2 zigzag scales and pull-out teeth.

For Bear: (see *Step Right Up, p. 103)* Use tip 2 to outline and fill in ears, paws and muzzle. Pipe tip 2 dot facial details.

Leaves and Trees

(see Animals of the Amazon, p. 107)
For leaves, tint 10 oz. fondant medium green; knead in 1 teaspoon Gum-Tex. Roll out 1/16 in. thick. Cut 24 large and 40 medium leaves using Cut-Outs. Use veining tool from set to mark details. Let dry 24 hours on large Flower Formers dusted with cornstarch (position 22 medium leaves inside Flower Formers to use around cakes). **For trees,** tint 4 oz. fondant brown. Roll out ⅛ in. thick. Cut 5 x 1 in. strips to cover top 5 in. of each dowel rod for tree trunk; smooth with hands. Use veining tool to add details. Set trunks and leaves for tops in refrigerator to chill 3-5 minutes to help candy set faster. Assemble trees using melted green candy. Attach 3 medium leaves first; let set. Add 3 large leaves; let set.

Pleated Swags

(see Step Right Up!, p. 103)
Cut fondant strips following instructions. Form pleats in fondant by placing a plastic dowel rod under bottom edge of fondant strip and one on top, next to the first. Repeat with more rods to form pleats. Remove dowel rods, gather ends together and brush with water to secure. Let dry on cornstarch dusted surface.

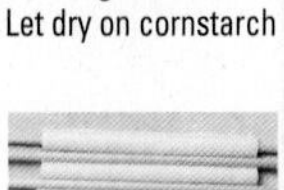

Form pleats in fondant by placing a dowel rod under bottom edge of fondant strip and one on top, next to the first dowel rod. For looser pleats, use wooden or plastic dowel rods. For tighter pleats, use wooden skewers or lollipop sticks. Repeat with more dowel rods to form pleats. Remove dowel rods, gather ends together and brush with water to secure.

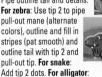

Candy Making Techniques

USING CANDY MELTS

Fast-melting confectionery coating wafers are the key to easy candy making. Smooth texture and great taste make Candy Melts your most convenient option for molding. Check out all the great colors on p. 194.

To Melt

Chocolate Pro Electric Melting Pot (p. 194): The most convenient way to melt—no microwave or double boiler needed! Melts large amounts of Candy Melts in minutes.

Double boiler method: Fill lower pan with water to below level of top pan. Bring water to simmer, then remove from heat. Put Candy Melts in top pan and set in position on lower pan. Stir constantly, without beating, until smooth and completely melted.

Microwave method: In microwave-safe container, microwave 1 package Candy Melts at 50% power or defrost setting for 1 minute. Stir thoroughly. Continue to microwave and stir at 30 second intervals until smooth and completely melted. Candy Melts may also be melted in Candy Decorating Bags (p. 194). Melt as described above, squeezing bag between heating intervals to blend Candy Melts together. When completely melted, snip off end of bag and squeeze melted Candy Melts into molds. Throw away bag when empty.

NOTE: Confectionery coating will lose its pouring and dipping consistency if overheated, or if water or other liquid is added. If coating is overheated, add 2 teaspoons hydrogenated vegetable shortening per 14 oz. Candy Melts.

To Mold (1 color candies)

Pour melted candy into clean, dry mold; tap lightly to remove air bubbles. Place mold on level surface in refrigerator until bottom of mold appears frosty or until candy is firm. Pop out candy. For lollipops, fill molds, tap to remove air bubbles, then position sticks in mold. Rotate sticks to thoroughly cover with candy so they remain securely in place. Chill to set then unmold.

To Color

Add Candy Colors (p. 195) to melted Candy Melts a little at a time. Mix thoroughly before adding more color. Colors tend to deepen as they're mixed. Pastel colored candies are most appetizing, so keep this in mind.

Multi-colored candy

"Painting" Method: Before filling mold cavity, use a decorator brush dipped in melted Candy Melts to paint features or desired details; let set. Fill mold and chill until firm as described above.

Piping Method: Use a parchment or Candy Decorating Bag filled halfway with melted candy. Cut small hole in tip of bag and gently squeeze to add candy detail to mold; let set. Fill mold and Chill until firm as described above.

Layering Method

Pour melted Candy Melts into dry molds to desired height. Chill until partially set. Pour melted contrasting color to desired height. Chill until partially set. Repeat until desired number of layers are formed; chill until firm and unmold.

Marbleizing Method

Separately melt 2 different colors of Candy Melts. Stir colors together, using a lollipop stick to draw lines in mixture. Do not overmix. Quickly spoon or place into molds while mixture is still soft. Tap. Chill until firm; unmold.

SPECIALTY TECHNIQUES

Candy Shells

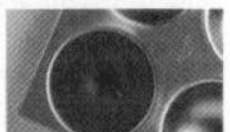

Fill pan cavity to the top edge with melted candy. Tap on counter to remove air bubbles. Let chill for 8 to 10 minutes or until a ⅛ to ¼ in. shell has formed. Pour out excess candy then return shell to refrigerator to chill completely. Carefully unmold shells (if you have difficulty removing shells, place pan in freezer for 2-3 minutes, then unmold). Smooth top edges by sliding across warmed cookie sheet or warming plate. Excess candy can be reheated and reused.

Candy Shells in Baking Cups

Spoon or pipe 1 to 2 tablespoons of melted candy into the bottom of a standard baking cup. Brush candy up sides, to desired height, forming an even edge. Chill 5 to 8 minutes. Repeat process if a thicker shell is needed. Chill until firm. Carefully peel baking cup off candy shell.

Covering Cakes and Cookies with Candy Melts or Poured Icings

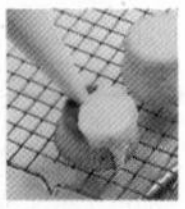

For Candy Melts, melt following package directions. For icing recipes, follow recipe directions to reach pouring consistency. For canned icing, heat in microwave at Defrost setting (30% power) for 20-30 seconds; stir. Repeat until consistency of icing will pour. Place cooled cakes or cookies on cooling grid positioned over cookie sheet or pan. Pour or pipe candy or icing on center of item, continue covering top so that candy or icing drips down and covers sides. Let dry.

CANDY PLAQUES

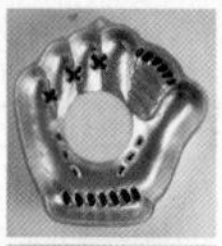

You can use pans as candy molds to make solid decorative plaques. If your pan has detail, it may be painted or filled in desired colors as you would for any candy mold.

Pour melted candy into center of pan cavity. Tap pan gently on counter to eliminate bubbles. Candy should be ¼ to ¾ in. thick, depending on project instructions. Place pan in refrigerator for about 30-40 minutes until firm (check occasionally; if candy becomes too chilled, it may crack). Unmold onto hand or soft towel (tap gently if necessary).

Mickey Candy Plaque

(see Engineering a Great Birthday, p. 28)

Tint 14 oz. Dark Cocoa Candy Melts black. Tint 21 oz. Mickey face color using orange candy color. Tint 3 oz. red. Reserve 4 oz. white. Pipe details into pan using melted candy in cut parchment bags (p. 128). Pipe tongue; chill until firm. Pipe pupils, nose and mouth; chill. Pipe whites of eyes; chill. Fill face area; tap to settle, chill until firm. Fill with remaining black candy. Tap to settle; chill until firm. Unmold. Position on cut-to-fit, foil-wrapped Cake Board.

Transformers Candy Plaque

(see Tracking the Transformers, p. 39)

Tint candy per instructions. Using Painting or Piping Method (p. 128), fill in black areas around eyes; chill until firm. Fill in light blue under eyes; chill. Pour in candy for gray mask area. Tap to settle; chill until firm. Pour in dark blue to complete plaque. Tap to settle; chill until firm. Use dots of melted candy to attach plaque to foil-covered, cut-to-fit Cake Board.

Spiderman Candy Plaque

(see Spidey's Bird's-Eye View, p. 38)

Make plaque using melted candy in cut parchment bags. Melt white candy; tint 18 oz. blue/violet, 6 oz. black; reserve 4 oz. white. Fill in blue areas of design (no webbing). Tap to settle; chill until firm. Fill in whites of eyes and black spider on chest; chill until firm. Melt red candy; fill in plaque to ¾ in. deep. Tap to settle; chill until firm. Unmold onto waxed paper-covered board. Use melted black candy to pipe webbing and figure details. Chill until firm

Elmo Candy Plaque

(see Elmo on Safari Cake, p. 33)

Divide and melt 1 pk. white candy; reserve 2 oz. white for eyes, tint 2 oz. orange for nose, 2 oz. black for mouth and pupils. In pan, mold mouth, nose and pupils; chill until set. Mold whites of eyes; chill. Mold remainder of face using 2 pks. of melted red candy. Chill until firm. Unmold.

Monkey Candy Plaque

(see Birthday Monkey Shines, p. 109)

Pipe details into Monkey Pan using melted candy in cut parchment bags. Tint 2 oz. candy black. Fill in pupils. Using melted Peanut Butter candy, fill in muzzle and inside of ears. Chill until firm. Fill in whites of eyes; chill until firm. Fill in body using 2 packages of melted light cocoa Candy Melts. Tap to settle; chill until firm. Add dot highlights to eyes after unmolding.

Elephant Candy Plaque

(see Trunk Talking, p. 106)

Reserve 3 oz. white Candy Melts. Mix and melt 2 packs of blue with remainder of 1 pack white. Add blue and a little black Candy Color to make gray shown. Pour into pan. Tap to settle; chill until firm. Use craft knife to carefully remove background area inside curve of trunk. Set plaque on waxed paper-covered board. Pipe details using royal icing. Fill in ears with tip 8; pat smooth with finger dipped in cornstarch. Pipe tip 2 outline tongue. Ice smooth background area within tail. Use tip 5 to fill in toes; pat smooth. Use tip 10 to pipe bead hair and outline tail; flatten slightly. Use tip 10 to fill in eyes; pat smooth. Pipe tip 5 dot pupils (flatten slightly) with tip 2 dot highlights. Let dry overnight.

Candy Mushroom and Base

(see 'Shroom with a View, p. 12)

For base, set Comfort-Grip cutter on cookie sheet. Fill ¼ in. deep with melted green candy. Tap to settle; chill until firm. **For mushroom stem,** use candy mold to make yellow cordial cup shells. Chill until firm. **For mushroom cap,** set Ball Pan in freezer for 15 minutes or more. Use light pink candy in cut parchment bag to pipe dots (if candy starts to drip, return pan to freezer to rechill). Chill until firm. Spoon in dark pink candy to make candy shell (p. 128); brush up sides, stopping ½ in. from top edge. Chill until firm.

Octopus Candy Shell

(see Grabbing All the Goodies, p. 21)

Melt 2 packages Candy Melts in microwave safe bowl or glass measuring cup (p. 128). Pour about ⅓ into Sports Ball Pan half. Rotate pan to evenly distribute candy; pour excess back into cup. Tap pan to settle candy; chill until firm. Using other half of pan, repeat process. Repeat process 2 more times so each pan half has 3 layers of candy forming a shell about ¼ in. thick. Before unmolding, place pans in freezer for 5-10 minutes. Unmold onto soft surface. Run edge of shells over warming tray or warm cookie sheet; attach shell halves. Let set. Run bottom of head over warming tray or warm cookie sheet for a flat bottom. Let set.

Village Pond and Bridge

(see Skating Village, p. 59)

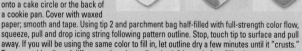

For pond: Prepare ½ cup melted very pale blue candy and place in cut parchment bag. Outline and pipe in a free form pond shape, approx. 9 x 5 in. at widest points, on Non-Stick Cookie Sheet. Chill until firm. Carefully lift and turn over. Brush smooth side with mixture of blue and white Pearl Dust. Move to waxed paper-covered board. Pipe ⅜ in. wide border on pond edge using melted white candy; immediately sprinkle on Sparkling Sugar. Chill until firm.

For bridge: Make bridge. Cut 1 x 3 in. strip of freezer paper. Pipe melted white candy on shiny side; smooth with spatula about ⅛ in. thick. Wait until candy begins to lose its shine (about 1 minute) then place inside large flower former (paper side down) to shape curve. Chill until firm then remove paper. Pipe white candy zigzag on edges; cover with Sparkling Sugar.

COLOR FLOW

Working With Color Flow

1. Trace your design pattern onto parchment paper, then tape paper onto a cake circle or the back of a cookie pan. Cover with waxed paper; smooth and tape. Using tip 2 and parchment bag half-filled with full-strength color flow, squeeze, pull and drop icing string following pattern outline. Stop, touch tip to surface and pull away. If you will be using the same color to fill in, let outline dry a few minutes until it "crusts." To prevent bleeding of different colors, let outline dry 1-2 hours before filling in.

2. Thin color flow mixture with water. Cut opening in parchment bag to the size of tip 2. Fill in design with thinned color flow.

3. Let decorations air dry thoroughly, at least 48 hours. To remove, cut away waxed paper from board, then turn over and peel waxed paper off the color flow piece.

Hint: For curved decorations, dry pieces on flower formers. To easily remove dried color flow, pull waxed paper backing over the edge of a table with one hand, while holding decoration with other hand. Waxed paper will pull off naturally. Or, with dried color flow resting on cookie sheet, place cardboard sheet over color flow, lift and turn over so that top of decoration rests on cardboard. Lift off waxed paper.

Since any moist icing will break down color flow, either position color flow decorations on cake shortly before serving or place on sugar cubes, attaching with full-strength Color Flow.

Wilton Disposable Decorating Bags.
The brand you can depend on!

Only Wilton
Disposable Decorating Bags
are made with our
exclusive blend of materials—
preferred by decorators
for their more comfortable
and feel" and superior strength.
Each batch is tested in
the Wilton Test Kitchen
o meet our quality standards.
n fact, Wilton disposable bags
outperform the competition
r superior breakage resistance
in test after test.
Not convinced?
Read why our customers
swear by Wilton Disposable
Decorating Bags!

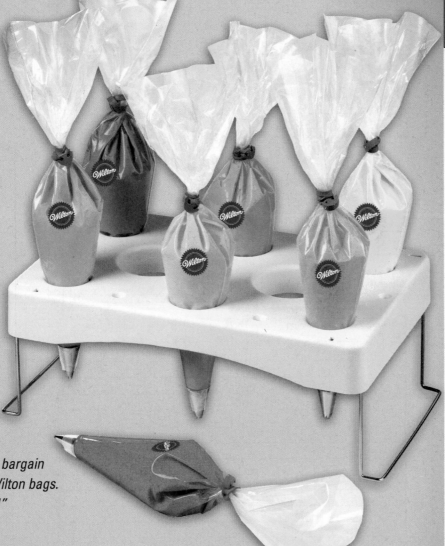

*hate to admit, but I have tried other bargain
ds, but they just don't hold up like Wilton bags.
Wilton's quality is exceptional!!"*
Sheryl G., Aiken, SC

*have used other disposable decorating bags,
t none have come close in quality to Wilton.
e bags are sturdy enough to resist tears, yet
exible enough to make decorating a breeze."*
Jamie Z., Erie, PA

*on Disposable Decorating Bags are of top-notch
ity and feel great in your hand no matter what
consistency of icing you are working with."*
Martina F., Vaughan, Ontario, CN

*"Wilton Disposable Decorating Bags are perfect
for piping practically anything. The bags are durable
and won't break or split apart on you. And the best
feature—clean up is a no-brainer."*
Christina M., Albuquerque, NM

*"Wilton Disposable Decorating Bags are the only bags
that I will use. They are the most durable bag on the
market. I love the option of sizes and know
I'll be using them for years to come!"*
Jennifer K., Lewis Center, OH

See the complete selection of Wilton Disposable Decorating Bags on page 136.

Retail Order Form

**Will Not Be
Delivered
Without Proper
Postage**

Caller Service No. 1604
2240 West 75th Street
Woodridge, IL 60517-0750

FROM

Name

Address   Apt. No.

City

State   Zip

Save mailing time!
Call 800/794-5866

Ask for mail order when phoning in your charge order.
Sé Habla Español!
Para mas informacion, marque 800-436-5778

Or, fax your order, Toll-Free:
888/824-9520
Only VISA, MasterCard, Discover Card or American Express are accepted.

Or order from our website:
www.wilton.com

HOW TO ORDER

1 Print your name, address and phone number clearly. (We do not sell our phone lists. A phone number is required in case of shipping difficulties.) If you wish for your order to be sent to another address, be sure to include that information in the area designated "SHIP TO."

2 PAY BY CREDIT CARD ONLY.
Only VISA, MasterCard, Discover Card or American Express accepted. SORRY, NO C.O.D. ORDERS, CHECKS OR MONEY ORDERS ACCEPTED.

To charge an order to your VISA, MasterCard, Discover Card or American Express, enter your charge card number and credit card identification number in the boxes. Supply card expiration date and your signature. Orders will not be processed without this information.

3 Fill in the number of items desired. If an item includes more than one piece, DO NOT list number of pieces. Example: 14 piece set is listed as 1 item under quantity.

4 Fill in stock number of item.

5 Enter page number on which item is shown.

6 Fill in name of item.

7 Total your order.

8 Determine tax required, depending on **your shipping destination**. See categories below. Wilton Enterprises is required by law to collect state taxes where applicable.

No tax added in Alaska, Delaware, Hawaii, Idaho, Nevada, New Hampshire, North Dakota, Montana, Oregon, Wyoming and the District of Columbia.

Group 1 States:
Add sales tax for merchandise only (no tax on shipping charges) using tax rates listed for your shipping destination.* Add tax on line 8.

Alabama 6%; Arizona 6%; California 9%; Colorado 4.1%; Florida 7%; Illinois 7.75%; Iowa 6%; Louisiana 4%; Maine 5%; Maryland 6%; Massachusetts 6.25%; Oklahoma 8.5%; Utah 6.25%; Virginia 5%.

Group 2 States:
Add tax for total of merchandise and shipping charges using tax rates listed for your shipping destination.* Add tax on line 11.

Arkansas 8.5%; Connecticut 6%; Georgia 7%; Indiana 7%; Kansas 7%; Kentucky 6%; Michigan 6%; Minnesota 7.125%; Mississippi 7%; Missouri 5.225%; Nebraska 6.5%; North Carolina 7.75%; New Jersey 7%; New Mexico 5%; New York 8.5%; Ohio 6.75%; Pennsylvania 6%; Rhode Island 7%; South Carolina 7%; South Dakota 6%; Tennessee 9.25%; Texas 8.25%; Vermont 6%; Washington 8.6%; Wisconsin 5.5%; West Virginia 6%

***Tax rates are subject to change according to individual state legislation without notice and are the responsibility of the consumer.**

9 Add appropriate amount to your order for shipping and postage. (See chart inside Order Form to determine charges.) Wilton ships via Federal Express Ground Service to the continental United States, Alaska, Hawaii and Puerto Rico. Shipments will arrive in approximately 10 days after we receive the order. Please allow 1-2 extra days for shipments to Alaska, Hawaii and Puerto Rico. Shipments to Guam and the Virgin Islands ship via standard Parcel Post through the U.S. Post Office. Please allow 4-6 weeks for delivery. We do not ship outside of the U.S.

10 EXPRESS AIR DELIVERY. Phone orders placed by noon CST will be delivered in 3 to 5 business days for an additional $15.00. This service is available upon request for retail customers only in the continental United States.

11 Total tax for Group 2 states if applicable. See above.

12 Total your Order.

When Your Order Arrives . . . Should you be missing an item from your order (1) check to be sure you have not overlooked the merchandise (2) check over your receipted order form. If any items are temporarily out of stock, we will notify you of the date you may reorder those items. Your credit card will be charged only for merchandise shipped.

Wilton Return Policy: Inspect all merchandise upon arrival. If you're dissatisfied in any way with any item, notify Wilton Customer Service in writing with a copy of your invoice and all available information regarding your order before returning merchandise. ALL MERCHANDISE MUST BE RETURNED WITHIN **60 DAYS.** Handle returns promptly. Returns will be credited to the original credit card.

For inquiries on your previous order, send all available information and a copy of your invoice to: Wilton Industries, MS9A, 2240 West 75th Street, Woodridge, IL 60517.

RETAIL ORDER FORM

Retail Customers Only:
Phone in Your Charge Order Toll-Free: 800/794-5866
Fax or Internet Ordering 24 hours a day, 7 days a week
By Toll-Free Fax: 888-824-9520
From Our Web Site: www.wilton.com
Caller Service No. 1604; 2240 West 75th Street, Woodridge, IL 60517-0750

1 **SOLD TO:** (PLEASE PRINT PLAINLY)

NAME ___ First ___ Middle Initial ___ Last

ADDRESS

CITY ___ STATE ___ ZIP

(AREA CODE) DAYTIME PHONE NO. (Required)

E-MAIL

SHIP TO: (FILL IN ONLY IF DIFFERENT FROM SOLD TO)

NAME ___ First ___ Middle Initial ___ Last

ADDRESS

CITY ___ STATE ___ ZIP

(AREA CODE) DAYTIME PHONE NO. (Required)

E-MAIL

2 **CREDIT CARD INFORMATION** (ONLY CREDIT CARD ORDERS ACCEPTED)
Use Visa, MasterCard , Discover Card or American Express
Fill in the boxes:

☐ VISA ☐ MasterCard ☐ DISCOVER ☐ AMERICAN EXPRESS

Credit Card Number

(REQUIRED) CREDIT CARD IDENTIFICATION NUMBER
3 digit number appears on back of card in signature area after your credit card number.

Expiration Month/Year ___ **Signature**

3 How Many	**4** Stock Number		**5** Page	**6** Description	Price of One	**Total Price** Dollars	Cents
1701	W	3506	132	2011 Yearbook (NO shipping charge)	$12.99		

Shipping Charges (See No. 8)
Orders up to $15.99 . . . . add $7.00
Orders from $16.00-30.99 . . . . add $8.75
Orders from $31.00-40.99 . . . . add $10.00
Orders from $41.00-50.99 . . . . add $11.50
Orders from $51.00-75.99 . . . . add $14.00
Orders from $76.00-100.99 . . . . add $16.75
Orders from $101.00-150.99 . . . . add $21.00
Orders from $151.00 and above . . . . . add $27.50
Enjoy quick delivery!

Wilton orders shipped via Federal Express will arrive within approximately 10 working days after we receive them.
Please allow 4-6 weeks for orders shipped via U.S. Post Office.

7 TOTAL MERCHANDISE →
8 GROUP 1 STATES - STATE AND LOCAL TAXES - SEE NOTE #8 →
9 ADD SHIPPING & POSTAGE CHARGE →
NOTE: Find the amount you pay at left.
10 EXPRESS AIR DELIVERY (optional) →
Add $15.00 to standard shipping charges for Federal Express delivery only.
SUBTOTAL →
ADJUSTMENTS/CERTIFICATES TOTAL →
11 GROUP 2 STATES - Total tax for merchandise and shipping - SEE NOTE #8 →
12 ORDER TOTAL →

Prices in this Yearbook were accurate at the time of printing and supersede all previous Wilton publications. Due to dynamic market conditions, the price of some items may have changed. Please check **www.wilton.com** for the most up-to-date prices before placing an order.

RETAIL ORDER FORM

Retail Customers Only:
Phone in Your Charge Order Toll-Free: 800/794-5866
Fax or Internet Ordering 24 hours a day, 7 days a week
By Toll-Free Fax: 888-824-9520
From Our Web Site: www.wilton.com
Caller Service No. 1604; 2240 West 75th Street, Woodridge, IL 60517-0750

---

❶ SOLD TO: (PLEASE PRINT PLAINLY)

NAME
First   Middle Initial   Last

ADDRESS

CITY   STATE   ZIP

(AREA CODE) DAYTIME PHONE NO. (Required)

E-MAIL

SHIP TO: (FILL IN ONLY IF DIFFERENT FROM SOLD TO)

NAME
First   Middle Initial   Last

ADDRESS

CITY   STATE   ZIP

(AREA CODE) DAYTIME PHONE NO. (Required)

E-MAIL

---

❷ CREDIT CARD INFORMATION (ONLY CREDIT CARD ORDERS ACCEPTED)
Use Visa, MasterCard , Discover Card or American Express
Fill in the boxes:

☐ VISA   ☐ MasterCard   ☐ DISCOVER   ☐ AMERICAN EXPRESS

Credit Card Number

(REQUIRED) CREDIT CARD IDENTIFICATION NUMBER
3 digit number appears on back of card in signature area after your credit card number.

Expiration Month/Year   **Signature**

❸ How Many	❹ Stock Number			❺ Page	❻ Description	Price of One	Total Price Dollars	Cents
	1701	W	3506	132	2011 Yearbook (NO shipping charge)	$12.99		

Shipping Charges (See No. 8)
Orders up to $15.99 . . . . add $7.00
Orders from $16.00-30.99 . . . . add $8.75
Orders from $31.00-40.99 . . . . add $10.00
Orders from $41.00-50.99 . . . . add $11.50
Orders from $51.00-75.99 . . . . add $14.00
Orders from $76.00-100.99 . . . . add $16.75
Orders from $101.00-150.99 . . . . add $21.00
Orders from $151.00 and above . . . . . add $27.50
Enjoy quick delivery!
Wilton orders shipped via Federal Express will arrive within approximately 10 working days after we receive them. Please allow 4-6 weeks for orders shipped via U.S. Post Office.

Prices in this Yearbook were accurate at the time of printing and supersede all previous Wilton publications. Due to dynamic market conditions, the price of some items may have changed. Please check **www.wilton.com** for the most up-to-date prices before placing an order.

❼ TOTAL MERCHANDISE ⟶
❽ GROUP 1 STATES - STATE AND LOCAL TAXES - SEE NOTE #8 ⟶
❾ ADD SHIPPING & POSTAGE CHARGE ⟶
NOTE: Find the amount you pay at left.
❿ EXPRESS AIR DELIVERY (optional)
Add $15.00 to standard shipping charges for Federal Express delivery only.
SUBTOTAL
ADJUSTMENTS/CERTIFICATES TOTAL ⟶
⓫ GROUP 2 STATES - Total tax for merchandise and shipping - SEE NOTE #8 ⟶
⓬ ORDER TOTAL

HOW TO ORDER

❶ Print your name, address and phone number clearly. (We do not sell our phone lists. A phone number is required in case of shipping difficulties.) If you wish for your order to be sent to another address, be sure to include that information in the area designated "SHIP TO."

❷ PAY BY CREDIT CARD ONLY.
Only VISA, MasterCard, Discover Card or American Express accepted. SORRY, NO C.O.D. ORDERS, CHECKS OR MONEY ORDERS ACCEPTED.
To charge an order to your VISA, MasterCard, Discover Card or American Express, enter your charge card number and credit card identification number in the boxes. Supply card expiration date and your signature. Orders will not be processed without this information.

❸ Fill in the number of items desired. If an item includes more than one piece, DO NOT list number of pieces. Example: 14 piece set is listed as 1 item under quantity.

❹ Fill in stock number of item.

❺ Enter page number on which item is shown.

❻ Fill in name of item.

❼ Total your order.

❽ Determine tax required, depending on **your shipping destination.** See categories below. Wilton Enterprises is required by law to collect state taxes where applicable.

No tax added in Alaska, Delaware, Hawaii, Idaho, Nevada, New Hampshire, North Dakota, Montana, Oregon, Wyoming and the District of Columbia.

Group 1 States:
Add sales tax for merchandise only (no tax on shipping charges) using tax rates listed for your shipping destination.* Add tax on line 8.

Alabama 6%; Arizona 6%; California 9%; Colorado 4.1%; Florida 7%; Illinois 7.75%; Iowa 6%; Louisiana 4%; Maine 5%; Maryland 6%; Massachusetts 6.25%; Oklahoma 8.5%; Utah 6.25%; Virginia 5%.

Group 2 States:
Add tax for total of merchandise and shipping charges using tax rates listed for your shipping destination.* Add tax on line 11.

Arkansas 8.5%; Connecticut 6%; Georgia 7%; Indiana 7%; Kansas 7%; Kentucky 6%; Michigan 6%; Minnesota 7.125%; Mississippi 7%; Missouri 5.225%; Nebraska 6.5%; North Carolina 7.75%; New Jersey 7%; New Mexico 5%; New York 8.5%; Ohio 6.75%; Pennsylvania 6%; Rhode Island 7%; South Carolina 7%; South Dakota 6%; Tennessee 9.25%; Texas 8.25%; Vermont 6%; Washington 8.6%; Wisconsin 5.5%; West Virginia 6%

*Tax rates are subject to change according to individual state legislation without notice and are the responsibility of the consumer.

❾ Add appropriate amount to your order for shipping and postage. (See chart inside Order Form to determine charges.) Wilton ships via Federal Express Ground Service to the continental United States, Alaska, Hawaii and Puerto Rico. Shipments will arrive in approximately 10 days after we receive the order. Please allow 1-2 extra days for shipments to Alaska, Hawaii and Puerto Rico. Shipments to Guam and the Virgin Islands ship via standard Parcel Post through the U.S. Post Office. Please allow 4-6 weeks for delivery. We do not ship outside of the U.S.

❿ EXPRESS AIR DELIVERY. Phone orders placed by noon CST will be delivered in 3 to 5 business days for an additional $15.00. This service is available upon request for retail customers only in the continental United States.

⓫ Total tax for Group 2 states if applicable. See above.

⓬ Total your Order.
When Your Order Arrives . . . Should you be missing an item from your order (1) check to be sure you have not overlooked the merchandise (2) check over your receipted order form. If any items are temporarily out of stock, we will notify you of the date you may reorder those items. Your credit card will be charged only for merchandise shipped.

Wilton Return Policy: Inspect all merchandise upon arrival. If you're dissatisfied in any way with any item, notify Wilton Customer Service in writing with a copy of your invoice and all available information regarding your order before returning merchandise. ALL MERCHANDISE MUST BE RETURNED WITHIN **60 DAYS.** Handle returns promptly. Returns will be credited to the original credit card.

For inquiries on your previous order, send all available information and a copy of your invoice to: Wilton Industries, MS9A, 2240 West 75th Street, Woodridge, IL 60517.

Retail Order Form

Wilton Featherweight Bags can handle the pressure!

Wilton Featherweight Bags are built to be the longest-lasting bags you can buy. Strong, resilient seams help them perform year after year; our exclusive polyester material becomes softer the more you use them. Don't take our word for it—listen to our customers:

"I love the Featherweight Bags. Wilton is ahead in the ongoing "Green" process with these Featherweight Bags. They are reusable and durable. They clean up easily."
Melissa B. Buffalo, NY

18 in.
Featherweight™
Decorating Bag

16 in.
Featherweight™
Decorating Bag

14 in.
Featherweight™
Decorating Bag

12 in.
Featherweight™
Decorating Bag

10 in.
Featherweight™
Decorating Bag

8 in.
Featherweight™
Decorating Bag

"Easy clean-up, great feel, and a wide assortment of sizes make these bags my favorite. My decorating caddy is filled with Wilton Featherweight Bags—as a cake decorator, you can never have enough!"
Amy C. Jackson Springs, NC

"The Featherweight Bags are a joy to use. Soft, pliable and clean exceptionally well. A delight to use for beginners to us old pros!!! Kudos to you."
Natalie A. Winterset, IA

"The Featherweight Bags are great — ease of use, hassle-free washing, long lasting (10 years!!) and definitely durable. Thank you for this great product."
Aney M. Doha, Qatar

"I love using these decorating bags! They make decorating so much easier and therefore more fun!!"
Karen H. Friendswood, TX

See the complete selection of Wilton Featherweight Decorating Bags on page 136.

2011 PRODUCT SHOPS

FIND IT FAST...
ORDER WITH EASE!

Welcome to the most complete selection of cake decorating products anywhere! Here you'll find all the great Wilton tools, ingredients, accents and more you need to create every design in this Yearbook.

Go ahead and browse! Our shops are conveniently organized to help you find what you need fast. Whether you're decorating a batch of holiday cookies or creating a 3-tiered wedding cake, it's easy to find everything on your list.

When you're ready to buy, we make it a breeze! Charge your order 4 easy ways at your convenience:

PHONE TOLL-FREE
800-794-5866
8:00 am-4:30 pm, Monday-Friday CST
(RETAIL CUSTOMERS ONLY)

FAX TOLL-FREE
888-824-9520
24 HOURS A DAY/7 DAYS A WEEK

ORDER ON-LINE
www.wilton.com
24 HOURS A DAY/7 DAYS A WEEK

MAIL YOUR ORDER
Use the convenient retail order form in this book.

¡Se Habla Español!
Para mas informacion,
marque 800-436-5778

Instructional

Find inspiration with Wilton how-to books and videos. There's something perfect for your next celebration, from kids' birthday cakes to multi-tiered wedding designs.

Specialty Publications

Cookie Exchange

A cookie exchange is the perfect way to kick off the holiday season and this is the book you need to make it a success! Whether you're hosting or simply attending, Wilton *Cookie Exchange* is filled with ideas to inspire you. Discover hundreds of festive cookie designs, including a Gallery section with more than 150 easy ideas in 6 favorite seasonal shapes. Sharing favorite recipes is always a cookie exchange highlight, so you'll want to check all the great tastes inside. From melt-in-your-mouth almond snowballs to cool crème de menthe bars, there are so many great recipes to try, along with a baking basics section to ensure your cookies turn out just right. If you're hosting the party, we'll help you plan the entire event, from invitations and room decorations to festive presentation ideas. With Wilton *Cookie Exchange*, you can make it a celebration to look forward to every holiday season! Soft cover, 96 pages.
902-W-1102 $14.99

The complete guide to creating the perfect cookie exchange, with delicious recipes, festive cookie designs and fun party ideas

Brownie Fun!

Brownie Fun! is packed with over 140 easy-to-make designs and delicious recipes for brownies and mini treats. You'll find fun shapes like flowers, footballs, burgers, volcanos and space aliens that are perfect for kids' birthday parties. Create perfect brownies for every holiday, too. From stand-up Easter eggs and Halloween witches' brooms to candy-topped Christmas ornaments and shaped snowflakes, you can enjoy Brownie Fun all year long. You'll even find brownies elegant enough to serve at weddings, showers and other special occasions,. We'll also show you how to mix, bake and decorate the perfect brownies using the complete line of Wilton brownie products. With the *Brownie Fun!* book and our unique pans, cutters and toppings, it's easy to make brownies everyone will remember! Soft cover, 112 pages.
902-W-1105 $14.99

Cupcake Fun!

Wilton presents today's hottest party dessert like you've never seen it before. This all-new collection features over 150 exciting cupcake and treat ideas for all occasions, with complete baking and decorating instructions to make them easy. Discover captivating new shapes from coffee cups to flying saucers, plus a great recipe section with delicious surprises like Key Lime Cupcakes, Mocha Icing and more. Great baking and decorating products, too! *Cupcake Fun!* is the book you need to create the ultimate cupcake celebration. Look for many more great cupcake ideas and recipes at www.cupcakefun.com. Soft cover, 128 pages.
902-W-795 $12.99

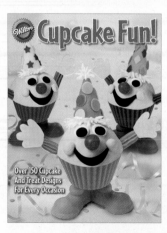

Over 150 Cupcake And Treat Designs For Every Occasion

2011 Yearbook of Cake Decorating

Start planning a year of amazing celebrations with the new edition of the Wilton Yearbook. In 2011, the Yearbook is packed with more cake and dessert ideas than ever before! You'll find more than 240 exciting designs for every occasion, in tune with today's most exciting themes and colors. Our Party Animals special section features a wild world of unforgettable cakes, starting with our sensational circus cover scene. It's a 3-tier, 3-ring circus, with colorful fondant pop animals, clowns and ringmaster complemented by a dazzling carousel cake with a whirl of colorful fondant ponies and stars. What a perfect way to top off a birthday—and it's just the beginning! You'll also find the best in traditional and contemporary wedding designs, festive holiday desserts, today's hottest character cakes, wonderful cupcake creations and more. As always, the Yearbook features step-by-step instructions, technique resource guide, complete product section and a website link to more great designs with techniques featured in Wilton Method Cake Decorating Courses. Soft cover. 240 pages.

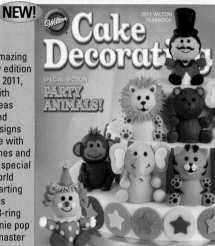

English 1701-W-3506 $12.99
Spanish 1701-W-3508 $12.99

2011 Pattern Book

Duplicate many of the beautiful cake designs featured in the *2011 Yearbook* and on the Wilton website. Includes over 160 decorating outlines to transfer to your cake. Easy-to-follow instructions. Soft cover; 48 pages of patterns.
408-W-2011 $8.99

Cake Decorating Beginner's Guide

• How to bake and ice perfect cakes
• How to mix any color icing with ease
• 15 fantastic cake ideas to decorate in 6 steps or less
• Step-by-step decorating instructions for stars, rosettes, drop flowers and more

Wilton, the #1 name in cake decorating, shows beginners everything they need to know, step-by-step. The *Beginner's Guide* makes decorating easy to learn and fun to do for everyone! Soft cover, 40 pages.
902-W-1232 $3.99

Candy Making Beginner's Guide

• 20 incredible candy ideas—all made in a few easy steps
• Easy ways to melt perfectly every time
• Painting color details in candy
• How to make classic creme-filled and dipped candies
• Great candy gift and favor ideas

You'll be amazed at the fantastic candies you can make using this book. The possibilities are endless, using the great selection of Wilton Candy Melts and Candy Molds. The *Beginner's Guide* shows you how, step-by-step, so you will make great-looking candies your very first time. The *Beginner's Guide* has the information you need to start making candy like a pro. Soft cover, 40 pages.
902-W-1231 $3.99

Wedding Publications

Wilton Wedding Style

From the experts in cake decorating, this is the book that shows you the full spectrum of wedding color possibilities from white to bright. In each color-themed section, you'll see how to incorporate your signature color into every part of the day—including exciting invitations, cakes that capture the moment and favors your guests will always remember. Wilton Wedding Style gives you: 100-plus ideas for invitations, favors, tabletop décor and more; 18 dream cakes plus petits fours, cupcakes and edible favors; Step-by-step project instructions with materials checklists; Hundreds of decorating ideas for ceremonies and receptions. Soft cover, 124 pages.
902-W-1101 $14.99

Wilton Tiered Cakes

The most contemporary looks in reception cakes! In *Wilton Tiered Cakes,* you'll see how to mix colors on a wedding cake using textured fondant or floral accents. Discover our cute teddy bear tower with fondant baby blocks used as separators. It's all here—38 amazing cake designs—along with complete instructions, techniques, construction and cutting guides, plus great Wilton products. Soft cover, 128 pages.
902-W-1108 $14.99

Wilton Wedding Cakes—A Romantic Portfolio

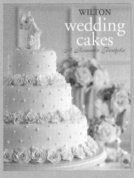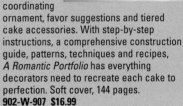

A Romantic Portfolio sets the bride's imagination free, with 38 exquisite cakes, along with coordinating ornament, favor suggestions and tiered cake accessories. With step-by-step instructions, a comprehensive construction guide, patterns, techniques and recipes, *A Romantic Portfolio* has everything decorators need to recreate each cake to perfection. Soft cover, 144 pages.
902-W-907 $16.99

Celebrate! With Fondant

It's the first book to feature fondant done the Wilton way—using our exciting cake designs, step-by-step instructions and convenient fondant products. More than 40 terrific cakes, along with alternate ways to decorate every design. Soft cover, 120 pages.
902-W-911 $14.99

Gifts from the Kitchen

Wilton Gifts from the Kitchen shows you dozens of great ways to package and present a food gift that is as welcoming and tasteful as the good things inside. This book makes it easy, using supplies you may already have on hand, along with convenient Wilton accents. *Wilton Gifts from the Kitchen* is also a great recipe book, with over 50 easy-to-prepare foods. Soft cover, 96 pages.
902-W-1225 $12.99

The Wilton School— Decorating Cakes

This book presents what Wilton has learned in 80 years of teaching cake decorating, including 30 exciting cakes with complete instructions and product listings; 103 techniques with instructions; helpful recipes, plus in-depth sections on baking cakes, preparing icing, and more. Complete product guide. Soft cover, 116 pages.
902-W-904 $14.99

Instructional Videos

BAKE DECORATE CELEBRATE! Seasons 1-3 on DVD!

It's the ultimate introduction to cake and dessert decorating on video! Each boxed set includes a complete 13-episode season of the popular Telly Award-winning Public Television series, which makes it easy for anyone to create something great to serve. In every episode, hosts Nancy Siler and Melanie Glasscock focus on a specific theme, such as Kids' Birthdays, Shaped Pans or Whimsical Cupcakes. They'll decorate specialty projects based on that theme and give you related decorating ideas to make the celebration complete. Special segments in each episode include Decorating Basics, featuring essential techniques, and Decorating Tips, with a variety of designs made using one specific tip. Each set includes 4 DVDs, approx. 6 hours total.

Season 1
Garden Party Desserts, Chocolate Treats, Fruits, Easy Flowers and more. Set/4.
901-W-121 $39.99

Season 2
Roses, Tarts, Pool & Beach, Patriotic and more. Closed captioned. Set/4.
901-W-131 $39.99

Season 3
Apples, Apples, Apples, Tropical & Tasty, Critters You Can Eat, Quick Change Cakes and more. Closed captioned. Set/4.
901-W-132 $39.99

Cake Decorating Basics

See and learn the essentials of creating amazing cakes and desserts, step by step! Everything from tools to icings, baking perfect cakes, decorating stars, shells, flowers and more, is covered in this 60-minute DVD.
901-W-120 $19.99

How to Make Icing Flowers

Learn how to make roses, Easter lilies, violets, pansies, daisies, poinsettias and more! Five cake designs incorporate all the flowers included in this 60-minute DVD.
901-W-258 $19.99

How to Make Wedding Cakes

Invaluable lessons on how to design and assemble tiered cakes for weddings, showers, anniversaries and other special occasions. Hints for transporting and serving are also included in this 60-minute DVD.
901-W-256 $19.99

Uses of Decorating Tips

Valuable quick reference and idea book for any decorator. Features five of the most popular decorating tip families and explains what each does. Shows the versatility of many tips by presenting varied cake designs. Soft cover, 48 pages.
902-W-1375 $9.99

Cake Decorating

Wilton products are designed by decorators for decorators. We've been helping people make amazing cakes since 1929—and we continue to create the innovative products you need to succeed. From ready-to-use icing that's the ideal consistency to our exclusively formulated bags and tips, Wilton quality makes a difference in the cakes you serve.

Decorating Sets

Convenient sets of decorating essentials give you instant versatility! From the perfect assortment of tips and bags for decorating your first cakes to comprehensive collections of tools and supplies in easy-to-carry caddies, Wilton has a set that's right for you. Each features Wilton precise high-quality tips for achieving many of the most popular techniques.

NEW!

ULTIMATE Decorating Set

Everything you need for every Wilton Method Course and more! With the Ultimate Decorating Set, you get the world's best decorating caddy, loaded with the world's best cake decorating tools from Wilton. It's our most extensive collection of the essential tools for every decorating need! For buttercream and royal icing, you get 17 precision metal tips, reusable and disposable bags, 4 stainless steel spatulas, flower-making supplies including nails, template stickers and stamens, plus the time-tested Practice Board Set for perfecting every technique learned in our Decorating Basics Course. You also get over 30 tools for gum paste and fondant decorating, including our exclusive Ribbon Cutter/Embosser Set, which cuts textured fondant strips in a variety of widths, plus flower cutters, shaping and modeling tools and more. With this set, you can do it all! Set/177.
2109-W-0200 $199.99

LOOK AT ALL YOU GET!

For Buttercream and Royal Icing:
- 17 Decorating Tips: Round 1, 3, 5, 12; Star 1M, 14, 16, 18, 21; Petal 59s, 101, 104; Leaf 352, 366; Bismarck 230; Drop Flower 2D; Multi-Opening 233
- 9 and 11 in. Straight Spatulas
- 9 and 13 in. Angled Spatulas
- 2 10 in. Featherweight® Decorating Bags
- 50 12 in. Disposable Decorating Bags
- 6 15 in. Parchment Triangles
- 4 Standard Couplers
- 6 Silicone Tip Covers
- 4 Pc. Decorating Nail Set
- Two 2-Pc. Lily Nail Sets
- 180 Lily Stamens
- 48 Flower Nail Template Stickers
- 6 Foil Squares
- Wave Flower Former Set
- 6 Flower Forming Cups
- Tip/Coupler Dishwasher and Storage Bag
- Practice Board with Stand and Patterns

For Fondant and Gum Paste:
- Button Flower Fondant Cut & Press Set
- Fondant Ribbon Cutter/Embosser Set
- Pansy Cutter
- Thick and Thin Fondant Shaping Foam
- 3 Decorating Brushes
- Dusting Pouch
- Thick and Thin Modeling Tools
- Ball Tool
- Veining Tool
- 2 Dowel Rods
- 2 Pc. Mum Cutter Set
- 3 Pc. Round Cut-Outs Set
- 5 Pc. Stepsaving Rose Flower Cutter Set
- 1 Calla Lily Cutter
- 6 Calla Lily Formers
- Straight Scallop Cutter
- 9 in. Rolling Pin with 4 Rings (two ⅛ in., two 1/16 in.)
- Easy-Glide Fondant Smoother
- 8 in. Cake Circle

Plus—The ULTIMATE Tool Caddy to store it all neatly!

$250 value!

Everything you need for all 3 Wilton Method Decorating Courses!

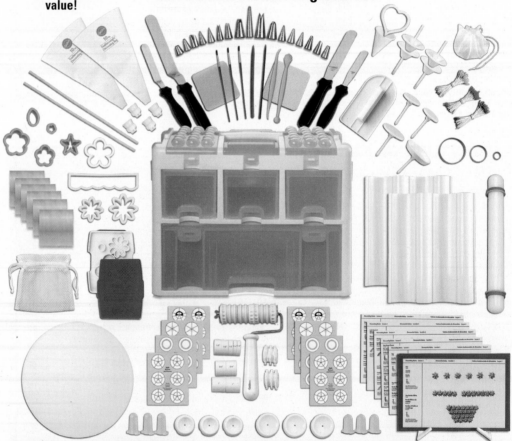

Ultimate Tool Caddy (unfilled)

The only caddy custom-made for Wilton tools. With the Ultimate Tool Caddy, all your Wilton tools are in the perfect place. All its specialized spaces keep your supplies protected and organized! Pegs stack tips upright for easy identification. Flip-top holders provide easy access to couplers and other tip supplies. 3-section drawers give you 9 spaces to organize any way you want! Icing color drawer cradles each jar to prevent spills. Oversized drawer with dividers—store large items or create 3 new compartments! Spatula slots keep blades straight and stable.
409-W-623 $59.99

ORDER TOLL FREE: 800-794-5866

101 Piece Tool Caddy Collection

This convenient caddy contains our most complete collection of tools, colors and flavors for the cake decorator. It's a great way to organize, carry and store the essentials—tips, couplers, colors, spatulas and more. Lift-out tray holds tips, couplers, brushes and colors securely. Upright storage prevents spills and makes it easy to find what you need. Generous storage area keeps books, spatulas, bags and other large supplies neatly organized. Set/101.

2109-W-861 $144.99

Save over $40
Compared to individual prices

Includes These Tools:
- Eight .5 oz. Icing Colors: Golden Yellow, No-Taste Red, Brown, Violet, Pink, Royal Blue, Black, Kelly Green
- 3 Couplers (2 standard, 1 large)
- 2 Tip/Coupler Dishwasher and Storage Bags
- Tip Cleaning Brush
- 24 Disposable 12 in. Decorating Bags
- 3 Professional Reusable Decorating Bags (8, 10 and 16 in.)
- 4 Tip Covers
- Tip Saver
- 1½ in. Flower Nail No. 7
- Flower Lifter

- 3 Spatulas (8 and 13 in. Angled, 8 in. Tapered)
- Garland Marker
- *Decorating Cakes* Book
- 20 All-Purpose Disposable Decorating Gloves
- Practice Board with Patterns
- 2 Bake-Even Strips
- 8 oz. Clear Vanilla and No-Color Butter Flavors
- Cake Leveler
- Quick Ease Roller
- Easy-Glide Fondant Smoother
- Decorating Brush

Plus 18 Tips:
- Round: 1, 2, 2A, 3, 12
- Star: 16, 18, 21, 32
- Basketweave: 48
- Leaf: 67, 352
- Petal: 102, 103, 104, 125
- Drop Flower: 2D
- Cake Icer: 789

---

50 Piece Tool Caddy Decorating Set

We've put together the perfect set for both beginning and advanced decorators. The generous selection of tips, colors and tools gives you the flexibility to decorate virtually any kind of cake. There's also plenty of room to add new items and keep everything organized to save you time. Set includes all tools specified as needed in our Course I class. Set/50.

2109-W-859 $61.99

Save $26
Compared to individual prices

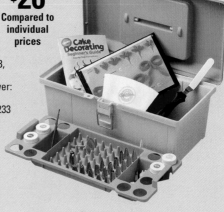

Includes These Tools:
- Tip Brush
- Decorating Brush
- 1½ in. Flower Nail No. 7
- 2 Standard Couplers
- 18 Disposable 12 in. Bags
- One 10 in. Professional Bag

- 8 in. Angled Spatula
- Four .5 oz. Icing Colors: Lemon Yellow, Christmas Red, Royal Blue, Leaf Green
- Practice Board with Stand
- *Cake Decorating Beginner's Guide*

Plus 19 Tips:
- Round: 2, 3, 5, 7, 12
- Leaf: 67, 352
- Drop Flower: 225
- Closed Star: 133
- Basketweave: 47
- Petal: 101, 103, 104
- Open Star: 16, 18, 21, 32
- Large Drop Flower: 2004 (2D)
- Multi-Opening: 233

Classic Tool Caddy

Lift out tray keeps 48 tips and 12 color jars within reach (tips and colors not included). Stores colors upright to prevent spilling. Plastic.

409-W-860 $26.99

53 Piece Cake Decorating Set

The works! Decorate many advanced wedding, floral and basketweave cakes as well as basic cakes. Set includes: metal decorating tips 2, 3, 5, 7, 12, 16, 18, 21, 32, 48, 67, 101, 103, 104, 129, 225, 349 and 352; 24 disposable 12 in. decorating bags, two tip couplers; 5 icing colors (.5 oz. each: Golden Yellow, Moss Green, Rose Petal Pink, Cornflower Blue, Violet); one 1¼ in. flower nail No. 9; 8 in. angled spatula; storage tray; and 40-page Cake Decorating Beginner's Guide. Set/53.

2104-W-2546 $32.99

25 Piece Cake Decorating Set

A solid foundation set for decorating. Set includes: metal decorating tips 3, 16, 32, 104 and 352; 12 disposable 12 in. decorating bags; two tip couplers; 4 icing colors (.5 oz. each: Lemon Yellow, Pink, Sky Blue, Violet, Leaf Green); 1¼ in. flower nail No. 9; instruction booklet. Set/25.

2104-W-2536 $12.99

18 Piece Cake Decorating Set

Perfect for Wilton character cakes! Set includes: metal decorating tips 4, 12, 18 and 103; 6 disposable 12 in. decorating bags; 2 tip couplers; 5 liquid color packets (.067 fl. oz. each: Yellow, Red, Green, Orange, Blue); instruction booklet. Set/18.

2104-W-2530 $7.99

12 Piece Cupcake Decorating Set

Create all kinds of fun cupcake designs perfect for celebrations or everyday treats! Includes star tips 1M (rosettes, stars, drop flowers), star tip 22 (zigzags, pull-out stars), round tip 12 (outlines, dots, messages) and Bismarck tip 230 for exciting filled cupcakes, plus 8 disposable bags, instruction booklet. Set/12.

2104-W-6667 $8.99

Decorating Tips

Presenting the best quality tips on the market, used by decorators throughout the world. Wilton tips are made to hold their shape and create precise decorations year after year. Rust-proof and dishwasher safe tips are tested for consistent performance in the Wilton Test Kitchen. All tips work with standard bags and couplers, unless otherwise indicated.

ROUND TIPS

Outline, lettering, dots, balls, beads, stringwork, lattice, lacework.

 #1 402-W-1 $0.99

 #6 402-W-6 $0.99

 #2A Smaller version of 1A. 402-W-2001* $1.69

 #1L 402-W-901** $1.89

 #7 402-W-7 $0.99

 #1A Bold borders, figure piping. 402-W-1001* $1.89

 #1s 402-W-1009 $1.59

 #8 402-W-8 $0.99

 #2 402-W-2 $0.99

#9 402-W-9 $0.99

 #230 Fill eclairs and bismarcks. 402-W-230** $2.19

#3 402-W-3 $0.99

#10 402-W-10 $0.99

#55 402-W-55 $0.99

#4 402-W-4 $0.99

#11 402-W-11 $0.99

#57 402-W-57 $0.99

#5 402-W-5 $0.99

#12 402-W-12 $0.99

#301 For flat lettering. 402-W-301 $0.99

DROP FLOWER TIPS

Small (106-225); medium (131-194); large (2C-1G, great for cookie dough).

 #106 402-W-106 $1.69

#225 402-W-225 $1.69

#140 402-W-140 $1.89

#1B 402-W-1002* $1.89

 #107 402-W-107 $1.69

#131 402-W-131 $1.69

#195 402-W-195** $1.69

#1C 402-W-1003* $1.89

#108 402-W-108** $1.69

#190 402-W-190** $1.89

#2C 402-W-2003* $1.69

#1E 402-W-1005* $1.89

#109 402-W-109** $1.89

#191 402-W-191 $1.69

#2D 402-W-2004* $1.69

#1F 402-W-1006* $1.89

#129 402-W-129 $1.69

#193 402-W-193 $1.69

#2E 402-W-2005* $1.69

#224 402-W-224 $1.69

#194 402-W-194** $1.89

#2F 402-W-2006* $1.69

#1G 402-W-1007* $1.89

MULTI-OPENING TIPS

Rows and clusters of strings, beads, stars, (Use 233 for grass).

 #42 402-W-42 $0.99

#233 402-W-233 $1.69

#235 402-W-235* $1.69

 #89 402-W-89 $0.99

#234 402-W-234* $1.89

TRIPLE STAR Triple Star* 402-W-2010 $2.89

 #134 402-W-134** $1.89

CLOSED STAR TIPS

Create deeply grooved shells, stars and fleurs de lis.

 #24 402-W-24 $0.99

#28 402-W-28 $0.99

#31 402-W-31 $0.99

#133 402-W-133 $0.99

 #26 402-W-26 $0.99

#29 402-W-29 $0.99

#33 402-W-33 $0.99

#54 402-W-54 $0.99

 #27 402-W-27 $0.99

#30 402-W-30 $0.99

#35 402-W-35 $0.99

PETAL TIPS

Realistic flower petals, dramatic ruffles, drapes, swags and bows.

 #59s/59 402-W-594 $0.99

 #97 402-W-97 $0.99

#150 402-W-150 $1.69

#125 402-W-125* $1.69

 #59 402-W-59 $0.99

#101s 402-W-1019 $1.59

#116 402-W-116* $1.69

#126 402-W-126* $1.69

 #60 402-W-60 $0.99

#101 402-W-101 $0.99

#121 402-W-121* $1.69

#127 402-W-127* $1.69

#61 402-W-61 $0.99

#102 402-W-102 $0.99

#123 402-W-123* $1.69

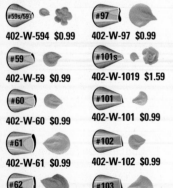 #127D Giant Rose** 402-W-1274 $1.89

#62 402-W-62 $0.99

#103 402-W-103 $0.99

#124 402-W-124* $1.69

#64 402-W-64 $0.99

#104 402-W-104 $0.99

BASKETWEAVE TIPS

Tips 44, 45 make only smooth stripes; rest of basketweave tips and Cake Icer make both smooth and ribbed stripes.

 #44 402-W-44 $0.99

#1D 402-W-1004** $1.89

 #45 402-W-45 $0.99

#2B 402-W-2002* $1.69

#46 402-W-46 $0.99

#47 402-W-47 $0.99

#789 Cake Icer** 409-W-789 $3.29

#48 402-W-48 $0.99

*Fits large coupler.   **Tip does not work with coupler. Use with parchment or uncut bags only. Cake Icer Tip should be used with bags 14 in. or larger.

Tip Sets

Be ready for virtually any decorating need with these generous sets. Each includes a great variety of tips in the most popular families—round, petal, drop flower, leaf, open star and more—stored upright in a convenient locking case.

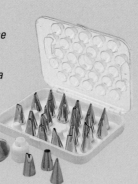

Deluxe
Includes: 26 metal decorating tips (2, 4, 7, 13, 16, 17, 18, 30, 42, 46, 47, 61, 65, 66, 67, 74, 78, 97, 98, 101, 102, 103, 104, 106, 107 and 199); 1¼ in. flower nail No. 9; tip coupler; plastic tipsaver case. Set/28.
2104-W-6666 $28.99

Master
Includes: 52 metal decorating tips: (1, 2, 3, 4, 6, 7, 12, 13, 16, 17, 18, 22, 24, 27, 30, 31, 32, 42, 45, 46, 47, 48, 54, 59, 61, 65, 66, 67, 68, 69, 70, 73, 74, 78, 96, 97, 98, 101, 102, 103, 104, 106, 108, 109, 123, 124, 129, 134, 136, 195, 199 and 2C); two standard tip couplers; two 1¼ in. flower nails No. 9; plastic tipsaver case. Set/56.
2104-W-7778 $49.99

OPEN STAR TIPS

Star techniques, drop flowers; the finely cut teeth of 199 through 364 create decorations with many ridges; use 6B and 8B with pastry dough too.

 #13
402-W-13 $0.99

 #14
402-W-14 $0.99

#15
402-W-15 $0.99

#16
402-W-16 $0.99

#17
402-W-17 $0.99

#18
402-W-18 $0.99

#19
402-W-19 $0.99

#20
402-W-20 $0.99

 #21
402-W-21 $0.99

 #22
402-W-22 $0.99

 **#32**
402-W-32 $0.99

#199
402-W-199 $1.69

#362
402-W-362 $1.69

#363
402-W-363 $1.69

#364
402-W-364 $1.69

#172
402-W-172** $1.69

#1M (2110)
402-W-2110* $1.69

#4B
402-W-4400** $1.69

#6B
402-W-6600** $1.69

#8B
402-W-8800** $1.89

LEAF TIPS

So realistic! Ideal for shell-motion borders too.

 #65s
402-W-659 $1.59

#66
402-W-66 $0.99

#68
402-W-68 $0.99

#73
402-W-73 $0.99

#75
402-W-75 $0.99

#352
402-W-352 $1.59

#70
402-W-70 $0.99

#65
402-W-65 $0.99

#67
402-W-67 $0.99

#69
402-W-69 $0.99

#74
402-W-74 $0.99

349/ 352s
402-W-349 $1.59

#326
402-W-326 $1.59

#112
402-W-112** $1.69

#113
402-W-113* $1.69

#115
402-W-115* $1.69

#366
Makes leaves for larger flowers.
402-W-366* $1.89

† For left-handers.   *Fits large coupler.

SPECIALTY TIPS

Shells, ropes, hearts, Christmas trees, ring candle holders!

#98
402-W-98 $0.99

#347
402-W-347 $1.69

#136
402-W-136 $1.89

#77
402-W-77 $0.99

#78
402-W-78 $0.99

#83
402-W-83 $0.99

#96
402-W-96 $0.99

#79
402-W-79 $0.99

#105
402-W-105 $0.99

#80
402-W-80 $0.99

#81
402-W-81 $0.99

#250
402-W-250* $1.89

#252
402-W-252* $1.89

#95
402-W-95 $0.99

RUFFLE TIPS

Plain, fluted, shell-border, special effects.

#86
402-W-86 $0.99

#87
402-W-87† $0.99

#88
402-W-88† $0.99

#100
402-W-100 $0.99

#353
402-W-353 $1.59

#340
402-W-340 $1.59

#401
402-W-401 $1.59

#402
402-W-402* $1.69

#406
402-W-406* $1.89

#403
402-W-403** $1.89

LEFT-HANDED TIP SETS

LEFT-HAND

Now left-handers can achieve the same beautiful flowers as right-handed decorators! Tips fit standard bags and couplers.

Drop Flower Set
Includes Left tips 106 and 107 for making small swirled flowers. Set/2.
#106L
#107L
418-W-613† $3.29

Petal Set
Includes Left tip 59° for violets, Left tip 97 for Victorian roses and Left tip 116** for large Wilton roses. Set/3.
#59°L
#97L
#116L
418-W-612† $3.29

Decorating Bags

All decorating bags are not the same! Wilton bags are tested to be the best. They simply feel better in your hand—soft and strong to provide decorating performance you can count on. From pure parchment triangles to our convenient Disposable or premium reusable Featherweight styles, Wilton bags are made to our strict specifications for consistent quality.

Featherweight Decorating Bags

The best quality bags for decorating, with strong resilient seams to help them last for years! Featherweight bags feel soft and comfortable in the hand—the polyester material becomes softer the more the bags are used. Lightweight, strong and flexible, they'll never get stiff. Coated to prevent grease from seeping through. Each batch is tested in the Wilton Test Kitchen to meet our exacting standards. Dishwasher safe. Instructions included; sold singly.

8 in.	404-W-5087	$3.29
10 in.	404-W-5109	$4.79
12 in.	404-W-5125	$5.79
14 in.	404-W-5140	$6.79
16 in.	404-W-5168	$8.49
18 in.	404-W-5184	$9.49

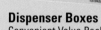

Dispenser Boxes

Convenient Value Packs make it easy to pull out one bag at a time, so you can keep your decorating space uncluttered. Instructions included.
Pk./50
2104-W-1273 $13.19
Pk./100
2104-W-1249 $20.99

15 in. Parchment Triangles

Authentic parchment paper is the professional's choice for convenience and quick bag preparation. Make use-and-toss decorating bags ideal for small amounts of icing or brush striping. Excellent wet strength for candy or a variety of icings. Also great for smoothing iced cakes and transferring patterns. Pk./100.
2104-W-1508 $6.99

12 in. Disposable Decorating Bags

Wilton's strict testing standards ensure the highest quality disposable bags you can buy. Our proprietary blend of materials helps Wilton bags feel more comfortable and outperform competitive bags. They can be used with or without a coupler and work great for microwave-melting and piping of Candy Melts. Fits standard tips and couplers. Just use, then toss! Instructions included.
Pk./12 2104-W-358 $4.19
Pk./24 2104-W-1358 $6.79

16 in. Disposable Decorating Bags

Larger size lets you decorate longer without refilling the bag—great for piping borders on large cakes. It's the only size bag to use with Cake Icer Tip 789, for covering cakes fast. Just use, then toss. Strong flexible plastic; fits standard tips and couplers. Also perfect for microwave-melting and piping of Candy Melts. Instructions included. Pk./12.
2104-W-1357 $5.29

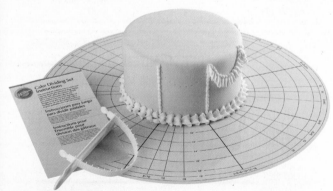

Cake Dividing Set

Measures equal sections of your cake for precise placement of garlands, stringwork and other designs. Cake Dividing Wheel marks up to 16 divisions on cakes up to 20 in. diameter. Garland Marker adjusts to 7 widths. Instructions included. Set/2.
409-W-806 $9.99

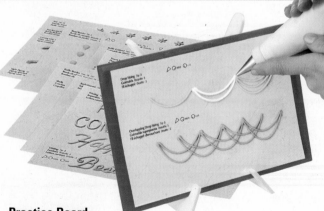

Practice Board with Patterns Set

The time-tested way to perfect decorating techniques. Includes stand and 20 full-size patterns. 9 x 6 in.
406-W-9464 $7.99

ORDER TOLL FREE: 800-794-5866

Decorating Tools & Accessories

Saves decorating space and time!

Decorating Bag Holder
Keep your icing bags close at hand and organize your decorating space with this convenient stand. Great for Wilton Featherweight, Disposable or Parchment Bags! The 2 large and 6 small spaces hold bags upright so they'll be easy to grab. Use the smallest openings to hold flower and cupcake nails. To prevent air from drying out icing, we suggest using Wilton Silicone Decorating Tip Covers below or placing a damp towel that touches tip ends under the Bag Holder. 11.5 x 7.25 x 4.5 in. Patent pending.
417-W-115 $9.99

Bags, ties, tips and tip covers shown sold separately.

Silicone Decorating Tip Cover Set
With convenient silicone covers, icing won't dry out in your bag between uses. They fit snugly over all standard and most large tips to keep air out. Top rack dishwasher safe. Pk./6.
414-W-916 $5.99

Icing Bag Ties
Convenient bands wrap around the twist of your decorating bag, then lock to prevent icing from oozing out of the top. As you squeeze out icing, slide the tie down to maintain the pressure. Pk./12.
417-W-173 $4.49

Tip/Coupler Dishwasher and Storage Bag
Place nylon mesh bag in dishwasher silverware rack for easy tip and coupler cleaning. Tips not included. 5¾ x 6 in. Pk./2.
417-W-1640 $3.29

Tip Brush
Great for cleaning small tip openings. Plastic bristles. ¼ x 4 in. long.
418-W-1123 $1.59

Decorating Couplers
Couplers make it easy to change decorating tips on the same icing bag.

Standard
Fits all decorating bags and standard tips.
411-W-1987 $0.69

Large
Use with large decorating tips and 14 to 18 in. Featherweight Bags.
411-W-1006 $1.69

Tipsaver Cases
Small case holds 26 tips; large case holds 52 tips Tips not included.
Small 405-W-8773 $6.99
Large 405-W-7777 $8.49

Tip Saver
Restores bent tips to their proper shape; opens clogged tips. Place tip over pointed or cone-shaped end, put on cover and twist back and forth to reshape. Heavy-duty plastic.
414-W-909 $3.29

Decorating Tools & Accessories

Decorating Nail Set
A great selection of sizes for creating virtually any size nail flower! Includes a cupcake nail, with a recessed platform for finishing a standard cupcake with a perfectly-swirled top. Includes 1.5, 2, 2.5 in. Flower Nails and 2.25 x 2.5 in. Cupcake Nail. Stems insert easily in nails to create a secure platform. Top rack dishwasher safe. Pk./4.
417-W-107 $6.99

Flower Lifter
Easily transfers buttercream flowers from nail to cake without damage. Angled design keeps your hands from touching the cake. Detachable blades for easy cleaning. Plastic. 5¼ in. long.
**417-W-1199
$3.29**

Flower Nail No. 7
For basic flower making. Provides the control you need when piping icing flowers. Just rotate the nail between your thumb and fingers as you pipe a flower on the head. Stainless steel. 1½ in. wide.
402-W-3007 $1.29

Pre-Cut Icing Flower Squares
No more cutting! Perfectly sized waxed paper squares attach to your flower nail with a dot of icing for easy piping and transfer of flowers. Save work and get a fresh flat surface every time. Pk./50.
414-W-920 $1.99

Lily Nail Set
Essential for making cup flowers. Includes ½, 1¼, 1⅝ and 2½ in. diameter cups. Set/8.
403-W-9444 $2.29

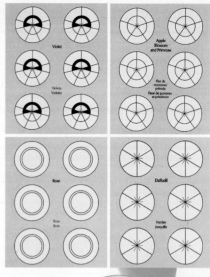

Flower Nail Templates **NEW!**
Convenient stickers guide you to create perfectly formed flowers! Stick a template on your nail, add a waxed paper square and you're ready to decorate. The guidelines help you achieve the ideal petal position and size. Includes 4 template styles used to create 5 popular icing flowers including Daffodils, Apple Blossoms and Primroses, Violets and Roses (2 sheets, 12 templates of each design). Set/48.
414-W-1000 $3.99

STAMENS
Finish your royal icing or gum paste flowers with these lovely stamen styles. Cut stamens to desired size and insert in flower center.

NEW!

Lily Stamen Set
Create lifelike lilies with trim-to-fit lily stamen clusters in 3 natural colors! Simply place in royal icing or gum paste flower centers before drying. Includes 10 each pink, yellow and brown. 2.125 in. long. Pk./30.
1005-W-4451 $3.29

NEW!

Color Stamen Set
Finish your flowers with beautiful, natural looking stamens in 3 pretty colors. Includes 60 each yellow, white and orange. 2.125 in. long. Pk./180
1005-W-4452 $3.29

Flower Stamen Assortment
Includes 60 each Pearl, Fluffy and Glitter. May be tinted (except Pearl) with Wilton Icing Colors added to vanilla. 2.5 in. long. Pk./180.
1005-W-410 $3.29

Wave Flower Former Set **NEW!**
Use this convenient connecting platform to dry flowers, leaves and other decorations in royal icing, gum paste or fondant. Wave shape makes it easy to dry concave or convex shapes; large drying area is great for ribbons, bows and streamers. 14.5 x 9 in. assembled. Patent pending. Set/2.
1907-W-1320 $6.99

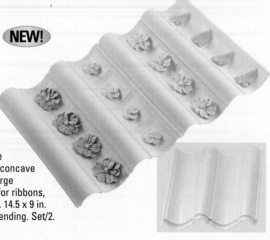

Flower Former Set
Dry icing leaves and flowers in a convex or concave shape. Three each of 1½, 2 and 2½ in. wide holders, all 11 in. long. Set/9.
417-W-9500 $6.29

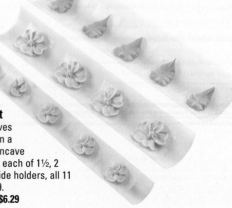

Cake Decorating Turntables

A quality cake turntable is a must for easy decorating. Turntables lift your cake off the work surface so you can create borders conveniently. And they rotate, allowing you to decorate all the way around the cake without straining.

It tilts! Decorate any part of your cake conveniently!

Trim 'N Turn ULTRA Cake Turntable
Experience the ultimate in turntable control. The Trim 'N Turn ULTRA combines an extra-high smooth-turning platform with non-slip detail for secure performance. The easy-locking platform keeps your cake steady as you create delicate flowers and writing. Platform turns in either direction for easy icing, borders, combing and leveling. Great for left-hand or right-hand users.
- Non-slip design with soft-grip ring molded into platform to keep cake in place
- 3 in. raised base with arched sides for easy grip
- Hidden ball bearing track for smooth turning
- Lock platform with ease using the pull-out tab
- 12 in. platform removes from base for easy cleaning
- Holds cakes up to 11 in. with platform visible—holds larger cakes if needed

307-W-301 $20.99

Trim 'N Turn PLUS Cake Turntable
Decorate with more convenience and control with the Trim 'N Turn PLUS. Its smooth-turning performance puts your cake in the ideal position for decorating beautiful borders and icing sides perfectly smooth.
- Non-slip base is raised for better control.
- Arched sides for easy lifting
- Removable 12 in. platform for easy cleaning
- Hidden ball-bearing track for smooth turning
- Holds cakes up to 11 in. with platform visible—holds larger cakes if needed

307-W-303 $13.99

Professional Turntable
Extra strength and effortless turning for decorating tiered wedding cakes. Heavy-duty aluminum stand is 4½ in. high with 12 in. diameter plate. Holds cakes up to 16 in. diameter.

307-W-2501 $69.99

Tilting Cake Turntable
The Tilting Cake Turntable moves to 3 preset angles (12°, 24°, and level) and locks in place, making every decorating technique easier! 6 in. high turntable smoothly rotates in any of the angled positions for effortless decorating of top borders, stringwork, lettering on top and sides of cake, more. Includes lock to prevent rotation. Non-slip bottom, 12 in. diameter.

307-W-894 $69.99

Ergonomic Spatulas

Wilton gives decorators more choice—a variety of spatula styles and sizes to fit every need. All have stainless steel blades for strength and flexibility. Decorate with greater comfort, more control and less fatigue, thanks to the ergonomic handle with finger pad. Keep a variety on hand for icing and filling cakes of every size, bag striping and more.

WHITE HANDLES
Nylon weighted handles give you greater control. Can hang for convenient storage.

Straight
Great for spreading and smoothing fillings, all-around kitchen use.
9 in.
409-W-6045 $7.99
11 in.
409-W-6046 $9.99
15 in.
409-W-6047 $13.99

Angled
Ideal angle for smoothing cake sides and spreading fillings.
9 in.
409-W-6040 $7.99
13 in.
409-W-6041 $9.99
15 in.
409-W-6042 $13.99

Tapered
Easily ices hard-to-reach spots on your cake.
9 in.
409-W-6057 $7.99

Cake Knife/Spatula
This stainless steel knife is perfect for torting cakes— it cuts layers cleanly and has the width you need to transfer layers without breakage. Use the smooth edge for spreading icing or filling on cake layers. It's easy to control, with a lightweight nylon handle that is comfortable in any hand. 15 in. long.
409-W-6048 $9.99

BLACK HANDLES
Contoured handle with finger pad provides an excellent grip and superior control.

Straight Blade
9 in.
409-W-6006 $4.29
11 in.
409-W-6018 $6.29
15 in.
409-W-6030 $10.49

Angled Blade
9 in.
409-W-6012 $4.79
13 in.
409-W-6024 $6.79
15 in.
409-W-6036 $10.49

Tapered Blade
9 in.
409-W-6003 $4.29

Press Sets

Block Message Press Set
Includes Best, Happy, Wishes, Anniversary, Birthday and Congratulations. Message holder. Word height ⅞ in. Set/6.
2104-W-2077 $4.09

Make-Any-Message Letter Press Set
Imprint the perfect sentiment! Press words up to 10½ in. wide, letters ¾ in. high. Includes letter holder. Set/56.
2104-W-10 $8.99

Italic Make-Any-Message Press Set
Pretty and sophisticated letters for a custom message. Press words up to 10½ in. wide, letters ¾ in. high. Includes letter holder. Set/58.
2104-W-2277 $8.99

Decorator Favorites Pattern Press Set
Includes: fleur-de-lis; double heart; medallion; open heart; closed scroll; heart; large, medium and small C-scrolls; crest; double scroll; vine. Set/12.
2104-W-3160 $6.99

Designer Pattern Press Set
Imprints elegant designs for easy overpiping. Includes: symmetrical swirl; small and large fleurs de lis; corner flourish; flower; heart bow; scroll; curlicues. Set/8.
2104-W-3112 $6.99

Script Message Press Set
Combine the words Best, Happy, Wishes, Birthday, Anniversary, and Congratulations. Word height ⅞ in. Set/6.
2104-W-2061 $4.09

Cake Stencils Variety Pack
Our collection of 4 stencil designs gives you several ways to make birthday and everyday cakes more festive. It's so easy —just place on your iced cake, then sprinkle with Wilton Cake Sparkles, add exciting Wilton Sugars in a rainbow of colors or use Color Mist Food Color Spray. Also works beautifully with Wilton Rolled Fondant—fill in designs with sugars or decorate with FoodWriter Markers. Includes Happy Birthday, Flower, Swirl and Heart designs. Pk./4.
417-W-148 $7.99

Garland Marker
Adjusts to 7 preset widths and varying depths to easily mark perfectly uniform garlands on cake sides. Instructions included.
409-W-812 $4.49

Decorating Triangle
Each side adds a different contoured effect to iced cakes. Easy to hold. Plastic, 5 x 5 in.
417-W-162 $1.29

Decorating Comb
Run edge across your iced cake to form perfect ridges. Plastic, 12 x 1½ in.
417-W-156 $1.69

ORDER TOLL FREE: 800-794-5866

Decorating Tools

NEW!

Dessert Decorator Plus

It's the easy-to-use tool for beautiful decorated desserts! One hand does it all—elegant shells, stars and leaves, beautiful script messages, pretty bows and flowers. Just press the thumb lever and icing will flow; release lever and icing stops. Changing tips is easy—simply unscrew the cap, insert a new tip and apply coupler onto the cylinder.
415-W-0906 $14.99

See-through Barrel
You'll know at a glance how much icing is left! Parts detach easily for filling and cleaning.

Rotating Cylinder
Places tip in the perfect decorating position with an easy turn.

Pull-Out Plunger
Inner ring pushes icing through cylinder.

Convenient Thumb Lever
Lets you hold tool and decorate with one hand.

Ergonomic Design
Finger-grip barrel is easy to handle in right or left hand.

Instruction Sheet
See how to create every decoration shown!

Dessert Decorator Plus includes all this:

2 Tip Couplers
Two sizes hold standard (small) and large tips.

| Round Tip | Star Tip | Petal Tip | Leaf Tip | Filling Tip |

5 Precision Tips
Produce perfectly-shaped decorations every time. Great for shells, beads, bows, leaves, filled cupcakes and more!

It's easy to add beautiful decorations to any dessert or appetizer in minutes! Designed for comfortable one-hand decorating and effortless tip positioning, this is the most convenient dessert tool you'll ever use. Create beautiful decorations—shells, stars, rosettes, leaves. The recipe book included is filled with fabulous ideas to tempt your family and friends. Decorate desserts with elegant whipped cream or icing designs. Dress up pastry shells with dramatic swirls of mousse. With Dessert Decorator Pro, you can do it all!
415-W-850 $31.49

Dessert decorator Pro®

Rotating Cylinder
Just turn to place the tip in the correct position for any decoration.

Ergonomic Design
Easy, comfortable grip for right or left hand. Outer sleeve fits your fingers like a glove.

Stainless Steel Cylinder
Preferred by pastry chefs because stainless won't transfer flavors and it maintains temperature of fillings.

Fits Virtually Any Tip/Coupler
Use with the tips included or with most other Wilton tips.

Pull-Out Plunger
Inner ring pushes filling smoothly through cylinder.

Convenient Thumb Lever
The ideal distance from cylinder for comfortable one-handed decorating.

Durable Construction
Cylinder and plunger are housed in an impact-resistant sleeve for years of great decorating performance.

Dessert Decorator Pro includes all this:

Two Tip Couplers
Two sizes to hold standard (small) and large tips.

| Tip 366 Leaf | Tip 4B Star | Tip 125 Petal | Tip 21 Star | Tip 1M Star | Tip 230 Bismarck |

Six Durable Nickel-Plated Tips
Quality metal tips produce perfectly-shaped decorations every time.

Tip/Coupler Dishwasher and Storage Bag
Just place nylon mesh bag with tips and couplers in your dishwasher silverware rack for easy tip and coupler cleaning.

Easy To Fill and Clean
Most parts detach with ease; wash in warm, soapy water.

Tips in bag for size reference only. Tips included are shown at left.

Recipes and Instructions
Includes delicious recipes and easy decorating instructions for elegant desserts and appetizers.

Icing Sculptor

Now your cakes can have an elegant sculpted finish that will give them a beautiful professional look. It's easy with the Icing Sculptor. Just insert any combination of the 64 design blades—mix and match between the 14 sculpting edges to create your favorite customized effects. Then glide the comb over the iced cake sides to create attractive ridges that will beautifully frame your design. Create hundreds of pattern combinations—wide or narrow ridges, dramatic swirls and vertical designs too. Also includes sculptor handle and complete instructions. This versatile tool has a Patent No. D489,582. Set/66.
2104-W-12 $13.99

So Easy!
Select the sculpting blades you want and slide into handle. Press sculptor into iced cake as you rotate cake on turntable.

So Versatile!
Mix and match between the 14 edge designs on 64 blades to achieve the perfect look for your cake.

Includes 8 of each 2-Sided Design Blade

Icings & Gels

All Wilton icings are formulated for easy decorating as well as great taste. Our convenient ready-to-use icings are the perfect medium consistency for decorating, so you don't need to worry about mixing or measuring.

TUBE ICINGS, GELS

Tube Decorating Icings

The same high quality as our Ready-To-Use Icings, in a convenient tube. Create flowers, borders and more. Ideal for small areas of color on character cakes. Use with the Tip Set or Coupler Ring Set (below) and any standard-size Wilton metal tip (not included). Colors match Wilton Icing Colors (p. 146). 4.25 oz. Certified Kosher. **$1.99**

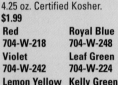

Red 704-W-218	**Royal Blue** 704-W-248
Violet 704-W-242	**Leaf Green** 704-W-224
Lemon Yellow 704-W-236	**Kelly Green** 704-W-227
Orange 704-W-212	**Chocolate** 704-W-254
Pink 704-W-230	**White** 704-W-200	**Black** 704-W-206

Coupler Ring Set

Attach Wilton standard size metal decorating tips onto Wilton tube icings to create any technique. Set/4.
411-W-1989 $2.29

Tip Set

Tips easily twist onto Wilton tube icings to create many decorating techniques. Includes Star, Round, Leaf and Petal Tips. Set/4.
418-W-621 $2.19

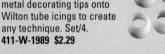

Tube Decorating Gels

Add colorful highlights to your decorating with these transparent gels. Create a beautiful stained-glass effect and add distinctive writing and printing. Great for cakes and cookies. Colors match Wilton Icing Colors (p. 146). .75 oz. Certified Kosher. **$1.49**

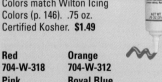

Red 704-W-318	**Orange** 704-W-312
Pink 704-W-330	**Royal Blue** 704-W-348
Violet 704-W-342	**Kelly Green** 704-W-324	**White** 704-W-302
Lemon Yellow 704-W-336	**Brown** 704-W-354	**Black** 704-W-306

STRIPED ICINGS

NEW!

Two dazzling colors come together every time you squeeze! Create exciting 2-tone decorations for party cakes and cupcakes. Use with the Tip Set or Coupler Ring Set (below) and standard-size Wilton metal tips (not included). The larger sized star, petal or leaf tips optimize the two-tone effect. 4.25 oz. Certified Kosher. **$2.49**

704-W-217 Pink/Lavender
704-W-203 Red/White
704-W-201 Green/Black
704-W-211 Blue/Yellow

SPARKLE GEL

Make your cake decorations more dynamic! Squeeze on sparkling color effects with our ready-to-use gel. Great for dots, messages, water effects and fondant accents. Try it on cookies, cupcakes and more! Resealable 3.5 oz. tubes. Certified Kosher. **$2.99**

Black 704-W-1061	**White** 704-W-107	**Gold** 704-W-1060	**Red** 704-W-112
Blue 704-W-110	**Yellow** 704-W-108	**Green** 704-W-111	**Pink** 704-W-356

Ready-To-Decorate Icing

Add an exciting finishing touch to treats, without mixing or mess. Just slip one of the four free tips over the nozzle and start the fun. Colors match Wilton Icing Colors (p. 146). 6.4 oz. Certified Kosher. **$4.29**

Red	710-W-4400
Green	710-W-4401
White	710-W-4402
Black	710-W-4404
Pink	710-W-4406
Blue	710-W-4407
Violet	710-W-4408
Yellow	710-W-4409
Orange	710-W-4410

Four FREE decorating tips included:

Small Round Tip
For dots and outlining

Leaf Tip
For basic and ruffled leaves

Large Round Tip
For writing and printing

Star Tip
For stars, swirls and pretty borders

Icing Writer

Squeeze colorful accents onto fondant and Wilton Cookie Icing with this ready-to-use icing! It's easy to control, just squeeze the bottle and icing flows smoothly from the built-in round tip. Dries to a smooth, satin finish. 3 oz. bottle. Certified Kosher. **$2.49**

Red	710-W-2225
Yellow	710-W-2226
Pink	710-W-2230
White	710-W-2228
Green	710-W-2229
Violet	710-W-2231
Blue	710-W-2227

Cookie Icing

Quick-setting microwavable icing covers cookies with a smooth finish— perfect for decorating with colorful Wilton Icing Writer accents or FoodWriter markers! Easy to use—just heat and squeeze onto cookies using the convenient cap. Sets smooth in just 1 hour. 10 oz. bottle covers approx. 12 cookies, 3 in. each. Certified Kosher. **$4.49**

White 704-W-481
Red 704-W-488
Green 704-W-493
Blue 704-W-444 **NEW!**

Drizzle Icing

Just heat and squeeze over brownies and other treats to add a ribbon of flavor. Use with Brownie Fudge Icing (p. 143) for exciting marbleized designs. 10 oz. bottle. Certified Kosher. **$4.99**

Vanilla Crème 704-W-151
Peanut Butter 704-W-150

ORDER TOLL FREE: 800-794-5866

READY-TO-USE ICINGS

Wilton makes the only ready-to-use icing that is the perfect consistency for decorating. The pure white color is best for creating true vivid colors using Wilton Icing Colors. Rich and creamy, with a delicious homemade taste.

Creamy Decorator Icing
Ideal thin-to-medium consistency for use in Wilton Method Cake Decorating Classes in a convenient easy-carry tub. Great for icing cakes, making borders, messages and more. Contains 9 cups—enough to decorate ten 8 or 9 in. round cake layers. Certified Kosher. 4.5 lb. tub.
White 704-W-680 $14.99

Decorator Icing
Ideal stiff consistency for making roses and flowers with upright petals. One 16 oz. can covers two 8 or 9 in. layers or one 9 x 13 in. cake. 16 oz. can.
White 710-W-118 $3.29
Chocolate 710-W-119 $3.29

Brownie Fudge Icing
Rich fudge flavor and velvety texture makes this the perfect icing for spreading on brownies. Heat it in the microwave for an easy glaze; use with Wilton Drizzle Icing (p. 142) to create delicious designs. 16 oz. can.
710-W-9700 $3.29

Color Flow Mix
Create dimensional flow-in designs for your cake. Just add water and confectioners' sugar. 4 oz. can makes ten 1½ cup batches. Certified Kosher.
701-W-47 $7.49

Piping Gel
Pipe messages and designs or glaze cakes before icing. Use clear or tint with icing color. 10 oz. Certified Kosher.
704-W-105 $3.99

NEW!

Vanilla Whipped Icing Mix
Our light, whipped icing provides the ideal texture for decorating in an easy-to-make, delicious mix. Just add ice water and it whips up velvety-smooth for icing or decorating. Light and delicate flavor. Makes 5 cups. Certified Kosher Dairy.
710-W-1241 $4.99

Creamy White Buttercream Icing Mix
Our convenient mix has the delicious taste and creamy texture of homemade buttercream icing. Use just as you would your favorite buttercream recipe. Makes 1½ to 2 cups. Enough to ice a 1-layer 8 in. cake. Certified Kosher Dairy.
710-W-112 $2.99

Royal Icing Mix
At last—a convenient mix for creating hard-drying flowers and other decorations! Great for making flowers in advance for Wilton Method Courses or your own decorated cakes. Top off petits fours with pretty floral accents, add brilliant color to cookies for all occasions or dress up desserts with drop flowers. Makes 2 cups—enough icing for about 280 drop flowers or 88 small roses. Certified Kosher Dairy.
710-W-1219 $4.99

Meringue Powder
Primary ingredient for royal icing. Stabilizes buttercream, adds body to boiled icing and meringue. Replaces egg whites in many recipes. Resealable top opens for easy measuring. 4 oz. can makes 5 recipes of royal icing; 8 oz. can makes 10 recipes. 16 oz. can makes 20 recipes. Certified Kosher.
4 oz. 702-W-6007 $5.29
8 oz. 702-W-6015 $8.49
16 oz. 702-W-6004 $16.99

Flavorings

Decorators trust Wilton flavorings for great taste that won't change icing consistency. Wilton flavors are concentrated— only a drop or two adds delicious taste to icings, cakes, beverages and other recipes.

Pure Vanilla Extract
The world's finest vanilla is from Madagascar. Unmatched flavor and aroma enhances cakes, puddings, pie fillings, custards and more. 4 fl. oz. Certified Kosher.
604-W-2270 $7.99

Clear Flavorings
Recommended and used in Wilton Method Classes, these delicious flavors won't change your icing color. Essential for making pure white icings for wedding cakes and maintaining vibrant colors in all your decorating. Certified Kosher.

Clear Vanilla Extract
2 fl. oz.
604-W-2237 $1.99
8 fl. oz.
604-W-2269 $4.99

Clear Butter Flavor
2 fl. oz.
604-W-2040 $1.99
8 fl. oz.
604-W-2067 $4.99

Clear Almond Extract
2 fl. oz.
604-W-2126 $1.99

Sprinkles & Sugars

You've never had more exciting ways to top your treats! Wilton makes decorating quick, easy and colorful with a great variety of toppings to give your iced cakes, cupcakes and cookies the perfect finishing touch. From glistening pearlized sugars and flavorful crunches to beautifully-detailed icing flowers, Wilton has a dazzling decoration for every occasion.

JUMBO SPRINKLES

Give your cupcakes a big finish! Top them with our Jumbo Sprinkles in exciting shapes and colors. These big and bold decorations are perfect for cupcakes, mini cakes, jumbo and king-size cupcakes, brownies and cookies. Certified Kosher. **$4.49**

Heart Drops
5.25 oz.
710-W-035

Jumbo Confetti
3.25 oz.
710-W-029

Jumbo Stars
3.25 oz.
710-W-026

Jumbo Hearts
3.25 oz.
710-W-032

Jumbo Rainbow Nonpareils
4.8 oz. **710-W-033**

Jumbo Daisies
3.25 oz.
710-W-028

SPRINKLES

Pour on the fun! Great shapes and colors add a dash of excitement to cakes, cupcakes, ice cream and more. Certified Kosher. **$2.29**

Rainbow Nonpareils
3 oz.
710-W-772

White Nonpareils
3 oz.
710-W-773

Cinnamon Drops
3 oz.
710-W-769

Chocolate Flavored Jimmies
2.5 oz. **710-W-774**
6.25 oz.
710-W-168 $4.49

Rainbow Jimmies
2.5 oz.
710-W-776
6.25 oz.
710-W-994 $4.49

Chocolate Hearts
2.5 oz. Naturally and artificially flavored.
710-W-622

SPARKLING SUGARS

Put extra dazzle in your decorating! These easy-pour sugars have a coarse texture and a brilliant sparkle that makes cupcakes, cookies and cakes really shine. Certified Kosher.

Blue
5.25 oz.
710-W-039 $3.99

Yellow
5.25 oz.
710-W-036 $3.99

Lavender
5.25 oz.
710-W-037 $3.99

Pink
5.25 oz.
710-W-038 $3.99

White
8 oz.
710-W-992 $4.49

Rainbow
8 oz.
710-W-991 $4.49

COLORED SUGARS

Wilton sugar is excellent for filling in brightly colored designs on cakes, cupcakes and cookies. 3.25 oz. bottle. Certified Kosher.
$2.29

Blue
710-W-750

Yellow
710-W-754

Orange
710-W-759

Pink
710-W-756

Red
710-W-766

Lavender
710-W-758

Light Green
710-W-752

Dark Green
710-W-764

Black
710-W-762

CRUNCHES

Add delicious flavor and a colossal crunch! Sprinkle over iced cupcakes. Certified Kosher. **$4.99**

Cookies 'N Cream
5 oz.
710-W-9702

Rainbow Chip
Certified Kosher Dairy. 5.25 oz.
710-W-9704

Turtle
5 oz.
710-W-9703

6-Mix Assortments

They're so convenient! Assorted fun shapes in an easy-pour flip-top bottle. Top cupcakes, ice cream and other goodies. Certified Kosher. **$4.99**

Flowerful Medley
Includes Confetti, Colorful Leaves, Daisies, Pastel Hearts, Wild Flowers, Butterflies. 2.2 oz. total.
710-W-4122

Animals and Stars
Includes Cows, Stars, Dinosaurs, Stars and Moons, Bears, Dolphins. 2.1 oz. total. **710-W-4123**

Nonpareils
Includes Pink, Orange, Green, Red, Yellow, Purple. 3 oz. total.
710-W-4125

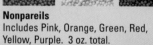

Jimmies
Includes Pink, Orange, Green, Red, Yellow, Blue. 2.52 oz. total.
710-W-4127

4-Mix Assortments

They're so convenient! Assorted sugars in an easy-pour flip-top bottle. Top cupcakes, ice cream and other goodies. 4.4 oz. total. Certified Kosher. **$4.99**

Bright Sugars
Includes Yellow, Light Green, Lavender, Pink. **710-W-651**

Primary Sugars
Includes Red, Dark Green, Blue, Yellow.
710-W-650

ORDER TOLL FREE: 800-794-5866

EDIBLE GLITTER

Wilton Edible Glitter adds a glimmering touch to treats. Perfect for use on iced cakes, cupcakes and cookies—or sprinkle on drinks for twinkling toasts! Thousands of pieces in every jar! Certified Kosher. **$5.99**

NEW!

Silver Stars
0.04 oz.
703-W-201

Gold Stars
0.04 oz.
703-W-200

Silver Hearts
0.06 oz.
703-W-204

Gold Hearts
0.06 oz.
703-W-203

Pink Hearts
0.06 oz.
703-W-205

CAKE SPARKLES

Brilliant edible glitter in a variety of colors, great for stencilling, snow scenes, highlighting messages. .25 oz. Certified Kosher. **$3.29**

Blue
703-W-1314

Yellow
703-W-1272

Orange
703-W-1308

Pink
703-W-1260

Red
703-W-1284

Purple
703-W-1266

Green
703-W-1278

Silver
703-W-1285

White
703-W-1290

Black
703-W-1302

PEARLIZED SPRINKLES

Create a color sensation on your cakes and cupcakes! Add the soft, shimmering look of Sugar Pearls in 5 glistening shades. Or, shake on the sparkle with dazzling Pearlized Sugars and Jimmies! Certified Kosher.

NEW!

Green Sugar Pearls
5 oz.
710-W-1130 $4.99

NEW!

Yellow Sugar Pearls
5 oz.
710-W-1131 $4.99

NEW!

Pink Sugar Pearls
5 oz.
710-W-1132 $4.99

NEW!

Blue Sugar Pearls
5 oz.
710-W-1133 $4.99

Sugar Pearls
5 oz.
710-W-044 $4.99

Pearlized Sugar
5.25 oz.
710-W-043 $4.49

Gold Pearlized Sugar
5.25 oz.
710-W-041 $4.49

Silver Pearlized Sugar
5.25 oz.
710-W-042 $4.49

Sapphire Pearlized Sugar
5.25 oz.
710-W-047 $4.49

Emerald Pearlized Sugar
5.25 oz.
710-W-048 $4.49

Ruby Pearlized Sugar
5.25 oz.
710-W-046 $4.49

Pearlized Jimmies
4.5 oz.
710-W-045 $4.49

ICING FLOWERS

Add breathtaking color and detail to your special cakes! Wilton Icing Flowers are the ideal time-saver, with beautifully-shaped petals that rival the best hand-piped flowers. They're the perfect way to dress up brownies, cupcakes and other treats for parties and gifts. With Wilton Icing Flowers, it's easy to create an impressive cake top bouquet in a variety of styles and colors. **$5.99**

NEW! **NEW!**

Leaves
4 large, 1.25 in.;
6 small, .875 in. Pk./10.
710-W-1100
All sizes are approximate.

Purple Posies
4 large, 1.25 in.;
6 small, 1 in. Pk./10.
710-W-1101

Daisies
4 large, 1.25 in.;
6 small, .875 in. Pk./10.
710-W-7157

Pink Posies
4 large, 1.25 in.;
6 small, .875 in. Pk./10.
710-W-7158

Red Roses

Small
.75 in. Pk./12.
710-W-7152

Medium
1.25 in. Pk./8.
710-W-7151

Large
1.75 in. Pk./6.
710-W-7150

White Roses

Small
.75 in. Pk./12.
710-W-7155

Medium
1.25 in. Pk./8.
710-W-7154

Large
1.75 in. Pk./6.
710-W-7153

Icing Colors

Produce deep, rich color with just a small amount using this fast-mixing gel. The Wilton exclusive concentrated gel formula was developed to help decorators achieve the exact shade desired without changing icing consistency. An unmatched color selection makes it easy for you to achieve virtually any shade.

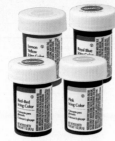

Single Bottles
1 oz. Certified Kosher.
$1.99

MIXING SKIN TONES

It's easy to create a wide variety of skin tones using various Wilton Icing Colors. Simply add desired color to white icing with a toothpick. If you wish to reach a shade lighter or darker than what is indicated, add slightly less or more of the icing color. Color listings for projects in this book reflect skintone shown; feel free to choose your own shade.

1. To reach desired skin tone color, start with enough icing to cover the entire area, as matching shades later may be difficult.

2. Dip the end of a toothpick into the color or colors indicated, and swirl into icing and blend well.

3. Add color a little at a time until you achieve the shade you desire. Always use a new toothpick each time you add color to keep icing out of your jar of color.

Skin tone	Icing Colors
	Copper
	Ivory with a touch of Red
	Brown
	Brown with a touch of Red
	More brown, with a touch of Red

*Note: Large amounts of these colors may affect icing taste.

Use No-Taste Red for large areas of red on a cake. When using Black, start with chocolate icing to limit the amount of color needed.

‡Daffodil Yellow is an all-natural color. It does not contain Yellow #5. The color remains very pale.

Ivory 610-W-208 · **Daffodil Yellow‡** 610-W-175 · **Buttercup Yellow** 610-W-216 · **Golden Yellow** 610-W-159 · **Lemon Yellow** 610-W-108 · **Copper** 610-W-450 · **Creamy Peach** 610-W-210 · **Rose Petal Pink** 610-W-410

Terra Cotta 610-W-206 · **Orange** 610-W-205 · **Red-Red*** 610-W-906 · **Christmas Red*** 610-W-302 · **Red (no-taste)** 610-W-998 · **Rose** 610-W-401 · **Burgundy** 610-W-698 · **Pink** 610-W-256 · **Violet** 610-W-604 · **Delphinium Blue** 610-W-228

Cornflower Blue 610-W-710 · **Royal Blue** 610-W-655 · **Sky Blue** 610-W-700 · **Teal** 610-W-207 · **Kelly Green** 610-W-752 · **Leaf Green** 610-W-809 · **Moss Green** 610-W-851 · **Juniper Green** 610-W-234 · **Brown** 610-W-507 · **Black*** 610-W-981

Primary 4-Icing Colors Set

Lemon Yellow, Sky Blue, Christmas Red, Brown in .5 oz. jars. Certified Kosher. Set/4.
601-W-5127 $4.99

8-Icing Colors Set

Lemon Yellow, Orange, Pink, Christmas Red, Violet, Sky Blue, Leaf Green and Brown in .5 oz. jars. Certified Kosher. Set/8.
601-W-5577 $9.99

12-Icing Colors Set

Our most popular collection creates the spectrum of primary colors plus light and dark skin tones, teal and burgundy. Lemon Yellow, Golden Yellow, Pink, No-Taste Red, Burgundy, Violet, Royal Blue, Teal, Kelly Green, Copper, Brown, Black in .5 oz. jars. Certified Kosher. Set/12.
601-W-5580 $13.99

Pastel 4-Icing Colors Set

Creamy Peach, Rose Petal Pink, Willow Green, Cornflower Blue in .5 oz. jars. Certified Kosher. Set/4.
601-W-25588 $4.99

Garden Tone 4-Icing Colors Set

Buttercup Yellow, Delphinium Blue, Aster Mauve, Juniper Green in .5 oz. jars. Certified Kosher. Set/4.
601-W-4240 $4.99

White-White Icing Color

Stir in to whiten icing made with butter or margarine. Perfect for wedding cakes. 2 fl. oz. Certified Kosher.
603-W-1236 $2.99

Glycerine

Stir into dried out icing color, fondant or gum paste to restore consistency. 2 fl. oz. Certified Kosher.
708-W-14 $1.99

COLOR MIST FOOD COLOR SPRAY

This easy-to-use spray gives decorators the versatility and dazzling effects of an airbrush in a convenient can! Creates a rainbow of excitement on so many desserts. Use it to transform a plain iced cake with sensational color, add splashes of holiday color to iced cookies and cupcakes. Great for party desserts—highlighting whipped topping or ice cream with color. No mess, taste-free formula; add a little color or a lot. Colors match Wilton Icing Colors above. 1.5 oz. Certified Kosher. **$3.29**

Red 710-W-5500	**Blue** 710-W-5501
Yellow 710-W-5502	**Green** 710-W-5503
Violet 710-W-5504	**Pink** 710-W-5505
Black 710-W-5506	**Orange** 710-W-5507

ORDER TOLL FREE: 800-794-5866

Rolled Fondant

White Ready-To-Use Rolled Fondant

Fondant has never been more convenient and easy to use for decorating! With Wilton Ready-To-Use Rolled Fondant, there's no mess, no guesswork. The 24 oz. (1.5 Lb.) package covers an 8 in. 2-layer cake plus decorations; the 80 oz. (5 Lb.) package covers a 2-layer 6 in., 8 in. and 10 in. round tiered cake plus decorations. Pure white. Certified Kosher.

24 oz. (1.5 Lb.) Pk.
710-W-2076 $6.79

80 oz. (5 Lb.) Pk.
710-W-2180 $22.99

1. Roll out.   **2. Layer over cake.**   **3. Trim and decorate.**

Color Fondant Multi Packs

Convenient four-pouch assortments are perfect for multicolored flowers and borders. Each 17.6 oz. package contains four 4.4 oz. packs. Certified Kosher. **$10.49**

Primary Colors
Green, Red, Yellow, Blue
710-W-445

Neon Colors
Purple, Orange, Yellow, Pink
710-W-446

Pastel Colors
Blue, Yellow, Pink, Green
710-W-447

Natural Colors
Light Brown, Dark Brown, Pink, Black
710-W-448

FoodWriter Edible Color Markers

Use like ink markers to add fun and dazzling color to countless foods. Kids love 'em! Decorate on fondant, color flow, Wilton Cookie Icing, royal icing, even directly on cookies. Brighten everyday foods like toaster pastries, cheese, fruit slices, bread and more. Each set includes five .07 oz. FoodWriter markers. Certified Kosher.

Primary Color Sets

| Yellow | Green | Red | Blue | Black |

Fine Tip Set/5. 609-W-100 $8.49
Bold Tip Set/5. 609-W-115 $8.49

Neon Color Set

| Purple | Orange | Pink | Light Green | Black |

Fine Tip Set/5. 609-W-116 $8.49

FINE TIP
BOLD TIP

Gum Paste and Ingredients

Create beautiful handmolded flowers right from the package.

Ready-To-Use Gum Paste

Now you can have gum paste on hand whenever you need it! With Ready-To-Use Gum Paste, there's no mixing, no mess—just tint, roll out and cut to create incredible floral bouquets for your cakes. Follow the easy instructions included and use with Wilton Gum Paste Decorating Sets to make roses, daisies, apple blossoms, tulips and many more beautiful blooms. Perfect for use with electronic cutting systems. 1 Lb. Certified Kosher.
707-W-130 $9.99

Gum Paste Mix
Just add water and knead. Workable, pliable dough-like mixture molds beautiful flowers and figures. 1 Lb. Certified Kosher.
707-W-124 $5.99

Gum-Tex
Makes fondant and gum paste pliable, elastic, easy to shape. Plastic resealable lid. 6 oz. Certified Kosher.
707-W-117 $7.99

Glucose
Essential ingredient for making fondant and gum paste from scratch. Use with Wilton Gum-Tex. 12 oz. Certified Kosher.
707-W-107 $3.99

Glycerine
Stir into dried out fondant, gum paste or icing color to restore consistency. 2 fl. oz. Certified Kosher.
708-W-14 $1.99

Fondant Mats, Rolling Pins and Accessories

FONDANT IMPRINT MATS

Imprint a beautiful recessed pattern to cover your cake! Just smooth your rolled fondant over the mat, place on your cake and peel back the mat. The recessed design imprinted in the fondant adds beautiful definition, so even white cakes stand out. Also great for textured fondant ribbons and edging. 20 x 20 in. **$19.99**

Star Power
409-W-416

Happy Birthday
409-W-417

Floral Fantasy
409-W-415

Graceful Vines
409-W-414

Using Fondant Imprint Mats

1. Roll out fondant ⅛ in. thick using rolling pin.

2. Lift fondant onto Fondant Imprint Mat using rolling pin. Or, place Fondant Imprint Mat on top of rolled fondant.
3. If fondant is on top of Fondant Imprint Mat, smooth by pressing firmly with Wilton Easy-Glide Fondant Smoother (below) or roll with rolling pin. If fondant is below Fondant Imprint Mat, roll with rolling pin.
4. Lift Fondant Imprint Mat with fondant attached and center imprinted fondant on cake. Peel back mat. Smooth fondant around cake by gently pressing with heel of hand.

Easy-Glide Fondant Smoother

Essential tool for shaping and smoothing rolled fondant on your cake. Works great on top, edges and sides! Shapes fondant to sides of cake so that no puffed areas appear. Trim off excess with a sharp knife. 6.25 x 3.35 in. wide.
1907-W-1200 $5.49

20 in. Rolling Pin

Its extra-wide, smooth design is perfect for covering cakes with rolled fondant. The non-stick surface makes handling large pieces of fondant easy—just dust the surface with confectioners' sugar and roll out fondant to the size you need, then use the Rolling Pin to lift the fondant from your work surface to the cake. Great for rolling out pastry dough and pie crusts too. 20 x 1.5 in. diameter. (Mat sold below.)
1907-W-1210 $21.99

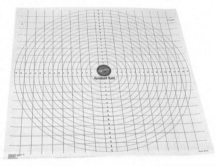

Roll & Cut Mat

For precise measuring, rolling and cutting of fondant or dough. Pre-marked circles for exact sizing. Square grid helps you cut precise strips. Non-stick surface for easy release. 20 in. square with circles from 3 in. to 19 in. diam.
409-W-412 $9.49

20 in. Rolling Pin Guide Rings

Slip these easy-to-use guide rings onto the ends of your 20 in. rolling pin to achieve the perfect thickness every time. Includes ¹⁄₁₆ in. (blue) for flower petals and leaves, ³⁄₁₆ in. (gold) for letters, numbers and appliqué shapes, ⅛ in. (orange) for shapes cut with Wilton Cut-Outs or cookie cutters and for covering cakes with fondant. Set/3.
1907-W-1010 $4.49

9 in. Rolling Pin

Roll out fondant evenly, in the perfect thickness for easy cutting and shaping, with this 3-piece non-stick roller. Roll to the perfect ⅛ or ¹⁄₁₆ in. height used for cutting many fondant decorations, using the slide-on guide rings. Easy to handle—just the right size for preparing small amounts of fondant to place on your cake. Perfect for use with Fondant Multi Packs and Cut-Outs. 9 x 1 in. diameter. Includes ⅛ and ¹⁄₁₆ in. rings.
1907-W-1205 $6.99

Quick Ease Roller

Makes it easy to prepare small pieces of fondant and gum paste for cutting flowers and designs. Wooden roller fits comfortably in palm of hand. 4.2 in. wide.
1907-W-1202 $5.49

ORDER TOLL FREE: 800-794-5866

Fondant Tools and Accessories

No one has more ways to decorate with rolled fondant than Wilton! We've developed a complete line of tools that make fondant easier than ever to shape, cut and imprint. Finish your decorations with a dazzling accent—brush on Pearl Dust to create colorful highlights for flowers, bows and swags.

PEARL DUST

Give your fondant, gum paste, royal icing and molded Candy Melts decorations a beautiful, glittering finish! Wilton Pearl Dust creates rich, lustrous highlights on flowers, bows, letters and more. Easy to use, just brush onto your decoration with a soft artist brush. Or, to paint decorations, pour a small amount of lemon extract into a a Color Tray cavity; stir in Pearl Dust and brush onto your decoration. Edible; Certified Kosher (except Orchid Pink and Lilac Purple). .05 oz. bottle. **$3.99**

Leaf Green 703-W-215	**Lilac Purple** 703-W-221	**Sapphire Blue** 703-W-222	**Ruby Red** 703-W-223	**Gold** 703-W-216
Yellow 703-W-213	**Bronze** 703-W-214	**Orchid Pink** 703-W-217	**Silver** 703-W-218	**White** 703-W-219

10-Pc. Fondant/Gum Paste Tool Set

Here are the tools every decorator needs to create breathtaking gum paste and fondant flowers, leaves and accents. Precise modeling tools feature comfortable grips for easy handling. Colored grips and numbered tip designs make tools easy to identify. Convenient case keeps the collection organized and handy. Includes large/small veining tool, shell tool/knife, large/small dogbone tool, serrated quilting/cutting wheel, umbrella tool with 5 and 6 divisions, scriber/cone tool, large/small ball tool, palette knife and modeling sticks #1 and #2. Set/10.
1907-W-1107 $29.99

Fondant Shaping Foam

Thick and thin squares are the ideal soft surface for shaping flowers, leaves and other fondant or gum paste cutouts. Use the thin square for thinning petal edges with a ball tool, carving vein lines on leaves and making ruffled petal strips. Use the thick square for cupping flower centers. Thin: 4 x 4 x .2 in. Thick: 4 x 4 x 1 in. Set/2.
1907-W-9704 $3.29

Dusting Pouches

Essential for rolling out gum paste or fondant! Fabric pouch dusts surfaces with a cornstarch/ confectioners' sugar mixture to prevent your rolling pin from sticking. Gathering cord closes pouch securely—just tap lightly on the pouch to sprinkle. 7 in. diameter. Pk./4.
417-W-106 $3.29

Flower Forming Cups

Curved round shape is ideal for drying gum paste, fondant and royal icing flowers and leaves. Openings in bottom center make it easy to pull wires through and adjust for the perfect drying position. Includes 2.5 and 3 in. diameter cups for drying everything from simple blossoms and briar roses to large daisies. Set/6.
1907-W-118 $5.49

Brush Set

Fine-bristle brushes in three tip designs (round, square and bevel) help you achieve different painted effects. Use with Icing Writer (p. 142); or attach fondant decorations with water or adhesive. Set/3.
1907-W-1207 $3.29

Wave Flower Former Set

NEW!

Use this convenient connecting platform to dry flowers, leaves and other decorations in royal icing, gum paste or fondant. Wave shape makes it easy to dry concave or convex shapes; large drying area is great for ribbons, bows and streamers. 14.5 x 9 in. assembled. Patent pending. Set/2.
1907-W-1320 $6.99

Flower Former Set

Dry fondant or icing leaves and flowers in a convex or concave shape. Three each of 1.5, 2 and 2.5 in. wide holders, all 11 in. long. Set/9.
417-W-9500 $6.29

STAMENS

Finish your royal icing or gum paste flowers with these lovely stamen styles. Cut stamens to desired size and insert in flower center.

NEW!

Lily Stamen Set

Create lifelike lilies with trim-to-fit lily stamen clusters in 3 natural colors! Simply place in royal icing or gum paste flower centers before drying. Includes 10 each pink, yellow and brown. 2.125 in. long. Pk./30.
1005-W-4451 $3.29

NEW!

Color Stamen Set

Finish your flowers with beautiful, natural looking stamens in 3 pretty colors. Includes 60 each yellow, white and orange. 2.125 in. long. Pk./180.
1005-W-4452 $3.29

Flower Stamen Assortment

Includes 60 each Pearl, Fluffy and Glitter. May be tinted (except Pearl) with Wilton Icing Colors added to vanilla. 2.5 in. long. Pk./180.
1005-W-410 $3.29

Fondant Tools and Accessories

Look at the fondant shapes you can add to your cakes! Fantasy flowers, floral bouquets, textured bows and geometric designs—they're all so easy to cut and shape with Wilton tools.

FONDANT CUT & PRESS SETS

Give your cake the perfect finish! Create a beautifully-textured fondant and/or gum paste design in seconds with the Fondant Cut & Press. It's easy—just roll out fondant, gum paste or a 50/50 mixture, cut with the rectangular cutting edge, then place on inside of press bottom, cover with top and press to imprint design. Includes 2 piece cutter/press, instructions.

Button Flower
1907-W-1306 $6.99

Rose Leaf
1907-W-1300 $6.99

NEW!

Calla Lily Former Set
Cut, shape and dry beautiful, deeply-cupped gum paste Calla Lilies with the cutter and formers in this set. Step-by-step instructions make it easy! Includes 1 cutter, 6 formers and complete instructions. Set/7
417-W-1109 $5.99

Just roll to cut and emboss textured fondant strips

Cutter/Embosser
Three detachable wheels (straight, wavy and ridged) for cutting and for embossing patterns on fondant. Light, easy-rolling design cuts at the perfect angle. Comfortable handle also stores wheels.
1907-W-1206 $4.49

Fondant Decorative Punch Set
Punch out fondant accents with elegant openwork shapes. As you punch, the disk imprints a detailed design that adds a pretty touch of texture. The comfortable angled handle holds 8 design disks. Disks turn to lock into place. Set/9.
1907-W-1204 $9.99

Add exciting 3-dimensional decorations in fondant

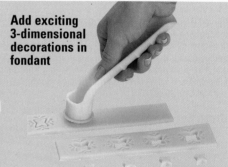

| Large Tulip with Leaves | Dutch Blossom | Paisley with Dots | Wide Diamond with Scrolls | Small Tulip with Leaves | Snapdragon with Leaves | 4-Leaf Clover with Dots | Narrow Diamond with Scrolls |

Fondant Ribbon Cutter/Embosser Set
Just choose the cutting and embossing wheel designs you want, slide the washer, core, wheels and spacers on the roller handle, and roll on fondant. Produces ribbon widths from ¼ in. to 3¾ in. when combining spacers. Complete set includes: 8 embossing wheels; 9 spacers; 9 cutting wheels; roller handle with detachable core; assembly hardware. Set/26.
1907-W-1203 $16.49

Add beautiful textured fondant ribbons, stripes and bows to your cake!

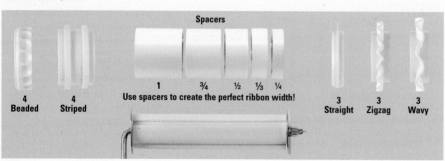

Spacers

1   ¾   ½   ⅓   ¼
Use spacers to create the perfect ribbon width!

4 Beaded   4 Striped   3 Straight   3 Zigzag   3 Wavy

Stepsaving Rose Bouquets Flower Cutter Set
Create gorgeous fondant and gum paste roses and forget-me-nots using book and cutters in this set. Cutters include large and small rose, rose leaf, calyx and forget-me-not. Set/6.
1907-W-1003 $8.99

Floral Garland Cutter/Ejector Set
Quickly and easily cuts and positions fondant or gum paste flowers on cakes. Includes ejector, 5 cutters and instructions. Set/7.
1907-W-1001 $10.99

Floral Collection Flower Making Set
Make incredibly lifelike gum paste flowers. Full-color how-to book includes many arranging ideas and step-by-step instructions. Kit includes 24 plastic cutters, 1 leaf mold, 3 wood modeling tools, protector flap, 40-page instruction book and 2 foam squares for modeling. Set/32.
1907-W-117 $21.99
Book only 907-W-117 $9.99

Letters & Numbers Gum Paste & Fondant Mold Set
With this set, it's easy to put the finishing touches on your cakes with a beautiful 3-dimensional message or monogram. Just fill molds with a 50/50 gum paste and fondant blend, press and smooth with tool included and release. Great for 2-tone letters and numbers, a perfect way to personalize cake and cupcakes. Includes 11 mold sheets with 52 alphabet molds (upper and lower case A-Z), 3 punctuation marks and 10 numeral molds, stainless steel smoothing/releasing tool, molding instructions. Set/13.
2104-W-3070 $21.99

CUT-OUTS
With Cut-Outs, it's easy to make fun 3-D shapes for your fondant cakes and cupcakes. Just roll out fondant and/or gum paste, press down with Cut-Out and lift away. Remove shapes with a small spatula. Stainless steel (except for plastic Daisy) shapes range from .6 in. to 2.5 in.

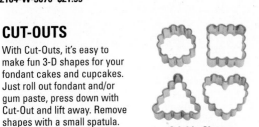

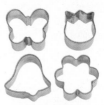

Crinkle Shapes
Circle, Square, Triangle, Heart.
1.25 in. Set/4.
417-W-444 $3.19

Fancy Shapes
Flower, Leaf, Oval, Heart
1.5 to 2 in. Set/4.
417-W-445 $3.19

Garden Shapes
Butterfly, Tulip, Bell, Flower
1.25 to 1.75 in. Set/4.
417-W-443 $3.19

Daisy
Durable plastic.
.75 to 2.5 in. Set/3.
417-W-439 $2.59

Oval
.625 to 2.25 in. Set/3.
417-W-438 $2.59

Round
.75 to 2.25 in. Set/3.
417-W-432 $2.59

Square
.625 to 2.25 in. Set/3.
417-W-431 $2.59

People
.75 to 1.35 in.
Set/6.
417-W-441 $4.19

Heart
.75 to 2.25 in. Set/3.
417-W-434 $2.59

Star
.625 to 2.1 in. Set/3.
417-W-433 $2.59

Flower
.625 to 2.1 in. Set/3.
417-W-435 $2.59

Funny Flower
.75 to 2.3 in. Set/3.
417-W-436 $2.59

Leaf
1 to 3 in. Set/3.
417-W-437 $2.59

Alphabet/Number
.75 to .875 in. Set/37.
417-W-442 $15.79

Baking Accessories

Bake Easy! Non-Stick Spray

For cakes that turn out beautifully every time, start by spraying pans with Bake Easy. This convenient non-stick spray helps your cakes release perfectly with fewer crumbs for easier icing and a flawless look for decorating. Just a light, even coating does the job. Use for all mixes and recipes, versatile for all types of baking and cooking. 6 oz.
702-W-6018 $3.49

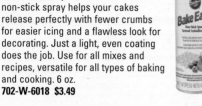

Cake Release

Another step-saving Wilton idea! No need to grease and flour your baking pan—Cake Release coats in one step. Simply spread Cake Release lightly on pan bottom and sides with a pastry brush and add batter. Cakes release perfectly every time without crumbs, giving you the ideal surface for decorating. In convenient dispensing bottle. 8 oz. Certified Kosher.
702-W-6016 $3.49

Bake-Even Strips

A Wilton innovation! Cakes bake perfectly level and moist, without cracking, when you wrap these strips around the outside of the pan before baking. Oven-safe, instructions and clips included.

Small Set
Two 1½ in. high strips, 30 in. long. Enough for two 8 or 9 in. round pans. Set/2.
415-W-260 $8.99

Large Set
Four 1½ in. high strips, 36, 43, 49 and 56 in. long. Enough for one each: 10, 12, 14, 16 in. round pans. Set/4.
415-W-262 $18.99

Cake Carriers

Cake Caddy

The 6 in. high see-through plastic dome has 3 locking latches that hold the base securely in place wherever you go. Convenient handle gives you a firm grip. The elegant base is approximately 13 in. diameter and holds and stores up to 10 in. round cake or pie, cupcakes, cookies and more. Pat. No. D522,813.
2105-W-9952 $14.99

ULTIMATE Cake Leveler

This feature-packed leveler makes it easier than ever to create perfectly straight cake tops and layers. The ULTIMATE Cake Leveler does it all—safe, precise cutting, easy height adjustment and convenient storage! Complete instructions included. Patent pending.
- Twist-lock feet raise and lower blade with ease
- Blade has 8 height adjustment positions for delicate torted cakes and for cutting off cake crowns.
- Sliding sleeve locks handle securely.
- Ergonomic handle gives you more control when cutting.
- Precision stainless steel blade for effortless cutting with fewer crumbs.
- Folds and stores in a snap! Just slide the handle sleeve to unlock and fold in the sides. Includes clamp to lock legs when folded and blade covers to store safely anywhere.

415-W-800 $24.99

NEW!

Cake Leveler

Make your cake top perfectly level for precise decorating—just place adjustable wire in notches to desired height up to 2 in. and glide through the cake. Makes torting easy, too! For cakes up to 10 in. wide.
415-W-815 $3.29

6-Piece Covered Mixing Bowl Set

Perfect for preparing decorating icings—clear lids snap on tight to keep icing the right texture. Includes one each 1, 2 and 3 quart nesting bowls with easy-grip handles and easy-pour spouts for better control. Rubberized base keeps bowls from sliding on countertops. Measurements clearly marked for precise mixing. Dishwasher safe. Set/6.
417-W-469 $13.99

Non-Stick Parchment Paper

Use Wilton silicone-treated non-stick parchment to line baking pans and cookie sheets—a non-fat alternative that saves cleanup time. Roll out cookie dough between 2 sheets, dough won't stick and will easily transfer to your cookie sheet. You can even reuse it for the next batch. Oven-safe to 400°F, great for conventional ovens, microwaves and the freezer. Double roll is 41 square feet, 15 in. wide. Certified Kosher.
415-W-680 $5.29

Pastry Mat

Non-stick mat with pre-marked measurements for easy rolling and precise cutting! Includes circles for pie, tart and pizza crusts from 6 to 16 in. diameter, pre-marked inches and centimeters for exact cutting of lattice strips. Delicious cookie and pie crust recipes are printed on the mat. Non-stick surface for easy release. 18 x 24 in.
409-W-413 $9.49

THE ULTIMATE 3-IN-1 CADDY

The versatile and safe way to carry cakes and desserts.

The Ultimate 3-In-1 Caddy features an exclusive reversible cupcake tray which holds 12 standard or 24 mini cupcakes. Or, remove the tray to carry up to a 9 x 13 in. decorated cake on the sturdy locking base. The see-through cover has higher sides to protect icing flowers and tall decorations. You can also use the caddy at home, to keep pies, cookies and brownies fresh for days after baking. 18 x 14⅛ x 5½ in. high. Patent No. D572,539.
2105-W-9958 $19.99

ORDER TOLL FREE: 800-794-5866

Better Baking Tools

Essential tools designed to do more! Wilton Better Baking Tools are designed with exclusive features that make baking easier:

- *The Egg Separator has a countertop cup design to collect and measure egg whites—makes pouring into recipes a breeze*
- *The Cake Tester has a storage cover to protect in drawer*
- *The Baker's Pastry Blender features a unique patented clip that slides along the wires to remove butter and dough*
- *The Cyclone Whisk has an innovative center spiral that incorporates more air into batters*
- *The Rolling Pin has removable handles making it fully submersible and dishwasher safe*

NEW!

Egg Separator
Separate eggs with less mess! Ideal for egg white omelets; cup holds up to 10 egg whites.
2103-W-391 $6.99

NEW!

Cake Tester
Reusable pick comes out clean when cake is ready.
2103-W-434 $3.99

Scoop It Measuring Spoons
Set/5.
2103-W-325 $5.99

Scoop It Measuring Cups
Set/4.
2103-W-324 $7.99

2 Cup Liquid Measure
Patent Pending.
2103-W-334 $7.99

4 Cup Liquid Measure
Patent Pending.
2103-W-335 $9.99

Cake Lifter
2103-W-307 $9.99

Baker's Blade
Patent No. D587,538.
2103-W-310 $7.99

Silicone Spoon Scraper
Patent No. D584,927.
2103-W-328 $6.99

Silicone Stand Mixer Scraper
Patent No. D587,537.
2103-W-329 $6.99

Silicone Universal Scraper
Patent No. D586,630.
2103-W-327 $6.99

Cyclone Whisk
Patent No. D582,223.
2103-W-317 $9.99

Baker's Pastry Blender
2103-W-313 $6.99

Tilt 'n Mix 3-Pc. Bowl Set
2103-W-306 $29.99

12 in. Rolling Pin
2103-W-301 $24.99

Kitchen Tools

Make decorating and kitchen tasks easier! Lightweight, comfortable tools with contoured handles and quality blades of stainless steel and silicone heads suited for the task.

Pastry Wheel
Create crisp straight or graceful scalloped edges with this smooth-rolling pastry wheel. Comfortable handle with finger/thumb guard. 6.5 in. long.
2103-W-315 $8.99

Pastry Brush
Flexible silicone bristles are great for brushing on Cake Release, shortening or hot glazes. More durable than nylon bristles. Comfortable ergonomic handle. 8.5 in. long.
409-W-6056 $5.99

Cookie Spatula
Angled stainless steel blade moves cookies from pan to plate with ease. Slides easily under cookies—great for serving brownies and bar cookies too. Comfortable ergonomic handle with thumb rest. 9 in. long.
409-W-6054 $6.99

Cake and Pie Server
Slice and serve with greater control. The comfortable ergonomic handle with thumb rest and angled blade makes lifting every slice easier. Serrated stainless steel blade cuts even the first slice cleanly. 9 in. long.
409-W-6058 $6.99

All-Purpose Spatula
Blend and mix with greater comfort, more control and less fatigue, thanks to the contoured Comfort Grip handle. Flexible silicone blade is ideal for blending and removing icing from bowls or containers—great for all-around kitchen use. Stain and odor resistant.
9 in. 409-W-6050 $7.99

Bakeware

In Wilton decorating classes, we've shown millions of students that to get a beautiful cake for decorating, you have to start with a quality pan. That's why Wilton designs bakeware with more features to promote perfect baking every time.

NEW!

ULTRAGOLD™
PREMIUM ALUMINUM BAKEWARE

Creates Cakes Perfect for Decorating

The decorating experts at Wilton have designed every UltraGold pan with features that provide the perfect baking results decorators demand. With UltraGold Bakeware, your cakes and desserts turn out beautifully.

PREMIUM ALUMINUM
Our high quality aluminum requires a more precise manufacturing process to ensure a perfect shape and better baking results for you.

DURABLE ANODIZED SURFACE
Anodizing creates a more consistent surface finish. This means that UltraGold's signature golden finish will look great and bake beautifully for years to come.

LIMITED LIFETIME WARRANTY
Wilton is so confident of the quality, we back UltraGold Bakeware with a Limited Lifetime Warranty.

OVERSIZED HANDLES FOR EASY LIFTING
You'll always get a good grip with UltraGold. Convenient extended handles help you lift the pan safely and easily every time. Pan dimensions are stamped on the handles for easy identification.

EVEN HEATING, WON'T WARP
UltraGold heats more evenly and holds its shape like no other brand. Our premium aluminum distributes heat evenly for a light, golden brown cake surface that is ideal for decorating.

ORDER TOLL FREE: 800-794-5866

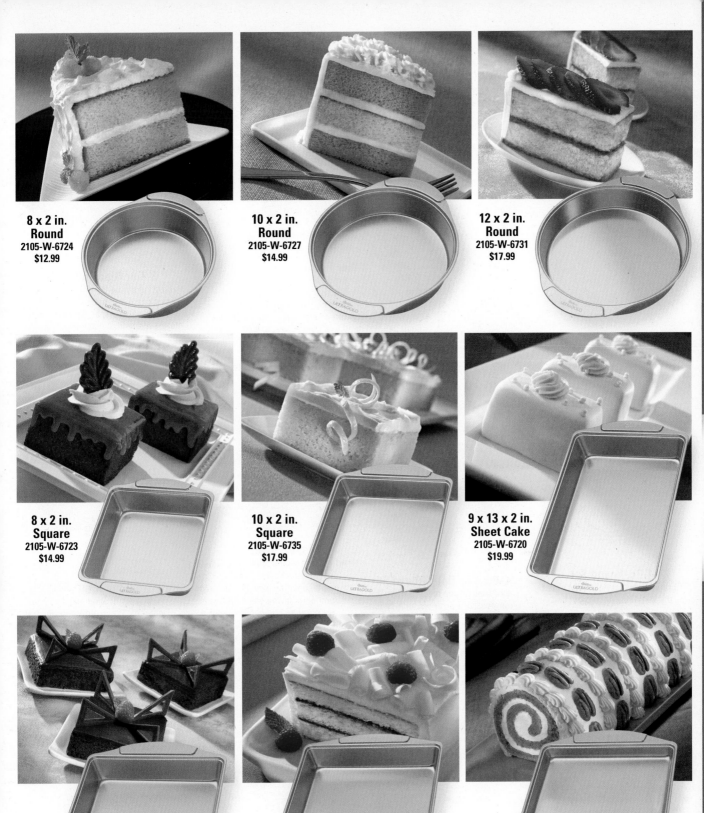

**8 x 2 in.
Round**
2105-W-6724
$12.99

**10 x 2 in.
Round**
2105-W-6727
$14.99

**12 x 2 in.
Round**
2105-W-6731
$17.99

**8 x 2 in.
Square**
2105-W-6723
$14.99

**10 x 2 in.
Square**
2105-W-6735
$17.99

**9 x 13 x 2 in.
Sheet Cake**
2105-W-6720
$19.99

11 x 15 x 2 in. Sheet Cake
2105-W-6718 $24.99

12 x 18 x 2 in. Sheet Cake
2105-W-6719 $29.99

11 x 17 x 1 in. Jelly Roll
2105-W-6721 $22.99

Pan Sets

Create a classic tiered cake with confidence when you start with Wilton even-baking aluminum pan sets. For generations, decorators have counted on Wilton quality pans to bake the light golden-brown surface essential for beautiful tiers. The precise lines and seamless baking surface of each pan helps you achieve a perfect cake for decorating. In addition to traditional tiered shapes such as rounds, squares and ovals, you'll find exciting new pillow, diamond and paisley shapes to help you create cakes that set any special occasion apart. Each pan is 2 inches deep, except where noted. Aluminum.

NEW!

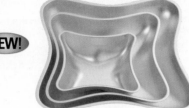

3-Tier Pillow Set
Create a romantic tiered wedding cake in a classic ring pillow shape. Stack the tiers for a dramatic presentation that looks sensational with fondant, especially when textured with Wilton Imprint Mats. Each pan will need to be baked twice, iced and stacked together to achieve the full pillow effect shown here. Set of 4 includes 6.75 x 6.75 x 2 in., 10 x 10 x 2 in. and 13.25 x 13.25 x 2 in. pans plus heating core for even baking in the largest pan.
2105-W-0575 $47.99

3-Tier Diamond Set
A dazzling shape for dramatic tiered cakes. Create a contemporary look for weddings, showers, anniversaries and more—the unique diamond design is ideal for rolled fondant cakes. Set of 3 includes 10.25 x 7.4 in., 15 x 11 in. and 19.25 x 14.25 in. pans*.
2105-W-4204 $47.99

4-Pc. Round Set
Our most popular collection offers the versatility of constructing classic wedding tiers or creating individual round party cakes in exactly the size you want. Set of 4 includes 6, 8, 10, 12 in. pans.*
2105-W-2101 $39.99

4-Pc. 3 in. Deep Round Set
Extra-tall design helps you create impressive 2-layer wedding tiers, 5 in. high. Set of 4 includes 8, 10, 12, 14 in. pans.*
2105-W-2932 $47.99

4-Pc. Oval Set
An elegant shape ideal for cascading arrangements. The large 16.5 in. pan also works well as a base for round tiers, giving you added space for floral arrangements or large decorations. Set of 4 includes 7.75 x 5.5 in., 10.75 x 7.8 in.; 13.5 x 9.8 in. and 16.5 x 12.38 in. pans.*
2105-W-2130 $47.99

4-Pc. Heart Set
A perfect fit when used with our Decorator Preferred Heart Separator Plates. Set of 4 includes 6, 10, 12 and 14 in. pans. Aluminum.
2105-W-606 $47.99

3-Pc. Square Set
A favorite graduated grouping, highlighted by a 16 in. pan for a dramatic base tier. Set of 3 includes 8, 12, 16 in. pans.*
2105-W-2132 $47.99

3-Pc. Paisley Set
Create a beautiful tiered cake with graceful curves unlike any other. Ideal for cascading floral arrangements—perfect for weddings, showers and more. Set of 3 includes 9 x 6 in., 12.75 x 9 in. and 17 x 12 in. pans.
2105-W-4039 $47.99

4-Pc. Petal Set
The lively curves of this best-selling tiered set tie in perfectly with floral-themed weddings and showers. Or, use one petal tier in combination with other shapes—the petal sections are a great way to add texture to your design. Set of 4 includes 6, 9, 12, 15 in. pans.*
2105-W-2134 $47.99

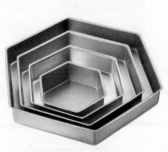

4-Pc. Hexagon Set
A great choice for fondant-covered designs. The sharp lines of our hexagon pans create a strong presence for weddings, religious occasions, graduations and more. Set of 4 includes 6, 9, 12, 15 in. pans.*
2105-W-3572 $47.99

*Heating Core (p. 159) is recommended for pans which are 10 in. diameter or larger.

ORDER TOLL FREE: 800-794-5866

Performance Pans

The classic aluminum pans—durable, even-heating and built to hold their shape through years of use. We named them Performance Pans because they perform beautifully. These are great all-purpose pans you'll use for casseroles, entrees, baked desserts and more. Wilton has sold millions of Performance Pans because decorators and bakers know they can depend on them.

Rounds

A great selection of sizes for the most popular cake shape of all. Put together your own set to create classic tiers or bake an individual round cake your guests will love. Even-heating aluminum for the best baking results.

6 x 2 in.
2105-W-2185 $7.99

8 x 2 in.
2105-W-2193 $8.99

10 x 2 in.
2105-W-2207 $9.99

12 x 2 in.
2105-W-2215 $12.99

14 x 2 in.
2105-W-3947 $16.49

16 x 2 in.
2105-W-3963 $19.99

2-Pan Round Set
9 x 2 in. deep
2105-W-7908 $14.49

Sheets
9 x 13 x 2 in. deep
2105-W-1308 $12.99

11 x 15 x 2 in. deep
2105-W-158 $17.99

12 x 18 x 2 in. deep
2105-W-182 $19.99

Covered Baking Pan
Clear, durable cover makes it easy to transport desserts and keep them fresh at home. 11 x 15 x 2 in.
2105-W-3849 $22.99

Squares

You'll call on this shape constantly for cakes, brownies and entrees—fortunately, our quality aluminum pans are built for years of great baking results. Find the right size for a single cake or a tiered masterpiece.

6 x 2 in.
507-W-2180 $7.99

8 x 2 in.
2105-W-8191 $9.99

10 x 2 in.
2105-W-8205 $11.99

12 x 2 in.
2105-W-8213 $16.49

14 x 2 in.
2105-W-8220 $20.99

16 x 2 in.
2105-W-8231 $22.99

SweetHeart
A gently curving shape gives the classic heart a more romantic flair. Whether you accent it with pretty icing flowers or pair it with bold fondant decorations, this cake will charm guests for birthdays, Mother's Day, Valentine's Day, showers and more. Takes 1 standard mix.
10.25 x 11 x 2 in.
2105-W-1197 $12.99

Specialty Pans

Classic Angel Food
If you're looking for a healthy dessert, you can't do better than angel food! It's delicious with a simple fresh fruit topping. Removable inner core sleeve, cooling legs. Aluminum.

7 x 4.5 in. deep.
Takes ½ standard mix.
2105-W-9311 $15.49

10 x 4 in. deep.
Takes 1 standard mix.
2105-W-2525 $18.99

Fancy Ring Mold
Beautiful sculpted pan, ideal for pound cakes, mousse and more! Takes 1 standard mix. 10 in. diameter x 3 in. Aluminum.
2105-W-5008 $12.99

Springform Pans

When shopping for a springform pan, you want strong construction and an easy-release design that will let you remove a perfect cheesecake every time. Wilton springform pans are built tough, with strong springlocks that hold up year after year. The removable waffle-textured bottom design keeps crusts from sticking while distributing heat evenly. Springlock releases sides. Aluminum.

6 x 3 in.
2105-W-4437 $12.99

8 x 3 in.
2105-W-8464 $14.49

9 x 3 in.
2105-W-5354 $15.49

10 x 3 in.
2105-W-8465 $16.99

Cookie Sheets and Pans

A warped sheet can ruin a batch of cookies. With Wilton Cookie Sheets, you won't worry about warping. The extra-thick aluminum heats evenly for perfectly browned bottoms. Versatile sheets are great for baking appetizers, turnovers and more.

Jumbo Aluminum Sheet
Extra-thick construction heats evenly for perfectly browned bottoms.

14 x 20 in.
2105-W-6213
$19.99

Insulated Aluminum Sheet
Two quality aluminum layers sandwich an insulating layer of air for perfect browning without burning.

14 x 16 in.
2105-W-2644
$20.99

Jelly Roll and Cookie Pans
Wilton pans are 1 in. deep for fuller-looking desserts.

10.5 x 15.5 x 1 in.
2105-W-1269 $14.49

12 x 18 x 1 in.
2105-W-4854 $16.49

Muffin Pans

With so many great Wilton muffin pans to choose from, you'll be making muffins and cupcakes more often. You'll love our mini pans for the perfect brunch muffins and the jumbo size pan for bakery-style muffins and cupcakes.

Jumbo Muffin
Make super-size cupcakes and muffins. Six cups, each 4 x 2 in. Aluminum.
2105-W-1820 $18.99

White Jumbo Baking Cups (shown on p. 184)
Microwave-safe paper. 2.25 in. diameter. Pk./50
415-W-2503 $1.99

Standard Muffin
Most popular size for morning muffins, after-school cupcakes and desserts. Twelve cups, each 3 in. diameter x 1 in. Aluminum.
2105-W-9310 $18.99

White Standard Baking Cups (shown on p. 184)
Microwave-safe paper. 2 in. diameter. Pk./75
415-W-2505 $1.99

Mini Muffin
Great for mini cheesecakes, brunches, large gatherings. Cups are 2 in. x .75 in. Aluminum.
12 Cup 2105-W-2125 $12.99
24 Cup 2105-W-9313 $19.99

White Mini Baking Cups (shown on p. 184)
Microwave-safe paper. 1.25 in. diameter. Pk./100
415-W-2507 $1.99

Loaf Pans

It's all in the crust. Wilton Loaf Pans bake bread with hearty, crisp crusts and soft, springy centers. Our superior anodized aluminum promotes better browning, resulting in the perfect texture for all your breads.

Petite Loaf
Great for single-size dessert cakes, frozen bread dough. Nine cavities, each 2.5 x 3.38 x 1.5 in. Aluminum.
2105-W-8466 $11.99

Mini Loaf
Everyone loves personal-sized nut breads or cakes. Six cavities are 4.5 x 2.5 x 1.5 in. Aluminum.
2105-W-9791 $11.99

9 x 5 in. Loaf
Favorite size for homemade breads and cakes. 2.75 in. Aluminum.
2105-W-3688 $8.49

Long Loaf
Legs provide support for cooling angel food cakes, breads or classic cakes. 16 x 4 x 4.5 in. deep. Aluminum.
2105-W-1588 $15.49

Mini Shaped Pans

One cake mix makes 12-14 mini cakes. Aluminum.

Mini Fluted Mold
Six cavity pan is 14.75 x 9.75 in.; individual cavities are 4 x 1.25 in. deep.
2105-W-2097 $20.99

Mini Star
Six cavity pan is 14.5 x 11 in.; individual cavities are 4.75 x 1.25 in. deep.
2105-W-1235 $14.49

Decorator Preferred®

Professional Aluminum Bakeware

Built with the most features to help decorators bake their best! Compare these benefits to any brand:

- **Straight Sides**—Bake perfect 90° corners for the precise look wedding cakes require.
- **Grip Lip Edges**—Extra-wide rims make heavy filled pans easy to handle.
- **Pure Aluminum**—The best material for baking cakes—creates a light, golden brown cake surface, beautiful for decorating.
- **Superior Thickness**—Thicker than ordinary bakeware, built to distribute heat evenly for more consistent baking.
- **Hand-Crafted Construction**—Sheets and squares are hand welded for excellent detail and durability.
- **Lifetime Warranty**—Superior construction and performance designed and guaranteed to last a lifetime.

Squares
Perfect 90° corners give you the flawless look necessary for wedding tiers.

8 x 2 in.	12 x 2 in.
2105-W-6142 $11.99	2105-W-6144 $19.99
10 x 2 in.	
2105-W-6143 $16.49	

Sheets
Extra-thick aluminum distributes heat efficiently on these large pans.

9 x 13 x 2 in.	12 x 18 x 2 in.
2105-W-6146 $18.99	2105-W-6148 $25.49
11 x 15 x 2 in.	
2105-W-6147 $20.99	

Rounds
What a selection of sizes —including the hard-to find 18 in. Half Round, which lets you bake and ice two halves to create one 18 in. round cake.

2 inch	3 inch
6 x 2 in.	6 x 3 in.
2105-W-6122 $7.99	2105-W-6106 $9.99
8 x 2 in.	8 x 3 in.
2105-W-6136 $8.99	2105-W-6105 $10.99
9 x 2 in.	10 x 3 in.
2105-W-6137 $9.99	2105-W-6104 $12.99
10 x 2 in.	12 x 3 in.
2105-W-6138 $11.99	2105-W-6103 $16.49
12 x 2 in.	14 x 3 in.
2105-W-6139 $14.49	2105-W-6102 $19.99
14 x 2 in.	16 x 3 in.
2105-W-6140 $19.99	2105-W-6101 $22.99
16 x 2 in.	18 x 3 in. Half Round
2105-W-6141 $21.99	2105-W-6100 $26.99

3-Pc. Round Set
6, 10 and 14 in. diameter x 3 in. deep. Set/3.
2105-W-6114 $44.99

Hearts
Ultimate heart cake is beautiful for showers, weddings, more!

6 x 2 in.	10 x 2 in.	14 x 2 in.
2105-W-600 $7.49	2105-W-602 $10.99	2105-W-604 $15.49
8 x 2 in.	12 x 2 in.	16 x 2 in.
2105-W-601 $8.49	2105-W-607 $12.99	2105-W-605 $17.99

Contour
Create cakes with an elegant, rounded top edge. This is the perfect shape for positioning rolled fondant. 9 x 3 in. deep.
2105-W-6121 $14.49

Heating Core
Distributes heat to bake large cakes evenly. Recommended for pans 10 in. diameter or larger. Releases easily from cake. 3.5 x 3.5 x 4 in. diameter.
417-W-6100 $8.49

BAKEWARE

Chrome-Plated Cooling Grids

Sturdy design will never rust. Great selection of popular sizes.

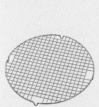

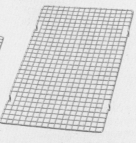

13 in. Round
2305-W-130 $8.99

10 x 16 in. Rectangle
2305-W-128 $6.99

14.5 x 20 in. Rectangle
2305-W-129 $9.99

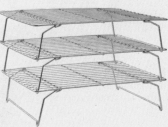

3-Tier Stackable
Use singly or stack to save space while cooling three cake layers, pies and tarts or batches of cookies at the same time. Individual grids are 13.5 x 9.75 x 3 in. high; stacked grids are 9.75 in. high.
2305-W-151 $14.49

Wonder Mold Pans

Classic Wonder Mold

Creates an elegant 3-D shape for decorating fabulous dress designs. Use with our Teen Doll Pick to make the doll of your dreams. Pan is 8 in. diameter x 5 in. deep; takes 5–6 cups of firm-textured batter. Heat-conducting rod assures even baking. Kit contains pan, rod, stand, 7 in. brunette doll pick and instructions. Aluminum/plastic.
2105-W-565 $19.99

Mini Wonder Mold

Use with Mini Doll Picks for a quartet of party treats. Great with the Wilton Classic Wonder Mold (at right) for a color-coordinated bridal party centerpiece. One cake mix makes 4 to 6 cakes. Pan is 10 x 10 x 3 in. deep. Individual cakes are 3.5 x 3 in. Aluminum.
2105-W-3020 $12.99

Mini Doll Picks

4.25 in. high with pick. Pk./4.
1511-W-1019 $6.49

Teen Doll Picks

Her hair and face are prettier than ever to give your Wonder Mold cakes a realism and sophistication unlike anything you've seen. 7.25 in. high with pick.
$3.29
Brunette **2815-W-101**
Blond **2815-W-102**

Ethnic Doll Pick

Beautiful face for realistic doll cakes. 7.75 in. high with pick.
2815-W-103
$3.29

Novelty Shaped Pans

Princess Carriage

Give it the royal treatment decorated in her favorite colors. Or, decorate a classic carriage cake for the bridal shower to match your colors. One-mix pan is 13.75 x 12 x 2 in. deep. Aluminum.
2105-W-1027 $12.99

Crown

This majestic crown cake is a fun way to honor both kids and adults alike—perfect for birthdays, school parties, Mother's and Father's Day, more! One-mix pan is 14.25 x 10.5 x 2 in. deep. Aluminum.
2105-W-1015 $12.99

Rocking Horse

It's a favorite kids shape that's also ideal for showers and play group parties. One-mix pan is 11 x 12.75 x 2 in. deep. Aluminum.
2105-W-2009 $12.99

#1

Great for kids' birthdays, first anniversary, contest winners, first place teams—or just to let someone know they're #1 with you! One-mix pan is 12.75 x 8.5 x 2 in. deep. Aluminum.
2105-W-1194 $12.99

Baby Buggy

It's a precious carriage design fit for royalty and ready to dress up for colorful cakes or elegant salads and gelatins. One-mix pan is 11.25 x 11.25 x 2 in. deep. Aluminum.
2105-W-3319 $12.99

3-D Rubber Ducky

A big splash for birthdays, baby showers and school celebrations. Five adorable designs included. Two-piece pan takes 5½ cups batter, 9 x 5 x 7 in. high. Aluminum.
2105-W-2094 $16.49

Novelty Shaped Pans

Monkey
He'll be the top banana at so many fun occasions! Kids will just love him at birthday parties, school celebrations and jungle-themed events. One-mix pan is 12.75 x 11.25 x 2 in. deep. Aluminum.
2105-W-1023 $12.99

Dinosaur
Our prehistoric party pal has a fun-loving look that's just right for kid's birthdays, school functions and animal-themed celebrations. One-mix pan is 12.75 x 11 x 2 in. deep. Aluminum.
2105-W-1022 $12.99

NEW!

Elephant
This fun-loving elephant will make a great guest at birthday parties, school celebrations, baby showers and many more special events. One-mix pan is 12 x 9.25 x 2 in. deep. Aluminum.
2105-W-0576 $12.99

Butterfly
A butterfly cake or molded salad is the perfect way to captivate! Go wild with fun colors. One-mix pan is 11 x 8.5 x 2 in. deep. Aluminum.
2105-W-2079 $12.99

Lady Bug
It's a pan that adapts to any environment—try it as a birthday bee, a Valentine love bug or even a friendly fly for that special gardener in your life. One-mix pan is 12 x 10 x 2 in. deep. Aluminum.
2105-W-3316 $12.99

Animal Crackers
Pick your favorite from the menagerie of critters on the box—pig, cat, giraffe or panda bear—or create a furry face of your own. One-mix pan is 10.75 x 9.25 x 2 in. deep. Aluminum.
2105-W-4945 $12.99

Party Pony
This proud pony is a sure bet for birthdays, race day parties and school celebrations. One-mix pan is 13.75 x 10.5 x 2 in. deep. Aluminum.
2105-W-1011 $12.99

Teddy Bear
This cutie will be busy all year 'round with birthdays, school parties and baby showers. One-mix pan is 13.5 x 12.25 x 2 in deep. Aluminum.
2105-W-1193 $12.99

Ballerina Bear
Decorate her to match your own little ballerina or cheerleader as a reward for a great performance! One-mix pan is 14.5 x 10 x 2 in. deep. Aluminum.
2105-W-1028 $12.99

Mini Stand-Up Bear Set
Includes baking stand, four clips and instructions. Two-piece pan takes 1 cup of batter; standard pound cake mix makes about 4 cakes. Assembled cakes are 4 x 3.25 x 4.75 in. high. Aluminum. Set/8.
2105-W-489 $14.49

Stand-Up Cuddly Bear Set
Five decorating ideas on the box! Two-piece pan takes 6.75 cups of firm-textured batter. Includes 6 clips, heat-conducting core and instructions. Pan is 9 x 6.75 x 8.5 in. high. Aluminum. Set/10.
2105-W-603 $26.99

Cupcake
Big enough for the whole crowd to eat. Bake and decorate it to look like your favorite party cupcake—only bigger! Create endless color and flavor combinations. One-mix pan is 9.75 x 9.5 x 2 in. deep. Aluminum.
2105-W-3318 $12.99

BAKEWARE

Novelty Shaped Pans

Skate
Keep the party fun rolling with a skate cake to decorate for your guest of honor. It puts a fun spin on birthdays, skating parties and competitions. One-mix pan is 11.5 x 8.5 x 2 in. deep. Aluminum.
2105-W-0848 $12.99

Baseball Mitt
Wait until your guests catch this exciting cake! It's the perfect treat for opening day, birthdays and team gatherings—for kids and adults alike. One-mix pan is 10 x 10.25 x 2 in. deep. Aluminum.
2105-W-0561 $12.99

Sports Ball Set
Use this four-piece set to create a perfect sports cake centerpiece. Includes two 6 in. diameter half-ball pans and two metal baking stands. Each pan half takes 2.5 cups batter. Aluminum. Set/4.
2105-W-6506 $12.99

Soccer Ball
A great way to reward a season or a game well done! One-mix pan is 8.75 x 8.75 x 3.5 in. deep. Aluminum.
2105-W-2044 $12.99

Mini Ball
Ice two mini balls and push together for a 3-D effect. One cake mix makes 10-12 mini balls. Six cavities, each 3.5 x 3.5 x 1.5 in. deep. Aluminum.
2105-W-1760 $12.99

First and Ten Football
Touching down at Super Bowl parties, award dinners, homecomings and much more. One-mix pan is 12 x 7.75 x 3 in. deep. Aluminum.
2105-W-6504 $12.99

Helmet
I's easy to create the ideal victory celebration cake, with school colors, stats or the final score. Great for tailgate parties, homecoming rallies or to honor the performer. One-mix pan is 12.75 x 10.5 x 2 in. deep. Aluminum.
2105-W-1029 $12.99

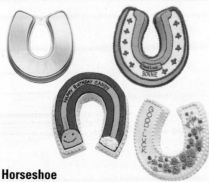

Golf Bag
For your favorite golfer's birthday, group golf outings, awards dinners and more. Whether decorated for men or women, it always shows perfect form. One-mix pan is 13.25 x 8.25 x 2 in. deep. Aluminum.
2105-W-1024 $12.99

Guitar
A guitar cake sets the tone for fun at your next party! Celebrate school band concerts, kid and adult birthdays! One-mix pan is 16.5 x 8.5 x 2 in. deep. Aluminum.
2105-W-570 $12.99

Star
Brighten birthdays, opening nights, even law enforcement occasions. One-mix pan is 12.75 x 12.75 x 1.8 in. deep. Aluminum.
2105-W-2512 $12.99

Horseshoe
Say "good luck" at birthdays, graduations, bon voyage parties! One-mix pan is 11.5 x 12 x 1.75 in. deep. Aluminum.
2105-W-3254 $12.99

Book
Serves up to 30. Three-mix pan is 15 x 11.5 x 2.75 in. deep. Aluminum.
2105-W-2521 $17.99

ORDER TOLL FREE: 800-794-5866

Novelty Shaped Pans

3-D Cruiser
Bake exciting 3-D cakes, ready to customize for all occasions. One-mix pan is 11 x 6.75 x 4 in. deep. Aluminum.
2105-W-2043 $12.99

Pirate Ship
A cargo of great decorating ideas on the label! Birthdays, movie parties and school celebrations provide a bounty of decorating opportunities. One-mix pan is 13.2 x 11.25 x 2 in. deep. Aluminum.
2105-W-1021 $12.99

NEW!

Dump Truck
This tough truck is the perfect vehicle for your birthday cake design. It carries loads of fun party memories, whether hauling cookie gifts or colorful candies. One-mix pan is 8 x 12 x 2 in. deep. Aluminum.
2105-W-0562 $12.99

Train
Load with delicious cargo! One-mix pan is 14 x 7.25 x 2 in. deep. Aluminum.
2105-W-2076 $12.99

Choo-Choo Train Set
Two-piece pan snaps together to create a cake 10 x 4 x 6 in. high. Takes 6 cups batter. Aluminum. Set/2.
2105-W-2861 $14.49

Firetruck
When the occasion calls for a five-alarm celebration. One-mix pan is 15.5 x 8.5 x 2 in. deep. Aluminum.
2105-W-2061 $12.99

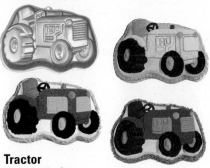

Tractor
Down on the farm has never been so much fun. One-mix pan is 13.5 x 9.5 x 2 in. deep. Aluminum.
2105-W-2063 $12.99

Stand-Up House
Haunted houses, Easter hutches, Christmas cottages, schools and dog houses are a few ideas for this pan. Cakes can stand up or lay flat. One-mix pan is 9 x 3 x 8.75 in. high. Aluminum.
2105-W-2070 $15.49

Enchanted Castle
Royal treat for little girls' birthdays or any event. Wonderful for molded sugar or ice cream. One-mix pan is 11.5 x 11.75 x 2 in. deep. Aluminum.
2105-W-2031 $12.99

Dancing Daisy
It's the perfect shape for cakes, molded gelatin and ice cream, brunch breads and more. Pick this daisy for Mother's Day, wedding showers and birthdays for any garden-lover. One-mix pan is 12 x 12 x 2 in. deep. Aluminum.
2105-W-1016 $12.99

Sunflower
Spread sunshine at the celebration! Ideal for cakes, mousse, gelatin and salad molds. Center can be filled with fruit and whipped topping. One-mix pan is 10 in. round x 2 in. deep. Aluminum.
2105-W-1019 $12.99

Topsy Turvy
Our topsy turvy "tiered" cake is just the right look for wacky birthdays, wild parties or special occasions. One-mix pan is 10.25 x 12 x 2 in. deep. Aluminum.
2105-W-4946 $12.99

Dimensions DECORATIVE BAKEWARE

You'll create one-of-a-kind cakes with amazing detail and definition, thanks to our heavyweight cast aluminum designs. Dimensions' extra-thick construction and premium non-stick coating mean these uniquely sculpted shapes will release from the pan perfectly. Lifetime Warranty.

Perennial
9.5 x 3.2 in.; 9 cup capacity.*
Patent No. D530,563.
2105-W-5031 $30.99

Tulip
9.5 x 4 in.; 11 cup capacity.*
Patent No. D526,529.
2105-W-5032 $30.99

4-Cavity Mini Snowflakes
Each 5 x 2.25 in.; 7 cup total capacity.*
Patent No. D543,413.
2105-W-5028 $30.99

Crown of Hearts
11 x 2.5 in.; 11 cup capacity.*
Patent No. D486,992.
2105-W-5011 $30.99

Antoinette
9 x 4 in.; 11 cup capacity.*
Patent No. D478,246.
2105-W-1189 $30.99

2-LAYER CAKE PANS
Assemble shaped top and bottom cake halves with a thin layer of icing.

Large Cupcake
Finished cake 8.25 x 7.5 in.; 10 cup total capacity.* Patent No. D575,097 and Patent Pending.
2105-W-5038 $30.99

Multi-Cavity Mini Cupcakes
Finished cakes 3.8 x 4 in.; 6 cup total capacity.* Patent No. D577,535 and Patent Pending.
2105-W-5043 $30.99

Multi-Cavity Mini Flower Baskets
Finished cakes 3.9 x 4.2 in.; 6 cup total capacity.*
Patent No. D579,562.
2105-W-5029 $30.99

Multi-Cavity Mini Pumpkins
Finished cakes 3.4 x 3.4 in.; 5 cup total capacity.*
Patent No. D574,663.
2105-W-1183 $30.99

6-Cavity Mini Hearts
Each 4 in. x 2 in.; 7 cup total capacity.*
Patent No. D487,211.
2105-W-5012 $30.99

Queen of Hearts
9 x 3.25 in.; 11 cup capacity.*
Patent No. D478,466.
2105-W-5001 $30.99

Cascade
9.5 x 4.75 in.; 11 cup capacity.*
Patent No. D478,249.
2105-W-1199 $30.99

Belle
9 x 3.75 in.; 11 cup capacity.*
Patent No. D478,250.
2105-W-1186 $30.99

*For cakes, fill pans ½ to ⅔ full.

NON-STICK CHECKERBOARD CAKE SET

With this unique baking set, you'll create cakes with an exciting multicolored pattern— there's style in every slice! Just place the Dividing Ring in one of the three 9 x 1.5 in. pans in the set and follow instructions for adding dark and light colors of batter in the divisions. Enjoy two tastes in one cake—try the Golden Yellow/ Chocolate recipe on the package. Great for colorful holiday cakes too! Three pans feature oversized handles for safe lifting from the oven; each takes 5½ cups batter. Non-stick steel pans; plastic Dividing Ring. Set/4.
2105-W-9961 $15.99

Non-Stick Bakeware

Our premium non-stick bakeware combines superior non-stick performance, serving convenience and elegant design, to provide the highest level of baking satisfaction.

• Oversized handles for safe lifting of the pan
• Pan dimensions permanently stamped into handles
• Heavy-duty steel construction prevents warping
• Durable, reinforced non-stick coating offers superior release and easy cleanup
• 10-Year Warranty

Cake and Pie Pans

9 x 1.5 in. Round Cake
2105-W-408 $9.99

9 x 9 x 2 in. Square Cake
2105-W-407 $10.99

11 x 7 x 1.5 in. Biscuit/Brownie
2105-W-443 $11.99

13 x 9 x 2 in. Oblong Cake
2105-W-411 $14.99

13 x 9 x 2 in. Oblong
Cake w/Plastic Cover
2105-W-423 $19.99

9 x 1.5 in. Pie
w/Fluted Edges
2105-W-438 $9.99

2105-W-408

2105-W-411

Muffin and Loaf Pans

6 Cup Regular Muffin
2105-W-405 $11.99

12 Cup Mini Muffin
2105-W-403 $8.99

12 Cup Regular Muffin
2105-W-406 $16.99

Large Loaf
9.25 x 5.25 x 2.75 in.
2105-W-402 $9.99

4 Cavity Mini Loaf
5.75 x 3 x 2.2 in.
2105-W-444 $21.49

2105-W-405

2105-W-402

Cookie Pans and Sheets

Small Cookie
13.25 x 9.25 x .5 in.
2105-W-436 $13.99

Medium Cookie
15.25 x 10.25 x .75 in.
2105-W-412 $14.99

Large Cookie/Jelly Roll
17.25 x 11.5 x 1 in.
2105-W-413 $16.99

Jumbo Air Insulated
Sheet
18 x 14 in.
2105-W-422 $23.99

2105-W-412

2105-W-422

Springform Pans

4 x 1.75 in. Round
2105-W-453 $6.99

6 x 2.75 in. Round
2105-W-447 $11.99

9 x 2.75 in. Round
2105-W-414 $16.99

10 x 2.75 in. Round
2105-W-435 $17.99

4 x 1.75 in. Heart
2105-W-457 $9.99

9 x 2.75 in. Heart
2105-W-419 $21.49

2105-W-435

2105-W-419

Tart/Quiche Pans

9 x 1.2 in. Round
2105-W-442 $11.99

11 x 1.2 in. Round
2105-W-450 $13.99

Round 3-Pc. Set
8 x 1.2 in., 9 x 1.2 in.,
and 10 x 1.2 in.
2105-W-451 $26.99

4 in. Tart/Quiche
6-Pc. Set 4 x .75 in. with removable bottom.
2105-W-441 $17.99

2105-W-450

Specialty Pans

Fluted Tube
9.75 x 3.4 in.
2105-W-416 $16.99

6 Cavity Mini Fluted
Tube 4.2 x 2 in.
2105-W-445 $21.49

Angel Food 9.4 x 4.25 in.
2105-W-415 $19.99

14 in. Pizza Crisper
14 x .5 in.
**2105-W-420
$16.99**

2105-W-445

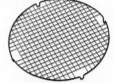

2105-W-420

Cooling Grids

10 x 16 in.
Rectangle
**2305-W-228
$9.99**

14.5 x 20 in.
Rectangle
**2305-W-229
$14.49**

13 in. Round
**2305-W-230
$10.49**

3-Tier
Stackable
15.8 x 9.8 in.
**2105-W-459
$11.99**

2305-W-228

2305-W-230

Filled Cake Pan Sets

The patented recessed design creates a contour you can fill with ice cream, fruit, mousse and more—just bake, fill, flip and frost! The premium non-stick coating provides easy release so cakes unmold perfectly from the pan. Also great for pasta and potato entrees, molded salads and appetizers.

Fanci-Fill
Set includes two 8.75 x 2 in. non-stick pans, bonus recipe booklet with 12 delicious ideas and complete instructions. Non-stick steel. Set/2.
2105-W-150 $17.99

Mini Tasty-Fill
Set includes four 4 x 1.25 in. non-stick pans, bonus recipe booklet with 12 delicious ideas and complete instructions. Non-stick steel. Set/4.
2105-W-155 $11.99

Heart Tasty-Fill
It's easy to create delicious cakes with a heart-shaped filled center! Set includes two 8.5 x 2.75 in. non-stick pans, bonus recipe book with delicious recipe ideas and complete instructions. Non-stick steel. Set/2.
2105-W-157 $17.99

Silicone Molds

Make treats in favorite party shapes using these colorful, easy-release molds! Great for baking mini cakes and brownies, molding ice cream, gelatin and more. Individual cavities are 2.5 x 2.5 x 1.25 in. deep. One cake mix makes 20 to 24 cakes.

Silicone Mini Stars
2105-W-4819 $9.99

Silicone Mini Hearts
2105-W-4824 $9.99

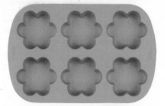

Silicone Mini Flowers
2105-W-4825 $9.99

Silicone Bakeware

Discover the convenience and easy release of flexible silicone bakeware!

- Exceptional baking performance for your favorite recipes
- Freezer, refrigerator, oven, microwave and dishwasher safe*
- Resists stains and odors
- Oven safe to 500°F
- Easy and convenient storage
- Limited lifetime warranty

EASY-Flex
SILICONE BAKEWARE

Flexible pans and tools for great baking performance

9 in. Round
2105-W-4800 $9.99

9 x 5 in. Loaf
2105-W-4804 $9.99

6-Cup Muffin
2105-W-4802 $9.99

12-Cup Mini Muffin
2105-W-4829 $9.99

Baking Mat
Line cookie sheets—protects against burned bottoms and cleans up with ease! Or, use as a pastry mat.
10 x 15 in. 2105-W-4808 $9.99
11 x 17 in. 2105-W-4809 $12.99

Standard Baking Cups
2 in. diameter.
Convenient fill line.
Pk./12.
415-W-9400 $9.99

*Always place silicone bakeware on a cookie sheet for easy removal from oven.

BROWNIE MOLDS

Shaped brownies on a stick are the perfect fun-to-eat treat for parties and favors! Just bake, cool, pop in a stick and decorate.

Blossom Brownie
One 8 x 8 in. size brownie mix makes 6 brownies.
2105-W-4924
$9.99

Round Brownie Pops
One 8 x 8 in. size brownie mix makes 24 brownies. Individual cavities are 1.75 x 1.75 x 1.75 in. deep.
2105-W-4925 $9.99

Bite-Size Brownie Squares
Little brownie bites— just the right size for parties and snacks. One 8 x 8 in. size brownie mix makes 40 to 42 brownies. Individual cavities are 1.5 x 1.5 x .75 in. deep.
2105-W-4923 $9.99

Non-Stick Oven Liner
Never Scrub Your Oven Again!

- **EASY TO CLEAN**
  Spills or burned-on foods wipe away with a soft, damp cloth.
- **CUT TO FIT**
  Use as is or trim with scissors to custom fit ovens.
- **OVEN-SAFE UP TO 500°F**
  Withstands high baking temperatures while maintaining non-stick performance.

Oven Liner
23 x 16.25 in.
2102-W-1021
$14.99

ORDER TOLL FREE: 800-794-5866

Cupcake Fun!

What makes Wilton cupcakes more fun? It's our exciting products, which make baking, decorating and serving one-of-a-kind cupcakes a pleasure! See www.cupcakefun.com for more great products and ideas!

Cupcake Fun!

Wilton presents today's hottest party dessert like you've never seen it before. This all-new collection features over 150 exciting cupcake and treat ideas for all occasions, with complete baking and decorating instructions to make them easy. Discover captivating shapes from coffee cups to flying saucers, plus a great recipe section with delicious surprises like Key Lime Cupcakes, Mocha Icing and more. Great baking and decorating products, too. *Cupcake Fun!* is the book you need to create the ultimate cupcake celebration. Soft cover, 128 pages.
902-W-795 $12.99

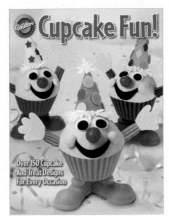

12-Piece Cupcake Decorating Set

Wait until you see how much fun cupcakes can be using the decorating tips in this set! You'll create all kinds of fun designs perfect for celebrations or everyday treats! Includes star tip 1M (rosettes, stars, drop flowers), star tip 22 (zigzags, pull-out stars), round tip 12 (outlines, dots, messages) and Bismarck tip 230 for exciting filled cupcakes; 8 disposable bags, instruction booklet. Set/12.
2104-W-6667 $8.99

CUPCAKES 'N MORE DESSERT STANDS

The look is fresh and fun, featuring bold silver-finished wire spirals to securely hold each cupcake. The twisting, towering design is perfect for any setting—showers, kids' birthdays, weddings, holidays and more.

13 Count Standard
9.25 in. high x 9 in. wide.
Holds 13 standard cupcakes.*
307-W-831 $13.69

24 Count Mini
10.5 in. high x 9 in. wide.
Holds 24 mini cupcakes.*
307-W-250 $15.79

19 Count Standard
18 in. high x 12 in. wide.
Holds 19 standard cupcakes.
307-W-666 $20.99

The Ultimate 3-in-1 Caddy

It's the most convenient way to take along cakes, cupcakes, muffins and more! The Ultimate 3-in-1 Caddy features an exclusive reversible cupcake tray which holds 12 standard or 24 mini cupcakes. Or, remove the tray to carry up to a 9 x 13 in. decorated cake on the sturdy locking base. The see-through cover has higher sides to protect icing flowers and tall decorations. You can also use the caddy at home, to keep pies, cookies and brownies fresh for days after baking. 18 x 14 x 6.75 in. high. Patent No. D572,539.
2105-W-9958 $19.99

23 Count Standard
12 in. high x 13 in. wide.
Holds 23 standard cupcakes.*†
307-W-826 $31.49

*Pat. No. 7,387,283. †Pat. No. D516,385.

38 Count Standard
15 in. high x 18 in. wide.
Holds 38 standard cupcakes.*
307-W-651 $41.99

4-Tier Stacked Dessert Tower

Great way to display cupcakes, appetizers, brownies and other party treats! Four plastic stacking sections with angled tiers for the best view of decorated desserts. Sections easily disassemble and nest for storage; assembled tower is 16.25 in. high x 12 in. wide. Holds 36 standard cupcakes. Pat. No. D560,974.
307-W-856 $19.99

Collapsible for easy storage

Puzzle Cakes!

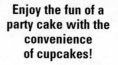

Enjoy the fun of a party cake with the convenience of cupcakes!

Transportation
415-W-9453

Animal
415-W-9452

SILICONE BUILD-A-CAKE SETS

Arrange the shaped silicone cups on a baking pan, fill and bake, then decorate and serve. Decorating Puzzle Cakes! is easy! Check the instructions inside for 3 fun designs you can create using simple icing techniques and colorful candies. Or, use your imagination and create more fun shapes of your own. Set/24. **$14.99**

SILICONE BAKING CUPS

Discover the convenience and easy release of flexible silicone! Reusable oven-safe cups in fun colors and exciting shapes are perfect for baking and serving. All have convenient batter fill line.

Silly-Critters!
Pink, Yellow, Blue, Brown. Cups are 2 in. diameter. 2.3 in. high with feet. Pk./4.
415-W-9451 **$9.99**

Bear Fun Cups
6 Tan, 6 Brown. 2 in. wide. Pk./12.
415-W-9449 **$9.99**

Silly-Feet!
Orange, Yellow, Blue, Purple. Cups are 2 in. diameter. 2.3 in. high with feet. Pk./4.
415-W-9428 **$9.99**

Flower Fun Cups
6 Yellow, 6 Pink. 2 in. wide. Pk./12.
415-W-9450 **$9.99**

Pastel Round
3 each pink, yellow, green, blue. 2 in. diameter. Pk./12.
415-W-9410 **$9.99**

Triangle
6 Pink, 6 Purple. 2.4 in. wide. Pk./12.
415-W-9423 **$9.99**

Square
6 Blue, 6 Green. 2 in. wide. Pk./12.
415-W-9424 **$9.99**

Heart
6 Pink, 6 Red. 2 in. wide. Pk./12.
415-W-9409 **$9.99**

JUMBO SPRINKLES

Give your cupcakes a big finish! Top them with Jumbo Sprinkles in exciting shapes and colors. These big and bold decorations are perfect for cupcakes, mini cakes, jumbo and king-size cupcakes, brownies and cookies. Innovative shapes for holiday, birthday or any celebration. Certified Kosher. **$4.49**

Jumbo Stars
3.25 oz. **710-W-026**

Jumbo Confetti
3.25 oz. **710-W-029**

Jumbo Daisies
3.25 oz. **710-W-028**

Jumbo Hearts
3.25 oz. **710-W-032**

Jumbo Rainbow Nonpareils
4.8 oz. **710-W-033**

Heart Drops
5.25 oz. **710-W-035**

6-Cup King-Size Muffin Pan

Create extra-tall treats! Great for cupcakes, ice cream, molded gelatin, mini angel food cakes, and mousse. Heavy-gauge premium non-stick for quick release and easy clean-up. Use with King-Size Baking Cups, p. 169.
2105-W-9921 **$9.99**

Jumbo Muffin Pan

Make super-size cupcakes and muffins. Six cups, each 4 x 2 in. Heavy-gauge premium non-stick for quick release and easy clean-up.
2105-W-955 **$6.99**

Cupcake Pedestals

Perfectly display cupcakes, muffins, party favors and more— or turn the pedestal over for the perfect ice cream cone holder!
5.2 in. high. Pk./4.
307-W-839 **$7.99**

Add-A-Message Fun Pix

Great for place markers, announcing awards and favorite sayings at banquets. Four fun colors to go with your favorite baking cups.
3 in. high. Pk./12.
2113-W-7611 **$2.29**

ORDER TOLL FREE: 800-794-5866

Baking Cups

The easiest way to dress up a cupcake! Ideal for holding candy and nuts, too.

Made of microwave-safe paper unless otherwise noted. Standard size, 2 in. dia., Mini size, 1.25 in. dia., Candy size, 1 in. dia., King size (3 in. high) and Jumbo size (2 in. high) are 2.25 in. dia.

NEW!

Be My Cupcake
$2.09
Standard Pk./75.
415-W-127
Mini Pk./100.
415-W-128

Cupcake Heaven
$2.09
Standard Pk./75.
415-W-422
Mini Pk./100.
415-W-426

Bubble Stripes
$2.09
Standard Pk./75.
415-W-114
Mini Pk./100.
415-W-115

Snappy Stripes
$2.09
Standard Pk./75.
415-W-5381
Mini Pk./100.
415-W-5380

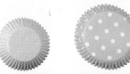

Lilac Polka Dots $2.09
Mini Pk./100.
120-W-168

Pink Polka Dots $2.09
Standard Pk./75.
120-W-169

Silver Foil
$1.99
Wax-laminated paper on foil.
Standard Pk./24.
415-W-207
Mini Pk./36.
415-W-1414

Gold Foil
$1.99
Wax-laminated paper on foil.
Standard Pk./24.
415-W-206
Mini Pk./36.
415-W-1413

White
$2.09
King-Size
Pk./24.
415-W-2118

White $1.99
Jumbo Pk./50.
415-W-2503
Standard Pk./75.
415-W-2505
Mini Pk./100.
415-W-2507

SPECIALTY BAKING CUPS

Exciting shapes and designs help your cupcakes make a grand entrance for any occasion. Scalloped cups are 2.31 in. diam.; all others are 2 in. diam. Patent pending.

Petal Cups
A pretty pastel flower in full bloom! Perfect for shower, Mother's Day and birthday cupcakes.
Standard Pk./24. $3.99

Pink
415-W-1375

Lavender
415-W-1442

Yellow
415-W-1443

Ruffled Cups
Gently flared edges and a softly puckered texture makes these a great alternative to crisply pleated cups.
Standard Pk./24. $3.99

White
415-W-1389

Teal
415-W-1390

Rose
415-W-1391

Scalloped Cups*
Straight-up fun—from the neatly scalloped top to the bold recipe motif on the straight sides.
Standard Pk./15. $3.99

Pleated Cups
A peaked and softly pleated style in rich colors creates a bold, breezy presentation.
Standard Pk./15. $3.99

Blue
415-W-1397

Teal
415-W-1398

Pink
415-W-1399

Blue
415-W-1381

Yellow
415-W-1382

Purple
415-W-1383

*Do not place in muffin pans. Place directly on cookie sheet and fill halfway with batter.

NEW!

Dazzling Dots $1.59
Standard Pk./50.
415-W-582
Mini Pk./75.
415-W-1141

Assorted Jewel $2.09
Assorted gold, purple, teal.
Standard Pk./75.
415-W-1078
Mini Pk./100.
415-W-1111

Assorted Primary $2.09
Assorted red, yellow, blue.
Standard Pk./75.
415-W-987
Mini Pk./100.
415-W-1110

Assorted Pastel $1.99
Assorted pink, yellow, blue-green.
Standard Pk./75.
415-W-394
Mini Pk./100.
415-W-2123

CUPCAKE BOXES

Brightly-patterned window boxes are the perfect way to hold and display your cupcakes! Each box includes an insert with recessed space to hold standard size cupcakes safely in place. Easy folding assembly; great for gifts and favors! Choose single, 4-cupcake size or 6-cupcake size.

Holds 4 standard cupcakes. Pk./3.
White
415-W-1215
$5.29

Cupcake Heaven

Holds 4 standard cupcakes. Pk./3.
415-W-1206
$5.29

Holds 4 standard cupcakes. Pk./3.
Silver
415-W-1359
$5.29

Holds 1 standard cupcake. Pk./3.
415-W-289
$3.29

Holds 6 standard cupcakes. Pk./2.
415-W-1207
$5.29

CUPCAKE FUN!

Brownie Fun!

Wilton is raising the bar for brownies, with a complete line of products that will help you create the best-looking, most delicious brownies ever!

Brownie Fun!

It's the book that proves brownies can be as colorful and fun as your favorite party treats! In *Brownie Fun!*, the fudgy treats everyone loves take on amazing new shapes and dazzling colors that will be the talk of your next celebration. *Brownie Fun!* is packed with over 140 easy-to-make designs and delicious recipes for brownies and mini treats. We'll also show you how to mix, bake and decorate the perfect brownies using the complete line of Wilton brownie products. Soft cover, 112 pages.
902-W-1105 $14.99

12 Piece Brownie Decorating Set

The ideal set for discovering the fun of cake and brownie decorating! Create most of the fun icing techniques in the *Brownie Fun!* book with the tips included—rosettes, stars, drop flowers, messages and more. Includes tips 5, 21, 352 and 2D, standard coupler, decorating triangle, 6 disposable decorating bags and instruction sheet.
2104-W-2533 $8.99

CRUNCHES

Add delicious flavor and a colossal crunch! **$4.99**

Cookies 'N Cream
Certified Kosher. 5 oz. **710-W-9702**

Turtle
Certified Kosher. 5 oz. **710-W-9703**

Rainbow Chip
Certified Kosher Dairy. 5.25 oz.
710-W-9704

Brownie Stencil Set

With 6 fun stencils, it's easy to make homemade brownies look great for the party or for giving. Decorate small, large pans or single brownies. Set/6.
417-W-1312 $7.99

ICING

Vanilla Crème
704-W-151

Peanut Butter
704-W-150

Brownie Fudge Icing
Rich fudge flavor and velvety texture make this the perfect icing for spreading on brownies. Heat it in the microwave for an easy glaze; use with Wilton Drizzle Icing (at left) to create delicious designs.
1 Lb. can.
710-W-9700 $3.29

Drizzle Icing

Just heat and squeeze over brownies to add a ribbon of flavor. Use with Brownie Fudge Icing (at right) for exciting marbleized designs. 10 oz. bottle. Certified Kosher. **$4.99**

Cutters

COMBO CUTTERS

Make multiple shapes with just one cut. Stainless steel Combo Cutters are divided into a neat space-saving square, which maximizes the number of treats you get from one pan. Each cutter approx. 4 x 2.5 x 2.75 in. deep. **$3.99**

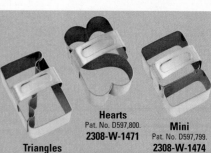

Triangles
Pat. No. D597,801.
2308-W-1473

Hearts
Pat. No. D597,800.
2308-W-1471

Mini
Pat. No. D597,799.
2308-W-1474

PUSH 'N POP! BROWNIE & TREAT CUTTER

Cut a sensational heart-shaped treat with the stainless steel cutter and pop it out with the built-in plunger.
4.5 x 3 x 3 in. deep.
2308-W-4074 $7.99

ORDER TOLL FREE: 800-794-5866

Brownie Tools

Easy-to-handle Brownie Tools from Wilton make mixing, cutting and serving brownies a breeze!

Brownie & Treat Cutter
Cut brownies and treats at a fun new angle! The zigzag blade cuts clean decorative edges. Great for crispy treats, pizza and sandwiches, too! 4.9 x 3.75 in.
2308-W-1480 $7.99

Perfect Cut Brownie Marker
No more messy edges! Just insert the stainless steel tines into a pan of warm brownies to score. When completely cool, break apart or cut with a knife for a perfect, clean edge. 4.9 x 3.75 in. Patent Pending.
570-W-1159 $7.99

Brownie Lifter
Move your brownies from pan to plate looking great! Its tapered nylon blade is set at the perfect angle for getting under brownies without breakage. 9 in. long.
570-W-1160 $6.99

Sugar Shaker
Shake up your brownies with color using powdered sugar and the Sugar Shaker! Easy-to-fill, easy-to-handle shaker is also great for dusting brownies and cakes with cocoa. Fine mesh strainer with color grip and fitted lid for easy use and storage. 10 oz. capacity.
2103-W-388 $8.99

Batter Blender
Mix thick brownie batter faster and with less effort. Silicone head is great for stirring, scraping and spreading batter. Scalloped tip breaks up clumps. 11 in. long. Pat. No. D600,510.
570-W-1158 $7.99

Bakeware
NON-STICK BAKEWARE

Our premium non-stick bakeware combines superior non-stick performance, serving convenience and elegant design, to provide the highest level of baking satisfaction.

9 in. Square Covered Brownie Pan
Perfect for taking homemade brownies to the party! Ideal size for most standard brownie mixes. 9 x 9 x 2 in.
2105-W-9199 $7.99

6-Cavity Dessert Shell Pan
Bakes edible individual dessert shells, great for brownie bowls, sponge cakes and more. One 8 x 8 in. size brownie mix makes 6 brownies. Individual cavities are 3.5 in. diameter x 1.5 in. deep.
2105-W-8600 $8.99

SILICONE BAKEWARE

Flexible silicone is ideal for releasing moist-textured brownies—they pop right out. Wilton silicone bakeware creates the perfect single servings in fun new shapes!

Round Brownie Pops 8-Cavity Silicone Mold
One 8 x 8 in. size brownie mix makes 24 brownies. Individual cavities are 1.75 x 1.75 x 1.75 in. deep.
2105-W-4925 $9.99

Bite-Size Brownie Squares 24-Cavity Silicone Mold
Little brownie bites—just the right size for parties and snacks. One 8 x 8 in. size brownie mix makes 40 to 42 brownies. Individual cavities are 1.5 x 1.5 x .75 in. deep.
2105-W-4923 $9.99

Blossom Brownie 6-Cavity Silicone Mold
One 8 x 8 in. size brownie mix makes 6 brownies. Individual cavities are 2.25 x 2.25 x 1 in. deep.
2105-W-4924 $9.99

12 in. Brownie Sticks
For fun brownie pops. Pk./20.
1912-W-1003 $3.99

Brownie Presentation
BROWNIE GIFT BOX KITS
Colorful window boxes, tissues and accents are the ideal way to present your gift of homemade brownies.

Small
Includes 3 boxes: 2 x 3.5 x 3.5 in., 3 tissue sheets: 4 x 4 in., 6 stickers: 1 in. diameter. Set/3.
415-W-9478 $2.99

Medium
Includes 3 boxes: 2 x 6.25 x 6.25 in., 3 bands: 1.5 ft. long, 3 tissue sheets: 10 x 10 in., 3 inserts, 1 sticker sheet. Set/3.
415-W-9477 $5.99

Brownie Envelope Kit
Create a fun brownie gift with envelopes, lace-look doilies and colorful seals. Just lay envelope flat and place doily and brownie in center; fold flaps toward center and secure with seals. Includes 6 envelopes: 4.5 x 4.5 in., 6 doilies: 4.5 in. diameter, 6 seals: 1.5 in. diameter. Set/6.
1912-W-1297 $3.99

BROWNIE FUN!

Party

You've written the guest list—now start your decorating list here! From baking cups to candles, cake toppers to treat bags, Wilton has the exciting and colorful party designs you want.

Theme Party Products

Give your party personality! See how easy it is to pull your look together with the great selection of Wilton theme party products. You'll discover favorite subjects including jungle animals, colorful flowers, over-the-hill tombstones and sports for every season. Find candles, party bags, baking cups, candy molds, cake pans and more—all with the Wilton touch of fun design and detail.

BIG TOP **NEW!**

Ladies and gentlemen, children of all ages—the greatest way to celebrate your special occasion is under the Big Top! Bright colors and fun designs delight kids and adults alike.

Elephant Cake Pan
This perky pachyderm is sure to please all your party guests. One-mix cake pan is 12.25 x 9 x 2 in. deep. Aluminum.
2105-W-0576 **$12.99**

Primary Colors Cake Stand Kit
Bright, primary colors highlight your cake and add fun to your celebration. Holds up to 10 in. round or 9 x 13 in. rectangle sizes. Includes cake server. 15 x 11 x 6 in. high.
1510-W-140 **$10.99**

Icing Decorations
Perfect for topping cakes, cupcakes and cookies! Pk./12.
710-W-1072 **$5.99**

Primary Colors Cupcake Stand Kit
It's an instant party, with a bright 3-tier cupcake stand, fun decorative topper, colorful baking cups and Fun Pix! Includes 12 x 17 in. high stand, 24 - 2 in. diameter cups and 24 - 3 in. high picks. Holds up to 24 cupcakes.
1510-W-135 **$10.99**

Baking Cups
Microwave-safe paper. Standard size, 2 in. diameter, Pk./75; mini size, 1.25 in. diameter, Pk./100. **$2.09**
Standard 415-W-1155
Mini 415-W-1162

Frame Cake Topper
Display your favorite face on top of the cake. Frame topper makes a great keepsake and scrapbook addition after the party. 4.25 x 5 in.
2113-W-1602 **$1.99**

CandyPick Mold
Create colorful candy toppers to transform plain cakes and cupcakes into exciting party treats! It's easy, using your favorite Candy Melts colors and this fun detailed mold. 2 designs, 8 cavities.
2115-W-2117 **$1.99**

Cupcake Wraps 'n Pix
Fun circus theme decorates cupcakes. Includes 12 wraps (2 in. diameter) and 24 pix, 2 designs (3 in. high). Baking cups sold separately. Pk./12.
415-W-1563 **$3.49**

Lollipop Mold
3 designs, 3 cavities.
2115-W-2116 **$1.99**

PRINCESS

The royal treatment for any birthday girl begins here, with colorful treats and cakes that rule!

Princess Carriage Pan
Create a birthday celebration fit for a princess! Give it dazzling windows and wheels decorated in her favorite colors. Or, decorate a classic carriage cake for the bridal shower, with flowers and accents to match your colors. One-mix pan is 12.25 x 9.5 x 2 in. deep. Aluminum.
2105-W-1027 $12.99

NEW!

Candles
Approx. 2.25 in. high. Set/4.
2811-W-1001 $3.99

NEW!

Icing Decorations
Perfect for topping cakes, cupcakes and cookies! Pk./12.
710-W-1074 $5.99

NEW!

Frame Cake Topper
Display your favorite face on top of the cake. Frame topper makes a great keepsake and scrapbook addition after the party. 4.25 x 5 in.
2113-W-1600 $1.99

NEW!

Baking Cups
Microwave-safe paper. Standard size, 2 in. diameter, Pk./75; mini size, 1.25 in. diameter, Pk./100. $2.09
Standard 415-W-1142
Mini 415-W-1145

Cupcake Combo Pack
Quick and colorful way to serve cupcakes that set the tone for your celebration. Contains 24 each 2 in. diameter baking cups and 3 in. high paper party picks. Pk./24.
415-W-1313 $2.29

NEW!

3 Pc. Cutter Set
Includes castle, crown and slipper, each approx. 3 to 3.5 in. Coated metal. Set/3.
2308-W-0915 $3.69

NEW!

Cupcake Wraps 'n Pix
Fairy tale fun for cupcakes! Includes 12 wraps (2 in. diameter) and 24 pix, 2 designs (3 in. high). Baking cups sold separately. Pk./12.
415-W-1561 $3.49

Fairy Tale Lollipop Mold
3 designs, 3 cavities.
2115-W-1033 $1.99

Romantic Castle Cake Set
Everything you need to transform your tiered cake into a fantasy castle is included: three sizes of detailed turret towers with removable peak pieces, lattice windows, a paneled door and roof pieces. Complete assembly and decorating ideas included. For design ideas visit www.wilton.com! Set/32.
301-W-910 $20.99

NEW!

Cake Stand Kit
Holds up to 10 in. round or 9 x 13 in. rectangle sizes. Includes cake server. 9 x 13 in. rectangle
1510-W-137 $10.99

Princess Cupcake Stand Kit
It's an instant princess party, with a bright 3-tier cupcake stand, fun decorative topper, colorful baking cups and Fun Pix! Includes 12 x 17 in. high stand, 24 - 2 in. diameter cups and 24 - 3 in. high picks. Holds up to 24 cupcakes.
1510-W-1008 $10.99

CandyPick Mold
Create colorful candy toppers to transform plain cakes and cupcakes into exciting party treats! It's easy, using your favorite Candy Melts colors and this fun detailed mold. 2 designs, 8 cavities.
2115-W-2113 $1.99

NEW!

WHEELS

Kids just love a celebration on the move!. Perfect for birthdays, school parties and special events.

 NEW!

Icing Decorations
Perfect for topping cakes, cupcakes and cookies! Pk./12.
710-W-1075 $5.99

Frame Cake Topper
Display your favorite face on top of the cake. Frame topper makes a great keepsake and scrapbook addition after the party. 4.25 x 5 in.
2113-W-1601 $1.99

Cupcake Wraps 'n Pix
Cupcakes are ready to roll! Includes 12 wraps (2 in. diameter) and 24 pix, 2 designs (3 in. high). Baking cups sold separately. Pk./12.
415-W-1562 $3.49

Baking Cups
Microwave-safe paper. Standard size, 2 in. diameter, Pk./75; mini size, 1.25 in. diameter, Pk./100. **$2.09**
Standard 415-W-1147
Mini 415-W-1149

Construction Vehicles Candles
Approx. 1.75 in. long. Set/4.
2811-W-858 $3.99

Firetruck
When the occasion calls for a five-alarm celebration. One-mix pan is 15.5 x 8.5 x 2 in. deep. Aluminum.
2105-W-2061 $12.99

3 Pc. Cutter Set
Includes plane, train and race car, each approx. 3 to 3.5 in. Coated metal. Set/3.
2308-W-0946 $3.69

SWEET DOTS

The look is trendy, the result is amazing! Dots add fun to birthdays, holidays, and family events!

NEW!

Frame Cake Topper
Fun dots surround the star of the party. Frame topper makes a great keepsake and scrapbook addition after the party. 4.25 x 5 in.
2113-W-1605 $1.99

Icing Decorations
Perfect for topping cakes, cupcakes and cookies! Pk./12.
710-W-1077 $5.99

Cupcake Wraps 'n Pix
The party never ends with dressed-up, dotted cupcakes. Includes 12 wraps (2 in. diameter) and 24 pix, 2 designs (3 in. high). Baking cups sold separately. Pk./12.
415-W-1566 $3.49

Baking Cups
Microwave-safe paper. Standard size, 2 in. diameter, Pk./75; mini size, 1.25 in. diameter, Pk./100.
$2.09
Standard 415-W-1052
Mini 415-W-1183

CELEBRATION

What a great way to cap off any celebration, from birthdays to that New Year's Eve bash!

Topsy Turvy Pan
Our topsy turvy "tiered" cake is just the right look for wacky birthdays, wild parties or special occasions. One-mix pan is 10.25 x 12 x 2 in. deep. Aluminum.
2105-W-4946 $12.99

NEW!

Cake Stand Kit
The celebration begins as you display your cake in style. Holds up to 10 in. round or 9 x 13 in. rectangle sizes. Includes cake server. 15 x 11 x 6 in. high.
1510-W-139 $10.99

NEW!

Frame Cake Topper
Showcase the star of the party on top of the cake. Frame topper makes a great keepsake and scrapbook addition after the party. 4.25 x 5 in.
2113-W-1604 $1.99

NEW!

Icing Decorations
Perfect for topping cakes, cupcakes and cookies! Pk./12.
710-W-1076 $5.99

Party Icing Decorations
Perfect for topping cakes, cupcakes and cookies! Certified Kosher. Pk./9.
710-W-461 $2.29

NEW!

Cupcake Stand Kit
It's an instant party, with a 3 tier cupcake stand, fun decorative topper, colorful baking cups and Fun Pix. Includes 12 x 17 in. high stand, 24 each 2 in. diameter cups and 3 in. high picks. Holds up to 24 cupcakes.
1510-W-134 $10.99

Cupcake Combo Pack
Quick and colorful way to serve cupcakes that set the tone for your celebration. Contains 24 each 2 in. diameter baking cups and 3 in. high paper party picks. Pk./24.
415-W-1176 $2.29

NEW!

Baking Cups
Microwave-safe paper. Standard size, 2 in. diameter, Pk./75; mini size, 1.25 in. diameter, Pk./100. $2.09
Standard 415-W-986
Mini 415-W-1164

Candles
Approx. 1.5 in. high. Set/4.
2811-W-860 $3.99

4 Pc. Cutter Set
Set of 4 includes cake, cupcake, party hat and gift, each approx. 3 to 3.5 in. Coated metal.
2308-W-0909 $4.79

NEW!

NEW!

CandyPick Mold
Create colorful candy toppers to transform plain cakes and cupcakes into exciting party treats! It's easy, using your favorite Candy Melts colors and this fun detailed mold. 9 designs, 9 cavities.
2115-W-2110 $1.99

Cupcake Wraps 'n Pix
The party never ends with dressed-up, dotted cupcakes. Includes 12 wraps (2 in. diameter) and 12 pix (3 in. high). Baking cups sold separately. Pk./12.
415-W-1565 $3.49

NEW!

Party/Birthday Lollipop Mold
4 designs, 4 cavities.
2115-W-4434 $1.99

JUNGLE PALS

Kids will just love these adorable creatures for birthdays, school parties and special events.

NEW!

Frame Cake Topper
Honor the star of the party on top of the cake. Frame topper makes a great keepsake and scrapbook addition after the party. 4.25 x 5 in.
2113-W-1603 **$1.99**

Monkey Pan
He'll be the top banana at so many fun occasions! Kids will just love him at birthday parties, school celebrations and jungle-themed events. One-mix pan is 12.75 x 11.25 x 2 in. deep. Aluminum.
2105-W-1023 **$12.99**

NEW!

Icing Decorations
Perfect for topping cakes, cupcakes and cookies! Pk./12.
710-W-1073 **$5.99**

Fun Pix
Approx. 3.25 in. high. Set/24.
2113-W-1012
$2.29

Jungle Animals Topper Set
1.75 to 3 in. high. Set/4.
2113-W-2095 **$4.29**

NEW!

Baking Cups
Microwave-safe paper. Standard size, 2 in. diameter, Pk./75; mini size, 1.25 in. diameter, Pk./100.
$2.09
Standard 415-W-1324
Mini 415-W-1013

Baking Cups
Microwave-safe paper. Standard size, 2 in. diameter. Pk/50.
415-W-1012 **$1.59**

NEW!

Candle Picks
Approx. 2 in. high. Set/4.
2811-W-1012 **$3.99**

NEW!

3 Pc. Cutter Set
Includes elephant, lion and monkey each approx. 3 to 3.5 in. Coated metal. Set/3.
2308-W-0916 **$3.69**

NEW!

Cupcake Wraps 'n Pix
It's a jungle out there! Includes 12 wraps (2 in. diameter) and 24 pix, 2 designs (3 in. high). Baking cups sold separately. Pk./12.
415-W-1564 **$3.49**

Monkey Large Lollipop Mold
3 designs, 3 cavities.
2115-W-2100 **$1.99**

Animals Cookie Candy Molds
With Cookie Candy Molds and easy-melting Wilton Candy Melts, it's a breeze to add a great tasting and colorful candy design to your favorite cookies. Great for sandwich cream cookies or any round cookie 2 in. diameter or less. 4 designs, 8 cavities.
2115-W-1354 **$1.99**

PIRATES

Give kids a party to treasure with cakes and cupcakes that carry high seas excitement.

Cupcake Combo Pack
Quick and colorful way to serve cupcakes that set the tone for your celebration. Contains 24 each 2 in. diameter baking cups and 3 in. high paper party picks. Pk./24.
415-W-1015 $2.29

Pirate Ship
Your ship has come in with this favorite kids' shape and its cargo of great decorating ideas on the label! One-mix pan is 13.2 x 11.25 x 2 in. deep. Aluminum.
2105-W-1021 $12.99

NEW!

Lollipop Mold
3 designs, 3 cavities.
2115-W-2111 $1.99

NEW!

CandyPick Mold
Create colorful candy toppers to transform plain cakes and cupcakes into exciting party treats! It's easy, using your favorite Candy Melts colors and this fun detailed mold. 2 designs, 8 cavities.
2115-W-2112 $1.99

AGING GRACEFULLY

The secret of aging is keeping your sense of humor! These Wilton products help anyone face those big birthdays with a smile!

NEW!

Cupcake Combo Pack
Quick and colorful way to serve cupcakes. Contains 24 each 2 in. diameter baking cups and 3 in. high paper party picks. Pk./24.
415-W-1315 $2.29

Icon Candles
Candles that feature a fun hand-carved tombstone. Instant fun, great size for cupcakes too! 2.5 in. high. Pk./10.
2811-W-8417 $2.29

Candle
2.25 in. high.
2811-W-553 $2.29

Cake Stand Kit
Celebrate the status of old age as you display and serve your cake in style. Holds up to 10 in. round or 9 x 13 in. rectangle sizes. Includes cake server. 15 x 11 x 6 in. high.
1510-W-141 $10.99

Candle Picks
1.75 in. high.
Set/13.
2811-W-786 $2.29

SMILEY FACE

Have a nice party! This friendly face has a way of making everyone happy at birthdays, housewarmings and welcome home parties.

Pretzel Mold

Easy to mold; 1 design, 6 cavities.
2115-W-4437
$1.99

Chunky Candles
Thicker candles to energize any cake! They feature bold textured spirals and a fun hand-carved shape on top. 3.25 in. high. Pk./4. **$3.99**

Smiley Flames
2811-W-6326

Lollipop Mold
1 design, 10 cavities.
2115-W-1715 $1.99

Candles
1.5 in. high. Set/6.
2811-W-9351 $3.99

Smiley Stars
2811-W-6325

DANCING DAISY FLOWER

Pick this daisy for Mother's Day, wedding showers and birthdays for any garden-lover.

Pan
One perfect flower makes bunches of great cakes and desserts! One-mix pan is 12 x 12 x 2 in. deep. Aluminum.
2105-W-1016 $12.99

Flowers Cookie Candy Molds
Add a great tasting and colorful candy design to your favorite cookies. Great for sandwich cream cookies or any round cookie 2 in. diameter or less. 2 designs, 8 cavities.
2115-W-1351 $1.99

Lollipop Mold
1 design, 9 cavities.
2115-W-1430 $1.99

Icing Decorations
Certified Kosher. Pk./12.
710-W-353 $2.29

Party Bags
20 plastic bags, 20 ties included. 4 x 9.5 in. Pk./20.
1912-W-7813 $2.09

Baking Cups
Microwave-safe paper.
Standard 2 in. diameter. Pk./50.
415-W-7812 $1.59
Mini 1.25 in. diameter. Pk./100.
415-W-1088 $2.09

Daisy Comfort-Grip
Easy-grip stainless steel cutter with extra-deep sides approximately 4 x 4 x 1.75 in. Recipe included.
2310-W-619 $3.19

RUBBER DUCKY

This bathtime favorite will make the biggest splash for birthdays and baby showers.

NEW!

Candles
1.5 in. high. Set/6.
2811-W-9337 $3.99

Favor Accent*
Tie onto favors, gifts and decorations. .85 in. high. Pk/20.
1004-W-2850 $2.99

Candy Mold
1 design, 6 cavities.
2115-W-1565 $1.99

Ducky Baking Cups
Microwave-safe paper.
Standard 2 in. diameter. Pk/75.
415-W-1016 $2.09
Mini 1.25 in. diameter. Pk/100.
415-W-1017 $2.09

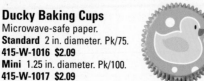

3-D Cake Pan
Five adorable designs included. Two-piece pan takes 5½ cups batter. Aluminum.
2105-W-2094 $16.49

ORDER TOLL FREE: 800-794-5866

GOLF

Great ways to top cakes with perfect form.

Golf Topper Set*

Includes 4.5 in. high golfer plus three each: 2.5 in. wide greens, 4 in. high flags, 5 in. clubs and golf balls. Set/13.
1306-W-7274
$3.29

Topper Set with Decals

Includes 1 topper, 6 candleholders, 6 - 2 in. high candles. 1 sheet of decals. Set/14.
2811-W-8420 $5.49

HOCKEY

When the goal is a great cake, here's the topper set to use!

Topper Set With Decals

Includes 1 topper, 6 candleholders, 6 - 2 in. high candles, 1 sheet of decals. Set/14.
2811-W-8422 $5.49

FISHING

Land the perfect cake for your angler, with bright candles and toppers.

Frustrated Fisherman Topper

4.5 in. high.
2113-W-2384
$3.79

Tropical Fish Candles

Approx. 1.5 in. high. Set/4.
2811-W-9333 $3.99

Metal Cutter

Cuts cleanly and releases with ease. Approximately 3 in.
2308-W-1017 $0.69

CAMOUFLAGE

Attention! That's what your cakes and cupcakes will get when you outfit them in our camouflage-pattern accents. Perfect for birthdays and coming-home celebrations.

Chunky Candles

Thicker candles to energize any cake! They feature a fun hand-carved shape on top. 2.25 in. high. Pk./4.
2811-W-1009 $3.99

Cupcake Combo Pack

Quick and colorful way to serve cupcakes. Contains 24 each 2 in. diameter baking cups and 3 in. high paper party picks. Pk./24.
415-W-1082 $2.29

Theme Party Products

SPORTS

Here's the perfect game plan for your next party, whatever sport you favor: Action-packed, colorful ways to serve cakes, cupcakes or treats.

Mini Ball Pan

Ice two mini balls and push together for a 3-D effect. One cake mix makes 10–12 mini balls. Six cavities, each 3.5 x 3.5 x 1.5 in. deep. Aluminum.
2105-W-1760
$12.99

Sports Ball Pan Set

Includes two 6 in. diameter half-ball pans and two metal baking stands. Each pan half takes 2½ cups batter. Aluminum. Set/4.
2105-W-6506 $12.99

Sports Lollipop Mold

Makes favorite sports balls from every season. 4 designs, 4 cavities.
2115-W-4432
$1.99

Sports Cookie Candy Mold

It's easy to add a great tasting and colorful candy design to your favorite cookies. Great for sandwich cream cookies or any round cookie 2 in. diameter or less. 4 designs, 8 cavities.
2115-W-1353 $1.99

Cupcake Combo Pack

Quick and colorful way to serve cupcakes that set the tone for your celebration. Contains 24 each 2 in. diameter baking cups and 3 in. high paper party picks. Pk./24.
415-W-1314 $2.29

BASKETBALL

Slam dunk winners! Create thrilling cakes and candies.

Topper Set with Decals

Includes 1 topper, 6 candleholders, 6 - 2 in. high candles. 1 sheet of decals. Set/14.
2811-W-8423 $5.49

Candle

1.75 in. high. Set/6.
2811-W-9323 $3.99

Basketball Topper Set*

Includes 1 forward, 2 centers, 3 guards and 1 hoop, 2.25 to 4 in. high. Set/7.
2113-W-2237 $3.29

Soccer Ball Pan

One-mix pan is 8.75 x 8.75 x 3.5 in. deep. Aluminum.
2105-W-2044 $12.99

SOCCER

A great way to reward a season or a game well played!

Topper Set with Decals

Includes 1 topper, 6 candleholders, 6 - 2 in. high candles, 1 sheet of decals. Set/14.
2811-W-8421 $5.49

Baking Cups

Microwave-safe paper. Standard size, 2 in. diameter. Pk./50.
415-W-296 $1.59

Icing Decorations

Certified Kosher. Pk./9.
710-W-477 $2.29

Candle

1 in. high. Set/6.
2811-W-9322
$3.99

Soccer Topper Set*

Seven players and two nets, 1.75 to 2 in. high. Set/9.
2113-W-9002 $3.29

Soccer Ball Pan

One-mix pan is 8.75 x 8.75 x 3.5 in. deep. Aluminum.
2105-W-2044 $12.99

⚠ *WARNING: CHOKING HAZARD
Small parts. Not for children under 3 years.

ORDER TOLL FREE: 800-794-5866

BASEBALL/SOFTBALL

From Little League to World Series celebrations, cover the bases with 3-D cakes and hit candles and toppers.

Topper Set with Decals
Includes 1 topper, 6 candleholders, 6 -2 in. high candles, 1 sheet of decals. Set/14.
2811-W-8425 $5.49

Soccer Ball Pan
One-mix pan is 8.75 x 8.75 x 3.5 in. deep. Aluminum.
2105-W-2044 $12.99

Baking Cups
Microwave-safe paper. Standard size, 2 in. diameter. Pk./50.
415-W-298 $1.59

Icing Decorations
Certified Kosher. Pk./9.
710-W-475 $2.29

Candle
2.75 in. high. Set/6.
2811-W-750 $3.99

Baseball Topper Set*
Batter, catcher, three fielders and pitcher, 2.1 to 2.75 in. high. Set/6.
2113-W-2155 $3.29

FOOTBALL

Touching down at Super Bowl parties, homecomings, award dinners and much more.

NEW!

Topper Set with Decals
Includes 1 topper, 6 candleholders, 6 - 2 in. high candles, 1 sheet of decals. Set/14.
2811-W-8424 $5.49

First and Ten Football Pan
One-mix pan is 12 x 7.75 x 3 in. deep. Aluminum.
2105-W-6504 $12.99

Baking Cups
Microwave-safe paper. Standard size, 2 in. diameter. Pk./75.
415-W-5152 $2.09

Icing Decorations
Certified Kosher. Pk./9.
710-W-478 $2.29

Candle
2 in. high. Set/6.
2811-W-757 $3.99

Mini Football Silicone Mold
Discover the convenience and easy release of flexible silicone bakeware! Freezer, refrigerator, microwave and dishwasher safe—oven safe to 500°F. One mix makes 20-24 footballs. 6 cavities, each 2.5 x 1.5 in. deep.
2105-W-4842 $9.99

4 Pc. Colored Metal Cutter Set
Built to last, they cut cleanly. Includes pennant, football, jersey, and helmet. Recipe included. Approx. 3 in. Set/4.
2308-W-1263 $4.79

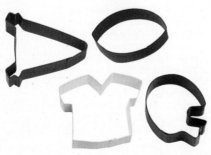

Football Topper Set*
Eight players and two goal posts, 1½ to 4½ in. high. Set/10.
2113-W-2236 $3.29

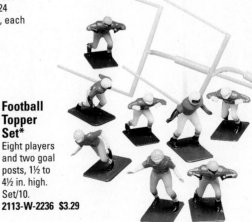

⚠ *WARNING: CHOKING HAZARD
Small parts. Not for children under 3 years.

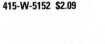

PARTY

Candles

NOVELTY

White
2811-W-773

Multicolor
2811-W-777

Longs
Sized right for larger cakes or for making a bold statement on any cake. 5.875 in. high. Pk./12. **$2.29**

Slenders
6.5 in. high. Pk./24.
2811-W-1188 **$0.99**

Assorted
2811-W-1230

Red & Blue
2811-W-704

"Trick" Sparklers
Blow 'em out—they relight! 6.5 in. high. Pk./18. **$1.29**

Glow-in-the-Dark
These luminous candles will lend an extra touch of fun to any celebration. Assorted colors: white, yellow, green, blue. 2.5 in. high. Pk./10. 2811-W-165 **$2.29**

CANDLE SETS

Wilton gives you more choices! Top your cake with candles in the perfect colors—and check out our exciting designs.

Home Improvement Tools
Approx. 2.25 in. high. Set/5.
2811-W-9136 **$3.99**

Construction Vehicles
Approx. 1.75 in. long. Set/4.
2811-W-858 **$3.99**

Race Cars
Approx. 1.75 in. high. Set/4.
2811-W-9135 **$3.99**

Firefighting
Approx. 1.5 in. high. Set/4
2811-W-9339 **$3.99**

Farm
Approx. 1.625 in. high. Set/4.
2811-W-9347 **$3.99**

Fiesta
Approx. 1.75 in. high. Set/4.
2811-W-9345 **$3.99**

Baby Things
Approx. 2 in. high. Set/4.
2811-W-855 **$3.99**

Beach Sandals
.375 in. high, .875 in. long. Set/6.
2811-W-9352 **$3.99**

Margaritas
1.25 in. high. Set/6.
2811-W-9343 **$3.99**

Champagne Bottles
2 in. high. Set/6.
2811-W-163 **$3.99**

Beer Cans
1.75 in. high. Set/6.
2811-W-9326 **$3.99**

PICK SETS

Put your celebration message in lights! These bright candle picks are a unique and easy way to pick up the party theme on your cake top. Fun colors are just right for the occasion.

Happy Birthday
1.75 in. high. Set/15.
2811-W-785 **$2.29**

Congratulations
1.75 in. high. Set/15.
2811-W-787 **$2.29**

COLOR FLAME CANDLES

Candle and flame are colored the same!

Color Flame Candles give your cake that extra dash of excitement and fun. Includes 4 vivid colors— blue, red, orange and green. They make a plain iced cake a party treat to remember. 2 in. high. Pk./12. **$2.99**
Assorted 2811-W-1011
Blue 2811-W-1017
Red 2811-W-1019

Add-A-Message Fun Pix
Serve party cupcakes in an exciting new way —clip on messages, pictures and more with these colorful plastic picks! Great for place markers, announcing awards at banquets and favorite sayings. Four fun colors to go with your favorite baking cups. 3 in. high. Pk./12.
2113-W-7611 **$2.29**

Musical Candle
Plays "Happy Birthday To You". 4.75 in. high.
2811-W-1231 **$4.29**

ORDER TOLL FREE: 800-794-5866

Classic Candles

Pearlized Multicolor
Watch them shimmer from the moment you light them! 2.5 in. high. Pk./10. **$2.29**
2811-W-3665

Glitter
2.5 in. high. Pk./10. **$1.29**
White 2811-W-248
Pink 2811-W-244
Blue 2811-W-246
Black 2811-W-247

Celebration
2.5 in. high. Pk./24. **$0.79**
White 2811-W-207
Pink 2811-W-213
Red 2811-W-209
Blue 2811-W-210
Black 2811-W-224

Assorted Celebration
Classic spirals in attractive two-tones. 2.5 in. high. Pk./24.
2811-W-215 **$0.79**

"Trick"
Blow 'em out—they relight! 2.5 in. high. Asst: White, Yellow, Pink, Blue. Pk./24.
2811-W-220 **$1.29**

Silver and Gold
2.25 in. high. Pk./10. **$1.79**
Silver 2811-W-9123
Gold 2811-W-9122

Numerals
Festive way to mark age or year. Edged in green unless specified. 3 in. high. **$0.89**

#1 2811-W-9101	Pink #1 2811-W-240	Blue #1 2811-W-241

#2 2811-W-9102	#7 2811-W-9107
#3 2811-W-9103	#8 2811-W-9108
#4 2811-W-9104	#9 2811-W-9109
#5 2811-W-9105	#0 2811-W-9100
#6 2811-W-9106	? 2811-W-9110

RAINBOW COLORS

Shimmer
2.5 in. high. Pk./10.
2811-W-3663 **$2.29**

Tricolor
2.5 in. high. Pk./10.
2811-W-779 **$2.29**

Rounds
2.5 in. high. Pk./24.
2811-W-284 **$0.79**

Crayons
3.25 in. high. Pk./8.
2811-W-226 **$1.79**

Party Thins
8 in. high. Pk./20.
2811-W-239 **$1.29**

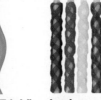

Triangle "Trick" Sparklers
2.5 in. high. Pk./9.
2811-W-278 **$1.29**

Wavy "Trick" Sparklers
2.5 in. high. Pk./10.
2811-W-272 **$2.29**

Lattice
2.5 in. high. Pk./10.
2811-W-3656 **$2.29**

Curly
3 in. high. Pk./12.
2811-W-9127 **$1.79**

SOFT COLORS

Shimmer
2.5 in. high. Pk./10.
2811-W-3664 **$2.29**

Tricolor
2.5 in. high. Pk./10.
2811-W-782 **$2.29**

Party Thins
8 in. high. Pk./20.
2811-W-255 **$1.29**

Rounds
2.5 in. high. Pk./24.
2811-W-291 **$0.79**

Triangle "Trick" Sparklers
2.5 in. high. Pk./9.
2811-W-288 **$1.29**

HOT COLORS

Shimmer
2.5 in. high. Pk./10.
2811-W-3662 **$2.29**

Tricolor
2.5 in. high. Pk./10.
2811-W-781 **$2.29**

Rounds
2.5 in. high. Pk./24.
2811-W-225 **$0.79**

Crayons
3.25 in. high. Pk./8.
2811-W-282 **$1.79**

Party Thins
8 in. high. Pk./20.
2811-W-237 **$1.29**

Triangle "Trick" Sparklers
2.5 in. high. Pk./9.
2811-W-276 **$1.29**

Wavy "Trick" Sparklers
2.5 in. high. Pk./10.
2811-W-270 **$2.29**

Lattice
2.5 in. high. Pk./10.
2811-W-3655 **$2.29**

Twist
2.5 in. high. Pk./8.
2811-W-3659 **$2.99**

Icing Decorations

Wilton Icing Decorations are perfect for adding messages to cakes, cupcakes, cookies and more. Edible shapes are Certified Kosher.

NEW!

Happy Birthday
Certified Kosher. Pk./22.
710-W-2735 **$2.29**

NEW!

Alphabet/Numerals
Certified Kosher. Pk./71.
710-W-2734 **$2.29**

Baking Cups

The easiest way to dress up a cupcake! Ideal for holding candy and nuts, too.
Made of microwave-safe paper unless otherwise noted. Jumbo cups are 2.25 in. diameter, standard cups are 2 in. diameter, mini cups are 1.25 in. diameter, candy cups are 1 in. diameter.

NEW!

SPECIALTY BAKING CUPS

Exciting shapes and designs for any occasion help your cupcakes make a grand entrance. Scalloped cups are 2.31 in. diam.; all others are 2 in. diam. Patent pending.

Petal Cups
A pretty pastel flower in full bloom! Perfect for shower, Mother's Day and birthday cupcakes. Standard Pk./24. **$3.99**

Pink
415-W-1375

Lavender
415-W-1442

Yellow
415-W-1443

Ruffled Cups
Gently flared edges and a softly puckered texture makes these a great alternative to crisply pleated cups. Standard Pk./24. **$3.99**

White
415-W-1389

Teal
415-W-1390

Rose
415-W-1391

Scalloped Cups*
Straight-up fun—from the neatly scalloped top to the bold recipe motif on the straight sides. Standard Pk./15. **$3.99**

Blue
415-W-1397

Teal
415-W-1398

Pink
415-W-1399

Pleated Cups
A peaked and softly pleated style in rich colors creates a bold breezy presentation. Standard Pk./15. **$3.99**

Blue
415-W-1381

Yellow
415-W-1382

Purple
415-W-1383

*Do not place in muffin pans. Place directly on cookie sheet and fill halfway with batter.

Be My Cupcake
$2.09
Standard Pk./75.
415-W-127
Mini Pk./100.
415-W-128

Cupcake Heaven
$2.09
Standard Pk./75.
415-W-422
Mini Pk./100.
415-W-426

Bubble Stripes
$2.09
Standard Pk./75.
415-W-114
Mini Pk./100.
415-W-115

Snappy Stripes
$2.09
Standard Pk./75.
415-W-5381
Mini Pk./100.
415-W-5380

Assorted Pastel $1.99
Assorted pink, yellow, blue-green.
Standard Pk./75. 415-W-394
Mini Pk./100. 415-W-2123

Pastel Silicone Baking Cups
Bake and serve in reusable oven-safe cups. 3 each pink, yellow, green, blue. Standard size, 2 in. diameter. Pk./12.
415-W-9410 **$9.99**

Dazzling Dots $1.59
Standard Pk./50.
415-W-582
Mini Pk./75.
415-W-1141

Pink Polka Dots
$2.09
Standard Pk./75.
120-W-169

Lilac Polka Dots
$2.09
Mini Pk./100.
120-W-168

NEW!
Assorted Jewel
$2.09
Assorted gold, purple, teal.
Standard Pk./75.
415-W-1078
Mini Pk./100.
415-W-1111

Assorted Primary $2.09
Assorted red, yellow, blue.
Standard Pk./75.
415-W-987
Mini Pk./100.
415-W-1110

Party Bags
Wrap up cookies, candies, favors and more!
Contains 20, 4 x 9.5 in. bags and 20 twist ties, unless otherwise noted. **$2.09**

Red
1912-W-2357

Gold Foil
$1.99
Wax-laminated paper on foil.
Standard
Pk./24.
415-W-206
Mini Pk./36.
415-W-1413

Silver Foil
$1.99
Wax-laminated paper on foil.
Standard
Pk./24.
415-W-207
Mini Pk./36.
415-W-1414

White
$1.99
Jumbo Pk./50.
415-W-2503
Standard
Pk./75.
415-W-2505
Mini Pk./100.
415-W-2507

White Petite Loaf Cups
Microwave-safe paper. Pk./50.
415-W-450 **$1.59**
Petite Loaf Cups (3.25 x 2 in.) fit Petite Loaf Pan p. 158.

White Nut and Party Cups
Mini 1.25 oz. Pk./36.
415-W-500 **$1.99**
Standard
3.25 oz. Pk./24.
415-W-400 **$1.99**

Dazzling Dots
1912-W-1090

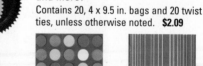
Snappy Stripes
1912-W-1089

Colorful Stars
1912-W-2362

Clear Party Bags
4 x 9.5 in. Each pack contains 25 bags and 25 ties.
1912-W-1240 **$2.09**
Mega pack 50 Ct.
1912-W-1239 **$3.19**
4 x 6 in. Mini Bags
Mega pack 100 Ct.
1912-W-1294 **$4.19**

Clear Shaped Party Bags
4.5 x 7.25 in. Each pack contains 100 bags and 100 ties.
1912-W-1112 **$4.19**

ORDER TOLL FREE: 800-794-5866

Cake Toppers and Stands

With Wilton toppers, a decorated cake is just minutes away! The excellent detail you expect from Wilton is evident in every design.

Musical Light Show Topper

The birthday message flashes brightly while the "Happy Birthday" song is played for everyone to join in. Convenient ON/OFF switch. Requires four AG13 or LR44 Alkaline Button Cell Batteries; 8 batteries included. Each set of 4 batteries lasts for 28 minutes of playing time.
2113-W-3465 $6.49

NEW!

Carousel Cake Display Set

Decorate a grand carousel to match your celebration cake—perfect for birthdays and holidays. Everything you need to transform your tiered cake into a nostalgic carousel is included: 10 in. base plate, carousel canopy top, 4 pillars, 4 horses and a blossom finial on top. Complete assembly and decorating ideas included.
301-W-1335 $24.99

DOLL PICKS

Derby Clowns Set*

2 in. high with pick. Set/6.
2113-W-2759 $2.29

⚠ *WARNING: CHOKING HAZARD Small parts. Not for children under 3 years.

Brunette
2815-W-101

Blond
2815-W-102

Ethnic
2815-W-103

Teen Doll Pick

Her hair and face are prettier than ever—she'll give your Wonder Mold cakes a realism and sophistication unlike anything you've seen. 7.75 in. high with pick. **$3.29**

Mini Doll Pick Set

4.25 in. high with pick. Set/4.
1511-W-1019 $6.49

Entertaining

Every big event needs a main attraction—the Wilton Chocolate Pro Fountain will be the most popular stop at the party!

CHOCOLATE PRO CHOCOLATE FOUNTAIN

• Holds 4 lbs. of melted chocolate
• Tiers come apart for easy cleaning
• Three adjustable feet, plus bubble level, allow perfect leveling from all angles

Bring the excitement of chocolate dipping to your next party! The Chocolate Pro Chocolate Fountain makes it easy to enjoy delicious hand-dipped desserts any time! The graceful canopy style creates an elegant flow from all 3 levels; the bowl is designed to keep chocolate melted and flowing. With the Chocolate Pro, any celebration becomes more special. Let your guests dip cake and cookies for a flavorful finishing touch. Great for fruit, or try a sweet and salty combination by dipping potato chips and pretzels. 120V; UL listed.
2104-W-9008 $109.99

CHOCOLATE PRO FOUNTAIN AND FONDUE CHOCOLATE

The best real melting chocolate for fountains and fondues is here! Made from premium ingredients for superior melting and a delicious chocolate taste. Ideal texture and rich flavor for making dipped desserts. No tempering needed! 2 Lbs.
2104-W-2618 $17.99

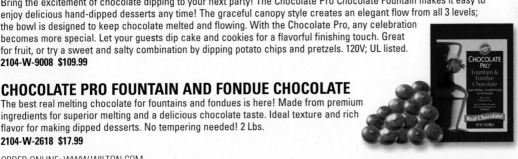

Famous Favorites

Wilton helps you make kids feel like stars! We have a great cast of today's favorite faces and themes on fun party products for cakes, cookies and more.

NEW!

Disney

MICKEY MOUSE CLUBHOUSE

Cake Pan
It's always exciting when *Mickey Mouse* joins the party! Fun design is perfect for kids and adults alike. One-mix pan is 13 x 12 x 2 in. deep. Aluminum.
2105-W-7070 $14.49

Toppers
Top your party treats with *Mickey's* charm and a wink! Plastic toppers are great on cupcakes, brownies, cakes and more. 1.5 in. high. Set/8.
2113-W-7070 $4.49

Candle
Always a party favorite, *Mickey Mouse* candle is handpainted with fun details. Clean-burning. 3 in. high.
2811-W-7070 $4.49

Let's Celebrate!

©Disney
www.DisneyChannel.com

Icing Decorations
Edible sugar shapes to decorate cupcakes, cookies, ice cream and cake. Certified Kosher. Pk./9.
710-W-7070 $2.49

Icing Color Set
Includes four .5 oz. jars: Peach, *Mickey* Skin Tone and 2 Black. Certified Kosher. Set/4.
601-W-7070 $5.99

Baking Cups
Standard size, microwave-safe paper. 2 in. diameter. Pk./50.
415-W-7070 $1.79

Treat Bags
Fill with candy, cookies and other goodies; great for gifts and surprises, too! Includes sixteen 4 x 9.5 in. bags with twist ties. Pk./16.
1912-W-7070 $2.09

ORDER TOLL FREE: 800-794-5866

 NEW!

Cake Pan
Send your celebration "To infinity, and beyond!" *Buzz Lightyear* is simply the coolest space ranger, and this cake is sure to please everyone at the party. One-mix pan is 13 x 10.25 x 2 in. deep. Aluminum.
2105-W-8080 $14.49

Toppers
Exciting *Disney/Pixar Toy Story* characters add more fun to party treats. Plastic toppers are great on cupcakes, brownies, cakes and more. 1.5 in. high. Set/8.
2113-W-8080 $4.49

Baking Cups
Standard size, microwave-safe paper. 2 in. diameter. Pk./50.
415-W-8080 $1.79

Icing Decorations
Edible sugar shapes to decorate cupcakes, cookies, ice cream and cake. Certified Kosher. Pk./12.
710-W-8080 $2.49

Candle
Buzz Lightyear lights up the party. Handpainted candle has colorful, fun details. 3.25 in. high.
2811-W-8080 $4.49

Icing Color Set
Includes four .5 oz. jars: Green, *Buzz Lightyear* Skin Tone, Purple and Black. Certified Kosher. Set/4.
601-W-8080 $5.99

Treat Bags
Fill with candy, cookies and other goodies; great for gifts and surprises too! Includes sixteen 4 x 9.5 in. bags with twist ties. Pk./16.
1912-W-8080 $2.09

©Disney/Pixar
www.ToyStory.com

HELLO KITTY ®

 NEW!

Cake Pan
Hello birthday fun! *Hello Kitty* makes birthday wishes come true with a bright and special celebration cake. Perfect for friends of all ages, this pan creates a cake as sweet as Hello Kitty herself! One-mix pan is 10.5 x 9.25 x 2 in. deep. Aluminum.
2105-W-7575 $14.49

Toppers
Top your treats with *Hello Kitty*! Plastic toppers are great on cupcakes, brownies, cakes and more. 1.4 in. high. Set/8.
2113-W-7575 $4.49

Icing Decorations
Edible sugar shapes to decorate cupcakes, cookies, ice cream and cake. Certified Kosher. Pk./12.
710-W-7575 $2.49

Baking Cups
Standard size, microwave-safe paper. 2 in. diameter. Pk./50.
415-W-7575 $1.79

Candle
Hello Kitty brightens the celebration. Detailed candle is handpainted and clean-burning. 2.2 in. high.
2811-W-7575 $4.49

Icing Color Set
Includes four .5 oz. jars: Red, Pink, Yellow, and Black. Certified Kosher. Set/4.
601-W-7575 $5.99

Treat Bags
Fill with candy, cookies and other goodies; great for gifts and surprises too! Includes sixteen 4 x 9.5 in. bags with twist ties. Pk./16.
1912-W-7575 $2.09

SIL-34223

ORDER TOLL FREE: 800-794-5866

SPONGEBOB SQUAREPANTS™

NEW!

Cake Pan
Everyone's favorite porous pal puts extra excitement in the party. One-mix pan is 11 x 12 x 2 in. deep. Aluminum.
2105-W-5135 **$14.49**

Toppers
SpongeBob takes the cake (and other goodies) with these handpainted plastic toppers. Use on cupcakes, brownies, cakes and other treats. 2 in. high. Set/6.
2113-W-5130 **$4.49**

NEW!

Candle
SpongeBob serves up the best birthday celebration! Handpainted, clean-burning with colorful details. 2.62 in. high.
2811-W-5135 **$4.49**

Icing Decorations
Edible sugar shapes to decorate cupcakes, cookies, ice cream and cake. Certified Kosher. Pk./9.
710-W-5130 **$2.49**

Baking Cups
Standard size, microwave-safe paper. 2 in. diameter. Pk./50.
415-W-5130 **$1.79**

NEW!

Icing Color Set
Includes four .5 oz. jars: Yellow, Red, Blue and Brown. Certified Kosher. Set/4.
601-W-5135 **$5.99**

Treat Bags
Fill with candy, cookies and other goodies; great for gifts and surprises too! Includes sixteen 4 x 9.5 in. bags with twist ties. Pk./16.
1912-W-5130 **$2.09**

Cake Pan
Any party is a joy ride when you serve a cake starring *Lightning McQueen*! All the fun details you love on the big screen are here. One-mix pan is 13.75 x 6.25 x 2.75 in. Aluminum.
2105-W-6400 $14.49

Toppers
Rev up the fun with treats topped with your favorites from *Disney/Pixar Cars*! Handpainted plastic toppers are great on cupcakes, brownies, cakes and other treats. 1.25 in. high. Set/6.
2113-W-6400 $4.49

Icing Decorations
Edible sugar shapes to decorate cupcakes, cookies, ice cream and cake. Certified Kosher. Pk./9.
710-W-6400 $2.49

Baking Cups
Standard size, microwave-safe paper. 2 in. diameter. Pk./50.
415-W-6400 $1.79

Candle
Handpainted, clean-burning with fun details. 3.5 in. high.
2811-W-6400 $4.49

Icing Color Set
Includes four .5 oz. jars: Red, Blue, Yellow, Black. Certified Kosher. Set/4.
601-W-6400 $5.99

Treat Bags
Fill with candy, cookies and other goodies; great for gifts and surprises too! Includes sixteen 4 x 9.5 in. bags with twist ties. Pk./16.
1912-W-6400 $2.09

ORDER TOLL FREE: 800-794-5866

Cake Pan

Enter *Ariel's* world of enchantment under the sea! Her sweet look will captivate kids and bring all the thrills of *The Little Mermaid* story to your celebration. One-mix pan is 10.5 x 11.75 x 2 in. Aluminum.
2105-W-4355 $14.49

Toppers

When *Ariel* surfaces on party desserts, there's a new wave of birthday excitement! Handpainted plastic toppers are great on cupcakes, brownies, cakes and other treats. 1.75 in. high. Set/6.
2113-W-4355 $4.49

© Disney   DisneyPrincess.com

Icing Decorations

Edible sugar shapes to decorate cupcakes, cookies, ice cream and cake. Certified Kosher. Pk./9.
710-W-4355 $2.49

Candle

Handpainted, clean-burning with fun details. 3 in. high.
2811-W-4355 $4.49

Baking Cups

Standard size, microwave-safe paper. 2 in. diameter. Pk./50.
415-W-4355 $1.79

Icing Color Set

Includes four .5 oz. jars: *Ariel* Skin Tone, Teal, Lavender and Red. Certified Kosher. Set/4.
601-W-4355 $5.99

Cake Pan

Tinker Bell makes birthday wishes come true! She brings fun to the celebration on a cake that captures the twinkle in her eye and the magic in her smile. One-mix pan is 10.5 x 12 x 2 in. Aluminum.
2105-W-5110 $14.49

Toppers

Top your treats with *Tinker Bell* and create enchantment! Handpainted food-safe plastic is great on cupcakes, brownies, cakes and other treats. 2¼ in. high. Set/6.
2113-W-5110 $4.49

© Disney
DisneyFairies.com

Icing Decorations

Edible sugar shapes to decorate cupcakes, cookies, ice cream and cake. Certified Kosher. Pk./9.
710-W-5110 $2.49

Candle

Adorable *Tinker Bell* illuminates your cake! Handpainted, clean-burning with colorful details. 3 in. high.
2811-W-5110 $4.49

Baking Cups

Standard size, microwave-safe paper. 2 in. diameter. Pk./50.
415-W-5110 $1.79

Icing Color Set

Includes four .5 oz. jars: Blue, Yellow, Red, *Tinker Bell* Skin Tone. Certified Kosher. Set/4.
601-W-5110 $5.99

SPIDER SENSE SPIDER-MAN™

Icing Decorations
Edible sugar shapes to decorate cupcakes, cookies, ice cream and cake. Certified Kosher. Pk./11.
710-W-5062 $2.49

Cake Pan
When *Spidey* drops in for the party, kids will be captivated! This exciting pan features everyone's favorite web-slinger landing right in the center of the action, for a cake that will be the talk of the celebration. One-mix pan is 13 x 12.75 x 2 in. Aluminum.
2105-W-5062 $14.49

Candle
Handpainted, clean-burning with exciting details. 3 in. high.
2811-W-5062 $4.49

Baking Cups
Standard size, microwave-safe paper. 2 in. diameter. Pk./50.
415-W-5062 $1.79

Toppers
Spider-Man finishes on top again—and he'll complete your treats with excitement! Handpainted plastic toppers are great on cupcakes, brownies, cakes and more. 1.62 in. high. Set/6.
2113-W-5062 $4.49

Icing Color Set
Includes four .5 oz. jars: Blue, 2 Red and Black. Certified Kosher. Set/4.
601-W-5062 $5.99

Treat Bags
Fill with candy, cookies and other goodies; great for gifts and surprises too! Includes sixteen 4 x 9.5 in. bags with twist ties. Pk./16.
1912-W-5062 $2.09

TRANSFORMERS

Cake Pan
Optimus Prime transforms any birthday party into an action-packed celebration! The Transformers have been a smash everywhere they go and now they're here on an energy-charged cake pan kids will love. One-mix pan is 9 x 12 x 2 in. deep. Aluminum.
2105-W-5060 $14.49

Cake Decoration
Handpainted with fun details. 2.75 in. high.
2811-W-5060 $4.49

Baking Cups
Standard size, microwave-safe paper. 2 in. diameter. Pk./50.
415-W-5060 $1.79

Icing Decorations
Edible sugar shapes to decorate cupcakes, cookies, ice cream and cake. Certified Kosher. Pk./9.
710-W-5060 $2.49

Toppers
These robotic aliens capture all the thrills and excitement you'll want at the party. Lenticular image; plastic toppers are great on cupcakes, brownies, cakes and more. 1.5 in. high. Set/6.
2113-W-5060 $4.49

Icing Color Set
Includes four .5 oz. jars: Blue, Dark Blue, Gray and Black. Certified Kosher. Set/4.
601-W-5060 $5.99

Treat Bags
Fill with candy, cookies and other goodies; great for gifts and surprises too! Includes sixteen 4 x 9.5 in. bags with closures. Pk./16.
1912-W-5060 $2.09

ORDER TOLL FREE: 800-794-5866

Icing Decorations
Edible sugar shapes to decorate cupcakes, cookies, ice cream and cakes. Certified Kosher. Pk./9.
710-W-3460 $2.49

NEW!

Cupcake Toppers
Elmo always adds fun to your celebration. Top your party cupcakes, treats, brownies, and more with Elmo's bright smile! 1.5 in. high. Pk./8
2113-W-3461 $4.49

Baking Cups
Standard size, microwave-safe paper. 2 in. diameter. Pk./50.
**415-W-3461
$1.79**

NEW!

Elmo Face
Cake Pan
He's sweet, lovable and popular with kids of all ages. One-mix pan is 13.5 x 10.5 x 2 in. Aluminum.
2105-W-3461 $14.49

Elmo Birthday Candle
Elmo brings smiles to the party. Handpainted, clean-burning with colorful details. 3.12 in. high.
2811-W-3464 $4.49

Treat Bags
Fill with candy, cookies and other goodies; great for gifts and surprises too! Includes sixteen 4 x 9.5 in. bags with closures. Pk./16.
**1912-W-3461
$2.09**

Icing Decorations
Edible sugar shapes to decorate cupcakes, cookies, ice cream and cake. Certified Kosher. Pk./8.
710-W-6300 $2.49

DORA the EXPLORER™

NEW!

Cake Pan
¡Vámonos! Travel along with Dora to make the best birthday cake for your celebration. The bright design is perfect for all ages. One mix pan is 11 x 11 x 2 in. deep. Aluminum.
2105-W-6305 $14.49

NEW!

Candle
Dora puts the finishing touch on your cake with bright colors and adventure. Detailed, handpainted and clean-burning. 2.6 in. high.
2811-W-6305 $4.49

NEW!

Baking Cups
Standard size, microwave-safe paper. 2 in. diameter. Pk./50.
**415-W-6305
$1.79**

NEW!

Treat Bags
Fill with candy, cookies and other goodies; great for gifts and surprises too! Includes sixteen 4 x 9.5 in. bags with twist ties. Pk./16.
**1912-W-6305
$2.09**

Toppers
Dora is ready to top your delightful party treats! Handpainted plastic toppers are great on cupcakes, brownies, cakes and other treats. 2.25 in. high. Set/6.
2113-W-6300 $4.49

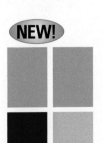

NEW!

Icing Color Set
Includes four .5 oz. jars: Purple, Pink, Brown and Dora Skin Tone. Certified Kosher. Set/4.
**601-W-6305
$5.99**

Candy Making

Let Wilton show you how much fun candy making can be! Use our Candy Melts and molds for beautiful candy in 3 easy steps—just melt, mold and serve!

Candy Melts

Delicious, creamy, easy-to-melt wafers are ideal for all your candy making—molding, dipping or drizzling.
14 oz. bag. Certified Kosher Dairy.
$2.99

NEW!

Pastels
1911-W-490

Brights
1911-W-491

Colorburst Candy Melts

Capture a rainbow of color in every candy you mold with Colorburst Candy Melts! Brilliant flecks of color are blended into each easy-melting wafer, for candies that will look great for showers, receptions, holidays and more. 10 oz. bag. Certified Kosher Dairy.
$2.99

Dark Cocoa
1911-W-358

Light Cocoa
1911-W-544

Dark Cocoa Mint
1911-W-1920

Peanut Butter
1911-W-481

Green
1911-W-405

Blue
1911-W-448

Yellow
1911-W-463

Orange
1911-W-1631

Red
1911-W-499

Pink
1911-W-447

Lavender
1911-W-403

White
1911-W-498

Candy Melts Decorating Pen Set

Give your homemade candies a delicious touch of color with these easy-melting candy pens. Just melt in hot water and squeeze into detailed areas of candy mold. The snip-off tip makes it easy to control the flow and add great-looking details. Includes 1.6 oz. tubes of Red, Yellow, Blue and White. Set/4.
1914-W-1285 $10.99

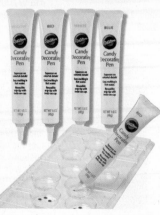

Candy Decorating Bags

The convenient way to melt small amounts of Candy Melts and pipe color detail in your molds! Or, drizzle candy designs over molded candies and desserts. Flexible 12 in. plastic bags—just use, then toss. Pk./12.
2104-W-4825 $4.29

Candy Melting Accessories

CHOCOLATE PRO ELECTRIC MELTING POT

The fast and easy way to melt chocolate and Candy Melts!
• Melting base stays cool to the touch
• Removeable non-stick Melting Pot holds 2½ cups
• Easy-pour spout
• Non-skid feet keep Chocolate Pro steady
It's the fast and fun way to mold candies like a pro. With the Chocolate Pro, you'll be able to mold lollipops and fancy dipped-center candies. Serve elegant dipped desserts like fruit, cake, cookies and fondue. Add the great taste of chocolate to potato chips and pretzels. Create flavored chocolate sauces for ice cream or silky ganache glaze to pour over cakes. 120 volts. cUL Listed.
2104-W-9004 $32.99

CANDY MELTS STAY-WARM CERAMIC MELTING CUPS & BOWLS

Ceramic keeps candy melted longer for easier candy-making because microwave-safe ceramic retains heat. Great for heating and pouring dessert toppings too.

Melting Cups
Cups are great for melting colors separately. Use them like an art palette for painting colors. Holds heat up to ½ hour. Includes 6 cups (2 x 1.5 in. deep) and 6 decorating brushes. Set/12.
1904-W-1067 $10.99

Melting Bowls
Ideal for filling all types of Wilton molds. Take them to the table for easy dipping. Holds heat up to 1 hour. Two, 4 x 3.5 in. deep. Set/2.
1904-W-1076 $10.99

Pretzel Molds

Easy to mold: add your favorite melted Candy Melts, position pretzel rod and chill to set. **$1.99**

Race Car
2 designs,
6 cavities.
2115-W-1034

Baby
2 designs, 6 cavities.
2115-W-2101

Butterfly
2 designs, 6 cavities.
2115-W-1032

Smiley Face
1 design, 6 cavities.
2115-W-4437

Flowers
1 design, 6 cavities.
2115-W-4436

Presents
1 design, 6 cavities.
2115-W-4442

Candy Color Sets

Primary Candy Color Set

Concentrated oil-based colors blend easily with Candy Melts. Includes Yellow, Orange, Red and Blue in .25 oz. jars. Certified Kosher. Set/4.
1913-W-1299 $3.99

Garden Candy Color Set

Create pretty pastel colors! Concentrated oil-based colors blend easily with Candy Melts. Includes Pink, Green, Violet and Black in .25 oz. jars. Certified Kosher. Set/4.
1913-W-1298 $3.99

Cookie Candy Molds

Turn store-bought cookies into candy-coated treats! With Cookie Candy Molds and easy-melting Wilton Candy Melts, it's a breeze to add a great tasting and colorful candy design to your favorite cookies. Just brush colored candy details in the mold, let set, then add more melted candy and position your cookie in the mold. Great for sandwich cream cookies or any round cookie 2 in. diameter or less. **$1.99**

Animals
4 designs, 8 cavities.
2115-W-1354

Sports
4 designs, 8 cavities.
2115-W-1353

Flowers
2 designs, 8 cavities.
2115-W-1351

Hearts
2 designs, 8 cavities.
2115-W-1352

Classic Candy Molds

Wilton has a great selection of traditional shapes to create elegant gift assortments and party trays.

Dessert Accents

Finish your signature dessert with flair—top it with a dramatic candy shape using this exciting mold. Swirls, scrolls, zigzags, triangles and leaves add 5-star style. 5 designs, 10 cavities.
2115-W-2102 $1.99

Dessert Shells

2-piece mold.
1 design,
3 cavities.
2115-W-1035
$2.99

Truffles
1 design, 14 cavities.
2115-W-1521 $1.99

Peanut Butter Cups
1 design, 11 cavities.
2115-W-1522 $1.99

Deep Heart Truffles
1 design, 8 cavities.
2117-W-100 $1.99

Cordial Cups
Mold a candy "glass" for dessert liqueurs, or fill with whipped cream and float in cocoa or coffee. 1 design, 6 cavities.
2115-W-1535 $1.99

Mint Discs
1 design, 18 cavities.
2115-W-1739 $1.99

Gift Truffles
1 design, 15 cavities.
2115-W-1728 $1.99

CANDY MAKING

Candy Molds

More fun shapes and greater detail make Wilton Candy Molds the perfect way to create candy. Look at the variety! You can do it all, from exciting kids' party treats to elegant wedding and shower favors. Molding and coloring couldn't be easier when you use Candy Melts. Look for terrific design ideas and molding instructions on every mold package. For specific Holiday designs, see our Seasonal Section, p. 204-227

LARGE LOLLIPOP MOLDS

NEW!

Big Top
3 designs, 3 cavities.
2115-W-2116 $1.99

NEW!

Pirate
3 designs, 3 cavities.
2115-W-2111 $1.99

Monkey
3 designs, 3 cavities.
2115-W-2100 $1.99

Fairy Tale
3 designs, 3 cavities.
2115-W-1033 $1.99

Party/Birthday
4 designs, 4 cavities.
2115-W-4434 $1.99

Pinwheel
2 designs, 3 cavities.
2115-W-4443 $1.99

Sports
4 designs, 4 cavities.
2115-W-4432 $1.99

Double Heart
2 designs, 4 cavities.
2115-W-4440 $1.99

CANDYPICK MOLDS

NEW!

Create colorful candy toppers to transform plain cakes and cupcakes into exciting party treats! It's easy, using your favorite Candy Melts colors and these detailed molds in 4 fun themes.

Happy Birthday
9 designs, 9 cavities.
2115-W-2110 $1.99

Big Top
2 designs, 8 cavities.
2115-W-2117 $1.99

Pirate
2 designs, 8 cavities.
2115-W-2112 $1.99

Princess
2 designs, 8 cavities.
2115-W-2113 $1.99

2-PACK CANDY MOLD SETS

Girl Power
10 designs, 10 cavities. Pk./2.
2115-W-1604 $2.99

Baby
10 designs, 10 cavities. Pk./2.
2115-W-1605 $2.99

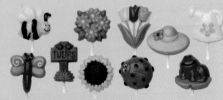

Garden Goodies Lollipop
10 designs, 10 cavities. Pk./2.
2115-W-1607 $2.99

CANDY & LOLLIPOP MOLDS

Stars
1 design, 12 cavities,
2115-W-1554 $1.99

Roses in Bloom
1 design, 10 cavities.
2115-W-1738 $1.99

Hearts
1 design, 15 cavities.
2115-W-1712 $1.99

Dancing Daisies Lollipop
1 design, 9 cavities.
2115-W-1430 $1.99

Smiley Face Lollipop
1 design, 10 cavities.
2115-W-1715 $1.99

Rubber Ducky
1 design, 6 cavities.
2115-W-1565 $1.99

Sea Creatures Lollipop
5 designs, 5 cavities.
2115-W-1414 $1.99

Seashells
5 designs, 11 cavities.
2115-W-1561 $1.99

Baby Treats
5 designs, 5 cavities.
2115-W-4447 $1.99

Wedding Shower Lollipop
5 designs, 10 cavities.
(4 lollipop, 6 candy).
2115-W-1711 $1.99

Wedding Favor
3 designs, 6 cavities.
2115-W-4446 $1.99

Roses & Buds Lollipop
3 designs, 9 cavities.
(4 lollipop, 5 candy).
2115-W-1708 $1.99

10-PACK CANDY MOLD SET

Be ready for any celebration with this great variety of theme molds! Includes 72 total shapes and 114 total cavities for fun candy messages, sports treats, flowers and more. Pk./10.
2115-W-1724 $9.99

Alphabet
26 designs, 26 cavities

Numbers
10 designs, 10 cavities

Transportation
6 designs, 7 cavities

Sports Champ
7 designs, 7 cavities

Celebration
5 designs, 10 cavities

Hearts
1 design, 15 cavities

Peanut Butter Cups
1 design, 11 cavities

Snack Time
6 designs, 12 cavities

Fruit Lollipop
5 designs, 5 cavities

Garden Flowers
5 designs, 11 cavities

Candy Making Tools

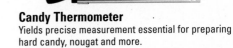

Candy Thermometer
Yields precise measurement essential for preparing hard candy, nougat and more.
1904-W-1200 $14.99

Candy Dipping Set
Easy-handling spoon and fork, each 7.75 in. long. Set/2.
1904-W-3230 $3.29

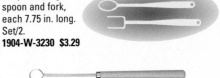

Metal Dipping Set
Professional-quality stainless steel with wooden handles. 8.75 in. long. Set/2.
1904-W-925 $10.99

Easy-Pour Funnel
Push-button controls flow of candy. 5 x 4 in. diameter, nylon.
1904-W-552 $4.29

Squeeze Bottles
Melt candy with ease, then fill your mold without mess! Our convenient bottles are available in 3 sizes so you can melt just the amount of Candy Melts you need, right in the bottle. Great way to store and reheat leftover candy.

Regular
12 oz.
1904-W-1189 $1.99

Mini
6 oz. Pk./2.
1904-W-1166 $1.99

Candy Melting Plate
Microwave-melt up to 11 Candy Melts colors at one time with less mess! Plastic with non-slip grip edge. Includes decorating brush.
1904-W-8016 $3.29

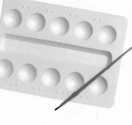

Decorator Brush Set
Plastic, durable bristles, easy-to-hold handle. Set/3.
2104-W-9355 $1.69

Candy Wraps and Boxes

Your homemade candy deserves a beautiful presentation. Wilton has everything you need to wrap and package your candy gifts like a pro.

Accessories

Create the perfect pop with sticks in every size. Clear wrappers and tags make giving easy.

Pretzel Candy Gift Boxes

Your tempting pretzel pop gifts show through the front window. Tented design holds pretzels upright to protect against breakage. 3 x 2 x 9.5 in. high. White. Pk./3.
1904-W-2000 $2.99

Tented Candy Gift Boxes

Stand-up design with front window will give your homemade candy gift the ideal showcase. 3.25 x 1.6 x 5.75 in. high. White. Pk./3.
1904-W-1087 $2.29

Lollipop Tags

Write a name or a message, then slide the tag onto your lollipop stick. Perfect for party lollipops, cookie pops and more. Pk./12.
$2.29
Flower 1904-W-1071
Star   1904-W-1089

Drawstring Lollipop Bags

Fill with your favorite candies, then pull the drawstring to close—a fun way to give your goodies. Clear bags are also great for cookies, nuts and other treats. 4.5 x 5.5 in. Pk./15.
1912-W-9469 $2.29

Candy Gift Boxes

For attractive gift giving.
1 Lb. White Candy Boxes
Pk./3. **$2.99**
1904-W-1172
½ Lb. Candy Boxes
Pk./3. **$2.29**
White 1904-W-1150
Red 1904-W-1152

"Home Made" Box Seals

Let everyone know the care you put into your candy gift with these embossed seals. Add this "homemade" touch whenever you give baked goods too! Pk./24.
1904-W-8936 $1.29

Love Chocolate Candy Gift Boxes

Bright, fun pattern makes your gift even sweeter! Pk./3.
½ Lb. Candy Boxes 1904-W-4242 $2.29

Truffle Boxes

An elegant look, with a lock-close top that forms a perfect "bow." Holds 2-3 pieces of candy. Pk./4. **$2.29**
White 1904-W-1154
Gold 1904-W-1156

Lollipop Wrapping Kit

Cover your candy lollipops and special treats for gift-giving! Contains 18 sticks, (4 in.) 18 bags (3 x 4 in.), 18 twist ties.
1904-W-1193 $2.29

Clear Treat Bags Only
3 x 4 in. Pk./50.
1912-W-2347 $2.89

Glassine Candy Cups

Crisply-pleated, just like professionals use. White glassine-coated paper. **$1.79**
1.25 in. Diameter
Pk./75.
1912-W-1245
1 in. Diameter
Pk./100.
1912-W-1243

Pretzel Bags

See-through bags are ideal for showing off your candy-coated pretzels—great for favors and gifts. 20 plastic bags, 20 twist ties. 2.25 x 9.75 in. Pk./20.
1912-W-5911 $2.29

Foil Wrappers

Bright, shiny coverings for candy and lollipops! 4 x 4 in. squares. Pk./50.
$1.99
Gold   1904-W-1197
Silver 1904-W-1196
Red   1904-W-1198

Foil Candy Cups

Crisply-pleated, just like professionals use. Wax-laminated paper on foil. Pk./75.
$1.79
Red   415-W-314
Blue   415-W-313
Pink   415-W-315
Gold   415-W-306
Silver 415-W-307

Lollipop Sticks

Sturdy paper sticks in 4 sizes. Not for oven use.
4 in. Pk./50.
1912-W-1006 $1.99
6 in. Pk./35.
1912-W-1007 $1.99
8 in. Pk./25.
1912-W-9320 $1.99
11¾ in. Pk./20.
1912-W-1212 $3.99

ORDER TOLL FREE: 800-794-5866

Cookie Making

Wilton has just what you need to make cookies fun! Easy-to-use presses, colossal cutter sets, fun stencils, colorful icings and unique toppings sure to create unforgettable cookies!

Cookie Presses

Wilton has the best selection of feature-packed presses anywhere! From our Comfort Grip Press, designed for easy handling and filling, to our powerful cordless Cookie Master Plus, spritz cookie-making has never been easier!

Making traditional spritz cookies has never been so easy! Cookie Pro Ultra II is designed to be the easiest to fill, most comfortable press you've ever used. And, with 12 terrific shapes, plus 4 fun mini cookie designs, your holiday cookie baskets will be more festive than ever! Includes complete instructions and delicious recipes. Set/17.
2104-W-4018 $24.99

Twelve Disks in Festive Shapes

Plus 4 BONUS Disks For Mini Cookies!

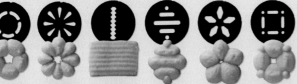

COOKIE MASTER *Plus*
Cordless Cookie Press

Our cordless cookie press is so powerful and easy to operate, you'll use it all year to create cookies, appetizers, desserts and more. Exclusive patented reverse action means there's no need to take press apart for refilling. Ergonomic design is shaped to fit in your hand for excellent comfort.

Includes 12 aluminum disks in classic and seasonal shapes, 4 accent tips for decorating and filling and 2 bonus recipe booklets—sweet and savory. Uses 4 AA batteries, not included. Patent Nos. D484,755; 6,701,828. Set/19.
2104-W-4008 $39.99

4 Accent Tips

12 Disk Designs

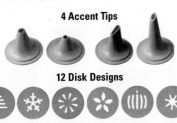

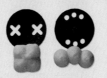

COMFORT GRIP
Cookie Press

Experience a classic press that is truly comfortable. Its ergonomic handle feels great in your hand and the easy-squeeze action releases perfectly shaped dough. Clear barrel takes the guesswork out of refilling. Fluted bottom raises press off the cookie sheet for better-defined shapes. Includes 12 cookie disks in a variety of shapes and our classic spritz recipe. Set/13.
2104-W-4011 $12.99

12 Disk Designs

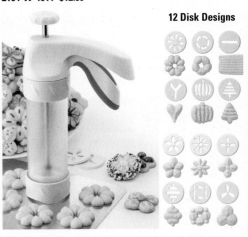

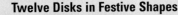

Comfort-Grip Cutters

Easy-grip stainless steel cutters with extra-deep sides are perfect for cutting so many favorite foods into spectacular shapes. Ideal for brownies, biscuits, sandwiches, sheet cakes, cheese, crispy rice treats, fudge and much more. The cushion grip gives you comfortable control even when cutting into thick desserts. Each approximately 4 x 4 x 1.75 in. Recipe included. **Each $3.19**

Heart
2310-W-616

Round
2310-W-608

Flower
2310-W-613

Teddy Bear
2310-W-609

Double Heart
2310-W-647

Daisy
2310-W-619

Butterfly
2310-W-614

Star
2310-W-605

Cookie Decorating Accents

Add that extra touch that makes cookies more exciting. With Wilton products it's easy! Squeeze on the fun with Wilton Cookie Icing and Icing Writer, for colorful decorations with a satin finish. Or let kids draw designs and messages in cool colors with FoodWriter Edible Color Markers.

FOODWRITER EDIBLE COLOR MARKERS

Use edible markers to add fun and dazzling color to countless foods. Kids love 'em! Decorate on Wilton Cookie Icing, fondant, color flow and royal icing designs. Brighten everyday foods like toaster pastries, cheese, fruit slices, bread, more. Each set includes five .07 oz. FoodWriter pens. Certified Kosher. Set/5. **$8.49**

Primary Colors Sets

Yellow Green Red

Blue Black

Bold Tip 609-W-115
Fine Tip 609-W-100

Neon Colors Set

Purple Orange Pink Light Green Black

Fine Tip 609-W-116

FINE TIP   **BOLD TIP**

COOKIE ICING

Use this quick-setting microwavable icing to cover your cookies with a smooth finish—perfect for decorating with colorful Wilton Icing Writer accents! Easy to use—just heat and squeeze onto cookies using the convenient cap. Sets smooth in just 1 hour. 10 oz. bottle covers approximately 12 (3 in.) cookies. Certified Kosher. **$4.49**

White 704-W-481
Red   704-W-488
Green 704-W-493
Blue   704-W-444

ICING WRITER

Squeeze colorful accents onto fondant and Wilton Cookie Icing with this ready-to-use icing! It's easy to control, just squeeze the bottle and icing flows smoothly from the built-in round tip. Dries to a smooth, satin finish. 3 oz. bottle. Certified Kosher. **$2.49**

Yellow   **Pink**
710-W-2226   710-W-2230

Red   **White**
710-W-2225   710-W-2228

Green   **Violet**   **Blue**
710-W-2229   710-W-2231   710-W-2227

Cookie Sprinkles & Sugars

6-MIX COLORED SPRINKLE ASSORTMENTS

They're so convenient! Assorted fun shapes in an easy-pour flip-top bottle. Top cupcakes, ice cream and other goodies. Certified Kosher. **$4.99**

4-MIX COLORED SUGAR ASSORTMENTS

Brighten up plain cookies fast with our colorful decorating sugars. Just sprinkle these extra-fine sugars on your sweet treats before baking, or after cookies are iced. Certified Kosher. **$4.99**

Nonpareils
Includes Pink, Orange, Green, Red, Yellow, Purple. 3 oz. total.
710-W-4125

Jimmies
Includes Pink, Orange, Green, Red, Yellow, Blue. 2.52 oz. total.
710-W-4127

Brights 4-Mix
Contains Pink, Yellow, Light Green, Lavender. 4.4 oz. total.
710-W-651

Primary 4-Mix
Contains Red, Dark Green, Blue, Yellow. 4.4 oz. total.
710-W-650

Cookie Cutters

Wilton has more cutter shapes than anyone—and we've gathered your favorites in convenient sets. From our big 101 Cookie Cutters Set, with a variety of popular themes to specialty collections of animals, flowers, letters and more, Wilton has a set perfect for any occasion.

PLASTIC CUTTER SETS

101 Cookie Cutters

With this set, you're covered! Make cookies featuring popular holiday and theme shapes like sports, flowers, animals and more. Or use the complete alphabet and numeral collections included to create the perfect cookie message. Great for cutting all kinds of food into fun shapes—perfect for crafting, too. Average cutter size approx. 3.5 x 3.5 in. Recipe included. Set/101.
2304-W-1050 $14.99

Animal Pals 50-Piece Cutter Set

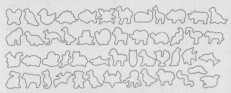

Everyone will go wild for cookies, foods and crafts made with this menagerie of favorite animal shapes. Shapes include fish, dog, cat, birds, butterflies, reptiles and more. Average cutter size approx. 3.5 x 3.5 in. Recipe included. Set/50.
2304-W-1055 $8.99

A-B-C and 1-2-3 50-Piece Cutter Set

Complete alphabet and numeral collection, great for cookies, brownies, gelatin treats, learning games, crafts and more. Average cutter size approx. 3.5 x 3.5 in. Recipe included. Set/50.
2304-W-1054 $8.99

Plastic Cutters

With our large variety of brightly-colored cutter shapes, the making is as much fun as the eating! Child-safe design means kids can help. Each approx. 3 x 4 in. **Each $0.69**

Fish 2303-W-128	**Dinosaur** 2303-W-112	**Teddy Bear** 2303-W-133	**Butterfly** 2303-W-116	**Puppy** 2303-W-137	**Dog Bone** 2303-W-123

Star 2303-W-135	**Hand** 2303-W-147	**Foot** 2303-W-113	**Girl** 2303-W-120	**Boy** 2303-W-124	**Airplane** 2303-W-101	**Flower** 2303-W-117

Locomotive Engine 2303-W-139	**Cat** 2303-W-118	**Heart** 2303-W-100	**Duck** 2303-W-148	**Four-Leaf Clover** 2303-W-134	**Cross** 2303-W-141

Plastic Nesting Cutter Sets

Your favorites in child-safe, graduated shapes. Discover all the fun ways to use our cutters—for bread shapes, stencils, sun catchers and so much more.

Blossom
1.2 to 4.5 in.
Set/6.
2304-W-116 $2.99

Heart
1.5 to 4.2 in.
Set/6.
2304-W-115 $2.99

Star
1.6 to 4.6 in.
Set/6.
2304-W-111 $2.99

Cookie Cutters

COLORED METAL CUTTER SETS

Multi-piece sets represent popular themes. Built to last, they cut cleanly and release easily. Recipe included. Each approx. 3 in.

 NEW!

Flower
Tulip, butterfly, and daisy. Set/3.
2308-W-0948
$3.69

NEW!

Pet
Paw, bone, doghouse, and dog. Set/4.
2308-W-0910
$4.79

NEW!

Party
Cake, cupcake, present, and party hat. Set/4.
2308-W-0909
$4.79

Wedding
Cake, dress, bells and double heart. Set/4.
2308-W-1071
$4.79

Baby
Carriage, rocking horse, teddy bear, and onesie. Set/4.
2308-W-1067
$4.79

Football
Pennant, football, jersey, and helmet. Set/4.
2308-W-1263
$4.79

METAL CUTTER SETS

Multi-piece sets add variety. Built to last, they cut cleanly and release easily. Recipe included.

Mini Romantic
Butterfly, heart, bell, crinkled heart, tulip, and blossom. Each approx. 1.5 in. Set/6.
2308-W-1225 $3.29

Mini Noah's Ark
Horse, ark, elephant, bear, giraffe and lion. Each approx. 1.5 in. Set/6.
2308-W-1206 $3.29

Mini Geometric Crinkle
Square, circle, heart, diamond, oval and triangle. Each approx. 1.5 in. Set/6.
2308-W-1205 $3.29

Classic
Geometric, crinkle diamond, heart, half moon, star and flower. Each approx. 3 in. Set/6.
2308-W-1235 $5.29

Bug Buddies
Caterpillar, dragonfly, spider, butterfly, bee and ladybug. Each approx. 3 in. Set/6.
2308-W-1245 $5.29

Hearts
Seven different heart cutter designs from stylized to traditional. Sizes range from 1.5 to 3 in. Set/7.
2308-W-1237 $5.29

Nesting From The Heart
Two crinkled, two smooth. Largest is approx. 5 in. Set/4.
2308-W-1203 $4.79

NEW!

Nesting Circles
You'll use every size in this classic shape! Largest is approx. 5 in. Set/4.
2308-W-0914 $4.79

NEW!

Nesting Butterflies
Fluttering fun in four sizes. Largest is approx. 5 in. Set/4.
2308-W-1119 $4.79

Nesting Stars
For holidays and more! Largest is approx. 5 in. Set/4.
2308-W-1215 $4.79

Nesting Blossoms
Flowers in four sizes. Largest is approx. 5 in. Set/4.
2308-W-1204 $4.79

METAL CUTTERS

Metal cutters from Wilton are built to last through years of cookie making; they cut cleanly and release with ease. Each shape is approximately 3 in.
Each $0.69

Daisy
2308-W-1007

Butterfly
2308-W-1015

Chick
2308-W-1000

Heart
2308-W-1003

Fish
2308-W-1017

Shamrock
2308-W-1011

Star
2308-W-1008

Gingerbread Boy
2308-W-1002

Bear
2308-W-1009

Bell
2308-W-1006

Circle
2308-W-1010

Cross
2308-W-1018

Cookie Bakeware and Accessories

Cookie Treat Pans

Cookie treats on a stick are so easy! Just press cookie dough into pan, insert a cookie stick, then bake, cool and decorate. Create your own cookie blossoms for that special someone; also great for rice cereal treats and candy. Recipe included. Each pan makes 6 individual treats, 3.5 in. x .25 in. deep. Aluminum.
Each $9.99

Star
2105-W-8102

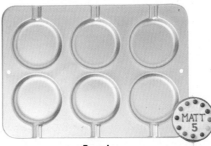

Round
2105-W-8105

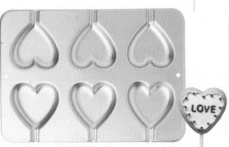

Heart
2105-W-0580

Blossom
2105-W-8109

Cookie Treat Sticks
For fun cookie pops.
6 in. Pk./20.
1912-W-9319 $1.99
8 in. Pk./20.
1912-W-9318 $2.99

Clear Party Bags
4 x 9.5 in. Each pack contains 25 bags and 25 ties.
1912-W-1240 $2.09

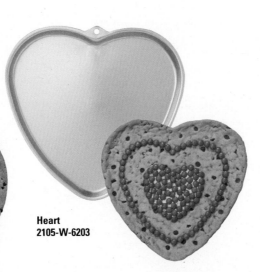

Round
2105-W-6201

Heart
2105-W-6203

Giant Cookie Pans
Our Giant Cookie Pans help you create a jumbo pan cookie in a shape that will be a big hit for any occasion. Specially designed for one package of refrigerated dough, they are also great for brownies and pizza! Each shape is approximately .75 in. deep and can be used with recipes that call for a standard 13 x 9 in. pan. Aluminum. **Each $7.49**

Cookie Sheets
Wilton Cookie Sheets are extra thick aluminum to heat evenly for perfect browning.

Aluminum
Extra-thick construction.
Jumbo 14 x 20 in.
2105-W-6213 $19.99

Insulated Aluminum
Two quality aluminum layers sandwich an insulating layer of air for perfect browning without burning.
16 x 14 in.
2105-W-2644 $20.99

Cooling Grids
Chrome
Sturdy design will never rust.
13 in. Round
2305-W-130 $8.99
10 x 16 in.
2305-W-128 $6.99
14.5 x 20 in.
2305-W-129 $9.99

Non-Stick
Cookies and cakes won't stick with our slick non-stick coating.
13 in. Round
2305-W-230 $10.49
10 x 16 in.
2305-W-228 $9.99
14.5 x 20 in.
2305-W-229 $14.49

3-Pc. Stackable Chrome-Plated
Use singly or stack to save space while cooling three batches of cookies at the same time. Individual grids are 13.5 x 9.75 x 3 in. high; stacked grids are 9.75 in. high.
2305-W-151 $14.49

See p. 154-166 for the full line of Wilton Bakeware.

Non-Stick Parchment Paper
Use Wilton silicone-treated non-stick parchment to line baking pans and cookie sheets—a non-fat alternative that saves cleanup time. Oven-safe to 400°F, great for conventional ovens, microwaves and the freezer. Double roll is 41 square feet, 15 in. wide. Certified Kosher.
415-W-680 $5.29

Cookie Spatula
Angled stainless steel blade moves cookies from pan to plate with ease. Slides easily under cookies—great for serving brownies and bar cookies too. Comfortable ergonomic handle with thumb rest. 9 in. long.
409-W-6054 $6.99

Jumbo Cookie Spatula
Generously-sized spatula is great for handling multiple or oversized cookies, brownies, pastries and large treat bars. The easy-grip handle helps balance large cookies and desserts. Stainless steel; dishwasher safe. 11 in. long.
570-W-2018 $6.99

COOKIE MAKING

Seasonal

Wilton makes every time of year worth celebrating! With so many fun ways to serve cakes, cookies and other treats, it's easy to let everyone taste the excitement of each season.

HALLOWEEN

Bakeware

NON-STICK MINI CAKE PANS

Bake fun single-size cakes, brownies and more. Non-stick steel releases treats easily. One mix makes 24-28 treats, each 3.75 x 1.25 in. deep.
$11.99

Jack-O-Lantern
2105-W-1541

Skulls
2105-W-1511

NEW!

Iridescents! Jack-O-Lantern Pan

This bright, colorful shape is as much fun for serving party treats as it is for baking! Designed for quick, easy cake decorating. Also ideal for crisped rice cereal treats, molded gelatin, bread dough and more. One-mix pan is 11.75 x 11.2 x 2 in. deep. Aluminum.
2105-W-2059 $7.49

Petite Jack-O-Lantern Pan

Make personal petite smiling pumpkins. One mix makes 9-13 dozen jack-o-lanterns. 12 cavities, each 2 x 1.2 in. deep. Aluminum.
2105-W-8462 $11.99

SILICONE MOLDS

Discover the convenience and easy release of flexible silicone bakeware! Freezer, refrigerator, microwave and dishwasher safe— oven safe to 500°F. One mix makes 20-24 treats. 6 cavities, each 2.5 x 1.5 in. deep.
$9.99

Mini Jack-O-Lantern Faces
2105-W-4939

Mini Scary Skulls
2105-W-4899

NEW!

Icings

See Color Guide at right.

Striped Icing

Create fun 2-color decorations in colors perfect for the season. Tubes can be used with our Tip and Nail Set or Coupler Ring Set (p. 142) and Wilton metal tips. The larger sized star, petal or leaf tips optimize the two-tone effect. 4.25 oz. Certified Kosher. **$2.49**
Orange/Black **704-W-202**
Green/Black **704-W-201**

Tube Decorating Icing

Tubes can be used with our Tip and Nail Set or Coupler Ring Set (p. 142) and any standard size Wilton metal tip. Colors match Wilton Icing Colors (p. 146). 4.25 oz. Certified Kosher. **$1.99**
Orange   **704-W-212**
Black   **704-W-206**
Violet   **704-W-242**
White   **704-W-200**

Tube Decorating Gel

Transparent gels are great for writing messages and decorating cakes and cookies. Colors match Wilton Icing Colors (p. 146). .75 oz. Certified Kosher. **$1.49**
Orange   **704-W-312**
Black   **704-W-306**
Violet   **704-W-342**
White   **704-W-302**

Sparkle Gel

Squeeze on sparkling color effects with our ready-to-use gel. Great for dots, messages and fondant accents. Resealable 3.5 oz. tube. Certified Kosher. **$2.99**
Orange **704-W-109**
Black   **704-W-1061**
White   **704-W-107**

Cookie Icing

Easy to use—just heat and squeeze onto cookies using the convenient cap. Sets smooth in just 1 hour. 10 oz. bottle covers approximately 12 cookies, 3 in. each. Certified Kosher. **$4.49**
White   **704-W-481**
Orange **704-W-496**
Black   **704-W-205**

Ready-to-Decorate Icing

Anyone can decorate with Wilton Ready-to-Decorate Icing! Our brilliant colors and 4 decorating tips make it a breeze to add an exciting finishing touch to treats—without mixing or mess. 6.4 oz. Certified Kosher. **$4.29**
Orange   **710-W-4410**
Black   **710-W-4404**
Violet   **710-W-4408**
White   **710-W-4402**

Colors

HALLOWEEN COLOR GUIDE

| Orange | Black | Violet | White |

Halloween Icing Colors Set

.5 oz. jars of Black and Orange. Certified Kosher. Set/2
601-W-3010 $2.99

FoodWriter Edible Ink Markers

Add fun, dazzling color to foods. Decorate on fondant, color flow, royal icing designs and cookie icing. Includes Black and Orange markers (.07 oz. each). Certified Kosher. Set/2.
609-W-101 $4.29

Color Mist Food Color Spray

Gives decorators the versatility and dazzling effects of an airbrush in a convenient can! Use it to add sensational color to iced cookies and cupcakes. No mess, taste-free formula. 1.5 oz. Certified Kosher.
$3.29
Orange **710-W-5507**
Black   **710-W-5506**
Violet **710-W-5504**

Party

Baking Cups

Microwave-safe paper. Standard size, 2 in. diameter, Pk./75. Mini size, 1.25 in. diameter, Pk./100. $2.09

NEW!

Polka Dot Pumpkin
Standard **415-W-1270**
Mini **415-W-1271**

Skulls & Scrolls
Standard **415-W-1267**
Mini **415-W-1268**

Haunted Manor
Standard **415-W-1114**
Mini **415-W-1116**

Party Bags

Colorful Halloween designs for candy and cookie treats. Unless otherwise noted, 20 plastic bags, 20 ties included. 4 x 9.5 in. Pk./20. $2.09

NEW! **NEW!**

Polka Dot Pumpkin
1912-W-1064

Skulls & Scrolls
1912-W-1068

Haunted Manor
1912-W-1028

Shaped Bags with Ties

Large bags are 6 x 9 in. 15 plastic bags, 15 ties included. Pk./15. $2.09

NEW! **NEW!**

Polka Dot Pumpkin
1912-W-1065

Skulls & Scrolls
1912-W-1070

Haunted Manor
1912-W-1031

Icing Decorations

Perfect for topping cakes, cupcakes and cookies. Certified Kosher. $2.29

  NEW!

Smiling Pumpkins
Pk./12.
710-W-7200

Skull & Bones
Pk./12.
710-W-234

Polka Dot Pumpkin Cupcake Combo Pack

Quick and colorful way to serve cupcakes. Contains 24 each 2 in. diameter baking cups and 3 in. high paper party picks. Pk./24.
415-W-1265 $2.29

NEW!

NEW!

Haunted Manor Cupcake Wraps 'N Pix

Spooky cupcakes in an instant. Includes 12 wraps (2 in. diameter) and 24 pix, 2 designs (3 in. high). Baking cups sold separately. Patent pending. Pk./12.
415-W-1712 $3.99

Sprinkles

INDIVIDUAL BOTTLES

Shake up your Halloween treats. Plastic bottles for convenient pouring and storing. Certified Kosher.

Jumbo Ghost
3 oz. bottle.
710-W-567 $4.49

NEW!

Metallic Jimmies
4.5 oz. bottle.
710-W-189 $4.49

Spider Mix
2.5 oz. bottle.
710-W-186 $2.29

Hallow Pumpkin Mix
2.5 oz. bottle.
710-W-182 $2.29

Halloween Nonpareils
3 oz. bottle.
710-W-584 $2.29
5.25 oz. bottle.
710-W-183 $3.29

Orange Sugar
3.25 oz. bottle.
710-W-759
$2.29

Black Sugar
3.25 oz. bottle.
710-W-762
$2.29

Lavender Sugar
3.25 oz. bottle.
710-W-758
$2.29

Cake Sparkles

Edible glitter, .25 oz. bottle. Certified Kosher. **$3.29**

Orange
703-W-1308

Black
703-W-1302

Purple
703-W-1266

White
703-W-1290

6-Mix Halloween Pumpkin

Includes Black and Orange Nonpareils, Halloween Confetti, Hallow Pumpkin Mix, Black, Orange and Purple Sugars. 7.1 oz. Certified Kosher.
710-W-185 $5.99

NEW!

Haunted Manor Treat Boxes

Create a spooky gift with black boxes and colorful stickers. Includes 3 boxes (3 x 6.25 x 6.25 in.) and 1 sticker sheet. Pk./3.
415-W-1239 $5.29

Pre-Baked Cookie Kits

No baking, just fun! Everything you need is included to make great haunted designs.

Pre-Baked and Pre-Assembled Halloween Cookie House Kit

It's perfect for home, school or office celebrations—so easy and fun to make. Includes pre-baked, pre-assembled cookie house (measures 7 x 4 x 8 in. high), orange and black decorating icing mixes, colorful candy (Halloween mini round candies, orange, yellow and black jelly beans, purple round candies), 1 ghost icing decoration, 2 round decorating tips, 2 disposable decorating bags, cardboard base and complete decorating instructions.
2104-W-4319 $16.49

Pre-Baked Halloween Cookie House Kit

Easy to assemble and fun to decorate—it's the ideal family activity for Halloween. Includes 10 pre-baked gingerbread house pieces (assembled house measures 7 x 4 x 8 in. high), orange and black decorating icing mixes, 1 ghost icing decoration, colorful candy (Halloween mini round candies, jelly beans and candy corn), 2 decorating tips, 2 disposable decorating bags, cardboard base, complete assembly and decorating instructions.
2104-W-4318 $16.49

Candy

NEW!

NEW!

NEW!

Eyeballs
3-D Candy Mold
Makes 5 creepy
3D eyeballs!
1 design, 10 cavities.
2115-W-1422 $1.99

Skulls
3-D Candy Mold
Makes 4 spooky 3D
skulls!
1 design, 8 cavities.
2115-W-1421 $1.99

Creepy Tombstone
3-D Candy Mold
Makes 3 creepy
tombstones with
interchangeable bases.
2115-W-1415 $1.99

Skeleton Fingers
Pretzel Mold
1 design,
6 cavities.
2115-W-1418
$1.99

Witch Fingers
Pretzel Mold
2 designs,
6 cavities.
2115-W-1616
$1.99

Mummies
Pretzel Mold
1 design,
6 cavities.
2115-W-1783
$1.99

Smiling Pumpkins
Lollipop Mold
1 design,
7 cavities.
2115-W-1750
$1.99

Halloween Candy Kit for Pretzels

NEW!

Transform store-bought pretzels into
candy-coated treats! It's Halloween
fun for everyone with lots of spooky
shapes and colorful Candy Melts.
Everything you need is here—just add
pretzels! Includes 3 molds: Rats (1
design, 4 cavities), Skeleton & Spider (2
designs, 6 cavities), Pumpkin & Bats (2
designs, 6 cavities); 16 oz. Candy Melts
(4 oz. each Light Cocoa and artificially
vanilla flavored White, Orange and
Green); 4 disposable decorating bags, 1
decorating brush, 20 clear pretzel bags
with ties. Certified Kosher Dairy.
2104-W-3256 $9.99

Halloween Candy Kit MEGA PACK

NEW!

Everything you need to have a howling
good time making dozens of Halloween
lollipops and candies. Spooky shaped
molds and a great assortment of Candy
Melts colors help you create the
coolest treats in town. Includes 3 molds:
Graveyard Large Lollipop (3 designs,
4 cavities), Vampire Treats Lollipop
(2 designs, 6 cavities), Frightening
Candy (4 designs, 8 cavities); 16 oz.
Wilton Candy Melts (4 oz. each Light
Cocoa and artificially vanilla flavored
Orange, White and Red); 20 (6 in.)
Lollipop Sticks; 4 Disposable Decorating
Bags; 1 Decorating Brush; 20 party bags
with ties (10 each Purple and Orange).
Certified Kosher Dairy.
2104-W-3255 $9.99

Candy Melts

Ideal for molding, dipping or
coating. Artificially vanilla
flavored unless otherwise
indicated. 14 oz. bag.
Certified Kosher Dairy. **$2.99**

Orange	1911-W-1631
Yellow	1911-W-463
Dark Green	1911-W-405
Dark Cocoa	1911-W-358
Light Cocoa	1911-W-544
Dark Cocoa Mint	1911-W-1920
White	1911-W-498
Lavender	1911-W-403

Spooky Green
10 oz.
1911-W-488

Midnight Black
10 oz.
1911-W-489

See pages 194-198 for more Wilton candy items.

HALLOWEEN CANDY NECKLACE KITS*

NEW!

It's the perfect party
activity—each
kit makes 8 tasty
necklaces! Easy to
make, fun to wear
and eat!
$3.99

Skull & Bones
2104-W-4464

Pumpkin
2104-W-1274

*Recommended for children 3+ years.

Cookie Cutters

COMFORT-GRIP CUTTERS

These easy-grip cutters with extra-deep sides are perfect for cutting so many favorite foods into spectacular shapes.
The cushion grip gives you comfortable control even when cutting thick desserts. Recipe included. Stainless steel
sides, 4.5 x 4.5 x 1.5 in. deep. **$3.19**

NEW!

Tombstone
2310-W-599

Ghost
2310-W-607

Bat
2310-W-661

Pumpkin
2310-W-600

Witch's Hat
2310-W-630

4 PC. GRIPPY CUTTER SET

Safe, easy cutting, with a comfortable
grip and deep plastic sides. Four shapes
include cat, ghost, pumpkin and bat,
approx. 3.5 in. Set/4.
2311-W-257 $4.49

ORDER TOLL FREE: 800-794-5866

Cookie

Halloween Cookie Shapes Non-Stick Pan
Includes 12 classic shapes for your Halloween cookies and single-serving molded desserts. 12 cavities, each approximately 2.75 x 2.25 x .25 in. deep.
2105-W-8131 $11.99

Halloween Cupcake and Cookie Stencils
Just place one of the fun designs over your iced treat, then sprinkle with Wilton Cake Sparkles or Colored Sugars (p. 205) or spray with Color Mist Food Color Spray (p. 204). 8 designs.
417-W-499 $2.19

Halloween Push 'N Print Cutter Set
Serve cookies that make a great impression—use Push 'N Print Cutters to emboss a fun design before baking! It's so easy! Load one of the 3 imprint disks in the cutter, cut the cookie, then press the plunger with disk still in place to imprint the design. Bake, cool and serve a treat that's perfect for celebrations and cookie gift baskets. Great for embossed fondant decorations too! Disks are 2.9 in. diameter. Recipe included. Set/4.
2308-W-4002 $7.99

METAL CUTTERS
Put variety in your cookie making with fun Halloween multi-shape sets. There are styles to please everyone. Recipe included.

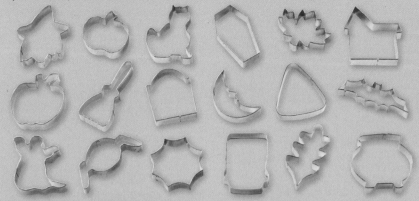

18 Pc. Halloween Cutter Set
Set of 18 includes witch, pumpkin, cat, coffin, maple leaf, house, apple, witch's broom, tombstone, moon, candy corn, bat, ghost, spider, spider web, Frankenstein, oak leaf and cauldron, each approx. 3 in. Set/18.
2308-W-1131 $10.49

3 Pc. Haunted Halloween Cutter Set   NEW!
Set of 3 includes cat face, skull and tombstone. Each approx. 3 in. Coated metal. Set/3.
2308-W-1092 $3.69

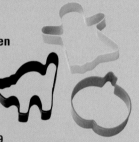

3 Pc. Halloween Cutter Set
Set of 3 includes pumpkin, ghost and cat. Each approx. 3 in. Coated metal. Set/3.
2308-W-1265 $3.69

12 Pc. Halloween Mini Cutter Set
Set includes pumpkin, skull, witch's hat, tombstone, bat, acorn, cat, house, maple leaf, moon, oak leaf and ghost, each approx. 1.5 to 2.25 in. Set/12.
2308-W-1246 $5.29

6 Pc. Halloween Mini Cutter Set
Set includes cat, pumpkin, bat, skull, ghost and moon, each approx. 1.5 in. Set/6.
2308-W-1211 $3.29

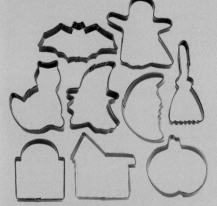

9 Pc. Halloween Cutter Set
Set includes bat, ghost, cat, witch, moon, witch's broom, tombstone, house and pumpkin, each approx. 3 to 3.75 in. Colored aluminum. Set/9.
2308-W-2501 $10.49

4 Pc. Spooky Shapes Cutter Set
Set includes moon, pumpkin, witch and ghost, each approx. 3 in. Coated metal. Set/4.
2308-W-1200 $4.79

4 Pc. Nesting Cutter Sets
Create boo-tiful Halloween treats in 4 sizes. Each cuts neatly and is easy to handle. Sizes from 2.25 to 4.5 in. Set/4. **$4.79**

Ghosts
2308-W-1238

Pumpkins
2308-W-1210

SEASONAL

Bakeware

Silicone Mini Leaf and Pumpkin Mold
Freezer, refrigerator, microwave and dishwasher safe; oven safe to 500°F. One mix makes 20-24 cakes. 6 cavities, each 2.6 x 2.5 x 1.5 in. deep.
2105-W-4874 $9.99

Pumpkin Pie Pan
Holds one 15 oz. can of pumpkin pie filling. Use for apple, peach and cherry pies, too! Ideal for ready-to-bake pie crusts. 9 x 1.5 in. deep. Aluminum.
2105-W-3970 $8.49

Candy

Scarecrows Lollipop Mold
2 designs, 4 cavities.
2115-W-1613 $1.99

Pumpkin Harvest Pretzel Mold
2 designs, 6 cavities.
2115-W-1420 $1.99

Candy Melts
Ideal for all your candy making, molding, dipping or coating. Artificially vanilla flavored unless otherwise indicated. 14 oz. bag. Certified Kosher Dairy. $2.99

Red	1911-W-499	Dark Cocoa	1911-W-358
Light Cocoa	1911-W-544	Dark Cocoa	
Orange	1911-W-1631	Mint	1911-W-1920
Yellow	1911-W-463	White	1911-W-498
Dark Green	1911-W-405	Peanut Butter	1911-W-481

See pages 194-198 for more Wilton candy items.

Sprinkles

Individual Bottles
Plastic bottles for convenient pouring and storing. Certified Kosher.

Jumbo Leaves Mix
3.25 oz. bottle.
710-W-565 $4.49

Leaves Mix
2.5 oz. bottle.
710-W-787 $2.29

Red Sugar
3.25 oz. bottle.
710-W-766 $2.29

Dark Green Sugar
3.25 oz. bottle.
710-W-764 $2.29

Cake Sparkles
Edible glitter in .25 oz. bottle. Certified Kosher.
$3.29

Red
703-W-1284

Dark Green
703-W-1278

Orange
703-W-1308

Yellow
703-W-1272

6-Mix Assortment
Includes Yellow, Red, Orange and Light Green Sugar, Leaves Mix and Chocolate Jimmies. 7.2 oz. Certified Kosher.
710-W-751 $5.99

DIMENSIONS DECORATIVE BAKEWARE
With Dimensions Non-Stick Cast Aluminum Bakeware, anyone can create desserts with elegant shapes and spectacular detail. Heavyweight cast aluminum conducts heat extremely evenly. Premium non-stick surface for easy release and cleanup. Aluminum.

Multi-Cavity Pumpkin
Finished cakes 3.4 x 3.4 in. 5 cup total capacity. Patent No. D574,663
2105-W-1183 $30.99

Cookie

Comfort-Grip Cutters
Cushion grip cutters have extra-deep stainless steel sides. Great for cutting, cushion grip gives comfortable control. Recipe included. Approx. 4.5 x 1.5 in. deep.
$3.19

Maple Leaf
2310-W-632

Oak Leaf
2310-W-633

METAL CUTTERS
Sure-to-please shapes. Recipe included.

3 Pc. Harvest Cutter Set
Includes turkey, pumpkin and leaf, each approx. 3 to 3.5 in. Coated metal. Set/3.
2308-W-1264 $3.69

6 Pc. Harvest Mini Cutter Set
Oak leaf, maple leaf, apple, pumpkin, elm leaf and acorn, approx. 1.5 in. Set/6.
2308-W-1217 $3.29

9 Pc. Leaves and Acorns Nesting Cutter Set
Graduated acorns, oak and maple leaves, (3 each). 1.75 to 3.75 in. Set/9.
2308-W-2000 $6.29

Party

Baking Cups
Microwave-safe paper. Standard size, 2 in. diameter, Pk./75. Mini size, 1.25 in. diameter, Pk./100.
$2.09

Autumn Leaves
Standard 415-W-431
Mini 415-W-433

Party Bags
Colorful Autumn designs for candy and cookie treats. 20 plastic bags, 20 ties included. 4 x 9.5 in. Pk./20.
$2.09

Autumn Leaves
1912-W-1430

Icing Decorations
Wilton Icing Decorations are perfect for topping cakes, cupcakes and cookies. Certified Kosher. Pk./18.
$2.29

Mini Pumpkins
710-W-538

Autumn Cupcake & Cookie Stencils
Just place one of the fun designs over your baked treat, then sprinkle with Wilton Cake Sparkles or Colored Sugars (shown at left) or spray with Color Mist Food Color Spray (p. 148). 8 designs.
417-W-495 $2.19

CHRISTMAS
Bakeware

Iridescents! Tree Pan
This bright, colorful shape is as much fun for serving party treats as it is for baking! Designed for quick, easy decorating. Also ideal for crisped rice cereal treats, molded gelatin, bread dough and more. One-mix pan is 14 x 10 x 2 in. deep. Aluminum.
2105-W-2081 $7.49

Gingerbread Boys and Trees Non-Stick Mini Cakes Pan
Non-stick steel releases treats easily and delivers great detail. One mix makes 16 gingerbread boys and trees. 6 cavities, each approximately 2.8 x 3.7 x 1.3 in. deep.
2105-W-1515 $11.99

SILICONE MOLDS
Discover the convenience and easy release of flexible silicone bakeware! Freezer, refrigerator, microwave and dishwasher safe—oven safe to 500°F. **$9.99**

Bite-Size Gingerbread Boy Mold
NEW!
One mix makes approximately 80 gingerbread boys. 24 cavities, each 1.75 x 1.6 x .75 in. deep.
2105-W-4901

Bite-Size Tree Mold
NEW!
One mix makes approximately 80 trees. 24 cavities, each 2.25 x 1.75 x .75 in. deep
2105-W-4902

Petite Tree Mold
One mix makes 40-48 trees. 12 cavities, each 2 x 1 in. deep.
2105-W-4898

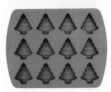

Mini Gingerbread Boy/Stocking/Tree Mold
One mix makes 20-24 stockings/ gingerbread boys and trees, each approximately 2.5 x 1.5 in. deep.
2105-W-4893

Mini Snowflake Mold
One mix makes 20-24 snowflakes. 6 cavities, each 2.5 x 1.5 in. deep.
2105-W-4831

Icings
See Color Guide below.

Striped Icing
Create fun 2-color decorations in colors perfect for the season. Tubes can be used with our Tip and Nail Set or Coupler Ring Set (p. 142) and Wilton metal tips. The larger sized star, petal or leaf tips optimize the two-tone effect. 4.25 oz. Certified Kosher.
Green/Red 704-W-204 $2.49
Red/White 704-W-203 $2.49

Tube Decorating Icing
Can be used with our Tip and Nail Set or Coupler Ring Set (p. 142) and any standard size Wilton metal tip. Colors match Wilton Icing Colors (p. 146). 4.25 oz. Certified Kosher. **$1.99**
Kelly Green 704-W-227
Red   704-W-218
Leaf Green   704-W-224
White   704-W-200

Sparkle Gel
Squeeze on sparkling color effects with our ready-to-use gel. Great for dots, messages and fondant accents. Resealable 3.5 oz. tube. Certified Kosher. **$2.99**
Green 704-W-111
Red 704-W-112
White 704-W-107
Gold 704-W-1060

Ready-to-Decorate Icing
Anyone can decorate with Wilton Ready-to-Decorate Icing! Our brilliant colors and four decorating tips make it a breeze to add an exciting finishing touch to treats—without mixing or mess. 6.4 oz. Certified Kosher. **$4.29**
Green 710-W-4401
Red   710-W-4400
White 710-W-4402

Cookie Icing
Easy to use—just heat and squeeze onto cookies using the convenient cap. Sets smooth in just 1 hour. 10 oz. bottle covers approximately 12 cookies, 3 in. each. Certified Kosher. **$4.49**
Green 704-W-493
White 704-W-481
Red   704-W-488

Tube Decorating Gel
Transparent gels are great for writing messages and decorating cakes and cookies. Colors match Wilton Icing Colors (p. 146). .75 oz. Certified Kosher. **$1.49**
Green 704-W-324
Red   704-W-318
White 704-W-302

Colors

CHRISTMAS COLOR GUIDE
Red   Kelly Green   Leaf Green   White

Holiday Icing Colors Set
Red-Red and Kelly Green in .5 oz. jars. Certified Kosher. Set/2.
601-W-3011 $2.99

FoodWriter Edible Color Markers
Add fun, dazzling color to countless foods. Kids love 'em! Decorate on fondant, color flow, royal icing designs and cookie icing. Includes Green and Red markers (.07 oz. each). Certified Kosher. Set/2.
609-W-102 $4.29

Color Mist Food Color Spray
The dazzling effects of an airbrush in a convenient can! Use it to add sensational color to iced cakes, cookies and cupcakes. No mess, taste-free formula. 1.5 oz. Certified Kosher. **$3.29**
Green 710-W-5503
Red   710-W-5500

SEASONAL

Party

Baking Cups
Microwave-safe paper. Standard size, 2 in. diameter, Pk./75. Mini size, 1.25 in. diameter, Pk./100. **$2.09**

Woodland Friends
Standard **415-W-1579**
Mini **415-W-1580**

Jolly Fun
Standard **415-W-4797**
Mini **415-W-4798**

Snowflake Wishes
Standard **415-W-1245**
Mini **415-W-1246**

Party Bags
Colorful Christmas designs for candy and cookie treats. Unless otherwise noted, 20 plastic bags, 20 ties included. 4 x 9.5 in. Pk./20. **$2.09**

Woodland Friends
1912-W-1314

Jolly Fun
1912-W-1077

Snowflake Wishes
1912-W-1309

Shaped Bags with Ties
Large bags are 6 x 9 in. 15 plastic bags, 15 ties included. Pk./15. **$2.09**

Woodland Friends
1912-W-1313

Jolly Fun
1912-W-1078

Snowflake Wishes
1912-W-1310

Icing Decorations
Perfect for topping cakes, cupcakes and cookies. Certified Kosher. **$2.29**

Gingerbread Boys
Pk./18.
710-W-464

Snowflakes
Pk./12.
710-W-543

Woodland Friends Cupcake Combo Pack
Quick and colorful way to serve cupcakes. Contains 24 each 2 in. diameter baking cups and 3 in. high paper party picks. Pk./24.
415-W-1581
$2.29

Candy Cups
Perfect for holiday sweets! 1 in. dia. Pk./75. **$1.79**
Red Foil 415-W-314
Silver Foil 415-W-307
Gold Foil 415-W-306

Red/Green Candy Cups
Mixed, glassine paper. 1 in. Pk./72.
1912-W-1247 $1.79

Petite Loaf Baking Cups
For gift breads. White paper. Fits Petite Loaf Pan (p.158). Pk./50.
415-W-450
$1.59

6-Mix Assortment
Includes Christmas Nonpareils, Confetti, Twinkling Trees Mix, Green and Red Sugar and Christmas Jimmies. 6.8 oz. Certified Kosher.
710-W-755 $5.99

Sprinkles

Jumbo Sprinkles
Try our Jumbo Sprinkles—big bold toppers perfect for cookies, brownies and more. Plastic bottles for convenient pouring and storing. Certified Kosher. **$4.49**

Snowflakes
2.6 oz. bottle.
710-W-569

Gingerbread Boys
2.75 oz. bottle.
710-W-586

Individual Bottles
Shake up your holiday treats with fun colors and designs. Plastic bottles for convenient pouring and storing. Certified Kosher.

White Sugar Pearls
5 oz. bottle.
710-W-044 $4.99

Metallic Jimmies
4.5 oz. bottle.
710-W-095 $4.49

Snowflake Mix
2.5 oz. bottle.
710-W-797 $2.29

Christmas Confetti
2 oz. bottle.
710-W-172 $2.29

Christmas Nonpareils
3 oz. **710-W-585 $2.29**
5.25 oz. **710-W-173 $3.29**

Cinnamon Drops
3 oz. bottle.
710-W-769 $2.29

Chocolate Jimmies
2.5 oz. bottle.
710-W-774 $2.29

Red Sugar
3.25 oz. bottle.
710-W-766 $2.29

Dark Green Sugar
3.25 oz. bottle.
710-W-764 $2.29

Sparkling Sugars
Easy-pour sugars have a coarse texture and brilliant sparkle. 8 oz. bottle. Certified Kosher. **$4.49**

Holiday Mix
710-W-308

Red/White
710-W-998

Green/White
710-W-997

Cake Sparkles
Edible glitter in .25 oz. bottle. Certified Kosher. **$3.29**

Red
703-W-1284

Green
703-W-1278

White
703-W-1290

ORDER TOLL FREE: 800-794-5866

Candy

NEW!

Snowflake Large Lollipop Mold
3 designs,
3 cavities.
2115-W-1571
$1.99

Santa Lollipop Mold
1 design,
9 cavities.
2115-W-1706
$1.99

Santa/Reindeer Pretzel Mold
2 designs,
6 cavities.
2115-W-1572
$1.99

Christmas Trees Pretzel Mold
1 design,
6 cavities.
2115-W-1747
$1.99

Holiday
2115-W-1359

Winter
2115-W-1360

Candy Cane Molds
Add a new twist to store-bought candy canes by molding a fun candy character on them! Fill mold cavities with your favorite melted Candy Melts, position candy cane and refrigerate to set. **$1.99**

Santa Claus Candy Cane Mold
2 designs,
2 cavities.
2115-W-1575

Frosty Friends Candy Cane Mold
2 designs,
2 cavities.
2115-W-1573

Cookie Candy Molds
Turn store-bought cookies into candy-coated treats! With Cookie Candy Molds and easy-melting Wilton Candy Melts, it's a breeze to add a great tasting and colorful candy design to your favorite cookies. Just brush colored candy details in the mold, let set, then add more melted candy and position your cookie in the mold. Great for sandwich cream cookies or any round cookie 2 in. diameter or less. 2 designs, 8 cavities. **$1.99**

Christmas Candy Kits for Pretzels

NEW!

Transform store-bought pretzels into candy-coated treats! It's holiday fun for everyone with lots of merry designs and colorful Candy Melts. Everything you need is here— just add pretzels. Includes 3 molds: Candy Cane & Snowflake (2 designs, 6 cavities), Bulbs & Snowmen (2 designs, 6 cavities), Santa (1 design, 6 cavities); 16 oz. Wilton Candy Melts (4 oz. each Light Cocoa and artificially vanilla flavored White, Red and Green); 4 Disposable Decorating Bags, 1 Decorating Brush, 20 pretzel bags with ties. Certified Kosher Dairy.
2104-W-3258 $9.99

Christmas Candy Kit MEGA PACK

NEW!

Everything you need to have a jolly time making dozens of Christmas lollipops and candies. Festive shaped molds and a great assortment of Candy Melts colors help you create the coolest treats in town. Includes 3 molds: Stocking and Santa Large Lollipop (3 designs, 3 cavities), Ornaments Lollipop (3 designs, 6 cavities), Gifts Candy (4 designs, 12 cavities); 16 oz. Wilton Candy Melts (4 oz. each Light Cocoa and artificially vanilla flavored White, Red and Green); 20 (6 in.) Lollipop Sticks; 4 Disposable Decorating Bags, 1 Decorating Brush, 20 party bags with ties (10 each red and green). Certified Kosher Dairy.
2104-W-3257 $9.99

Candy Melts
Ideal for molding, dipping or coating. Artificially vanilla flavored unless otherwise indicated. 14 oz. bag. Certified Kosher Dairy. **$2.99**

Red	1911-W-499	Dark Cocoa	1911-W-358
White	1911-W-498	Dark Cocoa	
Dark Green	1911-W-405	Mint	1911-W-1920
Light Cocoa	1911-W-544	Yellow	1911-W-463

Colorburst Brights Candy Melts
Brilliant flecks of color are blended into each easy-melting wafer, for candies that will look great for showers, receptions, holidays and more. 10 oz. bag. Certified Kosher Dairy.
1911-W-491 $2.99

See pages 194-198 for more Wilton candy items.

Cookie Cutters

Christmas Push 'N Print Cutter Set
Serve cookies that make a great impression—use Push 'N Print Cutters to emboss a fun design before baking! It's so easy! Load one of the 3 imprint disks in the cutter, cut the cookie, then press the plunger with disk still in place to imprint the design. Bake, cool and serve a treat that's perfect for celebrations and cookie gift baskets. Great for embossed fondant decorations too! Disks are 2.9 in. diameter. Recipe included. Set/4.
2308-W-4003 $7.99

Christmas Cupcake and Cookie Stencils
Turn plain treats into holiday visions. Just place 1 of the 8 fun designs over your iced treat, then sprinkle with Wilton Cake Sparkles or Colored Sugars (p. 210) or use FoodWriter Edible Ink Markers or Color Mist Food Color Spray (p. 209). 8 designs.
417-W-510 $2.19

5-Pt. Star
2303-W-135

Christmas Tree
2303-W-132

Plastic Cutters
Great shapes for end-of-year celebrations! 3 x 4 in. high.
$0.69

METAL CUTTERS

Put variety in your cookie-making with fun Christmas multi-shape sets. There are styles to please everyone. Recipe included.

18 Pc. Holiday Cutter Set
Snowflake, holly leaf, gingerbread girl, star, sleigh, tree, stocking, snowman, reindeer, ornament, candy cane, Santa hat, angel, bell, gift, wreath, gingerbread boy and mitten. Each approx. 3 in. Set/18.
2308-W-1132 $10.49

3 Pc. Christmas Cutter Set
Set of 3 includes snowflake, gingerbread boy and tree, each approx. 3 to 3.75 in. Coated metal. Set/3.
2308-W-1266 $3.69

9 Pc. Holiday Cutter Set
Candy cane, gingerbread girl, stocking, angel, star, bell, snowman, tree and gingerbread boy, each approx. 3 to 3.75 in. Colored aluminum. Set/9.
2308-W-2500 $10.49

4 Pc. Jolly Shapes Cutter Set
Stocking, star, tree and candy cane, each approx. 3 in. Coated metal. Set/4.
2308-W-1201 $4.79

3 Pc. Holiday Cutter Set
Set of 3 includes present, star and ornament, each approx. 2.5 to 3.25 in. Coated metal. Set/3.
2308-W-1118 $3.69

12 Pc. Holiday Mini Cutter Set
Star, angel, gingerbread girl, stocking, candy cane, teddy bear, bell, holly leaf, tree, gingerbread boy, ornament and sleigh. Each approx. 1.5 in. Set/12.
2308-W-1250 $5.29

6 Pc. Holiday Mini Cutter Set
Bell, gingerbread boy, holly leaf, tree, candy cane and angel, each approx. 1.5 in. Set/6.
2308-W-1214 $3.29

4 Pc. Nesting Cutter Sets
Bake your favorite holiday shapes in four fun sizes! Quality metal cuts neatly and is easy to handle. Sizes from 5 to 2.5 in. Set/4.
$4.79

Snowflakes
2308-W-1244

Gingerbread Boys
2308-W-1239

3 Pc. Snowflake Cutter Set
Set of 3 includes stylized, wavy and straight-edge, each approx. 3 in. Coated metal. Set/3.
2308-W-1106 $3.69

3 Pc. Trees Cutter Set NEW!
Set of 3 includes triangle tree, startop tree and classic fir, each approx. 3 in. Coated metal. Set/3.
2308-W-1103 $3.69

3 Pc. Gingerbread Cutter Set NEW!
Set of 3 includes boy, girl and house, each approx. 3 in. Coated metal. Set/3.
2308-W-1102 $3.69

3 Pc. Snowflake Wishes Cutter Set NEW!
Set of 3 includes present, reindeer and Santa, each approx. 3 in. Coated metal. Set/3.
2308-W-1104 $3.69

6 Pc. Snowflake Wishes Mini Cutter Set NEW!
Reindeer, Santa, 3 ornaments, and present. Each approx. 1.5 to 2 in. Set/6.
2308-W-1109 $3.29

SCOOPS

Stainless Steel Cookie Scoops NEW!
Scoops uniform portions of dough; spring handle for easy release.
Regular
417-W-141 $5.99
Large
417-W-139 $6.99

Holiday Red Cookie Scoop
Festive color and convenient design make holiday baking more fun! Scoops and releases approx. 1 tablespoon of dough with ease. Dishwasher safe plastic.
417-W-320 $2.99

Cookie Presses

Cookie Pro ULTRA II

Making traditional spritz cookies has never been so easy! Cookie Pro Ultra II is designed to be the easiest to fill, most comfortable press you've ever used. And, with 12 terrific shapes, plus 4 fun mini cookie designs, your holiday cookie baskets will be more festive than ever! Includes complete instructions and delicious recipes. Set/17.
2104-W-4018 $24.99

Twelve Disks in Festive Shapes

Plus 4 BONUS Disks For Mini Cookies!

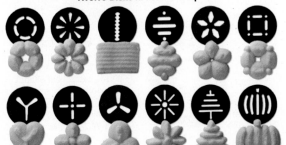

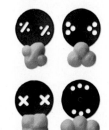

COOKIE MASTER Plus

Cordless Cookie Press

Our cordless cookie press is so powerful and easy to operate, you'll use it all year to create cookies, appetizers, desserts and more. Exclusive patented reverse action means there's no need to take press apart for refilling. Ergonomic design is shaped to fit in your hand for excellent comfort.

Includes 12 aluminum disks in classic and seasonal shapes, 4 accent tips for decorating and filling and 2 bonus recipe booklets—sweet and savory. Uses 4 AA batteries, not included. Patent Nos. D484,755, 6,701,828. Set/19.
2104-W-4008 $39.99

12 Disk Designs

4 Accent Tips

COMFORT GRIP.

Cookie Press

Experience a classic press that is truly comfortable. Its ergonomic handle feels great in your hand and the easy-squeeze action releases perfectly shaped dough. Clear barrel takes the guesswork out of refilling. Fluted bottom raises press off the cookie sheet for better-defined shapes. Includes 12 cookie disks in a variety of shapes and our classic spritz recipe. Set/13.
2104-W-4011 $12.99

12 Disk Designs

Bakeware

Recipe Right Non-Stick

Built with all the right qualities for better baking results. Pan dimensions are embossed on handles for easy reference. Heavy-gauge construction means pans spread heat evenly and won't warp. Non-stick coating provides exceptionally quick release and easy cleanup. 5-year warranty. Aluminum.

Non-Stick Parchment Paper

Use Wilton silicone-treated non-stick parchment to line baking pans and cookie sheets—a non-fat alternative that saves cleanup time. Double roll is 41 square feet, 15 in. wide. Certified Kosher.
415-W-680 $5.29

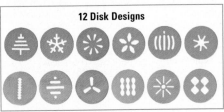

15 x 10 in. Cookie Sheet
2105-W-967 $5.49

12 Cup Muffin Pan
2105-W-954 $6.99

24 Cup Mini Muffin Pan
2105-W-914 $10.99

Bake Easy! Non-Stick Spray

This convenient non-stick spray helps your baked goods release perfectly. Just a light, even coating does the job. Use Bake Easy! for all mixes and recipes —cookies, muffins, cupcakes, brownies, breads and more. Versatile for all types of baking and cooking. 6 oz.
702-W-6018 $3.49

SEASONAL

Cookie Cutters

COMFORT-GRIP CUTTERS

These easy-grip cutters with extra-deep sides are perfect for cutting so many favorite foods into spectacular shapes. The cushion grip gives you comfortable control even when cutting thick desserts. Recipe included. Stainless steel sides, 4.5 x 4.5 x 1.5 in. deep. **$3.19**

NEW!

Snowflake
2310-W-592

Gingerbread House
2310-W-662

Gingerbread Boy
2310-W-602

Candy Cane
2310-W-644

4-Pc. Grippy Cutter Set
Safe, easy cutting, with a comfortable grip and deep plastic sides. Four shapes include stocking, tree, star and gingerbread boy, each approx. 3.5 in. Set/4.
2311-W-260 $4.49

Mitten
2310-W-639

Christmas Tree
2310-W-604

Star
2310-W-631

Snowman
2310-W-634

Gingerbread Accessories

Time for some home improvement! We have the perfect add-ons for your gingerbread projects— easy-mix icing to complete construction and decorate, fun candies to brighten the look.

NEW!

NEW!

NEW!

NEW!

NEW!

Gingerbread Mix
It's easy to achieve perfect gingerbread house pieces with our unique gingerbread mix. This specially formulated mix holds its shape as it bakes, without spreading! Mix makes a house approx. 7.5 x 7 x 6.5 in. Or use Gingerbread Mix to make cookies and ornaments. 24 oz.
2104-W-6011 $6.99

Frosty White Icing Mix
Mixes to the perfect texture for assembling and decorating gingerbread! Sets up and dries quickly for great results. Excellent for lattice, garland, icicle and scallop details on houses. 14 oz.
2104-W-6001 $4.49

Handmade Icing Decorations
Delightful details add charm! Eight fun shapes include: penguin, snowman, reindeer, elf, Santa, tree, wreath and sign. Pk./8.
2104-W-6004 $5.99

Holiday Candies Assortment
Dress up your gingerbread! Four bright shapes include mini light bulbs, stars, mini gum drops and mini sugared gum drops; 3 oz. of each candy. Decorating instructions included on package.
2104-W-6007 $6.49

Gingerbread Cookie Bag Kit
A wonderful way to gift wrap your gingerbread. Clear bags printed with bright snowflakes, gift tag to personalize and ribbon tie. Includes: 8 bags (6 x 11 in.); 8 shaped gift tags; 8 ribbons (1.5 ft. long).
1912-W-9801 $3.49

NEW!

NEW!

6 Cavity Gingerbread House
2105-W-8147

12 Cavity Holiday
2105-W-8122

Cookie Shapes Pans
Includes classic shapes for your single-serving holiday cookies and molded desserts. 6 cavities, each approximately 3.5 x 4 x .25 in. deep. 12 cavities, each approximately 2.75 x 2.25 x .25 in. deep. **$11.99**

3 Pc. Gingerbread House Cutter Set
Cut, bake and build a merry gingerbread house! It's easy to create perfectly-sized cookies using these cutters. For easy preparation, use our Gingerbread Mix and Frosty White Icing Mix (sold above). Includes: 3 cutters (5.5 x 6 in., 8.875 x 7 in.; 2.875 x 5.5 in.).
2308-W-1096 $7.99

Christmas Cookie Tree Cutter Kit
Kit includes 10 plastic star cookie cutters in graduated sizes, 3 disposable decorating bags, round decorating tip, cookie and icing recipes, baking and decorating instructions for 4 designs. Tree measures approx. 8 x 11 in. high when assembled.
2104-W-1555 $7.99

ORDER TOLL FREE: 800-794-5866

Gingerbread Kits

NEW!

Gingerbread Mini Village Kit
Ready to assemble and decorate. Make this wonderful holiday village come to life and create a family tradition, too. Use our comprehensive kit to decorate 5 enchanting houses. Includes 5 easy-to-assemble individual sets of gingerbread house panels (assembled houses measure between 3 and 4 in. high), lots of colorful candy, icing mix, red liquid color packet, 2 decorating bags and tips, cardboard bases, complete instructions. Houses measure approx. 2.75 - 3.75 in. high x 2.5 - 3 in. wide x 1.5 - 3 in. deep.
2104-W-1901 $16.49

GIANT Gingerbread House Kit
Everything you need is inside—6 pre-baked house pieces and 2 pre-baked gingerbread kids, 3 packets of icing mix, 3 decorating bags and 2 tips, loads of candy for decorating and complete instructions for assembling and decorating. House measures 8.25 in. high x 9 in. wide x 8.5 in. deep.
2104-W-4689 $39.99

Gingerbread House Kit
Includes pre-baked gingerbread pieces, icing mix, assorted candies, decorating bag and tip, cardboard base, complete instructions and decorating ideas. House measures 8 x 7 x 6.5 in. high.
2104-W-1509 $16.49

Pre-Assembled Gingerbread House Kit
Includes assembled house cookies with cardboard base, icing mix, candies, decorating bag and tip, complete instructions and decorating ideas. House measures 5.5 x 5.5 x 4.5 in. high.
2104-W-1904 $16.49

Gingerbread House Kit
Includes pre-baked house pieces, icing mix, assorted candies, decorating bag and tip, cardboard base, complete instructions and decorating ideas. House measures 5.25 x 5.5 x 4.75 in. high.
2104-W-1903 $12.99

NEW!

Gingerpops Cookie Kit
Build and decorate 10 jolly gingerpops to share with friends! Everything you need is included: 20 pre-baked gingersnaps cookies (approx. 2.25 x 2 in.), creamy white icing mix, red liquid icing color packet, 3 types of colorful candy, 10 sticks, 10 treat bags, 10 gift stickers, 2 decorating bags, 2 decorating tips and complete instructions for assembly and decorating.
2104-W-5313 $12.99

Gingerbread Boy Cookie Decorating Kit
Decorate 8 fun cookies! Great for gifts or special treats. Includes cookies, icing mix, colorful candies, decorating bag, tip and complete instructions.
2104-W-1090 $12.99

Gingerbread Tree Kit
Just stack pre-baked star cookies, decorate with icing and candy and add the star icing decoration tree top! Includes cookies, white and green icing mix, icing decorations, candies, 2 decorating tips, 2 decorating bags and complete instructions. Tree measures 5.5 x 8.25 in. high.
2104-W-1905 $12.99

SEASONAL

Cookie Exchange

This party is the perfect way to kick off the holiday season— and Wilton has the products you need to make it festive and fun! Start with the great decorating and presentation ideas in our Cookie Exchange Book and put together an event to remember!

NEW!

NEW!

Cookie Exchange

Whether you're hosting or simply attending, Wilton *Cookie Exchange* is filled with ideas to inspire you. Discover hundreds of festive cookie designs, including a Gallery section with more than 150 easy ideas in 6 favorite seasonal shapes. Sharing favorite recipes is always a cookie exchange highlight, so you'll want to check all the great tastes inside. From melt-in-your-mouth almond snowballs to cool crème de menthe bars, there are so many great recipes to try, along with a baking basics section to ensure your cookies turn out just right. If you're hosting the party, we'll help you plan the entire event, from invitations and room decorations to festive presentation ideas. With Wilton *Cookie Exchange*, you can make it a celebration to look forward to every holiday season! Soft cover, 96 pages.
902-W-1102 $14.99

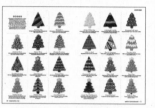

13-Pc. Cookie Decorating Set

A great start to your cookie exchange decorating. Just cut out your favorite Wilton Christmas cookies and decorate them with your choice of icing colors and decorations. Includes: 5 tips (Round: #2, 3, 5; Star: #18; Leaf: #352); 6 disposable decorating bags; 2 Pc. Stencil Set (Tree and Gingerbread Boy); complete instruction sheet.
2104-W-2538 $8.39

NEW!

NEW!

NEW!

NEW!

Snowflake Wishes Stackable Treat Box Kit

Festive cookie boxes ready to fill and give as gifts to family and friends. A beautiful presentation when stacked and tied with included ribbon. Includes 3 boxes (3 x 9.5 x 6.5 in., 2.5 x 8.5 x 5.5 in., 2 x 7.5 x 4.5 in.); 1 red ribbon (4.75 ft.).
415-W-1310 $5.29

Snowflake Wishes Small Treat Box Kit

Window boxes covered with bright holiday dots and snowflakes. Just add your favorite homemade treats, attach the included stickers and your holiday cheer is ready to share. Includes 3 boxes (each 3 x. 4.5 x 4.5 in.); 1 sticker sheet.
415-W-1307 $3.29

Snowflake Wishes Large Treat Box Kit

Boldly-striped boxes are just brimming with holiday fun. Large boxes fit more of your favorite homemade cookies and treats, attach the included stickers and share your tasty treasures. Includes 2 boxes (each 3 x 9.5 x 6.5 in.); 1 sticker sheet.
415-W-1309 $5.29

Snowflake Wishes Rectangular Treat Box Kit

Great shape for a row of large cookies or stack smaller treats and cookies. Fill and personalize with assorted stickers included. Includes 3 boxes (each 2.5 x 8 x 3.25 in.); 1 sticker sheet.
415-W-1306 $5.29

NEW!

NEW!

NEW!

Snowflake Wishes Treat Boxes

A charming little holiday house, complete with Santa and his reindeer. Ready to personalize and fill with treats or candy to give to family and friends. Includes 6 boxes (each 4 x 3.75 x 3 in.).
415-W-1403 $4.19

Holiday Parchment Sheets

Make your holiday food gifts merrier with these festively patterned, silicone-treated Parchment Sheets. The colors look great with Wilton gift boxes. Or, line candy and cookie gift bags, snack bowls, roll baskets. 1 ft. x 10.75 in. sheets. Pk./50.
415-W-1001 $7.99

Jumbo Cookie Spatula

Generously-sized spatula is great for handling multiple or oversized cookies, brownies, pastries and treat bars. Easy-grip handle helps balance large desserts. Stainless steel; dishwasher safe. 11 in. long.
570-W-1161 $6.99

Gifts from the Kitchen

Your homemade treats are even more welcome when packaged in our boxes, bags and accessories. We make it easy to present your delicious foods with pride!

GIFT-GIVING CONTAINERS

Create a custom food gift with our crisp white containers! Add color and flair with your own gift wrap, ribbon, tissue and tags.

Treat Cups
Present all your uniquely-shaped desserts in these great treat cups. Greaseproof coating for added strength and easy cleanup. Not recommended for baking. **$1.99**

 NEW!

Round
2.5 x .5 in.
Pk./18.
415-W-908

Rectangular
2.5 x 3.75 x .75 in.
Pk./12.
415-W-909

Treat Boxes
Create the perfect gift with window boxes. Great for candies or 3.5 in. cookies. Pk./3.

Small
Includes seals/sticker sheet. 4.5 x 4.5 x 1.5 in.
415-W-102 $3.29

Medium
Includes insert for 4 cupcakes. 6.25 x 6.25 x 3 in.
White 415-W-1215 $5.29
Silver 415-W-1359 $5.99

NEW!

 **NEW!**

Compartment Box
3 boxes (6.25 x 6.25 x 2 in. high) with 12 removable trays (3.2 x 3.2 x 1.8 in. high).
415-W-1431 $5.29

 **NEW!**

Rectangle Box
8 x 3.25 x 3.25 in. high. Pk./3.
415-W-1433 $5.29

 **NEW!**

Large Treat Box
Window boxes show off your delicious treats and small cakes. 4 x 8 x 8 in. Pk./3.
415-W-9490 $5.29

 **NEW!**

Gable Box
4.5 x 3.5 x 7 in. high. Pk./3.
415-W-1430 $5.29

Hexagon Treat Boxes
Self-closing top forms a pretty petal box top. Great for cookies, candy and favors. 4 x 6.25 in. high. Pk./4.
415-W-105 $5.29

Ribbon and trims shown above not included.

Popcorn Treat Boxes
Classic shape stands up tall to hold popcorn, nuts and other snacks. 3.75 x 2.25 x 5.25 in. high. Pk./4.
1904-W-1141 $3.29

Treat Basket
Roomy handled basket is ideal for your gifts. Great for muffins, mini loaves and more. 6.5 x 6.5 x 3 in. Pk./2.
415-W-104 $5.29

CLEAR TREAT BAGS
Find the perfect size to wrap up any treats.

10 x 16 in. Treat Bags
Wrap up bread loaves, smaller bowls and plates of treats. Includes 4 - 10 x 16 in. bags; 4 - 18 in. ribbons, 4 gift tags.
1912-W-1142 $3.29

16 x 20 in. Treat Bags
Ideal size for Treat Baskets above filled with muffins. Great for a cookie platter, pie, scones and more. Includes 3 - 16 x 20 in. bags; 3 - 18 in. ribbons, 3 gift tags.
1912-W-1143 $4.29

SEASONAL

VALENTINE

Bakeware
DIMENSIONS
DECORATIVE BAKEWARE

With Dimensions Non-Stick Cast Aluminum Bakeware, everyone can create Valentine desserts with elegant shapes and spectacular detail. Heavyweight cast aluminum conducts heat evenly. Premium non-stick surface for easy release and cleanup.

Mini Heart
Each heart is 4 x 2 in. deep. Six 1 cup cavities. Pat. No. D487,211.
2105-W-5012 $30.99

Queen Of Hearts
9 x 3.25 in. deep. 10 cup total capacity. Pat. No. D478,466.
2105-W-5001 $30.99

SweetHeart Pan
Its gently curving shape gives the classic heart a more romantic flair. One-mix pan is 10.25 x 2 in. deep. Aluminum.
2105-W-1197 $12.99

Silicone Heart Molds
Discover the convenience and easy release of flexible silicone bakeware! Freezer, refrigerator, microwave and dishwasher safe—oven safe to 500°F. One mix makes 40-48 petite hearts; 20-24 mini hearts. Petite hearts each 1.5 x 1.5 x 1 in. deep. Mini hearts each 2.6 x 2.5 x 1.5 in. deep.

Ruffled Mini Heart Mold
2105-W-4861 $9.99

Mini Heart Mold
2105-W-4012 $9.99

Petite Heart Mold
2105-W-4860
$9.99

9 in. Non-Stick Heart Pan
Your classic heart cake will release perfectly. Cleanup is easy too. 9 x 2.25 in. deep. Non-stick steel.
2105-W-410 $13.99

Heart Pans
For graceful expressions of love on Valentine's Day or anytime, in just the size you need. 2 in. deep. Aluminum.

6 in.	2105-W-600	$7.49
9 in.	2105-W-5176	$8.99
12 in.	2105-W-607	$12.99

Non-Stick Mini Heart Pan
Perfect size for party petits fours, molded salads and more. Non-stick steel releases treats easily. One mix makes 20-24 hearts; 6 cavities, each 2.25 x 2.4 x 1.25 in. deep.
2105-W-1539 $8.99

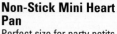

Mini Heart Pan
Great size for petits fours, individual brownies and more. One mix makes 12-18 hearts. 6 cavities, each 3.5 x 1 in. deep. Aluminum.
2105-W-11044 $12.99

Petite Heart Pan
Bite-size muffins, brownies and cookies will win hearts. One mix makes 10-15 dozen hearts. 12 cavities, each 1.75 x 1.6 x .5 in. deep. Aluminum.
2105-W-2432 $11.99

Heart Springform Pans
Create elegant Valentine cheesecakes with these easy-releasing non-stick pans. Springlock sides, removable bottom for easy serving. Non-stick steel.

9 x 2.75 in.
Standard
2105-W-419
$21.49

4 x 1.75 in.
Mini
2105-W-457 $9.99

Icings

VALENTINE COLOR GUIDE

Red	Pink	Violet	White

Ready-to-Decorate Icing
Includes 4 decorating tips! Anyone can decorate with Wilton Ready-to-Decorate Icing. Add an exciting finishing touch to treats without mixing or mess. 6.4 oz. Certified Kosher.
$4.29

Red	710-W-4400
Pink	710-W-4406
Violet	710-W-4408
White	710-W-4402

Sparkle Gel
Squeeze on sparkling color effects with our ready-to-use gel. Great for dots, messages, water effects and fondant accents. Resealable 3.5 oz. tubes. Certified Kosher.
$2.99

Red	704-W-112
Pink	704-W-356
White	704-W-107

Striped Icing
Create fun 2-color decorations in colors perfect for the season. Tubes can be used with our Tip and Nail Set or Coupler Ring Set (p. 142) and Wilton metal tips. The larger sized star, petal or leaf tips optimize the two-tone effect. 4.25 oz. Certified Kosher.
Pink/Red 704-W-216 $2.49

Cookie Icing
Just heat and squeeze onto cookies using the convenient cap. Sets smooth in just 1 hour. 10 oz. bottle covers approximately 12 cookies, 3 in. each. Certified Kosher. **$4.49**

White	704-W-481
Red	704-W-488
Pink	704-W-486

NEW!

Tube Decorating Icing
Tubes can be used with our Tip and Nail Set or Coupler Ring Set (p. 142) and any standard size Wilton metal tip. Colors match Wilton Icing Colors (p. 146). 4.25 oz. Certified Kosher. **$1.99**

Red	704-W-218
Pink	704-W-230
Violet	704-W-242
White	704-W-200

Tube Decorating Gel
Transparent gels are great for writing messages and decorating cakes and cookies. Colors match Wilton Icing Colors (p. 146). .75 oz. Certified Kosher.
$1.49

Red	704-W-318
Pink	704-W-330
Violet	704-W-342
White	704-W-302

Party

NEW!

Baking Cups

Microwave-safe paper. Standard size, 2 in. diameter, Pk./75. Mini size, 1.25 in. diameter, Pk./100. **$2.09**

Valentine Standard
415-W-1096
Mini 415-W-1093

Hearts Standard
415-W-517
Mini 415-W-414

Heart Silicone Baking Cups

No muffin pan needed! Bake and serve in these reusable oven-safe cups. Pk./12, 6 red, 6 pink.

Standard
415-W-9409 **$9.99**
Mini 415-W-9425 **$7.99**

Candy Cups

Wax-laminated paper on red foil. 1 in. diameter. Pk./75.
415-W-314 **$1.79**

NEW!

Party Bags

Colorful solid red and Valentine designs for candy and cookie treats. Unless otherwise noted, 20 plastic bags, 20 ties included. 4 x 9.5 in. Pk./20. **$2.09**

Red Party Bags
(not shown.)
1912-W-2357

Valentine
1912-W-1117

Hearts
1912-W-1269

NEW!

Treat Boxes

Give the special ones in your life a sweet treat with colorful window boxes that hold candies, cookies or 4 cupcakes. Pretty eyelet lace pattern creates a Valentine gift that will show how much you care! Includes 3 boxes (3 x 6.25 x 6.25 in.) and 3 cupcake inserts. Pk./3.
415-W-1335 **$5.29**

Hearts Remembered Icing Decorations

Perfect for topping cakes, cupcakes and cookies. Certified Kosher. Pk./18.
710-W-824 **$2.29**

NEW!

Cupcake Combo Pack

Colorful baking cups and picks are the ideal match for your Valentine cupcakes! Cups are microwave-safe paper, 2 in. diameter; picks are 3 in. high. Pk./24.
415-W-1097 **$2.29**

Color

Color Mist Food Color Spray

Gives decorators the versatility and dazzling effects of an airbrush in a convenient can! Use it to add sensational color to cakes, iced cookies and cupcakes. No mess, taste-free formula. 1.5 oz. Certified Kosher. **$3.29**

Red **710-W-5500**
Pink **710-W-5505**
Violet **710-W-5504**

See Color Guide p. 218.

Candy

Love Pretzel Mold
2 designs, 6 cavities.
2115-W-1451 **$1.99**

Heart Pretzel Mold
1 design, 6 cavities.
2115-W-3025 **$1.99**

Kissy Lips Candy Mold
1 design, 8 cavities.
2115-W-1450 **$1.99**

Double Heart Large Lollipop Mold
2 designs, 4 cavities.
2115-W-4440 **$1.99**

Roses and Buds Lollipop Mold
3 designs, 9 cavities.
2115-W-1708 **$1.99**

Hearts Candy Mold
1 design, 15 cavities.
2115-W-1712 **$1.99**

Heart Candy Necklace Kit

It's the perfect party activity—kit makes 8 tasty necklaces! Kids will love the cool colors and great flavors—and stringing the candy beads and charm is a breeze. Includes 8 individual necklace packs; each pack contains over 50 candy beads, 1 heart shaped charm and 17.5 in elastic string.
2104-W-1058 **$3.99**

Valentine Candy Making Kit MEGA PACK

NEW!

Lots of fun shapes and colorful Candy Melts make this kit just what you need to create the cutest candies for everyone you love. Kit includes: Lovely Flowers Large Lollipop Mold (2 designs, 3 cavities), Hearts Lollipop Mold (3 designs, 6 cavities), Love Bugs Candy Mold (3 designs, 8 cavities); 16 oz. Candy Melts brand confectionery coating (4 oz. each light cocoa, white, red and pink); 20 lollipop sticks (6 in.); 4 disposable decorating bags; decorating brush and 20 party bags/ties. Certified Kosher Dairy.
2104-W-3267 **$9.99**

Candy Melts

Ideal for molding, dipping or coating. Artificially vanilla flavored unless otherwise indicated. 14 oz. bag. Certified Kosher Dairy. **$2.99**

Red **1911-W-499**
Pink **1911-W-447**
White **1911-W-498**
Light Cocoa **1911-W-544**
Dark Cocoa **1911-W-358**

See pages 194-198 for more Wilton candy items.

SEASONAL

VALENTINE
Sprinkles

Individual Bottles
Shake up your Valentine treats with fun colors and designs. Plastic bottles for convenient pouring and storing. Certified Kosher.

Jumbo Hearts
3.25 oz. bottle.
710-W-032
$4.49

Micro Hearts
3.5 oz. bottle.
710-W-096
$4.49

Fill Your Heart Mix
3 oz. bottle.
710-W-099 $4.49

Hearts Mix
2.5 oz. bottle.
710-W-854
$2.29

Valentine Nonpareils
3 oz. bottle.
710-W-625
$2.29
5.25 oz. bottle.
710-W-558
$3.29

Chocolate Hearts Mix
Naturally and artificially flavored.
2.5 oz. bottle.
710-W-622 $2.29
3.75 oz. bottle.
710-W-6315 $3.29

Sugars
3.25 oz. bottle. Certified Kosher. **$2.29**

Red
710-W-766

Pink
710-W-756

Lavender
710-W-758

Cake Sparkles
Edible glitter, .25 oz. bottle. Certified Kosher. **$3.29**

Red
703-W-1284

Pink
703-W-1260

Purple
703-W-1266

6-Mix Assortment
Includes 2 Heart Mixes, Sweetheart Nonpareils, Pink, Red and Lavender Sugars. 7.2 oz. Certified Kosher.
710-W-738 $5.99

Valentine Push 'N Print Cutter Set
Emboss a fun design in cookies before baking! Load one of the 3 imprint disks in the cutter, cut the cookie, then press the plunger with disk still in place to imprint the design. Disks are 2.9 in. wide. Recipe included. Set/4.
2308-W-4000
$7.99

METAL CUTTERS
Put variety in your cookie-making with fun Valentine multi-shape sets. Recipe included.

9 Pc. Valentine Cutter Collection
Great variety of hearts, hugs and kisses designs from 1 to 5 in. Colored aluminum. Set/9.
2308-W-2502
$10.49

4 Pc. From The Heart Nesting Cutter Set
Includes 2 crinkled shapes. Largest cutter is approx. 5 in. Metal and coated metal. Set/4.
2308-W-1203 $4.79

Heart Cutters
Cuts neatly and is easy to handle. 3 in. wide.
Metal 2308-W-1003 $0.69
Red Metal 2308-W-1322 $0.79

 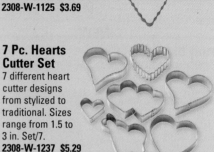

3 Pc. Hearts Cutter Set
Includes smooth-edge, curved and scalloped shapes, each approx. 3 to 3.5 in. Coated metal.
2308-W-1125 $3.69

7 Pc. Hearts Cutter Set
7 different heart cutter designs from stylized to traditional. Sizes range from 1.5 to 3 in. Set/7.
2308-W-1237 $5.29

6 Pc. Valentine Mini Cutter Set
Double heart, crinkle heart, heart with arrow, heart, O and X, each approx. 1.5 in. Set/6.
2308-W-1255 $3.29

Comfort-Grip Cutters
Cushion-grip cutters with extra-deep stainless steel sides. The cushion grip gives you comfortable control even when cutting into thick desserts. Recipe included.
4.5 x 4.5 x 1.5 in. deep.
$3.19

Heart
2310-W-616

Lips
2310-W-646

Double Heart
2310-W-647

6 Pc. Hearts Nesting Cutter Set
Great for cookies, imprinting patterns in icing, cutting bread shapes and more. Plastic in sizes from 2.25 to 4.2 in. Set/6.
2304-W-115 $2.99

Heart Cookie Treat Pan
Just press cookie dough into pan, insert a cookie stick, then bake, cool and decorate. Also great for adding fun shapes to other goodies like rice cereal treats and candy pops. Each treat is 3.5 in. x .25 in. deep. Aluminum.
2105-W-0580 $9.99

Cookie Treat Sticks
6 in. Pk./20. **1912-W-9319 $1.99**   8 in. Pk./20. **1912-W-9318 $2.99**

Cookie Pans

Valentine Cookie Shapes Non-Stick Pan
Includes 12 classic shapes for your holiday cookies and single-serving molded desserts. 12 cavities, each approximately 2.75 x 2.25 x .25 in. deep.
2105-W-8139 $11.99

Heart Giant Cookie Pan
Create a giant-sized pan cookie or brownie in a heart shape. Ideal for refrigerated dough and brownie mix. Recipe included. Pan is 11.5 x 10.5 x .5 in. deep. Aluminum.
2105-W-6203 $7.49

ORDER TOLL FREE: 800-794-5866

EASTER
Bakeware

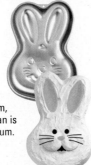

Step-By-Step Bunny Pan
Get springtime celebrations hopping—just bake, ice and decorate! He's also perfect for molding gelatin, ice cream, salads and more. One-mix pan is 9.75 x 14 x 2 in. deep. Aluminum.
2105-W-2074 $7.49

3-D Bunny Pan
Instructions for 5 different decorating ideas included. Two-piece pan bakes bunny approx. 7.25 x 4.75 x 7 in. high. Pan takes 4½ cups of pound cake batter. No heating core needed. Aluminum. Set/2.
2105-W-2042 $14.49

Stand-Up Lamb Pan
This 3-D lamb will charm everyone at your Easter table. Two-piece pan makes lamb 10 x 4.5 x 7 in. high; takes 6 cups of pound cake batter. Instructions included. Aluminum. Set/2.
2105-W-2010 $14.49

3-D Egg Pan

Hatch a great Easter centerpiece! Two-piece pan takes just one cake mix. Includes 2 ring bases for level baking of each half. Each half is 9 x 6 x 2.75 in. Aluminum. Set/4.
2105-W-4793 $14.49

6-Cavity Non-Stick Mini Cake Pans
Mini cakes are fun to serve at Easter brunch or wrap them up and add to baskets. Easy-release, easy-clean non-stick steel bakes cakes with great detail. Also excellent for brownies, ice cream molds, muffins and more.

Flower
Each cavity 4 x 4 x 1.5 in. deep. One mix makes about 14 cakes.
2105-W-5490 $11.99

Decorated Egg
Each cavity 4.2 x 2.9 x 1.5 in. deep. One mix makes about 14 cakes.
2105-W-1550 $11.99

Bunny
Each cavity 4 x 2.6 x 1.2 in. deep. One mix makes about 18 cakes.
2105-W-1551 $11.99

Cross Pan
Truly inspiring for holidays, Christenings and other religious occasions. Bevel design is excellent with rolled fondant. One-mix pan is 14.5 x 11.2 x 2 in. deep. Instructions included. Aluminum.
2105-W-2509 $9.99

Silicone Molds
Discover the convenience and easy release of flexible silicone bakeware! Freezer, refrigerator, microwave and dishwasher safe; oven safe to 500°F.

Mini Bunny/Basket
Six cavities, each approx. 3 x 1.5 in. deep. One mix makes 20-24 treats.
2105-W-1052 $9.99

Mini Decorated Egg
Six cavities, each 3.5 x 1.5 in. deep. One mix makes 20-24 eggs.
2105-W-4847 $9.99

Petite Easter Egg
Twelve cavities, each 1.75 x 1.5 in. deep. One mix makes 40-48 eggs.
2105-W-4864 $9.99

EASTER COLOR GUIDE

Pink	Violet	Yellow	Green/Leaf Green	White

Color Mist Food Color Spray
Gives decorators the versatility and dazzling effects of an airbrush in a convenient can! Use it to add sensational color to cakes, iced cookies and cupcakes. No mess, taste-free formula. 1.5 oz. Certified Kosher. **$3.29**

Pink	710-W-5505
Violet	710-W-5504
Yellow	710-W-5502
Green	710-W-5503

Easter Icings
See Color Guide above right.

Ready-to-Decorate Icing
Includes 4 decorating tips! Anyone can decorate with Wilton Ready-to-Decorate Icing. Add an exciting finishing touch to treats without mixing or mess. 6.4 oz. Certified Kosher. **$4.29**

Pink	710-W-4406
Violet	710-W-4408
Yellow	710-W-4409
Green	710-W-4401
White	710-W-4402

Sparkle Gel
Squeeze on sparkling color effects with our ready-to-use gel. Great for dots, messages, water effects and fondant accents. Resealable 3.5 oz. tubes. Certified Kosher. **$2.99**

Pink	704-W-356
White	704-W-107
Yellow	704-W-108
Green	704-W-111

Striped Icing **NEW!**
Create fun 2-color decorations in colors perfect for the season. Tubes can be used with our Tip and Nail Set or Coupler Ring Set (p. 142) and Wilton metal tips. The larger sized star, petal or leaf tips optimize the two-tone effect. 4.25 oz. Certified Kosher. **$2.49**

Pink/Lavender 704-W-217
Blue/Yellow 704-W-211

Cookie Icing
Just heat and squeeze onto cookies using the convenient cap. Sets smooth in just 1 hour. 10 oz. bottle covers approximately 12 cookies, 3 in. each. Certified Kosher. **$4.49**

Pink	704-W-486
Yellow	704-W-487
White	704-W-481

Tube Decorating Icing
Tubes can be used with our Tip and Nail Set or Coupler Ring Set (p. 142) and any standard size Wilton metal tip. Colors match Wilton Icing Colors (p. 146). 4.25 oz. Certified Kosher. **$1.99**

Pink	704-W-230
Violet	704-W-242
Yellow	704-W-236
Leaf Green	704-W-224
White	704-W-200

Tube Decorating Gel
Great for decorating cakes and cookies and writing messages. Colors match Wilton Icing Colors (p. 146). .75 oz. Certified Kosher. **$1.49**

Pink	704-W-330
Green	704-W-324
Violet	704-W-342
White	704-W-302
Yellow	704-W-336

SEASONAL

Party

NEW!

Hop 'n Tweet Baking Cups
Microwave-safe paper. Standard size, 2 in. diameter, Pk./75. Mini size, 1.25 in. diameter, Pk./100. **$2.09**
Standard   415-W-1126
Mini   415-W-1125

Hop 'n Tweet Cupcake Combo Pack
NEW!
Colorful baking cups and picks are the ideal match for your Easter cupcakes! Cups are microwave-safe paper, 2 in. diameter; picks are 3 in. high. Pk./24.
415-W-1124 $2.29

NEW!

Hop 'n Tweet Party Bags
Colorful Easter designs for candy and cookie treats. 20 plastic bags, 20 ties included. 4 x 9.5 in. Pk./20.
1912-W-1176 $2.09

Hop 'n Tweet Treat & Egg Stand
It's the colorful centerpiece that will get your Easter celebration hopping! The ideal way to display eggs after coloring, with a frisky bunny topper that sets the tone for springtime fun. Sturdy, easy-to-assemble stand with locking tabs that keep plates in place. Holds 16 eggs, mini cupcakes, cereal treats or other small goodies. Stand measures 10 x 11.25 in. high. Instructions included.
1512-W-118 $4.99

Candy

Hoppy Easter Pretzel Mold
2 designs, 6 cavities.
2115-W-1419 $1.99

Hatching Chick Pretzel Mold
2 designs, 6 cavities.
2115-W-1495 $1.99

Bunny Basket Mold
1 design, 2 cavities.
2115-W-1416 $1.99

Hoppy Easter Lollipop Mold
8 designs, 9 cavities.
2115-W-1718 $1.99

Fuzzy Bunny Lollipop Mold
4 designs, 4 cavities.
2115-W-1496 $1.99

NEW!

Easter Candy Making Kit MEGA PACK
Lots of fun springtime shapes and colorful Candy Melts make this kit just what you need to create the cutest candies for everyone's Easter basket. Kit includes: Spring Friends Large Lollipop Mold (3 designs, 3 cavities), Fun Flowers Lollipop Mold (11 designs, 11 cavities), Egg Candy Mold (5 designs, 11 cavities); 16 oz. Candy Melts brand confectionery coating (4 oz. each light cocoa, white, pink and yellow); 20 lollipop sticks (6 in.); 4 disposable decorating bags; decorating brush and 20 party bags/ties. Certified Kosher Dairy.
2104-W-3259 $9.99

Candy Melts
Ideal for molding, dipping or coating. Artificially vanilla flavored unless otherwise indicated. 14 oz. bag. Certified Kosher Dairy. **$2.99**

Pink	1911-W-447	White	1911-W-498
Lavender	1911-W-403	Dark Cocoa Mint	1911-W-1920
Yellow	1911-W-463	Light Cocoa	1911-W-544
Blue	1911-W-448	Dark Cocoa	1911-W-358

See pages 194-198 for more Wilton candy items.

Sprinkles

Individual Bottles
Shake up your Easter treats! Plastic bottles for convenient pouring and storing. Certified Kosher.

NEW!

Easter Micro Mix
3 oz. bottle.
710-W-1018 $4.49

Spring Confetti
2 oz. bottle.
710-W-1278 $2.29
3 oz. bottle.
710-W-970 $3.29

Colorful Egg Mix
2.5 oz. bottle.
710-W-7486 $2.29
3.75 oz. bottle.
710-W-716 $3.29

6-Mix Assortment
Includes Bunny Sprinkle Mix, Colorful Egg Mix, Spring Confetti, Lavender, Pink and Yellow Sugars. 6.8 oz. Certified Kosher.
710-W-1017 $5.99

Cookie

Easter Cupcake & Cookie Stencils
Just place one of the 8 fun designs over your baked or iced treat, then sprinkle with Wilton Cake Sparkles or Colored Sugars or spray with Color Mist Food Color Spray (p. 221). Set/8.
417-W-496 $2.19

Cookie

METAL CUTTERS

Put variety in your cookie-making with fun Easter multi-shape sets. There are styles to please everyone. Recipe included.

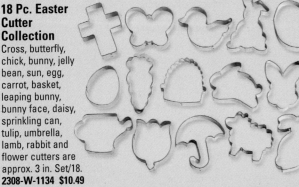

18 Pc. Easter Cutter Collection
Cross, butterfly, chick, bunny, jelly bean, sun, egg, carrot, basket, leaping bunny, bunny face, daisy, sprinkling can, tulip, umbrella, lamb, rabbit and flower cutters are approx. 3 in. Set/18.
2308-W-1134 $10.49

12 Pc. Easter Mini Cutter Collection
Bunny face, egg, cross, flower, tulip, sun, carrot, chick, butterfly, sprinkling can, umbrella and bunny cutters are approx. 1.5 in. Set/12.
2308-W-1254 $5.29

6 Pc. Easter Mini Cutter Set
Butterfly, daisy, tulip, bunny face, chick and bunny, each approx. 1.5 in. Set/6.
2308-W-1209 $3.29

Colorful Cutter Sets
Our metal cutters look great with their bright colors and fun shapes. Perfect for hanging until your next cookie-baking bash.

3 Pc. Spring Cutter Set
Set of 3 includes carrot, hopping bunny and flower, each approx. 3 to 3.5 in. Coated metal. Set/3.
2308-W-1328 $3.69

NEW!

3 Pc. Easter Cutter Set
Set of 3 includes bunny, butterfly and tulip, each approx. 3 to 3.5 in. Coated metal. Set/3.
2308-W-1216 $3.69

4 Pc. Hoppy Easter Cutter Set
Springtime favorites in pastels of the season. Tulip, egg, butterfly and bunny. Coated metal. Each approx. 3.5 in. Set/4.
2308-W-1207 $4.79

9 Pc. Easter Cutter Collection
Lamb, tulip, flower, bunny, chick, egg, butterfly, bunny face, and carrot cutters are approx. 3 in. Colored aluminum. Set/9.
2308-W-2503 $10.49

COMFORT-GRIP CUTTERS
Cushion-grip cutters with extra-deep stainless steel sides. Recipe included. Approx. 4.5 x 1.5 in. deep. **$3.19**

Bunny 2310-W-659
Chick 2310-W-625
Egg 2310-W-649
Bunny Face 2310-W-626

4 PC. GRIPPY CUTTER SET
Includes butterfly, flower, egg, and bunny face, approx. 3.5 in. Set/4.
2311-W-258 $4.49

Easter Push 'N Print Cutter Set
Emboss a fun design before baking! It's so easy! Load one of the 3 imprint disks in the cutter, cut the cookie, then press the plunger with disk still in place to imprint the design. Disks are 2.9 in. wide. Recipe included. Set/4.
2308-W-4001 $7.99

Cookie Pans

Easter Cookie Shapes Non-Stick Pan
Includes 12 classic shapes for your holiday cookies and single-serving molded desserts. 12 cavities, each approximately 2.75 x 2.25 x .25 in. deep.
2105-W-8129 $11.99

Bunny Cookie Treat Pan
Just press cookie dough into pan, insert a cookie stick, then bake, cool and decorate. Each treat is 3.5 x 2.75 x .25 in. deep. Aluminum.
2105-W-8106 $9.99

Cookie Treat Sticks
6 in. Pk./20. **1912-W-9319 $1.99**
8 in. Pk./20. **1912-W-9318 $2.99**

PLASTIC CUTTERS
Child-safe design means kids can have a great time helping. And remember all the fun ways to use our cutters—for bread shapes, stencils, sun catchers and so much more.

Individual Cutters
Each approx. 3 x 4 in. **$0.69**

 Cross 2303-W-141
 Duck 2303-W-148
Egg 2303-W-119

10 Pc. Easter Egg Canister Cutter Set
A fun and convenient egg canister holds 10 cutters, each approx. 3.5 in. Set/10.
2304-W-95 $5.99

SEASONAL

COMMUNION

Cross Pan
Beveled design is excellent with rolled fondant. One-mix pan is 14.5 x 11.2 x 2 in. deep. Instructions included. Aluminum.
2105-W-2509 **$9.99**

Faith Cross Stationery
Beautifully designed in white 80 lb. card stock with white pearlized trim. Professionally print at home at **www.wiltonprint.com**.

Cross/Bible Lollipop Mold
4 designs, 6 cavities (2 lollipop, 4 candy).
2115-W-4435 **$1.99**

Cross Seals
Self adhesive, silver tone, 1 in. diameter. Pk./50.
1008-W-2337 **$2.99**

Invitations
Border and cross accent. Invitation: 5.5 x 8.5 in.; envelope: 5.75 x 8.75 in. Pk./12.
1008-W-775 **$4.99**

ST. PATRICK'S DAY

NEW!

Silicone Mini Shamrock Mold
Microwave, freezer, refrigerator, and dishwasher safe; oven safe to 500°F. One mix makes 20-24 shamrocks. 6 cavities, each 2.6 x 2.5 x 1.5 in. deep.
2105-W-1286 **$9.99**

Shamrock Pretzel Mold
2 designs, 6 cavities.
2115-W-1499 **$1.99**

Shamrock Shower Baking Cups
Microwave-safe paper. Standard size, 2 in. diameter, Pk./75. Mini size, 1.25 in. diameter, Pk./100.
$2.09
Standard 415-W-1322
Mini 415-W-1068

NEW!

Shamrock Shower Party Bags
Colorful design for candy and cookie treats. 20 plastic bags, 20 ties included. 4 x 9.5 in. Pk./20.
1912-W-1099 **$2.09**

NEW!

Shamrock Lollipop Mold
1 design, 5 cavities.
2115-W-1545 **$1.99**

Shamrock Foil Fun Pix
Add a shimmering, lucky touch to cakes, cupcakes, ice cream and more. Approx. 3½ in. high. Pk./12.
2113-W-1347 **$2.49**

Shamrock Comfort-Grip Cutter
Cushion-grip with extra-deep stainless steel sides gives you comfortable control even when cutting into thick desserts. Recipe included. 4.5 x 1.5 in. deep.
2310-W-648 **$3.19**

Shamrock Pan
Celebrate St. Patrick's Day with this fun symbol of joy and celebration. Also great for school parties, birthdays, sports celebrations and much more. One-mix pan is 11.75 x 2 in. deep. Aluminum.
2105-W-185 **$9.99**

Shamrock Sprinkle Mix
Shake up your St. Patrick's Day treats! Plastic 2.5 oz. bottle for convenient pouring and storing. Certified Kosher.
710-W-7485 **$2.29**

Shamrock Icing Decorations
Perfect for topping cakes, cupcakes and cookies. Certified Kosher. Pk./9.
710-W-286 **$2.29**

Shamrock Green Metal Cookie Cutter
Quality metal cuts neatly. Approx. 3 in.
2308-W-1320 **$0.79**

Sparkle Gel
Squeeze on sparkling color effects with our ready-to-use gel. Great for dots, messages, water effects and fondant accents. Resealable 3.5 oz. tubes. Certified Kosher.
$2.99
Green 704-W-111
White 704-W-107

Cookie Icing
Just heat and squeeze onto cookies using the convenient cap. Sets smooth in just 1 hour. 10 oz. bottle covers approximately 12 cookies 3 in. each; Certified Kosher. **$4.49**
White 704-W-481
Green 704-W-493

4-Leaf Clover Cookie Cutter
Cut cookies, sandwiches and use in crafts. Plastic; 3 in. wide.
2303-W-134 **$0.69**

ORDER TOLL FREE: 800-794-5866

PATRIOTIC
Bakeware

Stars and Stripes Pan
Decorate a grand old flag cake perfect for that July 4th cookout. Accent Old Glory with Piping Gel and fresh summer fruit. One-mix pan is 13 x 9 x 2 in. Aluminum.
2105-W-183 $9.99

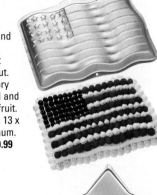

Star Pan
Your colorful star cake will set off sparks on the 4th and brighten parties all year long. One-mix pan is 12.75 x 1.9 in. deep. Aluminum.
2105-W-2512
$12.99

Mini Star Pan
One mix makes 12-16 stars. 6 cavities, 4.75 x 1 in. deep. Aluminum.
2105-W-1235
$14.49

Silicone Mini Star Mold
Microwave, freezer, refrigerator, and dishwasher safe; oven safe to 500°F. One mix makes 20-24 stars. 6 cavities, each 2.6 x 2.5 x 1.5 in. deep.
2105-W-4819 $9.99

Cookie

3 Pc. Red, White and Blue Cutter Set
Bake a star-studded salute to the USA with colorful cutters in sizes from 3.25 to 5 in. Coated metal. Set/3.
2308-W-1240 $4.19

3 Pc. Patriotic Cutter Set
Set of 3 includes flag, star and USA, each approx. 3 to 3.5 in. Coated metal. Set/3.
2308-W-0903 $3.69

Comfort-Grip Star Cutter
Cushion-grip cutters with extra-deep stainless steel sides perfect for cutting so many favorite foods into patriotic shapes. The cushion grip gives you comfortable control even when cutting into thick desserts. Recipe included. 4.5 x 1.5 in. deep.
2310-W-605 $3.19

4 Pc. Nesting Stars Metal Cutter Set
A parade of small to large stars to create fun cookies for the 4th or all year long. Sizes from 5 to 2.5 in. Set/4.
2308-W-1215 $4.79

Star Metal Cookie Cutter
Quality metal is clean-cutting and easy to handle. 3 in.
2308-W-1008 $0.69

6 Pc. Nesting Stars Cutter Set
Plastic. 1.6 to 4.6 in. Set/6.
2304-W-704 $2.99

Star Cookie Treat Pan
Press cookie dough into pan, insert a cookie stick, then bake, cool and decorate. Makes 6 individual treats, 3.5 x .25 in. deep. Aluminum.
2105-W-8102 $9.99

Cookie Treat Sticks
6 in. Pk./20. 1912-W-9319 $1.99
8 in. Pk./20. 1912-W-9318 $2.99

Icings

PATRIOTIC COLOR GUIDE
Red   White   Blue

Ready-to-Decorate Icing
Includes 4 decorating tips! Anyone can decorate with Wilton Ready-to-Decorate Icing! Our brilliant colors add an exciting finishing touch to treats without mixing or mess. 6.4 oz. Certified Kosher. $4.29
Red   710-W-4400
White   710-W-4402
Blue   710-W-4407

Cookie Icing
Just heat and squeeze onto cookies using the convenient cap. Sets smooth in just 1 hour. 10 oz. bottle covers approx. 12 cookies 3 in. each. Certified Kosher.
$4.49
White   704-W-481
Red   704-W-488
Blue   704-W-444

Sparkle Gel
Squeeze on sparkling color effects with our ready-to-use gel. Great for dots, messages, water effects and fondant accents. Resealable 3.5 oz. tubes. Certified Kosher.
$2.99
Red   704-W-112
Blue   704-W-110
White 704-W-107

Tube Decorating Icing
Tubes can be used with our Tip and Nail Set or Coupler Ring Set (p. 142) and any standard size Wilton metal tip. Colors match Wilton Icing Colors (p. 146). 4.25 oz. Certified Kosher. $1.99
Red   704-W-218
White   704-W-200
Royal Blue   704-W-248

Tube Decorating Gel
Transparent gels are great for writing messages and decorating cakes and cookies. Colors match Wilton Icing Colors (p. 146). .75 oz. Certified Kosher.
$1.49
Red   704-W-318
White   704-W-302
Royal Blue   704-W-348

SEASONAL

Party

NEW!

Patriotic Baking Cups
Microwave-safe paper. Standard size, 2 in. diameter, Pk./75.
415-W-1196 $2.09

NEW!

Patriotic Cupcake Combo Pack
Colorful baking cups and picks are the ideal match for your patriotic cupcakes! Cups are microwave-safe paper, 2 in. diameter; picks are 3 in. high. Pk./24.
415-W-1198 $2.29

Patriotic Foil Pix
Looks like a dazzling fireworks display on your holiday treats! Great for cakes, cupcakes. 4 in. high. Pk./12
2113-W-712 $2.49

Stars and Stripes Party Picks
2.75 in. high mini flags. Paper. Pk./40.
2113-W-704 $1.79

Beer Cans
1¾ in. high. Pk./6.
2811-W-9326 $3.99

Red and Blue Sparklers
6½ in. high. Pk./18.
2811-W-704 $1.29

NEW!

Stars & Flags Icing Decorations
Perfect for topping cakes, cupcakes, cookies. Certified Kosher. Pk./15.
710-W-1040 $2.29

NEW!

Patriotic Party Bags
Colorful stars & stripes design for candy and cookie treats. 20 plastic bags, 20 ties included. 4 x 9.5 in. Pk./20.
1912-W-1198 $2.09

Cupcakes 'N More Dessert Stands
Individually decorated cupcakes are the perfect way to add a personal touch to celebrations. Now, with Cupcakes 'N More, you have the perfect way to serve them, featuring wire spirals to securely hold each cupcake.

38 Count Standard
15 x 18 in. wide.
Holds 38 cupcakes.*
307-W-651 $41.99

23 Count Standard
12 x 13 in. wide.
Holds 23 standard cupcakes.*†
307-W-826 $31.49

13 Count Standard (shown)
9.25 x 9 in. wide. Holds 13 standard cupcakes.*
307-W-831 $13.69

24 Count Mini
10.5 x 9 in. wide.
Holds 24 mini cupcakes.*
307-W-250 $15.79

*Pat. No. 7,387,283. †Pat. No. D516,385.

Sprinkles

Individual Bottles
Plastic bottles for easy pouring and storing. Certified Kosher. **$2.29**

Patriotic Mix
2.5 oz. bottle.
710-W-786

Red Sugar
3.25 oz. bottle.
710-W-766

Blue Sugar
3.25 oz. bottle.
710-W-750

Cake Sparkles
Edible glitter, .25 oz. bottle. Certified Kosher. **$3.29**

Red
703-W-1284

Blue
703-W-1314

Colors

Color Mist Food Color Spray
Dazzling effects of an airbrush in a convenient can! Add sensational color to iced cakes, cookies and cupcakes. No mess, taste-free formula. 1.5 oz. Certified Kosher.
$3.29
Red 710-W-5500
Blue 710-W-5501

Candy

Graduation Pretzel Mold
3 designs, 6 cavities.
2115-W-1445 $1.99

Graduation Lollipop Mold
6 designs, 8 cavities.
2115-W-1729 $1.99

Candy Melts
Ideal for all your candy molding, dipping or coating. Artificially vanilla flavored unless otherwise indicated. 14 oz. bag. Certified Kosher Dairy. **$2.99**

Yellow	1911-W-463
White	1911-W-498
Blue	1911-W-448
Dark Cocoa Mint	1911-W-1920
Light Cocoa	1911-W-544
Dark Cocoa	1911-W-358

See pages 194-198 for more Wilton candy items.

ORDER TOLL FREE: 800-794-5866

GRADUATION

Silicone Mini Mortarboard Mold
Microwave, freezer, refrigerator, and dishwasher safe; oven safe to 500°F. One mix makes 20-24 caps. 6 cavities, each 2.7 x 2.7 x 1.25 in. deep.
2105-W-4907 $9.99

Topping Off Success Pan
Decorate in your grad's school colors. One-mix pan is 14.75 x 11.75 x 2 in. deep. Aluminum.
2105-W-2038 $9.99

Book Pan
Detail any of life's important chapters, including graduation. 11.5 x 15 x 2.75 in. deep. Three-mix pan serves up to 30. Aluminum.
2105-W-2521 $17.99

Party

NEW!

Graduation Baking Cups
Microwave-safe paper. Standard size, 2 in. diameter, Pk./75.
415-W-1352 $2.09

NEW!

Graduation Cupcake Combo Pack
Lively baking cups and picks are the ideal match for your graduation cupcakes! Cups are microwave-safe paper, 2 in. diameter; picks are 3 in. high. Pk./24.
415-W-1354 $2.29

NEW!

Graduation Party Bags
Fun cap and star designs for candy and cookie treats. 20 plastic bags, 20 ties included. 4 x 9.5 in. Pk./20.
1912-W-1200 $2.09

NEW!

Graduation Class Cupcake Stand
Greet the grad with cupcakes and treats served on this fun centerpiece stand. In minutes, you can create an exciting 3-tiered cupcake stand with a graduation topper. Your cupcakes will look perfect for the party. Stand measures 1 ft. wide x 1.5 ft. high. Instructions included.
1510-W-1048 $5.99

Candles

Candle Set
3 caps, 3 diplomas, ½ to 2 in. high. Set/6.
2811-W-1800 $3.99

Champagne Bottle Candles
2 in. high. Set/6.
2811-W-163 $3.99

NEW!

Graduation Add-A-Message Fun Pix
Serve party cupcakes in an exciting new way—clip on pictures, messages and more with these fun plastic picks! Great for place markers, too! 3 in. high. Pk./24.
2113-W-1008 $2.29

Cookie

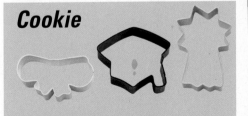

3 Pc. Graduation Cutter Set
Set of 3 includes diploma, graduation cap and star ribbon, each approx. 3 to 3.5 in. Coated metal. Set/3.
2308-W-1491 $3.69

SEASONAL

Wedding Style

Wilton has a beautiful selection of products for today's bride. From invitations to toasting glasses to favors, we'll help you design the wedding day of your dreams!

Wedding Ensembles

Fulfill your wedding day dreams with the finest coordinated wedding accessories. A complete collection makes a beautiful gift. Or choose individual accessories that personalize and accessorize the wedding day perfectly!

TIE THE KNOT

NEW!

A lavish taffeta bow decorates each of these accessory pieces.
A. Ring Bearer's Pillow 120-W-1039 **$14.99**
B. Guest Book/Pen Set 120-W-1041 **$19.99**
C. Flower Basket 120-W-1040 **$9.99**

SWIRL

NEW!

Bands of contrast beautifully encircle accessories. Candles feature faux rhinestone embellishment. Cake Knife & Server have stainless steel blades.
A. Cake Knife/Server Set and Toasting Glasses 120-W-445 **$39.99**
B. Unity Candle and Taper Candle Set 120-W-065 **$29.99**

GARDENIA

NEW!

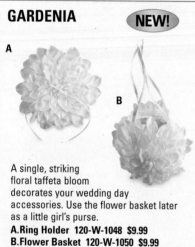

A single, striking floral taffeta bloom decorates your wedding day accessories. Use the flower basket later as a little girl's purse.
A. Ring Holder 120-W-1048 **$9.99**
B. Flower Basket 120-W-1050 **$9.99**

SWEETHEART

NEW!

The traditional symbol of true love adorns your favorite wedding day items.
Cake Knife/Server Set
120-W-125 **$19.99**

SIMPLICITY

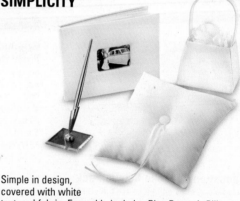

Simple in design, covered with white textured fabric. Ensemble includes Ring Bearer's Pillow, Flower Basket, Guest Book, Pen and Holder.
120-W-1244 **$59.99**

TIMELESS

Cake Knife/ Server Set
Lovely, opulent look with sophisticated detailing.
120-W-4004 **$29.99**

HEART SILVER

Toasting Glasses and Serving Ensemble
Bring the ultimate look of romance to your celebration. Silver-plated. Set/4.
120-W-232 **$49.99**

TOASTING GLASSES

Fluted
Fluted glasses toast the bride and groom on their special day. Set/2.
120-W-784 **$21.99**

TRADITIONAL

Guest Book & Pen
Guest book with attached pen creates a beautiful display at the reception table. Crafted in pearlized paper.
120-W-082 **$14.99**

ORDER TOLL FREE: 800-794-5866

Print Your Own Stationery

Create your own distinctive invitations and more with professional results right at home. It's easy to do—simply go to www.wiltonprint.com and see how. All stationery includes test sheets for perfect printing!

POCKET INVITATIONS

Today's trend in wedding stationery—the invitation and accessory cards are displayed and tucked into the pocket.

NEW!

NEW!

Embossed Flower
Bronze embossed shimmer paper.
Set of 25 Includes:
•25 Invitations and Mailing Envelopes
•25 Pocket Folders
•25 All-Purpose Cards
•25 Reply Cards & Envelopes
1008-W-1520 $34.99

Bronze Photo
Bronze shimmer paper.
Set of 25 Includes:
• 25 Invitations and Mailing Envelopes
• 25 Pocket Folders
• 50 All-Purpose Cards
• 25 Reply Cards & Envelopes
• 25 Gold Seals
1008-W-1516 $34.99

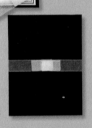

String of Pearls
White with Pearlized trim.
Set of 25 Includes:
•25 Invitations and Mailing Envelopes
•25 Pocket Folders
•50 All-Purpose Cards
•25 Reply Cards & Envelopes
•25 Printable Seals
1008-W-177 $34.99

Black & White Elegance
White with Black trim.
Set of 25 Includes:
•25 Invitations and Mailing Envelopes
•50 All-Purpose Cards
•25 Reply Cards & Envelopes
•25 Pockets
•75 Foam Adhesives
•25 White Organza Ribbons & Bows
1008-W-186 $34.99

Vintage Ivy
Ivory and Brown.
Set of 25 Includes:
•25 Invitations and Mailing Envelopes
•25 Pocket Folders
•50 All-Purpose Cards
•25 Reply Cards & Envelopes
•25 Adhesives, Ribbons & Pre-Tied Bows
1008-W-178 $34.99

NEW!

Black & White Scroll Delight
Black and white.
Set of 25 Includes:
•25 Invitations and Mailing Envelopes
•25 Reply Cards, 25 Envelopes
•25 Belly Bands
•25 Bows, Ribbons, Adhesives
1008-W-1519 $24.99

NEW!

Calla Lily Bouquet
White and ivory.
Set of 25 Includes:
•25 Invitations and Mailing Envelopes
•25 Vellum Wraps
•25 Reply Cards and Envelopes
•25 Pre-Tied Bows, Adhesives
1008-W-1565 $24.99

Glitz and Glamour
White/Pearlized White/Glittered Vellum Wrap.
Set of 25 Includes:
•25 Invitations and Mailing Envelopes
•25 Vellum Wraps
•25 Reply Cards and Envelopes
•25 Ribbon and Flower Embellishments, Adhesives
1008-W-314 $24.99

Happy Day
White with White/Glittered Vellum Pocket.
Set of 25 Includes:
•25 Invitations and Mailing Envelopes
•25 Reply Cards and Envelopes
•25 Pre-Tied Bows with Faux Rhinestone Trim, Adhesives
1008-W-711 $24.99

Scroll Bi-Fold Program
Ivory with Gold trim.
Includes:
• 50 Programs
1008-W-1555 $14.99

NEW!

Bridal Shower Fun
Pink and coordinating colors.
Set of 12 Includes:
• 12 Invitations and Mailing Envelopes
• 36 Icons
• 36 Adhesives
1008-W-1542 $5.99

Bride
White and Blue.
Set of 12 Includes:
• 12 Invitations and Mailing Envelopes
• 12 Tulle and Pre-Tied Bow Embellishments, Adhesives
1008-W-789 $9.99

NEW!

Save-the-Date Postcards
Pink and brown.
Set of 12 Includes:
• 12 Postcards
• 12 Print-Your-Own-Cards
• 12 Magnets
1008-W-1522 $5.99

Wedding Day Accessories

FLOWER-SHAPED PETALS

Fill the flower girl's basket, scatter on the cake table, decorate favors. Lifelike 2.5 in. diameter flower petals. Approx. 300 petals. **$9.99**

French Rose Wedding Bouquet

Perfect, beautiful blooms to keep or to use during the bouquet toss. Hand-crafted, fine faux flowers. Bouquet measures approx. 9.5 in. diameter x 7.5 in. **120-W-1013 $24.99**

Pink Rose
1006-W-984

Red Rose
1006-W-944

White Stephanotis
1006-W-952

Wedding Day Décor

Aisle Runner

Decorate the wedding aisle with a floral runner that adds a touch of elegance to the wedding ceremony. Aisle Runner also ensures that the bride's dress stays clean on the walk down the aisle! With pull cord for even unrolling; runner measures 100 ft. long x 3 ft. wide.
1006-W-996 $29.99

BRIDAL GARLANDS

Drape on pews and line the aisles, place along table edges and around the cake, wrap around pillars.

Lighted White Rose
Adds a soft glow! Uses 2 D Batteries, not included. 6 ft. length.
1006-W-350 $23.99

Rose Garland
Life-like roses strung together by organza ribbon. 6 ft. length. Non-lighting.
1006-W-917 $9.99

Flameless Votives

Add the romantic glow of candlelight with safe, no flame candles. Includes: 8 flameless votives (with 8 replaceable CR2032 batteries included), 8 holders. Average battery life: 24 hours. Set/8.
1006-W-7137 $15.99

RECEPTION GIFT CARD HOLDERS

Attractively keep the wedding gift cards together at the reception. Tulle, ribbon, flowers and cards not included.

Gift Shape

Whimsical gift box design of sturdy metal construction with faux gem trim. Extra long slot for envelopes, box opens from the top, heart-shaped lock and key. 10.75 in. high x 8 in. wide x 8 in. deep
120-W-220 $24.99

Mailbox

Personalize the flag with a photo or saying at www.wiltonprint.com. Includes easy to assemble mailbox, 2 printable labels, 1 test sheet. White printed cardboard. 12 in. high x 15.25 in. wide x 10.25 in. deep.
1006-W-396 $14.99

Wishing Well

A charming display for any shower, wedding, or anniversary celebration. White printed cardboard, easy to assemble. 30.5 in. high x 16 in. wide x 14 in. deep.
1006-W-395 $14.99

Celebration Tree

Use it as a party decoration, or as a centerpiece. Easy to assemble. Metal. Approx. 14 in. high x 11 in. wide. (Favors and decorations shown not included.)
1006-W-571 $9.99

ORDER TOLL FREE: 800-794-5866

Send-Off Favors

Wedding Style
Newest wedding book from Wilton features color-themed ideas for invitations, favors, decorations. Includes step-by-step instructions and materials checklists. Wilton Wedding Style gives you:
- 100-plus ideas for invitations, favors, tabletop décor and more
- 18 dream cakes plus petits fours, cupcakes and edible favors
- Step-by-step project instructions with materials checklists
- Hundreds of decorating ideas for ceremonies and receptions

Soft cover, 124 pages.
902-W-1101 $14.99

Ribbon Wands
Celebrate the bride and groom with a wave of these ribbon wands. Adds a festive flair to the celebration and great photo opportunities at send-off! Can be personalized with your wedding colors. Pk./24.
1006-W-9099 $19.99

Wedding Banner
Beautiful fabric banner announces the bride's arrival. Reverse side displays the just married message. Banner can be personalized with bride and groom's names or wedding date. Messages are embroidered on 100% polyester. 20 in. wide x 24 in. high.
1006-W-9100 $19.99

Car Decorating Kit
Eye-catching decorations trim the bride and groom's getaway vehicle with style! Includes: magnetic "Just Married" sign, window clings, pre-fluffed pom-poms, streamers, balloons. Crafted of weather-resistant materials, reusable (except balloons).
1006-W-483 $15.79

Pop Out Streamers
Great for weddings, graduations, birthdays, New Year's celebrations, surprise parties. Just aim and press lever. Each contains ten silver foil streamers that stay attached to tube for easy disposal. Streamers are over 10 feet long. Spring loaded, the streamers do not contain gunpowder or other explosives. Pk./14.
1006-W-932 $24.99

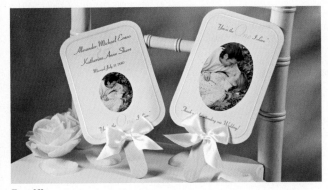

Fan Kit
Create a distinctive favor for your special day! Wedding fans not only keep guests comfortable, but let guests wave their approval of the bride and groom! Personalize the fan front and back with photos, special messages, and wedding day details online at www.wiltonprint.com, then print at home. Assembled fan measures approximately 10 in. long. Includes 24 fans, 24 ribbon bows, 24 fan handles, 24 adhesive strips. Pk./24.
120-W-516 $9.99

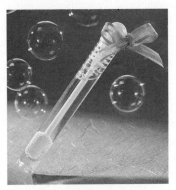

Love Knot Bubble Wands
Use after the ceremony or at the reception. 36 wands are packed in a convenient tray for reception table use. Each wand contains .16 fl. oz. bubble solution. Ribbon not included. Pat. Nos. D485,584 and D536,395. Pk./36.
1007-W-8017 $9.99

Silver-Tone Celebration Bells
Ring for a special kiss after the ceremony and at the reception. Hand to guests or place one at each setting at the reception. Contains 24 metal bells, poem tags and ties. Bell measures 1.25 in. tall. Pk./24.
1007-W-8012 $6.49

Favor- Making Kits

Fun and festive kits make it easy to personalize your favors online, at www.wiltonprint.com. Just download the template and print out the tags or labels. Each kit includes instructions and 2 test sheets. Candy not included.

Goblet Favor Kit
Raise the goblet favors and toast the bride and groom! Add a tulle circle, fill with your favorite candy, add a personalized tag and place one at each guest's place setting. Goblets measure 2.75 in. high. Includes 24 each favor containers, satin ribbons, tulle circles, printable tags. Pk./24.
1006-W-923 $24.99

Love Potion Favor Kit
Fill to match your celebration theme and surprise your guests. Bottles measure 2.75 in. high. Kit includes 24 glass bottles with slotted corks. 24 (12 in.) satin ribbon lengths, funnel for easy filling, 24 printable labels. Pk./24.
1006-W-1009 $24.99

Martini Glass Favor Kit
Create a favor that toasts your guests with a treat and a personalized message. Martini glasses measure 3.5 in. high. Includes 24 each favor containers, satin ribbons, tulle circles, printable tags. Pk./24.
120-W-518 $24.99

Champagne Bottle Favor Kit
Create a shower or reception favor that toasts your guests with a treat and a personalized message. Bottles measure 4 in. high. Includes 24 each favor containers, satin ribbons, printable labels. Pk./24.
120-W-519 $24.99

Favor Tin Kit
Create personalized favor tins for your celebration using your computer, or hand design. Includes 25 tins, 25 adhesive labels and strips. Tins measure 2 in. diameter. Pk./25.
1006-W-8038 $19.99

Umbrella Favor Kit
Shower your guests with a favor that carries a personalized message. Use as a place card, add an announcement or a thank you. Umbrellas measure 4 in. high. Includes 24 each favor containers, satin ribbons, printable tags. Pk./24.
120-W-520 $24.99

Heart Favor Kit
Fill with your favorite candy, wrap in the tulle, add a personalized tag to make beautiful favors for bridal shower and wedding reception. Hearts measure 2.5 in. wide x 1 in. deep. Includes 24 each favor containers, satin ribbons, tulle circles, printable tags. Pk./24.
1006-W-924 $24.99

Silver-Tone Bell Favor Kit
Set a bell at each place setting, guests will ring for the newlyweds to kiss. Bells measure 2.25 in. high. Includes 20 metal favor bells, 20 (12 in.) satin ribbon lengths, 20 printable place cards. Pk./20.
1006-W-1136 $24.99

Favor Accents

Romantic accents add sparkling beauty and elegance to favors, table decorations!

Engagement Rings
Add sparkle to favors, centerpieces, table decorations. "Faux diamond" approx. .25 in. diameter. Metal. Pk./12.
1006-W-115 $1.99

Sweetheart Charms
Shows the sweet, sentimental sign of love.Stamped tin. Measures 1.25 x .75 in. Pk./12.
1006-W-411 $1.99

Thank You Tags
Send a message of gratitude —tie to favor boxes or bags. Stamped tin. Measures 1.75 in. diameter. Pk./12.
1006-W-987 $1.99

White Pearl Beading
Molded on one continuous 5-yard strand. Plastic. Large (6 mm).
211-W-1990 $3.99

ORDER TOLL FREE: 800-794-5866

Favor Containers

These beautiful containers hold favors for shower, wedding and anniversary celebrations. Perfect for mints, almonds, potpourri and small gifts.

Flirty Fleur Favor Boxes
2.25 in. high x 2.25 in. wide. Paper.
Pk./10.
1006-W-936 $4.99

Sweet Heart Ribbon Favor Bags
6 in. high x 3.25 wide x 1.75 in. deep.
Includes sheer white ribbon. Paper.
Pk./10.
1006-W-940 $4.99

Flirty Fleur Ribbon Favor Bags
6 in. high x 3.25 wide x 1.75 in. deep.
Includes sheer white ribbon. Paper.
Pk./10.
1006-W-941 $4.99

Cake Slice Boxes
Bakery style boxes measure
5 in. square x 3.5 in. high.
Pk./5.
415-W-955 $3.99

Cookie Cutters

Bride's favorite cutter shapes are perfect for cookie making or as favors for guests at the shower and reception.

4 Pc. Wedding Cutter Set
Shapes include tiered cake, wedding dress, wedding bells, joined hearts. Recipe included. Each approx. 3 in. Coated metal. Set/4.
2308-W-1071 $4.79

Favor Candy

Trendy and traditional candies make great fillers for favors, candy buffets and candy dishes at showers, weddings, and celebrations!

Bling Rings
30 pieces per package. Sweet/tart fruit flavored. Each measures 1.12 in. high x 1 wide.
1006-W-6173 $4.29

Love Mix
Sweet/tart flavored.
12 oz. bag.
1006-W-9041 $6.29

Classic Doves
Sweet/tart flavored.
12 oz. bag.
1006-W-9052 $6.29

Pastel Jelly Beans
Fruit flavored.
12 oz. bag.
1006-W-9050 $4.29

Hearts
Sweet/tart strawberry flavored. 12 oz. bag.
1006-W-9053 $6.29

Pastel Pearls
Fruit flavored.
10 oz. bag.
Certified Kosher.
1006-W-904 $4.29

Wedding Bells
Sweet/tart flavored.
12 oz. bag.
1006-W-1140 $6.29

Mint Drops
Pastel. Certified Kosher
Dairy. 14 oz. bag.
1006-W-788 $6.29
32 oz. bag.
1006-W-3710 $13.99

Peppermint Pearls
10 oz. bag.
Certified Kosher.
1006-W-9401 $4.29

Pillow Mints
10 oz. bag. Pastel.
1006-W-858 $4.29
48 oz. bag. Pastel.
1006-W-379 $20.99
48 oz. bag. White.
1006-W-3711 $20.99

Jordan Almonds
Certified Kosher.
16 oz. bag. Pastel.
1006-W-779 $7.99
16 oz. bag. White.
1006-W-778 $7.99
44 oz. bag. Pastel.
1006-W-1133 $21.99
44 oz. bag. White.
1006-W-1134 $21.99

Wedding Cakes

The beautiful cake designs Wilton is famous for are just the beginning of your dream wedding presentation. Richly detailed Wilton cake toppers, accents, stands and separators complement your design to capture the moment forever.

Wedding Toppers

Discover the unmatched detail that has made Wilton figurines the perfect finishing touch for generations. The rich, sculpted crafting, realistic detailing and romantic designs make these figurines perfect wedding day keepsakes.

NEW!

Clay Topper
Height: 6.44 in.
Base: 3.5 x 2.25 in.
Material: Polymer clay.
202-W-100 $24.99

NEW!

Monogram Topper
Height: 5.875 in.
Base: 3.75 x 2.5 in.
Material: Acrylic.
202-W-103 $24.99

First Kiss
Height: 6.75 in.
Base: 3 in. diameter.
Material: Bonded marble.
202-W-258 $24.99

Clear Bianca
Height: 5.5 in.
Base: 3.75 x 3.5 in.
Material: Acrylic.
202-W-424 $24.99

Threshold of Happiness
Height: 5 in. Base: 3.25 x 2 in.
Material: Resin.
202-W-202 $24.99

Our Day
Height: 4.75 in.
Base: 2 x 1.75 in.
Material: Resin.
202-W-409 $6.99

Lasting Love
Height: 4.5 in.
Base: 2.25 x 1.75 in.
Material: Resin.
202-W-302 $6.99

Two Rings
Height: 5.5 in. Base: 3.75 in. diameter.
Material: Plastic, resin.
1006-W-1121 $34.99

Simple Joys
Height: 8 in.
Base: 4.5 in. diameter.
Material: Plastic, fabric flowers, fabric.
103-W-150 $24.99

Petite Spring Song
Height: 7 in.
Base: 3.25 in. diameter.
Material: Plastic, fabric flowers.
106-W-159 $12.99

HUMOROUS WEDDING FIGURINES

Add a lighthearted touch to the celebration. Great for pre-wedding events such as showers, these figurines are sure to bring a smile to the face of anyone who has ever planned a wedding!

Oh No You Don't
Height: 4.25 in. Base: 6 x 3 in.
Material: Resin.
115-W-102 $19.99 **Ethnic 115-W-104 $19.99**

Now I Have You
Height: 4.25 in. Base: 4.25 x 3.75 in.
Material: Resin.
115-W-101 $19.99

Ball and Chain
Height: 2.25 in. Base: 3.5 in.
Material: Resin.
1006-W-7143 $19.99

ORDER TOLL FREE: 800-794-5866

CAKE PICKS

The new look—stunning picks draw attention to your celebration—perfect for cake tops, floral arrangements, bouquets and centerpieces. Beautifully appointed with rhinestones, crafted of painted resin.

Decorative
Perfect for wedding and anniversary celebrations.

I Do
3.5 in. high, 7 in. wide.
120-W-928 $14.99

Double Hearts
5 in. high, 4.5 in. wide.
1006-W-985 $14.99

Anniversary
Delicately detailed picks with the look of silver or gold create a cake to remember.

Silver 25th
5 in. high, 4 in. wide.
1008-W-758 $14.99

Gold 50th
5.25 in. high, 4.25 in. wide.
1008-W-762 $14.99

Cake Displays

Stunning Wilton Cake Displays are the perfect way to show off your special wedding cake. Take a look—there's one perfectly suited to your wedding cake size and design.

NEW!

Cake and Treat Display Set

Elegance and versatility all in one cake stand set! Three different stand sizes and removable scroll legs allow multiple combinations of cake set-ups. The elegant white finish and clear plates will complement any cake design for perfect creative display. Also a beautiful way to serve cupcakes, appetizers and other party foods. Set includes: 3 coated metal support rings (8.25 in dia. x 8.25 in. high, 10.25 in. dia. x 6.25 in. high, 12.25 in. dia. x 4 in. high), 3 clear plastic plates (8, 10, 12 in. dia.), coated metal scrolled legs [3 each small (3.5 in.), medium (6.75 in.) and large (8.25 in.)]. Set/15.
307-W-352 $39.99

3 Tier Pillar Cake Stand

A distinctive display, featuring locking pillars in a secure base, providing dramatic tier heights and stable support. Its unique design and clean construction complements any setting—great for cakes, mini cakes, appetizers and more. Set includes 15.75 in. off-white plastic base; 3 pillars—5.75 in., 12.75 in. and 19.5 in. high; 3 plate supports and plates (10 in., 12 in. and 14 in. plates hold 10 in., 12 in. and 14 in. round cakes).
307-W-350 $59.99

Graceful Tiers Cake Stand

Ideal for garden-themed wedding cakes, but also perfect to display cupcakes, muffins, candies, fruit and more. The three-tiered, scrollwork stand features crystal-clear plates which nest securely in each section. Set includes cream-colored powder-coated metal stand, 14.5 in. wide x 29.5 in. high; 3 clear separator plates, 8, 10 and 12 in. diameter; 1 wrench, all hardware; assembly instructions.
307-W-841 $54.99

Replacement Plate Set
302-W-7925 $10.49

Fancy Scrolls Cake Stand

The perfect way to display your party cakes or fancy desserts. Slide the two scrolled base pieces together to form the base and place the 12 in. plate on top for a secure cake presentation. After the party, the base pieces easily disassemble and lock into the plate for compact storage.
307-W-854 $14.99

Cake Displays

Round Floating Tiers Cake Stands (Collapsible)

The beautiful illusion of floating tiers makes a grand display for your cakes. Includes tier support rings, ring support bars, connector bar, 8, 12, and 16 in. separator plates. Assembly required. Instructions and all hardware included. Disassembles for easy storage.
307-W-710 $77.99

Replacement plates are available at www.wilton.com

Candlelight Cake Stand

Elegant scrollwork and soft candlelight show off your cake design. Flameless votives are convenient and safe. Stand supports 40 lbs., use with 14 in. smooth or scallop edge separator plate (not included). Set includes 21.5 in. diameter x 5 in. high stand, 4 flameless votives (with 4 replaceable CR2032 batteries included), 4 glass holders. Average battery life: 24 hours.
307-W-351 $44.99

Cakes 'N More 3-Tier Party Stand

Contemporary stairstep stand with crystal-clear plates puts the focus where it belongs—on your stunning cake and desserts! Constructed in metal with chrome-plated finish, stand holds 3 different size cake plates—8, 10 and 12 in. (included).
307-W-859 $31.49
Replacement Plates Set/3. 302-W-7925 $10.49

CUPCAKES 'N MORE DESSERT STANDS

Individually decorated cupcakes are the perfect way to add a personal touch to celebrations. Now, with Cupcakes 'N More, you have the perfect way to serve them, featuring wire spirals to securely hold each cupcake.

38 Count Standard
15 in. high x 18 in. wide. Holds 38 cupcakes.* (shown) 307-W-651 $41.99
23 Count Standard
12 in. high x 13 in. wide. Holds 23 cupcakes.*†
307-W-826 $31.49
13 Count Standard
9.25 in. high x 9 in. wide. Holds 13 cupcakes.*
307-W-831 $13.69
24 Count Mini
10.5 in. high x 9 in. wide. Holds 24 mini cupcakes.*
307-W-250 $15.79
*Pat. No. 7,387,283. †Pat. No. D516,385.

Romantic Castle Cake Set

Create a fairy tale for your wedding. Everything you need to transform your tiered cake into a fantasy castle is included: three sizes of detailed turret towers with removable peak pieces, lattice windows, a paneled door and roof pieces. Complete assembly and decorating ideas included. For design ideas visit www.wilton.com! Set/32.
301-W-910 $20.99

ORDER TOLL FREE: 800-794-5866

Separator Plates

Decorator Preferred Smooth Edge Plates
Built for unmatched stability, with patented Circles of Strength design.

6 in.	302-W-4101	$2.39
8 in.	302-W-4102	$3.29
10 in.	302-W-4103	$4.29
12 in.	302-W-4104	$5.29
14 in.	302-W-4105	$6.29
16 in.	302-W-4106	$9.49
18 in.	302-W-4107	$12.59

Decorator Preferred Square Plates
Clean lines, smooth edges, unmatched strength. Features patented Circles of Strength design.

6 in.	302-W-1801	$3.19
8 in.	302-W-1802	$4.19
10 in.	302-W-1803	$5.29
12 in.	302-W-1804	$6.29
14 in.	302-W-1805	$7.39
16 in.	302-W-1806	$10.49
18 in.	302-W-1807	$13.69

Decorator Preferred Scalloped Plates
Built for unmatched stability, with patented Circles of Strength design.

6 in.	302-W-6	$2.39	12 in.	302-W-12	$5.29
7 in.	302-W-7	$2.59	13 in.	302-W-13	$5.79
8 in.	302-W-8	$3.29	14 in.	302-W-14	$6.29
9 in.	302-W-9	$3.69	15 in.	302-W-15	$7.39
10 in.	302-W-10	$4.29	16 in.	302-W-16	$9.49
11 in.	302-W-11	$4.79	18 in.	302-W-18	$12.59

Crystal-Look Plates
Wilton Crystal-Look plates have an elegance like no other, with ridged sides that look like cut crystal. Use with Crystal-Look pillars (sold below).

7 in.	302-W-2013	$4.19	13 in. 302-W-2078	$8.39
9 in.	302-W-2035	$5.29	*17 in. 302-W-1810	$15.79
11 in.	302-W-2051	$6.29		

*Use only with 13.75 in. Crystal-Look pillars (sold below).

17 in. Crystal-Look Plate and Pillar Set
Contains four 13.75 in. pillars and two 17 in. plates. (not shown)

301-W-1387 $48.29

FILLABLE PILLARS
Fill pillars with colorful gems, ribbon or decorative stones to personalize your cake design! A great way to add reception colors or themes to a classic wedding cake design. Pillars are designed to be used with Wilton Decorator Preferred Separator Plates in a variety of sizes and shapes. Sets include 4 pillars, 8 pedestals. Not recommended to be filled with any type of liquid. Plastic. Pk./12.

4 in. Fillable Pillars
303-W-801 $7.99

6 in. Fillable Pillars
303-W-802 $9.99

Separator Pillars

"Hidden" Pillars
Separate cake tiers and create a floating illusion. Pushed into tiers as dowel rods, they fit onto all Decorator Preferred separator plates. Trimmable, hollow plastic. 6 in. high. Pk./4.

303-W-8 $3.19

Crystal-Look Pillars
Contemporary cut crystal look. Pk./4.

3 in.	303-W-2171	$3.69
5 in.	303-W-2196	$4.79
7 in.	303-W-2197	$5.29
*13.75 in. (not shown)	303-W-2242	$4.19

*Sold singly. Use only with 17 in. Crystal-Look plate (sold above).

Grecian Pillars
Elegantly scrolled and ribbed. Pk./4.

3 in.	303-W-3606	$3.29
5 in.	303-W-3703	$4.29
7 in.	303-W-3705	$5.49

Crystal-Look Spiked Pillars
For single plate cake construction. Pk./4.

7 in.	303-W-2322	$4.79
9 in.	303-W-2324	$5.79

Grecian Spiked Pillars
For single plate cake construction. Wide base increases stability. Pk./4.

5 in.	303-W-3708	$2.59
7 in.	303-W-3710	$3.69
9 in.	303-W-3712	$4.79

Baker's Best Disposable Pillars with Rings
For single plate cake construction. Pk./4.

7 in.	303-W-4000	$3.19
9 in.	303-W-4001	$3.69

Roman Columns
Handsome pillars may be used with 16 and 18 in. plates. Pk./2.

10.25 in.	303-W-8136	$6.29
13.75 in.	303-W-2130	$7.39

Cake Assembly Sets

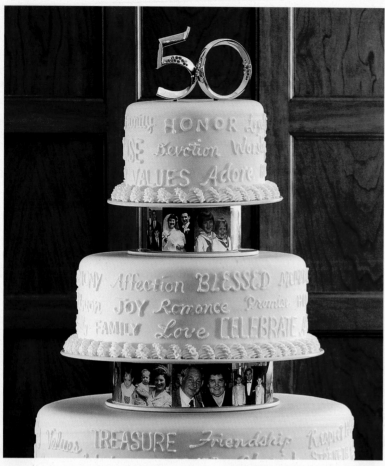

Globe Pillar and Base Sets

The 2 and 2.5 in. Pillar Sets are positioned between tiers, as globes fit over hidden pillars to provide strong support. The 3 in. Base Set features a reinforced center channel which fits over separator plate feet to hold your base cake. Sets include four globes and four 9 in. pillars. Globe Base Set includes 4 pillar globe bases.

2 in. Globe Pillar Set/8.
303-W-822 $8.39
2.5 in. Globe Pillar Set/8.
303-W-824 $10.49
3 in. Globe Base Set/4.
303-W-825 $10.49
9 in. Replacement Pillars Set/4.
303-W-4005 $4.19

Tailored Tiers Cake Display Set

The elegant patterned fabric complements most wedding, shower and anniversary designs. As an added bonus, use the included acetate photo wraps to customize the separators with treasured family photos, wrapping paper or an alternate fabric. Set includes 2 satin brocade wrapped craft foam separators (4.25 and 7.25 in. diameter x 2 in. high), 4 smooth-edge spiked separator plates (one 6 in., two 8 in., one 12 in. diameter) and 2 acetate photo wraps. Set/8.
304-W-8174 $31.49

Spiral Separator Set

Add an elegant touch to your special occasion cakes with this beautifully scrolled separator. Setup could not be simpler—the smooth-edge plates are spiked to fit inside the top and bottom rings for a secure presentation. 10 in. Set Includes 7 x 4.25 in. high wire separator ring, 2 smooth-edge separator plates, 8 and 10 in. diameter. Set/3.
303-W-8176 $20.99

Fluted Bowl Separator Set

Simply fill it with fresh or silk flowers, tulle or patterned fabric, or use it on its own. Setup could not be simpler—spiked separator plates fit inside the top and bottom openings of the bowl for a secure presentation. Set includes 4 in. high fluted bowl and 2 smooth-edge separator plates (6 and 10 in. diameter). Set/3.
303-W-823 $20.99

Roman Column Tier Set

Stately Roman pillars and scalloped-edge plates create beautiful settings for all tiered cakes. Includes 8 pieces: six 13.75 in. Roman columns and two 18 in. round Decorator Preferred separator plates. Set/8.
301-W-1981 $44.99

Tall Tier Cake Stand

Display your multi-tiered cakes up to 6 tiers high with this majestic stand. Lace-look plates enhance every cake design and hold tiers from 6 to 16 in. diameter. The twist-together center columns and strong, interchangeable plates provide stability.

Basic Set

Includes: 5 columns, 6.5 in. high; top nut and bottom bolt; 18 in. footed base plate; 8, 10, 12, 14 and 16 in. separator plates. Set/13.
304-W-7915 $49.99

Crystal-Clear Cake Divider Set

Sparkling twist legs push through the cake, rest on plate below and beautifully accent your cake design. (Dowel rods not needed). Includes 6, 8, 10, 12, 14 and 16 in. separator plates, and 24 7.5 in. twist legs. Set/30.
301-W-9450 $52.49

Additional Plates

6 in.	**302-W-9730**	**$3.19**
8 in.	**302-W-9749**	**$4.19**
10 in.	**302-W-9757**	**$5.29**
12 in.	**302-W-9765**	**$7.39**
14 in.	**302-W-9773**	**$9.49**
16 in.	**302-W-9780**	**$11.59**

7.5 in. Twist Legs

Pk./4. **303-W-9794 $4.19**

9 in. Twist Legs

Pk./4. **303-W-977 $5.29**

Dowel Rods and Pegs

Wooden Dowel Rods

Cut and sharpen with strong shears or serrated knife. Length: 12 in. Diam.: .25 in. Pk./12.
399-W-1009 $3.29

Plastic Dowel Rods

Heavy-duty hollow plastic provides strong, stable support. Cut with serrated knife or strong shears to desired length. Length: 12.25 in. Diam.: .75 in. Pk./4.
399-W-801 $2.59

Plastic Pegs

Insure that cake layers and separator plates atop cakes stay in place. Pegs do not add support; dowel rod cake properly before using. Length: 4 in. Pk./12.
399-W-762 $1.49

Cake Accessories

Flower Display Cups

Blossom-shaped display cups are a creative way to add the beauty of fresh flowers to cake designs. Flower Cups help with the arrangement of flowers by keeping them in place while displayed on the cake surface. Bottom spike holds cup in place on fondant or buttercream icing; top spike can hold a ball of fondant for easy insertion of stems. Plastic. Pk./3.
205-W-8504 $6.99

Fresh Flower Cake Spikes

The perfect way to display fresh flowers on cakes. Spike is topped by a silicone cap to prevent spills and hold flowers in place. Also ideal holders for wired icing flowers and artificial flower displays. Plastic. Pk./6.
205-W-8501 $6.99

Flower Holder Ring

Use at the base of Fanci Fountain. 12.5 in. diameter x 2 in. high. 1.75 in. wide opening; inside ring diameter is 8.5 in. Plastic.
305-W-435 $5.49

Fanci Fountain Cake Fountain

Add the drama of flowing water to your wedding cake design. The crystal-clear design enhances any tiered cake. Adjustable, smooth water flow. Use with 16 or 18 in. scalloped edge plates; or 18 in. smooth edge plate (p. 237). Set-up instructions included. Height: 12 in. Diameter: 10 in.
306-W-2000 $73.49

Replacement Parts for Fanci Fountain are available at www.wilton.com.

Crystal Bridge and Graceful Stairway Set

Bridge the gap between lavish tiers. Includes two stairways (16.75 in. long) and one platform (4.75 x 5 in.). Plastic. Set/3.
205-W-2311 $16.99

Silver Cake Platters

Grease-resistant platters serve party cakes, pastries and appetizers with style! Strong corrugated board features a shining silver-tone surface and elegant scalloped shape.

NEW!

12 in. Round
Pk./8.
2104-W-1166 $8.49

14 in. Round
Pk./6.
2104-W-1167 $8.49

13 x 19 in. Rectangle
Pk./4.
2104-W-1169 $8.99

ORDER TOLL FREE: 800-794-5866

Cake Boards and Accents

Your cake will look its best when presented with quality Wilton boards, doilies and ruffled trims.

Cake Boards

Shaped cakes look best on boards cut to fit! Strong corrugated cardboard, generously-sized in rectangular shapes. Perfect for sheet and square cakes. For shaped cakes, use the pan as a pattern and cut out board to fit cake (see p. 110).

10 x 14 in. Pk./6. **2104-W-554 $5.99**
13 x 19 in. Pk./6. **2104-W-552 $5.99**

Cake Circles

Corrugated cardboard for strength and stability.

6 in. diameter Pk./10.	**2104-W-64**	**$3.99**
8 in. diameter Pk./12.	**2104-W-80**	**$4.79**
10 in. diameter Pk./12.	**2104-W-102**	**$5.99**
12 in. diameter Pk./8.	**2104-W-129**	**$5.99**
14 in. diameter Pk./6.	**2104-W-145**	**$6.29**
16 in. diameter Pk./6.	**2104-W-160**	**$6.99**

Silver Cake Bases

Convenient .5 in. thick silver foil-covered bases are grease-resistant, food-safe and reusable. Strong to hold heavy decorated cakes without an additional serving plate. Perfect for all types of cakes and craft creations.

10 in. Round Pk./2.	**2104-W-1187**	**$7.99**
12 in. Round Pk./2.	**2104-W-1188**	**$8.99**
14 in. Round Pk./2.	**2104-W-1189**	**$10.99**
16 in. Round Pk./2.	**2104-W-1190**	**$12.99**

Show 'N Serve Cake Boards

Scalloped edge has the look of intricate lace. Food-safe, grease-resistant coating.

10 in. diameter Pk./10.	**2104-W-1168**	**$4.99**
12 in. diameter Pk./8.	**2104-W-1176**	**$5.49**
14 in. diameter Pk./6.	**2104-W-1184**	**$5.99**
14 x 20 in. Rectangle Pk./6.	**2104-W-1230**	**$6.99**

Ruffle Boards

Ready-to-use cake board and ruffle in one. Bleached white board and all-white ruffling complement any cake.

8 in. (for 6 in. round cake)	**415-W-950**	**$2.79**
10 in. (for 8 in. round cake)	**415-W-960**	**$3.29**
12 in. (for 10 in. round cake)	**415-W-970**	**$4.49**
14 in. (for 12 in. round cake)	**415-W-980**	**$4.99**
16 in. (for 14 in. round cake)	**415-W-990**	**$5.99**
18 in. (for 16 in. round cake)	**415-W-1000**	**$8.49**

Tuk-'N-Ruffle

A pretty touch that attaches to edge of your serving tray or board with royal icing or tape. White.
60 ft. bolt per box.
802-W-1008 $16.49
6 ft. pkg.
802-W-1991 $3.29

Fanci-Foil Wrap

Serving side has a non-toxic grease-resistant surface.
Continuous roll:
20 in. x 15 ft.
White
804-W-191 $8.99
Gold
804-W-183 $8.99
Silver
804-W-167 $8.99

Cake Doilies

Add instant elegance to cake plates, dessert trays, entrée and sandwich servings. Use under table centerpieces and plants, for decorations and crafts, too.

Cake Accents

Romantic accents add a sparkling beauty and elegance to cakes.

Silver Foil

4 in. Round Pk./12.
2104-W-90404 $2.49
6 in. Round Pk./18.
2104-W-90116 $2.49
8 in. Round Pk./12.
2104-W-90006 $2.49
10 in. Round Pk./6.
2104-W-90007 $2.49
12 in. Round Pk./4.
2104-W-90412 $2.49

Gold Foil

4 in. Round Pk./12.
2104-W-90304 $2.49
6 in. Round Pk./18.
2104-W-90306 $2.49
8 in. Round Pk./12.
2104-W-90308 $2.49
10 in. Round Pk./6.
2104-W-90310 $2.49
12 in. Round Pk./4.
2104-W-90312 $2.49

Greaseproof White

4 in. Round Pk./30.	**2104-W-90204**	**$1.99**
6 in. Round Pk./30.	**2104-W-90206**	**$1.99**
8 in. Round Pk./16.	**2104-W-90208**	**$1.99**
10 in. Round Pk./10.	**2104-W-90210**	**$1.99**
12 in. Round Pk./6.	**2104-W-90212**	**$1.99**
14 in. Round Pk./4.	**2104-W-90214**	**$1.99**
10 x 14 in. Rectangle Pk./6.	**2104-W-90224**	**$1.99**

White Pearl Beading

Molded on one continuous 5-yard strand. Remove before cutting and serving cake. 6 mm beads.
211-W-1990 $3.99

Baby

Start planning the party! From pink to blue, and themes in between, this dazzling array of Wilton products will inspire you to make the cutest things for your baby celebration.

Shower Accessories

Decorate, entertain and celebrate the new baby with a selection of clever shower accessories and gifts!

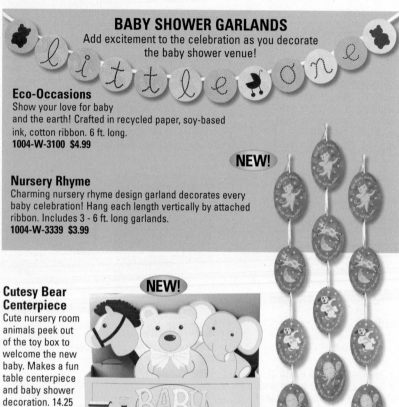

BABY SHOWER GARLANDS
Add excitement to the celebration as you decorate the baby shower venue!

NEW!

Eco-Occasions
Show your love for baby and the earth! Crafted in recycled paper, soy-based ink, cotton ribbon. 6 ft. long.
1004-W-3100 **$4.99**

NEW!

Nursery Rhyme
Charming nursery rhyme design garland decorates every baby celebration! Hang each length vertically by attached ribbon. Includes 3 - 6 ft. long garlands.
1004-W-3339 **$3.99**

NEW!

Cutesy Bear Centerpiece
Cute nursery room animals peek out of the toy box to welcome the new baby. Makes a fun table centerpiece and baby shower decoration. 14.25 x 6 x 9 in. high.
1004-W-3149 **$3.99**

NEW!

Baby Feet Diaper Cake Kit
Create and decorate an impressive, fun and functional diaper cake that will be the talk of the baby shower. Includes 7, 6, and 5 ft. ribbon lengths, 10 baby feet cut-outs, 3 blocks, base, adhesives, instructions. Diapers not included.
1004-W-3140 **$6.99**

Tummy Belt Baby Shower Game
Good-natured game gives everyone a chance to guess mom-to-be's tummy size by cutting off a length of sash. Sash measures 150 ft. long.
1004-W-1041 **$3.99**

Mommy-to-Be Sash
Honorary sash lets the Mommy–to-Be know she is special. Polyester. 8 ft. long.
1003-W-1007 **$4.99**

Autograph Mat
Holds a 5 x 7 in. photo, with room for autographs and good wishes all around from friends and family. Few gifts touch so many like this one! For use in an 11 x 14 in. frame. Pen included.
1009-W-1106 **$5.99**

Decorate-A-Bib Shower Game
Fun shower activity entertains guests as they create personalized bibs for the new baby. Includes 6 cotton bibs (6.25 x 5.75 in.) and 6 permanent color markers. Pk./6.
1003-W-1072 **$9.99**

Trivia Coasters
Fun baby shower game—20 clever baby-related trivia questions printed on drink coasters. Play the game and see which guest table has the most correct answers. Pk./20.
1003-W-2501 **$5.99**

ORDER TOLL FREE: 800-794-5866

Baby Feet Cupcake Stand

NEW!

Celebrate the new baby with cupcakes and treats served on this cute centerpiece stand. In minutes, you will create a colorful 3-tier cupcake stand with a fun decorative topper. Holds up to 24 cupcakes (baking cups not included). Stand - 1 ft. wide x 1.46 ft. high; topper - 7 in. high.
1004-W-1492 $6.99

NEW!

Baby Feet Wraps 'n Pix

Celebrate the pitter-patter of little feet in an instant. Includes 12 wraps (2 in. diameter) and 24 pix (12 pacifiers - 1.5 in high, 12 baby bottles 2.5 in. high).
1004-W-1493 $3.99

Baking Cups

Microwave-safe paper. Standard size, 2 in. diameter, pack 75; mini size, 1.25 in. diameter, pack 100. **$2.09**

Baby Feet
Standard
415-W-113
Mini
415-W-112

Ducky
Standard
415-W-1016
Mini
415-W-1017

Baby Feet Party Bags

Fill with candy, cookies and other goodies; great for gifts and surprises, too! 20 plastic bags, 20 ties included. 4 x 9.5 in. Pk./20.
1912-W-1100 $2.09

Favor-Making Kits

Oh-so-cute baby shower favors add so much to the celebration. Conveniently packaged in larger quantities to complete your favor making in no time at all. Personalize the tags at **www.wiltonprint.com**; *it's easy to do, just download the template and print! Use as a place card, add an announcement or a thank you note. Add your favorite candy (sold on p. 244), and your favors are ready for the party!*

Baby Bottle Favor Kit

Mom-to-be will love these adorable favor containers. Bottles measure 4 in. high. Multicolor pastel assortment includes: 24 favor containers, 24 ribbons, 24 print-your-own tags, 2 test sheets. Bear accent not included. Pk./24.
1006-W-577 $24.99
Bottles Only Pk./6.
1006-W-696 $5.99

Pail Favor Kit

Perfect for the baby celebration. Pails measure 2 in. high and are all white. Includes: 18 favor containers, 18 ribbons, 18 print-your-own tags, 2 test sheets. Tulle and safety pin accent not included. Pk./18.
1006-W-916 $24.99
Pail Only
1006-W-915 $1.29 each

Baby Block Favor Kit

Favorite baby icon celebrates the big occasion. Blocks measure 1.75 x 1.75 x 1.75 in. square. Multicolor pastel assortment includes: 20 favor containers, 20 ribbons, 20 print-your-own tags, 2 test sheets. Tulle not included. Pk./20.
1006-W-284 $24.99

Pacifier Favor Kit

Perfect for fun baby celebrations! Pacifiers measure 2.5 in. long. Multicolor pastel assortment includes: 20 favor containers, 20 ribbons, 20 print-your-own tags, 2 test sheets. Pk./20.
1003-W-1062 $24.99

Rattle Favor Kit

Looks so sweet at each place setting. Rattles measure 4 in. long. Multicolor pastel assortment includes: 20 favor containers, 20 ribbons, 20 print-your-own tags, 2 test sheets. Pk./20.
1006-W-572 $24.99

BABY

Celebrate the New Baby with Special Stationery!

Announce the birth, and invite guests to baby's first milestone events.

NEW!

NEW!

Faith Cross Stationery

Inspiring design adds a beautiful touch to spiritual events. Beautifully crafted in white 80 lb. card stock with white pearlized trim. Professionally print at home at www.wiltonprint.com.

Invitations
White with white border and cross accent. Invitation: 5.5 x 8.5 in.; envelope: 5.75 x 8.75 in. Pk./12.
1008-W-775 $4.99

Cross Seals
Self adhesive, silvertone, 1 in. diameter. Pk./50.
1008-W-2337 $2.99

Over The Moon Invitations

Imaginative words and drawings decorate quality card stock invitations. Professionally print at home at www.wiltonprint.com. 5.5 x 8.5 in. invitations; 5.75 x 8.75 in. envelopes. Pk/12.
1008-W-1548 $4.99

Baby Block Invitations

Iconic baby design decorates quality 80 lb. card stock invitations. Professionally print at home at www.wiltonprint.com. 5.5 x 8.5 in. invitations; 5.75 x 8.75 in. envelopes. Pk./12.
1008-W-127 $4.99

Baby Feet Invitations

Beautifully designed in white 80 lb. card stock with pastel and white pearlized baby feet embossed trim. Professionally print at home at www.wiltonprint.com. 5.5 x 8.5 in. invitations; 5.75 x 8.75 in. envelopes. Pk./12.
1008-W-8135 $4.99

Favor Containers

Package up a sweet treat for the baby shower guests!

NEW!

Nursery Rhyme Favor Boxes
Charming nursery rhyme design filled with candy or small gifts makes this perfect for the baby shower. Boxes are 2.5 x 2 x 3.3 in. high; ribbons 1 ft. long. Pk./12.
1004-W-3337 $5.99

Eco-Occasions Favor Boxes
Crafted in recycled paper, soy-based ink, cotton ribbon. 2 x 2 x 2 in. Pk./6.
1004-W-3105 $5.99

Favor Boxes
Each box has 2 acetate windows. 2 x 2 x 2 in. square paper boxes are easy to assemble. Candy sold below. Pk./12.
1003-W-1017 $5.99

Favor Tote Bags
Fill with your favorite baby shower candy or a small gift. Paper bags measure 3 x 2.25 x 5.5 in. Candy sold below. Pk./12.
1003-W-1055 $5.99

Ribbon Favor Bags
Paper bags hold treats and small gifts. Thread the ribbon through the holes at top of bag to close. 2.75 x 1.4 x 4.5 in. Includes 12 - 12 in. ribbons. Pk./12.
1003-W-1053 $5.99

Favor Accents

Add special touches to your baby favors, gift tie-ons and table decorations.

Ducky* **NEW!**
Yellow. .85 high. Pk./20
1004-W-2850 $2.99

Newborn Baby Figurines*
1 in. high. Pk./6.
1103-W-62 $1.99

Baby Bracelets
Pink, blue, yellow, mint green. 1.25 in. high. Pk./6.
1103-W-56 $2.99

Mini Clothes Pins*
Pink, lavender, blue, yellow, mint green. 1.3 in. high. Pk./20.
1103-W-27 $1.99

Mini Baby Bottles*
Pink, lavender, blue, yellow, mint green. 1.25 in. high. Pk./20.
1103-W-16 $1.99

Shower Rattles
Pink, lavender, blue, yellow, mint green. 3.75 in. high. Pk./6.
1103-W-29 $2.99

Pacifiers*
Pink, lavender, blue, yellow, mint green. .75 in. high. Pk./20.
1003-W-1086 $2.99

Safety Pins*
1.5 in. long. Pk./20. $1.99
Pink 1103-W-21
Blue 1103-W-26

⚠ ***WARNING: CHOKING HAZARD**
Small parts. Not for children under 3 years.

Favor Candy

Fun shapes, beautiful colors, great flavors! Wilton candy makes the perfect filler for favors, treat bags, and candy dishes.

Baby Feet
Sweet/tart fruit flavored. 12 oz. bag.
1006-W-9047 $6.29

Mini Pacifiers
Sweet/tart fruit flavored. 12 oz. bag.
1006-W-540 $6.29

Baby Talk
Fruit flavored. 10 oz. bag.
1006-W-1115 $4.29

Mint Drops
Pastel. Certified Kosher Dairy. 14 oz. bag.
1006-W-788 $6.29
32 oz. bag.
1006-W-3710 $13.99

Pastel Pearls
Fruit flavored. 10 oz. bag. Certified Kosher.
1006-W-904 $4.29

Pastel Jelly Beans
Fruit flavored. 12 oz. bag.
1006-W-9050 $4.29

Pillow Mints
10 oz. bag. Pastel.
1006-W-858 $4.29
48 oz. bag. Pastel.
1006-W-379 $20.99
48 oz. bag. White.
1006-W-3711 $20.99

Jordan Almonds
Certified Kosher.
16 oz. bag. Pastel.
1006-W-779 $7.99
16 oz. bag. White.
1006-W-778 $7.99
44 oz. bag. Pastel.
1006-W-1133 $21.99
44 oz. bag. White.
1006-W-1134 $21.99

ORDER TOLL FREE: 800-794-5866

Bakeware

Rocking Horse

This happy hobby horse sets the pace for a birthday that rocks! It's a favorite kids shape that's also ideal for showers and playgroup parties. One-mix pan is 11 x 12.75 x 2 in. deep. Aluminum.
2105-W-2009 $12.99

#1

Add the #1 cake to all the important first celebrations. One-mix pan is 12.75 x 8.5 x 2 in. deep. Aluminum.
2105-W-1194 $12.99

Baby Buggy

It's a precious carriage design for shower and christening, for cakes or elegant salads and gelatins. One-mix pan is 11.25 x 11.25 x 2 in. deep. Aluminum.
2105-W-3319 $12.99

3-D Rubber Ducky

This bathtime favorite will make a big splash at baby showers. Five adorable designs included. Two-piece pan takes 5½ cups batter. 9 x 5 x 7 in. high. Aluminum.
2105-W-2094 $16.49

Teddy Bear

Everybody just loves teddy bears. This cutie will be busy all year 'round with birthdays, school parties and baby showers. No time for hibernating with all these fun events on the agenda. One-mix pan is 13.5 x 12.25 x 2 in deep. Aluminum.
2105-W-1193 $12.99

Cake Server

Whimsical stacked blocks spell out B-A-B-Y on the handle. Crafted in plastic with serrated edge. 10 in. long.
1006-W-1312 $5.99

Cookie Cutters

4-Pc. Baby Cutter Set

Carriage, rocking horse, bear, onesie, each approximately 3 in. Coated metal. Set/4.
2308-W-1067 $4.79

BABY

Candles

Wilton gives you more choices! Top your cake with candles in the perfect colors. Check out our handpainted details and clean-burning, matching designs.

Rubber Ducky
1.5 in. high. Set/6.
2811-W-9337 $3.99

Baby Things
Approx. 2 in. high. Set/4.
2811-W-855 $3.99

Shimmer
2.5 in. high. Pk./10.
2811-W-3664 $2.29

Tricolor
2.5 in. high. Pk./10.
2811-W-782 $2.29

Candy Molds

Fun-shaped, reusable molds celebrate baby over and over again. Making candy is easy to do, complete directions are included! Use with Wilton Candy Melts brand confectionery coating. **$1.99**

Candy Melts
Ideal for molding, dipping or coating. Artificial vanilla flavored unless otherwise indicated. 14 oz. bag. Certified Kosher Dairy.
$2.99

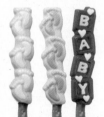

Baby Pretzel Mold
Position pretzel rod and refrigerate to set. 2 designs, 6 cavities.
2115-W-2101

Baby Treats
5 designs, 5 cavities.
2115-W-4447

Baby Bottles Lollipop
1 design, 6 cavities.
2115-W-1560

Baby Shower
4 designs, 11 cavities.
2115-W-1710

Mini Baby Icons
5 designs, 20 cavities.
2115-W-1537

Rubber Ducky
1 design, 6 cavities.
2115-W-1565

Orange 1911-W-1631	**White** 1911-W-498	**Dark Cocoa Mint** 1911-W-1920
Yellow 1911-W-463	**Dark Cocoa** 1911-W-358	
Pink 1911-W-447	**Light Cocoa** 1911-W-544	
Blue 1911-W-448		
Lavender 1911-W-403	**Colorburst Pastels** 10 oz. bag. 1911-W-490	

NEW!

See pages 194-198 for more Wilton candy items.